Apprentice in Budapest

Memories of a World That Is No More

Raphael Patai

LEXINGTON BOOKS
Lanham • Boulder • New York • Oxford

943.912
P 27 a

LEXINGTON BOOKS

Published in the United States of America
by Lexington Books
4720 Boston Way, Lanham, Maryland 20706

12 Hid's Copse Road
Cumnor Hill, Oxford OX2 9JJ, England

Copyright © 2000 by Lexington Books
Originally published in 1988 by University of Utah Press

British Library Cataloguing in Publication Information Available

Library of Congress Cataloging-in-Publication Data

Patai, Raphael, 1910–1996
   Apprentice in Budapest : memories of a world that is no more / Raphael Patai.
      p. cm.
   Includes index.
   ISBN 0-7391-0210-9 (paper : alk. paper)
      1. Patai, Raphael, 1910—Childhood and youth. 2. Jews—Hungary—
   Budapest—Biography. 3. Jewish scholars—Biography. 4. Folklorists—
   Biography. 5. Budapest (Hungary)—Biography. I. Title.

DS135.H93 P377 2000
943.9'12004924'0092—dc21
[B]   00-061200

Printed in the United States of America

⊖™ The paper used in this publication meets the minimum requirements of American
National Standard for Information Sciences—Permanence of Paper for Printed Library
Materials, ANSI/NISO Z39.48–1992.

To My Sister Évi

My Best and Most Constant Friend

Contents

Preface

In writing this account I have had to rely, especially in connection with the earliest years of my life, on my memory, which was practically the only source of information about what I felt and did, and what happened to me, in my first ten or fifteen years. Since this forced me to contemplate problems presented by the unevenness of my memory, manifested in such occurrences as its alternation between total recall and total oblivion, I inevitably became interested in the phenomenon of memory itself, and could not keep myself from occasionally sidestepping into a consideration of the nature, the characteristics, the workings of memory, as I could ascertain, or at least glimpse, them, from delving into my own head, so to speak.

As this whole book testifies, in writing it I was again and again bemused and puzzled by memory as a psychological function. Repeatedly, in the course of writing these pages I was prompted to marvel at the seemingly arbitrary selectivity of my memory, at its retention of what appeared to be insignificant little events and details and, conversely, at its letting the waters of Lethe swallow up other events and sequences that I *know* must have happened and must have influenced the course of my life, and yet of which I have retained absolutely nothing. As the number of examples of this contrary behavior of my memory multiplied, I became more and more aware of it, was more and more puzzled by it, and began to suspect that the workings of memory must have their own rules, even if we, or at least I, do not understand them. But I did recognize this much: if one's memory retains an incident, a feeling, a place, a face, the mere fact of such retention endows those items with a significance that must not be doubted even if it is not readily apparent.

In pondering this issue I found that the fact of remembrance itself supplies the most reliable yardstick with which to measure the significance of such past occurrences, and especially those of a life's distant past. If an event, an utterance, a scene, a feeling manages to embed itself in one's consciousness to the extent of maintaining itself there in the form of a distinct memory-fragment, and over a time-span of fifty or sixty years, then it inevitably follows that, in order to accomplish this feat, it must have had considerable intrinsic meaning for the psyche of the person concerned, and has therewith earned the right to full disclosure.

In addition to my memory, and in supplementation of it, I relied on written sources, both printed and surviving in manuscript, in the reconstruction of the story of my apprentice years in Budapest. This often meant the necessity of making a mental jump—from delving into myself and trying to bring up from the depths of the mental files I carried in me things that had lain dormant and hidden for many decades, to the very different world of the present with its books, catalogs, files, letters, and papers, to peruse the like of which had been my métier for many a decade. Occasionally I felt that the manner in which I presented the two types of information, one next to the other, made for rough transition, and that the two types of sources resisted melding, so that the resultant narration turned out to be patchy; but I could not help it. On the positive side, I think that in every case the more systematic factual data I dug up by research in the libraries and in my own personal archives significantly supplemented the more haphazard bounty caught in the net of my memory, and this justified the occasional inclusion of the former, even at the cost of interrupting the flow of the latter.

I wish to thank, as I did on many a previous occasion, Dr. Leonard Gold, head of the Jewish Division of the New York Public Library, and his knowledgeable staff for their unfailing courtesy in helping me locate hard-to-find sources in the vast holdings of that invaluable treasure house. I owe a different kind of indebtedness to members of my family. My sister, Mrs. Éva (Évi) Koigen, of Givatayim, Israel, with whom I repeatedly discussed our common childhood experiences, passed away in February 1987. Shortly before her death she interviewed for me our cousin, Mrs. Judith Molnár-Zaran, of Ramat Gan, Israel, about the last years in the life of our grandparents in Budapest, which she witnessed. My brother, Saul Patai, of Jerusalem, Israel, read most of the manuscript and made several valuable corrections where his memory was more accurate than mine. My elder daughter, Jennifer, of Tucson, Arizona, took keen interest in the story of her ancestors and the early years of her father, providing a great stimulus for working on this book and giving me the feeling that I was writing something that ultimately could be a link tying her children with their remote Jewish forebears in faraway Europe. My younger daughter, Daphne, despite being deeply involved in writing her own books, read the entire manuscript and made many suggestions that I subsequently incorporated into my text. I am also grateful to the staff of the University of Utah Press, whose enthusiastic readiness to undertake the publication of this book before even seeing the manuscript greatly encouraged me to persevere in working on it.

At the age of seventy-six no man can be sure of how much more time he has to accomplish additional works. Should I be granted a few more years, I shall try to write another book about the fifteen years, 1933–1947, that I spent in Palestine. I intend to title it *Journeyman in Jerusalem*.

Raphael Patai

Forest Hills, September 5, 1987

1

Infancy and Early Childhood: 1910–1916

Earliest Memory-Flashes

The first childhood memory emerges from the night of unremembrance like a nocturnal landscape that is, for a moment, flooded by the glare of lightning that streaks overhead. Where there was but a moment earlier nothing, not even the dimmest suggestion of a shape, suddenly a hundred details spring into sight, colors glow, and manifest reality takes the place of lost nonbeing—only to be, a second later, obliterated again as the bolt of memory fades away as fast as it struck. The phantom world it conjured up sinks back into a total obscurity that will again yield its secrets only to another streak of lightning illuminating a scene separated from the first by a passage of months or perhaps years. Such a flash of recollection, preceded by nothing and followed by nothing, shows me to myself at a time when I could not have been more than one year old.

One day, when I was unable to walk as yet, I managed to negotiate the three flights of wide stone stairs that led from my parents' apartment to the street. I did this by the simple expedient of letting my backside bump down step after step. Having arrived by this primitive method of locomotion at the bottom of the stairs, I crawled to the street door of the house, proceeded to cross the sidewalk, and moved out into the roadway. There I sat down to pause between the two rails of the tramline that passed in front of the house. As I looked around, I noticed a frightening black object towering over me at the curb. It was a squarish column that seemed to me much taller than a man. There was something unspeakably sinister and threatening about it. What it actually was I do not know to this day, nor do I recall ever having seen it again, although we continued to live in the same house until my late teens. The sight of that black stele made me first freeze with fright, then break into tears. The next thing I remember is that I was swept up into the arms of my mother, who carried me upstairs to the safety of our apartment. Not for at least another year thereafter does my memory again illuminate a scene from my childhood.

This first adventure of mine as a one-year-old explorer of the unknown was, of course, later recounted to me by my mother. She told me how they discovered suddenly that I was missing, how they searched all the rooms of our apartment and those of my grandparents who lived next door on the same floor, until, near desperation, she thought of the seemingly impossible — that I might have managed to get down the stairs — and how she flew down, glanced into the courtyard, then rushed through the front door, and snatched me from between the rails at the very last moment, just before the wheels of a streetcar that was rapidly approaching would have cut me to pieces.

Much later I learned that mothers like to tell their children what the latter did when they were small, and that in this manner children build up a store of pseudomemories about the first years of their lives. One therefore often wonders whether one actually remembers an early event or only thinks that one remembers it because one was told about it later, perhaps many years later. This being the case, I, too, would feel inclined to doubt that that first flash of my memory illuminates the actual scene with my one-year-old self in the center, rather than its subsequent recall and recount with motherly solicitude. There is, however, one detail in that scene that nobody else but I could have known: the paralyzing terror that sinister stele struck into my one-year-old heart. Of all the details of that little adventure, precisely *that* is the one I remember with the greatest clarity. Perhaps the image of that black pilaster is the only thing I truly and unquestionably remember of the event itself, and all the rest — my sliding down the stairs, my being rescued by my mother — was supplied by subsequent stories that she told me. But that one image, and my reaction to it, are, I feel sure, my own authentic recollections from the age of one.

Another such isolated piece of early childhood memory illuminates a scene that must have taken place a year or so later. One morning, I remember, I woke up in my crib with a strong urge to urinate. I was alone in the room, and called out for Mother. I called repeatedly, and with increasing urgency, but to no avail. For some reason that I can no longer recall, it seemed impossible for me to go to the lavatory, which was but a few steps away. Instead, I got down from the crib, and relieved myself on the floor under it. What happened next I no longer know.

My fright at seeing that sinister, threatening black pilaster must have been the source of my childhood fear of dark corners, which, I remember, haunted me perhaps to the age of five or six. In our apartment there was a long entrance hall that led from the front door to the rooms. In the darkest corner of this hall, next to the door paneled with frosted glass that opened into the living room, there was a box about the height of a table with a door at the front. It housed, as I found out later, the gas meter. This box with its mysterious content filled me with fear, and whenever I had to pass it — which I had to do several times a day on the way to and from my room — I hastened to put a safe distance between it and myself as quickly as possible. At the same time, I remember, I was vexed by a curiosity to find out what exactly was contained in the box and how it looked; but I was never able to overcome my fear to the extent of stopping in front of it, opening it, and looking inside. Occasionally, however, the door stood ajar; and at such times, as I ran past it, I could espy in its depth a black, drumlike shape before I hurried on to remove myself from its dangerous vicinity.

Even before I rid myself of this fear there arose another, much more serious, danger to plague me in the evenings before I would fall asleep. The nursery in which my sister and I slept had two large windows facing onto the long loggia that led from the stairway to the entrance door of our apartment. How I got the idea I have long since forgotten, but somehow I came to believe that, after dark, malicious and loathsome demons were lurking in this loggia, crouching under the windows, and trying to climb through them into the room. On occasion I imagined I could even see their horrible hands with clawlike fingers reaching up and grasping the windowsill. Had they succeeded in entering, I knew, they would have fallen upon me and tortured me to death. Fortunately, I was well prepared to prevent their entry, and even to banish them from beneath the window for the duration of the night. All I had to do was to recite, voicelessly, but with my lips moving so as to enunciate clearly every word, the *Shema'* prayer in the original Hebrew, which I did whenever the

occasion required it. I must have been about three when my grandmother taught me this basic prayer of Judaism. In the evenings after
I had gone to bed, she would come in, sit down next to me, recite
the prayer, and bid me repeat it after her word by word: *Shema'—
Yisroel—Adonay—Eloheinu—Adonay—Ekhod* (Hear, O Israel, the
Lord our God, the Lord is One), and so on to the final words, *al
mezüzays beisekho uvishorekho* (on the doorposts of your houses
and in your gates)—I still remember clearly how she pronounced
them.

It seemed to me quite a lengthy prayer, and I was eager to reach
its end. After a while, long before I knew all of it by heart, I recognized the word *mezüzays* (this is how Grandmother pronounced
mezuzot, doorposts), and knew that it was followed by only two
more words. This always made me smile happily in anticipation. For
many years thereafter the word *mezuzot* never failed to evoke in me
a feeling of mirth. When the prayer was finished, Grandma would
make sure that the net I had to wear over my head was in place so
that my ears, which stood away like wings, would be trained to lie
flat against its sides. (Only recently I read in the autobiography of a
British author that this contraption, which he, too, had to wear in
his childhood, was called a "scrum-cap.") Then she would kiss me
good-night, and say, "Now turn to the wall, and go to sleep!"

What the words of the *Shema'* prayer meant, I had, of course,
no idea. My grandmother never bothered to translate or explain
them to me—possibly she herself was not quite sure of their meaning—but that they were very sacred and very potent words had been
deeply impressed upon me by her demeanor and the obviously exceedingly great importance she attached to teaching them to me and to
making sure I recited them every night. Neither do I remember how
long it took me to learn the whole prayer by heart, but I can recall
that it was its first sentence that served as my powerful weapon against
the demons of the night lurking outside the window. As soon as I
would become aware that they had arrived, I would recite that first
sentence with great fervor. Its sacred force would make the evil ones
draw back and fade away, and by the time I enunciated the last of
its six magic words, they would be gone.

Sometimes, however, my demons would be in an especially ugly
and pugnacious mood, and though the words of the *Shema'* would
beat them back momentarily, they would soon take courage again
and resume their efforts to scale the window. When this happened I

knew that I had to hurl more powerful missiles against them, that is, utter (always voicelessly) words even more sacred than the *Shema'*. Again, how fortunate, I did know such words. I no longer remember who taught them to me, and I suspect that I learned them at a later age than the *Shema'*, but certainly before I was taught the Hebrew alphabet at the age of five. That more powerful and more sacred incantation consisted of the words *Adonay, Adonay, El Raḥum weḤanun* (Lord, Lord, God merciful and compassionate). I had no idea of the meaning of these words either, except for *Adonay* and *El*, which I knew were the Hebrew words for God. Only much later did I discover that these were the words Moses uttered when God appeared to him on Mount Sinai (cf. Exodus 34:6), and that they were recited several times in the High Holy Day services. In any case, these most powerful words would never fail to work their magic: the demons, and with them my fears of the night, would disappear for good, and I would fall peacefully asleep.

My fears of dark corners and nocturnal demons, and the frequent combats in which I marshaled my secret arsenal of sacred weapons against them, were parts of my very own most private world. I was never even tempted to tell anybody about them. True, I myself was not too much bothered by them either. They were nothing but fleeting moments of anguish in an otherwise happy childhood of sunny days spent in pleasurable activities. My companion in everything was my sister Évi, eighteen months younger than I, with whom I shared the nursery and spent my days, going to "the island" and the zoo, and playing in the apartment, in the loggias that hugged the courtyard side of each floor of the four-story building, or in the courtyard itself, or running wildly up and down the stairs.

The earliest memory in which my sister figures dates from a time when she was between one and a half and two years old. On the floor of the nursery I built myself a "castle" consisting of a cushion and two or three cardboard folding picture books that I stood on edge and arranged in a circle so as to form a wall around it. I seated myself in this domain, and my sister, still barely able to speak, approached timidly and asked, "Dudu, can I sit?" I graciously granted her permission, moving aside one or two folds of a book to enable her to step into the area I had staked out for myself, and she plumped down happily on the cushion next to me. This little game must have been played by us several times, and did not escape the attention of our mother, who would later tell me of it as a proof of the devotion my sister had for me from her earliest age.

Of course, all was not always this sweet and smooth between my sister and me. As we grew older we quarreled, and I suspect that in most cases I must have been the aggressor, and must have tyrannized her whenever the mood struck me. However, Mother was always there to protect her, and, if need be, to mete out stern retribution.

As a small child I had a very strong attachment to my mother, which continued until it gradually diminished in adolescence. Whenever she would go out on an errand and leave me at home—not alone, of course, but in the care of the maid—I would desperately hang on to her skirt until the very moment she went out the front door of our apartment and pulled it shut behind her. Then I would remain standing there behind the door, crying and pressing my face against the lowest of its many glass panels, which I could barely reach, and follow her receding figure with my eyes as she walked along the loggia, until she turned right at its end and disappeared down the stairway.

The German Fräulein

About the time I was four or five, our parents, both of whom spoke German as fluently as Hungarian, decided that we children must be taught German. German was considered the key to European culture by middle-class Hungarians, and especially those of the "Israelite" persuasion. Hungary had been subjoined to Austria as a theoretically equal partner in the Austro-Hungarian Empire since the 1867 accord, but its intelligentsia could never escape feeling inferior to Austria with its fabulous *Kaiserstadt* Vienna, which was not only a great metropolis but also a world-famous center of German culture. And beyond Austria there was the larger, more powerful, and culturally even more important German *Reich*, surrounded, in turn, by a ring of smaller countries in which all educated people spoke German. To know only Hungarian meant to be confined to a small language area, to be limited in one's cultural horizon to Hungarian literature plus those foreign works that happened to be translated and published in Hungarian, that is, to remain in effect condemned to lifelong cultural provincialism. To know German, on the other hand, meant to be an *Europäer*, a citizen, culturally speaking, of the great civilized world.

Considerations such as these must have motivated my parents, as they did many middle-class Jewish parents, to engage a *deutsches Fräulein*, a German governess, into whose care we were forthwith delivered. For seven or eight years thereafter, the Fräulein remained a fixture in our household. During that period we must have had several, but I cannot remember a single one of them. What I do recall is that the Fräulein had complete charge of my sister and me (and later, when our brother was born, of him, too, of course). She lived in, although I cannot now imagine where she slept in our relatively small apartment, which consisted of nothing more than four rooms (a living-dining room, Father's study, our parents' bedroom, and the nursery), a bathroom, a kitchen, a maid's room (which was only big enough for the maid herself), and a small larder, known as the *shpayz*, raiding which, as I shall tell later, was to become one of my great childhood pleasures.

Being with the Fräulein from the moment we woke up in the morning until we went to sleep in the evening, and she knowing only German—ignorance of Hungarian was a prime prerequisite for a young woman who wanted to be a German governess in Budapest—we had no choice but to learn German, which we did with the astounding speed with which children pick up a new language. Soon Father was able to introduce the iron rule of speaking only German at the lunch table, around which—lunch being the main meal of the day—the family would regularly gather between one and two o'clock in the afternoon. Whenever we children would be noisy at the table, engage in loud prattle, or banter in Hungarian, Father would quelch our chatter by admonishing us, humorously but with a sternness that brooked no objection: *Schweig still und sprich Deutsch!*—"Be quiet and speak German!"

Some years later, when I developed an inclination for drawing, I sketched out the sentence *Bitte deutsch zu schprechen* (Please speak German) on a large sheet of drawing paper in beautiful Gothic script, which I copied meticulously from a book. I filled in the letters carefully with India ink, and placed the completed masterwork on top of the sideboard in the dining room, leaning it against the wall. I was very proud of my handiwork, until somebody—I no longer remember who it was—pointed out that I had misspelled the last word, which should have read *sprechen*. I never again engaged in German calligraphy.

The Island and the Zoo

We lived within about half an hour's walking distance from two places that, as long as the weather was clement, were the favorite haunts of children under the supervision of governesses. One was the *Margitsziget*, Margaret Island, the other the zoo. The island, as it was referred to by everybody, was one large park. It lay in the middle of the Danube, and was joined by the Margaret Bridge to the city spread out on both banks of the river. To cross the bridge one had first to buy at a tollbooth a large, thin, embossed brass token, then, a few steps farther, deposit it in a box in front of another booth guarded by another uniformed official. This second guard was usually asleep, sitting there in the cool depths of his stone tollbooth, and the story went that if a person duly deposited his token, which would drop with a loud clatter to the bottom of the box, the guard would continue to sleep peacefully; but if somebody would try to sneak by without putting his token into the slot, the guard would immediately awaken, and then—woe to the culprit.

This widely current myth, instead of intimidating me, became a challenge. Each time we passed the booth I tried to get away with one of the three tokens that the Fräulein had purchased for the three of us, and then, at my insistence, handed to me. I cannot recall ever having been caught by the sleeping Cerberus, but I do remember that I had accumulated quite a collection of these tokens when, one day, the bridge toll was abolished.

After reaching the midway point between the two banks of the river, we would make a right turn and walk down the ramp that at this juncture led from the bridge to the tip of the long, fish-shaped island. The Fräulein would seek out a pleasant shady spot, sit down on a bench, and strike up conversation with other expatriate German governesses, while we children could roam about freely as long as we remained within her sight. If there was another boy around of more or less my own age, we would approach each other, hesitantly but with simulated nonchalance, and then one of us would, somewhat timidly, take the initiative by uttering the ritually approved polite formula of inviting a peer to play: *Kisfiu, jön játszani?* (literally: little boy, will he come to play?). Since we were properly brought up children, we would not use the familiar second person singular (Hungarian has an equivalent of the German *du*, or French *tu*), but the polite third person (corresponding to the German *Sie*) used as a sign of respect between adults not intimately acquainted. My parents, for instance, addressed each other and us children as *du*, but we addressed our parents with *Sie*. Since the two "little boys" did not know each other, the correct form of address was *Sie*. If the answer was yes, as it usually was, we would play hopscotch, or some other game in which the participation of two or more partners was essential.

When we got tired of playing we would begin gathering wild chestnuts, which in the summer and fall were always found in ample supply under the huge, gnarled old trees of the island. We would have with us one or two satchels in which the Fräulein would bring along our ten o'clock snack. This usually consisted of a large sandwich: two slices of bread spread with butter and marmalade, or butter and cheese, or goose fat and a slice of goose liver, or goose fat and smoked tongue. Since our parents kept a kosher home, goose fat with cheese, or any other mixing of meat and milk products, was, of course, strictly forbidden. As a dessert we usually had some fruit, of which Hungary had a rich variety and great abundance. If we were thirsty, there were always the ornamental taps, from which we could take a pure and cold drink.

There were, of course, not only boys but also girls around. But boys and girls never played together, and for a boy to approach a girl and ask her to join in a game was simply unheard of. Yet I do remember that I would ogle the girls from a distance, that they seemed to me very peculiar creatures, very different from us boys, and, in particular, that they seemed to have very long legs. This impression, as I gradually came to realize, was simply due to the fact that they wore very short skirts that left most of their thighs uncovered.

By the time we had to leave the island to get home for the midday meal, our satchels would be filled with wild chestnuts. I still remember the keen esthetic pleasure I had in gathering this beautiful, hard, round, albeit inedible, fruit, with its shiny auburn skin, and the large greyish spot on one side. Occasionally, as the wild chestnuts dropped from the trees, they were still encased in their green, thorny outer coats, so that one had to be most careful in removing this encumbrance without hurting one's fingers.

After lunch I would thread some of the wild chestnuts on a string. I would borrow one of Mother's long and thin U-shaped hairpins, straighten it, then rebend it so that one side was longer than the other, tie the string to it, and proceed to pierce with it one chestnut after the other until I had a long enough chain to hang on the wall of the nursery, or around one of the large wardrobes in which our clothes were kept. Once, I remember, the hairpin, after I forced it through a hard chestnut, went straight through my left thumb. I jumped up to run to the bathroom, to remove the pin from my thumb under the tap. But, as I ran out of the room, the other chestnuts that were already strung up got caught under the door, and the pin was jerked out of my thumb as inadvertently and as suddenly as it had pierced it. I proceeded to the bathroom and let cold water flow on the two small holes in my thumb — and therewith the flash of memory disappears.

Our main purpose, however, in gathering wild chestnuts was not to decorate the nursery but to feed them to the animals in the zoo. Our excursions to the Margaret Island alternated with visits to the zoo. Rules of not feeding the animals either did not exist or were blithely disregarded, and once we arrived at the open-air enclosures with our satchels full of chestnuts we proceeded to throw them as deftly as we could to the various beasts. Of all the animals that were regular chestnut consumers I remember the elephant and the hippopotamus in particular. When feeding the elephant, the more daring children would place a chestnut on the open palm of their hand, reach in across the outer of the two railings as far as they could, and let the big beast pick up the chestnut from their hand with the end of its trunk, which it stuck through the heavy bars of its enclosure. But I liked most to feed the hippopotamus. It would open wide its enormous mouth, and we children would bombard it with chestnuts. When the hippo had accumulated a few pounds of them in its huge maw, it would snap it shut with a loud smack, masticate, swallow — and then the fearsome jaws would open again, ready to receive another helping.

Before long the chestnuts would all be gone, and we would continue to roam about in that latter-day Garden of Eden where all the animals seemed to live peacefully in the immediate vicinity of one another and of children. The lions were housed in a large, artificial grottolike rocky structure whose front part had no railing at all but was separated from the people by a deep ditch that, we were assured, was wide enough so that even the most athletic lion could not jump over it. Behind the lions' cave the rocks rose steeply to form what appeared to me to be a high mountain, which was the abode of mountain goats. The lions could not climb up to the goats, but, so we were told, once it happened that a goat lost its foothold, fell down among the lions, and was promptly devoured by them. I shuddered when I heard the story.

Next I remember the cage of the squirrels, in which the main attraction was a squirrel-exercise contraption, consisting of two parallel wheels rotating on a common axis, with their outer rims connected by a series of sticks. One of the squirrels would always get in between the two wheels and try to run upward on the connecting sticks, which would make the wheels turn with great speed while the squirrel itself would remain always in the same spot at the bottom. Each of the animals had its fascination, but I no longer remember them in detail, except for the peacock, which had the freedom of the zoo, and which I would watch, and follow if necessary, in the hope of seeing it open its magnificent tail.

What I do remember most clearly are the thrills of various pleasure rides we children could take in the zoo. One was on the back of an elephant, another on the back of a camel, the third on a little choo-choo train that rolled around the whole zoo whistling loudly and frequently, and the fourth was the so-called cave train, whose locomotive had the shape of a gilded dragon, which went into a cave where it slowly passed all kinds of marvels: mechanically animated fairies, dwarfs, monsters, and figures from Hungarian folklore, which alternatingly delighted and frightened us for the duration of the fifteen-minute ride. I can even remember how we got on the back of the elephant. After the Fräulein paid for our ride, we went up some wooden stairs to one of two platforms between which there was just enough room for the elephant to stand and pass through. Along the back of the elephant were fastened two benches with footholds in front of them. All we had to do was to step over, sit down on the bench, and let ourselves be lashed in by the attendant. When all was secure, the elephant driver who sat across the neck of the great beast (only much much later did I learn that he was the Hungarian version of the Indian mahout) did something, I don't know what, that made the elephant start its perambulation on its appointed round. I shall never forget the sensation of being rocked, rolled, shaken, and swung to and fro on that big grey back.

An integral part of good middle-class Jewish upbringing in Budapest was to teach the children some music, which in most cases meant piano lessons. Mother played the piano—she herself having received the same kind of education a generation earlier when it was still a daring innovation for religious Jewish families—and so an upright piano graced our living room ready to receive our attention. I remember nothing of the first piano teacher whom our parents engaged to teach my sister and me except that she was a woman. But I can recall very clearly that my musical career lasted through exactly one lesson. The teacher bid me place my two hands over the keyboard and instructed me to imitate the position she made her own hands assume: wrists down, knuckles up, fingers rounded and pointing downward. I was unable to conform, whereupon she tried to mold my hands into the required position. I offered resistance; she tried to apply force, which turned my resistance into resentment. At the end of the lesson I resolutely announced to my mother that my hands were unable to perform the contortions the teacher demanded, that she had tried to break my fingers, and that I would simply not go on with these lessons. Mother, probably after due consultation with Father, accepted the decision. What musical talent was forever lost during that single unsuccessful lesson I shall never know. The hands of my sister must have been more supple, for her piano lessons continued, and many years later, I remember, I often begged her to play for me a Beethoven sonata or a piece by Grieg, to which I would listen with great pleasure.

Echoes of the Great War

I was not yet four years old when World War I broke out. In the summer of 1914 my parents took my sister and me to Abbazia on the Adriatic for a seaside vacation. We must have left Budapest by train in the morning, arrived at Fiume (which at the time was part of Hungary, today Rijuka, Yugoslavia) in the evening, and then took the boat from Fiume to Abbazia. Of this trip I remember only the boat ride. We are sitting aboard ship, it is dark, and in the distance I can see the lights of the shore, seemingly motionless. I am, if not exactly afraid, made uneasy by the dark, the strange surroundings, and the great expanse of black water. Of our sojourn in Abbazia I recall nothing, but years later I had in my possession a snapshot that I subsequently lost in the course of my moves from place to place, showing my father standing hip deep in the water and holding me on his shoulder.

I have some vague recollection of the day on which our vacation was cut short by the outbreak of the war. Suddenly my parents were packing, and we rushed back to Budapest. Historical data help me pinpoint the date of our return. The Archduke Francis Ferdinand and his wife were assassinated in Sarajevo, Bosnia, on June 28, 1914. On July 23 Austria-Hungary, in a ten-point ultimatum, accused Serbia of responsibility for the murder. This was followed on July 28 by the Austro-Hungarian declaration of war against Serbia. I can therefore assume that our return from Abbazia to Budapest must have taken place within a few days after July 28.

As far as I could perceive, the war had little or no immediate effect on the life of our family or of Budapest as a whole. I remember being lifted once up to the window so as to be able to see a detachment of soldiers march down the street. And another occasion, on which my grandfather came into our apartment and said with great enthusiasm to Mother: "What do you say to the Germans?" This, of course, must have been the general reaction in Hungary to the early German victories. And as for the Jews, they had a special reason to rejoice over every Russian defeat, of which at the time I was, of course, not aware: Russia, the land of pogroms and Jew-baiting, received only what it so richly deserved. No other impressions of the great "war to end all wars" were left in my memory. Whatever else I seem to remember about it is certainly reconstruction from later information. Thus I know that none of those members of my family in whose proximity I lived was called up. Grandfather was too old; Father was a high school teacher and thus exempted from service; Mother's only brother was a lawyer and was assigned some job in one of the many offices of the army. But three of my father's brothers were in the Hungarian army, and one of them was wounded in action. I was also told later that my mother and grandmother, like all other housewives, had to donate their heavy brass kitchen mortars and pestles to the war effort—the metal was needed to make guns and bullets. I can no longer tell whether my memory of the first line of a Hungarian patriotic anti-Serbian song, *Vigyázz, vigyázz, kutya Szerbia* (Beware, beware, dog Serbia), goes back to the period itself or is based on accounts of those days I was given later.

Study and Play

My father very rarely spoke to me about his childhood, but I gathered that when he was three years old his father began teaching him the Hebrew alphabet, and that when he was four he was sent to the *ḥeder*, the Hebrew school, in the village of Gyöngyöspata. I shall later speak in greater detail of my father's childhood. He did not try to repeat with me this early introduction to Hebrew, but when I reached the ripe age of five he thought it was high time for me to be initiated into Hebrew studies. However, while his own father was his first teacher, he on his part did not have the time to teach me, and it was not until I reached my Bar Mitzva that he began to instruct me in the Talmud. He led an extremely busy life, which explains not only why he could not himself teach me Hebrew, but also why I have no direct recollection of him, with the exception of a few incidents, until I reached ritual maturity at the age of thirteen.

In any case, my first Hebrew teacher was a young woman, in connection with whom I remember only one single thing. I was told in advance that she would come to teach me, and when I heard the doorbell ring, and then heard her talking to Mother in the entrance hall, I quickly hid under a table in the nursery. Then Mother and the teacher came in, and Mother literally had to pull me out from under the table. She warned me to behave, but I nevertheless dared to put up some resistance, as a result of which the lady Hebrew teacher lasted only a short while. However, Father's conviction that I must learn Hebrew was too strong for me to buck. The lady teacher was replaced by a man, better able to cope with an unwilling pupil. I still remember his name, Moses Wachsberger, because in later years I would meet him on and off. He was the author of a Hebrew-language textbook in Hungarian, and one of the well-known Hebrew pedagogues in Budapest. I might add that before long I resigned myself to the inevitable, and Mr. Wachsberger had no trouble in leading me deeper and deeper into the mysteries of Hebrew.

Although the Hebrew lessons cut into my play activities, I was still able to spend most of my time in walks to the island and the zoo, under the supervision of the Fräulein; or else, without her supervision, in exploring the nooks and crannies of our apartment house. In these activities my sister and I were often joined by our second (or third?) cousins, Szonyi (Sonya) and Ada, daughters of Dr. Joseph Jacobi, our family physician, who lived, and had his office, on the second floor of our building. Szonyi was perhaps a year older than I; Ada was my sister's age. Their company stimulated me to some fool-hardy acts. To show off, I would climb over the balustrade of the loggia and stand outside it on the narrow ledge, hanging on for dear life and trying not to look down into the abyss gaping two or three floors below. Szonyi liked to eat raw green peas, and would bring along a few pods, crack them open, and offer some to all of us. Impressed by whatever an older girl did, I, too, would munch some of the hard peas, although I did not like them at all.

Under the house there was a cellar, divided by wooden partitions into twelve compartments corresponding to the number of apartments in the building. These sections served as storage bins for the coal and wood used to make fires in the kitchen range and in the large square tile stoves, one of which stood in a corner of each room. I would occasionally venture down into that netherworld, which, strangely, inspired me with much less fear than the dark corner in the hall of our own apartment. Each tenant also had a section in the attic in which old furniture, trunks, and the like were kept. This area, too, was the object of my occasional explorations. These, however, remained of necessity superficial, for each section in both the cellar and the attic had a door of its own that was always kept locked by its owner, so that all I could do was walk along the passageway and try to espy in the dim available light, through the open wooden slats of the doors, the secrets that lay behind them.

While telling about my explorations in our building let me speak briefly of another scene that I remember, although I cannot with certainty place it in my preschool years. In addition to the super, of whom I shall have to say a little more later, the house staff consisted of an under-janitress (this is the nearest I can come to translating the Hungarian *viciné*), whose task it was to clean the public areas in the building, that is, the stairs and the loggias. This woman lived with her daughter in a small room on the first floor under the main stairway. I don't remember the woman, but I do remember her daughter, who must have been about my age, but was of very small stature. I no longer know how and where, but somehow I heard about hypnosis, and I thought I would try it out on her. I see myself talking to her on one of the landings of the stairway. She wears a calf-length dress, but neither shoes nor stockings. I tell her to close her eyes and do as I say. She is willing, closes her eyes. I tell her, "Turn around." She turns around. I tell her, "Raise your arm." She raises her arm. "Take a step sideways." She does it. She follows my instructions beautifully, and I am convinced that I have the knack of hypnotism. Then I tell her, "Raise up your dress." Thereupon she opens her eyes, gives a decisive "No," and runs away. I look after her. I observe that the soles of her bare feet are black with dirt. My experiment with hypnosis is an evident failure.

The Kurländer Cousins

When casting back my memory to my preschool years, what strikes me is not so much the discontinuity and brevity of the memory-flashes separated by long intervals of absolute darkness as the seeming haphazardness of the items retained or the scenes I am able to recall after seven decades, as against the total loss of even the faintest traces of events that in my present judgment were much more important and hence would have warranted retention by the mind's secret mechanism of memory selection, but of which I know only because my mother later told me about them. I am driven to the conclusion that a child's mind (and perhaps the human mind in general) has a set of criteria of its own that, in an unconscious process, is constantly at work selecting some items for preservation while rejecting others, many others, and thus breaking up the continuous flow of impressions that a person absorbs all the time he is awake, and which are reflected in his dreams as well, into a few disparate and disjointed snapshots whose very *raison d'être*, or, rather, reason of retention, remains hidden to consciousness. Only rarely can one guess or understand why a certain event makes such a strong impression on the infant that three score and ten years later, after he has grown old, he still sees it vividly before his mind's eye.

One such understandable flash of memory, that of the excursion on my backside down three flights of steps to the rails of the electric streetcar line, has remained with me not because of the trip itself, although it was quite a feat for a one-year-old, but because of the shock of fright I sustained when, sitting there, I looked around and noticed that tall black column hovering over me at the curb in sinister, awesome majesty. This was undoubtedly the peg upon which were hung all the other details of that early adventure. I remember distinctly that years later, when I was a pupil at the elementary school, on my way to or from the school, I would occasionally glance around, half fearfully and half curiously, to see whether I could again catch a glimpse of that threatening apparition. The fact that each time I had to conclude that the ogre, or whatever it was, had gone away did not prevent me from thinking of it again and again, looking for it, and remembering that I had seen it and that it had somehow threatened me.

One of the psychologically less explicable memory-flashes of my early childhood is connected with the Feast of Purim. On that feast it was customary to let children dress up as the main characters in the story told in the biblical Book of Esther and visit relatives who, in turn, were supposed to treat them to some cookies or sweets. The costumes were, of course, based on pure fantasy, and the faces of the children, as if to emphasize that they were acting out fabulous characters, were painted lavishly. One Purim, when I could not have been more than three or four, the two children of Mother's uncle Ede came to our house, all dressed up in garish costumes, with masks on their faces. The older one, Lili, was about thirteen, her brother Bandi some two years younger. Mother received them with the customary expressions of delight, and treated them to *Homentashn* (literally, Haman's bags), the favorite Purim pastry, which consisted of prune jam and poppy seeds wrapped into triangular envelopes of dough. Lili and Bandi removed their masks in order to be able to enjoy the pastry, and I noticed that their faces were painted flaming red. Now, everything I have thus far told about the scene could be nothing more than logical reconstruction flowing from the one unquestionably authentic memory of that event. What I do remember with unmistakable clarity is my reaction when I saw my big cousins' brightly painted faces. I felt that they had done something very naughty by painting their faces red, and I wagged my finger at them admonishingly. Why should I remember such an insignificant little gesture?

While thinking of this scene, later memories of Lili and Bandi push themselves into my mind. I am now seventeen or eighteen. Lili is a pianist, the wife of Zoltán Bán, a concert manager, whose services Father used in organizing "cultural evenings" for his journal, about which I shall have more to say later. Zoltán Bán, in turn, had Lili accompany on the piano the singers who appeared in those recitals. She was an uncommonly beautiful woman, but far from being a first-rate accompanist. At one of the concerts—and this is what I see clearly before me—she accompanies Maria Basilides, the great contralto of the Budapest Opera. When the Basilides gives her the nod, she starts in the wrong key. Basilides turns to her; she stops, starts again, and again in the wrong key. The contralto now makes a right turn, steps over to Lili, bends over her shoulder, points out to her something in the notes, and then moves back to her place in front of the piano. She is smiling all the time. At the third attempt Lili gets it right. It is a painful scene, but the diva carries it off like a grande dame. In the midst of thunderous applause she takes Lili's hand and makes her take a bow together with her. I last heard about Lili in 1983. She still lived in Budapest. She was in her early or mid-eighties. Those who saw her recently told me that she was still a beautiful woman.

I have no recollection of what Lili's brother did as a young man, but I remember that in his twenties he was an amateur boxer. Once he gave me a photograph showing him in his white boxing trunks, in a typical boxer's pose, with his two hands, bulblike in their thick padded gloves, raised in front of him. He bends somewhat forward and has a glowering expression on his face. I still have this picture in one of my photo albums. Bandi owned a heavy motorcycle, I believe it was a Harley-Davidson, and once or twice he took me for a spin. He was involved in a serious accident, from which he retained a scar on his forehead. In 1944 he was deported and killed by the Nazis.

Their father Ede (Edward), my grandmother's brother, was a character. He had earned his doctorate in law, but, as far as I know, never practiced it. I remember him as he was in the late 1920s: a tall, sparse, elderly man, with a prominent nose and pronounced nostrils, grey eyes, and a permanent sneer. As a young man he had married a beautiful woman, of whom I know only that her name was Malvin, who, by the time I knew him, had divorced him. Lili evidently inherited her looks from her. They lived for a while in Nagyvárad (today Oradea Mare in Rumania), where his parents lived, and where, as my mother told me, their acquaintances nicknamed Lili and Bandi "the eaglets," in reference to the Grand Hotel Eagle, which was owned by their grandfather and of which they were the presumptive heirs. In 1927 Uncle Ede launched a small biweekly titled (in Hungarian) *Sabbath: Dr. Ede Kenéz-Kurländer's Review*, which, as evil tongues would have it, earned him a living not with what he published in it but with what he did not publish; in other words, it was what was called in Hungarian a "revolver paper." Whether this was true or not I never bothered to ascertain, being satisfied with the fact that Uncle Ede was loyal to my family and, on a few occasions, gave even me favorable mention. Thus when my long article on the history of the Jews in Hungary appeared in the *Jüdisches Lexikon*, Uncle Ede published a brief but very laudatory review of it, written by another uncle of mine, Dr. Ernő Molnár, husband of my mother's sister Dóra (*Szombat*, December 20, 1930).

Two months later (February 18, 1931, issue) Uncle Ede himself gave me the honor of devoting a note to me in his column "I Read—I Don't Read," which he used for ruthless criticism of unwelcome phenomena in Jewish life. Under the heading "I Don't Read" he pointed out that a recent article in *Egyenlőség* (Equality), the anti-Zionist Jewish weekly with which my father had a long-standing feud,

> enumerated the Hungarian students presently at the Breslau Rabbinical Seminary. And, wonder of wonders, I don't read among them the name of George Patai, although he has just now published a Hebrew study that was received with great acclaim not only in Breslau in the circle of his teachers, but also in Budapest. Why was he omitted? It is not difficult to explain. George Patai is the son of Joseph Patai, editor-in-chief of *Mult és Jövő*. Even though the *Egyenlőség* only recently went to bat for the explanation of Uncle Donath according to which the [biblical phrase] *poked avon ovaus al bonim* does not mean "He avenges the sins of the fathers on the sons," but "he takes into consideration. . . ." Well, the *Egyenlőség* really did take them into consideration. . . .

Only those who were in the know understood that this note accused the editor of *Egyenlőség* of having omitted my name from among the Hungarian students attending the Breslau Seminary in order to hurt my father. Incidentally, Uncle Ede was guilty of an inaccuracy and of a journalistic invention. I published at that time no Hebrew study, but only the article in German on the history of the Jews of Hungary. And, to the best of my knowledge, nowhere was that article received "with great acclaim."

As for Uncle Donath mentioned in the note, he was Benjamin Donath, seventy-three years old at the time, an autodidact philologist, who in those years created quite a stir by "proving" that the phrase mentioned (see Exodus 20:5) meant, contrary to the current translations, that God takes into consideration the sins of the fathers when He judges the sons, in the sense that He regards the former as a mitigating circumstance, because if a son grows up in the house of a sinful father, he inevitably is influenced by what he sees there, and thus has less of a chance to become an honest, upright man. Uncle Donath was totally obsessed with the mission of removing this blemish from the face of the Jewish God, presented his views to the Vatican, and demanded that in the new Latin translation of the Bible that was being prepared at that time by the Roman Curia the text should be changed accordingly.

Grandfather's Tales

But I have allowed myself to be enticed into speaking of things that were to take place many years after my early childhood, which is the subject of this chapter. To return to those years, there is one more incident I remember from my preschool days. It is my painful run-in with a boy of about my own age who lived with his parents on our floor. From the entrance to our apartment to that of this boy—his name and everything else about him have long since escaped me—ran a long and narrow balcony that formed a right angle with the wider loggia that connected the staircase with our entrance door. It was on this balcony that the encounter between us took place. I see him standing near the entrance door to his apartment, and myself near our own door, at a distance of several yards from him. He holds a long whisk broom in his hands, while I have nothing in mine. Some exchange of words takes place between us. He flings taunts and insults at me. I get enraged and begin to walk toward him with the intention of teaching him a lesson, but as I reach a distance of perhaps six feet from him he raises the broom with both hands and lets it drop on my head. Despite the numbing pain, I manage to take another step or two toward him, determined to have my revenge, but after a second I cannot help bursting into tears. Crying means complete loss of self control, and all I am able to do is turn around and run sobbing to Mother for help and comfort.

I have a vague recollection that the same incident took place several times, at any rate more than once. Peculiarly, all my early childhood memories, with the exception of the very first one, cover incidents that occurred repeatedly. Perhaps it is precisely their repetitiousness that reinforced the impression they left in my mind to the extent of enabling me to remember them today, seventy years later.

In addition to the rage and the frustration that my defeat by the neighbor's boy caused me, I also remember the disappointment I felt with my mother over her reaction to my distress. I expected her to go over to the neighbors and administer a good thrashing to the boy who dealt so basely with her son. Once, I remember, she actually did go over, trailing me after her, but all she did was to talk to the boy's mother. Seeing that there was no justice in the adults' world, I resolved to take bloody revenge myself on that unspeakable kid as soon as I was big enough to be able to tackle him. Soon, however, his family moved away, and a couple of elderly women moved into their place. Although my tormentor thus disappeared from the horizon, years later I still hoped that one day I would meet him in the street, would, of course, have no problem in recognizing him, and would administer severe but just retribution.

When I was about five or six years old, my grandfather who lived next door to us used to entertain my sister and me with Hungarian and Jewish folktales that he himself must have picked up in his childhood. A favorite figure of Hungarian Jewish folklore was Yosele Tégláser, better known as Yosele Kakas. Yosele is the diminutive of the Hebrew name Yosef (Joseph), the surname Tégláser indicates that he was from a locality called Téglás, while Kakas means cock in Hungarian. Kakas evidently was not Yosele's family name— for how could a Jew have had such a racy Hungarian name?—but an epithet given to him by the Jews who enjoyed telling stories about him and listening to the tales of his exploits.

It seems that Yosele was a man of extraordinary strength, a modern Samson. To my regret, at the age of five or six I was not yet a folklorist, and thus made no effort to record the stories Grandfather told us about Yosele, or even to retain their details in my memory. I remember only two episodes, and even these only in bare outline. Once, it seems, Yosele was challenged to break twenty panes of glass at one stroke. He stood the panes up vertically, stacking them tightly one next to the other and leaning them slightly against a wall. Then he stepped away, to a distance of several yards, fished out a *forint* (florin) from his pocket, and hurled the coin against the glass. The bystanders did not at first understand what had happened, but then they saw that the coin went clean through all the twenty glass panes and remained embedded in the wall. This was a feat of strength bordering on the miraculous.

The second story concerned Yosele's death. One day his enemies taunted him, and, pointing at a huge barrel whose cover was tightly nailed down, said to him: "Look, here is this barrel full of lead. We bet you cannot lift it." Yosele looked at the barrel for a moment, then, summoning all his enormous strength, bent down to heave it from the ground. But his enemies had played a mean trick on him: the barrel was empty. Thus all the power Yosele prepared to pick up the barrel found no resistance and no outlet. The barrel shot up into the air, and Yosele fell dead, killed by the energy that, since it could not be expended, turned inward and destroyed him. I may add that many years later Avigdor Hameiri, the Israeli Hebrew poet and novelist, who in his youth had been a disciple of my father in Hungary, wrote up the adventures of Yosele Kakas in a long folk-epic, which, however, I have so far not been able to see.

Grandfather's other favorite folk-hero was *Dávid cigány*, that is, Gypsy David. Gypsy David was a cesspool cleaner. Grandfather described to us with visible enjoyment how, when Gypsy David was called to clean out the night soil from a big cesspit, he would undress down to his underpants, and then jump straight into the pit and go to work, singing all the time, "O how good it is in this pit!" When he was finished, he washed as thoroughly as he could, and then doused himself with a full bottle of eau de cologne to get rid of, or mask, the lingering foul smell. One day Gypsy David did something wrong—I am sure Grandfather described in detail what he did, but I cannot remember it—whereupon the people got hold of him, pulled off his pants, and gave him a thorough thrashing. But Gypsy David was too proud to let them know that they hurt him, and so in desperation he sang as loudly as he could, "O how good it is on the bum! O how good it is on the bum!" For "bum" Grandfather used the Hungarian children's term *popsi*. This story impressed my sister and me greatly, and when Grandfather finished telling it, we went to bed in considerable hilarity, which remained with us the next morning. When we awoke, at a rather early hour, my sister and I climbed on the table in the middle of the nursery, and began to cry out in a loud singsong, "O how good it is on the bum! O how good it is on the bum!" We carried on like this for a while, when suddenly the door opened, and through it stormed Father, dressed in an ankle-length nightgown; without as much as a word he administered a good beating, first on my bum and then on my sister's. Then he said, "And now be quiet!" and went back to his bedroom. I remained hurt by the injustice in this world: all we did was to repeat the very words Grandfather told us the night before, and, lo and behold, we get thrashed for it!

My respect for my father, then and later as well, was so great that on the very rare occasions, such as the one recounted above, when he administered physical punishment, and even when I knew that he was approaching me with the intention of doing so, I stood still and waited passively while the inevitable overtook me. The spanking was always mild, consisting of nothing worse than a few claps with his open palm on my buttocks. Only once, as far as I can remember, did he lose control, and in his anger threw a chair at me. That must have happened much later, and I must have been guilty of a very serious offense to outrage him to such an extent.

Although I respected and even feared my father, I also had complete, absolute trust in him. He was for me like a rock, the foundation on which I could always rely, come what may. He could do no wrong, even inadvertently. I remember an incident that either created or confirmed this feeling in me. Father taught me how to skate, and in the winter months he occasionally took me to the skating rink. I would hold on to him, and, compared to my wobbly floundering, his stately, solid way of gliding over the ice seemed to me like security itself. I used to fall often, and once, as I fell and flung my hands down on the ice, one of Father's skates went over my fingers. I felt their pressure, but he must have noticed in the nick of time what was happening, for he was able to raise his skate just enough to glide over my hand without hurting it. While I got up I thought, "This is my Daddy! Anybody else would surely have cut my fingers straight off!"

I did not stand in the same awe of Mother, whom I loved dearly, certainly more than I loved Father, and with whom I was on much more familiar terms. When Mother wanted to punish me, I simply ran away, and I remember occasions when she chased me around the dining room table in a vain effort to catch and slap me. However, her verbal admonishments, which she administered much more frequently than Father, were effective enough, and I always heeded them, or at least resolved to heed them.

The occasion of one of the most serious dressings-down I got from Mother was an innocent comment I made once when the wife of Uncle Yóshka, Mother's cousin and our family physician, visited us. I don't know why I was present on that occasion, but after looking at her, I suddenly piped up, "Aunt Liza has a crooked mouth!" Aunt Liza rose magnificently to the occasion; she hugged me to her bosom and said, "You are absolutely right, Gyurikám." Mother sternly ordered me out of the room, and after Aunt Liza left I got an earful from her about my inexcusable rudeness.

Another occasion on which I spoke out of line was in the company of guests. When we had guests, Mother would wait in the nursery until several of them assembled, leaving their reception and entertainment to Father. Then she would make her entry, and after opening the door connecting the nursery and the living room, she would, while crossing over the threshold, turn back and say to us children, "Yes," even though we had asked no questions. Then she would step into the living room, and greet the guests. Even as a child I understood that by saying "Yes" to us at the very moment she left us to join the guests, she intended to create the impression that she had been busy with her children up to the last minute and therefore could not come in earlier to receive her guests. What psychological motivations lay behind her preference for going in to greet her guests in this belated fashion, I, of course, did not ask myself at that early age, and if I ask it today I do not know the answer. In any case, after a while, whenever my parents had guests, I waited for the moment Mother would open the door, turn back and say, "Yes," and then sweep into the living room to greet her friends. Once, after spending some time with the guests, Mother called me in to present me to them, and I, after bowing from the waist as I was taught to, suddenly was impelled to speak up and say, "Daddy plays the stock market." Mother considered this a terrible breach of etiquette. I was instantly banished to my room, and later came Mother's verbal chastisement.

A third occasion on which I did something even less excusable was when a seamstress was in our house working on some dresses for Mother. Grandmother and Aunt Dóra came in to inspect and approve the finished products, and as the seamstress was leaving, they all, one after the other, said to her, "God bless you!" I found the repetition of the same phrase tedious, and when my turn came to say good-bye to the woman, I said, "God strike you!" Before I had time to turn away, I was struck, not by God, but by Grandmother, who gave me a resounding slap in the face. She used to say about herself, "You know, Grandma has a quick hand," and she certainly proved it that time.

The only other occasion on which I remember having been slapped by Grandmother was many years later, when I was a student at the Seminary. At home we never spoke Yiddish, German being the inviolable rule, but at the Seminary I did pick up some Yiddish expressions from one or the other of my colleagues. Once, while talking to Grandmother, I used a Yiddish idiom, whereupon she slapped me and said, "Never again dare to say a Jargon word to me!" I don't remember what my reaction was at the time, whether I became aware of having done something wrong, but from today's vantage point I find it characteristic, and remarkable, that a thoroughly religious woman like my grandmother should have considered Yiddish such a base language that to be spoken to in that tongue was for her a serious affront. Characteristic, because a contempt for Yiddish was the general attitude of the majority of Hungarian Jews, whether Orthodox or Neolog, and remarkable, because Grandmother's own father, having come from Kurland in the Baltic to Transylvania, certainly had Yiddish as his mother tongue.

2

Ancestral Gleanings

As soon as I was old enough to relate to my parents and other members of my family, they, inadvertently or consciously, began to transmit to me attitudes, concepts, beliefs, and rules of behavior many of which they themselves had acquired years earlier, in their own childhood, from their forebears. This chain of transmission became stronger as I grew and as my understanding developed. When I was one year old all Mother could do for me was to take care of my bodily needs and shelter me in her bosom. At three, my grandmother thought me mature enough to be taught my first Hebrew prayer, a heritage of millennia in Judaism. At five, Father, motivated by values he himself had absorbed in his own childhood, saw to it that I begin to learn Hebrew. At the same age, my grandfather, in his desire to entertain his oldest grandchild, acquainted me with fragments of Hungarian and Jewish folklore that he must have retained from his own childhood.

This sequence of my personal experiences exemplifies the manner in which we all become products, not only of the immediate environment in which we grow up but also of the influences that molded that environment and that go back for uncounted generations. This being the case, it seems appropriate to interrupt at this point my childhood reminiscences and speak about the ancestry whose product I was, not only genetically but also intellectually and culturally. What follows in this chapter is based primarily on library research and to a lesser extent on information my parents, grandparents, and other relatives imparted to me on various occasions.

A Jew, as a rule, knows the identity of his ancestors only if they left books behind. And since, until the Jewish enlightenment of the nineteenth century, Jewish books meant, with a very few exceptions, rabbinical writings, only rabbis who were also authors left behind them their memory for their descendants to cherish. Exceptions to this rule were few and far between, and they consisted, in the first place, of communal leaders and of men who had influence in royal and princely courts, and who used their position to help and protect their communities from indignities, injustices, attacks, and persecutions, to which the Jews were only too frequently exposed in the course of their long history in the Diaspora. Characteristically, however, in many cases the names and records of these Jewish potentates—a designation most fitting because they often wielded great power over their coreligionists—survived not so much in Jewish writings as in documents preserved in state and city archives. The earliest of my known paternal ancestors happened to belong to this exceptional category.

While from a long-range historical-secular perspective my father's ancestry was more prominent than that of my mother, both Father and Mother knew much more of her rabbinic forebears than of his ancestors who were communal leaders. That Father's line of descent went back to the Mendel Thebens of Pressburg, and through them to the fifteenth-century Jewish prefects of the Mendel family, was unknown not only to Mother but also to Father, who never took much interest in the history of the Jews in Hungary in general and that of his own family in particular. I myself discovered this long paternal family line only very recently, when I began to think of including a family history in my memoirs.

On the other hand, I learned while still a child that my maternal grandfather, R. Moshe (Mór) Ehrenfeld, was a descendant of the "Khasam Sayfer" (as he himself pronounced the name of his illustrious ancestor), and of Rabbi Akiba Eger, who were the greatest talmudic luminaries of their age. Over my maternal grandfather's desk there hung a row of small framed portraits—partly photographs and partly reproductions of hand drawings—of ten or twelve of his famous ancestors, including those two, as well as his own father, grandfather, uncles, great uncles, and so forth. Inevitably, I asked at an early age who those forbidding-looking men were, all with flowing beards, and some with large fur hats, and was duly instructed as to their identities and my grandfather's relationship to them. As against this, of Father's ancestors I knew only his father, and even my father himself, I believe, knew only the identity of his two grandfathers. The Jewish custom in Hungary was to give children two sets of names: one or more Hungarian names, which were entered into the municipal birth register and then appeared in all official personal documents, and one or more Hebrew names, which were used only in an inner-Jewish context, especially in the synagogue. The Hebrew given names were invariably those of recently deceased ancestors. If, when a boy child was born, one of his two grandfathers was dead, it was *de rigueur* to give him the name of that dead grandfather. If both of his grandfathers were alive, the choice had to be among the names of his four great-grandfathers, with the paternal line given preference.

The Hungarian names given to me were Ervin György (Erwin George), and as long as I lived in Hungary I was called Gyuri, a diminutive of György. I remember being worried as a small child about this name: Gyuri was clearly a child's name, and I could not imagine how I could be called by this name once I grew up. Raphael, the Hebrew name I was given, was that of my mother's mother's father, whose full name was Raphael Kurländer. My sister, who was born just after Mother's maternal grandmother had died, was called after her Sarah, and in Hungarian Éva. My brother was given the Hungarian names Gusztáv Frigyes (Gustav Frederick), and the Hebrew name Shaul (Saul), after Mother's father's father, Rabbi Shaul Ehrenfeld of Szikszó. The very fact that all three of us were given Hebrew names borne by Mother's ancestors speaks volumes of the difference in *yiḥes* (prestigious descent) between Mother's and Father's ancestry.

My Father's Ancestors

The earliest ancestors to whom I can trace my descent on Father's side consist of the Mendel family, which in the fifteenth and sixteenth centuries filled in Hungary the position of *prefectus Judeorum universalium*, or prefect of all the Jews, an office not unlike that of the *Resh G'luta*, or exilarch, in Babylonia that had come to an end some two centuries earlier. The first incumbent of this office of the chieftainship of all Jews in Hungary was Judah Mendel, referred to in a contemporary document as *Menndl Jud*, who in 1476 led the Jewish delegation paying respects to Matthias Corvinus (r. 1458–1490), the great Renaissance King of Hungary. In that year Matthias and his fiancée Beatrix came to Buda to celebrate their wedding, and the first to greet the royal retinue outside the gates of the fortified city were the Jews. The chronicler Johann Seybold describes the scene:

> At the head of the Jews rode their aged chief on horseback, with a drawn sword from which was suspended a basket containing ten pounds of silver. Next to him rode his son, likewise with a sword and a silver basket. They were followed by twenty-four horsemen, all in purple full dress, with three ostrich feathers on their heads. After them came two hundred Jews on foot, with a red flag embroidered with a five-clawed owl's foot, with two golden stars under it, and surmounted by a golden tiara. All of them had the *ephod* [i.e., tallith, or prayer shawl] on their heads. The elders stood in the middle under a canopy, the young ones around them. When the king approached, they took a Tora-scroll to the queen, singing aloud, and broke into great jubilation. . . . They possibly did this because they expected no small profit from it.[1]

After Judah Mendel, the office of *prefectus Judeorum* remained in his family, passing from father to son for five generations, until it was abolished under Ferdinand I. The following list shows the succession and the dates of incumbency of these dignitaries, to whom a French ambassador to Hungary referred as *princes des juifz*:[2]

Judah Mendel (1460?–1482)
Jacob Mendel I (1482–1502)
Jacob Judah Mendel (1502–1512)
Jacob Mendel II (1512–1523)
Israel Mendel (1523–1526)
Isaac Mendel (1526–?)[3]

In addition to the above, another son of Jacob Mendel II, by the name of Tobias Mendel, is mentioned in an official document dated May 18, 1531, as the prefect of the Jews.[4]

The Mendels figure in a large number of royal rescripts and other documents in which the incumbent prefect is called *prefectus Judeorum nostrorum* (prefect of our Jews), or *princeps Judeorum* (principal of the Jews), or *prefectus Judeorum regni nostri* (prefect of the Jews of our kingdom). In a 1520 document Jacob Mendel II undertakes in the name of all the Jews of Hungary to pay the Palatine of the kingdom of Hungary, Stephanus Báthory, a lifelong tribute of 400 florins annually in exchange for his protection, and writes, *Nos Jacobus Mandel prefectus ceterique primates et Universitas Judeorum in hoc Regno Hungarie constitutorum et commorantium* (We the prefect Jacob Mandel and the other leaders of the entire community of the Jews who are settled and sojourning anywhere in this kingdom of Hungary). On the cover of the same document he is referred to as *Jacobus Mandel Supremus Judeorum* (Jacob Mandel chief of the Jews).[5]

What were the duties and the rights or privileges of the Jewish prefect? He represented the interests of both the king and the Jews. He was responsible for collecting the Jew-tax, which amounted to several thousand (according to one source 20,000) gold ducats. Responsibility for this huge amount was allocated by the Jews themselves among individual householders, and if there were complaints about it, the prefect of the Jews had to adjudicate them. Since the Jews were considered property of the Crown, their prefect was an officer of the Crown. As such, he had direct access to the king, to whom he reported about current affairs, and from whom he received his instructions. He had to be available to the king at all times, and therefore as a rule lived in Buda, the royal capital.

The king, on his part, was interested in securing the cooperation of both Jews and Christians with the Jewish prefect in order to enable him to fulfill his assigned tasks, and to make sure that there was no hitch in the collection of the taxes. Therefore the king often ordered the local authorities to obey the Jewish prefect. As a mark of his leading position, the Jewish prefect and members of his family were exempt from wearing the Jewish badge. The king made sure that this privilege of his Jewish prefect was honored abroad as well, whenever the prefect had to leave the country in pursuance of the kingdom's affairs. On festive occasions, such as coronation ceremonies, the Jewish prefect appeared at the head of a troop of horsemen, clad in fine armor. A German chronicler, describing the coronation of Ulászló (Ladislas) II in 1490, mentions that Mendel Jude (i.e., the Jew Mendel—the reference is to Jacob Mendel I) had twenty-four horsemen and such a valuable armor that nobody had ever seen anything like it.[6] A sword of the same Jacob Mendel, inscribed in Hebrew with silver inlay letters, reading "O God, the Lord, the strength of my salvation" and "Blessed be the name of the Lord" (Psalms 140:8 and 113:2) survived until the nineteenth century.[7]

The Jewish prefect had almost limitless powers over the Jews. In Buda he had at his disposal a special jail in which those Jews who disobeyed him or committed any crime, whether domiciled in Buda or in other parts of the country, were incarcerated at his order. In the same building were deposited for safekeeping the valuable objects pawned to Jews, against which they lent money. The prefect also had command of mercenary troops hired as guards by the Jews of Buda. He had deputies whom he would dispatch to various communities to see to it that his instructions and decisions were obeyed. In larger communities, such as Pressburg, he had permanent representatives.

In effect, the prefect of the Jews controlled Jewish life all over the country. The royal decrees pertaining to the Jewish communities were addressed to him, and it was his duty to see to it that they were forwarded to the communities and were obeyed. On the other hand, he represented the Jews of the country in negotiations, and signed contracts in their name. If there were disagreements within a Jewish community, he mediated them, and, if need be, settled them by decree. If, as it often happened, a conflict arose between a Jewish community and the town authorities, again he was the mediator. Even the appointment of a chief rabbi lay within the powers of the prefect. There is an extant document from before 1516 in which King Ladislas II orders all the Jews of Hungary to accept that Jewish "Pharisee" (i.e., rabbi) from abroad whom Jacob Mendel appointed, because Jacob and his predecessors were given the right to do so by Ladislas II and previous kings.[8]

Whenever Jews suffered abridgment of their rights or privileges anywhere in the country, they turned to their prefect, and he presented their claims to the king, usually orally, and in most cases obtained satisfaction. Numerous documents preserved in town archives show with what emphasis the king, after intervention by the prefect, ordered the local authorities to remedy the situation. The arguments the prefect used to convince the king of the justice of the Jews' cause varied, but in most cases they consisted of pointing out that the royal rights or the interests of the treasury would be harmed if the Jews were oppressed or made to suffer. This argument is reflected in many royal decrees: he who disturbs or hurts the Jews in their business indirectly causes damage to the treasury, because if money is extorted from the Jews or they are forced to sustain losses, they will be unable to defray their various taxes or will be able to do so only with great difficulties. Since the taxation of the Jews was totally in the hands of the prefect, he was able to use this situation for the protection of his coreligionists. If the need arose, he even threatened, and insisted on royal protection. He could, and did, intimate that if the wrongs suffered by the Jews were not remedied, they would leave the royal towns and move to the domains of a nobleman, which would mean a loss of revenue for the royal treasury.[9]

The most painful part of the prefect's job undoubtedly was to see to it that the taxes imposed upon the Jews were actually collected. The royal treasury decided upon the total amount, and the prefect, in consultation with the heads of the communities, had to allocate the sums payable by each of them. The communal leaders would come and present him with their case, and he had to find a balance among the many arguments, all of which aimed at one and the same thing: to reduce, or at least not to increase, the tax burden of their particular community. Then the prefect had to send out his tax collectors, who were helped in their difficult task by the Jewish judge of each town in conjunction with the civil authorities. It often happened that the prefect had to use force, and in some cases the recalcitrant leaders of a Jewish community had to be dragged off by the prefect's men to Buda, where they were kept by him as hostages.[10]

Not only the king but also the great nobles of the realm made use of the services of the Jewish prefect in connection with their business dealings. In 1529–1530, when George Margrave of Brandenburg, who was the uncle and guardian of the Hungarian king Louis II, planned to sell the castle and domain of Hunyad, the ancestral seat of the royal Hunyadi family, he entrusted the negotiations with the prospective buyer, Peter Perényi, the *voivod* (i.e., prince) of Transylvania, to the Jew Mendel of Buda, probably Isaac Mendel.[11] And, needless to say, the Mendels were among the major suppliers of money to the royal treasury and household, in the form of very substantial loans and credits.

The end to the office of Jewish prefect came during the reign of Ferdinand II (r. 1526–1564), emperor of the Holy Roman Empire. Ferdinand succeeded his brother-in-law, Louis II, as king of Hungary after the latter's death in the Mohács Disaster, which brought most of Hungary under the control of the Turks for some 170 years. From that time on there is a gap of a century and a half in the Mendel family history. Historical sources again appear, as far as the Mendel family is concerned, in the latter half of the seventeenth century with the appearance of a certain David Eben whose surname was Diviniensis, that is, "of Divin," Hungarian Dévény, German Theben, a town not far from Pozsony (German Pressburg; today

Bratislava, Czechoslovakia). He was the first known member of the Theben-Mendel family, which in the seventeenth and eighteenth centuries played a role in Hungarian Jewish life similar to that of the earlier Mendels in the fifteenth and sixteenth centuries, albeit on a smaller scale.[12] That David Eben of Theben was a descendant of the earlier Mendels of Buda was a family tradition. In the eighteenth century the family name of Mendel was gradually replaced by Theben, the name of the town where, it seems, they had their family seat.

The son of David Eben was Menaḥem Mendel Theben (d. 1730), a leader of the Pressburg Jewish community.[13] Menaḥem's son was Abraham Mendel Theben (d. 1768), who for forty years had the monopoly of buying the entire output of the imperial cloth factory, and thus had close relations with the Vienna court and the Austrian aristocracy. He is described in Jewish sources as *manhig ufarnas ham'dina*, leader and chief of the country, the title the Jews gave their foremost leader. He used his influence for the good of the Jews of Hungary, and intervened with Empress Maria Theresa (r. 1740–1780) on the occasion of the blood libel of Orkuta. That event bears retelling.

On June 3, 1764, a five-year-old Christian boy, named István Balla, disappeared from the village of Orkuta, in County Sáros. Two days later his naked body, with a rope around his neck, was found just outside the village. The Jews thereupon were accused of having killed the boy in order to use his blood for ritual purposes—an invariant repetition of the old ritual blood libel, against which already Josephus Flavius, the first-century C.E. Jewish historian, had to defend his coreligionists, and which was used in medieval times again and again as a pretext to persecute and kill Jews. In Hungary, the blood libel of Orkuta was neither the first nor the last of such accusations, nor were, in the course of its prosecution, more cruelties committed than in other places and at other times. But it had a special twist: witnesses were produced who testified that they had seen Hebrew letters tattooed on the body of the boy. The authorities sent troops to surround the synagogue in the neighboring village Szedikert, in which the Jews were assembled in celebration of Shavu'ot, the Feast of Weeks, and thirty of them were arrested. The judge had a life-size painting made of the murdered child's body, and sent it to Vienna to the Hungarian court chancellery. Empress Maria Theresa herself had a look at the painting, which thereafter was deposited in the National Archives.

Two months later, twenty-one of those arrested were released, while nine were indicted and retained in prison. The Jews of Szedikert sent a delegation to Pressburg to ask for the help of that influential Jewish community. Abraham Mendel Theben, its president, went to Vienna and was received in an audience by the empress, who, although consistently inimical to the Jews, was well disposed toward him and listened to his spirited defense of his people. Nevertheless, the legal proceedings continued. Several of the accused Jews converted to Christianity, whereupon they were released. Two others, Moses Josefovitch and Jacob Joseph Lefkovitch, were tortured by the notorious executioner of Eperjes for ten consecutive hours on January 25, 1765; the first survived, the second died on the rack. A few weeks later sentence was passed: it stated that the two who were tortured had received the punishment due to them; the rest were found not guilty. This, incidentally, was the last time torture was used in legal proceedings in Hungary.[14]

I don't know whether historical research could ascertain what influence, if any, Abraham Mendel Theben's intervention with the empress had on these juridical proceedings. I can only guess that the judges' awareness of the evident goodwill of the empress toward the head of the Hungarian Jews and of the audience she granted him in the matter before them could have been a moderating factor in their inquisitorial zeal.

Before passing on to a brief presentation of the life and work of Abraham's son Koppel (diminutive of Jacob), who was one of the most important *shtadlans* (interceders) of the eighteenth century, a few words are in order about a daughter of Abraham who was married to Mordekhai Eybeschuetz, son of the famous talmudist and kabbalist Jonathan Eybeschuetz (1690/95–1764), and one of the two central figures in a celebrated Shabbataian controversy. Leopold Löw (1811–1875), the great Hungarian rabbi, scholar, and religious reformer, tells about this marriage in a somewhat scornful manner: "Abraham Theben, the richest and most respected member of the Pressburg Jewish community, decided to make a fine *baḥur*, i.e., an outstanding Talmud student, happy with the hand of his daughter. Among the many suitors, of whom, of course, there was no dearth, Mordekhai Eybeschuetz was given the preference. . . . He was the son of R. Jonathan, who had thousands of pupils and whose name was celebrated all over Israel!"

1. The Mendel-Theben and Braun Genealogy

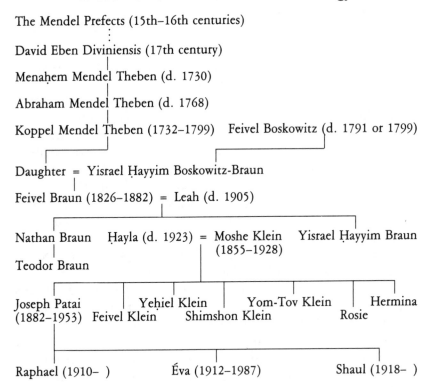

The Mendel Prefects (15th–16th centuries)

David Eben Diviniensis (17th century)

Menahem Mendel Theben (d. 1730)

Abraham Mendel Theben (d. 1768)

Koppel Mendel Theben (1732–1799)   Feivel Boskowitz (d. 1791 or 1799)

Daughter = Yisrael Hayyim Boskowitz-Braun

Feivel Braun (1826–1882) = Leah (d. 1905)

Nathan Braun   Hayla (d. 1923) = Moshe Klein   Yisrael Hayyim Braun
                                 (1855–1928)
Teodor Braun

Joseph Patai   Yehiel Klein   Yom-Tov Klein   Hermina
(1882–1953) Feivel Klein   Shimshon Klein   Rosie

Raphael (1910–)   Éva (1912–1987)   Shaul (1918–)

The wedding took place in Pressburg with all due pomp and circumstance, but before long trouble started. Young Eybeschuetz became suspected of Shabbataism, that is, of belief in the Messiahship of Shabbatai Zevi (1626–1676), whom some of his followers continued to consider the Messiah despite his patent failure to restore the throne of David in Jerusalem. Worse than that, Shabbatai Zevi in 1666 converted to Islam in order to save his life, and a group of his disciples followed him even in this act of apostasy, giving it a mystical meaning. Although Jonathan Eybeschuetz was among the Prague rabbis who in 1725 excommunicated the Shabbataian sect, later in his life, when he served as rabbi of the "Three Communities" of Altona, Hamburg, and Wandsbek, he himself was suspected of Shabbataism. This gave rise to a great public controversy between him and his chief opponent, R. Jacob Emden (1697–1776), which did not end even after Eybeschuetz's death in 1764. In its very midst, Eybeschuetz's younger son Wolf presented himself as a Shabbataian prophet, and more than a shadow of suspicion of Shabbataian sympathies fell on his elder brother Mordekhai. Despite the influence of Abraham Theben, in the spring of 1761 Samuel Sabel (Zanvil) Leidesdorfer, the president of the Pressburg Jewish community, had Mordekhai Eybeschuetz imprisoned. Eybeschuetz appealed to Empress Maria Theresa, and subsequently Leidesdorfer himself admitted that Mordekhai was innocent. Somewhat later both Mordekhai and Wolf Eybeschuetz moved to Dresden, where they founded a synagogue.[15]

Abraham's son Koppel (Jacob) Mendel Theben (born Pressburg, 1732; died Prague, 1799) joined his father in the firm that thereafter became known as Abraham Koppel Mendel. In 1773 he became president of the Jewish community of Pressburg, and a spokesman of the Jews of Hungary as a whole. But he was more than the run-of-the-mill *shtadlan*, Jewish interceder in high places. He used his position and fortune to help the Jews in every way he could. Thus, for instance, he used his own money to support hundreds of Jews who were forced to flee from various parts of Hungary. When Emperor Joseph II (r. 1780–1790), who intended to modernize and secularize the Jews of his realm, issued a decree prohibiting the wearing of beards, Koppel made use of his influence to achieve its repeal (on April 28, 1783). When the bridge toll was made twice as high for the Jews as it was for Gentiles, Koppel bought the total bridge revenues for a considerable amount, and then reduced the humiliating extra toll. On the occasion of the coronation of Leopold II (1791), Koppel led the Jewish delegation to Pressburg, and the king awarded him a gold medal weighing sixteen ducats.[16]

But over and above these measures, which were well along the beaten path followed by the usual *shtadlan*, Koppel conceived an idea that in his days was unheard of and that had to wait for more than a century before it could be realized. He dreamt of, and made efforts to achieve, equal rights for the Jews. It was this aspect of Koppel's work that interested me while I was a senior in Budapest to the extent of doing research and writing an article about him on the occasion of his 200th birthday. My essay, written in German, was published in several papers.[17] In it I dramatized Koppel's audience with Emperor Francis I (r. 1792–1835), which seems to have brought about, or hastened, the *shtadlan*'s demise. In 1799 Koppel appeared before the emperor bearing a gift of 21,000 gold ducats, entrusted to him by the Jews of Hungary, in order to lend weight to their request that the emperor graciously refrain from repealing their old exemption from military duty. But, instead of putting this humble request before the emperor, Koppel had the temerity to ask that His Majesty grant equal rights to the Jews. If the Jews, Koppel argued, were fit to serve in His Majesty's army like his other subjects, they should also be allowed to enjoy the rights His Majesty's subjects had. Koppel, who had fasted all day long before the audience, got so carried away by his emotions that, in his impassioned plea, he could not refrain from raising his voice.

According to the account of this audience given by Ignaz Reich, it took place in 1795 (not in 1799), and in it Koppel lost self-control to the extent of being unable to refrain from uttering what was in his mind and saying to the emperor, "One thing I can tell Your Majesty in all humility: until now no oppressor of the Jews came to a good end: thus Pharaoh, Nebuchadnezzar, Haman, Titus, and . . ."[18]

At this point the excitement was too much for Koppel Theben. He lost consciousness, and fell flat on his face. The attendants present quickly carried him out, and had him taken home. And, barely an hour later, an imperial messenger brought him the decision of His Majesty: the Jews were to continue to be exempt from military duty.

The community considered this outcome of the audience a great victory, but for Koppel Theben it was the most bitter defeat of his life. Something in him broke; he suffered a stroke, and was taken, at his doctor's advice, to Karlsbad for a cure. But his condition deteriorated while on the way, and he died in Prague. My article concludes: "He was the first who felt the breath of freedom, the first in whom the thought germinated, the first who dared not only to yearn but also to act. He took up the fight against the stiff resistance of the old regime, and implanted into the Jewish soul the hope and the expectation of freedom. His is the undying merit of having paved the way, and his is the eternal tragedy of the paver of the way."[19]

According to my great-uncle, R. Yisrael Hayyim Braun (he was the brother of my paternal grandmother), his grandfather, R. Yisrael Hayyim Boskowitz-Braun, married a daughter of Koppel Theben. This earlier Yisrael Hayyim was the son of R. Feivel Boskowitz, who was rabbi in the city of Gyöngyös, Hungary, in the late eighteenth century. A son of R. Yisrael Hayyim Boskowitz-Braun was Feivel Braun (1826–1882), among whose children was Hayla (d. 1923), my paternal grandmother, who became the wife of R. Moshe Klein (d. 1928), my paternal grandfather.[20]

About my paternal grandparents R. Yisrael Hayyim Braun has this to say: "[R. Feivel Braun] gave his daughter, my sister . . . Hayla, in marriage to the famous scholar, the man of great piety, who performs works of charity, etc., R. Moshe Klein of Gyöngyöspata, near the holy community of Gyöngyös."

About his own mother, Leah (my great-grandmother), he writes: "My mother, my teacher, the saintly one, the talent of whose acts who can tell, the Mistress Leah . . . who for about twelve years sat fasting every Monday and Thursday for her sons, my brothers—may they live long, the dear ones and the pleasant ones, all are equal in goodness and excel in wisdom and piety—that they be saved from eating nonkosher food, and her lips were [engaged] in prayer and supplication for her offspring. Amen."

About his father, Feivel, he says that "he shed tears like a river in his prayers, and fasted many many fasts. . . . "

After the death of my grandmother, his sister, he eulogized her in the preface of another of his books:

> Just as I was to send this book to the printer, the news reached me that my dear sister, the saintly, modest, and lovely one, the wreath of all the qualities, the honest and upright, the crown of her husband and the glory of her family, etc., the Mistress Hayla Klein, peace be upon her, ascended suddenly to the House of our Father, to heaven, on the 19th of Adar, 1923, in the holy community of Szatmár. Woe for those who are lost and are found no more. Splendor is her garment, and she laughs at the Last Day. My words are broken, and my sayings are moved, when I try to describe even a small part of her piety and the ability of her heart. May her soul be bound in the bundle of life.[21]

Rarely has an old man eulogized his sister in more moving words. Of my father's paternal grandfather I could discover very little. His name was Hayyim David Klein, and he lived in the town of Eszeny, on the banks of the upper reaches of the Tisza, the second largest river of Hungary, which cuts through the country from north to south. Once, shortly before he left Hungary for Palestine, Father visited that town, and there, in the Jewish cemetery, he found the tombstone of his grandfather, which carried the following Hebrew inscription: "Man of God, rich in deeds, he loved to gather, he sat in fasting, upright, feared sin. He enjoyed the labor of his hands, in purity of hands. He made himself strong like a lion to immerse himself under the ice. He drew forth and gave his sons the word of the Lord to drink, spurred them on always to stand at the threshold of the Tora of God. Our master, the saintly rabbi Ḥayyim David, son of our master the rabbi Joseph of blessed memory."

The whole inscription, like R. Yisrael Ḥayyim Braun's eulogy of his sister, is typical of the old-fashioned "Musive" style of Hebrew in which practically every phrase is a quotation from a biblical passage without whose knowledge the text can barely be understood. Thus the phrase "he loved to gather" echoes the many biblical passages in which God promises that He will gather the exiles of His people. In the phrase "always to stand at the threshold" there is a reference to Psalm 84:11, "I had rather stand at the threshold of the House of my God than dwell in the tents of wickedness."

As for immersion under the ice (evidently in the river Tisza), to perform a series of daily immersions, irrespective of the weather, was considered an act of great piety among certain Hasidic Jews. Father told me that he was told by his father that in the winter R. Ḥayyim David took an axe, went to the river, cut a hole in the ice, and submerged. To do this, he certainly had to make himself strong like a lion.

Father reprinted this gravestone inscription in the original Hebrew as a footnote to a poem he wrote about his grandfather. The poem is titled (in Hungarian) "My Grandfather on the Bank of the Tisza," and it tells about Ḥayyim David Klein a number of details that must have been part of the family tradition. It seems that he participated in the Hungarian revolutionary war of 1848, paid taxes in 1875, worked the land, made vinegar, and lived throughout his life in that same town of Eszeny. Father also mentions that the name of his grandmother was Leah.[22]

Of my paternal grandfather, R. Moshe Klein, I knew for a long time only what Father wrote in his small book *The Middle Gate: The Life of a Small Boy and a Big Book*, which he published in Hungarian in 1927, and which subsequently also appeared in German in installments in the Berlin *Jüdische Rundschau*, and finally in Hebrew in Father's own translation. In that book Father gives a highly romanticized, idyllic picture of his life as a child of six in the house of his parents in the village of Pata, some six miles from the city of Gyöngyös, capital of County Heves in Hungary. His parents made their livelihood from a small general store that occupied the front room in their house and was minded mostly by Grandmother, while Grandfather sat in a back room and studied the Talmud. There were some five or six Jewish families in the village, and they employed a *melamed* (teacher), who taught their children to read and write Hebrew, to recite the prayers, to translate into Yiddish the five books of Moses with the commentary of Rashi, and, at a more advanced stage, to find their way in the less difficult parts of the Talmud. The children gathered in a room in the *melamed's* house, and spent their day there from early morning until evening. Such rudimentary one-room schools went under the name *ḥeder* (literally, room) in all the East European Jewish communities. When Father was four he started to go to the *ḥeder*, and when he was six he started to study the tractate *Bava Metzia* (Middle Gate) of the Babylonian Talmud — whence the title of his autobiographical book.

If one reads that book critically, it appears that, despite the highly idealized picture it gives of the small boy's life in the bosom of his family and the *ḥeder*, Grandfather must have been a strict and hard taskmaster. This impression is created, first of all, by the fact that Father says in the whole book almost nothing about the relationship between him and his father. One of the very few things he tells about his father is that he was a "Hebraist and a talmudic scholar," and that it was his father who taught him to read Hebrew when he was three years old. Once Yosele (as he was called by his parents) knew how to read, he had to read aloud the daily prayers, while his father listened from the store, and if he caught the child skipping a word or not pronouncing it clearly, he cried, *"Gehüpert!* [Skipped!] Pay attention!"

On another occasion he describes how his father presided over the baking of the *matzot*, the unleavened bread, for Passover.

> I was filled with a peculiar pride when I saw my father sitting in front of the oven. The erupting flames lent a peculiar shine to his eyes, forehead, beard, whole face. I somehow felt that he was doing a most dangerous job, when, with outstretched arms, holding a thin wooden rod, he reached into the depths of the oven, put in the *matzot*, turned them, patted them down, and then took them up and out. I admired each of his movements as if he were a biblical miraculous Abraham who escaped from the fiery furnace of the Chaldeans. And yet, my father encompassed everything with one glance, and in a stentorian voice ordered about the other *bale batim* (householders) — becoming greatly enraged if he found that something was not in order. [23]

Sabbath afternoons, to keep track of his progress in his studies, Grandfather would examine him: "Yosele," he would call, "bring here the *Gemore* [Talmud]! What did you learn this week?" These few references to his relationship with his father are the only ones contained in Father's childhood reminiscences, and they all show his father in a censorious role.

About his mother he has much more to say, and what he says is suffused with warmth:

> My mother did not play the piano, did not strum the guitar, did not wear Biedermeier dresses, and did not read Goethe and Schiller. Still, to this day I have not known a more cultured woman. Like a veritable scholar, she explained the holy books, not only to us children, but also to the women who would gather around her, coming to her as to some miracle-working rabbi. She had a ready answer to everything, from the Bible, the Midrash, the *Kav haYashar* or the *Sefer haMussar*, or simply from *Seforim*, "books," which she would thus quote, without a title. She had sovereign mastery over a great and many-sided literature, a literature whose language is difficult of access, but whose contents are full of life, of wise and valuable vital relationships. We children liked the *Tzene Rene* most. This, too, is a book, and one of the best, to boot. Full of legends, full of fantasy, and full of beautiful teachings. When, on Sabbath afternoons, while my father napped—for "sleep on the Sabbath is a pleasure"—my good mother took me on her lap and read from the *Tzene Rene*, or told a tale without a book, I was the most happy child in the world.[24]

A note is in place here on the three books Father mentions as the favorites of his mother. *Kav haYashar* (The Measure of Righteousness), written in Hebrew and then translated into Yiddish by Zevi Hirsch Koidonover (d. 1712), a Polish rabbi and ethical writer, was first published in 1705. It reflects the vigorous and mystical spirit of Polish Jewry, and is full of wondrous tales depicting the rewards of the righteous and the punishment of the wicked.

As for the *Sefer haMussar*, I think Father made a mistake, and that the book liked by my grandmother must have been the *Sefer haMaggid* (Book of the Preacher), a Yiddish translation of the Prophets and the Hagiographa, with a paraphrase of Rashi's commentary, similar in nature to the *Tzene Rene* (see below), to whose author it was mistakenly attributed. It is highly unlikely that my grandmother was able to read a Hebrew philosophical book like the *Sefer haMussar* (Book of Ethics), which was written by the Provençal Jewish philosopher Joseph ben Kaspi (1279–1340) in the form of an ethical will.

Finally, the book whose title was popularly pronounced *Tzene Rene* (literally, *Tz'ena uR'ena*, meaning "Go forth and see," an abridged quotation from the Song of Songs 3:11) is an exegetical Yiddish rendering of topics or passages from the Five Books of Moses, the Haftarot, and the Scrolls, composed by Jacob ben Isaac Ashkenazi in the late sixteenth century. It became the greatest favorite among the East European pious Jewish women who could read only Yiddish.

From the fact that the only words Father remembered or mentioned as having been uttered by his father were words of command or reproach I suspect that my grandfather was a grouch and a Tartar. But Father never volunteered any information about his childhood, and his overt attitude to his father, as far as I could gather from the rare occasions on which he referred to him, was one of respect and love, so that in my youth I never became aware of the true character of my grandfather, and believed that he was as much a loving father to his sons as my father was to me.

Years later, I got a very different picture of the personality of my grandfather and of his attitude to his children from my uncle Philip (Feivel) Klein in New York. Reb Feivel, as I used to call him, was just about a year younger than Father, who was the oldest son. There had been an older sister, but she died in early childhood, as mentioned in Father's book. Overtly, Reb Feivel had the same admiring and respectful attitude to Grandfather as Father. But one did not have to use critical acumen to understand from Reb Feivel's stories that Grandfather was nothing less than a tyrant who ruled harshly over his children, and whose religious rigor was matched only by his unbending educational principles. My uncle Feivel remained to his death a simple, unsophisticated religious Jew, and when he described to me revealing scenes from his childhood he was totally unaware that they showed his father in a rather unfavorable light.

When he was about four and Father five, Reb Feivel told me, they would go to the *heder* together every morning. In the winter, while it was still pitch dark, Grandfather, who had been up for hours studying the Talmud, would call out, "Yosele, Feivel, *oyfshtayn* [get up]!" And woe to the child who was not out of bed by the time the last word of the brief alert was pronounced. When they were ready to go, Father, being older, was given a paraffin lamp to enable them to find their way in the dark. Once, Reb Feivel remembered, there was such heavy snowfall during the night that the children, when they reached the brook that they had to cross to get to the *ḥeder*, could not find the plank leading from one bank to the other, and fell into the water. There was but a thin layer of ice under the snow, and the children, of course, broke through it as they fell; the water was not deep, so that all that happened was that they got thoroughly wet. But the lamp went out, so they groped their way back home. Grandmother made them take off their wet clothes, dried off their bodies, and gave them a new set of clothes. In the meantime Grandfather dried the lamp, adjusted the wick, lit it, then gave it back to Yosele, and sent them off again. However, the same mishap occurred a second time. This time, after the children were provided with yet another change of clothes, Grandfather himself took the lamp in one hand and a shovel in the other, and went out with the children. When they reached the brook, he bid Yosele hold the lamp high, and went to work with the shovel to clear away the snow from the plank. When he finished, he said to the children, "Now go to the *ḥeder*!"

Father, too, remembered something of such incidents, but he sugarcoated them in his book:

> The two tractates, *Bovo Kammo* (The First Gate) and *Bovo Metzio* (The Middle Gate) of the Talmud were bound together, and it was quite a physical effort to carry the big and heavy folio from home to the *ḥeder*. True, the distance was not great, especially if instead of going around the mill we made a little turn and crossed the brook, over which a narrow plank led to the other bank. We, of course, always chose the forbidden and "dangerous" route, and, to be sure, it would happen that the heavy Talmud folio upset the balance and we fell into the brook. However, even that was no major mishap. The water was only knee deep, and we could easily wade out of it. And, anyway, after Passover every regular child already went barefoot. . . . [25]

Another incident, of which my uncle Feivel told me, had to do with a herring, and its victim was Yeḥiel ("Ḥile"), the third-oldest son of my grandparents. In poor households herring was a staple and appeared frequently on the dinner table. But Ḥile, unfortunately, could not stand herring, while Feivel loved it. Feivel's assigned task in the house every evening was to clean the boots of all members of the family, which was no easy job considering the amount of mud that covered the streets of the village whenever it rained. So Ḥile and Feivel struck a deal: Ḥile would pass his portion of herring, surreptitiously of course, to Feivel, who would eat it with relish;

and, in exchange for this favor from Feivel, Hile would relieve Feivel of the unpleasant job of scrubbing, scraping, and cleaning the boots. For a while this arrangement worked fine, until one day Grandfather noticed what was going on. He said to Hile, "Eat your herring." Hile said, "I cannot." Grandfather repeated, "Eat your herring." Hile did not dare to disobey his father, swallowed his piece of herring, and instantly threw up. Grandfather said nothing, but next time herring was served he again ordered Hile to eat it. Hile did so, and with great difficulty managed to keep it down. The third time Grandfather did not have to say anything, only to look at Hile, to make him eat his herring. "Before long," Uncle Feivel concluded his story, "herring became a favorite of Hile, and I had to go back to cleaning the boots."

As for Father's attitude to his father, I learned a little more about it when, after Grandfather's death, Father wrote an article about him entitled "A Righteous Man Passed Away," which he published in the September 1928 issue of his monthly *Mult és Jövő* (Past and Future). In it Father mentions that his father was born in Eszeny, on the banks of the Tisza, and that in his childhood he was a pupil of Moses Schick (1805–1879), known as Maharam Schick, a famous rabbinical authority, whose yeshiva in Huszt, Hungary, attracted students from many parts of Europe. Later Grandfather studied under R. Nathan Müller of Szécsény, the author of the responsa *Avne Hoshen*, published in Paks in 1912. When R. Feivel Braun of Pata, a descendant of famous rabbis and a highly respected man in his own right, was looking for a *shiddukh* (match) for his only daughter, the *gaon* of Szécsény hired a carriage and personally took to him Moshe Klein, his most outstanding student. This is how my grandfather Klein happened to settle in Pata, where he was to spend forty years of his life.

From Father's 1928 eulogy and from his autobiographical book I also know that the house in which Father spent the first twelve years of his life, although extremely modest (when I visited it at the age of sixteen I found that it was a simple, square, whitewashed, one-story building with a thatched roof), was the center of whatever Jewish life existed in Pata. In the courtyard there was a small synagogue in which the men of the six Jewish families assembled daily for the morning prayers, and again for the afternoon-evening devotions. On the Sabbath, when it was necessary to have a *minyan* (quorum) of ten male adults in order to hold a full service with the reading of the weekly portion from the Pentateuch, the Jews of the smaller neighboring village of Szűcsi, located at a distance of a little over a mile from Pata, would walk over, and the two contingents together would constitute a *minyan*. When the Szűcsi group was espied in the distance, coming over the crest of the hill separating the two villages, somebody would announce, "The Szűcsiers are coming," and the Pataers would immediately start the service with the Sabbath songs for whose recital no quorum was required. And if, despite the arrival of the Szűcsiers, there was no quorum of ten adults, they would put a prayer book under the arm of Yosele, Reb Moyshe's oldest son, thus promoting him to an honorary adult, and counted him as a member of the *minyan*.

In Reb Moyshe's house, Father tells in his article, there was a room set aside and always ready, in case a poor wayfarer, an *ayrekh*, should turn up, even though this meant that the Klein family, blessed with many children, had to sleep in cramped quarters. Occasionally, such a visitor would stay on for several weks, but Reb Moyshe's wife patiently fed him and served him. The wayfarer, in turn, repaid the hospitality by staying up half the night and studying the Talmud with Reb Moyshe, for whom this was the greatest treat.

Reb Moyshe Klein, according to Father's reminiscences, was a modest man whose great talmudic knowledge never became known in public. He wrote many glosses and *novellae (ḥiddushim)* on the Talmud, but they remained unpublished and ultimately got lost. Being not only a talmudist but also a kabbalist, he studied the *Zohar* on the Sabbath. All his life he yearned to go to Jerusalem, and he achieved this dream only three years prior to his death. After World War I, when Hungary was seized with the anti-Semitic contagion, Reb Moyshe's house in Pata was attacked, stones were flung at its windows, and he and Grandmother Ḥayla had to flee to their son Shimson, who lived in the nearby city of Gyöngyös. Although soon thereafter their neighbors from Pata came to assure them of their friendship and to ask them to return, Reb Moyshe remained inexorable in his disillusionment with the village in which he had spent forty years of his life, and instead moved to Szatmár (Satu Mare), by then part of Rumania, to be near his beloved *tzaddiq*, the Szatmarer Rebbe.

Satu Mare proved to be Grandmother's Samarkand: she was killed there in 1923 by a team of horses that ran wild, mounted the sidewalk, crushed her, and trampled her to death. Shortly thereafter my grandfather moved to Jerusalem, to join two of his sons, Yeḥiel (Hile) and Yom-Tov (Yantev), who had been living there for several years with their families. Grandfather moved into a one-room apartment without private facilities in the *Bote Ungarn* (Hungarian Houses) of the *Me'a Sh'arim* (Hundred Gates) quarter in Jerusalem, where only extremely religious Hasidic Jews lived, most of whom even there maintained their allegiance to the Szatmarer Rebbe. Adjoining the room was a shack that was used as the kitchen. A common toilet in the courtyard served several such apartments. There was no bathroom, for which the communal *miqve* (ritual bath) substituted. Once Grandfather settled there he remarried, because, as Father later explained to me, he could not cook for himself, his pride prevented him from eating at the table of his sons, and for a Hasidic Jew it was impossible, in fact, forbidden, according to his religious rules, to have a housekeeper who would come in daily to clean and cook for him: for such an ultra-Orthodox Jew it is sinful to be alone in a room with a woman who is not his wife or first-degree relative. Therefore, Grandfather remarried, taking a simple woman of his own age and religious convictions to wife, and thus Father, in his forties, suddenly had a stepmother. He was utterly respectful and considerate of his father's new wife, and even after Grandfather's death he visited her each time he was in Jerusalem, and contributed to her living expenses until she herself passed away.

When Father received the cable from his brother Yeḥiel saying *Avinu met* (Our father died), he was in Budapest taking care of his editorial responsibilities, while we children were with Mother at a resort on the shores of Lake Balaton. During the seven days of deep mourning one is not supposed to leave the house, and, being alone at home (the maid was with us at the lake), Father had nobody to prepare meals for him. Therefore he moved over, for the duration of the *shive* (literally, *shiv'a*, i.e., seven [days of mourning]), to my uncle Berti's house, which was spacious enough to accommodate him. To visit a mourner during the *shive* is an important *mitzve* (religious duty), so Mother sent me off to Budapest—it was a train ride of about three hours—to pay Father a visit of condolence. As was (and is) customary, in addition to the male members of the family, friends and acquaintances would come twice a day to constitute a quorum, in the morning for the *shaḥarit* (morning) prayers, and again at dusk for the combined *minḥa* (afternoon) and *ma'ariv* (evening) prayers, required so the mourners can recite the kaddish (the prayer for the dead) in public. I could not stay for the prayers, for Mother insisted that I take an early afternoon train back to Lake Balaton, but somebody told me that Uncle Berti did not attend the prayers, which, for such a near relative, was considered religiously improper behavior. The reason that my uncle absented himself from the prayers, I was told, was that in the morning he had riding lessons scheduled, and in the afternoon he was still at work.

I was at the time, and have remained throughout my life, acutely uncomfortable in the presence of people just bereaved of a loved one. This feeling is the only thing I remember from that visit of condolence to my father. I must, of course, have obeyed the traditional rules of behavior, such as not greeting a mourner either coming or going, for saying "good day" or the like to a person in deep grief would be most inappropriate, and reciting instead the traditional Hebrew words, "May the Place [i.e., God] comfort you among the rest of the mourners of Zion and Jerusalem." It is remarkable, as I now come to think of it, how Jewish tradition subordinates personal bereavement to the national bereavement suffered by the people as a whole with the destruction of Jerusalem, and how comforting a mourner is tied to the hoped-for comfort God will give the mourners of Zion when He, at long last, sends them the Messiah.

The duty to perform a ritual, whether acted or spoken, is a great help in easing the tensions occasioned when a family member reaches the great stages of life: birth, puberty, marriage, sickness, death. At the time I was not yet acquainted with Van Gennep's *Rites de passage*, but I distinctly remember that having to recite that traditional saying made it easier for me to enter the room where Father sat on the floor, as the mourning ritual required, and to act as demanded by our traditions, which have the proper prescription for every human contingency. Given the restrained relationship between Father and me, it would have been quite impossible to do what I would have liked to: to sit down next to him on the floor, to embrace him, and to say to him something personal that would have expressed the pain I felt seeing my father stricken by the loss of his father. But in my imagination a picture flashed across my field of vision, and I saw myself in the future, many years thence, sitting on the floor and mourning the death of my father, which I knew inevitably would have to come sooner or later. As things stood between Father and me, the only source that gave me an inkling of how he felt when his father died was the article I mentioned above, which, when I read it, moved me to tears.

It was not until 1983 that I found out the year of birth and the marriage date of my grandfather Moshe Klein. In October of that year I was invited to give a series of lectures at Brigham Young University in Provo, Utah, and at the University of Utah in Salt Lake City. While in Provo, I met again Eldin Ricks, who, some thirty years earlier, had been a student of mine at Dropsie College in Philadelphia. He was now professor emeritus of Bible studies at BYU. With him was his wife, who, it turned out, worked several days a week as a volunteer in the Genealogical Library of the Mormon Church. She told me about the unique collection of genealogical records that library had, and said that practically any person could find there information about the birth, marriage, and death of his ancestors. My curiosity was awakened, and I told her that I would be most interested to know whether they would have any trace of my paternal grandfather, who was a simple Jewish grocer in a Hungarian village, had never published any book, and lived a totally anonymous life. She assured me that they would, and made an appointment to meet me at the library a few days later.

The library occupied several floors of the huge office building of the Church of Jesus Christ of Latter-day Saints in the center of Salt Lake City, and in its large reading room there must have been, when I arrived there, more than a hundred people searching big ledger-registers or viewing microfilms, evidently engaged in a quest similar to mine. Mrs. Ricks met me, and at her request one of the librarians produced, within a surprisingly short time, several reels that contained microfilm copies of the pages of the official birth and marriage registers of the Jewish community of Gyöngyös, the city next to which the village of Gyöngyöspata is located. Originally, it seems, the name of the village was Pata. This is how it appears in the 1880 survey map of Hungary. Later its name was changed to Gyöngyös Pata, and still later to Gyöngyöspata.

I put the films into a microfilm reader, and soon I found the entry stating that on November 1, 1879, Mór Klein, grocer, who was born in Eszeny, County Szabolcs, and was twenty-four years of age, wedded Johanna Braun, born in Gyöngyös Pata, age left blank. The wedding took place in Gyöngyös Pata, performed by surrogate rabbi Mór Raab, with József Kálmán and his wife, and Samuel Rosenfeld and his wife, as witnesses. The entry also stated that the name of the bridegroom's father was David Klein, mother's name not stated, and that the bride's parents were Fülöp Braun and Lujza Blumenthál. Thus I discovered for the first time that my grandfather was born in 1855, and was seventy-three when he died in Jerusalem in 1928.

In another microfilm reel, containing the birth register of the Jewish communities of Gyöngyös and the nearby villages, I found the entry for my father's birth. It stated that he was born in Gyöngyös Pata on January 5, 1882, was legitimate, father's name Mór Klein, mother's name Hani (this seems to be a short form for Johanna) Braun. Parents' residence: Gyöngyös Pata. Midwife's name: Borbála Kitkai; names of the godparents or witnesses: Mór Rabb (evidently a variant spelling of Raab), and Zsiga Grünfeld. Circumcision was performed on January 13, 1882, by Emánuel Rosenzweig in Gy. Pata. Borbála Kitkai is definitely not a Jewish name, and I was surprised to learn that my rigidly religious grandfather gave his consent to having a Christian midwife assist at the birth of his child, which he, of course, did only because no Jewish midwife was available. In the column "Remarks" there is an additional entry that reads: "The change of the last name of József Klein to 'Patai' was approved by order no. 11856 of the Royal Hungarian Minister of the Interior on March 14, 1904."

My Mother's Forebears

On my mother's side I am a descendant of King David. That is, if credence can be given — which I doubt — to the assertions made by several of my second and third cousins, each a recognized rabbinical authority in his own right, who wrote about our common ancestors and made this claim of Davidic descent, without, however, attempting to adduce hard data to substantiate it, or trying to draw up a family tree or a genealogical chain. Typical of these claims is the one contained in the book *K'tov Zot Zikkaron* (Write This as a Memorial) written by Avraham Sh'muel Binyamin Sofer-Schreiber and published in New York in 1957. In it the author asserts that Moses Sofer (1762–1839), to whom both he and I can trace our descent with complete accuracy, and who is the central figure in this section, was a descendant of Shim'on of Frankfurt, the thirteenth-century author of the great Hebrew Midrash-collection known as *Yalqut Shim'oni*. This Shim'on, says R. Sofer-Schreiber, was a descendant of Rashi (Rabbi Sh'lomo ben Yitzhaq, 1040–1105), who, I may add, was the greatest biblical and talmudic commentator of all times, and lived in Troyes, France. Rashi, in turn, traced his descent to R. Yohanan haSandlar (2nd century C.E.), a famous Palestinian *tanna* (Mishnaic master), who counted himself a descendant of King David.[26]

Leaving aside this claim, which cannot be substantiated and which serves as an example of the traditional rabbinical pride of descent, I shall confine myself in the following pages to my actually traceable ancestry on my mother's side, which reaches back into the sixteenth century. Even so, so much is known of so many of my maternal ancestors, who constituted several interlocking rabbinical families of great renown and prolific authorship, that I must be highly selective in speaking of them, choosing only a few for presentation, although many of them were interesting characters who would deserve at least a brief biographical sketch.

In contrast to my father's ancestors, who lived in Hungary at least since the fifteenth century, my mother's forebears came partly from Germany, partly from Poland, and partly from Kurland (today part of Latvia). Many of them, at least many of those whose memory has been preserved, were rabbis, in fact great rabbinical luminaries, who wrote many books and had many children. Official Jewish family names did not exist until the late eighteenth century, and in most cases a man was identified by his first name and patronym (e.g., Moses ben Samuel), to which was added, especially in the case of newcomers to a locality, the name of the town or place he came from. Thus my great-grandfather, after whom I was named Raphael, was known in Nagyvárad, where he arrived in his youth and lived all the rest of his life, as Raphael Kurländer because he had come from Kurland.

Nor were family names strictly adhered to and transmitted from father to son. On the contrary, they were frequently changed due to any of a number of circumstances, as we shall see. Still, my maternal ancestors can, by and large, be grouped under three names: the Egers, the Sofers, and the Ehrenfelds, and I shall treat them under these headings.

The Egers

The earliest known members of this branch of my maternal ancestors were known as Gins or Ginsman (also spelled Günz, Günzmann). A Mayer Ginsman was *shtadlan* (interceder) in Halberstadt, Germany, where he died in 1674. His son Elijah (d. 1705) adopted the surname Eger. Elijah Eger's son was Yehuda Löb Eger (d. 1750), whose son was Simḥa Bunim Eger (d. 1764). The latter's son was Akiba Eger, who was born in Halberstadt ca. 1720, and died there at the young age of thirty-eight, in 1758. To distinguish him from his grandson, also named Akiba Eger, he is usually referred to as Akiba Eger the Elder.

Akiba Eger the Elder became rabbi in Zuelz, Silesia (today Biala in southwest Poland), and then in Halberstadt. Despite his short life, he left behind important talmudic studies, among them a book of *novellae* on the Talmud and responsa titled *Mishna diRabbi Akiba* (printed in Fürth, 1781). In the last two years of his life he was head of the yeshiva in Pozsony (Pressburg), Hungary, at the very time when my paternal ancestors, the Mendel Thebens, were the secular leaders of that community and of Hungarian Jews in general.

Akiba Eger the Elder's sons became famous rabbis, and his only daughter Gitel married Moses Güns or Günz (d. 1790). Their son Akiba (1761–1837) was born in Eisenstadt, one of the "Seven Communities" of Burgenland, western Hungary, and adopted the name of his maternal grandfather Eger. To distinguish between him and the latter, he is usually referred to as Akiba Eger the Younger. His younger brother Simḥa Bunim (1770–1819) was known by both surnames, Eger and Güns, as well as by a third one, Schlesinger. The sons of Akiba Eger the Younger returned to the family name of their paternal grandfather and were known as Ginz or Genz.

Akiba Eger the Younger outshone his grandfather in talmudic learning and authorship. He wrote a large number of *novellae* on the Talmud, notes on the *Shulḥan 'Arukh*, responsa, and many other religio-legal works. He served as rabbi in Märkish Friedland in West Prussia, and then, for twenty-three years, in the important community of Posen.

For R. Akiba Eger the Younger we have something that is rare in Jewish historical documents: a description of how he looked, how he acted, how he spent his day, and even what he ate. He was, it is reported,

> small of stature, his head large in relation to his body, his nose long-ish, his eyes sending forth fiery sparks, his forehead high-arched and broad. His facial features radiated seriousness and dignity. About his lips hovered a graceful smile, often accompanied by a sweet melancholy. In general, his somewhat delicate face gave the impression of ill health, silent suffering, and a pious and patient resignation.

2. The Genealogy of Moses Günz

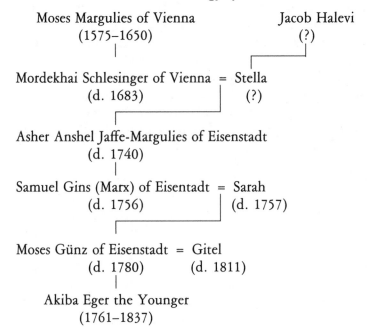

Moses Margulies of Vienna
(1575–1650)

Jacob Halevi
(?)

Mordekhai Schlesinger of Vienna = Stella
(d. 1683)   (?)

Asher Anshel Jaffe-Margulies of Eisenstadt
(d. 1740)

Samuel Gins (Marx) of Eisentadt = Sarah
(d. 1756)   (d. 1757)

Moses Günz of Eisenstadt = Gitel
(d. 1780)   (d. 1811)

Akiba Eger the Younger
(1761–1837)

For more than 25 years he went to bed at midnight and got up at 4 A.M. to study the Mishna until 6. From 6 to 7 he instructed members of his community. From 7 to 8 he recited the morning prayers. Then, from 8 to 9, he took breakfast with his family, whom otherwise he never saw all day long. His breakfast consisted of a cup of coffee without sugar. From 9 to 10 he studied the Bible, from 10 to 12 he held a collegium, and from 12 to 1 he recapitulated what he had lectured about. He never sat down to lunch; instead, a simple soup was given to him while he studied the Talmud. From 1 to 2, while resting on a sofa, he looked over, with pencil in hand, the new books that were presented him by the booksellers. At 2 he went to the *beth din* [rabbinical law court] or to a meeting of the congregation that used to take place at that time and last until 4 P.M. Returning home, he drank a small cup of wine, and immediately went out again to visit the sick and the mourners, accompanied by a servant of the *Hevra Qadisha* [Holy Society, whose main purpose consisted of visiting the sick and burying the dead]. He visited *all* mourners and all the sick without differentiating as to rank and status. In order to be able to pray also the *minha* [afternoon] prayer with the *tefillin* [phylacteries], he recited that prayer at 4 P.M., after which he lectured to some members of the community on the *Magen Avraham* [R. Abraham Gombiner's commentary on the *Shulhan 'Arukh*, the Jewish law code]. In the *ma'ariv*

3. *The Eger Genealogy*

Mayer Ginsman
(d. Halberstadt, 1674)
|
Elijah Eger
(d. Halberstadt, 1705)
|
Yehuda Löb Eger
(d. Halberstadt, 1750)
|
Simḥa Bunem Eger = Tzippora
(d. Halberstadt, 1764)
|
Akiba Eger the Elder
(b. Halberstadt ca. 1720, d. Pressburg, 1758)

Gitel = Moshe Günz (Ginz, d. 1790)
(d. 1811)

Akiba Eger the Younger = 1. Glikche; 2. Brendel (d. 1836)
(b. Eisenstadt, 1761, d. Frankfurt, 1837)

Sorel (Sarah) = Moshe (IV) Sofer
(1787–1832)   (b. Frankfurt, 1762,
              d. Pressburg, 1839)

prayer he always included a prayer for the sick. From 8 to 10 he took care of his correspondence, and then, until midnight, he "studied" [the Talmud]. Since in large congregations the poor were rarely accompanied on their last journey to the cemetery by many people, he instructed the *Hevra Qadisha* to have all burials in the morning, and to pass his *beth haMidrash* [house of study] with the coffin, and he would join the funeral procession at the head of his two- to three-hundred students. Friday afternoon he took a bath, and then took a walk until the arrival of the Sabbath. The Sabbath was the only day on which he sat down to a meal at a set table. He also functioned as a *mohel* [ritual circumciser], and thus entered thousands into the Covenant of Abraham.[27]

R. Akiba Eger the Younger struggled valiantly against the *Haskala* and the reform movement, both of which he considered a threat to traditional Judaism. The changing times, however, forced him to make at least some concessions. For instance, he countenanced the use of German instead of the traditional Yiddish as the medium of instruction in Judaism. While opposed to secular learning, when compulsory secular education for Jewish children was introduced by the Prussian authorities, he compromised and allowed one or two hours daily for that purpose. During the 1831 cholera epidemic he fearlessly cared for the sick, for which he received a royal message of thanks from Frederick Wilhelm III. He established several welfare institutions that continued to exist until World War II. He was a man of great modesty and humility, humanity and beneficence, and was universally beloved. His sons, Abraham and Solomon, and others after them, wrote his biography.

The Sofers

The first husband of Sorel (Sarah), the daughter of R. Akiba Eger the Younger, died when she was twenty-four, and left her with two small daughters. Soon thereafter she became the wife of Moshe Sofer (Moses Schreiber, 1762–1839), who himself had lost his first wife shortly before (in 1812). Moshe Sofer had no children by his first wife, who was a widow when he married her and was much older than he. He was fifty when he married Sorel, who was twenty-five years younger. Their marriage was a happy and fruitful one: it was blessed with no less than eleven children, of whom four were sons and seven daughters. The incessant childbearing—two children by the age of twenty-four and then eleven more within twenty years—took its toll on Sorel, and she died when she was forty-five, in 1832. After her death the seventy-year-old Moshe Sofer married a third time, again choosing a widow.

I was able to trace the ancestry of Moshe Sofer—disregarding the claim of Davidic descent—back seven generations to a Moshe (I) who was born in the middle of the sixteenth century, lived in Frankfurt on Main, and died there ca. 1620. His son was Shim'on (I) of Frankfurt, who died in 1656. His son was Moshe (II) of Frankfurt, who must have been born after the death of his paternal grandfather, for, as was (and still is) the custom, he was named after him. Moshe (II) died in 1688. His son was Shim'on (II), who was born in Frankfurt after the death of his paternal grandfather, and died in

1738. Shim'on (II)'s son was Moshe (III), who was born in Frankfurt after the death of his paternal grandfather Moshe (II) and was named after him. He married a daughter of R. Sh'muel Schotten haKohen, known as the "Maharshashak" from the initials of Morenu HaRav Sh'muel Schotten haKohen. R. Sh'muel Schotten was at first rabbi in Darmstadt, then *av beth din* (head of the rabbinical court) in Frankfurt, and author of the book *Kos Y'shu'ot* (Cup of Salvation), which was printed in Frankfurt in 1711. He died in 1709. Sh'muel Schotten's wife was a daughter of Yisrael Yosef Sh'muel of Cracow, who was head of the rabbinical court in Frankfurt from 1689 until his death in 1704.

Moshe (III) died in 1722 at a very young age—he must have been less than thirty-four years old, since his grandfather, after whom he was named, died in 1688. The son of Moshe (III) was Sh'muel Sofer, who was named after his maternal grandfather, since his paternal grandfather was still alive when he was born; that is, he must have been born after 1709, the year in which his maternal grandfather died. He married, in 1751, Reizel, the daughter of R. Elhanan of Frankfurt, the author of a kabbalistic prayer book. Sh'muel Sofer died in 1779, and Reizel in 1822. Their son, Moshe (IV) Sofer, born after ten years of childlessness, died in 1839.

Sh'muel Sofer was a scribe, a copyist of the Tora, termed *sofer* in Hebrew; hence his surname, which was also taken over by his son Moshe (IV), who also called himself "Moshe of Frankfurt," and also Schreiber, which is the German translation of Sofer. Sh'muel Sofer's wife Reizel was known for her many charitable works, and was called *Reizel Tzadekes*, Reizel the saintly.

The birth of Moshe (IV) Sofer, to whom I shall henceforward refer simply as Moshe, came to be embroidered with legend, as is the case with the birth of many a hero. These legends, as well as those that were woven around his later life, were collected by his grandson Solomon Sofer (1855–1930) in a book entitled *Ḥut haM'shullash* (The Threefold Thread), first printed in Munkacs in 1893, the second time in Drohobicz in 1908, and a third time in Tel Aviv in 1963. The pious author, whose avowed purpose is to glorify his grandfather, does not distinguish among historical fact, family tradition, and legend, but even so his book has considerable value as a source on the life and personality of Moshe Sofer.

According to family tradition, when the marriage of Sh'muel Sofer and his wife Reizel had remained childless for more than ten years, he was on the point of divorcing her, as he was expected to do by Jewish traditional law, so as to enable both his wife and himself to enter into new marriages and thus fulfill the commandment "Be fruitful and multiply" (Gen. 1:28). At the very last minute, however—thus Solomon Sofer relates—a mysterious visitor appeared in the house of Sh'muel Sofer in the person of a saintly relative of Reizel, and said to her: "Cry not, and let not your face fall, for let it be known to you that tonight you will be blessed by a 'seed of permanence.'" Thereupon Reizel went to the *miqve* (ritual bath), "and sanctified herself in great sanctity, and from there issued light for the whole House of Israel, and was born my grandfather of blessed memory. And this was a miracle."[28] Solomon Sofer continues:

> God remembered her for good, and she conceived, and bore a son on the 7th day of Tishri 5523 [1762], on the eve of the Sabbath, near the ushering in of the Bride [Sabbath]. And it came to pass as she knelt down to give birth, that she sent a messenger to the rabbi, the master of the locality, the great sage R. Abish Ḥasid of blessed memory, and her soul was in her request and her petition was with her, that they should wait in the synagogue with the ushering in of the Sabbath until she gave birth, lest, God forbid, the holy Sabbath be desecrated through her travail. And the sage, the Ḥasid, hearkened to her request saying in his holy spirit that it was a worthy thing to wait for, for the son who was about to be born to this woman would give light to the eyes of the sages with his Tora, and would succor Israel with his prayer, and his name would be called Moshe.[29]

The child Moshe manifested an extraordinary keenness of mind at a very early age. When he was four, he asked some critical questions in connection with the text of the Book of Genesis he was being taught in the *ḥeder*, which enraged his teacher so much that he hit the child. Moshe's father thereupon complained to R. Nathan Adler (1741–1800), the great rabbinical luminary of Frankfurt, and Rabbi Adler advised him to teach his son himself. This, incidentally, was how the child genius first came to the attention of Rabbi Adler. Under his father's tutelage the child Moshe made such great strides in his studies that when he reached six there was nothing more his father could teach him, and he sent the boy to study with another teacher.

Rabbi Adler must have kept an eye on the boy, and when Moshe was ten, Rabbi Adler offered to take over his instruction.[30] Rabbi Adler was not only a great talmudist, but also a fervent kabbalist, equally at home in the theoretical and the practical Kabbala—according to later testimony from Moshe Sofer he was capable of performing miraculous acts. In addition, he was a man of great warmth, and he grew extremely fond of the child prodigy placed under his care. Moshe, on his part, conceived a great love for his master that was to remain with him all his life.

In the yeshiva of R. Nathan Adler, Moshe soon became the star pupil, and the master's favorite student. One day, when Moshe was ten years old, R. Adler asked him to give a discourse on a talmudic problem, and during his presentation, Moshe ventured to say that his great-grandfather R. Sh'muel Schotten had erred in discussing a certain point that actually was very simple. When Moshe's father heard this, he became enraged over the lack of respect the child showed his illustrious ancestor, and slapped him. When this incident became known to Rabbi Adler, he ordered Moshe not to speak thenceforth to his father, for, as Solomon Sofer delicately puts it, he was afraid that if his father continued to discipline Moshe in a like manner, the child's ardor for study would cool. From that day on Moshe spoke not a word to his father. In the circumstances it was evidently painful for the child to live under the same roof with his father, and R. Adler took him to live in his house, thereby practically adopting him.

This situation went on for close to four years, and Moshe found it increasingly difficult to live in the same city as his father, whom he would encounter in the street without being able to exchange a word with him. Thus, at the age of fourteen he went, with the approval of R. Adler, to the city of Mainz to become a student of R. Jacob Moses David ben Mikhal Scheuer (d. 1782). He stayed there for two years, studying not only Talmud, but also German, French, and Latin, as well as general history and secular sciences. However, his longing for his mother and his master R. Nathan Adler became too strong to resist, and he returned to Frankfurt and again took up residence in the house of Rabbi Adler, with whom his relationship became even closer thereafter.

Soon after his return to Frankfurt, the sixteen-year-old Moshe finished studying the entire Talmud, quite an unusual feat for so young a boy. When he asked Rabbi Adler how he should celebrate this event (it was customary in the yeshivot to celebrate such a *siyyum* [completion] with a joyous feast), his master's answer was, "Fast three days!"—which Moshe unfailingly did.

The year thereafter (1779) Moshe's father died. I found no answer in the sources I was able to peruse to the question that arose in my mind—namely, whether Moshe thereupon moved back from the house of his master to that of his widowed mother, whom, according to all indication, he venerated and loved dearly. The next move in Moshe's life came three years later, when the relationship between R. Nathan Adler and the Frankfurt community deteriorated, in which development R. Adler's Kabbalism was an important factor. In any case, R. Adler at that juncture accepted an invitation from the important Moravian community of Boskowitz (today Boskovice in Czechoslovakia) to be its rabbi, and young Moshe, by then in his twentieth year, followed him there, and again lived in his house, for another three years. While in Boskowitz Moshe was also instructed by R. Adler in the Kabbala, and learned from him how to write *qame'ot* (amulets), whose texts he later entered in a special notebook.

This quasi-filial intimate relationship with R. Adler came to an end in 1785, when Adler returned to Frankfurt, and made it known to Moshe that the time had come for him to be independent of his master. Thus, after traveling together to Vienna, Moshe said goodbye to his beloved master, and, instead of returning with him to Frankfurt, where his mother certainly would have more than welcomed him, went to Prossnitz, where he married Sarah, the widowed daughter of R. Moshe Jerwitz, who was many years his senior. His wife's brother undertook to support the couple, while Moshe served in the honorary position of head of the local yeshiva. Two years later his brother-in-law became impoverished, and so Moshe was forced to accept (in 1789) an invitation to serve as rabbi of Dresnitz, Moravia, staying there for nine years. In 1798 he became rabbi of Mattersdorf, Hungary, and in 1803 rabbi of Pressburg, one of the most important Jewish communities in Central Europe. In 1812 Moshe's wife Sarah died, and within a year he married a second time. His bride was another Sarah, the daughter of R. Akiba Eger the Younger, likewise a widow, but twenty-five years younger: he was fifty-one, and she twenty-six.

Years later his son Shim'on Sofer (1820–1883), who served as rabbi in Mattersdorf from 1848, and in Cracow from 1861, asked his father why he did not obey the advice of the talmudic sages, according to which a man should marry at eighteen. Moshe Sofer answered him: "I know, I know. Believe me, I had myself bled a lot because of this, to weaken my body and to silence the hot seething of

youth. . . . Every month I had myself bled in order to weaken my
strength . . . and now I feel weak because of this. . . ."[31]

In his earlier years Moshe Sofer kept to a regimen that amounted
to nothing less than a constant mortification of the flesh, in which
he could persist only because he had inherited a sturdy constitution
and possessed extraordinary willpower. His grandson Solomon reports
that for decades he used to study standing, and never lay down to
sleep in a bed. If he became sleepy, he would put his feet in cold
water; and if he felt that sleep was about to overwhelm him, he
leaned his forehead on a key—when the key dropped, he woke up.[32]
Only from his middle years on did he allow himself to relax somewhat this more than Spartan regimen.

The influence of R. Nathan Adler remained with Moshe Sofer
all his life. He absorbed from his revered master the latter's appreciation of the Sephardic *nusah* (version) of the prayers, and venera-
tion of Isaac Luria, the great sixteenth-century Safed kabbalist, whose
kawwanot (sacred concentrations) remained an integral part of the
Sephardic and Ashkenazic ritual alike.[33] More than that: Moshe Sofer
remained convinced all his life that Nathan Adler was able to perform miracles with the "Holy Names." He refers to all three features
in one of his responsa, which contains these passages (in my translation from the Hebrew):

> Moreover, I say that prayer in the Sephardic version is not inferior to
> the Ashkenazic version, since the Tora has been received by them [i.e.,
> the Sephardim] from the first fathers. Therefore he who wants to con-
> centrate [*l'khawwen*] and does not know how, must pray according to
> the *nusah* of the ARI [R. Isaac Lurie]. And I shall speak for another
> moment [and say] that the Holy Names are of real effect, as I have seen
> with my own eyes [done] by the man of miracles, my teacher the True
> Cohen of blessed memory [i.e., Nathan Adler], and from that with
> which our sages of blessed memory occupied themselves in the *Sefer
> Yetzira* [Book of Creation, an early mystical treatise]. . . . In any case,
> the power of the Above prevails over nature. . . .[34]

While Moshe Sofer himself did not claim to have miraculous
powers, the fact that he kept a notebook into which he entered the
texts of amulets indicates that he did believe in their efficacy. Moreover, as his grandson Solomon reports with tantalizing brevity, "he
used to have visions both while asleep and while awake."[35] This
seems to have been an aspect of Moshe Sofer's personality that his
descendants, in their implacable opposition to Hasidism and Kabbal-

ism, wished to underplay. Thus no more than two or three of his visions found their way into the family tradition, visions that were of a totally innocuous kind, such as having had dreams that were portents of some disaster that occurred in a faraway place. One of these dreams indicated to him that his mother had died in Frankfurt. This happened in 1822, when his mother was about ninety years old, and Moshe Sofer himself was sixty.

Moshe Sofer continued to cherish the memory of his mother long after she died. Characteristic is an incident reported by his grandson Solomon: "Once Moshe, my grandfather, after recovering from an illness, preached a sermon in the synagogue, and in it he mentioned several of the great qualities of his mother, and praised her greatly. And, thereafter, he said to my uncle, 'The Holy One, blessed be He, never performed a great act in the world without revealing it to my mother in a dream.' "36

What an accolade from the mouth of a deeply God-fearing man! From this statement it also appears that Moshe Sofer must have inherited from his mother the proclivity for having visions.

About three years prior to his death Moshe Sofer wrote an ethical will addressed to his children and the community leaders of Pressburg, in which the main subjects were admonitions to lead a strict, moral, religious, and modest life. "If God gives you greatness [he uses the old Hebrew phrase "if God raises up your horn"] and has mercy upon you, as I hope, with the help of God, blessed be He, do not raise your head in pride and haughtiness of heart against any kosher man, God forbid. . . . "

On a different level, he forbids his "sons, daughters, sons-in-law, grandchildren, and their children" to read foreign books and to go to the theater. Then, addressing his daughters and daughters-in-law, he warns them, "Take heed that, heaven forfend, you uncover not even a handbreadth of your body by wearing short clothes as is customary" among the Gentiles. "Heaven forfend, there should not be a thing like this among those who grow up in my house. And all the more so must you beware of the evil of bad women, who let their hair be seen, and even if it be a wig I forbid it to you most strictly. . . ."37 Many of Moshe Sofer's descendants obeyed the strictures of his will most scrupulously. My own maternal grandfather, who was a great-grandson of Moshe Sofer, for instance, never set foot in a theater.

4. The Genealogy of Moshe Sofer

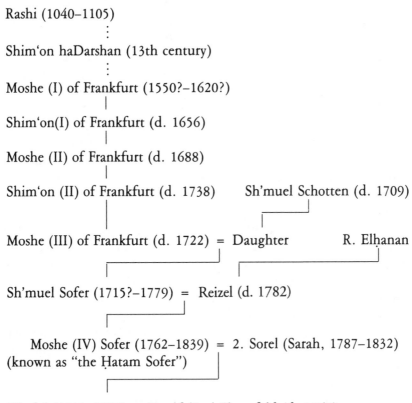

Rashi (1040–1105)
⋮
Shim'on haDarshan (13th century)
⋮
Moshe (I) of Frankfurt (1550?–1620?)
|
Shim'on(I) of Frankfurt (d. 1656)
|
Moshe (II) of Frankfurt (d. 1688)
|
Shim'on (II) of Frankfurt (d. 1738)   Sh'muel Schotten (d. 1709)

Moshe (III) of Frankfurt (d. 1722) = Daughter   R. Elhanan

Sh'muel Sofer (1715?–1779) = Reizel (d. 1782)

Moshe (IV) Sofer (1762–1839) = 2. Sorel (Sarah, 1787–1832)
(known as "the Ḥatam Sofer")

Hindel (1813–1879) = David Zevi Ehrenfeld (d. 1861)

Moshe Sofer died in 1839 at the age of seventy-seven. For several decades after his death his influence increased due to the work of his descendants and disciples who carried his teachings into numerous communities. His children, says the *Encyclopaedia Judaica*, "formed one of the best known rabbinic families." They served as rabbis in many countries, including Hungary, Galicia, Greece, Italy, and Israel. One of them was a teacher at the Jewish Theological Seminary in New York, another became a member of Parliament in Vienna. A third one died in Auschwitz.

In his spirited defense of Jewish tradition, which he considered inviolable, Moshe Sofer coined many pithy sayings and *bons mots* that became slogans of the Orthodox in their fight against Reform. Perhaps the best known is his use of a talmudic dictum, *ḥadash asur min haTora*, which in the original context meant "new [produce] is forbidden by the Tora" before the second day of Passover (i.e., the 16th of Nissan), when the priest presented the 'Omer in the Sanctuary. This saying was used by Moshe Sofer in the sense "[religious] innovation is forbidden by the Tora." His position was that any innovation, even one unimportant from the halakhic point of view, was forbidden simply because it was an innovation.

It is interesting to note that despite his unbending rigorism, innovation was a factor that accompanied Moshe Sofer all his life. While he was inexorably opposed to any innovation introduced or proposed by religious reformers, there was a huge area of innovations in which his principal teacher, Nathan Adler, and he himself even more so, engaged, and which he considered not only legitimate but the highest-ranking religio-scholarly activity.

When Nathan Adler's innovations and deviations from the accepted custom of Frankfurt led to increasing quarrels between him and the Frankfurt community, Moshe Sofer unhesitatingly sided with his master. In 1779 the innovations introduced by Rabbi Adler were so intolerable to the Frankfurt community that the *beth din* [rabbinical court] forbade him to conduct religious services in his home and forbade members of the community from attending such services. It even went so far as to threaten Rabbi Adler with excommunication.

Of the many works written by Moshe Sofer, the most acclaimed was the multivolume collection entitled *Hiddushe Torat Moshe Sofer* (*Novellae* [innovations] of the Tora of Moshe Sofer).[38] It was from the acrostic of this title that Moshe Sofer became known as "the Hatam Sofer." Thus the great fighter against religious innovation himself became known primarily for his own religious innovations. But, of course, there are innovations and innovations. The innovations fought against by Moshe Sofer were religious reforms that, on the whole, tended to abolish, or lighten, the many ritual prohibitions and positive religious commandments contained in the *Halakha*. The underlying philosophy of these reformist innovations was the conviction that all these minutiae of ritual, while they may have had their justification and may have been meaningful at the time they were promulgated, had become obsolete, and therefore had lost their justification and their mandatory character. This view and the innovations based on it were, of course, anathema to Moshe Sofer and his followers.

Moshe Sofer's own *ḥiddushim* were in sharp contrast with these innovations. They were all anchored in the unshakable belief in the eternal validity of the *Halakha*, the complex structure built up, in the course of centuries, upon the succinct biblical commandments, kept in many cases in most general terms that demanded interpretation. Hence rabbinical scholars were expected — in fact, duty bound — to continue that same traditional building process: by using their knowledge of the vast halakhic literature and their acumen, they reached conclusions as to further refinements of ritual "do's" and "don'ts." These, as a rule, fell in the general category of erecting a fence around existing *mitzvot* (commandments), and were never, or almost never, intended to permit something that was forbidden by the *Halakha*, while frequently prohibiting things, acts, or words that, up to that point, had been permitted by it.

Brief references to the work that made Moshe Sofer the foremost rabbinical authority of his age will have to suffice. Despite his familiarity with the languages and sciences of the Gentiles, he remained all his life uncompromisingly orthodox. During the thirty-three years of his tenure in Pressburg, he fought relentlessly against the Jewish Reform movement, and against the Jewish Enlightenment, the *Haskala*. He opposed with all his influence the emancipation of the Jews, because he feared that the granting of equal rights to them would ultimately lead to a weakening of the hold religion had over them. He built up in Pressburg the greatest yeshiva of the age, an institution of talmudic learning the like of which had not existed since the demise of the central yeshivot of Babylonia-Iraq many centuries earlier.

His literary production amounts to some one hundred volumes, most of them of a halakhic, and all of them of a religious character, only a few of which were published in his lifetime. Although he was opposed to the use of the languages of the Gentiles, when the need arose he wrote expert opinions in an elegant literary German and in a beautiful Gothic hand, signing his name as "Moyses Schreiber." He also wrote Hebrew poetry, and while his verses cannot be said to be possessed of a high poetic quality, they invariably express deep religious feelings, sometimes of a mystical bent, as illustrated by these lines, given in my literal translation:

> Embers of fire, the flame of God, is the love of my Lover,
> He cleaved to me, desired me, and encompassed me on the day of *Sh'mini 'Atzeret*,

The King spoke to me and thus addressed me: Be thou my Mistress.[39]

"Lover" and "King" are, of course, kabbalistic designations of God, and *Sh'mini 'Atzeret* is the last day of the Feast of Sukkot (Tabernacles), the joyous festival of love between Israel and the Tora.

In addition to his mystical inclination, it is his love of the Land of Israel that I find endearing in this most illustrious of my ancestors. He was a strong supporter of Jewish settlement in the Holy Land, and although he himself never visited Palestine, he encouraged his disciples to settle there. He was entrusted with what is called in contemporary sources "the presidency of the Holy Land," that is, the headship of the collection of monies in support of the religious Jews who lived in Jerusalem and the other three holy cities. On that occasion they sent him a piece of the tree under which, according to tradition, the three angels who visited Abraham rested (Gen. 18). Moshe Sofer was overjoyed with the precious gift and made of it a case for one of his most cherished possessions: the knife used by his master R. Nathan Adler to circumcise children. He had the case decorated with silver and engraved with the words "and lo, three men stood over against him" (Gen. 18:2).[40]

When Napoleon issued his proclamation (April 20, 1799) offering the Jews the land of their fathers, Moshe Sofer was filled with enthusiasm, and wrote a poem praising — not Napoleon, but God, who, he trusted, would lead him into freedom[41]

There used to be no greater honor in traditional rabbinical circles than to have one's *hagahot* (comments or notes) included in the standard printed editions of the Talmud. Very few even among the greatest rabbinical authorities merited such signal recognition. Among them is Moshe Sofer. I still have in my possession the twelve-volume set of the Talmud from which Father used to teach me when I was a teenager. It is one of the finest editions of the Talmud, printed in Vienna, from 1860 on. The title page of each volume lists the commentators whose notes are included in it, beginning with Rashi, and ending with "old notes copied from the manuscript of our master the *gaon*, the author of Hatam Sofer of blessed memory."

The Ehrenfelds

Hindel (1813–1879), the oldest daughter of Moshe Sofer, was given in marriage to David Zevi Ehrenfeld, a young rabbi in Pressburg.

David Zevi's father was Shaul (I) Ehrenfeld, of whom little is known except that he lived in northern Hungary and was a man of means and influence. All that the family chronicler found to say about him was that "he was a great prince" (*nagid*) and "influential with royalty" (*m'qorav lamalkhut*), the meaning of which remains doubtful.[42] When he sent off his son David Zevi to study in the yeshiva of Szerdahely, Hungary, he allegedly said to him: "If you will study diligently, you are mine; and if not, you will not be considered as one of my sons. . . ."[43]

David Zevi Ehrenfeld was exceptional among the members of the Sofer and Ehrenfeld families in that he wrote no books, although he must have been a man of great talmudic learning—otherwise Moshe Sofer would not have selected him for the honor of becoming one of his sons-in law. That he was a considerable talmudic scholar is attested by excerpts from his writings included in the works of his son Samuel. David Zevi died in 1861, leaving five sons, of whom Samuel (1835–1883) became best known for his responsa that he titled *Hatan Sofer*, meaning "Son-in-law of [Moshe] Sofer," but actually an acrostic of *Hiddushe Torat Nekhed Sofer* (*Novellae* of the Tora of the Grandson of [Moshe] Sofer, published in 1874). He established a pattern that was involuntarily to be followed by several members of the Sofer-Ehrenfeld family: after spending years in studying in various famous yeshivot, they would go into business, fail in it, and thereupon accept a rabbinical position. In 1866 Samuel Ehrenfeld became rabbi of Bethlen (now Beclean, Rumania); from 1868 to 1877 he was rabbi in Szikszó, Hungary, which had a respectable yeshiva; and from 1877 to his death he was rabbi in Mattersdorf, where his grandfather Moshe Sofer had served before him.

It is nothing short of remarkable how the biblical motif of protracted parental barrenness that precedes the birth of a hero (Abraham and Sarah, Jacob and Rachel) recurs in the Sofer-Ehrenfeld family tradition. We have heard above that Moshe Sofer reputedly was born after his parents had been married for more than ten years. About Hindel, the daughter of Moshe Sofer, and her husband David Zevi Ehrenfeld the family tradition records a similar sequence of events. They married in 1828, when Hindel was fifteen years old, and remained childless for six years. Hindel was close to despair, and went crying to her father, who had the reputation of possessing saintly powers. Moshe Sofer said to her, "Don't cry, my daughter," and reassured her that God would remember her with compassion.

In fact, within a year a son was born to her, and the happy parents sent a special messenger to bring the glad tidings to her father, who happened to be in Roggendorf at the time.[44] When the messenger told him that his first grandson was born, the seventy-three year-old Moshe Sofer was overwhelmed with joy that God let him live to see a grandchild, and said, "Let him be named Sh'muel after my father."

The grandson's first days in this world were beset with dangers. His mother was unable to breast-feed him — we are not told why — and in the whole city of Pressburg they could find no wet nurse. His father ran in despair to Moshe Sofer, whose role in connection with these family troubles resembles that of a Hasidic rabbi, a *tzaddiq*, and appealed for his help. Moshe Sofer said, "What can I do my son, trust in God and He will help." These few words seem to have been enough to produce a miracle. At that hour there was a bad storm, the rain came down in streams, and not a soul could be seen in the streets. But suddenly a poor woman in tattered clothes appeared at the door of the Sofer house, and asked whether they needed a wet nurse. "It is for you that we are waiting," said the young parents happily and ushered her in. The strange woman remained there, without asking about the payment she would receive, and from that day on took care of the infant Sh'muel. She spent nine months with him, the usual duration of breast-feeding a child, and never asked for, or even mentioned, money. When the nine months were up, she disappeared, as suddenly as she had come, and nobody knew where she had come from and where she went. After her disappearance the family understood that this was a miraculous event. As for Moshe Sofer, who had only four more years to live, he derived great pleasure from playing with his grandson, and shortly before he died "his holy hands held him to lead him to the House of Study."[45]

The 1848 revolutionary wars caused great hardships for the Jews of Pressburg in general, and for the grocery on which the Ehrenfeld family's livelihood depended in particular. Without giving up his yeshiva studies, young Sh'muel had to lend a hand in the store. His father would continue, as was his wont, to discuss talmudic problems with the scholars who came to the store, while Sh'muel would take care of the customers. On one occasion a customer came and asked for a sugar loaf, and young Sh'muel had to climb up the ladder to fetch it from a high shelf. While he was perched on top of the ladder, his father called up to him, "You know, Sh'muel, after all, the Maharsha is right!" They had been discussing a difficult passage in the talmudic supercommentary of Morenu HaRav Sh'muel Adels, known as Maharsha, and it was at that moment that David Zevi understood the precise meaning of the passage in question. And the customers wondered about such merchants, for whom the words of the Tora were sweeter than honey.[46]

But to return from legend to history, in 1877, when Sh'muel Ehrenfeld left Szikszó for Mattersdorf, the community invited his younger brother Shaul, my great-grandfather, to become their rabbi.

A brief biographical sketch of Shaul Ehrenfeld (b. Pressburg, 1839, d. Szikszó, 1905) is contained in the family album compiled by another member of the Sofer-Schreiber family, R. Avraham Sh'muel Binyamin Sofer-Schreiber, under the title *K'tov Zot Zikkaron* (Write This as a Memorial).[47] It states that Shaul Ehrenfeld was a man of great mental sharpness, "was wonderfully deep, and could uproot mountains with his logic. Our master the [author of] *K'tav Sofer* [a son of Moshe Sofer and uncle of Shaul Ehrenfeld], said of him that he envied him for the great sharpness of his mind and his crystal clear knowledge."[48]

Shaul Ehrenfeld married the daughter of a well-to-do Jewish merchant in Nagyvárad (German Grosswardein, today Oradea Mare in Rumania), and for a number of years lived, as was customary for young talmudic prodigies, in the house of his father-in-law, who took care of all his needs so that he would be able to spend all his time studying the Talmud. The method of study in places where there was no yeshiva was to join with a partner, so that the two scholars could discuss difficult passages and sharpen each other's wits by discussion and argument. Shaul Ehrenfeld's study partner was Mordekhai Loeb (Leopold) Winkler, who was five years younger than Shaul, and who subsequently became rabbi of Mád, Hungary, and the author of a collection of responsa, *L'vushe Binyamin* (The Garments of Benjamin).[49] According to the family tradition, the two young scholars "many times continued to study all night, and fought great battles over the Tora, one raising a problem, the other solving it. The [future] *gaon* of Mád with his wonderful erudition, and the gaon R. Shaul with his sharp-wittedness. . . . [50]

After a time Shaul Ehrenfeld moved to Pest (it was not until 1870 that the twin cities of Pest and Buda were united into Budapest). There he opened a bookstore, which occupation "enabled him to sit without being disturbed, and he sat all day immersed in his holy books." We recognize, of course, the pattern established by his father and grandfather, for whom—when not having a rabbinical position—ownership of a store was the best available alternative of making a living and yet being able to devote most of their time to talmudic study.

Soon after Shaul Ehrenfeld settled in Pest, that city hosted the Hungarian Jewish Congress, convened on December 14, 1868, at the behest of the government for the purpose of regulating the organizational and educational affairs of Hungarian Jewry. Having granted emancipation to the Jews in 1867 (to the great dismay of the Orthodox among them, led by the descendants of Moshe Sofer), the government considered it imperative that the Jewish denomination become an autonomous body, similar to the Christian churches, and that a countrywide framework be established for the Jewish religious and educational institutions. The eventual results of the congress were at variance with the intentions of the government. It led to the establishment of not one, but no less than three countrywide Jewish organizations: (1) the *Neolog* organization, which accepted the majority decisions of the congress, and which was similar in its religious outlook to American Conservative Judaism; (2) the *Orthodox* organization, consisting of those communities that refused to join the congressional organization and were more or less as tradition-abiding as Orthodox Jewry is today in America; and (3) the *Status Quo (Ante)* grouping, which refused to join either of the two former organizations, and insisted on maintaining the juridical status of the Jewish communities prior to the congress (hence its name), while adhering, in general, to a religious position somewhere between the Neolog and the Orthodox.

A great number of rabbis assembled in Pest for the congress, and many of them found respite from its tense controversies in Shaul Ehrenfeld's bookstore. They came to buy books, but were drawn into lively discussions on Tora and Jewish law by the learned Rabbi Shaul, "until the proprietor entirely forgot to sell any books." The *yiḥes* (ascribed status due to descent) Rabbi Shaul enjoyed as a grandson of Moshe Sofer was soon augmented by his own fame as an outstanding *ḥarif*, a sharp-witted scholar of the Talmud. Once, the family chronicler tells us, when "he sojourned in Galicia as the head of a rabbinical court, the greatest talmudic scholars of that country, who sat with him, were amazed at his extraordinary genius and sharp-wittedness."

When R. Shaul was about thirty-eight, his elder brother R. Sh'muel left Szikszó to become rabbi of Mattersdorf, whereupon he was invited to take his brother's place in Szikszó. He founded in that community a yeshiva that became an important center of talmudic learning in Hungary, and remained rabbi of Szikszó to the end of his life. As one of his biographers put it, "he ruled [*malakh*] there for about thirty years."[51]

Regrettably, almost nothing of R. Shaul's writings has survived. R. Sofer-Schreiber concludes his brief biography of R. Shaul by stating that he left behind a large number of "wonderful writings, full of Tora innovations, and it is a great pity that all of them were lost without seeing the light of day."[52] This being the case, the documentary basis for an evaluation of R. Shaul's thought and personality is also lost. Only scanty references to his teachings are found in books written by others, and these provide at least some meager insight into his mind. One of these sources quotes him as having given a novel interpretation to the biblical commandments:

> It is known that the commandments of the Tora themselves safeguard one against sinning, as Maimonides wrote at the end of the Laws of the Mezuza. And this is the difference between the laws of the nations and the laws of the Holy One, blessed be He: in the laws of the nations their "don'ts" have only one meaning: not to do that thing, but they don't have the power and the force to safeguard men from doing it. But the laws of the Holy One, blessed be He, have a twofold meaning, e.g., "Thou shalt not murder" or "Thou shalt not steal" have their simple meaning, but there is in them also a second meaning: the promise that if you want to observe them, the "don't" will safeguard you from murdering and stealing—this is the power and the force hidden and embedded in the "don'ts" of the Tora. No other law and statute has this, only the laws of God and His Tora. There is an allusion to this in the Bible: "And in all things that I have said unto you take ye heed" [*tishshameru*, Ex. 23:13], that is to say, in all things that I have said unto you to do or not to do you will be safeguarded [the Hebrew verb admits of this interpretation], for the commandments themselves will safeguard you that you don't sin. Likewise, "and make no mention of other Gods" [Ex. 23:13], that is to say, it is a commandment for you that you should not make mention of them, and, in fact, "it will not be heard out of thy mouth" [ibid.], for the "don't" of "make no mention" will in itself safeguard you that surely it will not be heard out of your mouth.[53]

In the sequel R. Shaul adduces more examples to show that the biblical commandments contain both "the warning not to do something, and the promise that, truly, it will not be done." Then he boldly generalizes and states that "in each of the 613 commandments there are two meanings: a meaning of command, and a meaning of promise. . . . "

For an outsider, that is, someone not standing within the traditional "four cubits of the Halakha," such interpretations of biblical commandments may appear forced, farfetched, and of little or no significance. But for the strictly tradition-directed thinking of the committed Orthodox world of which R. Shaul was part and for which each word, nay, each letter, of the biblical text is the repository of endless unfathomed meanings, a comment such as the above represents a major *ḥiddush*, innovation, in the most positive sense of the term: it opens up a new avenue to the understanding of the Bible, and especially of its laws, which are the eternal guidelines of the pious Jewish life.

Of the sons of Rabbi Shaul Ehrenfeld, Sofer-Schreiber mentions only Moshe (my grandfather), Solomon, and Samuel. He also mentions that one of his daughters married a certain Mr. Keller, and another a Mr. Friedman. A son of the latter was Dénes Friedman, my childhood tutor, and later chief rabbi of Ujpest, of whom I shall have more to say in another chapter. R. Sofer-Schreiber does not mention two other sons of R. Shaul, Simon and Benjamin, or his third daughter—I remember quite distinctly that my grandfather had three sisters, Sarah, Gisella, and Theresa, to whom we children would refer as Sóri, Gizi, and Rézi.

I know less of my maternal grandfather Moshe (Mór) Ehrenfeld than of several of my more remote ancestors. The reason for this is the simple fact that he never filled a rabbinical position, or authored any works, and therefore no written documentation of his life is available. Thus, in effect, all I know about him is based on the personal contact I had with him from the time I was old enough to listen to his stories to the time I left Budapest in 1933. I am not even sure of where and when he was born, although I suspect that he must have been born in Nagyvárad before his parents moved to Pest. As for his birth date, I have reason to believe that he was born in 1864, because shortly after my move to Jerusalem I remember having written him a letter congratulating him on his seventieth birthday, and telling him that on that occasion I gathered my friends and gave them an account of his life and of his illustrious ancestors. This must have been in 1934, and I imagine that my mother must have written me suggesting that I write a note to her father and wish him *bis hundert und zwanzig*, as goes the traditional Jewish saying, meaning "may you live to 120 years."

Let me see: I know that my grandfather was a rabbinical scholar, because occasionally he taught me a page in the Talmud. I assume that he must have attended in his youth the yeshiva headed by his father in Szikszó. I know that he went back from Budapest to Nagyvárad to marry, and I assume that he did so because his father had married a Nagyvárad girl and lived in that city in his youth and directed his son to do so. The girl he married was Theresa, the daughter of a leading citizen of Nagyvárad, Raphael Kurländer, after whom I was named Raphael.

5. The Ehrenfeld Genealogy

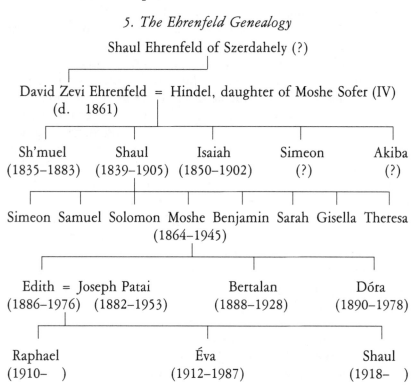

Shaul Ehrenfeld of Szerdahely (?)

David Zevi Ehrenfeld = Hindel, daughter of Moshe Sofer (IV)
(d. 1861)

Sh'muel (1835–1883)   Shaul (1839–1905)   Isaiah (1850–1902)   Simeon (?)   Akiba (?)

Simeon   Samuel   Solomon   Moshe   Benjamin   Sarah   Gisella   Theresa
(1864–1945)

Edith (1886–1976) = Joseph Patai (1882–1953)   Bertalan (1888–1928)   Dóra (1890–1978)

Raphael (1910–)   Éva (1912–1987)   Shaul (1918–)

The family traditions as to the origins of the Nagyvárad Kurländers are recorded by various genealogists in differing versions, occasionally contradictory, but the following sequence of events seems the most likely. In the late eighteenth century a young talmudist from Kurland in the Baltic (today part of Latvia) studied in the Prague yeshiva, where his best friend was Moses Stein of Topa, Hungary, a village near Nagyvárad. When the time came for the two friends to leave the yeshiva, they did not want to part and drew lots to decide in whose homeland both of them would settle. The lots favored Moses Stein, and so the two young talmudists settled in Nagyvárad, where the young man from Kurland, whose name was Raphael, became known as *der Kurländer Bokher*, that is, "the young man" or "the yeshiva-student" (the Hebrew word *baḥur*, colloquially *bokher*, means both) from Kurland. When the Emperor Joseph II (r. 1780–1790) ordered the Jews of Hungary to take on family names, the appellative was transformed into the young man's last name.

Raphael (I) Kurländer served as rabbi in various Hungarian towns, and died at a young age before 1823. He left behind several children, of whom the eldest was his son Isaac, whose Hebrew name was Y'hezq'el, who died in 1860. Isaac Kurländer became a well-to-do grain and spirits merchant in Nagyvárad, and the head of the Jewish community of the city. He owned a big house in the city center with stores fronting on the big marketplace. In 1858 he submitted the statutes of the Jewish Boys' Orphanage to the mayor of the city for approval. He married Johanna (Hentshi) Stein (d. 1883), who, according to family tradition, was the youngest sister of his father's best friend, Moses Stein. The parents of the Stein siblings were Gedalya Stein and Sarah Spitz of Szaniszló, County Bihar, Hungary. One of the brothers of Johanna Stein was Jacob Stein (1814–1866), who had a grocery store in Nagyvárad. According to one source, Raphael (II) Kurländer (1823–1899) was a brother of Isaac Kurländer; according to another, he was his son. In any case he had a big grocery and dry goods store in Nagyvárad, and was one of the most respected citizens of the community. The genealogists of the related Munk family term him "the very famous and greatly respected Raphael Kurländer," and state that he moved in the middle of the nineteenth century from Abony to Nagyvárad, where his big store was located in the Zöldfa Utca (Green Tree Street). Since Raphael (II) Kurländer was evidently named after his grandfather, it follows that he must have been the son, and not the brother, of Isaac Kurländer, and that his grandfather Raphael (I) must have died before he was born, that is, before 1823, and not in the 1830s as stated by one of the genealogists.

Raphael (II) Kurländer married Sarah (Záli, Szerén) Jacobi (1831–1911), daughter of Asher Anshel Jacobi (d. 1874 at a ripe old age), who was a leaseholder of the estates of Count Wesselényi and Count Degenfeld in Páncélcseh, County Szolnok-Doboka, Hungary. Asher Anshel had seven sons and three daughters. His father was Mendel Jacobi, a merchant in Páncélcseh, whose ancestors had come to Hungary from Germany in the seventeenth century.

After my grandfather Ehrenfeld married the daughter of Raphael Kurländer, the young couple lived in the spacious house of R. Raphael and were supported by him. They stayed in Nagyvárad for some ten to fifteen years, and all three of their children were born there. I do not know what my grandfather did during those years, but I suspect that, true to family tradition, he must have worked in some capacity in the big Kurländer store. To my great regret, at the time I taped a series of interviews with my mother in June 1968, when she was eighty-two (in the house of my sister in Givatayim, Israel), I did not ask her to tell me about the parents of her maternal grandparents. She made only a few remarks about the personality of her maternal grandmother:

> I always spent the vacations in Nagyvárad with my grandmother. Nagyvárad was for us like, how shall I put it, like paradise, we had it so good there. She was a wonderful woman. She had a great understanding for everything . . . a very good race. My grandfather was a much drier customer, but he adored small children. . . . He had a big dry goods store, where even the gypsies would come to buy, and my grandmother would occasionally sit at the cash register, to enable grandfather to spend time studying the Talmud. She was like a princess among the gypsies. She was simply wonderful. People came from afar just to have a look at her. She was a true aristocrat. She had a relative, Ármin Neumann, a member of Parliament, he and his wife once came especially to have a look at Mrs. Kurländer.

(I checked in the *Hungarian Jewish Lexicon*: Ármin Neumann, b. Nagyvárad, 1845, d. 1909, was a jurist, and author of books on law, and a member of the Hungarian Parliament from 1887 to 1903.)

From occasional remarks my mother made about her grandmother I can add a few more lines to her portrait. Mrs. Kurländer was a woman with very modern ideas for her times. She insisted that her children get a general secular education, which, in the case of her daughters, included learning French. In vain did her husband complain, *"Sorel, du shmadst mir die Kinder"* (Sorel, you are making renegades of my children)—the un-Jewish instruction continued. The son Ede (his Hebrew name was Y'ḥezq'el after his grandfather

Y'ḥezq'el-Isaac) was sent to high school, from which, after graduation, he went on to the university (I don't know in which city) to
study law. Despite her "modernistic" tendencies, Sarah Kurländer
was a deeply religious woman. My mother in her old age still remembered that on Yom Kippur eve her grandmother would stop the
great grandfather clock that stood in the room in which the women
of the family would assemble to pray—the men prayed in a neighboring room; a *gvir* (lord) like Raphael Kurländer did not go to the
synagogue on that most holy day of the Jewish year, but had services
held in his own house—and then took up a position in a corner of
the room and remained standing there praying, but otherwise motionless, until next evening, when the appearance of stars in the sky
signaled the end of the fast. My mother also told me that a few
months after I was born she took me to Nagyvárad to present me to
her grandmother. Her grandfather, after whom I was named, was of
course dead by that time. Soon thereafter Sarah Kurländer, too,
died, and when my sister Évi was born she was given the Hebrew
name Sarah after her.

By the time my mother, the eldest of Raphael Kurländer's
Ehrenfeld grandchildren, reached school age, there was no longer
any question that she would be given a general education. So she
went through elementary school, and started high school in Nagyvárad,
and even studied the piano in the Kurländer house. And the same
kind of education was also given to her younger brother and sister,
in addition to some rather rudimentary training in Hebrew, which
was considered the barest minimum to enable them to read the
Hebrew prayer book.

My mother kept until the end of her life a framed photograph
of her grandmother near her bed. There was quite a remarkable sim-
ilarity between her and her grandmother. The only difference I could
discern, apart from the obvious one in apparel—my great-
grandmother wears in the picture a tight, caplike head-covering that
completely hides her hair and ears, and her long-sleeved dress covers
her neck up to her chin—was that where my great-grandmother's
expression was severe, almost forbidding, my mother's mien was always
soft, friendly, and loving.

Of Raphael and Sarah Kurländer's children I know, in addition
to my grandmother, of one son and one daughter. Of the son, Dr.
Ede Kenéz-Kurländer, I shall speak in a later chapter. The daughter, Róza, married the head of the Orthodox Jewish community of

Nagyvárad, Isidor Ullman. They had two sons, Felix and Sándor (Alexander). Felix died relatively young; Sándor became the head of the community after his father's death. When my mother was a young girl, both courted her—so she remembered in her eighties— and wanted to marry her. When Isidor Ullman married Róza, his father-in-law took him in as a partner in his store, which from then on was called Kurländer and Ullmann.

My grandfather was twenty-one when he married Theresa Kurländer, who was seventeen at the time. Their first child, my mother, was born a year later, in 1886. They called her Edith in Hungarian and Esther in Hebrew. Two more children, a son Bertalan (Avraham) and a daughter Dóra, followed within four years.

6. *The Kurländer-Jacobi Genealogy*

Raphael (I) Kurländer   Mendel Jacobi

Isaac Kurländer (d. 1830?)   Asher Anshel Jacobi

Raphael (II) Kurländer = Sarah (Szerén, Záli) Jacobi
(1823–1899)   (1831–1911)

Theresa = Moshe Ehrenfeld   Ede   a daughter
(1868–1945)   (1864–1945)

Edith = Joseph Patai   Bertalan   Dóra
(1886–1976)   (1888–1928)   (1890–1978)

Everything else I know about my maternal grandparents is based on my own early childhood memories, and therefore the proper context of telling it is in connection with what I remember from those years. But, to bring their life story to a conclusion, I want to tell here of the last few months of their life in Budapest under German occupation, and their painful end, which came amidst the inhuman conditions in the Budapest ghetto before the city's liberation by the Russians and immediately following it. I shall do so in the words of my cousin Judith Molnár-Zaran, who dictated the following in Giva-tayim, Israel, on May 6, 1983, to my sister Évi, who, in turn, translated it from Hungarian into English and sent it to me. Judith (Juci) and her mother, my aunt Dóra, spent the war years with the grand-parents in Budapest, and her reminiscences, as far as I can judge, are a faithful eyewitness account of what happened.

In 1939 my aunt Edith and her husband [Joseph Patai] left Budapest for Palestine. My father, Rabbi Dr. Ernő Molnár, took over the editorship of the *Mult és Jövő*. In 1941 the "Jewish Law" put an end to the publication of the journal, and Gyula Virág, the office manager, remained in charge of winding up the finances. He was ready to give some of the money left to my grandfather, but he refused to accept anything for fear of violating the new laws. Since the Patais by then lived in Palestine, their money was regarded as alien property. Thus all that was left for my grandparents, parents, and me was the meager salary of my father that he received from the Jewish community of Pest. We had some preserves in the larder of our apartment at 68 Aréna Avenue where the five of us lived, but before long nothing was left.

On March 19, 1944, the Nazis entered Budapest, and our world, bad as it was until then, turned upside down. We had to leave our apartment and move to a small flat at 48 Dembinsky Street, which consisted of three rooms only. Into this small place were crowded, not only my grandparents, my parents, and I, but also my aunt Ruth and her two daughters, Alice, aged twenty, and Livia, aged seventeen. Her son Lorant had gone to live in London several years earlier. Within a few days also grandfather's brother, Uncle Solomon, moved in, bringing along with him a homeless sixteen-year-old boy. Thus, no less than ten of us lived in that small apartment. I no longer remember what was worse, the overcrowdedness or the lack of food. By that time we had long sold everything that was salable. I remember in particular the big carpet that Aunt Edith had given to my grandparents, and that Grandfather somehow managed to sell. Grandmother by that time already suffered from cancer and was bedridden. Once in a while a nurse came to treat her bedsores and other wounds. My mother and Aunt Ruth cooked, each of them separately. How Mother managed to find food no one knew. Despite her small stature she had real steel in her body, and was a pillar of strength in the most terrible situations. She begged and borrowed money and food, and literally kept us alive. As a rare treat, once or twice Grandfather even had his favorite food, goose liver.

The worst day for me was when, in October 1944, my father was "collected," and taken away by the Nazis. In the weeks thereafter I made several desperate attempts to find him, but they were of no avail. One day, at five in the morning, it was still pitch dark, several SS men and Arrow-Cross troopers came and rounded up the people in the apartment house. My mother and I escaped because a Christian neighbor, who hated the Nazis, hid us in his apartment. He took us into his bedroom, and left the door half open to show that no one was hidden there, and then invited the troopers for a drink, and drank with them until they were too inebriated to be able to count the number of people they were supposed to take in. So they left without me and my mother.

From October I worked in the Jewish Orphanage for Boys, which was protected by the International Red Cross. I was a medical gymnastics instructor. The same Gentile neighbor who had saved us wanted us to stay in his apartment, but the super of the building insisted that he would have to notify the police of the presence of two Jewish women in the building. We were desperate, we had nowhere to go. The solution, which seemed to me quite miraculous, was that Dr. Ottó Roboz, the director of the orphanage, took both of us into the institution. Thus we were saved, but the conditions in the orphanage were terrible. Daily more and more people had to be taken in, and there were constant fights for each few square inches of floor space to enable one to lie down. Every room was filled with mattresses from wall to wall, and once we lay down there was no room to turn, we lay so tightly packed.

After my mother and I moved into the orphanage, I saw my grandparents once more in the Dembinsky Street apartment where we left them. The Nazis did not bother with very old people, not even to the extent of taking them away. When I heard that they had started to take the Jews into the ghetto, I asked Dr. Roboz to help me, and he hired or bribed a soldier to escort me to the Dembinsky Street house. I found my grandmother horribly wasted away, shriveled, starved, looking like a ghost, nothing but skin and bones, the cancer eating away at her. My grandfather had turned into a shadow, he was bent and shaky, he who only a short while before was still so upright, so handsome, so youthful. He was eighty-one at the time, grandmother seventy-six. I remember Grandmother crying because of hunger pains, but there was nothing to eat . . . and I remember Grandfather feeding her with morsels, never taking a bite for himself . . .

In January 1945, when the Russians "liberated" Budapest and we went back to the Dembinsky Street apartment, we found only Uncle Solomon there, extremely sick. He told us that Grandmother had died some weeks before, and that Grandfather had been taken away, he did not know by whom or where. But my mother again performed a miracle: she hired two men to help her find Grandfather. They found him in a small dark closet or cubicle, suffering from dysentery and toxemia, lying in his blood and vomit, full of lice, delirious. The two men carried him back to our apartment, but it was too late to help him. He never regained full consciousness, only repeated three words again and again: "Ladyfingers, wine, Jucika; ladyfingers, wine, Jucika. . . ." He always had been a gourmet, and of all his grandchildren he loved me best. . . . Soon thereafter he died. He was buried in a mass grave, may he rest in peace.

3

My Parents

I know of the early life of my parents from a number of sources. One is my mother herself, who, beginning with my adolescence, and later especially in lengthy taped interviews in 1968 (when she was eighty-two), told me many things she remembered of her childhood and youth, of her first meeting with Father, and of their early life together. The second is the written reminiscences of my father, who wrote a small autobiographical portrait of himself as a six-year-old child in the house of his parents in Pata, and occasionally referred to his childhood and youth in his other writings as well. However, he never, or almost never, spoke to me about those early periods of his life. A realistic corrective to his highly idealized recollections was supplied in the 1950s by Father's brother Philip (Feivel) Klein in Brooklyn. Although sporadic and meager, the information I got from him constitutes an independent source, the third. The fourth is supplied by the poems, articles, notes, short stories, and books written by my father from the age of eighteen, and by the monthly and the weekly, both called *Mult és Jövő* (Past and Future), which he published and edited beginning with the year following my birth, and which represent an invaluable, albeit incomplete, chronicle of his life and work from 1911 to 1939. Despite diligent search I could discover only two external documents pertaining to Father's early poetic work, both written by Chief Rabbi Samuel Kohn of Budapest in 1904, when Father was twenty-two years old.

It is based on these sources that the story of my parents' early life is presented in this chapter. It will be complemented in the subsequent ones by my own recollections which, as the years passed, gradually grew more distinct and more numerous, and in which, for a long time, my parents occupied a dominant place.

My mother retained, to the end of her life, vivid and pleasant memories of her childhood and youth in Nagyvárad. She told me that she remembered the city as an important Hungarian cultural center. The *Magyar Zsidó Lexikon* (Hungarian Jewish Lexicon) informs me that around the turn of the century Nagyvárad had some 60,000 inhabitants, of whom between one-quarter and one-third were Jews. Most of the Jews belonged to the Orthodox congregation. The Neolog community, founded in 1870, was much smaller. One of its rabbis, from 1880 to 1884, was Alexander Kohut (1842–1894), who went from there to New York, where he became a founder and professor of the Jewish Theological Seminary of America. He was followed in the Neolog chief-rabbinate of Nagyvárad by Lipót (Leopold) Kecskeméti (1865–1936), whose major work, a three-volume study of the Prophet Jeremiah (published in Hungarian in 1932), I reviewed in my father's monthly. At one point in my review I commented on the splendid style of the work and said that, in addition to the most painstaking study that went into its making, it was apparent that for the actual writing the author had to wait for moments of inspiration. Dr. Kecskeméti was so delighted with this statement that he wrote to me that for that sentence he would have to kiss me on the forehead when he next saw me.

The Jews of Nagyvárad played an important role in the economic, social, and cultural life of the city, and several of the community's sons became outstanding in science, literature, law, journalism, and politics in Budapest and Berlin. My mother told me that in her youth Nagyvárad was called *a peceparti Párizs* (Paris on the banks of the Pece), and that, after she left for Budapest, on her regular summer return visits to the city she would occasionally catch a glimpse of Endre Ady (1877–1919), who, when he lived and worked as a journalist in Nagyvárad from 1900 to 1904, was already a celebrity and well on the way to becoming the foremost modern Hungarian poet. Ady himself called Nagyvárad "a city with a wonderful air, daring, conquering," while some decades earlier Lajos Kossuth (1802–1894), the great Hungarian patriot and statesman, called it "the Hungarian Birmingham."[1]

My mother also remembered that there was in Nagyvárad in those days a society of young writers, called *Holnaposok* (Those of Tomorrow) which published a literary review entitled *Holnap* (Tomorrow), and that once, when Father went there to visit Mother, he was asked either to contribute an article to it or to give a talk to the society—she was no longer sure which of the two invitations was tendered.

In Nagyvárad Mother was sent to a public school in which the language of instruction was Hungarian, but at home they spoke German. It seems that her parents, as well as her maternal grandmother, who was the dominant figure in the family, were quite liberal when it came to the education of their children. They even let Mother take piano lessons.

When my mother was about halfway through high school, her parents moved to Budapest. Here Grandfather Ehrenfeld, who up to that time had been supported, according to old Jewish custom, by his parents-in-law, had to earn a living. It is still a puzzle to me why, having received a fine rabbinical education in his father's yeshiva in Szikszó, he did not obtain a position as a rabbi. Unqualified as he was for secular professions, he became a salesman for a brush factory located in Debrecen, a big provincial city in Hungary. I think the name of the factory was Falk, and Grandfather became its sales representative in Budapest. I still remember seeing in my grandparents' apartment beautifully appointed trunks of various sizes, covered on the outside with black leather, which when opened revealed assortments of brushes, neatly strapped down each in its niche in a bed of luxurious red velvet. I loved to look at these sample cases, and Grandfather would occasionally give me one of the brushes as a present. When he was in his fifties, Grandfather lost his job, and thereafter, until his death some twenty-five years later, he never again earned a penny. His son, and his son-in-law, my father, supported him and his wife.

But to return to the years immediately after their arrival in Budapest, Mother completed her high school in a Budapest *gimnázium* in 1904 or 1905. *Gimnázium* was, and still is, the Hungarian term designating an eight-year secondary school, attended by students aged ten to eighteen, in which the emphasis is on languages, literatures, and history. She continued to study the piano, developed a marked talent for drawing and painting, and began to write poetry. In later years, of these artistic endeavors only poetry remained with her, and still later, when I myself began to take an interest in literature, I often wondered whether her poems were not superior to those of Father. In her old age, when she was about seventy, she returned to painting, and until her death at the age of ninety she produced many captivating pictures of flowers in vases, executed in brilliant watercolors. Soon after she finished the *gimnázium*, she met Father.

I described in the preceding chapter what I know about the early childhood of Father in the house of his parents in Pata. In a one-page handwritten autobiography, dated March 1, 1909—and, as shown by the 30-*fillér* revenue-stamp affixed to it, prepared for some official purpose—Father lists the institutions he attended from the age of ten to twenty-five:

> When I was ten and a half years old, my parents sent me to Kisvárda (County Szabolcs), to a Hebrew school, which I attended for two years. Thereafter, I was a pupil at the following higher Talmud schools: Sátoraljaujhely (three half-years), M. Huszt (three half-years), Nyitra (one half-year), and Szatmár (three half-years). In 1899 I came to Budapest, began to study the high school subjects, and, in the same year, on the basis of an entrance examination, I became a regular student at the National Rabbinical Seminary, where, at the end of the year, I was awarded a diploma of the fourth grade of the *gimnásium*. I left at the beginning of the next half-year, went to the Talmud school of the rabbi of Galgócz, and there simultaneously prepared myself for a combined examination of the fifth and sixth grades of the *gimnásium*, which I actually passed at the end of the year at the Roman Catholic *gimnásium* of Nyitra. In the same school I finished the seventh grade as a regular student. For the eighth-grade exam I again prepared privately while I worked in Zsitvaujfalu as a tutor. After my *matura* [high school exam] I came to Budapest and here I engaged in university studies. On May 31, 1907, I was awarded a doctorate, and in due course, after passing my basic, special, and pedagogic exams, I received, on May 16, 1908, my teacher's diploma in Hungarian and German literature. Since September 1908 I have worked as a substitute teacher in the municipal *real* school of the fourth district.

In another autobiographical note he wrote some fifteen years later (this one is two printed pages long, but I cannot identify the journal in which it was published) Father writes that in Kisvárda, where he went in his twelfth year, they studied fourteen to sixteen hours a day, that several students lived in one room that they themselves had to clean, that if they wanted to have heat they had to go out to the forest to gather wood, and that they had to get up every day at three in the morning. He also states that in Sátoraljaujhely he was given the distinction, as the best student, of becoming the repetitor of the rabbi's son, who was one year older than he. And finally he says that while in Szatmár, even before the age of seventeen, he began to take an interest in modern Hebrew literature and scholarship, and that, although it was strictly prohibited, he began to read Hungarian daily papers and literary magazines. This led him to the decision to seek admission to the Budapest Rabbinical Seminary, in which both Jewish and secular subjects were taught.

In his notes Father does not mention how and where the yeshiva students ate. But from occasional remarks he dropped in conversation with me I gathered that local Jewish families would have a yeshiva student eat one meal a week at their table. This was called *teg essen*, that is, "to eat days," and it meant that the students had to go to a different house every day of the week for that one daily meal. In one of his later articles Father describes the harshness, lovelessness, and disdain with which he and the other yeshiva students were treated in most of the homes in which they humbly appeared week after week to get their *kest* (food).

In Huszt, where his own father had been a yeshiva-*bokher* one generation earlier, Father was a student of Rabbi Moshe Grünwald, known from the title of his major books as "the *'Arugot haBosem*" (The Flower-Beds of Fragrance, published posthumously in Paks, in 1912–1913).

In 1910, when Rabbi Moshe Grünwald died, Father memorialized and eulogized him in an article full of love and sorrow.

> He was my master for three semesters, and during that time more than four hundred of us listened thirstily to the words of his mouth. We starved on dry bread, we shivered with cold in unheated rooms, only to be able to listen, twice a day, morning and evening, to his profound teachings, to be able to enjoy the radiance of his face reflecting the splendor of the *Shekhina*. We were at least twice as many as the number of the members of the congregation, and at least ten times the number of the well-to-do among them: from whom could we have expected help? But we suffered hunger and cold with patience for the sake of the Tora, to serve proudly one of her greatest masters, the phenomenal *gaon*, Rabbi Moshe Grünwald.

As Father's memory takes him back fifteen years, he sees himself listening to the Master who stands high above the four hundred, at the lectern, and teaches, explains, and throws out questions to his students.

> Suddenly there is deep silence. A difficult question flies out of the mouth of the Master like a heavy missile. Voiceless consternation. Who can answer the difficult question? A lanky boy, less than fourteen years of age, pushes himself to the front with his weak fists, and when he is

near enough he flings a few words toward the lectern. The Master catches them and cries happily:
"Little Yosele has it! Let him come near. Right up here to the lectern. Let him repeat aloud that which the big ones could not find!"
The Master is happy, and who could be happier than the boy. . . .
I can no longer recognize little Yosele. . . . But the image of the Master stands before me unchanged like a proud cedar of Lebanon. . . .

This happened in the first semester, and as a result the Master allowed Yosele to take home and copy some of his manuscript works, which, as long as he lived, he did not allow to be published. In the second semester the Master gave him the assignment to serve as *ḥazer-bokher*, that is, repetitor, for students who could not quite manage on their own, for which work he received a modest fee. As a rule this task was given only to older students, well advanced in their studies, and Father was made very happy by this distinction. But before long he began to move away from the world of the yeshiva. As he put it in 1910:

> Soon, however, some restlessness, which ever since my childhood had nestled in my breast, was to carry me along with the currents of other winds. I began to occupy myself with worldly studies, and mainly with philosophy, at first, of course, with the help of forbidden Hebrew books. But the Master, who was himself an educated, cultured man, did not reprimand me. He knew that "there is no man that hath power over the wind to retain the wind," as the wise Koheleth has said. When I went to take leave of him, he, full of concern, let his kindly eyes rest on me. He felt that I was lost to him. He knew that our ways were parting. He said sadly: "What a pity, Yosele, what a great pity. You could become a *godel* [a rabbinical authority]."
> He spoke no more. He gave me his hand, which I covered with kisses and tears. . . . I felt that I must go far, very far, from the rabbi of Huszt, but that there would be a point at which our souls would meet: the love of the Jewish people. And I felt that the great Master saw into my heart, clasped my hand, and said: "My son, after all, you cannot move off too far from me. . . . "[2]

When Father wrote this he was twenty-eight, and the event he described lay fifteen years in the past. This explains the mistake he made in placing his departure from the world of the yeshiva at the end of his sojourn in Huszt. The fact is, as his other notes make amply clear, that after Huszt he went on to the yeshiva of Nyitra, and only there did he begin to take an interest in the "outside world." In addition to its ultra-Orthodox Jews, Nyitra also had a large Neolog Jewish community — 3,000 of its 15,000 inhabitants were Jews—that maintained a junior high school and several other communal institutions. Nyitra was also the seat of a Catholic bishop; it had a seminary, and in it was located the *gimnázium* (high school) of great repute of the Piarist Teaching Order. It was an interesting town with several old historical castles and a number of imposing churches. It was the headquarters of the Cultural Society of Upper Hungary, and also boasted a beautiful theater building and a large amusement park. Evidently, it was a place where a youth with interest in the world outside the yeshiva would find many things to attract him.

In 1914, in an article he published in the April issue of *Mult és Jövő*, Father touched upon the circumstances in which he abandoned the world of the yeshiva for the greater outside world, and the subsequent intellectual road he was to take. The antecedents of this article were as follows. In 1913 *Alkotmány* (Constitution), the official daily of the parliamentary People's Party, which represented primarily Catholic interests (one must not forget that Hungary was a predominantly Catholic country!), published an attack on *Mult és Jövő*. It accused Father's monthly of fostering Jewish consciousness and separatism by presenting works of Jewish literature and art in an extremely attractive manner, and by preaching, in its essays and articles, Jewish self-esteem and Zionism. In response to this attack Father wrote a brief note in his column *Tollhegyről* (From the Pen-Point), which was a regular feature in his monthly. In it he stated that he welcomed the *Alkotmány* article, which pointed out, and brought to the attention of wider Christian circles, precisely what he intended to do in his journal.[3]

It seems that by 1913 the self-assured Jewishness and pro-Zionism of *Mult és Jövő* had attracted wide attention and provoked strong opposition and attacks in both anti-Semitic Hungarian and anti-Zionist Jewish circles. In the March 1914 issue (pp. 153–54) of his journal, in another note in the same column, Father ridiculed some of the accusations directed against him. There is, he writes, a group of "concerned" people who

> say pantingly, "The armies of the Zionists are breathing down our necks, they are rushing to win Palestine! They are conspiring against the Hungarian kingdom, selling the poor fatherland for pennies, they want to exchange the Hungarian tricolor for a kaftan with a mogen dovid [Star of David], and Joseph Patai wants to be king of Jews! He fights with fire and sword for the interests of the Jewish state, thus

trying to acquire merits for the throne of Jerusalem, which is all the
more dangerous in our midst, in fact, is outright *lèse-majesté*, since
His Majesty bears also the title 'King of Jerusalem' ". . . .

In the same month in which Father published this satirical rebut-
tal, the Hungarian Christian novelist Dezső Szabó (1879–1945) published an "Open Letter" addressed to Father in response to his first
note. Szabó, who was one of the most celebrated Hungarian novelists, acclaimed for his racy and spicy style and powerful characteriza-
tions, was of Transylvanian origin, and only a few years earlier had
taught at a high school in Nagyvárad. He was an intellectual anti-
Semite, although it was only after the fall of the 1919 Hungarian
Communist dictatorship that his anti-Semitism assumed a virulent
form. Soon thereafter he attacked the Horthy regime, and, from the
late 1930s on, he also turned against the Nyilaskeresztesek, the "Arrow-
Cross" party, as the Hungarian Nazis were called.

Dezső Szabó's open letter was published in the March 1914 issue
of *Huszadik Század* (Twentieth Century), the influential journal of
the Hungarian Sociological Society, which was a political rather than
scholarly group, largely responsible for the development of bourgeois radicalism in Hungary. In his letter Szabó argues that the solution of the Jewish question in Hungary was for the Jews to abandon
their separatism and become Hungarians like all the other Hungarians.

Father's reply, published in the April 1914 issue of *Mult és Jövő*,
is a spirited defense of Jewish tradition and Jewish values, which, he
asserts, more than justify the historical Jewish determination to preserve the Jewish cultural specificity:

> We lift out of the past everything that is future, that is cultural value,
> that is ethical purity, that is poetry, song, and beauty, and want to
> give it to life's Jewish wanderers as provision for their journey, so that,
> in the times of tired, grey twilights, they should be able to draw strength
> from it. . . .
> Modern Jewish literature and journalism proclaim no intransigent
> nationalism, no narrow backwardness, no monopoly on God, no miserly
> chauvinism, no aimless tradition. On the contrary, they want to present
> the eternal Jewish values that sparkle beyond ceremonies and partial-
> ity, want to implant into consciousness Judaism as a cultural concept;
> and while they take up a position of defense against external attacks,
> they strengthen the internal fortifications, and supply them with nour-
> ishment, weapons, gunpowder. And precisely because, as you yourself
> have said, Jewry is more radically betrothed to advancement, human-

ity, culture, than Faust's soul to the devil, precisely because Jewry's world view is itself progress, we must preserve, even for the sake of general culture, that idea-content that, with its millennial innervation, has anointed the Jews fighters for human progress.

Then, in response to Dezső Szabó's account of his "intellectual voyage," contained in his open letter, Father reveals something of his own path that led him away from the yeshiva, through a phase of militant antireligionism, to his total dedication to the fight for Jewish culture.

Let me, too, tell you about my own mental metamorphosis. My parents—may the Builder of the Universe bless them—belong to those Orthodox Jews whom you also value, and who nobly and heroically sacrifice all their joys in life to religion. They intended to make of me, too, such a holy sacrifice. At the age of three I prayed from the Hebrew prayer book, at four I translated the Bible in the *ḥeder*, at six I studied the Talmud, and from the age of ten to seventeen my restless blood drove me from one yeshiva to another. In Kisvárda and Sátoraljaujhely, in Szatmár and Mármaros-Huszt, I saturated my young soul with the sad talmudic chant, at the light of pale candles in endless nights, and this was its only spiritual nourishment. And it happened that the twilights that spelled farewell to the sun, the nights spent awake, and the mystical awakenings of the dawn pulled me to the Kabbala and to Hebrew poetry, which was a forbidden fruit in the yeshiva. This is why I had to leave Huszt, one of the yeshivot. Then in Nyitra, dazzled by the enticements of theater posters, I put on the clothes of my old landlady, combed my sidelocks to look like a woman's hairdo, and stole into the gallery of the theater to watch, intoxicated by the new world, *The Stripling*, if I remember correctly. This is why I had to leave that yeshiva. Finally in Szatmár, where allegedly I was caught in heresy, after the calvary of lengthy persecution in which stone-throwing and the purchase of a handgun had a role, I defiantly turned my back on the ghetto with the embitterment of a seventeen-year-old Uriel Acosta, and swore to be an apostle of a war of extermination against religion. This "apostleship" lasted three years, while I privately passed concentrated examinations to earn my high school diploma, and swung over from being a talmudist with sidecurls to being one of the so-called intellectuals. And then came my Damascus. I saw the spiritual desolation of the Jewish intellectuals, their spiritual beggarliness, I saw that they had nothing that would really be theirs, nothing that was not borrowed from, or cast off by, the true proprietors. I saw how that sacred energy was being destroyed here, day after day, which for thousands of years had implanted Jewry into the future with roots that could not be pulled up. I saw how the flowers and the fruits of our life-tree were falling, and not only the rotten ones or the wormy ones. And suddenly there shone into my eyes, like a great beacon, the aware-

ness that to declare war blindly against religion in the name of enlightenment stemmed from the same kind of prejudice as to declare war
blindly against enlightenment in the name of religion. Inquisition
remains inquisition whether it is black or red. What was needed here
was not a declaration of war and inquisition, but instruction and love.
And with eyes sensitized by the Greek and Latin classics, I began to
read the prophets, those first free thinkers of mankind whose books
contain the entire dictionary of today's progressive ideas. I became
acquainted with the vast Jewish literature, poetry, learned to recognize
the cultural values contained in Jewish religion, and began to rejoice
over the treasures I had acquired in those years that I had thought
sterile and wasted.

And two great redemptive tasks began to dawn in my mind: to
bring my racial brothers, who languished in the dimness of the ghetto,
nearer to culture with the gentle means of enlightenment; and to take
from the Jewish past all that is culture, all that is truly ours, all that we
can even today proudly claim as ours, all that has a future, and to save
it for the Jewish intellectuals, with the weapons of enlightenment. This
was my road through the *Egyenlőség, The Rivers of Babylon*, the
Hebrew Poets, to the *Mult és Jövő*.[4]

Father's response elicited an acknowledgment from Dezsö Szabó,
again in the *Huszadik Század*:

> Dr. Patai's article (*Mult és Jövő*, April 1914) moved me frankly,
> deeply. If any direction manifests itself in such humaneness, it becomes
> my own writing, and I feel that its representative is my brother. For
> the truth is not direction X or direction Y; it is every human trend, for
> opposing truths exclude each other only in logic; in life they presup-
> pose each other. Let Dr. Patai's truth be effective inasmuch as it pre-
> serves the forces of the Jewish race, its deep human values, and can
> make them influential. But let my truth be effective each time Jewish
> racism and confessionalism intend to attack, imply hatred against other
> human forms. By saying this I surely do not preach the desirability of
> uniformity! The questions raised are deep problems. And I dare say
> that our debate was endowed with a noble tone precisely because both
> of us were able to raise ourselves from our Judaism and Magyarism up
> to humanism.[5]

In 1968 Mother still remembered clearly Father's incognito visit
to the theater of Nyitra, and even added a psychological detail missing in Father's account.

> A theatrical company came to town and they announced that they
> would perform a light comedy, *A suhanc* (The Stripling). Father felt
> that he simply must, must, must [Mother repeated the word three
> times for emphasis] see this play, which for him represented the out-

side world. So he borrowed a dress from his landlady, combed his *payes* [sidelocks] to look like the hairdo of a girl, tied a kerchief around his head—he was still too young to have a moustache—and thus disguised went to see the play. But, he told me, all the time while he was in the theater he felt his rabbi's eyes on him, he felt he was committing a terrible sin. Next day, I don't know how, the news spread that he had been to the theater. The rabbi called him in. He was a saintly man, a true rabbi. He said to him: "What a pity! You could have become a great rabbi." While Father was with the rabbi the other students of the yeshiva gathered outside and waited for him to come out in order to beat him up. He had only one friend, Moses Braun, who later changed his name to Bolgár, and remained a lifelong friend of Father. He was a very strong, muscular boy, and he said to the others: "I shall lay flat anybody who dares to touch Yosele Klein!" So they left him alone. Soon thereafter Father left and entered the Rabbinical Seminary in Budapest.

What happened next was, again according to my mother, that "when Father's mother heard what he had done, that he was in Budapest in that terrible den of iniquity, she went to fetch him, took him by the hand, did not even let him gather his belongings, and brought him back home to Pata." This piece of information is supplemented by what Father himself told me, namely, that among the yeshiva students the rumor circulated that from the cellar of the Rabbinical Seminary in Budapest a door led straight into hell, and that as soon as a yeshiva-*bokher* arrived, they cut off his *payes* and forced him to eat pork.

According to the *Annual Reports* of the Seminary, Father was a regularly matriculated student in the 1899–1900 and the 1900–1901 school years. Also, from the datelines of his Hebrew poems, which he published in a small volume in 1902, it appears that Father was in Budapest in 1900–1901. In 1901 he went to Galgócz—some fifteen miles from Nyitra—where he worked as a tutor of the children of a Jewish family. In 1902 he took his final high school examination in Nyitra, and then went back to Budapest, where he was to remain until settling in Palestine in 1939.

This time his parents recognized that it would be in vain to try to drag him back to their home or to a yeshiva. They considered him lost to their world, which was for them the only Jewish world. Many years later I heard, either from Father or from Mother, that when his father found out that he had started studying at the university, he "sat *shive*" over him, that is, performed the traditional mourning ritual for a near relative of sitting for seven *shiv'a* days on the floor:

for him, a son who engaged in secular studies was dead. In 1968, when I asked Mother about this, she could no longer remember it.

In the "Piarist" Catholic high school in Nyitra Father had a Greek and Latin teacher whom both he and Mother remembered well in later years. Mother, of course, knew of him only from what Father had told her. His name was Gellért Váry. By the time my father was his pupil he was an old and sick man. He noticed Father's extraordinary sense and feeling for poetry, and often invited him to his cell, where he gave him private tutoring in Greek literature. There, and I quote Mother literally,

> Father was astonished by the primitivity of that cell, the absence of all comfort. There was nothing in it but a table, a chair, and a narrow hard pallet without even a pillow. "Why do you live in such conditions?" Father asked him. His teacher's answer was that the pampering of the body distracts one from the higher things. And Father suddenly remembered that his yeshiva master, the rabbi of Huszt, also slept like this, without a pillow, and he was struck by the similarity in spirit between the Catholic priest and the Jewish rabbi. . . .

Father himself did describe the ascetic way of life of the rabbi of Huszt in the article quoted above, but he did not, at least not in writing, draw the parallel mentioned by Mother between him and the Piarist.

What Father did tell me about his Piarist teacher referred to a later incident. As a young doctor of philosophy Father went to pay him a visit in Nyitra. When he entered, he introduced himself as Dr. Joseph Patai, and added immediately, "formerly Joseph Klein." Father Váry greeted him warmly, and apropos of Father's name change he told him that some time previously a big man had come to see him, introducing himself as Károly Szilágyi. The teacher could not remember any student by this name, nor could he recognize him by his looks. Thereupon Mr. Szilágyi exclaimed: "*O tempores o mora!*" The misplaced plural forms triggered the old teacher's memory, and he cried, "O, it is you, Schlesinger!"

Father himself changed his name soon after his arrival in Budapest the second time, when he began to publish poetry. In those days it was *de rigueur* for poets, writers, artists, and musicians to have Hungarian names, and since almost all the Jews had German names that were given them *volens nolens* in the days of Joseph II (1780–1790), they were foremost among the name Magyarizers. Father's original family name, Klein, was among the most common in Hungary, competing in frequency with Grosz, Weisz, Schwarz, Braun, Grün, and Roth, and thus he felt no special attachment to it. He chose the name of the village in which he was born and spent his childhood, appended to it the suffix *-i* which has the same function as the *-er* in English (as in "New Yorker" for instance), and thus became Patai. He first used this new name in the small volume of Hebrew poems he published in 1902—on the title page his name appears as "*Yosef haPatai*" (literally, Joseph of Pata). The *-i* suffix in Hebrew happens to have the same meaning as in Hungarian. Many Hungarians have names ending in *-i* and indicating places of origin. In the case of the nobility or gentry, the same suffix is spelled with a *y*, and there are Patays who are members of those classes. While I was still in Hungary, and occasionally even here in America, I have sometimes been asked whether I was related to X. or Y. Patai or Patay. I could always answer with absolute certainty: "If his name is Patai I can be sure he is no relative of mine. All my paternal relations are called Klein."

Father's book of Hebrew poems mentioned above was entitled *Sha'ashu'e 'Alumim* (Delights of Youth). He dedicated it to Wilhelm Bacher (1850–1913), the great master of Agada research and rector of the Budapest Rabbinical Seminary: "To my master and teacher . . . R. Benjamin Zeev Bachrach [this was the original name of Bacher], a gift of gratitude from his pupil, Y. haP." The first poem in the volume is a sonnet, "To My Teacher," in which the young poet addresses his master:

> You, my father, the researcher of Israel's glory,
> You are the pride of our people, my master and teacher. . . .
> . . . .
> You awakened my spirit, revealed the hidden,
> Accept this gift of mine that conveys my thanks. . . .

The volume opens with an introduction, written in high-flying poetical Hebrew prose by Moshe Ben-Zevi, who was none other than Moses Braun, later Bolgár, Father's best friend, born like him in 1882, and himself a Hebrew poet and writer. He studied law, but worked as editor of the Jewish weeklies *Zsidó Szemle* in Budapest and *Zsidó Néplap* in Ungvár (today Uzhorod in Czechoslovakia).

His friendship with Father lasted as long as Father lived in Hungary. Moses Bolgár was a happy-go-lucky fellow, who liked to drink and to sing, and in his attitude and behavior was more like a Hungarian peasant than like a Jew. Years later, when I got acquainted with the great Hebrew poet Saul Tchernichowsky, I was struck by the similarities between them: both had assimilated in personality to the Gentile environment in which they grew up; where Bolgár behaved and even looked like a Hungarian peasant, Tchernichowsky behaved and looked like a Russian peasant. And yet both of them carried in their soul the ancient flame of Hebrew poetry. One summer Moses Bolgár visited my parents in the spa to which our entire household was transplanted for the vacation months. Mother had with her her maid, a good-looking lass named Lina, to whom Uncle Mózsi took a liking. I remember him sitting around in the evening on the porch, with a bottle of wine before him, and merrily singing the praises of beautiful Lina, of course not in Hebrew but in fruity Hungarian. I could not have been more than ten at the time, and had no idea what Uncle Mózsi could have wanted with the girl.

In 1968 Mother, reminiscing about how Moses Bolgár in his youth had saved Father from being beaten up by his fellow yeshiva students, sighed and said: "Poor boy! He did protect Father, but," and here her memory made a jump of forty-five years, "he was unable to save himself. He was dragged away and gassed. Eyewitnesses reported that until the last minute he sat and read, as if nothing would concern him, even after they were concentrated in the place from which they were taken away. . . . "

In his introduction to Father's poems Moses Bolgár wrote, "You, man of delight, my friend, you clothed yourself in spirit and filled your soul with daring. You made your face like a rock, and heeded not the fools; and you came to this people to pour a new spirit into them. . . . Like a pillar of fire shall your book march to the four winds of the earth . . . and you will make yourself a great and glorious name for ever and ever."

Sixteen years after the publication of his Hebrew poems Father gave a lecture to the Israelite Hungarian Literary Society, the leading forum of Jewish cultural activity in Budapest, on "Hungarian Hebrew Poets," the text of which he subsequently included in the introductory first volume of the second, five-volume edition of his *Hebrew Poets* (Budapest: Mult és Jövő, 1921, 1:101–47), of which I shall have more to say below. In it he reviewed, among the works of several other Hungarian Hebrew poets, his own youthful efforts, of which by that time he was more critical than appreciative:

The volume of poems entitled *Sha'ashu'e 'Alumim* (Delights of Youth), by Joseph Patai, published in 1902, is more closely related to Simon Bacher and the old German and Italian schools than to the modern Hebrew poetry whose great flowering was as yet totally unknown to Patai, the young student. . . . Joseph Patai (born Gyöngyöspata, 1882) collected in this first book of his the poems he wrote as an adolescent in the yeshiva and the Seminary, and dedicated it to Vilmos Bacher in an introductory sonnet. We find in it two small biblical epics ("The Golden Calf" and "The Scapegoat") in the style of the lengthy Moses-epic of [Naphtali Herz] Wessely, which, alas, had everywhere become the model for Hebrew narrative poetry for almost a century. "The Golden Calf" places in the center of the tragedy the Midrashic legend, according to which the generation of the desert saw in a vision fiery angels carrying the coffin of Moses in the air. . . .

We also find in Patai's book one or two humorous and satirical poems about student life in Budapest ("Song of the Shoes"), a few lyrical memories ("Memories of Pest"), written when, at the urging of his parents, he left, after one year, the Budapest Seminary, and went to a yeshiva in Galgócz; a few poems of friendship and gratitude, one or two emotional outbursts ("The Prayer"), translations of Petőfi, Arany, and Vörösmarty [the three most outstanding Hungarian poets of the nineteenth century] ("Homer and Ossian," "The Bard," "On the Death of a Child," etc.), and, naturally, neither could laments on the destitution and humiliation of the Hebrew language be missing. The old complaint, which was a constant accompaniment of the age of Enlightenment, in the poetry of the Italian Luzzatto as much as in that of the German Letteris and the Russian Gordon, cast a gloom also over the soul of Patai. . . . [6]

Some time during, or perhaps immediately after, his university studies, Father had to enlist in the army. This was a duty for all young men in Hungary upon reaching the age of eighteen, but while all other recruits had to serve, I believe, for three years, this was reduced to one year for those few who were the proud possessors of a high school diploma. Although it was mandatory for them, too, to enlist, they were called *einjährig Freiwillige* (one-year volunteers)—the official language in the Austro-Hungarian army being German. I distinctly remember having seen in my youth a small photograph of Father showing him in the uniform of an army cadet. Although Father was in general reticent to talk to me about his youth, he did tell me a few anecdotes from his days as a "volunteer." Since he was a candidate for the doctor of philosophy degree, or perhaps already had it, his drill-sergeant, talking in German, used to address him contemptuously as *Sie von der Philosophie* (you of the philosophy).

When the sergeant found out that one of his trainees was a teacher of mathematics, he said to him, "So, you are a math teacher? Well, go and number the latrines!" Father also told me that when some of the peasant boys (who were, of course, not trained together with the intelligentsia) could not identify the terms "left" and "right" with their left and right feet, their drillmaster had them tie a bundle of straw to the left foot and a bundle of hay to the right foot, and then, instead of the usual command, "Left, right; left, right!" he would bark, "Straw foot, hay foot! Straw foot, hay foot!"

Soon after his arrival in Budapest, Father switched to writing poetry in Hungarian (he was to return to Hebrew only in his old age, after settling in Palestine), and before long he became known as a promising young Hungarian Jewish poet. It so happened that in those very years the Israelite Congregation of Pest planned to enhance the Sabbath and holiday services in its great Dohány Street synagogue, as well as in the many other synagogues it maintained all over the city, by having religious Hungarian poems, set to music, sung in alternation with the traditional Hebrew prayers. The chief rabbi, Dr. Samuel Kohn (1841–1920), was entrusted with the task of procuring suitable poems, and he, in turn, asked Father to write them. Two letters are extant in which Dr. Kohn asks the help of Joseph Bánóczi (1849–1926), principal of the Jewish Teachers Seminary and one of the most outstanding Hungarian literary critics, in judging the poems Father, twenty-two years old at the time, submitted to him in response to his request. They read as follows (in my translation from the Hungarian):

September 27, 1904

Dear Mr. Director:

Some time ago I received the official assignment to procure, in place of our present rather deficient synagogue songs, more suitable ones. After several frustrated attempts, finally I think I have found in Mr. Joseph Patai a Hungarian poet who possesses Jewish knowledge and Jewish sentiment, and I can expect him to solve this problem successfully. He has already actually written the songs. I looked them over several times with him, also Dr. Goldziher read them,[7] and Patai was kind enough to take our comments into account.

I would like to settle the matter as soon as possible, considering that these songs have to be set to music before they are printed.

In order to achieve this aim I turn to you with the respectful request that you go over the enclosed song texts, and communicate your comments and authoritative opinion to the author and to me, respectively.

The former will be useful for the author, the latter for me, inasmuch as I shall be able to refer to your opinion in my report to the council of our congregation, which, I know, will attribute great importance to it.

In the hope that you will be kind enough to fulfill my request in the interest of the matter,

I remain

Yours respectfully,

Dr. Samuel Kohn

Dr. Bánóczi replied immediately—regrettably, his letter is not extant—and the chief rabbi wrote to him a second time:

Sept. 30, 1904

Dear Mr. Director:

Please accept my thanks for having kindly taken care of my request so expeditiously.

In the interest of the matter and of Mr. Patai it would be desirable if Patai would rework the poems, or some stanzas, utilizing your comments and guidance that you communicated to him, and would thereafter again present them to you, and if you in turn would kindly express an opinion about the value of the thus reworked poems in general and in detail, so that I should be able to refer to your much valued opinion in my report that I shall submit, or possibly attach it.

Mr. Patai presented the [printed] poem, titled "From the Festal Liturgy," only as a sample; no mention was made of its inclusion among the songs.

Goldziher and I noticed a few unusual (possibly un-Hungarian) expressions and locutions, which, it seems, the author used for the sake of the rhyme and rhythm. Allow me to call your attention to these in particular.

Repeating my thanks, with cordial regards,

Yours,

Dr. Kohn[8]

Within a short time Father's *Templomi Énekek* (Temple Songs) were set to music, became part of the services in all the synagogues of the Pest community, and were sung by the choir to the accompaniment of the great organ of the Dohány Temple.

Once Bánóczi became acquainted with Father's work, he continued to take interest in it and in him, befriending the young poet and supporting his publishing ventures. Thus began a lifelong friendship between the two that only ended twenty years later with Bánóczi's death. When Father published the first issue of his monthly, the introductory article in it was written by Bánóczi, and subsequent issues also contain contributions by him.

In the early 1900s Father found employment as a staff writer for the Budapest Jewish political weekly *Egyenlőség* (Equality), published and edited by Miksa Szabolcsi (1857–1915). He also served for a while as Hebrew tutor of Szabolcsi's son, Lajos (1889–1943), who, after his father's death, became owner and editor of the paper. Father took the pen name "Secundus," thereby expressing his feelings of respect for Miksa Szabolcsi, whom he considered Primus.

Given Father's fervent Jewishness, it was inevitable that he should be attracted to Zionism. In 1903 he became one of the founders of the Budapest Maccabea, the organization of Zionist university students that was to develop into the hub of Zionist work in Hungary. His Zionism led to disagreements and clashes between him and Miksa Szabolcsi, who was a vociferous anti-Zionist and often attacked Zionism in his paper. Yet when Szabolcsi died, Father wrote an article about him in which he not only acknowledged his indebtedness to his former chief, but described him as an intrepid fighter for Jewry, and even tried to explain and excuse Szabolcsi's anti-Zionism as a position he was conditioned by his upbringing and environment to embrace.

> Szabolcsi rejoiced at the results Zionism achieved abroad, he loved Zionist literature and poetry, declared himself a cultural Zionist, loved the Jewish self-respect of the young Zionists and their Jewish enthusiasm, and waxed sentimental over the colonization of Palestine and the renaissance of the Hebrew language. But he had lived his youth in the days in which the Jews, who were educated in the Bach period, had to demonstrate their Hungarian patriotism in every direction, and even now he was afraid that Zionism, which, he felt, had assumed harmful "nationalistic airs," would endanger the position of Hungarian Jewry and give nourishment to anti-Semitism. While, of course, the fact is that, on the one hand, even the loudest patriotism and the most strident arguments will not convince the anti-Semites who simply do not want to be "convinced," and, on the other, today Hungarianism is already in the blood of the Hungarian Jewish youth, so that it is superfluous to make a constant show of patriotism, which can only arouse suspicions. After all, this generation was born Hungarian, Hungarian is its mother tongue, Hungarian are its songs, Hungarian is its culture — today it is only its Jewishness that is in need of saving. And nobody rejoiced more at this rescue work than Miksa Szabolcsi. At a Maccabea evening of the Zionist university students he stated in his

greeting that Zionism was his secret love, and that it pained him that he could not admit it openly, indeed had to turn against it in the outside world, because—this was what "politics" demanded.

Abandoning for a moment his reminiscences of Szabolcsi, Father used the opportunity to state clearly what his own views were about the matter:

> The adherence to this "policy," which was in any case futile outwardly, while inwardly it was sterile and brought atrophy, has become one of the greatest problems, of the most vital importance, for the whole of Hungarian Jewry. Hungarian Jewry has become a *corpus separatum*, has moved further and further from the roots, has withered, and become in the eyes of world Jewry notorious and ridiculous with its special chauvinism. The horoscope of the so-called liberal regime conjured up enchanting shores before the imagination of Hungarian Jewry, and showed it a new Canaan flowing with milk and honey from the Carpathians to the Adriatic, in which there were no more Jewish problems, no Jewish anxiety, no Jewish waiting for the Messiah. . . . This was the fatal mistake of Miksa Szabolcsi: to forget the many painful lessons of the past and the eternal fluctuation of historical events. The Jewish problem is not tied to time and to place; Zionism seeks a universal solution in both Palestine and the Diaspora. This is a question of the human dignity of Jewry that impassions those who are self-respecting and look to the future, and it would have deserved in this country a fighter of the stature of Miksa Szabolcsi. But it so happened that Miksa Szabolcsi, who planned visits to the Holy Land and wrote accounts of his travels in the Holy Land, who sang the praises of this or that Zionist colony, and for whom the Zionist hymn *Hatikva* was a household song, fought embittered battles against the Zionists. And Miksa Szabolcsi, the old fighter of Jewish self-respect, constantly opposed the young fighters of Jewish self-respect.

After taking to task the Hungarian Jewish establishment for having done nothing for Szabolcsi, for barely enabling him to make a living, and for looking down upon him because he served Jewry, Father describes at the end of the article his last visit to the sick man.

> I barely recognized in the broken, emaciated man the old, strong, fighting Szabolcsi. . . . I sat down next to his bed and I was seized with the image of Ben Yair about whom the Talmud relates that when he visited his dying master, Simon ben Yohai, he cried out, "Woe to me, my Master, that I must see you thus." And it seemed to me that I was hearing the answer of the martyr Ben Yohai: "Be glad and happy that you can see me thus, because all this came upon me for the sake of the Torah and Israel. . . . "

Miksa Szabolcsi motioned to his family to leave him alone with me for a moment. He reached for my hand with his two weak arms, and said with tears in his eyes: "My dear son, now that I have suffered so much I feel doubly what it means to hurt somebody, to cause suffering to somebody. It was a mistake, a misunderstanding, and I feel that I must make amends. We must forgive each other. We must work together in friendship for the sake of the Jewish people.[9]

A word seems in place about the reference Father makes to "the Bach period" in explanation of the origins of Miksa Szabolcsi's anti-Zionism. After the defeat of the Hungarian revolution of 1848 by Austria, the Viennese government, as represented by its minister of the interior, Baron Alexander Bach, imposed upon Hungary a regime of brutal repression of all patriotic manifestation and sentiment. The years between 1850 and 1859 became known as the Bach period, during which Baron Bach tried to transform the monarchy, which comprised many nationalities, into a unified, absolute, German-speaking empire, with the strictest censorship, oppression, and, where the need arose, open force. As a reaction to this ruthless regime, patriotism became the most cherished trait of the true Hungarians, at first *sub rosa*, and, after the fall of Bach in 1859, openly. During those years the Jews of Hungary felt that their greatest duty toward their homeland was to be demonstratively patriotic, which remained a major characteristic of Hungarian Jews down to the tragic days of World War II.

It was while working at Szabolcsi's weekly that Father met Mother. The office manager of *Egyenlöség* was Gyula (Julius) Virág, whose wife Szeréna was a second cousin of my mother. When Uncle Gyula (as I would later call him) told his wife about the young poet and journalist who had started working at the paper, and who, in addition, would soon have his doctorate, she decided that her young cousin Esztike must meet him. By that time Father had to his credit, in addition to his Hebrew poems, the liturgical songs, and he had begun to publish his Hungarian translations of medieval and modern Hebrew poetry. In 1905 he started to edit a modest series of books titled Hungarian Jewish Library, the third volume of which (preface dated November 1905), *Hebrew Poets*, contained his translations of poems by the eight most outstanding medieval Hebrew poets, Samuel Hanagid, Solomon ibn Gabirol, Moses ibn Ezra, Yehuda Halevi, Abraham ibn Ezra, Yehuda Alharizi, Immanuel of

Rome (Manoello), and Israel Najara. Two years later he published his doctoral dissertation entitled "Bajza and Lessing" in the foremost Hungarian literary review. It discussed the relationship of the Hungarian poet and critic Joseph Bajza (1804–1858) to the great German poet, dramatist, and critic Gotthold Ephraim Lessing (1729–1781). Bajza, incidentally, was born in Szűcsi, the village next to Pata, whose Jews were needed to form a quorum of ten adult men for the Sabbath prayers in grandfather Moshe Klein's house.

In connection with the circumstances in which she met Father, my mother told me in 1968 — more than sixty years after the event — about a legendlike occurrence that preceded their engagement. My paternal grandparents' house in Pata was always open to guests, the so-called *farers* or *ayrekhs*, pious, wandering Jews who went from place to place and were looked upon with religious awe as saintly, and somewhat mysterious, figures. One Friday afternoon, just as my grandmother was lighting the candles, which she always did well before dusk because it was a *mitzve*, a good deed in the religious sense, to usher in the Sabbath early, such a *farer* arrived. As he entered, he said *Mazel tov* (good luck). Grandfather, surprised, asked him, "For what?" The visitor answered, "Your eldest son is a bridegroom, and the name of his bride is Esther." Grandmother did not interrupt the candle-lighting ritual in the course of which she used to pray for all her seven children. She concluded the blessing over the candles with her usual solemnity, and then she turned to the stranger and said, "And now tell me about the *kalle* [bride]." But the *farer* could or would say nothing more. She understood his silence to mean that his mission was to say just what he had said, and that he could add nothing to it. After the Sabbath they wrote to their son, told him what had happened, and pressed him for particulars about his bride. But he answered them that, alas, he had not yet met the girl whom he desired to be his life's companion. However, within less than a year he and Mother, Esther, were engaged. When the story reached my mother's parents, it smoothed the way for the young couple to get their consent. Mother's father, religious Jew that he was, was originally opposed to the match because he would not agree that his daughter should marry an *epikayres*, an unbelieving Jew, which my father was known to be. But he saw in the incident a kind of higher blessing or approval: the *shiddakh* (match) must, after all, be from heaven. Mother's mother, on the other hand, who was "a really intelligent, 100 percent modern woman with a thinking head" (as Mother characterized her), explained the occurrence as nothing more than a case of news spreading from mouth to mouth and from place to place, often in an exaggerated and premature manner.

When I asked Mother (in 1968) how she herself viewed the event, she said that she was inclined to accept her mother's explanation. For even though Father might not yet have been ready to ask her for her hand — this is why he made his "alas" statement to his parents — he later confessed to her that the very first time they had met he had fallen in love with her. And the fact that thereafter they met frequently and went out together a lot may have been enough to engender the rumor that Joseph Patai had become engaged to marry Esther Ehrenfeld.

The first meeting between Father and Mother was preceded by a meeting between him and my mother's mother. Mother was in Nagyvárad where she used to spend her summer vacations, and her mother went with the Virágs to the theater. Grandfather, of course, never went to the theater because as a great-grandson of Moses Sofer he obeyed the injunctions of his illustrious forebear, who in his ethical testament placed the theater out of bounds for his descendants. But he did not, or could not, impose the same restriction on his wife. There in the theater Grandmother met Father. My grandparents lived at the time in the same house as the Virágs, at 42 Ó Street. According to what my mother remembered in 1968, she herself met Father the first time at Passover. If so, some eight months passed after the meeting of Grandmother and Father in the theater until the first meeting between Mother and Father, which seems to be too long a time even for those more leisurely days.

Mother could not recall the year in which that first meeting took place. However, it must have been in the spring of 1906, or perhaps a year earlier. I conclude this from the fact that in 1906 a volume of Father's poems (in Hungarian) was published, and in it, among the illustrations, there is one, printed twice (on pages 9 and 165), which was the work of Mother, identified only as "E. Ehrenfeld." It is a drawing of an eagle, shown soaring up toward the rays of an invisible sun. The volume, titled *Babylon Vizein* (On the Rivers of Babylon), contains mostly religious poems, including the synagogue songs mentioned before. At the time this book was published the relationship between Father and the editor of *Egyenlöség* was still good; the volume carries a dedication to Miksa Szabolcsi.

In any case, whether the year was 1905 or 1906, that Passover the Virágs and Father were invited by my grandparents to the Seder, the festive supper, surrounded by many prayers, songs, and rites. Grandfather, who conducted the observances, was dressed in the traditional *kittl*—this embroidered, long white linen gown is also worn in certain Jewish communities by the groom during the marriage ceremony, by all married men on the High Holy Days, and by the dead, who are garbed in it for their burial. Father, who, as he later confessed to her, was smitten by Mother at first sight, tried to engage her in conversation, but, as she told me in 1968, "I was used to following every word of the Seder, so that during that first meeting we did not speak at all."

When they did speak, at subsequent meetings, all did not go well at first. There were disturbing differences between the two young people in background, education, and views on art, religion, and life. There was Father's upbringing in the peasant environment of Pata, his barefoot childhood that stamped him with a certain mark of basic primitivity for the rest of his life. There were his rustic table manners, his loud slurping of the coffee or the soup, which Mother could not refrain from censuring occasionally at the dinner table years later, even in the presence of their adolescent children. There was Father's unrefined taste in food, about which Mother once told me in her typical half-humorous and half-embarrassed way that Father used to like having bread with herring and marmalade. For a young girl brought up in the refined atmosphere of a rich Jewish house in a city that was a cultural and artistic center, these peasantish traits must indeed have been difficult to tolerate.

More importantly, there was Father's rebellious irreligiosity, his outright rejection of all religious forms and rites, which clashed with Mother's outlook still anchored in traditional concepts and observances. He was, in addition, a socialist revolutionary, imbued with radical ideas and ideals to which he gave expression in his poems, two of which were published in 1905 in the Budapest daily *Népszava* (The People's Voice), the central organ of the Hungarian Social Democratic party, which for decades was to remain the only legal daily of the Hungarian workers' movement. These two, as far as I am able to ascertain, were the first of his original poems to be published in Hungarian. One is titled "Break the Lute," and its burden is: Break the lute that sings of frivolous things, of desires, loves, and lusts, and cries over the falsely pictured old times, for a new day is coming, a great struggle is in the making. . . . Break the lute that sings songs of pleasure to entertain the happy ones with flattery, in demeaning servitude, when the millions, yearning for freedom, already hammer on the iron walls of their prison, and the old world is about to collapse under the blows of a million fists. Break the lute, tear its sluggish chords, if even now it dares to sing of other things, when the lies fall into the dust, the sacred truth is victorious, and the triumphant, proud people steps up to its eternal throne. . . .

The second poem, entitled "The People's Judgment," is even more revolutionary. It calls for death to those who carry with blind pride the tawdry flag of tyranny, who do not hear the fearsome cries of woe of the tortured masses of slaves. . . . Already the waves billow, a million hills of water exult, sizzle, and the revolution dances its frightening dance over a thousand corpses. . . . Tremble! For here comes the people's judgment, rejuvenating the world. It comes to drive off the night shrouded in lies, and to light the eternal flame of truth.[10]

I can vividly imagine the shock my mild-hearted mother got when Father, undoubtedly proudly, showed her these poems. In her memory sixty-three years later Father's revolutionary idealism remained registered as an antifamily position:

> When we got acquainted, he told me that his feelings for his parents were the same as for any other poor people. As a socialist he had sympathy for all those who suffered. I was terribly upset by this. If there are such great differences in views between us, how can we hope to develop a harmony? . . . Once Father wrote to me that he was not created to protect only his own house; if a fire should break out, he would try to extinguish it not only in his own house but would try to save all Jewry. . . . My parents and I were at a summer resort when this letter came. I used to wait for the postman to see whether he brought something for me. When I read it, all my strength left me, I had to sit down on the nearest bench. I thought: is this, possibly, the beginning of his saying good-bye to me? If somebody feels that he must devote all his life to the Jewish people as a whole, how can he tie himself down to one woman? It seemed clear that despite his love, despite the great tenderness that radiated from his letter, his view was that he could not belong to one woman and one family only.

Then there were also differences between them in literary taste. Here it was Father who was far ahead of Mother, whose views on literature were at the time molded by nothing more than her high school classes in literary history, while Father, a young poet of stature in his own right, had a strong critical sense and uncompromisingly high standards. A critical ability to recognize value or the lack of it in a poem was for Father a basic manifestation of human intelligence. As Mother put it in 1968:

> There were many other things. He was not satisfied with my literary taste. The *Yearbook* of the Israelite Hungarian Literary Society published at that time a story in verse, a novel in the form of a long poem, I have forgotten who was the author. But I remember I told Father that it was beautiful. Well, he got terribly upset. His whole belief in our future happiness was shaken. . . . How, a girl who has so little literary taste? . . . It was terrible for him. . . . Later, of course, I, too, saw that it was really nothing but trash. . . .

It took time for difficulties and differences such as these to be ironed out. This explains, in part, why three or four years passed between my parents' first meeting and their marriage. Another reason was that my mother's parents, as well as the young couple, felt that first my father should have a position with a decent income. In June 1908 Father obtained his high school teacher's diploma, and in 1909 he was appointed to the faculty of the Budapest municipal *főreáliskola*, high school for modern languages and sciences, one of the finest educational institutions in the city. It so happened that this was the school at which Theodor Herzl was a student from 1870 to 1875. To be a teacher at such a school was an important position that carried considerable prestige as well as a comfortable salary. The wedding could now take place.

In 1968 Mother remembered very little of the time Father courted her. The Virágs seem to have been helpful in enabling them to meet, and whenever Father came to visit them, they immediately sent up word to Mother that "the black dog," as they referred to Father, more in fondness than in derision, was there. Thereupon Mother would go down to the Virágs' apartment, and there she and Father could converse, always, of course, chaperoned by Mrs. Virág. A little later Mother's parents moved to an apartment in Buda, with a view of the river, the Margaret Bridge, and the Margaret Island, and, looking out the window, Mother could espy Father walking across the bridge. She would recognize him from afar, even before she could discern his face, from his bushy black hair and the big black fluttering bow tie he sported. And, whenever Mother was away from the city, they wrote to each other frequently and at length. Mother remembered:

> Once Father wrote to me that my letters were beautiful. Well, this was for me as if he had dubbed me a knight. He wrote how much my letters gave him, how much I meant to him. He asked me why I did not address him as *Du* [the second person singular, the familiar form of address in Hungarian], whereupon I answered him that I could not yet say *Du* to him, that has to come by itself. I kept all his letters in a trunk that we jokingly called "the dirty laundry chest." When we came here [to Palestine, in 1939], I left it in Budapest. What a pity! The letters showed how difficult a road it was for us to become adjusted to each other. It was difficult because our backgrounds, our milieus, were so different.

Their official engagement took place in Nagyvárad. Mother was there for her usual vacation-time visit, and Father came after her and brought her an engagement ring. "It was a very cheap ring. When Malvin [the wife of Mother's uncle Ede Kurländer], who was a very malicious and evil-minded woman, as well as a stupid goose, saw it, she jeered at it. In fact, she was right, for that ring today would cost no more than perhaps three Israeli pounds. It was a piece of junk. At that time Father's esthetic sense was not yet highly developed. . . . "

I think it was sometime after his engagement to Mother that the reconciliation between Father and his parents took place. When Grandfather Klein learned that Father's intended was a religious girl from a good Jewish family, he relented. The son, whom he had pronounced dead some years earlier, had come back to life. Once engaged to Mother, Father felt that he wanted to do something for his parents. In his parents' house in Pata there was no running water, so that Grandfather had to go every day with his donkey to the village well, quite some distance away, to fetch water. This was no easy chore, for not only did he have to draw water from the well and fill the two barrels that were tied to the back of the donkey, but, after arriving back home, he had to lift off the heavy barrels from the back of the animal and place them in the kitchen. To save his father all this trouble, their resurrected son used whatever he could spare from his meager earnings to have a well dug in his parents' courtyard. Then, in order to make the life of his mother easier, too, Father had a porch built in front of the kitchen where his mother could do some of the preparations for the meals or simply take the air if she had time. Evidently, blood proved thicker than the water of all the revolutionary billows of which Father had sung with such abandon only a few years earlier.

After their engagement Father took Mother to meet his boss, Miksa Szabolcsi, and his family. Mother remembered the event some sixty years later:

> It was a delicate situation because the Szabolcsis would have liked Father to marry their daughter. That marriage would, of course, have assured Father's career: from being the chief contributor, he could immediately have been promoted to co-owner of *Egyenlőség*. So I went there with my heart leaping into my mouth. But they were people of culture. They received me well. Miksa Szabolcsi was a warmhearted man. He took me by the hand, led me to the window, looked into my eyes, and said: "With what did you enchant our Patai?" I did not yet have the facility for light repartee, and, besides, I thought that enchanting meant bewitching. So I answered simplemindedly, "That is not at all the case. I did not enchant him."

The wedding itself presented a problem. Mother's parents, being Orthodox, naturally wanted an Orthodox wedding. But this would have been embarrassing for Father as the chief contributor to the leading Neolog weekly. One must understand that in those days, only forty years after the Hungarian Jewish Congress split Hungarian Jewry into two mutually antagonistic camps, the Orthodox (or Conservative), and the Neolog (or Liberal), it would have been considered little less than treasonable for a Neolog intellectual leader to submit himself to an Orthodox religious ceremony. The solution found was to have a private wedding in Nagymaros, a resort on the banks of the Danube, and to ask Rabbi Israel Braun, Father's uncle, to officiate. Although Rabbi Braun was Orthodox, he was the rabbi of a small private congregation (that is, he was not a member of the official Orthodox establishment) and, besides, his being a close relative of the bridegroom superseded considerations of congregational affiliation. Moreover, if Rabbi Braun performed the marriage, it was sure to satisfy and reassure his sister, my father's mother, and her rigorist husband. Since a religious wedding was not recognized by the Hungarian authorities, it had to be, and was, preceded by a civil marriage at the Budapest city hall.

The question of a wedding trip was solved by the lucky coincidence of Father having received, shortly before his marriage, a fellowship from the Ministry of Education and Culture in recognition of his work as a translator of medieval Hebrew poets into Hungarian. The stated purpose of the fellowship was to enable him to do research at the British Museum Library in London and the Bodleian Library in Oxford, to locate unpublished manuscripts of Hebrew poets, and ultimately to translate and publish them in Hungarian. So in the summer of 1909 he and his bride set out for England, where they spent some eight weeks. Some of the poems he copied found their place in Father's Hungarian anthology entitled *Hebrew Poets*, some he published in Hebrew in *HaTzofe*, the scholarly journal edited by Professor Ludwig Blau, rector of the Budapest Rabbinical Seminary, and still others he published many years later in his Hebrew book *MiS'fune haShira* (From the Treasure House of Song), which was printed in Jerusalem in the 1940s. I take pride in the fact that Father dedicated this Hebrew book to me, saying, "To my first-born son Raphael, the first doctor of the Hebrew University of Jerusalem."

About my parents' trip to England I have three sources of information. One is the stories Mother told me while I was a teenager, the second, her reminiscences in 1968, and the third, Father's articles that he sent from the trip to *Egyenlőség*. As a teenager I was told that in the pension in which my parents stayed in London, they were served roast beef for breakfast which they put down as a curious local custom. (Needless to say, the pension kept a kosher kitchen.) Once they went rowing on the river (which river?), and, Father not being an adept at that sport, they found themselves drifting far downstream and had great difficulty in returning to the place where they had hired the boat. I must have been told of other adventures as well, but have long forgotten them.

In 1968 Mother told me that she did not consider the articles Father sent from England to his paper as being among his best work. Of Oxford she remembered another curiosity: no student there lived in one room. Every single student had two rooms, a living-dining room and a bedroom; no student would take any food, not even a cup of tea, in the room in which he slept. It was especially Father, who only a few years earlier had shared an unheated room with four other students in a poor section of Budapest, who was impressed by the comfort and luxury students enjoyed in Oxford. Conforming to local standards, my parents, too, took two rooms in the seven-room house of a merchant's clerk. Returning to London, they again boarded in the same Jewish pension, whose owner was, as Mother remembered, a very educated and many-sided person, who managed the boarding house with the help of his two sisters.

Quite rapidly an enormous sympathy developed between Father and that man. They would engage in hour-long conversations. One night I woke up, and saw that Father was not in his bed. I looked at the clock: it was two past midnight. I tiptoed down the stairs to see where he was, and saw him sitting in our landlord's study, deep in discussion with him. So I went up again and went back to sleep. Our landlord at the time published a yearbook for British Jews. I think there was a connection between that and Father's plan to publish a Hungarian Jewish almanac.

The last statement supplied an important clue to a question that had long bothered me: how did Father conceive the idea of publishing (in 1911) the *Magyar Zsidó Almanach* (Hungarian Jewish Almanac), that large, beautifully and luxuriously produced albumlike volume, which as an artistic and literary achievement has few equals to this day in any country? It would seem that the idea came to him in the course of his conversations with that anonymous editor of a British-Jewish yearbook.

From Father's articles that he sent from England and Holland to *Egyenlőség*, some of which he reprinted in 1920 in volume two of his collected essays,[11] I learned some additional details about his sojourn in England. In Oxford he became friendly with Moses Hirsch Segal (1876–1968), who was a tutor in biblical and Semitic studies at the university, and whom Father describes as a scholar of the Bible and the Mishna, and, at the same time, "the ritual slaughterer of the small Jewish congregation of Oxford." In Segal's home in Oxford Father also met Arye Leib Frumkin (1845–1916), Segal's father-in-law, a Jewish scholar of renown and pioneer of Jewish settlement in Palestine, who had built the first house in the first Jewish "colony," Petah Tiqva. After serving as rabbi in several British congregations, Segal became lecturer in Bible and Semitic langauges at the Hebrew University of Jerusalem. It was there that, several years later, I met him and his family, including his charming daughter Ettie. In 1936 he and I shared the Bialik Prize of the Tel Aviv Municipality, he for his book on the grammar of Mishnaic Hebrew, and I for my doctoral thesis on water in ancient Palestinian folklore, for which I earned the first Ph.D. degree to be awarded by the Hebrew University.

Apart from encounters such as these, Father's letters published in *Egyenlőség* contain no information on his life in England. I learned from them, however, that his view of British Jewish culture, and especially of the Anglo-Jewish press, was rather critical. On the other hand, he was impressed by the Zionism of British Jewry, and by its open avowal and assertion of its Judaism, which, as he pointedly stated in one of his letters, contrasted with the careful and painful hiding of Jewish identity he had observed in Hungary.

> According to British concepts it would be impossible for a Jew to deny his Jewishness, or to be flattered by being taken for a Christian. The Jewish gentleman would regard that as an incorrectness, a lack of character, not to mention conversion, which, in fact, occurs very rarely here. The noblest Jewish lords and ladies personally take the lead in the small organizations of the poorest Jews. They consider it quite natural that the forum of their charitable work should be Jewry, and the conviction that the essence of the real gentleman is a self-assured openness, and that the aristocrat, unless he is a parvenu, adheres quite naturally to the consequences of his birth, runs in their blood. And more than that: several of them emblazoned their coats of arms with Jewish motives: on the arms of Francis Abraham Montefiore one can read three times the word "Jerusalem" written in Hebrew characters. The coat of arms of Lord Swaythling displays a shield decorated with lion and palm motives, and carried by two Judean warriors. He himself visited Palestine twice to study the situation of the Jews there. In Hungary, first of all, to be concerned with Palestine is treason, and, moreover, not only would the Jewish "higher and lesser nobles" not put a Hebrew word on their coats of arms, but even the "common people" carefully wrap up their prayer books in newspaper when they go to the synagogue on the High Holy Days lest people recognize what they are from the golden Hebrew letters embossed on the bindings.

It must have been with quite some misgivings that the anti-Zionist Miksa Szabolcsi printed these lines, which pointed to a connection between the fear of Zionism and the hiding of Jewish identity and execrated equally both of these phenomena of Hungarian Jewish life.[12]

After a brief stopover in Amsterdam, my parents returned to Budapest and began to work on the realization of the idea of publishing a Hungarian Jewish almanac. Before long it became clear to them that the crux of the matter was finances. The publication of an extraordinarily luxurious large volume like the one my father envisaged would cost a lot of money. No publisher was willing to risk the investment in a venture that could well end up with a great deficit. When Father began to toy with the idea that he himself would publish the book, he consulted Miksa Szabolcsi, whose reaction was, as

Mother recalled in 1968, to warn him off most emphatically: "It will cost you your last pair of pants," he said. "To publish something like this! Are you crazy? Here in Hungary, where the Jews are even more red-white-green [the colors of the Hungarian flag] than the Christians?"

Finally, it was Mother's faith in Father and his plan that made the publication of the *Almanac* possible. The only money my parents had at the time was the dowry my mother had brought into the marriage. After thorough consultations and discussions they decided to invest it, all of it, into producing the *Almanac*. This much my mother told me, rather reluctantly, in 1968. She wanted me to stop the tape recorder while she was telling me about it:

> *Question*: From where did you have the money to publish the *Almanac*? It must have cost a fortune, such a luxurious, large volume. . . .
>
> *Answer*: I don't know. . . . It is not pleasant to talk about it. . . .
>
> *Question*: O, Mother, please!
>
> *Answer*: Well, Father got some dowry with me, and we used that money. . . . I think the promise was 10,000 florins, of which 5,000 was in cash, 2,500 went on buying furniture, and 2,500 remained as a debt. O, please, don't write about this. . . . It is unpleasant for me. . . .

This piece of information was a puzzle for me. Ten thousand florins was a respectable amount, and I knew that my grandfather Ehrenfeld never earned more money than was needed for a modest subsistence. My mother herself told me on another occasion, that once, when Grandmother was sick, Melissa Schlesinger, Mother's maternal first cousin, who was a rich woman, gave my grandparents a gift of 1,000 florins to tide them over. Still, seeing that the subject was a painful one for Mother, I did not raise the next logical question: how did her father have the money for such a dowry? Fifteen years later (1983) the puzzle was solved during a conversation I had with Aunt Ruth, the widow of Mother's brother, Bertalan Ehrenfeld. Although eighty-three years old, Aunt Ruth remembered clearly what she had learned about this issue when she became a member of the family more than sixty years earlier. What happened, she told me, was that Mother's dowry was provided by her grandmother Kurländer, who was still alive at the time, a widow and quite wealthy. In view of the fact that Mother was a great favorite of her grandmother, to whom she bore a striking resemblance, this explanation of the origin of Mother's dowry, and with it the finances for the *Almanac*, seems more than plausible.

Once the decision was made, Father and Mother jointly went to work on assembling the material for the *Almanac*. It was a major editorial undertaking, involving as it did the procurement of articles, short stories, poems, critical essays, and a rich assortment of illustrations from both Hungarian Jewish authors and artists and their colleagues abroad, whose writings, of course, had first to be translated into Hungarian. What Father intended to do was, as Mother recalled it in 1968, "to present to Jewry a work that did not reflect the spirit of oppressed Galuth Judaism. . . . He wanted to show Judaism in beauty. . . . This remained the central pillar of his entire life—to present Judaism in beauty, in art, in its ancient and revivified culture. . . . "

Looking back at the joint life of my father and mother from the historical distance of more than thirty years after my father's death, I believe that the close collaboration between them on the *Almanac* was a major factor that cemented their two lives, and created a closeness, a unity, a harmony between them that was to remain the foundation of their marriage for more than forty years.

As the foregoing remarks indicate, my parents' marriage was a happy one. I never witnessed a moment of discord between them, and they appeared to me to be always in complete harmony, with great concern for each other's well-being. If I knew more about the attitude of Mother toward Father than *vice versa*, this was due simply to the fact that she was much more outgoing in the expression of her feelings toward him, as she was also toward us children. She loved him dearly, and displayed in quite an unrestrained manner her concern for his safety and well-being. She worried about him, and whenever he was away from home, on a lecture tour in Hungarian towns, on trips to neighboring countries, or on a tour of Palestine, she trembled for his safety, and could barely wait for his return. As I grew older I recognized that beyond her complete devotion to Father, her overly intense fear and concern for him was basically the same feeling her own father had for members of his family, and that she exhibited the same anxiety where the well-being of her own children was concerned. But long before I reached this understanding, I developed an almost automatic reaction to her fear-studded sensitivity: I tried to conceal from her everything I felt would make her worry or become alarmed.

As for Mother's relations to Father, I am convinced not only that throughout their married life, which spanned forty-five years, she never took the slightest interest in any other man, but also that until the end, when his final illness enfeebled Father, he was for her the solid foundation and center of her very existence. Whether Father was similarly wrapped up emotionally in Mother I had no way of knowing because he spent so much time away from home and because, when at home, his behavior toward Mother was always extremely restrained.

However, there is incontrovertible evidence in the form of the many love poems Father wrote to Mother that his feelings toward her were those of the ardent lover toward the woman who is his muse and who inspires him with a love composed of a happy blend of the spiritual, the emotional, the intellectual, and the physical. In his verse he called her Sulamith, entitled the volume in which he collected his love poems *Sulamit, látod a Lángot?* (Sulamith, Seest Thou the Flame? (Budapest: *Mult és Jövő*, 1919), and dedicated it to "Edith, the Source of Songs." Several of the poems contained in this volume are as outspokenly erotic as was possible in the early twentieth century in Budapest. They attest to an aspect of his relationship to her that, on the basis of my own observation, I would never have suspected. What I saw led me to believe that he was rather cool toward her. I never saw him kissing or hugging or even touching her. I never heard him utter a word of endearment to her. I never even heard him call her by her name, while I remember clearly that she would call him Yóshka, a diminutive of Joseph, or Yóshkám, my Yóshka. That over and above the common interests they had in Judaism and Zionism, in Jewish art and culture, he appreciated her literary and poetic talent I know from the fact that he published her poems and critical essays in his journal, published a volume of her poetry and a novel of hers, and, in addition to these writings, published a small book of literary criticism of her poetry written by a poet-rabbi, Isaac Pap. Incidentally, no such volume of criticism was ever published about his own poetic work.

Several of Father's poems were set to music by Hungarian Jewish composers, such as Oszkár Dienzl and Hugó Kelen, and recited repeatedly at cultural evenings organized by Father and on various other occasions. I wish I were a poet and could translate some of these love poems with at least a faint resemblance to their original beauty. Regrettably, of Father's entire poetic output only four poems, all of a religious nature, and none of them among his best, were translated into English (published in the *Hebrew Standard* of New York and the *Jewish Independent* of Cleveland, Ohio), in the rather mediocre rendering of William N. Loew, of whom the only thing I know is that he was a brother of Immanuel Löw, the famous rabbi of Szeged, Hungary, and author of *Die Flora der Juden*. In his old age Father himself translated some of his poems into Hebrew, but these translations, too, lack the quality of the original.

While the *Almanac* was in the preparatory stage, Mother became pregnant, and just a few weeks before its appearance she brought me into this world on November 22, 1910. The birth took place, as was the custom at the time, at home, in the apartment my parents had in Munkácsy Street, not far from the place where my mother's parents lived. As she recalled in 1968:

> Everything went fine, everything was normal, it was easy. I was attended only by a madame [this was the term Mother used for a midwife]. If there were no complications, no doctor was needed. You weighed almost 5 kilos [about 11 pounds]. My other children were not quite that big. Évi was 4½ kilos, Guszti 4. It is much easier to bring up a big baby. I did not cry out, not even once. In the next room were Father and my mother. They heard not a sound. In the morning the neighbors asked, "What happened in your place last night that the lights were on all the time?" Nothing, only a man-child was born. Only when the madame told me it was a boy did I cry out happily, "A boy! A boy!"
>
> We moved to that apartment after I had become pregnant. Before that we lived on Lovag Street, in a very poor apartment. We called it *Wanzenburg* [Bedbug Castle]. We suffered tortures until we exterminated the bugs. I climbed up a ladder, and cleaned and cleaned. It was terrible. When the child was on the way that apartment was no longer good enough. There was no air, no terrace to put out the baby, no place to take him. So we moved to Munkácsy Street, near the city park. It was a much better apartment.

Simultaneously with me appeared the first of the two volumes of Father's anthology of Hebrew poets translated into Hungarian. It was published in 1910 by the Israelite Hungarian Literary Society, with the second volume following in 1912, just in time for the birth of my sister Évi. Among the poems contained in this anthology were several that had never before been published in any language, which Father had located and copied from the original Hebrew manuscripts in London and Oxford. Thus it came about that Hebrew poems by

Meshullam ben Solomon Da Piera (Gerona, early thirteenth century), Solomon ben Reuben Bonfed (Spain, fourteenth/fifteenth centuries), Saadya Longo (Salonika, early sixteenth century), David Onkineira (Turkey, sixteenth century), and others were first published in a language of whose existence they probably did not even know.

In the long introductory essay to the second edition of his anthology Father painted a fascinating picture of the life of poets in fifteenth/sixteenth-century Turkey:

> In the manuscript collection of the Bodleian Library I found a Hebrew volume that contains poems from the age of Israel Najara. The authors of these unknown poems lived in Salonika, Constantinople, and other cities of the Ottoman Empire, and, as one can learn from the notes in the volume, led a typical life of poets. They held bohemian meetings, went on sprees, and entered artistic competitions. Occasionally they made excursions, and vied with one another in singing the praises of a maiden they happened to meet, in deriding in song a creditor, or, in unmistakable Renaissance spirit, exulting in a grove or a wooded hill. Poor Saadya Longo, who pursued poetry as a profession, was the old master, the ancient bard, but many called him "old cantor" in mockery. David Onkineira, whose name appears here perhaps for the first time in a literary context, was the rich young man of the circle. At first he plagiarized, so as to be accepted by the bohemian group, but later he learned the ropes of versification, and wrote poems that are quite unusual and new in tone. The others, too, played the lute diligently. Still, they had enough time left for plotting a conspiracy against the Jewish duke of Naxos, whom the poets, it seems, did not like at all. But the very fact that it was possible for a Jew to become a duke, and for Jewish poets to live a rather free bohemian life, shows that in the Ottoman Empire the Jews were not segregated from the rest of the population to the extent they were in the ghettos of Christian countries. The Turkish Jews sang together with the people of the land, and thus Hebrew poetry became enriched by many popular songs. Najara complains that the Jewish youth constantly sing frivolous Turkish songs. This, in fact, was why he decided to write Hebrew love lyrics to the folk melodies: he intended them for the youth, but, of course, with a kabbalistic meaning.[13]

Father discusses his attitude to his work as a translator of Hebrew poems into Hungarian in the introduction to the first edition of his anthology:

> This two-part anthology is the first attempt to present in Hungarian the entire development of postbiblical Hebrew poetry. But for me, I must admit, this work was more than an attempt. I devoted the most

festive moments of many young years to the poems of these old and
new masters, the moments in which I felt that I myself was also a poet,
so as to transplant, with my own moods that I sacrificed, the kindred
moods of my Hebrew poets. This I consider the main and primary
precondition of true translation.[14]

Then he speaks of the difficulties the translator of medieval Hebrew
poetry has to face.

> The translator of Hebrew poets finds himself in quite a special posi-
> tion. The closer the phraseology of two languages to each other, the
> easier it is to transplant poetical products from the one into the other.
> But the phraseology of the Hebrew language is totally isolated. The
> medieval Hebrew poet wrote for a readership that was familiar with the
> Bible, remembered the prayers, and knew the Talmud. A stanza, a
> line, even a phrase or a word, would conjure up the mood of a prayer,
> echo some biblical verse, or contain an allusion to an agadic, or even
> halakhic, passage in the Talmud. If we translate it, bare and pale words
> stand before us, without any resonance. . . .
> Medieval Hebrew, even though enriched by a talmudic vocabulary,
> was rather poor, and often could express thoughts only by boldly strain-
> ing and wrenching word forms. Moreover, the texts, which were for
> long at the mercy of copyists and printers, are in many cases incom-
> plete or corrupt, and, with a few exceptions, have not yet been prop-
> erly edited. The translator, therefore, often must rely on a certain intu-
> ition in order to grasp the meaning and the mood of a poem, in order
> to be able to translate that which the poet wanted to express. . . .

Sixty years later Mother still remembered Father's feeling that he
had to sacrifice his own poetic creativity in devoting himself to the
translation of Hebrew poets: "His translations were marvelous. He
used to say that for him it was not work, not a task, but that he had
to sacrifice his own poetic fever. He translated only in those hours
when he himself could have written poetry . . . instead of which he
translated. . . . "

Speaking of Father's translations of Hebrew poets I must add a
comment of my own. After his death I once spent several hours
reading many of the poems in the original Hebrew and comparing
them with Father's translations. Although it may sound like an exag-
geration, I can say in all objectivity, and using all the critical faculties I possess, that all his translations do justice to the originals, and
that many are, to put it quite simply, much better poems than the
originals.

It was between the publication of the first and the second volume of Father's *Hebrew Poets* that the *Almanac* appeared. It was an

instant and resounding success, and met with an enthusiastic critical reception. It sold very well, and made Jewish culture what was called in Hungary *szalónképes*, that is, fit for good society. This was admitted even by the assimilants who constituted the majority of Budapest Jews. It demonstrated to a Jewry whose official leadership was strongly opposed to Zionism that all over the world Jews of the highest positions in governments, industry, and academe sympathized with, and actively supported, the Zionist endeavor of establishing a national home for the Jews in Palestine.

Within a few months after its publication Father decided, again with the emphatic concurrence of Mother, to publish, instead of subsequent volumes of the *Almanac*, a monthly to be called *Mult és Jövő (Past and Future: A Jewish Literary, Artistic, Social, and Critical Journal)*. He sent out circular letters that brought a positive response, and in January 1912 the first issue was published, carrying the added identification "Volume Two of the *Hungarian Jewish Almanac*." The banner also stated that the journal was published with the assistance of the Israelite Hungarian Literary Society, which was headed by Jewish religious leaders and by some of those Hungarian Jewish barons, noblemen, poets, professors, and so forth, who had not severed connections with Judaism. (I may mention that in the pre–World War I years there were some 300 Jewish families in Hungary that had been created barons or noblemen. Many others had the personal rank of court councillor, or governmental chief councillor, which entitled them to being addressed as *Méltóságos Uram*, literally, "Your Dignity," but roughly the equivalent of "Your Lordship.")

The literary and artistic level and the international-Jewish character of the monthly were such that it received an even greater critical acclaim than the *Almanac* the year before. The general daily papers and periodicals in Hungary, as well as quite a number of journals beyond the borders, published rave reviews. Father collected a few samples and published them in the March 1912 issue:

With its first issue, which is a veritable bulky album, *Mult és Jövő* entered the ranks of the most distinguished artistic journals of the world . . . (*Az Ujság*).

The first issue of *Mult és Jövő* is truly magnificent (Professor L. Stein, editor of *Nord und Süd*, Berlin).

The literary and artistic contents of Mult és Jövő stand on a high and modern level, and its makeup is a masterpiece of the Hungarian printing art (*Pester Lloyd*).

Mult és Jövő created a general sensation with its valuable literary contents and its superb artistic presentation (*Pesti Hirlap*).

• Never before, neither here nor abroad, has a Jewish journal been published with such rich content and artistic format (*Zsidó Szemle*).

There has never been such a cultural journal in Hungary (*Jövendő*).

In its July 21, 1916, issue, the *Hebrew Standard* of New York wrote:

There is probably no Jewry in any part of the world which can boast of an illustrated magazine of the beauty and splendor—typographically and artistically—of the *Mult és Jövő*, the "Past and Future," edited at Budapest by Dr. Joseph Patai, devoted to Jewish literature, fine arts, social life, and critics. It is a Jewish magazine par excellence; the illustrations are masterpieces of the engraver, etcher, photographer, printer, etc.

Twelve years later the *Hungarian Jewish Lexicon* had this to say (s.v. *Mult és Jövő*):

Jewish literary and artistic journal. Founded in 1911, and since then edited by Joseph Patai. Its contributors are prominent Hungarian Jewish and foreign scholars, writers, and artists. Each issue deals with a great Jewish creative value. Its illustrations are always of a high artistic level. It has had a considerable part in the popularization of Jewish literary and artistic knowledge. Its direction and tone are characterized by critical thoughtfulness, which is responsible for its great influence on the cultural life of Hungarian Jewry. By its exposure of Jewish problems that are independent of day-to-day politics it gave a more healthy direction to Jewish interests, and it is partly due to its work that today the Jewish and non-Jewish society of Hungary judges without prejudice the nonpolitical Palestine work, for whose furtherance a society, led by distinguished Jewish personalities, has been founded (*see* Pro Palestine Federation of Hungarian Jews). Its lead articles are exemplary in their objectivity, and its belletristic contributions are as a rule very valuable. The journal is well known abroad as well, and it is its great merit that it secured for Hungary the sympathy and interest of many significant foreign factors.

I have devoted some space to *Mult és Jövő* because it was the major slice of my father's life work, and because it had a profound influence on my own intellectual development from the time I learned to read until it ceased to appear, in World War II.

Most of Father's literary output—and he was an extremely prolific and versatile writer—appeared first on the pages of his monthly
before being published in book form. He wrote original poems, and
translated, as already mentioned, the great Hebrew poets into Hungarian; he wrote short stories, a short novel, memoirs of his childhood, a biography of Theodor Herzl, political articles, critiques of
what was going on in Hungary in general and within the Jewish
community in particular, book reviews, travel impressions gathered
while visiting many European countries, and, from 1929 on, the
young *yishuv* of Palestine. In addition, in a column entitled "Chronicle and Review," which he wrote single-handedly for thirty years, he
reported briefly on noteworthy events in Jewish life in Hungary and
abroad.

The last-mentioned column enabled him to publicize the books
he published, the lectures he gave, and the other communal activities he engaged in, and, coincidentally and fortunately for me as a
memoirist, it supplies data about his public life of which I would
never have known otherwise. On checking over the microfilm copy
of *Mult és Jövő* in the New York Public Library (my sister and I long
ago gave the complete set that Father originally kept at home to the
library of Tel Aviv University), I find that in the 1920s and 1930s
Father every month gave several lectures on Jewish cultural subjects,
on Jewish Palestine, on world Jewry, on Hebrew literature and poetry.
His lectures took him to the Jewish communities all over Hungary,
as well as to the neighboring countries, and especially to those parts
of Czechoslovakia, Rumania, and Yugoslavia that, until the end of
World War I, had been part of Hungary, and where the Jews, to a
greater extent than the Christian Hungarians, had retained their
Magyarism, and flocked to hear a Hungarian lecture given by the
illustrious editor of *Mult és Jövő*, of which many were faithful subscribers. I myself never heard Father speak outside Budapest, and all
I remember in connection with these lectures is that he was often
away from home.

Father also organized every winter season one or two "cultural
evenings" with the participation of some of the foremost Hungarian
Jewish and non-Jewish actors, singers, musicians, and important guests
from abroad. He himself used to introduce these evenings, which
took place in the largest concert halls of Budapest, with short addresses,
of which I remember only the feeling of pride I had when I saw my
father stand before an audience of two thousand, speaking beauti-

fully and passionately, and receiving the ovation that he never failed to elicit. Included in the programs of these evenings were, as a rule, one or more poems of Father's, recited by a celebrated member of one of Budapest's great theaters. Also, several of Father's poems, set to music by well-known Hungarian composers, would be sung by leading singers of the Budapest opera.

Inevitably, Father became a member of the executives of various Hungarian Jewish cultural and social organizations. In 1926 he initiated and organized the Pro Palestine Federation of Hungarian Jews to serve as a platform for those leaders of Hungarian Jewry who for political reasons did not want to be members of the Hungarian Zionist Organization but were nevertheless willing to support the cultural institutions of the *yishuv*, such as the Hebrew University of Jerusalem and other educational establishments, as well as the so-called Palestinian Jewish national funds, which financed urban and rural settlements. Father succeeded in enlisting the participation of some of the top leaders of Hungarian Jewry, including quite a few Jewish barons, industrial magnates, and university professors, and he himself served as chairman of the Federation's cultural section. In organizing the Pro Palestine, Father actually anticipated by three years what Chaim Weizmann did on a global scale in 1929 when he founded the enlarged Jewish Agency for Palestine with the participation of non-Zionist Jewish world leaders who were willing to work together with the Zionists for the upbuilding of Palestine. In fact, the Hungarian signatories of the charter of the Jewish Agency were all leading members of the Pro Palestine who had been recruited by Father.

From 1924 on Father every year led a group of tourists to Palestine and guided them all over the Holy Land. The only place in which he advertised these tours was his own journal, but the response was always sufficient to assemble groups of several dozens. The tours took place in the spring, and in some years there were even two. Their duration was about three weeks, and after Father saw his flock off in Haifa harbor, where they embarked for the homeward journey, he himself would remain in Palestine for another few weeks, lecturing at the Hebrew University, visiting and socializing with his friends on the faculty, and with the Hebrew poets of the country, or simply resting up. During his very first trip to the Holy Land he began to write up his travel impressions, which he later published, first in his journal and subsequently as a book, *A Föltámadó Szent-*

föld (The Renascent Holy Land). As a result of these frequent visits he became as well known in scholarly, literary, and artistic circles in Palestine as he was in Hungary.

From 1919 to 1923 Father also published and edited, in addition to his monthly, a Jewish political weekly likewise called *Mult és Jövő*. During the first two years of this weekly's four-year existence, he still continued to carry a full load as a teacher in the high school. That he managed to teach some twenty-four hours a week, carry the brunt of the editorial work for both his monthly and his weekly, write much of the material published in both, and, in addition, continue to write short stories, poems, polemical political articles, and I don't know what else, is nothing short of astounding. He certainly must have had quite an exceptional working ability. In 1921 he resigned from the school, or rather had himself retired (he received a pension from the city of Budapest until the outbreak of World War II).

I must go back to Father's early years as a high school teacher to recount an incident that throws some light on his relationship to his Christian colleagues and his humanitarian interest in his students. In 1968 Mother recalled that one of Father's colleagues was István Friedreich, a well-known writer who used the pen name Dénes Görcsöni.

> He was an anti-Semite, and Father and he had heated discussions on more than one occasion. Once Father wanted to fail a Jewish student in German, because the boy was so weak in the subject that it was impossible to give him a passing mark even with the best of will. Father had no personal contact with the boy, but Görcsöni, who was his home-room teacher, had, and knew about the extremely difficult situation of his family. After a faculty meeting Görcsöni took Father aside, told him about the boy's problems, and begged him to let him pass. "If so," said Father, "I shall tutor him privately." So the boy came twice a week to our apartment, and Father gave him German lessons, without pay, needless to say. Soon thereafter Görcsöni, who suffered from tuberculosis, died. Father wrote a beautiful obituary about him. [15]

On May 1, 1919, during the short-lived Communist regime in Hungary, all schools were ordered to have a celebration. For some reason that I can no longer ascertain after all these years, the principal of the school asked Father, the only Jew on the faculty, to give the festive address. It was a very delicate and even dangerous task, because the elimination of individuals who did something to incur the wrath of the government was an everyday occurrence during the rule of the Red commissars. Father nevertheless undertook the assignment, and chose as his subject the tension between nationalism and internationalism. He spoke of the great patriotic heroes of the Hungarian revolution of 1848, and said:

> We felt with deep pain that at the very time we paid homage to the memory of our heroes, neighboring nations branded as traitors, as despicable men, those who for us were so dear and saintly. And we felt and knew that, on the other hand, those whom we considered the despised hangmen of our national cause and whom we cursed were, in the memory of other nations, surrounded with the halo of saints. . . . Is it not, my brothers, a distressing thought that this condition should persist from generation to generation, and that this should be the eternal road of humankind?

And he concluded this part of his address by stressing that:

> All humankind, all the nations of the world, must join forces to shake off the rule of those who because of material interest, vain prejudice, or megalomania, incite nation against nation. If, instead of single classes, the people as a whole will everywhere constitute itself the nation, nothing will stand in the way of the brotherhood of peoples. Only this can be the meaning of internationalism.

Thus far he was on safe ground. But then he moved on to a hazardous criticism of the new Hungarian Communist regime. Internationalism, he said, cannot mean nationlessness. It cannot mean the rejection of the culture of a nation, of its historical values, its national traditions.

> Internationalism cannot aim at making the world one sheepfold, one red barracks, or a row of grey phalansteries. . . . This dreary picture cannot be an inspiring ideal. Man must be made free . . . but so that no true value should in the process be destroyed in the human soul. . . . A world culture can develop only from the individual cultures, that is, the national cultures of the various peoples. . . . All things that aim at separating peoples, at pitching peoples against one another, must disappear; but all things that project the rainbow of the human mind through new prisms must remain, and no color, no sound, must be lost from the resplendent orchestra of the human soul. Only this can be the ideal perspective of the Future. Only if it fights for the realization of this grandiose ideal does the labor movement, which strives for realistic interests, deserve that the soul of the youth that is enthused by ideal values should turn to it.

These were risky words in the days of the Hungarian Red Terror, when human lives did not count for much. Even more risky was the peroration:

"Proletarians of the World Unite" represents a value and not merely a new bloody alarm only if it teaches the elimination of all antagonistic interests, the cessation of all human wars, and the solidarity of all human endeavor. If it advances toward realization the dream of the prophets of the nations, the reveries of philosophers, the visions of poets about world freedom, the union of nations, and the messianic eternal peace. The preaching of the proletarian Internationale cannot be the proclamation of a new class rule; it must be the abolition of all tyranny, all oppression, so that there should be no more oppressed and oppressor, proletarian and bourgeois, but only man, man of a higher order, free, ideal. The slogan of "Proletarians of the World Unite" must be replaced by the redeeming new rallying-cry, "Humans of the World Unite!"[16]

Six years after the event, when Father published this speech in a volume of his collected articles, he recalled in the introductory statement that his colleagues and friends listened with dismay to his "counterrevolutionary" utterances, albeit in their hearts they approved of every word he had said. The principal of the school, Dr. Kopp, asked for its text in order to circulate it among a small group of the faculty. A Christian colleague said to him in true consternation: "How can a Jew be so stupid!? And you even handed it in in writing!" "It is in good hands," Father assured him. And he reassured himself with the thought that what he had said was his conviction that he could not hide, and would not hide in the future either.[17]

Barely a few months later Father got involved in another potentially hazardous situation. In July of 1919 the Hungarian Communist Revolutionary Governing Council found itself embroiled in fighting against Rumania, and, facing defeat, it resigned on August 1. Two days later the Rumanian army entered Budapest, and Admiral Miklós Horthy, heading the Hungarian National Army, began his leisurely advance from the south of the country toward the capital. By the late fall Horthy's army reached the resort town of Siófok on Lake Balaton, and at that juncture one of the leaders of the political department of the Ministry of Defense, a certain Colonel U., visited Father. The colonel told him that he was well aware of the uneasy mood of the Hungarian Jews, and that he thought it best that, in order to dispel it, a Jewish delegation should go to Siófok, to the temporary headquarters of the National Army, and hear a reassuring statement from the mouth of the commander-in-chief himself. The need for reassurance was, indeed, apparent, because after the fall of the Communist regime, in which the most powerful commissars were converted or nonconverted Jews, the Jewish leadership was apprehensive lest the reaction take the form of anti-Semitic excesses. In fact, by the time the delegation was assembled and set out for Siófok, quite a number of brutal attacks on Jews had taken place.

Father agreed that such a step could be useful, and undertook to assemble the delegation. Intensive consultations took place, and the following Jewish leaders agreed to join it: Jenő Polnay de Tiszasüly, a former minister of commerce; Baron Adolf Kohner, an industrialist and president of the Israelite National Office; Joseph Vészi, editor-in-chief of the *Pester Lloyd*, the most influential daily in the country; Adolf Frankl, president of the Orthodox Jewish National Office; and Father. Béla Feleki, vice-president of the Israelite Congregation of Pest, also declared himself ready to join, but his wife considered the undertaking too dangerous, and he withdrew at the last minute.

The five members of the delegation set out in a car early in November (I am unable to ascertain the exact date) of 1919 soon after sunrise. Budapest and the immediate vicinity were still occupied by the Rumanians, and when they reached the limits of the Rumanian-controlled area, they were subjected to a thorough search. All of Siófok was like a well-guarded military camp, but they had passes issued by the Ministry of Defense in Budapest, and were waved through all the checkpoints. Horthy received them immediately. Polnay, as the spokesman of the delegation, emphasized how much the Hungarian Jews had done for the economic upbuilding of the country, and how much they had to suffer under the Communist rule. Horthy responded at length, and then engaged all the members of the delegation in conversation. From what he said to them it was clear that he had been fed many anti-Semitic lies and calumnies, and the delegation did its best to disabuse him of them. At one point he asked: why did the "Maccabeans" arm themselves against the National Army? Father answered: "This, Your Excellency, is slander. As a student I was one of the founders of the Maccabea. We were never more than three or four dozen, our aims were cultural, we worked for the settlement of Palestine. During the war almost all of them enlisted, several died for the fatherland, others fell into captivity. Today they are very few. A small group that certainly cannot initiate an offensive." Horthy was visibly impressed by this and the other explanations. The members of the delegation felt that they had managed to clear the air. At the end of the meeting, which lasted two full hours, Horthy asked that it should not be publicized, and that the Jews should be notified only in the form of a confidential communication.

By the time they got back to Budapest it was late at night, but Father sat down to write up a communiqué, and early the next morning he cleared it with the other members of the delegation, and then cabled it to Siófok for approval. Of the approximately 150 lines of his write-up the censorship let stand no more than 10. Even those words of Horthy himself that showed a friendly attitude toward the Jews fell victim to the censor "in view of the public sentiment."

On November 16 the National Army entered Budapest, and a few days later Horthy again received the same delegation, this time augmented by Feleki. The main topic on this occasion was the Jews' complaints of the anti-Semitic atrocities that were taking place, referred to euphemistically as "individual undertakings." Horthy promised that he would have each case investigated. But, he said, to issue general orders for the protection of the Jews would not be advisable. "It would only create the opposite effect. They would say that I sold myself to the Jews. The nation has not yet totally recovered from its illness. But that, too, will come in time."[18]

This account affords some insight into the precarious situation of the Jews after the fall of the Communist government. While it lasted, the renegade Jews who were among its foremost leaders vented their wrath on the Jewish bourgeoisie without restraint. The Revolutionary Court, headed by a converted Jew, condemned to death, because of alleged counterrevolutionary activities, forty-four Jews, who were forthwith executed, and the decrees issued by the government council undermined the very foundations of the economic existence of the entire Jewish community. The Jews took an active part in the organization of the counterrevolutionary movement, the National Army was financed by Jewish money, and among the seventy-two counterrevolutionary officers there were fifteen Jews. Nevertheless, no sooner did the National Army, headed by Horthy, enter Budapest, and the national government, which elected Horthy regent of Hungary, consolidate its position, than the country was swept by anti-Jewish terror that Horthy either did not want or was unable to curb. Never before in their thousand-year history had the Hungarian Jews experienced a wave of anti-Semitism of a magnitude even remotely approximating the so-called White Terror. Jew-baiting was the order of the day, Jewish stores were looted, some 3,000 Jews were killed, and the corpses of many were simply thrown into the Danube. In view of these facts it is doubtful whether one can attribute any positive result to the Jewish delegation that Horthy received in Siófok and Budapest.

Father's role in that delegation has a puzzling aspect. Since he published his account, which I summarized above, at a time when all the members of the delegation were still alive and the Horthy regime was in full power, one can take it for granted that his report-ing of the events is accurate, and that his role in assembling the delegation and in participating in it was precisely as he described it. Also, quite apart from these external controls, he was not a man to claim credit where credit was not due. If so, why did the otherwise unidentified Colonel U. of the political department of the Ministry of Defense choose Father of all people to approach with the idea of the delegation? Father at the time was a young man of thirty-seven, and even though he was well known in Jewish circles as a poet and an editor, he had no official position in the Jewish establishment. Why was not one of the official leaders of the Jewish community the first to be sounded out? In the event, all the other members of the delegation were such leaders, men of advanced years and high posi-tion, well known for their journalistic, political, or economic work outside the community as well. Why was it felt necessary to use the services of Father as a middleman between the Ministry of Defense (or the army) and the Jews? I don't know the answer, and I cannot forgive myself that, during all the years when Father lived in semi-retirement in Jerusalem and I saw him very often, I never asked him to tell me about this incident, and, for that matter, about all the other events in his life in Hungary.

I mentioned above that from 1919 to 1923, for three and a half years, Father edited, in addition to his monthly, also a weekly, called *Mult és Jövő Hetilapja* (The Weekly of "Past and Future"). This was a political paper devoted essentially to fighting for Jewish rights in Hungary, and for Zionism within the Jewish community. The cen-sorship was rather unkind to this weekly. I still remember seeing the large blank spaces in the midst of its columns. Father once explained to me that the censors did not permit the closing up of these blanks and the filling up of the columns at the end of the articles with some other innocuous material; they insisted on the paper showing clearly that parts of a certain article were found offensive and were deleted; perhaps they did so in order to demonstrate to the public their vigilance and the thoroughness of the control they exercised. To stand up for Jewish rights in that virulently anti-Semitic environment in the years of the White Terror required not only total devotion to the Jewish cause but also extraordinary courage.

On March 29, 1923, the Royal Hungarian Ministry of the Interior issued an order suppressing the weekly *Mult és Jövő*. At first there was some confusion as to whether the monthly also had to cease publication, but this was soon cleared up, and Father could continue to publish it unhindered. In its May 1923 issue Father printed the text of the Ministry's order, which stated that the weekly was suppressed because "it discussed the events and legal measures with such a ruthless tendency that it imperiled public order and public safety in the greatest measure." The order was forwarded to Father with a covering letter signed by Dr. Városy, counselor of the Budapest municipality, who, I suspect, was none other than the father of a classmate of mine in the elementary school whom the teacher handled with kid gloves, and because of whom I got into trouble. I shall tell of the incident in the next chapter.

The above is, by and large, what I was able to gather in 1983, from the sources available in New York, about the life and work of my father until 1939, when he left Budapest for good and settled in Palestine. In subsequent chapters I shall add a good many more details on the basis of what I myself remember of him, beginning, roughly, with my thirteenth year, when he was about forty years old.

From the information I was able to locate, it becomes, I think, sufficiently clear that for several decades Father was a major force in Hungarian Jewish life. That he achieved such a position was due to several factors. In his monthly he created a forum in which the best of the cultural products of Hungarian-speaking Jews, numbering at the time about a million, could find an outlet. Moreover, the very existence of *Mult és Jövő* provided a stimulus for Jewish writers and artists to turn to Jewish subjects. Apart from this function, Father used his journal to make Hungarian Jewry aware of and acquainted with the existence of a rich, multifaceted, vibrant Jewish culture in other countries, and, particularly, in Palestine, and to show them that all over the world the cultural production of the Jews — recognized and extolled by the most exigent critics — was self-assuredly

Jewish and Zionist. With his original and translated poems he made the Hungarian language into a noble vehicle for the Jewish creative genius. By organizing cultural evenings, in which the most acclaimed Hungarian Christian actors recited and singers sang the works of Jewish poets and composers, he practically forced the Hungarian Jewish public to accept the value of Jewish culture and become its consumers. With his lectures he carried the message of Jewish culture into the most remote parts of Hungary and the territories detached from it after World War I. With the exhibitions he organized, and the appearance of Hebrew poets he invited from abroad, he enabled the Hungarian Jews to see and meet some of the works and persons of the most outstanding Jewish artists and writers. By conducting guided tours for Hungarian Jewish tourists in the Holy Land every year he made it possible for selected individuals to become personally acquainted with the achievements of the *yishuv*, and, upon their return to their hometowns, to act as disseminators of interest and concern for Jewish Palestine. He did all this because he was convinced that Jewish culture was the sole key to the survival of Jewry, and because he felt, as Mother quoted him in 1968, that "one must spread Jewish culture with fire and iron."

To appreciate the magnitude of the task he undertook as a young man in his early twenties, and persisted in until 1939, when, at the age of fifty-seven, he emigrated to Palestine, one must remember that Hungarian Jewry in the early twentieth century was living withdrawn into a state of self-isolation from world Jewry in general and from the Palestinian *yishuv* in particular. The Jews of Hungary were fearful that any expression of interest in what the Jews in other countries were doing, and any manifestation of a willingness to participate in general Jewish endeavors, would be taken by the powers that be in Hungary as a sign that the Jews were not good patriots. Ever since the defeat of the Hungarian revolution of 1848 by Austria, the Hungarian mind had been obsessed with patriotism. This trait was recognized and excoriated by a famous Hungarian (Christian) poet in a biting satire as early as the second half of the nineteenth century, and by many other thoughtful Hungarian critics of the national character. And as for the Jews, in strict conformity with the adage that the Jews are like the Gentiles only more so, in Hungary they were even more patriotic than the Christian Hungarians. In such an environment the odds were heavily against Father succeeding in his Jewish cultural and Zionist mission. Yet the cumulative effect of his untiring work was being felt more and more, so that, as the years rolled by, Hungarian Jewry ceased to be that "withered branch on the tree of world Jewry" that one of its greatest sons, Theodor Herzl, had felt it to be back in 1900.

Father's manifold activities yielded him an income well above the current expenses of his household. From his savings he was able to buy a plot of land in a prime residential location in Nyúl Utca (Rabbit Street) in Buda, which he later exchanged for a spacious apartment in a multifamily dwelling a building-contractor erected on it. Together with his friend Dr. Lajos Fodor, a lawyer in the city of Hatvan, Hungary, he invested some money in a ten-dunam (2½ acres or 10,000 square meters) piece of land in Shekhunat Boruchov (today Givatayim), near Tel Aviv, on part of which he later built two houses in which my sister Évi lived until her death, and her two daughters with their families still live today. He bought a six-story apartment house in Berlin, which for years yielded a respectable income. Less sound than these investments was his placement of 40,000 *pengő* in a second mortgage in Budapest, which he did upon the advice of a lawyer friend of his, and which proved a total loss when the owner was unable even to repay the first mortgage held by a bank. All his other investments, except those he made in Palestine, also were lost in the course of time. First his Berlin house went after the rise of Hitler in Germany; then, after he and Mother moved to Palestine (in 1939), his Budapest apartment, which he had transferred to Mother's sister, Mrs. Molnár, was taken by the Hungarian Nazis. At the same time, whatever value his journal and the books he had published represented also disappeared. Thus it was only due to the piece of land he had bought in Palestine, and the two houses he built on it, that he was not completely destitute when he arrived there.

Let me conclude this chapter with what Jenő Pintér wrote about Father in his multi-volume *History of Hungarian Literature*. The eighth volume of that magisterial work, dealing with Hungarian literature in the first third of the twentieth century, was published in 1941, and much of what Pintér wrote in it about Father was reprinted in his 1943 volume *Hungarian Literature of Our Century*. Pintér was the foremost historian of Hungarian literature, and already in the 1920s his books were considered the final authority on the subject. While I was still in high school there was a standing joke about his history of literature, which was published in many editions, full, abridged, and concise, to the effect that "the Pintér" came in various sizes: one pound, two pounds, five pounds, ten pounds, and two hundred pounds—the last figure, of course, referring to the rotund figure of the author rather than to his books. At the time Pintér wrote the 1941 version of his history, Father lived in Palestine, having left Hungary at the last minute before Italian shipping came to a halt, and Hungary was sealed off with no exit to the Mediterranean. With Father's settling in Palestine his literary work in Hungarian had come to an end. Whatever he wrote in the last years of his life consisted of translations of his own writings from Hungarian into Hebrew and of some new works in Hebrew. Thus Pintér's 1941 evaluation of Father as a Hungarian Jewish author can be considered a summation of the significance of his work as seen by the foremost Hungarian literary historian. He wrote:

> Joseph Patai (1882–) created an enthusiastic Jewish circle of writers around the journal *Mult és Jövő*. He wrote equally well in Hungarian and Hebrew, and both at home and abroad he presented systematically the aspirations of the Jewish spirit. His Hungarian poems open up to the Hungarian public an entirely unknown world: the mysterious world of Jewish religion, Oriental philosophizing, and ancient rites.
>
> Love the Holy Scripture—we read in Joseph Patai's poems—love the holy letters conceived in flames. Our ancestors went to their death for them, and bequeathed to us the restless life as a precious heirloom. There where the Jordan cries, the soul wanders sobbing; Carmel and Sharon murmur the baleful message: "The Temple is falling, Jerusalem is being destroyed!" But Judah laughs, as it laughed once upon a time, in vain does the prophet cry out into the gloomy night.
>
> The Zionist voice resounds with the faith that is concerned about the ancient traditions. This voice was heard in the Hungarian language most purely in the lyric poetry of Joseph Patai. The spirit of the Mosaic faith, the respect for the Hebrew national past, the enthusiasm for today's Palestine, the philosophical inclination rooted in talmudic study, the experiences and crises of modern European life—these are the components of the essence of his poetry. According to one of his Jewish critics, "Patai was educated in the spirit of the yeshiva, and whatever is ancestral value in that spirit, original Jewish value, Jewish knowledge that can never be acquired later in adulthood—of all that he forgot nothing, to all that he never became unfaithful after he entered the modern world. He did not sacrifice his original Judaism for the sake of Western culture. He was able to smelt down both of them in himself, and what he succeeded in doing he wanted to achieve for all Jewry. He wants to make Judaism presentable. He invites to us the strangers who sneer at us, and the Jews who pretend to be indifferent: look around,

we have treasures! You can look at everything, we have no secrets of which we are ashamed, only faults, just as any other people. We have our special literature with racial characteristics, we have great artists, scholars and heroes, dreamers and saints. He loves his people. Not only the highly cultured layer, the chosen of the spirit, but also the derided, despised Polish Jew."

Joseph Patai and his colleagues have kept their distance from that shallow frivolity that was so characteristic of some fashionable Jewish writers in Budapest. Love did not appear in their poems with sensuous undertones, their satire did not strike the note of political demagoguery. Their spirit was consanguineous with the Hebrew spirit, and maintained close ties with Yiddish literature.[19]

Pintér then goes on to discuss whether the writings of Jewish authors in Hungary manifest any specifically Jewish traits, Jewish consciousness, Jewish mood, and quotes a Jewish literary critic, Aladár Komlós, to the effect that some residual Jewishness can indeed be found in most of them. But then he concludes, "And most particularly in the poems of Joseph Patai, whose poetry reflects the first blush of the dawn of today's great rebirth of Jewish consciousness."[20]

Touching upon the question of whether the work of renegade Jewish authors belongs in the realm of universal Jewish literature, and, in that connection, discussing the meaning of the concept "Jewish literature," Pintér quotes Father, who, "referring to the opinion of the foremost Jewish scholars, asserted that also the works of the assimilated Jewish poets were Jewish literature, since assimilation was one of the intellectual trends in Judaism. Here in Hungary the *horror judaicus* was still alive, the fear that the belletrist who moved within the mental realm of Judaism would be stamped a denominational poet," although this had no justification at all. "The Jewish people is the only one in the world that has produced a multilingual literature, but that literature, even if written in Greek, Latin, Arabic, and other languages, is undoubtedly Jewish."

A few pages later Pintér gives Father's brief biography and then goes on to say: "Joseph Patai launched several literary enterprises, and organized numerous social movements, all of them with the aim of reviving racial self-consciousness among Hungarian Jews, and of stemming the process of the neglect of Jewish traditions." After enumerating Father's books, with a brief statement about the content of each, he concludes with a summary evaluation of Father's work:

Patai lives with his entire being in the Hebrew world of his coreligionists, he clings with every nerve to the sphere of thought of talmudic ideas. He filters his Weltanschauung through his orthodox Mosaic faith and Zionist point of view. It was he who made Palestine, the new Jewish state, popular among the Hungarian Jews, who with his indefatigable activity aroused interest even among the most indifferent in the cause of Hebrew nationalism. For decades he performed his work of wakening. The events proved him right. He did not delude himself with the illusion that Hungarian Jewry would assimilate to Magyardom. He saw clearly already at the time when the Neolog Jews and those who had converted to Christianity still believed fanatically in the rapid disappearance of the Jewish question.[21]

Although the attribution of *"racial* self-consciousness," "talmudic ideas," and "orthodox Mosaic faith" to Father is somewhat farfetched, it only shows that the Gentile Pintér was not too thoroughly grounded in questions of Jewish ideology. But his words about the Jewish mission of Joseph Patai among the Hungarian Jews are a fitting summary of Father's life work that was interrupted only with the outbreak of World War II.

In his chapter about the novel and the theater Pintér comes back once more to Father, and mentions members of his family as well:

Joseph Patai (1882–   ), editor of *Mult és Jövő.* About his literary career — see among the poets of the Jewish trend. His wife, Edith Patai, is a poet and novelist; his daughter Éva Patai, the author of a Hebrew Palestinian novel; his son, Raphael Patai, the first doctor of the Hebrew University of Jerusalem. Joseph Patai was many times feted in Palestine for his pioneering merits. The most outstanding Hebrew writers and scholars stated about him that from the point of view of Zionism his merits in Hungary had historical significance: with his journal he brought the air of Eretz Israel into assimilant Jewish homes; with his social activities he built a spiritual bridge between Hungary and Palestine; in his literary work his main goal was to serve artistically the Hebrew traditions, together with the endeavor to be of service, next to the common world of Jewry, also to his Hungarian homeland.[22]

A year after the publication of Pintér's *The Hungarian Literature of Our Century*, which contained these pages about Father, four-fifths of the Hungarian Jews were exterminated by the German Nazis and their Hungarian henchmen.

4

Early School Years: 1916–1920

I started to attend school in September 1916, when I was two months short of my sixth birthday. I have a vague recollection that for a long while—perhaps for two full years—I was taken to the school in the morning and fetched at noon, either by my mother or, more probably, by the Fräulein. It was a mere five minutes' walk from our home to the school, but it involved crossing Podmaniczky Street, which was a wide thoroughfare that the trolley tracks divided into three lanes. From the curb to the rails on our side of the street there was a distance of perhaps eight feet, then followed the rails, then a roadbed some twenty feet in width; on the other side of it were the rails of the trolley going in the opposite direction, separated by another eight feet from the curb on that side of the street. The trolley cars were bright yellow; they moved, as did all wheeled traffic in Budapest, on the left side of the street, and a typical train consisted of two cars: a larger and heavier one, which had the electric motor attached to its middle at the bottom between its two pairs of wheels, and a smaller one that it pulled after it.

Overhead, parallel to the rails, ran the wires from which the trolleys obtained their electricity by means of a large metal loop shaped somewhat like a Greek omega, which stuck out from their roofs and the top of which slid along the underside of the wire and was pushed up to it by a strong coiled spring visible only if one stood at some distance from the car. Occasionally I would see the motorman get off his car and pull this loop down—why, I do not know—by means of a rope that hung from it at the front of the trolley, adjust it, and then let it go up again. When the loop touched the overhead wire I could see a big bluish spark jump across. The motorman used to stand facing the front window of the car and

130

operate two handles that could be moved horizontally in a circular motion. One controlled the speed, and the other worked the brakes. When I became big enough to travel alone, my favorite place on the trolley was right next to the motorman, where I stood watching alternatingly the picture of the street rushing toward the trolley and the deft movements of his hands, which the car obeyed instantly. In front of the motorman there was also a large button that he would hit whenever he wanted to give a warning signal: it gave off one single loud clang like a high-pitched bell. This was the sound that all my life was to remain associated in my mind with streetcars.

Once we negotiated the crossing of Podmaniczky Street, we made a left turn into the narrower Nagymező (Great Field) Street, which also had its trolley lines, except that they ran next to each other in the middle of the street. This street, in contrast to ours, had shops on the ground floor of the buildings that lined it. At the second block we made another left turn onto Lovag (Chevalier) Street, which was a short and narrow residential street. The school was located on its right side, and in front of its entrance, at the curb, there was a heavy horizontal iron bar to prevent the children from running out into the roadway, although there was certainly no wheeled traffic to speak of on that street.

While I can recall much of what I saw during my daily walk from home to school and back—the candy store, the stationer, the tobacconist's shop—I remember very little of the school building itself, of my classroom, of my classmates, or of the teacher. That very little consists, essentially, of one incident and one smell. The incident, which was a painful one for me, indirectly involved one of my classmates whose name was Városy—we were called by our last names in school—and whose father, as I mentioned in the preceding chapter, was a man of some importance in the government. I noticed that the teacher—we had only one teacher, under whose stern eye we had to sit four or five hours daily, six days a week—treated Városy with special indulgence. For me to notice the matter, the teacher must have shown him some marked deference or at least unusual consideration. One day, when the teacher was again particularly nice to Városy, I whispered to the boy who shared with me a double bench: *A tanító úr kivételez* (The teacher plays favorites). Thereupon my bench-mate promptly raised his hand, and when the teacher recognized him, he stood up and said: "Patai says that the teacher plays favorites." I can still feel the astonished hurt with which I listened to this betrayal. The next moment the teacher called, "Patai!" I rose, stood at attention as we were required to, and was treated to a severe rebuke.

The smell I remember is that of the rubber eraser I used in correcting my early writing exercises. It is, of course, well known that smells have a peculiar power to bring back past scenes in one's mind. Decades later, whenever that particular smell would waft into my nostrils, I would instantly be transported back into my elementary school classroom, and see myself sitting at my desk with its dark, rough, wooden top all spotted and splattered with ink, my head tilted to the left, the tip of my tongue sticking out, diligently rubbing my eraser against the lined page of my copybook.

I remember no other event from my elementary school, not even the one circumstance that must have caused me difficulties, which, therefore, could be expected to have stuck in my memory. In my parents' home Jewish ritual laws were adhered to. Our kitchen was kosher, and we strictly observed the Sabbath rest. As far as we children were concerned, this meant quite a list of "don'ts": on the Sabbath we were not allowed to turn the electric lights on or off, to touch money, to use a vehicle, to tear paper, and, most importantly, to write. It is thus beyond any doubt that when I was first taken to school, Father or Mother explained to the teacher that while I would attend classes regularly on the Sabbath, I would not be allowed to write even as much as a single word on that Jewish day of rest. This must have led to quite a number of problems. How did I catch up with the work the class did on Saturday? What did the other boys do or say when they saw me sitting there without touching a pencil? Was I exposed to anti-Semitic remarks? Were there other boys in the class who shared my predicament? All this is a complete blank.

What I do recall from those first years in school are things one would consider unimportant and certainly not worth retaining in memory: that the walls of the classroom were painted a glossy greyish-green, and that next to the door that led from the corridor into the classroom there was a long row of coat hangers fastened to the wall not more than three feet from the floor so as to enable us to hang up our coats without any difficulty. But, above all, when I think back to that classroom, I remember the smell of that rubber eraser.

I am quite sure that the first elementary school I attended was located on Lovag Street. Had I not found among my papers a school certificate that states that I completed my fourth grade (when I was nine) in the Szemere Street elementary school, I could have sworn that I attended the Lovag Street school for the full four years' duration of my primary schooling. I have absolutely no recollection of having changed from one school to the other. Nor do I have, in contrast to the clear picture of the way from home to the Lovag Street school, any memory of the streets I passed going from home to the Szemere Street school.

I do remember, on the other hand, that a year or two after I had begun to go to school, as soon as I mastered the alphabet, I took to reading. I had loved to look at pictures in books long before, as witnessed by the many colored plates that I tore out of the *Meyers Konversations Lexikon*, the great German encyclopaedia whose many volumes took up two whole shelves in my father's library. Also, the first toys I remember having were picture books in the shape of folding cardboards, showing beautifully colored animals. But now the words I could decipher with rapidly increasing fluency added meaning and charm to the pictures.

The first two stories I read were Hungarian translations of the German children's classics *Struwwelpeter* (Shock-headed Peter) and *Max und Moritz*. I can still see before me the picture of the boy Struwwelpeter, weighed down by his distinguishing mark, the enormous shock of hair from which he got his name, standing stiffly with his arms stretched straight down and his fingers spread out. Of the many mischievous adventures of the twins Max and Moritz I loved most the one in which they got into a vat of flour, then fell into a baker's oven, and emerged baked into large child-shaped loaves. There was also a story in the same book about a boy who did not want to eat his soup and consequently, as graphically illustrated in the accompanying series of pictures, became thinner and thinner and, at the end, died. This story did not appeal to me too much, perhaps because I myself did not like soup. (I could not resist at this point getting the facts about these stories. My encyclopaedia informs me that it was Wilhelm Busch [1832–1908], the German poet and caricaturist, considered the father of the modern comic strip, who illustrated his poems for children by creating the two humorous characters of Max and Moritz in 1870.)

Once my appetite was whetted, I went through the entire fare of children's books of the period. I can recall specifically the tales of Andersen and the brothers Grimm, the adventures of Münchhausen, Gulliver, and Robinson Crusoe. But my favorite was *The Jungle*

Book, of which I was given a Hungarian translation illustrated with black-and-white line drawings. In between reading the stories I colored these drawings with crayons, and the thus embellished book remained my treasured possession until adolescence. I enjoyed *The Jungle Book* enormously. The book gave no indication as to the pronunciation of the names in the stories, so I read them in accordance with Hungarian phonetics, which is similar to Italian in that every individual letter always stands for the same individual phoneme. Thus the title of the book, which was left untranslated in the Hungarian edition, was for me *Yoongleh Bo-ok*; Mowgli was *Movglee*, Bagheera was *Bag-h-e-e-ra* (of course with the strong rolled Hungarian *r*), and so forth.

Thinking back on my enjoyment of *The Jungle Book*, I ask myself whether even at that early age I believed that animals can talk. My answer is a definite no. From my frequent visits to the zoo, I was quite familiar with all the animals constituting Kipling's jungle society. I had observed the wolf, the tiger, the bear, the black panther, the monkeys, and even the huge boa constrictor. I knew very well that the sounds these animals uttered were a far cry indeed from human speech, and I concluded with a natural certainty that just as these animals could not speak so the animal friends and foes of Mowgli in the jungle could not speak either. If I nevertheless enjoyed Kipling's masterpiece as greatly as I did, if I let myself be completely carried away by the wish to know what happened next, if I felt the same love for Mowgli that his friends of the wolf pack, Baloo the bear, and Bagheera the black panther had for him, I must have instinctively practiced what I much later learned was called "willing suspension of disbelief." So I read, and reread, and enjoyed the talk of the animals, the Laws of the Jungle they were fond of quoting, the loving endearments with which Mother Wolf addressed Mowgli, and all the other verbal expressions of the carefully layered animal society depicted by Kipling.

In the early spring of 1918, after Mother had become pregnant with her third child, she felt run down and consulted Uncle Yóshka, who prescribed mountain air and rest. Acting upon the doctor's advice, Mother wrote to her father's sister, who with her husband owned and ran a small hotel-pension in the resort town of Lőcse (today Levoča in Czechoslovakia) in the foothills of the northern Carpathians, and reserved a room. I don't know for what reason, but my parents decided that I would accompany Mother to Lőcse. My sister, who was not yet of school age, remained at home in the care of the Fräulein and the maid, and Father, Mother, and I set out for the mountains. Once Father saw that we were safely installed in the premises of Aunt Részka, he returned to Budapest.

From my sojourn in Lőcse, which must have lasted about two months, I remember a few details. One is the picture of the "White Lady of Lőcse," which, I believe, decorated the gate of the old castle. It showed a woman in a white dress and red shawl, placing one hand on the keyhole while beckoning with the other toward the fortifications as if calling the attackers. I must have been told the story that went with the picture, but have long forgotten it. However, prompted by my usual passion for facts, I have now looked up the entry about Lőcse and about its White Lady in the 1915 edition of the Hungarian Révay encyclopaedia, and in it I found a brief résumé of her tragic life. Born Juliana Géczy de Garamszeg about 1690, she became the wife of János Korponay and the lover of Baron István Andrássy, general of the army of Ferencz Rákóczi II and commander of the fortress of Lőcse. In 1709–1710, when Rákóczi rebelled against the Habsburgs, Lőcse was bombarded for three months by the Austrians, until, in February 1710, Juliana betrayed the defenders and helped the attackers conquer the city. It seems that Andrássy himself had something to do with this event, for immediately after the fall of Lőcse he became an adherent of the imperial party, and urged his brother, the commander of Krasnahorka, to surrender that castle as well. Juliana expected, and was promised, a royal reward for helping the imperial army take Lőcse, but fell under the suspicion of fraternizing with exiled members of the Rákóczi party; she was arrested in 1712, subjected to torture several times, and, on September 25, 1715, decapitated in the marketplace of the castle of Győr. The story of the White Lady of Lőcse forms the subject of a historical novel by Mór Jókai, which I read as a teenager without retaining any recollection of it.

The second thing I remember from Lőcse is the discomfort I felt at having to attend a new school in which I knew nobody and in which my classmates eyed me with the double suspicion accorded to a "new boy" who, in addition, had come from the big city. And finally I recall a scene in which I see myself walking with my mother and a man whom I did not know along a mountain path among tall and dark trees. I can visualize the man, turning halfway toward

Mother while walking beside her, and talking to her in an animated, persuasive manner. I found this strange, for never before—nor, for that matter, later—did I see Mother in the company of a man other than Father, and I had a vague feeling that, somehow, she was threatened by that man. Years later Mother was to tell me that the stranger in that picture was none other than Dezső Szabó, the novelist of whom I spoke in the preceding chapter. It seems that the polemic between Father and Dezső Szabó, which had taken place in 1914, had led to personal meetings between them in the course of which Szabó met my mother as well and, as their subsequent encounter in Lőcse shows, was taken by her beauty, charm, and intelligence. The meeting between Mother and Szabó in Lőcse was unquestionably sheer coincidence, but, having met her, he seems to have tried his honest best to seduce her. Perhaps as many as ten years later my mother spontaneously and impulsively supplied me with the facts of the event. One day she found me with a novel by Dezső Szabó in my hands, and this prompted her to tell me how the author of the book I was reading had importuned her years earlier in Lőcse. He was, it appeared, as direct and forceful in his approach to women as he was in his writing. "Imagine!" Mother said, her face flushing with indignation at the memory. "He had the effrontery to suggest that, since I was pregnant anyway, there could be no danger and no problem if I gave in to him. . . . "

Among the family papers I brought along with me to New York there are two letters Mother wrote to Father from Lőcse. She did not date her letters, and no postmark is visible on the first, which reads:

My dear, sweet Yóshka,

So far I have received only the postcard you sent while on the way, and so it is good that I heard over the phone that you had arrived safely. I calmed down after the mood of the parting, and, considering that now the spring has come to Lőcse, I am spending the time pleasantly, and, what is the main thing, usefully. We are much out in the open, and take walks twice every day, and I don't forego my walks even for the sake of the movie, the famous movie. Last evening I went only to the comedy, together with Gyuri, after having taken a stroll in the *Schiessplatz* [Shooting Place]. Gyuri is the sweetest on such occasions, when he has no opportunity to behave impertinently to anybody. He greatly enjoyed the sunset, the like of which he cannot see in Pest. This morning, although howling, he nevertheless went off to school, where we donated 5 crowns for charitable purposes.

Here, parallel with the spring, love blossoms, but still there are some dark sun spots. Gyuri is active about this, too, as an *enfant terrible*, and says things that highly amuse the whole table company. The money you left here with me will not be enough until the end, considering that I shall lay out 100 crowns for you, and, in addition, a respectable amount will be needed also for gloves and the resoling of shoes. For the time being only the first two weeks have been paid.

I hope to have some news from Pest before the day is over, and it is really not nice of you that despite your promise you sent no express letter.

With many hugs and kisses, yours,

Edith

The second letter, which bears the postmark with the date April 10, 1918, is written on a "closed post card," and reads:

My dear, good husband,

I was very glad that Lőcse did you a lot of good, because, even if you don't have to gain weight, a little reserve capital can do no harm. Your wife, too, tries to follow in your footsteps, and I hope that in the end the sojourn here will do me good. The weather is constantly fine, the window is open all day long, and, besides, we of course take walks twice daily. This morning, for instance, we went to the garden of Részka, which only a week ago would have been a great distance for me. But since you left I have been walking every day with really enormous energy, hoping that, after all, I shall get used to it, and, in fact, it already goes much better. As against this, my patience is already on the wane, although it is true that even in Pest nowadays the coming times are not precisely tranquil. But, still, things are different there. Today I wrote to Mrs. Mezei and Mrs. Lenkei, and I also comforted Szabina of Pressburg that she does not have to put down the pen. I don't remember the works of Sorel, and so, if I don't see the pictures it will be completely impossible for me to write about him. Please write more frequently, that belongs definitely to relaxation. Gyuri, thank God, feels splendid, at noon eats just as much as we do, and recently has been finishing even the soup and the vegetables. He goes to school, at times smiling, at times howling, but he has by now learned more or less to read German.

With many kisses, your loving wife

The references in these letters to me as a seven-year-old *enfant terrible* who is fresh to everybody and makes funny remarks to the amusement of the table company show to what extent memory is not only selective but also deceptive. Due to the selectivity of my memory I remember nothing of the incidents to which my mother's letters allude. Due to its deceptiveness, I see myself as a shy, timid child, who dares not open his mouth in the company of strangers, who clings to his mother's skirt and cries when she leaves him alone at home. This is a picture diametrically opposed to the one sketched by my mother. That her reports about my behavior are accurate cannot be doubted. Why, then, does the picture she paints of me remain strange and unbelievable to me? Can it be that once memory has created an image of the past, even if it did this selectively and deceptively, that image becomes a kind of unalterable subjective truth that supersedes whatever actually happened in the remote days of childhood? Or can it be that even then, while talking and acting freshly, as my mother describes it, inwardly I was shy, timid, and frightened, and that this was my own, private, true reality that has remained indelibly embedded in my memory?

Speaking of memory, a subject to which I shall have to return again and again, I must digress here for another moment to say a few words on a problem that has been bothering me practically from the very moment I began to write these memoirs. I find that while I am writing about one particular time or event in my life, my mind roams about, goes back to things that had happened earlier, or jumps ahead to happenings that took place later, often much, much later. This means that I find myself dwelling on, and dwelling in, several different periods simultaneously. This, of course, disturbs the flow of writing, since it is difficult, to say the least, to write about one specific event, and think at the same time of others, separated from it by many years or even decades. It would seem that this is a peculiar characteristic of memory: it can and does conjure up, and pull together, events or scenes that, when they actually occurred, were separated by long intervals.

These thoughts bring to my mind certain Renaissance painters who, on one large canvas, attempted to picture side by side events that represented a long historical sequence. They did this, for instance, in trying to illustrate the story told in the biblical Book of Esther. In one corner they show Queen Esther approaching her lord and master, King Ahasuerus; next to it Haman is seen entreating or threatening the queen; a little farther on Haman leads the horse on which Mordekhai rides triumphantly. Then, still on the same canvas, we are shown the gallows with Haman and his sons strung up, and finally we see the crowd of jubilant Jews in Susa saved by Esther. Even the best painter stumbled when trying thus to transform the time sequence of a narrative into a single picture in which the consecutive events cannot help appearing as if they were taking place simultaneously. To the viewer such a picture only makes sense if he knows the story that the painter is at pains to depict.

Memory's raw material consists, on the one hand, of all the events that make up the individual's life, however long a time-span they cover, and, on the other, of the loci, sceneries, and surroundings, immobile in themselves, within which those actions took place. Memory can thus achieve that which art can not: it can transpose action sequence into simultaneity. This is what I am learning as the memories of seventy years, all coming together, flood my mind and fill it with a mosaic whose little stones all dance together before my vision with movements complementing one another, even though their existence is anchored in times as far apart as the better part of a century. Of course, the moment one comes to set down these memory impressions in writing, one is instantly caught in the limitations of the narrative mode, and is compelled to retransform the simultaneity of memory into something like an orderly sequential presentation of bits and pieces, of events, feelings, experiences, thoughts, and acts.

Some weeks before my mother was due to give birth to either a brother or a second sister, I developed a rash. Mother instantly summoned Uncle Yóshka, who came, sat down at my bedside, examined me, and pronounced the verdict: scarlet fever. I had, he said, to be isolated from Mother lest the baby to be born suffer any harm. As for my sister, Uncle Yóshka said she might as well be put into bed right next to me, for it would be impossible in any case to prevent her getting infected. On that occasion, or perhaps at a subsequent visit of his, I remember having inadvertently touched his sleeve, whereupon he snatched his arm away, and gave a thorough rubbing with a wet towel to the spot I had touched.

So my mother went off to stay with her parents in their new apartment, located at a distance of about a mile from us. The reason for their moving away from the apartment they had next door to us was the marriage of my mother's sister Dóra, who was four years her junior. She married Dr. Ernő Molnár, a graduate of the Rabbinical Seminary of Budapest, who was a teacher of religion in the city's high schools and the editor of *Remény* (Hope), a monthly for Jewish youth. Aunt Dóra had lived with her parents, and after her marriage they all found it advisable that the young couple should continue matrilocal residence. This, however, required a larger apartment, which they found at 3 Magyar Street, in the central section of Budapest, called *Belváros* (Inner City). It was a spacious but very dark apartment from which all sunshine was effectively blocked by the hulking structure of the elegant Astoria Hotel across the extremely narrow street. To this apartment, then, my mother repaired to await her hour, while my sister and I remained at home under the care of the Fräulein.

She was still waiting when Uncle Yóshka pronounced me recovered and assured us that I was no longer a source of contagion. Thereupon, those being the days of summer vacation at school, I, too, was taken to my grandparents' apartment to stay there with Mother. The room that I had occupied during my illness had to be disinfected, which was done professionally. I do not know how it came about that I was present, but I remember very clearly that the disinfector sealed off the room by pasting strips of heavy paper around the frames of all the doors and windows; he then placed a fumigator in front of one door, and inserted a long, flexible brass tube into the keyhole. In this manner the germ-killing gas was blown from the fumigator into the room. Twenty-four hours later he came back, ordered everybody away, and opened the doors and the windows until all traces of the fumes were gone, after which the room was pronounced habitable again. At the same time he removed the large sign reading "Contagious Disease: Entrance Forbidden," which had been pasted on the front door of our apartment as soon as my illness was diagnosed. Thus the quarantine ended.

A few days later, on August 3, just as I awoke in the morning, the door to the room in which I slept opened, and in came my grandmother holding a very small and very red-faced, tightly bundled, and loudly crying baby in her arms. "This is your new little brother," she said. I quickly got out of bed to have a close look at the baby, but my grandmother did not allow me to touch him. "Go and say good morning to your mother," she motioned. I went in, and found Mother lying quietly in bed, with a smile on her face.

Much later, when I began to take interest in such things, and found out that the bearing of a child was a very painful process, I remembered that scene, and wondered how Mother could give birth to her child in the very next room, and keep so quiet that I did not even wake up. "Did you not scream, not even once, when you gave birth to Guszti?" I asked her. "No," she answered, "I never lost control to that extent."

A week or so after Guszti's birth we all moved back to our apartment, and, as far as I was concerned, life continued much as before. I dearly loved my baby brother, almost eight years younger than I, and would often lie down on my belly on the rug next to the baby carriage that served as his crib in the first few weeks or months of his life, and while engrossed in reading a book—by the age of eight I was a voracious and inveterate reader—I would rhythmically kick one of the large wheels of the carriage so as to keep it slightly swaying, which, I thought, would make the baby sleep. Once, I remember, I had the fright of my life as a result of this practice. I must have given the carriage a stronger kick than usual, and, to my horror, I felt the whole thing move. I thought I had caused the carriage to topple over, and imagined its frail contents falling to the floor and getting killed or maimed for life. I turned around as fast as I could, trying to stop the fall, and saw to my immense relief that the carriage had only rolled a few inches farther.

From the very moment of his birth Guszti became the favorite of the whole family. At the age of about one he developed a bad squint in one eye, which, however, only added to his charm in the eyes of all the rest of us. His standing epithet was *a kis édes*, "the little sweetie," and he was pampered by me and his big sister no less than by our parents. When Father worked, nobody was allowed to enter his study—except Guszti. He would crawl, and later totter, up to the big mahogany pedestal desk, and Father would lift him into his lap, or let him straddle his shoulders. Once, I remember, I caught a glimpse of the two of them through the open door of the study: Father was sitting at his desk and writing, with little Guszti straddling his neck and holding on to his head with one hand, while his other hand was tightly clenched around a pencil with which he was busily scribbling on Father's bald pate. Father himself began to write for him a series of children's stories, entitled "The Seven Tales of Gunczum-Bunczum" (Gunczum-Bunczum was the nickname by which Father, who found "little sweetie" too cloying, liked to address him), of which the first was published in Uncle Ernő's juvenile monthly. I do not think Father wrote more than that one; at least, no more were published.

One evening, when Guszti was, I believe, in his second year, he got a nosebleed that just did not want to stop. In panic, my mother summoned Uncle Yóshka, who managed to stop the bleeding but considered a possible recurrence so dangerous that he bedded down on the couch in our living room in order to be on hand if need be. Mother sat next to Guszti's crib and did not take her eyes off him all night. As far as I can remember—I must have received a detailed report from Mother the next morning—Uncle Yóshka's sleep did not have to be disturbed.

Another of my early memories of my brother is that one afternoon Father came home with Guszti, whose right eye was covered with a thick bandage wound around his head. I was present when the two of them entered, and thus witnessed the terrible fright with which Mother cried out, "Yóshka, what happened to the child?!" Father reassured her that nothing bad had happened, but that he had taken Guszti to the eye surgeon to have his squint corrected. Knowing how Mother feared for her children, he wanted to spare her anxiety, and had arranged for the operation without telling her.

In the spring of 1919 events took place in Budapest that shook the whole country, and had their reverberations on the European scene. My personal memories of them are extremely limited, but the outline of the events can easily be gleaned from any number of historical studies. When, at the end of World War I, the Central Powers were defeated, there followed a period of intense internal convulsions in Hungary, with several short-lived governments following one another. On March 21, 1919, a Communist Revolutionary Governing Council was installed, whose foreign commissar, the renegade Jew Béla Kún, was its *de facto* head. The Council entered into an alliance with Soviet Russia, and called upon the workers of the neighboring countries to join Hungary in its struggle against the "imperialist" powers. However, the Communist regime soon lost ground and had to resign, which it did on August 1, after having ruled for a little more than four months. This was followed by the Rumanian occupation of the capital, until, on November 16, 1919, the counterrevolutionary government led by Admiral Horthy took control. Horthy was next elected head of state with the title of regent, so that *de jure*, if not *de facto*, Hungary remained a kingdom. It was the Horthy government that signed the Trianon Peace Treaty (June 4, 1920), giving up about two-thirds of the territory Hungary had controlled until the end of World War I while it was part of the Austro-Hungarian dual monarchy. Transylvania was annexed by Rumania, northern Hungary by Czechoslovakia, southern Hungary by Yugoslovia, and, unkindest cut of all, part of western Hungary had to be ceded to Austria, Hungary's former sister-state and war ally.

Of all this I knew, of course, nothing at the time. What I did retain in my memory were a few visual impressions. I remember the great square in front of the Parliament building lavishly decorated in honor of May Day. Facing the Parliament, a beautiful neo-Gothic building somewhat reminiscent of the London Mother of Parliaments, the Communists set up a huge group of statues made of white plaster. Elsewhere they used the existing bronze statues of Hungarian historical figures as the core around which to build large red globes made of scaffolding and canvas. I can still visualize four of these huge, red, stationary balloons, each perhaps twenty feet in diameter, in four corners of a public park. Two months later, when the Communists were overthrown, the plaster statues were broken into pieces, and the canvas globes were torn to shreds. The debris of these short-lived Communist monuments littered the squares for a long time. And I remember leaning out the window of our apartment and watching fearfully the troops of the Rumanian enemy march down the street.

I also remember very vividly that one of my classmates at school, the son of a Communist commissar who must have been high up in the hierarchy of the regime, once invited me to visit him. He lived with his parents in a suite in the Danube Palace, the most elegant hotel in the city, which had been requisitioned by the government. How the mechanics of the visit were worked out I never knew, or have long forgotten, just as I have forgotten the name of my classmate. But I know that one day Father took me by the hand, and we walked from our home to the hotel. On each side of the entrance to the Danube Palace sat a uniformed soldier behind a machine gun trained on the street. It was the first time I had seen such an instrument of war and death, and I have no doubt that I must have been frightened. The next thing I remember is playing games with my classmate in his room—my father must have left. At one point my friend opened the door that led to the corridor, and asked the soldier who stood guard there to let him have his revolver. The soldier refused. When my father came to take me home, my classmate's father came out of the next room, shook hands with us, and tousled my hair. After the fall of the Communist regime I remember having been told that my classmate's father was apprehended, tried, convicted, sentenced to death, and executed.

The short-lived Communist regime in Hungary triggered a wave of anti-Semitism that, after the fall of Béla Kún in the summer of 1919, engulfed major sections of the Hungarian people. Father's outspoken articles in his journal on the internal and political problems of Hungarian Jewry provoked anger in anti-Semitic circles that was expressed in threatening or scurrilous missives, sent usually anonymously. One of these I have in my possession. It is a postcard, postmarked Budapest, May 4, 1919, and addressed to the Editorial Office of *Mult és Jövő*:

> You Patai Jew!
> Mind your mug, for if you write much about anti-Semitism we shall get hold of that small big nose of yours and shall take you with us to the front. We are telling you, shut up Jew, for there will be trouble. In the next issue write again about the Jews of Budapest.

On the reverse, next to the address, the anonymous writer added somewhat incongruously: "The Red Soldiers greet Joseph Patai."

Ignorant and innocent of the problems of the times, I lived through the Communist regime, its fall, the occupation of Budapest by the Rumanians, the establishment of the Horthy government, and the White Terror; I was preoccupied with my school, my Hebrew lessons, and the walks my sister and I took under the supervision of the Fräulein to the island and the zoo. If, because of the political upheavals, these walks had to be suspended, I do not remember any such thing. By the age of nine my passion for reading was firmly entrenched, and I remember vividly how at that age, and almost to the end of my high school years, I would be unable to tear myself away from the book I happened to be immersed in, even though it meant neglecting my homework. The total absorption in a novel, the burning urgency of knowing what happened next, the ardent love of the heroes and hate of the villains, the vivid conjuring up before my mind's eye of the scenes, places, and persons described in the book I was reading, all these were experiences that filled my childhood and adolescence with an intensity that was subsequently never again to be duplicated.

I was five months short of ten years of age when I finished my four years of elementary school. The certificate of the Szemere Street elementary school attests that I completed the fourth grade with the following results: Religious studies—excellent; writing—good; Hungarian language—good; arithmetic—good; geography—good; singing—good; drawing—good; gymnastics—good; external form of written papers—praiseworthy; conduct—praiseworthy; diligence—varying. The certificate also states that during the year I had fifty-five hours of excused absences, that is, about fourteen days, if the number of hours (periods) a day was four, which, I believe, was the case, from eight in the morning to twelve noon. The certificate is dated June 28, 1920.

5

High School Years: 1920–1924

The year before I finished elementary school the Jewish Congregation of Pest opened its high school for boys. The 215,000 Jews who lived in Budapest in 1920 had formed, after the 1870s, no less than five separate congregations, of which by far the largest was that of the Neolog community of Pest. Its official name was Israelite Congregation of Pest—Pest and not Budapest, because it was confined to the left, Pest, bank of the Danube. It maintained hospitals, orphanages, institutions for the blind and the handicapped, old people's homes, cultural institutions, numerous synagogues, and a network of elementary and lower secondary schools in which the curriculum was the same as in the municipal schools, with one difference. In the municipal schools two hours weekly were set aside for religious studies, for which the pupils were divided into three groups: Catholic, Protestant, and Jewish, with each receiving instruction in a separate classroom from a clergyman of its own faith. The courses in Jewish religion were given by graduates of the Jewish Teachers Institute or of the Rabbinical Seminary of Budapest.

As against this, in the Jewish congregational schools the number of weekly hours devoted to religious and Hebrew studies was increased to five, the maximum of weekly hours given to any subject. In the Hungarian school system elementary education lasted four years, for pupils aged six to ten, after which most of them would go on to a *polgári* (literally, civic) school, a kind of higher elementary, or lower secondary, school, for another four years. A minority would instead enter an academic high school, which awarded, after eight years of study and a rigorous final exam, a "maturity certificate," entitling the eighteen-year-old graduate to seek admission to a university.

146

In the fall of 1919 the high school of the Jewish Congregation of Pest admitted students to its first grade. That single class was housed in the building of the *polgári* school of the congregation, located in Wesselényi Street, not far from our home. This new Jewish high school, to be precise, was to be a *reálgimnázium*, that is, its curriculum was somewhere between that of a *gimnázium*, in which the accent was on humanities, including Latin and Greek, and a *reál* school, in which the sciences were emphasized. This meant that the Jewish *reálgimnázium* had Latin but not Greek, and had courses in mathematics, chemistry, and physics, as well as in Hungarian, German, and English, and, being a Jewish high school, also in Hebrew language, Bible studies, and Jewish religion. Once a student enrolled in the school—this was the system in all Hungarian schools—he could not choose among various courses but had to attend all the courses the school offered, year after year. Each period lasted fifty minutes, with a ten-minute break in between, except at eleven o'clock, when there was a twenty-minute break to enable the students to have their mid-morning snack, which each of them had to bring from home. Classes began at 8 A.M. and went on until 1 P.M. three days a week, and until 2 P.M. the other three. These three added hours were needed in order to accommodate the extra three periods of religious and Hebrew studies. Since it was a Jewish school, it rested on the Sabbath, with work going on as usual on Sundays. However, on Saturdays the students were required to attend morning service in the school synagogue.

Before a student could be admitted to any high school, the educational regulations of the country required that he pass an entrance examination. This, I still remember, caused me no small amount of trepidation. My father, too, seems to have felt that I was not quite up to passing the exam, and he hired a tutor to prepare me. The tutor he engaged was a first cousin of my mother, Dénes Friedman. His mother, Aunt Gizi, was a sister of my grandfather Ehrenfeld. I have to go to the *Encyclopaedia Judaica* to learn that Dénes was born in 1903, was ordained a rabbi in 1927, became rabbi of Ujpest, a large suburb of Budapest, joined the faculty of the Budapest Rabbinical Seminary in 1935, and published several scholarly studies. But I do remember that when he tutored me he was a very impressive, very tall and thin young man (he was in fact seventeen years old), and that he made me work hard. Of the things he taught me I remember, rather peculiarly, only one detail. He enumerated, and made me write down and memorize, the names of the countries that were big powers, medium powers, small powers, and "tiny" powers. I wondered how something can be tiny and yet a power, and I could not understand what was the point in all that. I don't think the matter came up in the course of the exam.

In later years I was to meet my cousin Dénes only once or twice. I was present in the synagogue of Ujpest when he was inaugurated as its rabbi. On another occasion he told me of a little incident that bears repetition because it throws some light on the tradition-bound and ancestry-oriented bent of mind of many Hungarian Jews. He was visiting, Dénes told me, a rabbi, and as he entered the other man's presence Dénes sat down without being asked to, and, in general, behaved with such a display of self-importance that the rabbi asked him, in Yiddish, *Epes a yikhes?* which can only be paraphrased in English as "Are you, by any chance, the descendant of important ancestors?" *Avade*, "certainly," answered Dénes, and proceeded to enlighten his interlocutor about his noble pedigree, which went back to the great Moshe Sofer. While doing so he conspicuously caressed his chin, thus calling the other rabbi's attention to his *lepkeszakáll* (butterfly beard), which is the Hungarian term for the type of beard growth that leaves two naked spots under the lips faintly resembling a butterfly with open wings. Contemporary sketches of Moshe Sofer and later photographs of his descendants show that they, indeed, had this kind of beard. Without sharing my cousin's pride in it, I may mention as a mere fact that I, too, have this feature in common with our illustrious ancestors, of which I became aware when, at the age of sixty, I let my beard grow. This incident shows not only that an inordinate pride in scholarly rabbinical ancestry was a characteristic of certain religious circles in Hungary, but also that such antecedents entitled one to respect and deference. After leaving Budapest for Jerusalem in 1933 I had no more contact with Dénes, and only when the war ended and details of the Hungarian Holocaust reached Palestine did I learn that, in 1944, when the Nazis invaded Hungary, he was deported to his death after witnessing the murder of his only son.

In 1920, when he tutored me, his tragic end was, of course, mercifully hidden behind the veils of the future. I passed the high school entrance exam on August 29, 1920, which I know because it was duly stamped, with the date, on the back of the fourth grade elementary school certificate that is still extant among my papers. In the fall of that year I started my high school studies by being admitted to the class of 1928 of the high school of the Jewish Congregation of Pest. That class consisted of two parallel forms, IA and IB, each with some forty or fifty students in it. I was placed in form IB. At the end of the fourth grade, when many students left the school, the two parallel forms were to merge into one to continue for another four years until graduation in the spring of 1928. By the time my sister reached high school age, two years behind me, the Jewish Congregation of Pest had established a high school for girls as well, and she became a student there.

I remember very little of my first years in the high school. I cannot recall the building at all, and if I do remember my teachers and classmates, I can no longer tell whether I remember them from the first few years, or from the later years when we were still together as a group and approached the age of eighteen and the dreaded final exam. I can still hear, though, the terrible din that filled the classroom during the intermissions between periods, the wild running about, the yelling, pushing, and shoving, the fist fights and the wrestling bouts, and then the sudden hush when the teacher entered. The school was an all-male institution—there were at the time no coeducational schools in Hungary—all the students, the teachers, and the other school personnel were males, and only in the principal's office did one solitary female secretary work. Throughout the eight years at that school I was rather shy, and mostly avoided the aggressive boys who created much of the noise and liked to throw their weight around. In fact, many of the boys were aggressive, some were outright hostile, and several of them annoyed me by calling me *Lópata* (horse hoof in Hungarian), instead of Patai. This, and the mockery some of the boys made of my Zionism, frequently resulted in fisticuffs between me and my classmates that usually ended in a draw or were interrupted by the entrance of the teacher.

Still, I had a few good friends whom I would meet after school or on Saturdays, with whom I would take walks in the many attractive places of the city, or whom I would invite over or visit. Among them I remember Dezső Stern, who was to become a doctor and was killed by the Nazis; László Schwarz, of whom I lost sight after graduation; László Salgó, who was to be my colleague at the Rabbinical Seminary and became chief rabbi of Budapest in the 1970s; and the brothers Sándor (Shanyi) and David (Duci) Rappaport, both of whom I was to meet again much later in America, where Shanyi worked as

a businessman and Duci became a famous psychologist. My friendship with the Rappaport boys lasted for several years; we were devoted
to one another, and visited each other frequently. The Rappaports
lived in Buda, and once, when Shanyi was sick with a cold and a
fever, and the weather was rather inclement, my mother tried to
persuade me to stay home instead of visiting him as I wanted to. I
insisted on going—this must have happened when I was too old to
be simply forbidden to go—and Mother in her frustration wrote a
satirical poem to me which began

> Up to Buda, my brave son Gyuri,
> To Rappaport who suffers from fever. . . .

The waters of Lethe have long since covered most of my experiences in the first few years in high school, but I remember with great
clarity and detail that in that period of my life I loved to eat, and
often went on foraging expeditions to get a snack in between the
regular five meals a day Mother gave us. I see myself sneaking into
the *Shpayz* (larder), that small storage-room next to the kitchen in
which were kept the conserves and the goose livers Mother prepared
in order to enrich the diet of her family. Toward the end of every
summer, after we returned from summer vacation, Mother would go
to the market with the maid, and purchase huge quantities of fruit—
apricots, black plums, greengage, and the like—and, assisted by the
maid, would prepare preserves. The fruit was peeled, cut up, and
cooked for a long time with lots of sugar in large pots, poured into
pint- or quart-sized jars, liberally topped with salicyl, a white salt-
like substance used to prevent the formation of mold, then tightly
closed with parchmentlike paper that was tied down around the
opening of the jar with a strong string. The jars were placed into
several very large pots, each of which could accommodate perhaps
six or eight of them, and the pots were filled with water so as to
cover the jars, and put on the stove to be boiled for a considerable
length of time. All these steps were considered necessary in order to
prevent spoilage. When the time came to open a jar, the top layer of
salicyl was first removed, then Mother would carefully inspect the
contents to see whether, despite all her precautions, they showed
signs of decay. Our larder contained dozens and dozens of such jars
filled with homemade preserves, which gradually diminished as the
season wore on, and the time approached for laying by a new sup-

ply. For the mid-morning snack, which we children took along to school, we usually got two hefty slices of bread generously topped with butter and one of Mother's marmalades. I loved them all, and I do not remember ever having left over even the smallest piece of these sandwiches.

However, my favorite among Mother's fruit preserves was the quince cheese. This consisted of quinces and sugar (and perhaps some spices as well?), boiled in water until the fruit was soft enough to be passed through a sieve, or rather squeezed through it with a large wooden spoon. Then the heavy purée was poured into brick-shaped forms and left to cool and harden. When ready to eat, this preserve had the consistency of hard cheese, and was cut with a knife into oblong slices that we children would be given to eat without bread, all by themselves.

Another great dish Mother used to prepare was goose liver. This was kept in a huge enameled bin that must have been at least two feet tall; it was round, wider at the bottom than at the top—that is, had the shape of a truncated cone—and had a tight-fitting lid attached by hinges at one side. The goose livers hidden in this treasure trove were embedded in goose fat, and were for me the greatest delicacies. Much later I learned that in order to make the liver of the geese increase in size, the poor birds were force-fed by the Hungarian peasant women. During the winter months the fat in the bin froze to the consistency of a thick and stiff paste. Many times, I still remember, I would sneak into the larder, open the lid of the bin, which reached up to my chest, and stick my fingers into the frozen fat, moving them around until I located a liver, from which I would tear off a sizable chunk and stuff it into my mouth then and there. I would not have been denied goose liver whenever I wanted it—in fact goose liver-and-fat sandwiches alternated with marmalade-and-butter sandwiches as our mid-morning snacks—but something must have prompted me to partake of this tasty stuff surreptitiously rather than to ask for it.

There were other delicacies, too, which Mother made and I loved. There was the sweet chestnut purée served either fluffy and topped with lots of whipped sweet cream or else shaped into little round patties and coated with transparent glazed sugar or with chocolate. Another of my favorite desserts was the *almásrétes*, apple turnover, which was prepared with great mastery by my grandmother. I used to watch her working the dough on a large kneading board, flattening it with a thick rolling pin, lifting it up with both hands so as to stretch it paper-thin, sprinkling more flour on it until finally satisfied, wrapping it around the peeled and cut up pieces of raw apple, forming it into a perfectly rounded long sausagelike tube about two to three inches thick, then cutting the unwieldy column into the proper length that could be accommodated in the baking pan, laying the pieces carefully side by side, and placing them in the stove over the fire, which was kept going with thick logs of wood, with shiny crystalline lumps of black coal, or with egg-shaped *koksz*, as the coke briquettes were called in Hungarian. What pleasure it was to bite into the warm pastry as soon as it came out of the oven, with its dough mantle flaking into many almost transparent, paper-thin layers, and the sweet apples within baked to a deliciously soft consistency.

I remember all these delicacies and my pleasure in eating them very clearly. What I do not remember is how old I was at the time to which these memories pertain. In any case, as I approached adolescence I lost my sweet tooth, and with it my appetite in general. Speaking of sweet tooth, by the time of my Bar Mitzva my unrestrained intake of sweets, candies, marmalades, and sugared and chocolated cookies and pastries had wrought havoc with my teeth—although my mother insisted that I brush them once a day—and I developed many cavities. Consequently, I became a patient of the family dentist, Dr. Hohenberg, who happened to live in the same building on Magyar Street as my grandparents. The last two of my lower molars, one on each side, could not be saved and were extracted; since in those days in Hungary the replacement of lost teeth was not customary, the lack of these two molars caused some malformation in the top row of teeth as well as a certain tilting of the adjacent lower molars. I was often plagued by toothache, and I remember occasions when, in acute pain, I would try to bury my head in the lap of my mother, who would hold me tight as if her protective nearness could bring me relief. She must have had endless patience and great love for me to be willing to serve as the cushion into which I pushed my head, often and who knows for how long each time, in the desperate hope of ridding myself of my toothache.

I of course hated to go to the dentist, who invariably caused me pain, but my visits to him had their compensation, for immediately after he saw me I would go up to the next floor where my grandparents lived, and receive some comfort from a piece of one of my grandmother's famous delicacies, which she always seemed to have in readiness. It was on the occasion of these visits that I would meet there my great-uncle Solomon Ehrenfeld, Grandfather's brother. Grandfather had several brothers and sisters, most of whom I never met. But I knew of their existence, and made up a rhyme composed of nothing but their names, and I still remember the first of the two lines: "Shimi, Shamu, Shalamon, Sóri, Gizi, Rézi. . . . "

The second line, which I forgot, ended with "Béni." Of these great-aunts and great-uncles I met only Solomon, Gizi (who was the mother of Dénes Friedman), and Rézi, that is Részka, in whose pension in Lőcse Mother and I spent several months in the spring of 1918. Of Shamu (Samuel) I knew that he was rabbi in Antwerp. Béni (Benő or Benjamin) lived somewhere in the Hungarian provinces, and his son Shanyi (Sándor, or Alexander) became a dentist in Budapest and later changed his family name to Máté. I know nothing of Shimi (Simon) and Sóri (Sarah).

Of all of them I knew best Uncle Solomon, whom I remember as a tall man of spare build, with straight silvery hair, deep-set blue eyes, the aquiline Roman — or rather, Jewish — nose of all the Ehrenfelds, an extremely handsome face, and the elegant bearing of a born aristocrat. What intrigued me most about him was that he was said to be living permanently in a hotel. How could a man live in a hotel, I wondered. Isn't a hotel a place where people stay for a few days when away from home? How can one's home be a hotel?

Years later I learned some additional facts about Uncle Solomon. He never married — in itself a most unusual thing for the scion of a great rabbinical family — had no visible means of support, and gave himself out to be a professor of mathematics, although in reality he never had any teaching position. He was a frequent lunch guest in the house of my grandparents. He would simply arrive shortly before lunchtime and, whether Grandmother liked it or not, he would stay for the midday meal, which was the main repast. After lunch, he and Grandfather, who was retired and therefore had nothing else to do, would often play chess, which inevitably gave rise to vehement altercations between them. I believe that Uncle Solomon must have received some financial aid from Grandfather, who himself was supported by his son and his son-in-law, my father.

Most intriguing about Uncle Solomon was that he was known by the entire family to be in love with a married woman, a distant relative, who was referred to in the family as "the Black Woman." I never knew, nor do I know to this day, why she was called by this name — I can only guess that she must have had a somewhat darkish skin — but I remember that her real name was Mrs. Shmulche Schreiber, which would make her husband an offspring of Moshe Sofer, whose descendants changed their name to Schreiber, and from whom both the Schreiber and the Ehrenfeld families traced their descent. Nor do I know what was the actual relationship between Uncle Solomon and "the Black Woman," although I suspect that, both being very religious, it remained a purely platonic affair.

I remember many details about our annual celebration of Passover. On the top shelves of the larder were kept the special Passover dishes, tableware, and pots and pans — a complete set of kitchen and table equipment — held in reserve throughout the year for the sole purpose of being used on the eight days of the Feast of *Matzot* (unleavened bread). A week or so before the holiday, which falls in the early spring, my mother and the maid would carry out an exceptionally thorough cleaning of the whole apartment; and once that was done, in the evening preceding Passover eve, Father would place a few crumbs of bread on the windowsills and on the floor along the wall and in the corners. Next morning would take place the rite of *b'diqat ḥametz* (searching for leaven), when Father, armed with a large wooden spoon and a small whisk made of goose feathers, would light a candle, give it to me to hold, and then go from room to room to locate and sweep into the spoon all the crumbs he had left around the night before. Then he would carefully wrap up the spoon with its contents and the whisk and burn them in the stove. This made the apartment *ḥametz*-free, and we were no longer allowed to eat bread until nine days later, when the holiday ended. Then followed a full day of hard work for Mother: she had to rid the kitchen range of its contamination by *ḥametz* by placing burning coals on top of it, and to cleanse the glasses by immersing them in boiling water. Then she would pack away the *ḥometzdig* kitchenware and tableware and replace them with their Pesaḥdig equivalents from the shelves in the larder. Immediately thereafter she began preparing the Seder meal.

As long as my parents and grandparents occupied two adjacent apartments at 6 Podmaniczky Street, we celebrated the Seders, the festive meals of the first two evenings of Passover, together with them. Grandfather, dressed in the traditional *kittl*, the long white embroidered robe, his head covered with a white silk cap bordered by a thin silvery ribbon, would conduct the rites. He would sit on a big easy chair, leaning against a soft cushion propped up in front of the backrest, in order to fulfill the traditional requirement that the participants at the festive Passover meal must sit *mesubbin*, reclining, as it says in the Haggada itself, "On other nights we eat either sitting or reclining, but this night we all recline." At the beginning of the evening I would be somewhat tense, because after the introductory benedictions and prayers my turn would come as the youngest male present—in later years my brother would take over the task from me—to ask the "Four Questions," in reply to which Grandfather, as the master of ceremonies, would recite the story of the Exodus as told in legendary form in the Passover Haggada.

One of the tasks of my early Hebrew teachers was to practice with me the reading of the questions, but after the first time they went easily. Once I performed my task, I could relax and enjoy the traditional melodies that, as the years passed, became more and more familiar to me and hence more and more enjoyable. While singing lustily I watched with eagle eyes when Grandfather broke in half one of the three *matzot* placed before him on the large Seder plate, wrapped it carefully in a white napkin, and hid it behind the pillow against which he leaned throughout the evening. This half *matzo*, called *afikoman*, or, as he pronounced it, *afikaymen*, was supposed to be eaten after the conclusion of the meal. And I was supposed, also by tradition, to steal it, hide it, and produce it only in return for a ransom Grandfather would have to pay for it. The opportunity to steal the *afikoman* would invariably arise when Grandfather got up and went to the bathroom to perform the ritual handwashing ceremony that preceded the benediction over, and the eating of, the first piece of *matzo* before the meal. That was my opportunity. I would jump up, run to Grandfather's temporarily vacated chair, extricate the *matzo* from behind the pillow, and hide it somewhere in a neighboring room. By the time Grandfather returned to his seat, I had reoccupied my own chair, and tried to keep a serious face while thinking about the gift I would ask from Grandfather as the price of restoring the *afikoman* to him after the meal.

The large china Seder dish, lavishly decorated with plant motifs, the Hebrew text of blessings, the sentence "This is the bread of affliction that our fathers ate in Egypt," and the names of the items of food that were placed on it, stood in front of Grandfather, and as he recited the answers to my "Four Questions" he would point to several of them. There were, in addition to the three *matzot* that were placed one on top of the other, a roasted egg and a bone as reminders of the paschal lamb that was offered up in the Jerusalem Temple; a dish of salt water symbolic of the tears of the Children of Israel suffering in Egyptian slavery; the *maror*, the bitter horserad-ish, freshly grated only an hour or two earlier so as to retain its full strength, reminiscent of the bitterness of the slavery; and the *ḥaroset* (pronounced by Grandfather *khrayses*), meaning clay, a paste made of grated almonds and apples diluted in wine, which was supposed to symbolize the mortar the Israelites used in building the cities of Pithom and Raamses under the lash of their cruel Egyptian taskmas-ters, but which was actually ingested together with the *maror* so as to neutralize to some extent its bite. When it came to the ritual eating of the *maror*, Grandfather would distribute small amounts of it to all of us sitting around the table, and then would himself swal-low such a massive portion that his eyes would instantly overflow with tears; he would gasp for air, and would have to wait a minute before he could continue with the recital.

The Seder meal itself would always begin with a hard-boiled egg that we ate from a saucer containing some salt water, which I loved. Then followed the chicken soup with several large *matze-kneydls* (*matzo* balls) in it, which Grandmother's culinary artistry knew how to make feather-light and very tasty; then came the *gefilte fish* in frozen jelly, then chicken and possibly some other meat, then des-sert, then fruit, and then, finally, came the turn of the *afikoman* that had to be the ritual conclusion of the meal. Grandfather would reach behind him, find to his perfectly simulated consternation that it was gone, and ask, "Who took the *afikaymen?*" I owned up, and he would ask, "Well, what do you want for it?" Interestingly, while I remember these details quite clearly, I have no recollection what-soever of what I ever asked as a ransom for producing the *afikoman*.

As against this I remember very clearly the Cup of Elijah. The drinking of a few glasses (for us children, sips) of red wine was part of the Seder, but in addition to our wine glasses there was a large silver cup, gilded on the inside and decorated with floral patterns on the outside, placed in the middle of the table and filled with wine. This was the Cup of Elijah, the famous fiery biblical prophet, who was supposed to come and drink from it. At one point in the course of the ritual recital, Grandfather would motion to me to open the door to enable Elijah to enter, and we would all recite in unison, "Pour out your wrath upon the nations which know You not, and did not call upon Your name . . . " At that moment Elijah was believed to enter, invisible of course, and drink some wine from his special cup. I was told to watch closely, for if I did, I would see how the wine diminished.

The after-meal part of the Haggada included several songs with merry melodies, each with recurring refrains, and an hour or so later we reached the last of them, the *Ḥad Gadya*, "One little kid," after which the evening closed with the threefold repetition of *Lashana Haba'a Birushalayim*, "Next year in Jerusalem!"

Grandfather's traditional piety included several beliefs whose superstitious nature was to become clear to me only many years later. When he saw me paring my nails before going to bed, he would say, "Don't do that in the evening!" I asked him why not, but he gave me no straight answer and said instead that one should pare one's nails only in the daytime. Years later I discovered that there was an old Jewish belief to the effect that if you pare your nails at night, demons can get hold of the parings and, being in possession of those parts of your body, can do you great harm. Evidently, Grandfather believed in this, but, at the same time, was ashamed to let me know that he did.

He also believed in the sanctity of pious and saintly rabbis, and in the possibility of obtaining what I later learned to be *baraka* through physical contact with them. Once he took me to the main Orthodox synagogue of Budapest, that of Rombach Street, of which the chief rabbi was R. Koppel Reich. It was summertime, and after the service Grandfather stood with me in the courtyard of the synagogue and we waited for Rabbi Reich to pass by. When he came, Grandfather told me to step forward and kiss the hand of the old rabbi, which I did.

When my uncle Berti died, at the age of forty, both of my grandparents were devastated, but Grandfather, sustained by his simple and unquestioning faith, recovered more rapidly and more fully than Grandmother, whose intelligence made it more difficult for her accept the tragic and untimely death of her only son as an event ordained by God.

In my preteen years I knew, more instinctively than cerebrally, that Hungarian Jews were intensely patriotic. Patriotism was perhaps the most salient feature in the Hungarian national character, and the Hungarian Jews were more patriotic than the non-Jewish Hungarians. I myself was, of course, not immune to these sentiments, which were inculcated in us, to begin with, in the elementary school. Back in the first grade we six-year-old children had to learn by heart a patriotic poem whose first stanza I still remember, and which, in literal English translation, read:

> May the Hungarian flag
> Stream high in the sky,
> May fame and glory wreathe it
> And good fortune accompany it.

As I write these lines, the picture of the Hungarian flag rises before my mind's eye as it was shown on the cover of a copybook, or perhaps of the primer that we used in the first grade. I am certain that the picture of the flag had something to do with the poem, for I can see before me, not the Hungarian flag itself, which, of course, I saw many times as long as I lived in Budapest, but that particular picture of the flag, which showed it fluttering in the wind, its three colors—red, white, and green—standing out clearly against the background of a light blue sky. And simultaneously I see myself posing in front of my family, among whom, I am quite sure, was Grandmother, and reciting that poem with great enthusiasm, projecting my voice as loudly as I am able to, my cheeks becoming flushed with patriotic fervor and my declamatory effort.

It was into this kind of red-white-green atmosphere that Father tried to infuse a feeling for Jewish culture, and to implant the recognition that to maintain contact with world Jewry was not unpatriotic and that to support the Zionist settlement work and the upbuilding of Jewish Palestine was a Jewish duty, in no way incompatible with the patriotic love Hungarian Jews had for their country.

Father's work frequently required meetings with Jewish scholars, artists, writers, and communal and political leaders. When I was ten or eleven Father began to take me along, and although I cannot remember anything that transpired in the course of his conversations with these men, I assume that the subjects discussed had something to do with articles Father wanted his interlocutors to write or planned to write about them. One of these visits was to Ignaz Goldziher, who had been acquainted with Father's work since 1904, and whose importance as one of the founders of the scholarly investigation of Islam I learned to appreciate only years later when I myself began to study Arabic. When we left him, Father said to me, "Don't ever forget that you shook hands with the greatest Orientalist alive." Since Goldziher died in 1921, this visit must have taken place before I was eleven years old. Goldziher's library was acquired by the Hebrew University of Jerusalem, where, from 1933 on, I had the privilege of perusing his books, which were full of his penciled marginal notes.

Another great Hungarian Jew with whom I shook hands shortly before his death was József Kiss (1843–1921), considered one of the greatest Hungarian poets, and this despite the fact that most of his poems had Jewish themes that could scarcely have appealed to Christian critics. Father published several of Kiss's poems in his monthly, and the visit must have had something to do with literary questions or plans.

I also remember having been taken along by Father on visits to two of his political acquaintances who, as I later learned, were more his opponents than friends. One was Vilmos Vázsonyi (1868–1926), of whom I knew nothing at the time, but who, as the *Hungarian Jewish Lexicon* informs me, was a leading politician in Budapest, and served for a number of years as minister of justice and minister of election rights in various Hungarian governments. The other was Pál Sándor (1860–1936), director of the Budapest municipal tramway company and member of Parliament, who (my source here is the *Encyclopaedia Judaica*) fought "somewhat defensively and apologetically" against the anti-Semitic policies of the government, the *numerus clausus*, and other discriminatory laws. He was an assimilationist, an outspoken opponent of Zionism, and Father wrote several strongly polemical articles against him in *Mult és Jövo*.

Another way in which Father introduced me about the same time to the great world that was Budapest was by taking me to the opera. The Budapest Opera, which still stands perfectly preserved (or rather, restored), is a beautiful baroque building whose planner was evidently influenced by both the Paris Opera and the Viennese State Opera. I remember how impressed I was by the great marble staircase, the spacious lobby with its many shining columns, and especially by the large horseshoe-shaped auditorium with its lavish gold and red velvet decoration. The first performance I was taken to was Mozart's *The Magic Flute*. I felt as if I had been transported into fairyland. I loved the scenery, the playful melodies—especially those sung by Papageno and Papagena, who were costumed like large birds—and I can even remember the name of one of the principal singers, Oszkár Kálmán, who sang the role of Sarastro, and whom I subsequently was to hear several more times when he appeared in the concerts organized by Father under the heading "Cultural Evenings of *Mult és Jövö.*" Later I learned that Kálmán, a Jew, was considered the greatest basso profundo in Hungary and perhaps all Europe.

The second opera my parents took me to was Halevy's *The Jewess.* The dramatic and tragic story gripped me, and I never forgot the great aria sung by Eliezer when struggling with himself whether or not to send his adopted daughter to her death. The opera was sung in Hungarian, in which the name of the daughter, Rachel, became for some reason Recha. I can still hear the melody and the words sung by the unfortunate Eliezer, which, translated literally from the Hungarian, were: "When Fate placed Recha into my hands, I swore that I would live only for you; and now shall I be the one to send you to grim death?" The mid-sentence change from third to second person did not bother me at the time in the slightest, but I remember I took logical exception to the huge red wig Recha wore in the opera. At the very end of the opera Recha is thrown into the fire—of which only the frightening reflection could be seen on the stage—she utters a bone-chilling scream, and Eliezer flings desperately and defiantly the words, "She is your daughter!" at the cardinal, his archenemy. I was thoroughly shaken by all this, but as we left I commented to my parents that, since Recha turned out not to be a Jewess after all, but the daughter of the cardinal, her presentation as a red-headed Jewish woman was misplaced.

I remember one more opera and one concert to which my father took me alone. I do not know why Mother did not come along on those occasions, and why my sister, who by that time was well advanced in her piano lessons, was not with us either. The opera was *Aïda,* my father's favorite. He told me that he loved this opera so much that he went to see it each season when it was performed. I, too, of course, was taken by the great melodies, the pageantry, the tragedy of this grandest of grand operas, and have seen it since several times in various cities. As a graduation present I took my daughter Ofra to see it at the Metropolitan Opera in New York, and told her that by doing so I was merely continuing an old family tradition.

The concert to which my father took me was a performance of Beethoven's *Missa Solemnis*, and while it did not make as deep an impression on me as the operas, undoubtedly because the visual element was missing, I did greatly enjoy it, and the experience became one of the sources of my enduring love of classical music. Of the four soloists I remember only the contralto, Maria Basilides, who, although not Jewish, appeared several times in the concerts organized by Father. A little detail that has remained in my memory in this connection is that Father wore his dinner jacket, which I did not see him do often.

From the age of twelve or thirteen I, with one of my classmate friends, used to go to the Hungarian National Theater, considered the finest theater in the country. It specialized in classical drama by both Hungarian and foreign playwrights. Since we did not have enough pocket money to purchase tickets, what we did was to go up to the third gallery, deposit our overcoats in the coatroom for the equivalent of a dime, and then give the usher, who usually was an old lady, something like a quarter, for which she allowed us to sit on the stairs. The entrance to the third gallery was at its very back and top, high up under the ceiling, and from there the stairs, and the rows of seats, led down to the front of the gallery that constituted the third, topmost, horseshoe of the auditorium. Occasionally it would happen that we did not have to sit on the stairs longer than the end of the first act; if we espied vacant seats after the intermission, we would occupy them and watch the rest of the play in comfort.

This is how I saw many of the great plays of Hungarian and world literature. Several of them impressed me so deeply that I never forgot them, and, if the occasion presented itself, went to see them again. Among my favorites was *The Tragedy of Man* by Imre Madách, the most celebrated Hungarian drama. It is a panoramic play, giving a rapid overview of world history in symbolic scenes, taking place in the Garden of Eden to begin with, then in ancient Egypt, Greece, and so forth down the centuries, and then on to the near future in which man is shown living in a phalanstery (I found out only much later that this scene drew heavily upon F. M. C. Fourier), and finally to the very end of man's existence in the distant future when the earth has become a ball of ice and its few surviving inhabitants are miserable Eskimos whose only concern is how to find food. "There are too many men and too few seals," says one of them. This whole millennial pageant is presented to Adam in a dream by Lucifer, whose purpose in doing so is to persuade him, by showing him mankind's tragic future, to commit suicide and thus prevent the human race from coming into being. In every scene Adam encounters a woman in whom, at the last moment, before Lucifer tears him away to lead him into a new era, he recognizes Eve. Adam's cry of "Eve! Eve!" tore at my heart, and the very romantic stage settings and lighting effects are something I can visualize to this day. In the last scene, which takes place once again in the Garden of Eden, Adam awakens from his dream vision, which spanned thousands of years, and runs to the edge of a cliff to throw himself down and thus to prevent the tragedy of man from taking place. But at that moment Eve tells him that she is pregnant, which makes Adam desist—it would be too late. God's voice is heard encouraging Adam, who takes heart but says, "Only that end, if only I could forget that!" The play concludes with the words of God, "I told you, Man, strive and trust!" so that what *The Tragedy of Man* actually says, as I understood it at the time, is that despite the chain of tragedies constituting human history, man's destiny is to forge ahead, to strive, to trust in God, and to conquer.

The deep impression the play made on me did not, however, prevent me from remarking to my friend who shared the experience with me that there was an obvious error in the ending of the play: even if Eve was pregnant, had Adam killed himself at that moment he would still have prevented mankind from coming into being since, even if Eve were to give birth to a boy child, he could not have had sex with his own mother, and the two of them would have remained the last two humans on earth. The possibility that a woman could be impregnated by her own son, and that thus mankind could be launched on its tragic road, never occurred to me.

Other favorites of mine were Calderón's *Life Is a Dream*, and Ibsen's *Peer Gynt*. The latter was performed with the full musical score by Grieg, whose melodies have remained with me all my life. Yet I liked most the scene in which Peer attaches a bolt to the door of the hut he builds in order to keep out the demons or demonic influences. I felt that this scene had a deep symbolic significance, although what this significance precisely was I could not say. Today I believe that I was affected by this scene because, without being aware of it, it touched in me the same chord whose vibrations years earlier had produced my imaginary struggles with the demons who tried to climb in through my window.

It was while sitting there on the stairs of the third balcony that I got acquainted with Shakespeare, Goethe's *Faust*, the great Greek tragedies, the social dramas of Ibsen and Strindberg, and I don't know what else. All in all, my attendance at the National Theater amounted to a veritable course in world drama. Later I occasionally wondered to what extent the slightly illicit manner in which I attended the plays contributed to my interest in them. It also appears puzzling in retrospect that I never went to any of the other theaters in Budapest, such as the Vigszinház (Comedy Theater), which presented the scintillating plays of Ferenc Molnár and other modern Hungarian and foreign playwrights. I knew of those plays, even read several of them, but never went to see them.

What I did do, as I grew and my self-assurance increased, was to explore the city. Budapest in the 1920s was for me a city full of fascination. I loved it so much that I often wondered how people could resign themselves to living in another city or any other part of the country. It was a beautiful place, especially on sunny days when its parks, its stately buildings, its monuments, its broad boulevards, and the hills of Buda with the grandiose royal palace sparkled and vibrated. I loved to take a stroll in the Inner City where splendid stores lined Váci Street and elegantly dressed men and women sat around in the sidewalk cafés and in front of the Gerbeaud, the most famous patisserie in town. I enjoyed walking along Teréz Boulevard with its movie theaters, then making a left turn onto Andrássy Avenue, in front of whose luxurious villas the roadbed was paved, not with cobblestones, but with brick-shaped wooden blocks so as to diminish the noise of the vehicles that otherwise might disturb the rich and therefore sensitive people who lived there.

Andrássy Avenue led to the greatest and most impressive monument of the city, erected on the occasion of the one-thousandth anniversary of the conquest of Hungary by the Magyar tribes led by Árpád. It consisted of a larger-than-life bronze equestrian statue of the great chieftain, flanked by the figures of the kings of the royal house founded by him standing under two great arches that stretched out like two huge arms to the right and left of him. At some distance behind this monument there was a lake on whose shore stood a replica on a reduced scale of the castle of Vajda-Hunyad, the ancestral seat of another great Hungarian royal family, the Hunyadis, whose most outstanding ruler, Matthias Corvinus, was the great Renaissance king of Hungary, and who appointed my first known ancestor prefect of the Jews of the country. Nearby was the entrance of the zoo, which, however, I avoided because I associated it with the childhood that I was eager to leave behind. In the same area were located the finest museums of the city, the large Museum of Fine Arts, with its beautifully proportioned front that looked like a Greek temple, and opposite it the Museum of Arts and Crafts, whose facade was covered with multicolored stones or bricks.

Somewhere not far from these museums was a separate building that housed one single painting, Árpád Feszty's huge cyclorama titled *Honfoglalás*, the conquest of Hungary. One entered the building through a street-level door, bought one's ticket, and then went up a flight of stairs that led into the middle of a large circular hall whose entire wall, artificially lighted, was taken up from floor to ceiling by one single oil painting done in a good old-fashioned academic style. It had no beginning and no end, but was one continuous circular picture, of which I remember only one figure: that of Chief Árpád sitting on a white horse that was standing motionless, in much the same manner as the equestrian statue showed him and his mount in the center of the millennial monument. However much I strain my memory to conjure up any other detail of the picture, I cannot get beyond the general and vague feeling that it was crowded with human figures—there must have been hundreds of them.

In the opposite direction from our apartment lay the Parliament building with its Gothic spires and needles and niches and arches and statues, and with the great dome in the middle topped by a slip spire, which to me looked exactly like an enlarged image of the military helmet worn by Kaiser Wilhelm and the officers of the German army in World War I. The rear of the Parliament building faced the Danube, and along its entire length there was an arcade that rose up straight from the lower quay and followed the ins and outs of the building itself, and was but partly covered by a series of flying buttresses. I loved to walk along this arcade, stopping frequently to watch a ship pass by, or simply to have a look at the view of the river, the Chain Bridge with its lions on the left, the Margaret Bridge with the island on the right, and the hills of Buda opposite with the royal palace looking down at the river and the row of old houses contemplating the view the Pest side of the city offered them. More than once I took along drawing paper and my colored crayons and drew sketches of what my eyes took in. Only two of these drawings are still in my possession today.

Walking from my parents' apartment to that of my grandparents in the Inner City I had to go along Kaiser Wilhelm Avenue, which passed directly by the back of the Basilica, as the largest Catholic church in the city was usually called. The back of the Basilica presented a circular aspect with heavy columns between its tall windows—it never occurred to me to scrutinize the columns closely enough to ascertain their style, but I believe they were Doric. Once or twice I went around the building so as to see its front—again large columns carrying a huge tympanum over the entrance. I was tempted to enter the church, just to see how it looked from the inside, but something kept me from following up my impulse—was it fear, or reluctance to enter the sanctuary of another faith? I have since been inside hundreds of churches in many countries, and during my last visit to Budapest in the 1970s I visited several churches there, too, but somehow I did not have the opportunity to go into the Basilica.

In peculiar contrast to these rather vivid memories of the city, I remember very little of my early years in the school itself. The lacunae in my memory are filled, at least to some extent, by a document that somehow survived my peregrinations from continent to continent, and which I still possess. It is my school report card, or, rather, report booklet, into which our homeroom teacher entered the grades I earned in each of the eight years of my attendance. From the semiannual reports contained in this booklet I learn quite a lot about the external circumstances of my life at school, and about the way I appeared in the eyes of my teachers during those eight crucially formative years of my life, between the ages of ten and eighteen.

First of all I learn that my "behavior"—the first entry on every semester report—was "laudable" in the first four years, which term was replaced by the equivalent "exemplary" in grades five to eight. Both terms denoted the highest mark. Similarly, I got the highest mark, "excellent," in religious and ethical studies, although I could swear that we never studied any such subject. In Hebrew language and literature, a course that consisted of translating selected passages from the Bible, I was also "excellent" for seven of the eight years, the exception being my second year when, because of illness, I got no grades at all in the first term and only "good" in the second. Other subjects we studied in the first year (when the students were ten or eleven) were Hungarian language and literature, Latin language and literature, geography, natural history, mathematics, geometry, calligraphy, and gymnastics, in all of which I was found to be "excellent," and singing, in which I only made "good" due to having no ear for music. In addition to these my report card contains the grade "neat" for "External Form of His Written Exercises," and the following entry under the rubric "Remarks Concerning the Mental Development, Diligence, Demeanor, Behavior, of the Pupil": "Very intelligent, has exemplary diligence, good behavior and demeanor."

The report card is signed by Dr. Bernard Heller, principal (who was later to play an important role in my life when I became his student at the Rabbinical Seminary), and by Dr. David Rafael Fuchs, form master. My relationship to Professor Heller in later years effectively blocked out all memories I otherwise might have retained about him from my first two years at the high school when he was its principal. As for Dr. Fuchs, the difficulty in remembering him in those early years is due to the fact that he remained my Latin teacher for eight full years, during each of which five hours weekly were devoted to that subject. But I do remember that he was a small, stocky man, with light blue eyes and short-cropped blond hair, given to wearing white neckties. He was a strict disciplinarian, and the whole form stood in awe of him. The school rules demanded that when the teacher entered the classroom, all the boys had to stand to attention next to their desks, and wait in complete silence until the teacher said, "Be seated!" The maintenance of complete silence and decorum throughout the period was mandatory, at least in principle. If the teacher called the name of a boy to ask him a question or to say something to him, the boy had to stand up and remain at attention until the teacher finished with him and told him to sit down. If a boy wanted to address the teacher, to ask him a question or to ask for permission "to go out," that is, to the lavatory, he had to hold up his hand with the index and middle fingers stretched out straight and the other three fingers bent tightly together, and wait until the teacher recognized him. Then he could stand up and say what he wanted to say.

Part of the period, usually the very beginning, was frequently used by the teacher to call upon two or three randomly selected pupils to come forward to the blackboard and answer questions covering the homework. For me, each of these impromptu mini-exams in front of the whole class and facing the stern Dr. Fuchs was a minor ordeal. I don't remember ever having discussed my feelings about Dr. Fuchs—or about any other of our teachers, for that matter—with my classmates, but judging from the complete quiet that reigned in the classroom when he was present—which contrasted rather drastically with the fidgeting and even unruly noisiness that some other teachers had to put up with—I would guess that all of us were thoroughly intimidated by him.

During my second high school year my health deteriorated. I was plagued by frequent toothaches, my temperature often rose somewhat higher than normal (it would hover around 37.2 or 37.3 degrees centigrade), and I was extremely thin. In retrospect it appears to me that as soon as these symptoms appeared, my health became one of the major preoccupations of my mother. She must have taken my temperature every morning, and whenever the thermometer climbed over the red 37-degree mark, she would keep me home from school. When it would have been time for me to get up, get dressed, have breakfast, and go to school, she would come into my room, and stick the thermometer under my arm. Ten minutes later she would come back to check what the thermometer showed. However, before she would come back, I would have a look for myself, and if I saw that my temperature was normal, and, for some reason, I did not want to go to school, I would dip the thermometer into the glass of hot chocolate that Mother had placed at my bedside, watch it climb up just a bit over 37, remove it, lick off the chocolate, and replace it under my arm. The underarm thermometers we had in those days were not very accurate, and once, in order to check the reliability of the one we had at home, Mother instructed me as I was going to our dentist, Dr. Hohenberg, to ask him to take my temperature with his thermometer. Dr. Hohenberg did better than that: he stuck a thermometer in each of my armpits.

Because of my frequent absences from school I got no grades at the end of the first term of my second year, and instead Dr. Fuchs wrote across the page in my report booklet: "Received no grades because of his illness." The page opposite this entry states that I was "absent with cause" for 456 hours that term, which, a quick calculation tells me, corresponded to about 90 school days I missed out of a total of 130. In the second term of that year I missed another 281 hours, or some 56 days, but still managed to get my grades, which, however, had deteriorated from "excellent" to merely "good." The card also says that I was exempted from gymnastics and singing. In the first term of the third year, although I missed only 181 periods (or 36 days), I again "received no grades because of illness," and at the end of the second term the very inferior grade "sufficient" appeared for the first time in my report card.

It must have been during the second year of my high school studies, when I was so frequently absent from school, that one day, toward evening, Dr. Fuchs paid us a visit. He came unannounced, just as I was being given a bath by Mother. When the maid came to announce the visitor, Mother bade him step into the bathroom, and Dr. Fuchs had an amiable chat with us while Mother finished bathing and drying me. Subsequently—I don't know when, where, or on what occasion—Dr. Fuchs reminded me of what he considered the exaggerated solicitude Mother exhibited on that occasion in trying to prevent me from catching a cold. It seems that while I stood there naked, and Mother was drying me with a big bath towel, Dr. Fuchs got up from his chair, whereupon Mother asked him not to move lest I catch cold from the breath of air his movements would create.

Years later, when I was in one of the upper forms and had to work quite hard on Latin syntax in order to satisfy the demands of Dr. Fuchs, I once screwed up enough courage to ask him why we had to spend so much time and effort on a subject of which, in all probability, we would never make use once we left school. His answer was that the study of Latin syntax sharpened the brain. I still don't know whether this is indeed the case, but now, when I am working on my studies on Jewish alchemists and must translate medieval Latin texts pertaining to that subject, I often bless the memory of Dr. Fuchs, who drilled us in Latin so thoroughly that even today, more than half a century later, I still remember what I learned then and can still use it.

In his classes Dr. Fuchs offered us philological explanations of Latin words only very rarely, and of them I remember only two. He told us that Latin *vir*, man, was derived from, or connected with, *vis*, strength, while the word for woman, *mulier*, was derived from *mollis*, soft, because the ancient Roman ideal was strength in men and softness in women.

There is one more thing I remember in connection with Dr. Fuchs. During the summer vacation of 1922 he got married, which we boys somehow found out when we returned to school that fall. A few weeks later he was absent from school for one day—the only time this happened during the entire eight years of my study. Several months thereafter we learned that his wife gave birth to a child—I have no recollection of the source of this intelligence either. But I remember that in my mind I made a connection between that one day of Dr. Fuchs's absence and the subsequent birth of his child. I imagined that he had to devote himself to his wife for one full day in order to make her pregnant. What exactly the role of a husband was in bringing about pregnancy in his wife I did not know, but I had some vague idea that close proximity between the two spouses for a certain period of time was a prerequisite.

I remember reading at about that time a novel by Mór Jókai, the most popular nineteenth-century Hungarian novelist, in which he describes, most discreetly and in a very veiled language, how a woman confronts a man and tells him, "This is your child," and reminds him that, years before, he and she had spent one night together somewhere on an island. I was very puzzled when I read this, for up to that time I had believed that pregnancy in a woman could result only from her living together in one house with her husband for a considerable period of time. Jókai's story indicated to me that one single night's togetherness between a man and a woman was enough to make her pregnant, but I still had no concept of any physical contact between man and wife. However, before long I was to do research on the subject and obtain authentic information.

Much later, long after graduating from high school, I learned that David Rafael Fuchs (b. 1884), who subsequently changed his name to David Fokos, was an outstanding Finno-Ugric philologist, a member of the Hungarian Academy of Sciences, who had made study trips among the Züryens (Syryens) of Central Asia, and authored several important books about them and about other Central Asian peoples and languages. When, after an absence of some thirty-five years, I first revisited Hungary in the 1970s, I asked about him, but he was no longer alive.

In the third year, my interest began to be selective, which was reflected in my year-end grades. I got "excellent" in religion, Hebrew, German, geography, and geometry; "good" in Hungarian, Latin, and arithmetic, but only "sufficient" in history. As for gymnastics, I was again exempted from taking it. I wonder how I spent those two weekly hours when the class was marched into the school's gymnasium and was put through its paces by our gym teacher, Zoltán Dückstein. Later, when I again took gymnastics like all the other boys, my interest in this kind of activity was, at best, lukewarm. We had to go through all kinds of exercises, knee bends, push-ups, bendings from the hip, running around the gymnasium, or, when the weather was warm enough, in the school's spacious courtyard, climbing up ropes, hanging upside down from rings, and the like. I was not good at any of these, and once Mr. Dückstein took me aside after class and tried to persuade me to pay more attention to developing my body. He pointed to a boy who was even more sparsely and flatly built than I, and yet was an excellent gymnast, and said, "Look at Springer. Have you ever seen a body less suitable for sports than his? And just watch what he has accomplished with interest, willpower, and perseverance." But his persuasion was of no avail—I just could not take any interest in gymnastics, and my marks in it slipped from a mediocre "good" to "sufficient," which was the lowest passing grade.

During my third year at the high school my somewhat higher than normal body temperature continued, and, finally, Uncle Yóshka came to the conclusion that it was caused by my tonsils, which were infected. I was taken to a throat specialist, Dr. Pollacsek, chief surgeon of throat diseases at, I believe, the Jewish Hospital, which was one of the best hospitals in the city. He recommended a tonsillectomy, which was duly performed within a short time. This time Mother knew in advance of the operation, came with me to the hospital, and waited—I am sure with great trepidation—in an adjoining room while the surgery was being performed. I was strapped into a chair and given local anesthetic—I still remember having gagged somewhat when the doctor shot the injections into the two sides of my throat—but thereafter the operation proceeded painlessly. All I felt was a pulling and tugging sensation as his instruments cut away the tonsils. When the second tonsil was out, and the doctor put it on a little table that stood at his right elbow, his assistant, who was standing right behind him, happened to sweep the tonsils to the floor with his sleeve; thereupon Dr. Pollacsek, who was famous for his wit, said to him, "What do you think you are doing? You can throw your own tonsils to the floor but not Gyuri's!" Then he went out to tell Mother that everything was fine, and, as she later reported to me, that I had behaved with extraordinary self-control.

I don't know in what manner Father paid Dr. Pollacsek for the operation, but I was told that artists usually paid their doctors by giving them one of their works. Father quoted Dr. Pollacsek as having told him that once he was invited to the home of a colleague, a heart specialist, where on the wall of the living room he saw a large painting by a well-known artist, who was also present on that occasion. Some time later another painter arrived, and when he saw the important painting decorating the doctor's wall, he turned to his artist friend and said, full of concern, "Poor fellow, you were *that* sick?"

After the operation I was kept in the hospital for a few days, and Mother stayed with me, sleeping in the other bed in the room. At first I was given only liquid food, then Dr. Pollacsek, who breezed in and out once a day, prescribed ice cream. "For once," he said, "you can eat as much ice cream as you want." But, as my luck would have it, swallowing was so painful that I could get down practically none of the precious ice cream that otherwise would have been the greatest treat for me. Father came to visit me in the hospital, sat down next to my bed, and, in order to entertain me, took one of the sheets of drawing paper that, together with crayons, Mother had brought along for me, and drew a large elephant, which he then proceeded to cut out. I never saw Father draw anything else but that elephant.

The removal of my tonsils seems to have done the trick, for afterward my temperature remained normal, which meant that my school attendance record improved. In the fourth year (1923–1924) I missed altogether only 204 hours (or 40 school days) and I was no longer excused from gymnastics, in which I got "good." However, in general, my interest in the school flagged, I did my homework half-heartedly at best, and at year's end I got "excellent" only in Hungarian language and literature and another subject called "graphic geometry," which, I guess, must have had more to do with drawing and sketching than with geometry. In Latin, German, arithmetic, religion, and Hebrew I got "good," while in history and natural history I had sunk to the "sufficient" level.

In the spring of 1923, as part of my work in the religion class, I had to prepare for a recitation of the *Haftara*, the brief prophetic portion from the Bible which follows the reading in the synagogue of the weekly portion from the Five Books of Moses every Sabbath. Although only Jewish men aged thirteen and over can be "called up" to the reading of the weekly portion of the Pentateuch, this rule is relaxed for the *Maftir*, the person for whom the last few verses of the weekly portion are repeated, and who, thereafter, is expected himself to read the *Haftara*. The introductory and closing benedictions, as well as the selections from the Prophets, have their own traditional cantillation, and, although my ear was not yet quite as unmusical as it was to become after puberty and after my boyish soprano changed to a manly baritone, I had quite some difficulty in mastering the strange lilting melodies. During the weeks preceding the Sabbath on which I was to be the *Maftir* I received special instruction, as did every *Maftir* boy in the school, from our teacher of religion and Hebrew, who also happened to be the teacher of German and Hungarian, Solomon Widder, a man all of us boys liked but did not fear, who nevertheless, precisely because we liked him, was able to keep us as quiet and disciplined as the much sterner Dr. Fuchs. Several times every week I stayed on at school for an additional hour or half hour, during which Mr. Widder made me repeat after him the age-old traditional chant of the benedictions and of the prophetic section that was to be the *Haftara* of my Sabbath. I don't know how well I mastered the melodies, but at the end Mr. Widder declared himself satisfied and me prepared. My *Haftara*, by the way, was Habbakuk 3:1–19, which is read on the second day of the Feast of Shavu'ot (Weeks) or Pentecost, in the spring, and to this day I remember, and can chant, albeit probably with no great musical accuracy, the benedictions and that *Haftara* itself.

At the age of eleven or twelve I was seized with a spirit of experimentation. I read or heard somewhere that if you fill an old electric bulb with water and drop it from any height, it will not break because the water in it will cushion the impact. In those days light bulbs were, I believe, made of considerably thicker glass than today, and at their very top they had a small, nipplelike protuberance. (Just a few days ago I happened to read in the *New York Times* that an American manufacturer has again begun to produce such bulbs, which are in demand because they are considered chic antiques, like old phones.) Nor, in those days (1922 or 1923) did a bulb live too long, for the filament tended to burn out after, I imagine, a few dozen hours of use. In any case, old bulbs were always easy to come by. I took hold of one, clipped off the nipple with a pair of tongs, and held the bulb under the tap until it slowly filled with water. Because of my inclination to be cautious, I went down to the second story of our house, which was just one flight of steps above the ground floor, and from its loggia I dropped the bulb onto the paved courtyard. It did not break. I went down to fetch it and took it up to the fourth floor to repeat the experiment—and it shattered. I do not recall whether I went down to recover or sweep up the pieces, but I still remember that after these negative results I said to myself, "You just can't believe everything you read or hear."

Another experiment I performed about the same time and in the same place also had to do with dropping, but this time not a bulb, but a cat. Again I read or heard somewhere that a cat will always land on its feet and come to no harm from whatever height it falls. A grey alley cat was a denizen of our courtyard, and one day I got hold of it, carried it up to the second floor, and threw it down into the courtyard. However, I hurled the animal away from me too energetically, so that it bumped against the wall, which at that point faced the loggia at a distance of some ten feet from where I stood. The cat used its claws to hold on to the wall, so that, instead of falling freely, it slid down alongside it, landing unhurt on the pavement of the courtyard. I did not repeat the experiment from the fourth floor, either because I took pity on the cat or because it did not let me catch it again.

Yet another, more successful experiment I undertook was to build an electric battery. I no longer remember where I read how to construct a simple storage battery, but I do remember that I purchased a zinc bar, a copper bar, and a bottle of a certain acid. I suspended the two metal bars from a wooden cover that I placed on top of a large china pot, attached a wire from each of the bars to a small flashlight bulb, carefully filled the pot with the acid—and, lo and behold!—it did work. I am not sure that I remember very accurately what the various parts were, but I still can distinctly recall the feeling of triumph I had when the bulb lit up, and kept burning hour after hour.

In connection with electricity I once performed what I felt was a heroic act, which, I was convinced, saved our apartment from being destroyed by fire. I noticed that an electric wire that ran along the top of a wall in our living room gave off a shower of sparks. I knew nothing of electric wiring, but it was clear to me that quick and determined action was required. I dragged in the ladder that was kept in the larder, climbed up, and with my pocketknife cut the wire with one quick and energetic stroke. I received no electric shock— I don't think I was aware that I was in danger of getting one, or, for that matter, that I knew what an electric shock was—and the sparks stopped. When I folded the knife to put it back into my pocket, I noticed with astonishment that its blade showed a semicircular notch where I had pressed it against the wire. I concluded that the electricity must have melted that part of the blade.

In the summer of 1923 our whole family went to Swinemünde on the Ost See (Baltic) coast of Germany. That was the year of the galloping inflation in Germany, and the Hungarian currency was worth more and more German marks every day. The Hungarian money, too, lost much of its value, but its decline was far from the precipitous decline of the mark. The Hungarian crown sank to one two-hundredth of its value between 1923 and 1924, of which I still have visible proof in my high school report book. Every year-end report has a revenue stamp affixed to the top of the page. The 1921 revenue stamp reads 1 crown and 50 fillérs (that is, 1.50 crowns); those of 1922 and 1923 — 5 crowns; that of 1924 — 1,000 crowns. It remained at 1,000 crowns for two more years, until the currency reform that introduced the pengő as the new monetary unit, worth 10,000 old crowns. Consequently, the 1927 revenue stamp reads 10 fillérs (that is, one-tenth of a pengő). In Germany the situation was much worse. There the inflation resulted in such unbelievable things as a postage stamp for an ordinary letter reading ten million marks. Since the value of the German mark declined day by day in relation to the Hungarian crown, the thing to do, of course, was to exchange every day just as many crowns as were needed for the expenses of that day.

We took the train from Budapest to Berlin, where we stayed a few days, and where my parents bought me a painting kit — a nice wooden box with an assortment of tubes of oil paint and brushes, several pretreated cardboard-mounted canvases, and a small portable tripod-shaped easel. For a number of years prior to that time I had shown some talent for — or, in any case, interest in — drawing, and would sketch primitive portraits of people who were willing to sit long enough for me to do so (among them was Grandfather, one of our maids, Father, Mother, and my sister and brother), and also did some landscapes in pencil and colored crayons. I still have in my possession a few of these "early Patais." Now I graduated to oil.

After the Berlin stopover we continued by train to Swinemünde, where we spent several weeks. Since we ate only kosher food, Father had taken along for the trip to Germany a little guidebook that contained a list of kosher restaurants, to which he used to refer jokingly as a kis piszkos, "the little dirty." In Swinemünde we stayed in a Jewish pension called Bajit Schalom (sic), which either was listed in that guide or was recommended to Father by the Hebrew poet Saul Tchernichowsky, who seems to have been a long-term guest there. Tchernichowsky was one of the many Jewish authors and artists with whom Father had contact, and whose works he published in his monthly. I have in my files a Hebrew postcard written to my father by Tchernichowsky from Swinemünde in which he discusses his poems set to music by Engel and Mirenburg and details of his planned visit to Budapest. In Swinemünde Father and Tchernichowsky were inseparable, and I still have in my possession a photograph showing them standing on the seashore, with my five-year-old brother Guszti posing in front of them, a toy pail in his hand. The picture was reproduced in the November 1923 issue of *Mult és Jövő*, and there is also a fourth person in it, Dr. Béla Vajda, chief rabbi of Losonc, Hungary, who was a well-known Jewish scholar and author.

The only thing I remember from our sojourn in Swinemünde is that I painted seascapes. I seem to have had no difficulty in mastering, in a manner of speaking, the technique of oil painting, but of the several pictures I must have painted only one survived, and it hangs today in my bedroom in Forest Hills. It shows a greenish-grey sea with foamy waves under a cloudy sky, a somewhat slanting horizon, a long jetty, and a steamer passing before it. It is a valiant effort for a twelve-year-old child in an unfamiliar medium.

Tchernichowsky's visit to Budapest materialized in January 1924. Father organized a literary evening in his honor, and Tchernichowsky was our house guest during his stay in Budapest. Although he was one of the most celebrated Hebrew poets, he looked like a Russian peasant. His non-Jewish looks, I thought at the time, fitted well with his adulation of classical Greece (one of his most famous poems was "Before the Statue of Apollo," which Father translated into Hungarian), and of the ancient pagan gods of Canaan who figured in his poems. He had a big shock of dark curly hair that he frequently fingered. Mother later told me that on one occasion, when she opened the door to the bathroom, which was left unlocked by Tchernichowsky, she found him standing before the mirror, combing his hair and pulling his locks down to his forehead. She found this manifestation of male vanity, completely absent in Father, rather amusing. Tchernichowsky was living at the time in Berlin, where he had no easy time trying to make a living as a Hebrew poet, and when he arrived in Budapest it turned out that he had no dinner jacket, which was a *sine qua non* for an appearance on a Budapest concert stage. So Father went down with him to Mr. Jakobi, his tailor, and had a tuxedo made for him posthaste.

The Tchernichowsky evening of *Mult és Jövő* took place on January 13, 1924, in the great hall of the Academy of Music. Father in his opening address spoke on "Tchernichowsky and the Jewish Renaissance," and subsequently published his speech in the February 1924 issue of his journal. Tchernichowsky's poems, in Father's Hungarian translation, were recited by Mari Jászai, the greatest tragedienne of the Hungarian stage, and by Gyula Gál, a leading member of the Hungarian National Theater, from both of whom I still have several letters addressed to Father. Other poems by Tchernichowsky, set to music, were sung by Dóra Bársony, soprano, and Oszkár Kálmán, basso, both of the Budapest Opera. Tchernichowsky himself, resplendent in his new tuxedo, read several of his poems in the Hebrew original. The evening was a resounding success, and was an important contribution to popularizing, and enhancing the prestige of, modern Hebrew literature in Hungary. Incidentally, it also provided Tchernichowsky with some much needed cash.

In November 1923 my parents celebrated my Bar Mitzva, the traditional Jewish coming-of-age of a boy. I remember nothing of my preparations for this event in school, but I do know that, as each of us boys reached his thirteenth birthday, we were "called up" in the school synagogue to the reading of the Tora for the first time as adults. This is the only traditionally established form of marking the fact that a boy has reached the age of responsibility as far as the observance of Jewish religious law is concerned. We all received special instruction in preparation for the great occasion, but it consisted of nothing more than teaching us how to recite, with the traditional cantillation, a passage from the large, handwritten Tora scroll, laid out on the *bima*, the podium with the lectern in the center of the synagogue to which we were "called up" on that occasion. This special instruction was given by Mr. Widder.

In retrospect it appears remarkable, nay strange, that neither at school nor at home were we taught anything about Jewish religion and about the religious duties we were supposed to shoulder from the day of our Bar Mitzva on. We were, it seems, expected to make our own deductions, to reach our own conclusions, as far as the doctrinary aspects of Judaism were concerned. I, for one, was never told anything directly about God, neither at home nor at school, and I have reason to assume that the other boys had the same experience at home. What was important in my religious education was, primarily, to learn and recite the prayers; secondarily, to observe the religious "do's" and "don'ts"; and finally, to understand the prayers. What conclusions could, or were to be, drawn from the prayers concerning God was entirely left to me. When I was three Grandmother had taught me the *Shema'* prayer; some years later one of my Hebrew tutors explained to me that it meant, "Hear, O Israel, the Lord our God, the Lord is one. Thou shalt love the Lord thy God with all thy heart. . . . " When I started to study the Book of Genesis, I found in it that God created heaven and earth in six days. But it was left entirely to me to piece together, without any help from parents, tutors, or teachers, my own image of God, and to draw my own conclusions as to the doctrines I as a Jew had to subscribe to. Not even on the occasion of my Bar Mitzva was I taught anything about these subjects. Instead, I was instructed in how to put on the phylacteries for the weekday morning prayers, and how to chant my section from the Pentateuch in the school synagogue, and nothing else. That I was nevertheless deeply impressed by the occasion, and full of a sense of self-importance as a Jew who has just reached the age of religious responsibility, must then be attributed solely to the subtle and subconscious influences the parental home exerted upon me in childhood.

These are, of course, not things I remember, but merely conclusions I reach now upon thinking back on those faraway days of childhood. What I do remember with great clarity are the preparations for the celebration of my Bar Mitzva at home, and the great event itself. By that time my Hebrew tutor was no longer Mr. Wachsberger, but a younger man, Mr. Jenő Eckstein. When Mr. Eckstein started to tutor me he used the Ashkenazic pronunciation of Hebrew, but even before the end of the first lesson Father told him to switch to Sephardic. In all the synagogues of Hungary all Hebrew texts (the Bible, the prayers) were read in the Ashkenazic pronunciation. The reason Father insisted on Sephardic was that it was the Hebrew pronunciation of the *yishuv* of Palestine, that is, the pronunciation of Hebrew as a living language, and that is what Father wanted Hebrew to be for me.

Mr. Eckstein was a religious Jew who wore a skullcap, and who probably required that I also wear one. Most of his instruction con-

sisted of teaching me to translate chapter after chapter of the biblical prophets, and religious Jews were (and are) firm in their conviction that while it was improper and irreligious for a Jew to be without
a head covering at any time, it was outright sinful to read the sacred
text unless one wore a hat or a skullcap. Mr. Eckstein was a somewhat corpulent man whose trousers were too tight for him and had a
yellowish stain in the front. His face was roundish with very light
skin, and he had blue eyes, an aquiline nose, and red lips. He was a
fine teacher, and under his tutelage I learned not only to know, but
also to love, the Hebrew prophets. I remember in particular how I
gradually grasped the great poetry of Isaiah, whose first ten chapters
Mr. Eckstein made me learn by heart, which was something I did
not relish at all at that time, but for which I am grateful to him to
this day.

When my Bar Mitzva was only a few weeks away, Father bought
me a pair of *tefillin*, phylacteries, and Mr. Eckstein taught me how
to place one of them on my forehead and wind the black leather
thong of the other around my left arm, hand, and fingers. After my
Bar Mitzva I prayed with the *tefillin* every weekday morning, never
missing a single day, for ten full years. Only after I went to Palestine
did I, under the influence of my new irreligious friends in Jerusalem,
give up the practice, never again to take it up. For the home celebration of my Bar Mitzva Mr. Eckstein composed for me a Hebrew
speech that I duly memorized. In contrast to the first ten chapters of
Isaiah, most of which I still remember, I cannot recall even a single
word or phrase of my Bar Mitzva speech, which I think is attribut-
able to the poorer quality of Mr. Eckstein's prose compared to Isaiah's
poetry. When the time came for me to deliver the speech—I know
that it did not contain the Hebrew equivalent of "Today I am a
man"—Mr. Eckstein sat behind me with the text in his hands, so as
to be able to prompt me if need be. I stood in front of him, facing
the assembled guests, and spoke. After I finished, which I did without a hitch, Mother hugged me, Father praised me, Grandfather
wiped a tear from his eye, and some of the guests predicted that I
would become a great orator.

I received many Bar Mitzva presents, but the one that meant
most to me was not a tangible gift but a poem written by my father.
It was long, consisting, appropriately, of thirteen stanzas of four
lines each. In the November 1923 issue of *Mult és Jövő* in which
Father published it, it filled the entire first page. It is titled *"Bár-*

Micvah" (the Hungarian spelling), and beneath its title it carries the line, "To my son Raphael." Although at the time my official name was Ervin György, for this festive poem Father used my Hebrew name. My first feeling, when I saw my name in print, was great pride; then, when I read it, my heart overflowed with love for my father. I had to read the poem slowly and several times because it was not easy to understand. Then I cut out the whole page and put it aside among the things I wanted to keep. And I have succeeded in keeping it to this day.

Just now I reread the poem. Its impact has not diminished in the sixty years since I read it as a proud Bar Mitzva boy. I tried my hand at translating it, but, not being a poet, I could not do it justice. I tried to render it in prose, but the results were disappointing. All I can do is indicate briefly its thought content. The poet addresses his son, tells him to wrap himself in the tallith, the prayer shawl, which will be shield and armor for him until old age. He encourages him to wear the *tefillin* as a proud diadem on his head, and to etch into his heart the love of our ancient letters. He warns him against forgetting, when pagan songs and strange magic will lure him, his father's words, the commands of ancestral tombs. "Fear not, my son," he says, "life is beautiful, full of joy, a myriad of stars will send you their rays, their power, but know that in the whirl of desires, over the furnace of raptures, the Law stands watch with its broadsword." He warns his son that God, whom he apostrophizes with the kabbalistic epithet "Ancient of Days," will carry us on the wings of time. Where to? Who knows? Search not! Who can find the key to the secrets of creation? . . . " And he concludes by saying to the Bar Mitzva boy, "Do you know, my son, that this white prayer shawl with the black stripes is our last attire, when we Jews are put to rest in the grave?"

I am sure that many thoughts and allusions contained in the poem were beyond my comprehension at the age of thirteen, but it was a poem addressed to me, and I certainly grasped that it enjoined me to learn about Judaism and to lead a Jewish life. I shall never know to what extent it influenced my journey through life.

Among the presents I received for my Bar Mitzva was a gold signet ring engraved with the initials of my Hungarian name, *P. Gy.* I kept this ring and wore it for seventeen years until I gave it in 1940 to my bride Naomi, just a few weeks prior to our wedding. Many years later Naomi gave the ring to our younger daughter Daphne, who still wears it today. The ring, when I last saw it, showed much wear and tear, and the edges of its oval seal were all worn away and rounded down, but the initials *P. Gy.* were still clearly visible. I don't know who gave me the ring originally.

Most of the presents I received for my Bar Mitzva were books. I must have been given dozens, but I remember only one of them. It was a large, album-sized volume, with a fancy binding, containing short stories by various authors, lavishly illustrated with color plates. The pictures in it had a peculiar, fairyland quality, and thinking back on them today I am reminded of the paintings of Burne-Jones, although I don't believe any of them were actually by him. I still see their vivid, jewel-like colors, clearly outlined figures, always standing before an overly busy background that itself consisted of multihued boughs, flowers, patterns, and the like. As for the stories, all I remember is one, and that only because I later encountered variants of it several times. It told about the miraculous healer who could cure the sadness and despair of all people by prescribing for them a visit to a performance of Harlequin, whose mirth was irresistible and who could dispel even the blackest gloom that ever beclouded a soul. One day the doctor is sought out by a man whose very image is that of utter misery. The doctor prescribes his medicine, which has never yet failed. "You must go and see a performance by Harlequin," he says. But the patient replies, "I cannot be helped by Harlequin." "Why not?" asks the doctor. "He has helped each and every one of my patients. Why should you precisely be the exception?" "Because," answers the patient, "I am Harlequin." This story, with its punch line, made such a deep impression on me that I never forgot it, and whenever I read, even decades later, another version of it, I was prompted to compare it in my mind with that first one, which I invariably found to be better.

I have a very vague recollection that my Bar Mitzva celebration in the home of my parents was attended by my paternal grandfather. He would, of course, not come to the Sabbath morning service in my school's synagogue at which I was "called up" to the reading of the Tora, because Hasidic Jews (my paternal grandfather was an adherent of the Szatmarer Rebbe) would not set foot in a Neolog synagogue, which for them was anathema. Even my maternal grandfather, who, although not a Hasid, was a strictly Orthodox Jew, would not enter a Neolog synagogue, and had never seen the inside of the great Dohány Street Temple, which was the largest synagogue in Europe. The very fact that the Dohány Temple, as it was referred to in common Jewish parlance, had an organ whose music was part of the Sabbath service (played, to be sure, by a Gentile organist, for Jews are forbidden to play a musical instrument on the Sabbath) was reason enough for my grandfather Ehrenfeld to avoid it like the plague.

My own attitude to religion as a teenager was characterized by a complacent acceptance of what I absorbed from living in the bosom of my family. Ours was an observant home in the sense that there was a code of behavior, consisting of a list of "do's" and "don'ts" that my parents followed and that they expected their children to observe. The "do's" were few in number, and involved primarily the duty of praying. There was the weekday morning prayer, the *shaḥarit*, which I had to recite with the tallith around my shoulder and the *tefillin* on my forehead and left arm, which I did with dispatch and in a greatly shortened form — yet to omit it would never have occurred to me. Even when I was sick and had to stay in bed, I would wrap myself in my prayer shawl, put on the phylacteries as prescribed, and recite my prayers without fail. Then there were the prescribed benedictions before partaking of food, the after-meal grace, the bed-time *Shema'* prayer in the evening, and the prayers of Friday night and Sabbath morning, as well as those of the annually recurring holy days for which attendance in a synagogue was required. I knew that these observances were a bare minimum, and that Jews more religious than my parents considered themselves obliged to recite many more daily prayers — my grandfather Ehrenfeld, for instance, never omitted the daily *minḥa* (afternoon) and the *ma'ariv* (evening) prayers, and his morning prayer was much longer than the *Shema'* and the Eighteen Benedictions to which my daily morning orisons were reduced — but I took it for granted that the extent to which I observed the duty of praying was just right and sufficient for me.

The other "do's" also concerned words, if not prayers. They included the study of the Bible and the Talmud, which I fulfilled amply under the guidance of first my Hebrew tutors, then my father, and still later my professors at the Rabbinical Seminaries of Budapest and Breslau. Yet in studying these sacred texts I did not feel that I was fulfilling a purely religious act or duty, but rather had a vague sense of doing something I should because I was a Jew and as such should know as much as I could about what my forebears wrote many centuries ago. This feeling was strengthened when my grandfather Ehrenfeld once or twice showed me in a volume of the Talmud the *ḥiddushim (novellae)* of Rabbi Moshe Sofer, his own great-grandfather, which gave me the feeling of a direct family connection between myself and the great masters of the Jewish past whose work was represented in the Talmud.

The "don'ts", of course, were much more numerous and more onerous to observe, although by no means exceedingly so. They included, first of all, the prohibition against eating nonkosher food, which meant not only that all restaurants, with the exception of the very few kosher ones, were out of bounds for us, but also that I could not eat in the homes of most of my classmates and friends, whose parents did not observe the dietary laws. They meant that even at home food could be eaten only within definite and strict limitations: we could never have milk, or any food made of milk, such as cream or cheese, as part of a meal in which meat was served. And even after lunch, which was the main meal of the day and always included meat, we were not allowed to drink milk or have butter for several hours.

As for wine, only that which was prepared under rabbinical supervision was permitted, but for us children this had only theoretical significance, for in practice the only wine we ever saw in our home was the single cup Father held in his hand while reciting the Friday evening *Qiddush* (sanctification), and then, twenty-four hours later, when performing the *havdala* (separation) ceremony, in which the Sabbath is bidden farewell and the weekdays are ushered in and welcomed. Even of those two cups Father took barely a sip. The association of wine with religious ritual was to remain with me for decades, and it was only when I entered the second half-century of my life that I began to enjoy a few glasses of wine with my dinners.

During the eight days of Passover we were not allowed to eat anything that was *ḥametz*, leavened, especially bread or other baked ware. On Yom Kippur, the Day of Atonement, it was prohibited to eat or drink anything at all for twenty-five hours. On *Tish'a be'Av*, the ninth of the month of Av, the traditional date of the destruction of the Temple of Jerusalem (both the First and the Second), we fasted only until midday, but Grandfather fasted all day long.

Most difficult for me of all the "don'ts" I had to observe were those that limited my activities on the Sabbath. There were so many things we were not allowed to do that I felt I was condemned to enforced idleness, and the Sabbath was for me a day of confinement and restriction rather than one of rest and pleasure. This was especially burdensome because I had to remember constantly what day it was, and that many motions I would perform automatically, such as taking up a pencil, or tearing a piece of paper, were forbidden.

Religion, of course, consists not only of commandments that prescribe what you must and must not do, but also of a set of creedal propositions. But, as already indicated above, I was never taught articles of faith. What I believed in, and what I knew about God and what He wanted of me, of the Jews in general, I absorbed incidentally, as it were, in the course of studying the Bible, the Talmud, and the prayers. All these texts are full of references to Him, His works, and the rules of behavior He imposed upon His chosen people. Thus, while I knew very well how I, as a Jew, was supposed to act, I was not consciously aware of what I believed, and even less so of what I was supposed to believe. For many years after my Bar Mitzva I still did not know that Judaism did have a belief system. Such a thing was never formulated for me by my teachers, and I never found written statements about it in any of the religious sources I studied. Only much later, when my scholarly interest in the creedal aspects of religion was awakened, did I discover that the thirteen principles of Jewish faith were formulated by Maimonides and that they were summarized in verse form in the poem *Yigdal Elohim*. Both of these texts are printed in the prayer book, among the many other pieces of liturgy whose sum total makes the morning prayer a very long one indeed, but, since I never recited the entire morning prayer, I did not know about them.

Judaism is definitely a nondogmatic, nondoctrinary, and noncatechistic religion. It does not teach a child (or an adult, for that matter) what he must *believe*, it teaches him what he must and must not *do*. In the course of my own formal Jewish education, which spanned close to twenty years, I was never taught Jewish beliefs. I was taught Jewish religious literature, some of which dealt with what certain prophets, poets, and philosophers believed about God, but never did I read in any of those texts, or hear any of my teachers say, "Therefore, we must believe that. . . . " It is indeed remarkable that although Judaism is the fountainhead of the two great creedal religions of the West, Christianity and Islam, Judaism itself is only implicitly creedal, and never confronts the individual Jew with explicit demands as to what he must believe. Many Jewish religious philosophers, it is true, formulated both before and after Maimonides what they considered the basic tenets of Judaism, but these efforts remained, by and large, of little interest for the average religious Jew, who knew what he had to do and not to do as a Jew, and was not concerned with what he had to believe. In fact, for Hasidic and other Orthodox Jews the entire literature of Jewish religious philosophy, much of which was written in the Middle Ages in Arabic and then translated into Hebrew, was (and is) suspect, and its study was discouraged or even anathema. Observations and discernments such as these were, of course, far beyond my horizon as a teenager, when Judaism was for me a natural condition of my life composed primarily of a set of "do's" and "don'ts."

About the time of my Bar Mitzva or soon thereafter my parents felt that my sister and I knew German well enough to be able to dispense with the services of the Fräulein. So the last German governess was dismissed, and in her place my parents engaged a French mademoiselle. Just as I remember nothing about any of the Fräuleins, so I remember nothing of the mademoiselle, except the series of incidents that led to her dismissal in short order. At the time my sister and I still slept in the same room, our old nursery, in two beds separated by the entire length of the room. I have no recollection about where the Fräuleins or the mademoiselle slept. Soon after her arrival, the mademoiselle, who must have been a woman in her twenties or perhaps thirties, began to come into our room after my sister and I had gone to bed, sit down on my bed, and tell us a story, or sing a song. While doing so, she began to caress me under the blanket. The first few evenings she caressed only my arm or my leg, but before long, when she thought that I had fallen asleep, she took to fondling my penis. I was surprised, but her touch gave me a pleasant sensation, although I was definitely aware of the forbidden nature of what she was doing, and I feigned sleep. The circumstance that fixes in my mind the time of these episodes is that I had not yet reached the stage of sexual development where my reaction would have been an erection; that is, I was definitely prepubertal, and could not have been much more than thirteen years old. After one or two evenings of this kind of special attention paid me by the mademoiselle, she bent down, pushed my blanket aside, and placed her cheek against my member, which created in me the desire to have her put it into her mouth. This was a purely physiological reaction, for at the time, although I may have had some knowledge of the mechanics of sexual intercourse, I certainly had no idea that such a thing as oral sex existed. I twisted and turned in my bed, as if I were restless in my sleep, with the purpose of bringing my penis into a position where she would put it into her mouth. But she did not.

This went on for a few more evenings, the mademoiselle fondling me, and I pretending to be asleep. Poor mademoiselle! She certainly must have had a sad case of sexual starvation to resort to such a poor substitute for normal satisfaction as fondling the undeveloped organ of a prepubertal boy. But, of course, as a thirteen-year-old I was very far from understanding her predicament. My compunction about the situation grew until I felt constrained to put an end to it. So one evening I pretended to wake up and to notice with great consternation what the mademoiselle was doing to me. I jumped out of the bed, flung my pillow at her head, and marched straight into the next room where my mother was sitting and reading. I was quite excited, and rapidly told Mother what had transpired. I have no recollection of Mother's reaction, but next morning, when I awoke, the mademoiselle was gone. The only other thing I remember in connection with this premature and aborted first experience with heterosexual sex is that on one occasion (when? in what context?) my mother praised me warmly for the character I showed in coming to her and telling her unhesitatingly what had happened. This, incidentally, was also the end of all governesses in our home.

As for my sexual enlightenment, it took place when I was about thirteen, in circumstances that, although I did not know it at the time, gave the first indication that I was destined to become a scholar and a researcher. Neither Father nor Mother ever spoke to me a word about sex. My best friend in school in those years, László (Laci) Schwarz, knew as little about it as I did. When our interest in finding out about sex awoke, we decided to turn to printed sources for information. I do not remember what data Laci was able to unearth, but I went about it systematically by starting to read the articles on the subject in the German *Meyers Konversations Lexikon*, the twenty-volume encyclopaedia that formed part of Father's library and with whose colored plates I was destructively familiar from my early infancy.

By the age of thirteen I was quite fluent in German, and the Gothic type in which the big *Meyers* was printed caused me no difficulty either. But since my knowledge of German did not include sexual terminology, the problem I had to overcome was how to discover the entry words under which I could find the information I sought. I solved it with the help of the big Hungarian-German dictionary that my father had and in which I looked up the German equivalents of the Hungarian terms for sex, sexual life, copulation, penis, vagina, pregnancy, childbirth, and so forth. Once I had the vocabulary, I went to the encyclopaedia and tried to find the articles about these subjects. Each time I found anything significant (and what was not significant for the curiosity of a thirteen-year-old boy?) I reported it to Laci, and thus, within a short time, I achieved a theoretical famil-iarity with "the facts of life," based on research and the utilization of reliable sources.

After writing the foregoing paragraph, curiosity again moved me to go back to the old *Meyers* and check what kind of information I was actually able to extract from it. In the New York Public Library I located the 1897 edition, which, in all probability, was the one my father had owned ever since my infant years. In it I found the fol-lowing entries (I am arranging them alphabetically): *Befruchtung* (Impregnation); *Begattung* (Copulation, which says, "the separated sexes are driven to copulation by an irresistible drive, the copulative or sexual drive, which awakens with maturity and is mostly tied to definite times [see Oestrus] . . . etc."); *Ejakulation* (ejaculation); *Embryo*; *Geburt* (Birth); *Geschlechtseigentümlichkeiten* (Sexual Char-acteristics); *Geschlechtskrankheiten* (Venereal Diseases); *Geschlechts-organe* (Genitals); *Geschlechtstrieb* (Sexual Instinct); *Penis*; *Puber-tät* (Puberty); *Same* (Semen); *Samenleiter* (Vas Deferens); *Schwangerschaft* (Pregnancy); *Sexualpsychologie*; *Wollustgefühl* (Sexual Pleasure, which begins, "A kind of general sensation that is brought about by the excitement of the sensitive nerves of the sexual apparatus or through imaginations of a sexual nature"); *Zeugung-vermögen* (Potency). The tone of the entries is dry and factual, but they do convey the gist of what was known in those pre-Freudian days of the world of sex. If I actually read them and if I understood what they said (some of the entries are long and rather technical), I certainly acquired a sound basis of sexology. Whether or not this was the case I no longer know, but I still remember vividly the excitement I felt while on this laborious literary voyage of research and discovery, and the conspiratorial atmosphere between me and Laci Schwarz when we shared and exchanged information.

About the same time I discovered in my uncle Ernő's library Wilhelm Bölsche's book *Love Life in Nature* in a Hungarian translation. Since I was ashamed to ask him to lend it to me, I read major portions of it standing in front of his bookcase, ready at any moment to put the book back on its shelf should anybody happen to come in. Although that book dealt only with the sex life of animals, and not of man, I was fascinated by the many curious details it contained, and obtained the impression that sex was a powerful force in the world of both animals and man, and this just before I felt its power in myself. Looking back at this adventure in sexual self-enlightenment, I feel I was lucky to have found this path rather than becoming exposed to or having to rely on the endless amount of misinformation that circulated among my classmates, some of which I, of course, overheard.

I said above that neither Father nor Mother ever spoke to me a word about sex. That remained the case throughout my adolescence. It would never have occurred to me to ask them any question concerning sex. We all behaved as if this realm of life simply did not exist. I can recall only one exception to this rule, and that came about through a mistake on my part. I was telling Mother that I had just started to read a classical epic (I forget which it was), and that I found its introductory part most interesting. I wanted to say prologue or perhaps proemium, but instead, by mistake, I said prostitution. Mother looked embarrassed as she corrected me. I asked, what then is prostitution, and she, even more embarrassed, explained that it meant the trade of a prostitute, a woman who sells her sexual services for money. Hearing this I got, if possible, even more embarrassed than she was, and immediately continued to talk about the epic I was reading.

Soon after my Bar Mitzva Father considered me sufficiently advanced in my Hebrew studies and ripe enough in mind to be introduced into the mysteries of the Talmud. He himself had started to study the Talmud at the age of six, and was kept in the *ḥeder* of Pata six days a week from dawn to nightfall. But that, of course, was a different generation and a different environment. For Father's father, Talmud was the *only* study a Jewish boy was supposed to engage in.

For my father, Talmud was one of the sources whose knowledge, he felt, was essential for the Jewish education of his son. So, instead of the seventy or eighty hours a week he had been kept at the Talmud from the age of six, he taught me, at the age of thirteen, three or four hours of Talmud, once a week. I can no longer recall when my private Hebrew lessons with Mr. Eckstein were discontinued, but I have written evidence they went on for several more years. Every Sabbath afternoon, soon after lunch, Father would call me into his study, take down from his red mahogany bookcase, from behind a glass-paneled door, a volume of his Talmud set, and begin to instruct me. I no longer remember what language of tuition he used, but since he normally insisted that we children talk to him in German, I imagine that he translated and explained the Talmud to me in that language.

Since by that time I was a truly avid reader of novels, his call invariably meant that I had to lay aside the book I was immersed in, always, of course, at a crucial point in the narrative when I was burning to know what would happen next, and instead force myself to pay attention to the intricacies of talmudic discussion. In addition to the difficulties presented by the subject matter, there was the problem of the language: much of the Talmud text is in Aramaic, which, while written in the same characters as Hebrew, bears only a slight resemblance to it, so that a prerequisite of studying the Talmud was (and is) the acquisition of a working knowledge of that ancient Semitic language. To study the Talmud required a considerable mental effort in several directions: I had to struggle to understand the Aramaic words and phrases, and, once Father explained them to me, I had to try to retain them in my memory. Then there was the difficulty caused by the total absence of punctuation: in the Talmudic text there are no commas, periods, or question marks, no quotation marks, no paragraphs; the text starts at the beginning of a chapter and runs on without any such reading aids to its very end. Additional problems are caused by the terse, laconic style, which often reads like the abridged minutes of a debate, where the *dramatis personae* are not identified, nor are their utterances kept apart by such stylistic devices as "Rabbi A. asked . . . ," "Rabbi B. answered . . . ," "Rabbi C. objected. . . . " Understanding a passage of the Talmud, unless it happened to recount a legend, in which case things were easier, meant keeping in mind the total context, and supplying from one's own knowledge a lot of detail without which the text would simply remain unintelligible. A taste of what I am talking about can be obtained from a randomly selected passage from the tractate *Berakhot*, of which I give here the translation exactly as it appears in the original:

> R. Abin the Levite said he who presses the hour hour presses him and he who gives way to the hour hour gives way to him from Rabba and Rav Yosef for Rav Yosef is Sinai and Rabba uproots mountains the hour needed them they sent there Sinai and uprooter of mountains which of them comes first they sent to them Sinai comes first for all need the master of wheats n. th. 1. Rav Yosef did not accept for the Chaldeans said to him you ruled two years Rabba ruled twenty-two years Rav Yosef ruled two and a half years (B. Berakhot 64a).

Not much sense can be made of this text without the commentary of Rashi and the oral explanations of a teacher. With them, one understands that the event told by Rabbi Abin was as follows: he who wants to seize the hour, the thing he wants to achieve escapes him, while he who refuses to seize the hour, the opportunity nevertheless offers itself to him. This we learn from what happened to Rabba and Rav Yosef. Rav Yosef was a master of a great store of knowledge ("Sinai"), while Rabba had such sharpness of mind that he could uproot mountains. The need arose for one of them to be appointed head of the yeshiva. The sages sent an inquiry to the sages of Palestine, asking them, "Between a 'Sinai' and an uprooter of mountains who is to be preferred?" They sent back word saying, "The 'Sinai' should be preferred for everybody is in need of a master who has accumulated much learning ('wheat')." Nevertheless (n. th. 1.) Rav Yosef did not accept the appointment, for the astrologers ("Chaldeans") had told him, "You will rule as head of the yeshiva for two years only, and then you will die." So Rabba ruled twenty-two years, and after him Rav Yosef ruled two and a half years.

As one can see, an intelligible translation-paraphrase of this passage requires twice as many words as are contained in the original. When it comes to differences of opinion in legal matters, the language of the Talmud is even more terse, and its understanding requires not only a familiarity with the style, but also a knowledge of the legal concepts and the methodology of talmudic argumentation and deduction.

I still remember vividly the acute reluctance with which, at Father's call, I laid aside the novel I happened to be engrossed in, went into his study, and sat down beside him at his great mahogany double-pedestal desk. I had, of course, no choice — the possibility of telling Father that just then I did not want to have a lesson in the Talmud never even entered my mind. I can no longer recall any particular part or subject in the Talmud that I studied under paternal guidance. What I do remember is that occasionally, very occasionally, Father himself was baffled for a while by the meaning of a talmudic sentence, when Rashi, whose commentary was part of our studies, did not supply, as he usually did, the key to the understanding of a passage, and Father would pull the large volume nearer in order to get enlightenment from the supercommentary of the *Tosafot*, or from the marginal notes that surrounded the page. At such moments I felt a special gratification at being taught something so difficult, so advanced, that it caused even Father to stop and make a palpable effort at understanding it. I also remember very definitely that, although Father had in his library the four-volume talmudic dictionary of Jacob Levy, he never consulted it because he did not understand a word. His knowledge of the Talmud was profound, although he had not studied it for more than twenty years when he began tutoring me in it.

What happened every time, every Sabbath afternoon, as I sat there next to Father and the world of the Talmud gradually unfolded itself to me, was that, within a few minutes after the beginning of the lesson, that world came alive for me, reached out and grabbed my attention, and held my interest to an extent as great as any adventure story. I was filled with an intense feeling of curiosity, a desire to find out what happened next, how the problem presented was resolved. These Sabbath afternoon lessons in the Talmud lasted several hours, usually as long as there was light enough to continue. Toward mid-afternoon Mother would open the door of the study, and without entering the room call in, "Yóshka, don't torture that child any longer!" And invariably it was I who protested and answered Mother that I wanted to go on.

I also remember that on those occasions when Father was away for the weekend, lecturing somewhere in the country, I would ask Grandfather Ehrenfeld, if he happened to visit us or if I went to see him in his apartment, to give me a Talmud lesson, which he did most willingly, and, having been a yeshiva student himself, most capably. Yet I could not help comparing his knowledge of the Talmud with that of Father and concluding that Father was unquestionably the greater talmudist. Thus, just as I am indebted to Mr.

Wachsberger for laying the foundations of my knowledge of Hebrew, and to Mr. Eckstein for introducing me to the biblical prophets, I have remained eternally grateful to Father for opening to me the gates of the Talmud, and imparting to me the ability to understand, to like, and even to admire that unique and great storehouse of Jewish life, law, and lore, the "great sea" of the Talmud.

Thus my Sabbaths were even more full of structured activity than my weekdays. Friday evenings Father would take me to the synagogue, then, after returning home, and before sitting down to the evening meal, he would give me the traditional paternal blessing. I would stand in front of him; he would place his hands on my head and recite, in Hebrew, the words with which Jewish fathers had blessed their sons for countless generations: "May the Lord make you as Ephraim and Manasseh." Then it was my sister's turn, and she, too, was blessed with the traditional words, "May the Lord make you as Sarah, Rebeccah, Rachel, and Leah." I don't know what my sister felt at that moment, but I felt a great surge of power, strength, and confidence pass from Father through his hands into me. Much later, when I got acquainted in the course of my folkloristic studies with the Arab concept of *baraka*, blessed virtue, as described by Edward Westermarck in his fascinating *Ritual and Belief in Morocco*, and by other students of popular Islam, I was to remember those Friday evening blessings and recognize that it was *baraka* that I absorbed from Father on those occasions.

These blessings were the main reason why Friday evenings were always very solemn times for me. Others were the two tall Sabbath candles that Mother lighted, just before we set out for the synagogue, in the two antique silver candlesticks on the middle of the table set for the meal, which were still burning when we returned. We all stood while Father pronounced the benediction over the red wine, filling his large silver goblet to the rim, and over the *ḥalla*, the plaited, white, somewhat sweetish bread with its shiny brown crust, of which each of us was given a piece after Father had dipped it into salt. Nor must I forget the Sabbath songs that we sang while sitting around the table and of which I liked most the one that bids welcome to the angels of peace. I think it was the repetitiousness of this song that endeared it to me.

My structured Sabbath busyness continued the next morning with the service in the synagogue of the school, and in the afternoon with the long Talmud lesson. After dark followed the *havdala* ceremony, performed by Father surrounded by the whole family. My memory of this ceremony goes back to my infancy, when I strained to hold up high the *havdala* candle, which was a large flat taper woven of many strands of wax each of a different color and each with a separate wick inside. The many wicks when lighted produced a broad wall of flame, much more impressive than the small single-wick flames of the two Sabbath candles lit the previous evening. Although the hot wax would drip down on my fingers, I would hold the *havdala* candle as high up as I could because I knew (from what source?) that I would grow as tall as the height of the flames. I also remember the swishing sound the flame made when Father extinguished it in the saucer that caught the overflow of the wine from the cup over which the appropriate benediction had been pronounced. And, of course, I remember with a sharp clarity the scent of the dry spices in the old silver filigree spice box shaped like a turret with a little flag at its top that could be turned all around. Father pronounced the prescribed benediction over the spices, the *besamim*, sniffed at it, and then passed it around so that we all could inhale its scent. The *havdala* concluded with the singing of the song *Shavu'a tov*, "Good week," which expressed the wish that we should all have a good, happy, and lucky week.

Although the theory and doctrine behind the Sabbath observances were to become known to me only much later, the practice of the Sabbath rites in which I participated from earliest childhood left an indelible impression on me. I enjoyed them more and more as the months and years passed. They gave ample compensation for the restrictions imposed on me by the "no work" rules of the Sabbath, and the better I came to know each word, each note, each movement as they followed one another in the same inexorably and deliciously repetitious order week after week, the more they came to mean to me, and the greater was the magic and enchantment that flowed out of them like a sequence of warm waves, which surrounded me like a protective caul with a sense of security and well-being.

It was about the time of my Bar Mitzva, or shortly after, that I first took interest in a girl. The name of my first love, to quote *The Tales of Hoffman*, was Lilla Rozsnyai. She was a beautiful little thing with very white skin, blue eyes, and red hair. She was a classmate of my sister, eleven or twelve years old at the time. I have a vague recollection that she was among the guests invited to my Bar Mitzva celebration. I never as much as spoke a word to her alone, but I was deeply in love with her for a while. Once, and only once, I screwed up enough courage to pay her an unannounced visit. I took one of my paintings, wrapped it up neatly, and asked my friend Laci Schwarz to come with me—I evidently needed moral support. We went together to the apartment of the Rozsnyais, and I timidly rang the bell, which was answered by Lilla's father, a tall man with a reddish moustache and something catlike in his countenance. I stammered something to the effect that we came to give a present to Lilla, whereupon he retreated and called his daughter, leaving us standing in front of the door. A minute later Lilla appeared. I said I brought her a gift, a picture I had painted, gave it to her, said good-bye, and left. I felt very daring and adventurous. I must have seen Lilla a few more times after this brief encounter, but if so, I remember nothing of those meetings. I think that upon finishing her fourth grade of high school she was one of the many who left the academic school, probably in order to learn a trade, perhaps as a secretary, and I never saw her again. Incidentally, Lilla was the name of the lady-love of the chevalier Mihály Csokonyai, the famous eighteenth-century Hungarian poet, whose poems celebrating Lilla we had to memorize, and this may have added to the romantic glamor of Lilla Rozsnyai in my eyes.

I was fond of books long before I could read. When, as a teenager, I would search the volumes of the *Meyers Konversations Lexikon* for sexual enlightenment or for any other information, as I soon acquired the habit of doing, I would often come across parts of pages that had been torn out. These mutilated pages usually contained colored illustrations, such as pictures of various animals, flags, soldiers in uniform, landscapes, ethnographic objects, and the like. When I asked my mother who was guilty of such barbarous treatment of our beautiful encyclopaedia, she explained that the culprit was none other than I, that as an infant of one or two my favorite pastime was to sit on the floor with a volume of the *Meyers* between my legs, to turn page after page, and to grab in my fist those pages that I liked. When she saw that I was ruining the books, she reproached me—probably rather mildly—but not being able to keep an eye on me all the time, she could not prevent me from continuing to give the books the same rough treatment. By the time I reached three, she said, I had learned to turn the pages and look at the pictures without damaging them.

My own memories about my reading habits do not reach further back than my sixth or seventh year, and it was not before I entered my teens that I began to read juvenile literature in earnest. Of the many authors I must have read as a young teenager I remember two whose works I devoured with passion and of whose books I tried to possess as many as I could. They were Karl May and Jules Verne. I read them, of course, in Hungarian translation, and since their names appeared on the title pages as May Károly and Verne Gyula, which read like good Hungarian names, and nowhere in the books was it mentioned that they were translated from the German and French respectively—or, at least, I did not notice that it was mentioned—it never even occurred to me that the authors could have been other than Hungarian. While reading their novels I was totally transported into the worlds they created, loved their heroes, hated their villains, and was so eager to know "what happens next" that I read on and on for hours, neglecting the only duty I had, namely, to do my homework for school. My favorite way of reading was to provide myself with a large slice of bread covered with butter and marmalade and sit crosswise in one of the large leather club chairs in the living room, leaning against one arm and swinging my legs over the other, reading and munching at the same time. It often happened that in the evening I could not tear myself away from the book I was reading, and since we children had to go to bed soon after supper, and the lights had to be turned out in the nursery, I took with me into bed the book and a flashlight, covered myself entirely with the blanket, and continued to read with the flashlight in the cozy and warm cave formed by the blanket over my head.

Of all the adventure stories of Karl May I liked most the one that took place in Arabia. I remember in particular one scene, told in first person, in which the author, whom the Arabs call Kara ben Nimsi, that is, "Karl, son of a German," finds a way to force them to recognize Jesus. The scene is set somewhere in the Arabian Desert. It is a stormy day, and the wind blows fiercely. A gust picks up the camel's litter in which the little son of the sheik sits, and deposits it in the middle of a large area of quicksand. The litter floats on the surface of the treacherous sand, and the boy cries for help, but the sheik and all his stalwarts are at a loss as to what to do. They try to approach the litter, but the quicksand threatens to swallow them up.

Kara, known to be the most resourceful of men among the Arabs just as he had been when as "Old Shatterhand" he outbraved, in other Karl May novels, all the braves of Indian chieftain Winnetou, is appealed to. "Save my son," says the sheik, "and I shall fulfill any wish of yours." Kara ben Nimsi, good Christian that he is, has been irked during all the time he has spent with his Arab friends by their contempt for Christianity and, in particular, Jesus Christ. Now he has the opportunity to score for Jesus against Allah and Mohammed, whom those Arabs constantly invoke. "If you and your men," answers Kara, "will say *Isa ben Mariam akbar* [I remember these words from the story, but not whether May translates them as "Jesus son of Mary is greater" or " . . . is the greatest," both of which would be correct], I shall save your son."

The sheik is horrified at the demand: how can he utter such blasphemous words? But then his love of his son prevails, he pronounces the revolting sentence that is the price he must pay for his son's life, his tribesmen repeat it after him, and Kara ben Nimsi gets to work. He takes his lasso, steps carefully to the edge of the quicksand, swings the lasso, lets it fly — and its noose catches the protruding corner post of the palanquin. Here, I remember, Karl May digresses in a lengthy paragraph to the effect that it was extremely fortunate that he was such a great expert at using the lasso — otherwise, who knows how often he would have had to try before succeeding in catching the post. Then he begins pulling the litter toward him, very, very slowly, telling the boy in the meantime to make no move lest he upset the delicate balance of the litter on the quicksand, which would be his end. I no longer remember what happens to Kara ben Nimsi after accomplishing this feat, but there can be no doubt that he emerges safely from the deserts of Arabia, and returns to his more favored hunting grounds among the North American Indians. I am aware that the above brief account of a typical Karl May scenario is unfair, for it reflects my present, critical reaction to a story that, to begin with, was intended for teenagers and impressed my precritical mind so deeply that sixty years later I still remember it down to little details.

None of the dozens of Jules Verne's novels I read can I recall in such detail. I remember, though, the opening lines of the novel

Robur the Conqueror, which tells about the adventures of the inventor of a "heavier-than-air flying machine." The accompanying illustrations depicted this imaginary machine in the shape of a big ship, from the deck of which protruded, instead of masts, dozens of vertical shafts, each with a horizontally mounted propeller at its top. While this airship was in flight, people promenaded on its deck as passengers would on a ship in balmy weather. The opening lines of this story tell about a duel fought with pistols by two people, both of whom heard some music coming down from the clouds (later we find out that the music had come from Robur's airship). One maintains that the melody is "Rule, Britannia," while the other argues that it is "Yankee Doodle," and it is this that they fight over. Neither of the two duelists gets hurt, but an innocent cow grazing nearby is hit by one of the bullets. I remember the end of the novel only vaguely. I think an enemy of Robur places explosives into his airship, and it crashes. I also think that the same hero returns in another Verne novel, titled *Lord of the World*, in which he has constructed a superior craft, which can ride on land like a car, travel on water like a ship, and fly in the air like an airplane.

I have similar general recollections of many other novels of Verne, among them *Castle in the Carpathians, Around the World in Eighty Days, Captain Nemo, Trip to the Moon, Twenty Thousand Leagues under the Sea, The Floating City, The Floating Island*—I am translating the Hungarian titles as I remember them; the English titles may be different. I had a full bookshelf of Verne's novels, all bound in the same beautiful cloth binding with lavish red and gold decoration.

Of the other authors whom I enjoyed in the early years of my reading career I remember de Amicis, whose *The Heart* tugged at my heart; Alphonse Daudet, with whose *The Little What D'ya Call Him* (the Hungarian translation of the French *Le petit chose*) I suffered greatly, especially when he did not dare to step down from his bed in his miserable room in Lyon because the floor was full of cockroaches; and Flammarion's *Stella*, which, as far as I can recall, tells the story of a youth and a maiden who manage to escape from a dying earth to a larger and younger planet, Jupiter, I believe.

About the same time I was briefly captivated by the Tarzan and Martian stories of Edgar Rice Burroughs, and then turned to Mór Jókai (1825–1904), the most popular and prolific Hungarian novelist, several of whose books (as I now find in the *Encyclopedia Amer-*

icana) have been translated into English. While I remember very clearly the fascination Jókai's masterfully spun stories exerted upon my mind, I can recall practically nothing of their contents, except that his protagonists were either entirely good or entirely evil, and, vaguely, one or two scenes, such as the aforementioned one-night union between a man and a woman that resulted in the birth of a child. I can also recall a scene from another Jókai novel in which a physician (an evil character) is beseeched by a woman to save the life of her child who is dying, and the doctor-villain asks her, in return, to give herself to him. The desperate mother, who loathes the doctor, has no choice but to give in, and the doctor possesses her then and there—I vaguely remember that the incident takes place in some strange place like a huge cave—and then treats the child, who actually recovers. I can recall in particular how the physician tells the mother that without his help the child has only a few minutes to live, and how the mother, after having sacrificed herself for her child, has a foreboding that the child, whose life she bought for such an unspeakable price, could not live long. Jókai has the child die within a few months. I cannot recall the title of the novel in which this scene occurs.

From another Jókai novel I remember a technical detail. Its title was *The Story of the Next Century*, and its hero invents and builds a flying machine made of a material that is transparent like glass but stronger than steel. I think the name Jókai gave that imaginary material was *ichor*, although I know, of course, that *ichor* is in Greek mythology the ethereal fluid flowing, instead of blood, in the veins of the gods. The flying machine is powered by electricity; its two wings, charged with identical electric current, slowly fold upward, and when they almost touch each other the electrical force in them pushes them apart and down with a mighty beat. Thus the machine flies like a huge bird, carried aloft and ahead by the rhythmical beat of its great transparent wings. Of the many characters who must have peopled the novel, and the airship, I remember only one: he is a black man, whom the inventor-owner takes along despite a warning given him by a wise man (?) that he should never allow aboard persons who have no beards—meaning women and blacks. Jókai seems to have believed that blacks were characterized by the absence of facial hair.

Another author whom I read with great enjoyment was Dmitri Merezhkovski. His collected works were published in a Hungarian translation in numerous blue-bound volumes, of which I somehow obtained a set. I recall his trilogy *Christ and Anti-Christ*, comprised of the novels *Julian the Apostate, Leonardo da Vinci*, and *Peter the Great*. Of all of them my inexplicably selective memory retained only two scenes. One again has to do with flying: Leonardo invents a flying machine, and despite his warning his famulus straps on the wings, jumps from a precipice, and—falls to his death. The other describes the arrival at the court of Peter the Great of a classical marble statue of Venus. As they are unpacking the statue, it threatens to topple over, whereupon Peter, who is described as a giant of a man, jumps forward and hugs the statue so as to steady it, and for a moment the tsar and the goddess are standing there as if in a tight embrace of love.

One of the volumes of the Merezhkovski series contained his essays, and of them I remember his captivating description of the radiant beauty of Greece, which concludes with something to this effect: "As I am writing these lines, I am sitting in my study, on a grey, cold, wintry Russian day. In front of me on my desk is a piece of white marble that I found on the Acropolis." For some reason, this sentence, or rather, the enchantment with Greece expressed in it, made such a deep impression on me that I retained it in my memory, and I conceived then and there an undying desire to see for myself the glories of Greece one day.

If I were to sit back and strain my memory, I could undoubtedly recall the names of many more Hungarian and foreign authors whose books I absorbed voraciously in my early teens, but the above list is long enough as it is. Instead of adding to it, let me say that, although at the age of about twelve I started to read German authors in the original, and at the age of fifteen I began to read English as well, as long as I lived in Hungary, that is, until my twenty-third year, I continued to read Hungarian, and enjoy the works of Hungarian authors, some of whom I consider even from my present-day perspective men of great talent whose writings deserve more recognition on the global scene than they have been given. No Hungarian author has so far been awarded the Nobel Prize in literature, and translations into English from Hungarian are far fewer than from the languages of other small European nations.

From my junior high school years dates my lifelong dislike of attending synagogue services. Part of our duties as students of the

Jewish high school was to attend the Sabbath morning services in the school synagogue, which lasted from ten to twelve. Many of the prayers were sung; those boys who had a good ear and a good voice sang solo pieces, while the rest of us constituted the choir. This is practically the only thing I remember from those services. The new premises into which the school moved when I was, I believe, in the fourth grade were at quite a distance from our home, so that six days a week I would take the trolley both ways, which was not too bad since it did not take more than half an hour. But on the Sabbath I was not allowed to use a wheeled conveyance, but had to walk, which took about an hour each way, and which was anything but pleasant, especially in the cold winter months. I had to leave home at about 9 A.M., and got back at 1 P.M., which meant that my whole morning was taken up, and I did not have a single weekly day of rest since Sunday was for us a regular school day like every other day of the week.

In addition, my father insisted that I go with him to a nearby synagogue for the Friday evening services, and, never daring to demur, I had to stop whatever activity I happened to be engaged in, and accompany him. When the High Holy Days rolled around, the endless hours I had to spend in the synagogue were even more burdensome. Out of family loyalty, my father would go, and take his family, to the small synagogue of which his uncle, Israel Hayyim Braun, was the rabbi. It was located in Szövetség Street, not too far from our home. One of the rooms in Uncle Braun's apartment, a room of about fifteen by twenty feet, on the third floor of a large apartment house, served as his prayer room, and behind an open door, the view through which was rendered hazy by a white semidiaphanous curtain, was another, smaller room in which sat the women. The pews in both rooms consisted of extremely uncomfortable, narrow planks of undressed wood, and similar wooden boards that served as backrests. After an hour or so I was barely able to remain seated. Even more unpleasant was the increasing foulness of the air in the unventilated room as the hours dragged on, and the exhalation of the tightly packed rows of praying, swaying, and sweating men filled the room. This was the synagogue where we went for the prayers on the evenings and mornings of the two days of Rosh Hashana (New Year), the evening and the whole day of Yom Kippur (Day of Atonement), as well as on the evenings and mornings of the Feast of

Sukkot (Tabernacles). I no longer remember how long the evening prayers lasted, but in the mornings of the two days of Rosh Hashana we were in the prayer room from about 8 A.M to 1 P.M.. The prayers on Yom Kippur eve took about three hours, and as for Yom Kippur day, we went to the synagogue at 8 in the morning and stayed there until after dark, that is, until 6 or 7 P.M..

Jewish tradition does not require a boy less than thirteen years old to fast on Yom Kippur, but in religious families it was customary to train the children gradually for the fasting, so that a ten-year-old would be made to fast until lunchtime, when a light snack would be given to him; next year this snack would be postponed to a later hour, and so forth, so that by the time he reached thirteen he was prepared to go without food or drink for twenty-four (actually twenty-five) hours. I still remember that more difficult than not eating anything from dusk until after dark on the next day was not to drink even a drop of water, for standing and sitting around in the overcrowded and stuffy prayer room made me extremely thirsty. The only thing the fasting people were allowed to do to alleviate their pangs of hunger and thirst was to lift to their noses a large raw quince that was studded all over with cloves, and to sniff at it so as to obtain some rather imaginary refreshment from its pleasant aroma.

As against the general discomfort of these High Holy Days there were also moments of elation, of emotional uplift, of catharsis. When it came to the confession of sins, which was recited several times, I would glance up at Father, who stood on my left, and saw on his face an expression of utter absorption and anguish as his lips murmured the sacred word and his right fist came down rhythmically upon his breast with every word: *oshamnu*, we sinned — and the fist beat, *bogadnu*, we were unfaithful — and the fist beat, and so on until the end of the alphabetically arranged list of all the transgressions of a moral nature of which the medieval rabbis could think and of which a person could possibly be guilty. I glanced at Grandfather Ehrenfeld on my right, and when I could catch a glimpse of his face, which as a rule he kept covered by his great tallith, which enveloped his head as well as his entire body, I saw in it the reflection of the same feelings as on Father's face, but with an even greater intensity and with less self-control, and I saw that he was crying, that his grey-blue eyes had turned red, and that the tears were running down his cheeks. To see these two men, whom I loved and looked up to, in the grip of such deep emotions had a powerful effect on me. I was shaken, and knew that by praying in unison with them, even if I myself was not crying, I faced, as they did, my Maker, and that my future life and happiness hung in the balance.

Every year on Yom Kippur my father led the *minḥa* (afternoon) prayer. Although he was not a trained *ḥazan* (cantor), he knew the melodies of the prayers, undoubtedly remembering them from his own childhood. He had a fine musical ear and a pleasant voice, and the ancient melodies poured forth from his lips in melancholy sweetness. As he chanted, standing there in front of the congregation, wrapped in his tallith, with his back toward us and facing east, the direction of the holy city of Jerusalem, I felt enormously proud of him, and my heart was filled with love. Finally, when evening fell, came the turn of the *neila* (concluding) prayer, and with the darkness the long fasting was over. Uncle Braun and his wife gave the adult members of the family a little schnapps, and us children some water with raspberry syrup, and then all of us got some light crumbly cookies, to give us strength for the walk home. And I was suffused with a great feeling of relief and accomplishment, and with the conviction that God had certainly heard me, rewarded me, and decided to let me have a good and happy year to come.

In the spring of 1924, when I was in the fourth grade of high school, Father visited Palestine for the first time. Thereafter he returned every year, until the late 1930s, each time taking with him a group of tourists whom he conducted across the length and breadth of the Holy Land. He described his early impressions of the *yishuv*, the Jewish community of Palestine, in a series of articles he published in his journal and then gathered in a book entitled *A Föltámadó Szentföld* (The Renascent Holy Land), which, when I read it as a fifteen-year-old, filled me with a great longing to go to Palestine, to live there, and to be part of that beautiful life that Father described so seductively in his book. However, eight years had to pass before my desire could be realized.

The first time Father left for Palestine his departure occasioned great worry for Mother. She feared for his safety, and I don't think she had a quiet moment until he returned, several weeks later, sunburned, vigorous, and overflowing with all the wonderful things he had seen in the Holy Land. Being fluent in Hebrew, he had felt immediately and totally at home in the *yishuv*, whose writers, artists, and scholars all had known about him, had received him as one of their peers, and had feted and honored him. The stories he told Mother and us children at the dinner table about his experiences in Palestine had to compensate her for the anxiety she suffered during the weeks of his absence. Mother had inherited her anxious nature from her father, whose favorite saying was, "Better afraid than frightened," and who, as my sister and I used to recall at a later age, when he had to catch a train, would go to the station two hours prior to departure time, and then stand on the platform with one foot on the stairs of the car to make sure that he would not miss it. But, quite apart from this congenital anxiety, Mother had in fact good reason to be apprehensive while Father was in Palestine. In 1924 Palestine was quite an undeveloped country in which malaria was endemic, so that all visitors were advised to take quinine three times a day. Jewish settlements were few and far between, and only three years had passed since the murderous Arab riots of 1921 in which several dozens of Jews were killed. The hygienic and sanitary conditions were unsatisfactory, diarrhea was almost inevitable, and, to cap all this, Father was known to be rash and impetuous and, Mother was convinced, not able really to take care of himself. I, of course, had no inkling of any of these things at the time, and all I remember is that after Father's return, when I heard and then read the accounts of his experiences, I became determined to go to Palestine one day.

After I finished the fourth grade of high school, Mother felt that I was in sufficiently good health to be allowed to go camping with the troop of boy scouts to which I belonged. The troop was organized under the aegis of the school, and, as far as I can remember, only boys of the fourth and fifth grades (the two highest of the school at the time) belonged to it. The "Camping Certificate," which I still happen to have, says that "György Patai participated in the second camping of our boy scouts' troop that we held on the György farm near Vasvár, from July 7 to 23, 1924, and he manifested during the entire time of this stationary camp the following boy scout qualities: orderliness, cleanliness, politeness, obedience, discipline, perseverance, willingness to help. Given in Budapest, August 1, 1924. [Signed] Géza Polgár." Mr. Polgár, the commander of the school's boy scouts, was one of the teachers. Had I not found this impressive document among my papers, I would certainly not have been able to recall either the time or the place of the camp. What I do remember is that we first traveled by train, walked quite a distance, then had to pitch our own tents in which we were to sleep for the duration of our camping. For several days it rained, at night it was cold, and, all in all, those sixteen days at camp were not the most enjoyable experience. In fact, I soon lost interest in scouting, and once we returned to school in the fall, I resigned from the troop.

I remember one more thing from those days in the camp. On Sabbath morning we marched to the nearby town, Vasvár, to attend the services in the local synagogue. When the time came for the reading of the Tora, several of the boys were "called up," which was a kind of honor given to the visitors. It was (and still is) the custom in many synagogues that the person honored by being called up to the Tora reading was given a blessing that was read out or, rather, chanted by the reader. Part of this blessing consisted of the words, "He who blessed our fathers . . . may He bless Mr." — and here the reader inserted the name of the person who had been called up and who stood next to him at the lectern — "for the sake of the amount of" — at which point the person to be blessed whispered into the ear of the reader the amount he wished to donate — "which he offered to" — one of the recognized charitable purposes connected with the synagogue or the congregation. These donations, and the payments for one's seat in the synagogue for the High Holy Days, took the place in Jewish congregations of passing around the baskets in Christian church services. Since Jews are forbidden to carry or even touch money on Sabbaths and holidays, their contributions, without which the synagogue could not survive, are given in this manner.

The first one of us boys to be called up was a Kohen, my classmate Fleischman, the son of well-to-do parents, and when his turn came to name his donation, he specified quite a sizable amount, which the reader repeated loudly and with evident satisfaction. After him another boy was called up, and then, by prearrangement, it was my turn. When I heard how much Fleischman donated, I felt I must beat him by giving more. I quickly calculated how much of my pocket money I still had, and figured that if I spent nothing during the remaining days, I could just top Fleischman's gift. I was quite determined to do so, when Mr. Polgár passed the word (we sat in the pews bunched around him) that he categorically forbade us to offer any more donations. Not to obey a scout commander was, of course, out of the question, and thus, when my turn came, I had to be content with being blessed by the reader for having given a *matone (matana)*, a "gift," to the synagogue, which in the traditional euphemistic phraseology of synagogue liturgy simply meant — nothing.

6

High School Years: 1924–1928

In 1924 news about a fabulous new invention reached Budapest. It was called radio, and it was said to be able to transmit the human voice and music over great distances, and without any wire such as was used by the telephone. One of the family journals to which Father subscribed for us carried an article describing in detail how to build a crystal radio receiver. The challenge was irresistible, and I felt I simply must try my hand at it. I bought the required parts, among them a cardboard cylinder, lots of thin insulated wire, heavy copper wire for the antenna, a slider, several other small parts, and, of course, the crystal. I was, however, unable to find a store that sold headphones. The whole thing was still so new that the parts were extremely difficult to come by. But I learned, I don't know any more from whom, that our physics teacher, Dr. Benő Strasser, was able to obtain headphones.

Strasser was a great actor whose lectures were full of flailing hand movements and other affected theatricals, all calculated to hold our attention; but he was also an excellent teacher, he knew how to control the class, and he explained his subject clearly, effectively, and in what I felt was a fascinating manner. It was due entirely to Dr. Strasser's personality and teaching methods that I got to like physics, while chemistry and mathematics, taught by teachers who were in every respect Strasser's opposites, were my least favored subjects. When I asked Dr. Strasser whether he could help me to get a pair of headphones, he looked at me sharply and said, "You mean to purchase?" "Yes, sir," I stammered. He said, "Well, I shall have them for you in a few days." When he brought the headphones to school, I paid for them, and took them home with great anticipation. I knew so little about the working of a radio that, before I began constructing the indoor antenna as per the instructions in the article, I asked Dr. Strasser whether, in order to be able to receive a broadcast, I would have to open the window of the room in which the antenna was located. Dr. Strasser made one of his characteristic sweeping gestures, and explained that the radio waves can easily penetrate closed windows, because. . . .

Although I did not understand what he was talking about, I was reassured, and proceeded with the construction of an antenna in my room (which, I think, I still shared with my sister, or was it my little brother by that time?). I pushed the table to the tall wardrobe that hugged one wall of the room, put a chair on the table, and so climbed up to the top of the wardrobe. From that positon I was able to hammer a large nail into the middle of the wall just a few inches below the ceiling, and then tied to it a string with five china insulators that I had prepared in advance. Then I repeated the same procedure at the middle of each of the remaining three walls, and, once done with this preparatory work, I stretched the copper wire through the holes in the insulator nuts going round the room five times, so that the wire formed a five-times-repeated quadrangle right under the ceiling. I must have worked hard on stretching and placing this elaborately constructed antenna just under the ceiling, because each time in order to thread the wire through the nuts I had first to reach them, which meant that I had to drag my makeshift scaffolding five times around the room. But finally the antenna was ready—five parallel squares of gleaming red wire, one inside the other, constituting a large diamond within the four walls of the room.

I don't remember much about how I constructed the receiver itself, but I know that one part of the job was to wind a thin wire tightly around the cardboard cylinder, in which I was assisted by my brother Guszti, six years old at the time. Then the slider had to be attached, the crystal mounted in its holder with its thin spring-mounted wire, with which one could touch the rough surface of the crystal at just about any place, and all the other requisite connections had to be made. When everything was ready, I clapped the headphones over my ears, and started to move the slider along the wire coil and at the same time to play with the crystal. To my great disappointment, all I could hear was a scraping sound as I moved the needle over the crystal, and nothing else. My set, the fruit of so many hours of hard work, just did not work. I thought that perhaps the antenna I constructed was not the right one, for I could not obtain the soft wire composed of several strands of thin wires woven together that the instructions called for, and substituted one thick and less flexible copper wire.

I went back to the store where I had bought all the stuff, and its owner opined that I should try to use the electric wires that brought the household current into our apartment as an antenna, and sold me a little gadget that could be plugged into any electrical outlet, but, he assured me, did not conduct any electricity and transmitted only the radio waves absorbed by the outdoor wires. When I tried out this patent, all I could hear was a steady hum. I was by that time quite discouraged, but was ashamed to admit defeat to my friends in class, to whom, of course, I had boasted of my project; and when shortly thereafter several of them came to our home one evening for a party (we occasionally gave such parties for classmates and friends), I tried to fake the results that had eluded me. I told one of my friends to put on the headphones, then went out of the room, and from behind the door began to speak in a muffled voice, imitating the style and manner of the announcer of Radio Budapest, whom I had heard somewhere over a functioning receiver. Some time later Father gave me money to buy a crystal set, and that was the end of my experimentation with electronics. One day, when returning from school, I found that the elaborate antenna with which I had deco-rated the ceiling of my room had disappeared—Mother must have instructed the maid to remove and discard it.

Perhaps a year or so later, at my instigation, my parents bought what I considered a real radio. It was made by Telefunken, a Ger-man firm, and was a large black box that could be plugged directly into the house current. It had, if I remember correctly, a built-in speaker, and it was powerful enough to pull in broadcasts originat-ing in the neighboring countries. For me this was a fascinating new toy, and I spent many evening hours listening to it and trying to identify the stations. At that time I no longer slept in my old nurs-ery, but in the living room on a *Schöberl*, that is to say, a large club chair that could be opened up and converted into a bed for the night. It was upholstered in dark red embossed velvet, and when opened up it was much higher than a regular bed. Next to it, on a little Biedermeier style table, which Father had bought in Germany together with several other pieces of antique furniture in 1923 or 1924, stood the Telefunken radio. After going to bed I could com-fortably reach its knobs, and once I found a program that interested me, I would lie back and listen. My favorites were operas, which were broadcast quite frequently, and to which I listened with rapture even though some performances ran late into the night.

My father did not like to see me listening to the radio. He would never interfere with my reading, but whenever he noticed that I was listening to the radio he would express a strong negative opinion about this activity. He did not go so far as to forbid it, but repeatedly told me that he thought it rendered one stupid. Despite this parental opinion, I continued to be an avid listener, but perhaps did not spend quite as much time with the radio as I would have otherwise. In a year or two I got over it altogether.

While I was still in the fourth grade, a new illustrated family weekly was launched in Budapest. Its title was *Aller Képes Családi Lapja* (Aller's Illustrated Family Paper). At the request of us children, Father subscribed to it. Both my sister and I found it interesting, and read most of the material it contained, although I remember nothing of its contents except for a single item that was not an article at all. One issue carried an insert of two or four pages, printed on thicker paper, that contained pictures of parts of a medieval castle, with instructions as to how to cut them out, fold them, paste them together, and thus construct a model castle. There were many turrets, crenellated walls, battlements, bay windows, and other features associated more with fairy-tale castles than with real ones. But in general it reminded me somewhat of the castle of Vajda-Hunyad in the City Park, which we children frequently saw. The task of building a paper castle intrigued me, but, looking closely at the cutouts, I saw that the model castle would be rather small, with which I was not satisfied. So I decided to "build" a larger castle, and proceeded to copy out each of the sections double the size. I used solid drawing paper, and carefully prepared an enlargement of each section exactly as it appeared in the journal. With my watercolors I painted in the walls, the windows, the doors, the towers, the roofs, copying from the original, then cut out the pieces, folded them according to the instructions, pasted them together, and assembled them. The result was a beautiful castle, much more impressive than the puny model contained in the paper.

The interest in childish construction projects as exemplified by the building of a crystal radio receiver and a paper castle was to remain with me for another year or two, at least in the form of an occasional relapse, even after my major preoccupation had become reading adult literature in Hungarian, German, and English. One example I remember is that, when I was about sixteen, on the occasion of a masked ball that I attended, I made myself a cardboard Roman helmet. I must have found the picture of a Roman helmet in one of the books in my father's library, and reproduced it as best I could, complete with a high crest, a visor, and two ear pieces. When I was satisfied with the shape of the thing, I pasted silverfoil all over it, and, lo, I had a shiny, glittering Roman helmet. As for the problem of what to wear over my shoulders, I solved it with ingenious simplicity. My mother had a floor-length red and black terry-cloth bath cape that I appropriated for the occasion. A small black silk mask over my eyes completed the costume, and I was convinced I cut a very impressive figure, especially since at that time I still considered it a distinct achievement that I had shot up to a height of six feet. I do not remember anything about the ball or the party for which I had prepared this outfit, except that in the course of the evening I was introduced to the younger sister of my aunt Ruth, Friedel Frank, who was perhaps three or four years my senior. Friedel wore no mask, and she asked me to take off mine so that she could see my face. I refused because I wanted to appear mysterious and to intrigue her.

I was in the fourth or fifth grade when the school moved into its new, as yet unfinished, building. It was a spacious, modern structure with a large yard, located on Abonyi Street, not far from the City Park. The distance from my home was about two miles, just a little too much to walk, especially in the snowy winter, loaded down with all the textbooks and copybooks I had to carry. However, the streetcar that stopped at our corner covered the distance in about thirty minutes. Once I got on the car without having a penny in my pocket. When the conductor came around to collect my fare, I searched desperately in all my pockets and then had to confess shamefacedly that I had lost my money. The conductor had evidently heard this excuse many times, for he bawled me out, told me that if he caught me again he would call a policeman, and ordered me off the car. It was a painful scene while it lasted, but when I was out in the street again I chalked it up as just one more experience.

On another occasion the spirit of exploration prompted me to try out a different means of transportation. At a distance of about half a mile from the school there was a train stop from which the train went on to the Western Railroad Station, which was quite near our apartment. Since I loved trains, I decided one day to go home by that train. I had to wait quite a while until the train came, and I arrived home late and got a scolding from my mother, but I enjoyed traveling by train alone for the first time.

In my fourteenth year I underwent the usual bodily and mental changes attendant on puberty. While I was in my eleventh and twelfth year, my sister, although eighteen months my junior, was taller than I, but now I shot up, overtook her, and by the time I was fifteen had attained my full height of six feet. However, I was extremely thin and very flat-chested, and, although my health was satisfactory, Mother worried a lot lest I fall victim to some debilitating and dangerous disease. In those days the generally held belief, which my mother shared, was that tall and thin youngsters were particularly suscepti-ble to tuberculosis, a dreaded, practically incurable, disease. The only preventive measure known was to put on weight, and for about two years the endlessly repeated refrain at the table was *Gyuri, egyél!* (Gyuri, eat!). But my appetite, which in earlier years had been excellent, was now minimal, and in vain did my good mother prepare the most enticing dishes—my food intake remained what she considered entirely inadequate.

Finally Mother felt constrained to do something about my thin-ness and lack of appetite. She first spoke to, and then sent me to, Uncle Yóshka, who looked me over, and decided that I needed a series of insulin injections. After he gave me the first shot, he said, "Now go back up home right away, for by the time you climb up the stairs you will be ravenously hungry, and will want to, and should, eat as much as you can." I went upstairs, sat down, and waited for the results, but—nothing happened. I was not able to eat more than on other days. Next day I reported to Uncle Yóshka about my fail-ure to react to his injection, but he was not discouraged at all. "No problem," he said, "I shall increase the dosage." Again there was no result. For a few more days thereafter I got my daily injection, with the amount of insulin increased each time, and each time with the same negative outcome, until Uncle Yóshka finally concluded that the dosage could not be increased any more, and that evidently I was a very unusual case—my organism did not react to insulin. So the injections were discontinued, and Mother went on begging and pestering me to eat and preparing the most enticing dishes, which, however, left me, or rather my appetite, unmoved.

Speaking of Uncle Yóshka, there are a few more things I remember about him. One is that once, while paying us a house call—I no longer remember who was sick—when he washed his hands and Mother passed him a towel, he told us, and demonstrated, what had to be done if your hands were wet and the towel hung high up on a hook. "You must reach upward," he said, and accompanied his words with a quick hand movement, "very quickly, snatch the towel, and bring it down. If you do it slowly, the water from your hands will flow back into your sleeve."

On another occasion he told us how, when he was a schoolboy, he would manage to get permission to leave the classroom. When he had not prepared his homework, and wanted to be sure not to be called upon by the teacher, he would take along to school a brush with hard bristles, give a smart tap with the bristles on his wrist right over the pulse, then swing his arm rapidly in a circle, which would result in a few drops of blood appearing on his wrist. Then he would ask permission to leave the classroom to take care of his wound. Needless to say, this was something I had to try out. I took along a brush to school, not doubting that Uncle Yóshka's patent would work. I selected the English class to carry out the experiment, which circumstance gives me the date, since it was in the fifth form, when I was fourteen, that we began to have English in school.

I remember very clearly not only our English teacher, but the very first period when we Hungarian boys first heard what to us appeared the twisted, peculiar sounds of English pronunciation. Most teachers in our school were men outstanding in their fields, but not all of them had mastered the secret of how to keep a bunch of fifty unruly adolescents quiet, how to dominate them, and how to make them respect, or even fear, them. Our English teacher, Dr. Hugó Latzkó, was totally unable to keep order in class. This we found out right away, but we never knew, nor would we have cared if we had known, about his scholarly accomplishments. Now, while writing these pages, I checked in the *Hungarian Jewish Lexicon* (published in 1929), and found that he was born in 1876, studied in Budapest, Berlin, Oxford, and Cambridge, was, prior to taking his job at our high school, a professor at the Commercial Academy of Budapest and a lecturer of English at Budapest University, and was the author of several books and studies on English literature, as well as English-language books and Hungarian-English dictionaries.

The first moment a new teacher confronted the class, there was a tense expectation, a momentary silence, followed on the part of the more daring boys by tentative moves to test whether the new teacher would tolerate breaches of discipline. The first few minutes were decisive in this contest between the teacher's purpose to keep order in class and the boys' desire to be unruly and to behave as noisily as possible. Once the boys sensed that the teacher tolerated no nonsense, once they saw that he clamped down hard on the slightest breach of discipline, they gave up, and from then on the teacher had no problems with them, provided, of course, that he remained vigilant and nipped in the bud any further attempt at unruliness. But woe to the teacher who lost the first battle, who proved weak, undetermined, or tolerant in those first few minutes of confrontation. He was lost, and from then on he had to spend his energy not on teaching his subject, but on desperate and unavailing efforts at trying to keep his wolf pack from howling too loudly and from turning the classroom into a bedlam. Today, in retrospect, I feel great pity and sympathy for those poor teachers who, while becoming experts and scholars in their chosen fields, did not master the tricks, or, shall we say, methods, of keeping a class in order. At that time, however, such sentiments were unknown to me, as they were to all my classmates, and there was not a single one of us who would have said to the others, "Hey, fellows, let's give this poor guy a break!"

I became aware of the existence of a technique of dominating a class when, on one occasion, my uncle Ernő Molnár substituted for our regular teacher of Hebrew and religion, who was absent because of illness. He entered the classroom quickly, with determined steps, and we stood at attention as we were required to. Then, just as he was about to pronounce the words "Be seated" one of the boys made a remark that he overheard. I forget what the remark was, but it was evident that it was a breach of discipline, and had Dr. Molnár overlooked it, as was done in a similar case by Dr. Latzkó when he first entered our classroom, he would have been lost as Dr. Latzkó was. But Dr. Molnár knew what he had to do. Instead of telling us to sit down, he made us remain standing, and asked, "Who said that?" There was no answer. He asked again, "Who said that?"; when there was still no answer, he said, "If the boy who spoke won't own up, you will spend the whole period standing up as you are." Under this pressure, finally and reluctantly, one boy raised his hand. "What's your name?" Dr. Molnár asked; when the boy gave him his name, he said to him, "If I hear one more sound out of you, down you go to the principal." Then, speaking to the class in general, he added, "And this holds good for all of you. Now you can sit down." Thereafter, there was complete silence for the whole period, and Dr. Molnár could proceed with his subject as he had planned, with proper cooperation on the part of the class. After this incident I looked at Uncle Ernő with new respect.

Unfortunately for Dr. Latzkó, this technique of keeping order in class was unknown to him. He entered the classroom, a bald, bespectacled, middle-aged man, with bow legs and a slight forward bend from the hips. He looked around with a glance that we in our ruthless quest for a weak spot in our quarry did not fail to recognize right away as expressive of meekness, mildness, and timidity. He introduced himself, and said that we would begin our course of English with a poem that he would write on the blackboard. To do so he had, of course, to turn his back to us, committing thereby the fatal mistake of letting the wolf pack out of his sight. He chalked up the title "The Mariners' Song," and under it the four lines of the poem that I still remember and that I quote here without checking my memory against a printed version.

> Our home is the ocean, our cradle the deep,
> We feel no emotion as on it we sleep,
> The waves are our pillow, our grave is the sea,
> The rougher the billow the happier we. . . .

While he was writing, the noise in the class gradually increased, but Dr. Latzkó did not or could not do anything about it. Then he proceeded to read aloud the lines he wrote, carefully enunciating each word, and asked us to repeat them after him. This, of course, was his second mistake, for it gave the boys an opportunity to shout all together, not in unison, but in a hilarious cacophony.

It is almost impossible to explain to English speakers how peculiar, in fact, how ridiculous, the English phonemes sounded to our Hungarian ears. True, by the time we were started on English we had already had four years of Latin and Hebrew, and two years of German. But the sounds of these three languages were pronounced by us, and, I suspect, by our teachers as well, as if they were Hungarian phonemes. Those three languages among them had only one single phoneme that did not have its equivalent in Hungarian. It was the one that in German is spelled *ch* (as in *ach*), and in Hebrew *ḥet* or *khaf*, which in both languages we were taught to pronounce like a hard fricative (which is much heard in Scotland), and which, for some reason, we found neither hard to learn nor strange. Nor did the German *ich* sound cause us any difficulty. But now, for the first time in our lives, we were confronted by a series of completely new, and for our ears very strange, phonemes, such as the *w*, the *ow*, the *r*, the *th*, which Dr. Latzkó asked us to repeat after him in a way very different from the pronunciation of their written equivalents in Hungarian, German, or Latin. (The Hungarian *r* is pronounced with a rolling of the tongue, as in Italian; the *w*, which does not exist in Hungarian but with whose written sign we were familiar from German and from such German Jewish names as Weisz, we were used to pronounce as *v*; diphthongs do not exist in Hungarian; and as for the *th*, there was nothing even remotely similar to it in Hungarian, German, Latin, or Hebrew.) I remember the efforts Dr. Latzkó made to demonstrate how the word *we* is pronounced: he contorted his mouth, pulled in his lips, in order to pronounce the *w* sound, then opened them for the *e*, and repeated this sequence several times, while his head shook slightly. All this caused considerable merriment in class, and by the time our first English period ended, we were triumphant in our savagery, and Dr. Latzkó must have been a wreck.

Well, it was this teacher whose class I chose for my experiment with Uncle Yóshka's method of drawing blood from the wrist. I took the brush from my school bag, hit my left wrist with it, and then, when Dr. Latzkó was not looking in my direction, started to swing my arm in a wide circle. But either the bristles were too soft—I think it was a clothes brush that I used—or I did not hit myself hard enough, but in any case no drops of blood appeared. I gave another, stronger tap to my wrist, and with my attention focused too much on my experiment to notice whether Dr. Latzkó was or was not looking toward me, I swung my arm around energetically, until I suddenly heard him call out, "Patai! What are you doing? Go down to the principal's office and tell him that I sent you down because of unruly behavior." So my experiment succeeded, after all, although not in the manner I intended: I managed to get out of the classroom, but earned a demerit for it. Nevertheless, as I now see from my report card for that year, the mark I got in "Behavior" remained "Exemplary."

In March 1925 Father organized an exhibition of the work of Abel Pann (1883-1963), who lived in Palestine and was a successful painter, biblical illustrator, and cartoonist. Pann had first caused a sensation with his drawings of Russian pogroms, and then became acclaimed for his imaginative illustrations of the Bible, for which he used local Oriental types to depict biblical characters. He was also one of the first teachers at the Bezalel Art School in Jerusalem, and his favorite medium was pastel. Pann was invited by Father to come to Budapest for the duration of the exhibition, which was to take place from March 15 to 25 in the Hungarian National Salon, the foremost art gallery in the city. Since my uncle Berti had only shortly before moved into his new and spacious villa on Maros Street in Buda, Father and he agreed that Pann would be his house guest. Because of difficulties in obtaining a Hungarian visa for Pann, who was of Russian birth, his arrival was delayed, and the opening of the exhibition, at which his presence was considered a *sine qua non*, had to be postponed for two weeks, but it finally did open on March 29. The exhibition was opened by Count Kuno Klebelsberg, the Hungarian minister of cultural affairs, and the Palestinian artist was welcomed by Count Gyula Andrássy in the name of the National Salon. With such names up front, the success of the exhibition among the Budapest Jews was practically guaranteed.

While staying with Uncle Berti and his wife Ruth, Pann, who had his pastels with him (he explained to me that he never traveled without them), painted a picture for him, and another for Father. The latter was a landscape, showing the Judean Desert with a spot of the Dead Sea visible in the distance, and above it the haze-covered Mountains of Moab. Once, when I entered his room, I saw that he was working on a picture. He was sitting on a chair, in front of another chair against the back of which he had propped up a drawing board with a sheet of grey paper fastened to it with thumbtacks. Under the board, covering both the seat of the chair and his own knees, was spread a sheet that served to catch the powder that kept drifting down as he was applying his pastels to the paper. A large box of pastels rested on a third chair to his left. I stopped at the door, but he bade me enter, and after I watched him for a while I could not help asking, "How can you paint a desert landscape while sitting here in the room?" He smiled and said, "Simple, I do it from memory." A few days later he brought the finished picture to my parents, who found a suitable place for it in their living room. Not until years later, when I myself saw the same view from the Mount Scopus campus of the Hebrew University, was I able to appreciate not only the artistic quality, but the uncanny verisimilitude of that picture, which hangs today in my sister's house in Givatayim.

The Abel Pann exhibition was a resounding success. After it closed, Béla Déry, the director of the National Salon, wrote Father telling him that the exhibition was not only a great artistic event, but also an important social one. No less than 87,864 people visited the exhibition, among them ministers of state, ambassadors, archdukes, generals, university professors, scholars, artists, and collectors, many of them returning seven or eight times. Many of the pictures were sold at high prices, and all the Budapest papers published rave reviews. Father published Déry's letter in the April 1925 issue of *Mult és Jövő*, and this is how I know about it.

Encouraged by the success of the exhibition in Budapest, Father organized another for Abel Pann at the prestigious Secession Art Gallery of Vienna, from August 1 to September 6, 1925, and a third one again at the Budapest National Salon from November 10 to 24, 1926.

The 1920s in general were a very busy time for Father. He was in his forties, enjoyed good health, was full of energy, and was a veritable cultural powerhouse. Barely six weeks after the Tchernichowsky evening, which I reported in the preceding chapter, he organized another cultural evening dedicated to the memory of the famous Yiddish poet Morris Rosenfeld (1862–1923), who had died shortly before in America. During those years, accompanied by the actor Arthur Fehér, he visited numerous cities in Hungary and the Hungarian-speaking parts of Czechoslovakia, Rumania, and Yugoslavia, he lecturing and Fehér reciting Patai poems and poems by Hebrew poets in Father's Hungarian translation. In the summer of 1925 he was a delegate to the Zionist Congress in Vienna. In February 1926 he organized an exhibition, again in the Hungarian National Salon, of the works of E. M. Lilien, the famous German Jewish graphic artist, who had been his friend for many years, and who had died shortly before.

Father's reputation as the cultural apostle of the Jewish renaissance grew and spread, and Hungarian-speaking Jews everywhere saw in him not only their cultural but also their spiritual leader. Yet at the same time the official Hungarian Jewish leadership continued to keep itself aloof from Zionism, and, in order to play down the popularity of Father as its spokesman, it attempted to present him as the representative of an undifferentiated and rather vague Judaism. Typical of this attitude were the words of greeting with which Rabbi Samuel Roth of Sátoraljaujhely introduced Father when he gave a lecture (on December 14, 1925) under the auspices of the local Israelite Girls' Association: "Patai's spirit shines in huts and palaces alike, his psalms have taken their place all over the country in our synagogues. There are those who say, with a certain tendency, that Joseph Patai is a *Zionist*. I say, Joseph Patai is a *Jew!*" (as reported in *Mult és Jövő*, January 1926, p. 39).

On December 14, 1926, took place what was called "Joseph Patai's Author's Evening" in the biggest concert hall of Budapest, the Vigadó, the municipal concert hall. An entire galaxy of Jewish and Gentile actors, singers, and musicians participated, and, as reported in the January 1927 issue of *Mult és Jövő*, (p. 38), the evening was a resounding success. It began with the recital of a long poem, written by the well-known Hungarian poet Béla Telekes, and presented by the actor Endre Bokor, which greeted not Father but his journal, and described in mellifluous cadences the cultural mission *Mult és Jövő* had been carrying out for the past fifteen years. Then followed recitals of Patai poems set to music by composers Rezső Máder, Hugó Kelen, Tibor Alpár, Oszkár Dienzl, and Béla Róth. The singers were members of the Budapest Opera and other leading Hungarian musical institutions, including Erzsi Sándor, Gabriella Relle, Ferenc Székelyhidi, Oszkár Kálmán, Dóra Bársony, and Erzsi Radnai.

Interspersed with the musical numbers were readings by outstanding *szavalóművészek* (declamationists), whose art was much sought after by the Budapest intelligentsia. Arthur Fehér recited Father's poem "In Thy Hands," and although this was a declamatory recital, it was accompanied by a large choir. Similarly, Judith Tordai read another of Father's poems, "Sulamith, Seest Thou the Flame?" in the Hebrew translation of Father's erstwhile disciple and lifelong friend Avigdor Hameiri, who by that time was an acclaimed poet in Palestine; Tordai's reading was accompanied by harp music. When Erzsi Sándor, a Gentile member of the Budapest Opera, sang a Hebrew song, the audience reacted with enthusiasm—that a Gentile Hungarian artist should sing in Hebrew was nothing short of a sensation. Zoltan Bán read Father's cycle of poems "Winter on the Sea," and the coloratura Stefi Sebők sang Father's poem "The White-Blue Ship." Margit Kiss, another elocutionist, read Father's poem "Be Comforted,

Be Comforted, My People," and the blind pianist Imre Ungár played the music written for Father's poem "In the Valley of Joshaphat." The report (which, I suspect, was written by Father himself) ends with these words: "Patai himself listened to the whole performance from the invisible depths of a loge, and despite the most enthusiastic "Author!" cries of the public refused to appear. Only at the end of the evening, responding to the persistent calls, did he appear on the stage together with Erzsi Sándor, and then again quickly withdrew amidst the thunderous applause of the audience."

At the age of fifteen I tried my hand at sculpture. At that time my father invited a young sculptor by the name of Wald to make busts of him and of Mother. First Mother sat for him, and then Father, and I was fascinated by his work. He rigged up a kind of podium in the middle of our living room, put a chair on it, and bade his model to sit, while he himself stood before his sculptor's stand, which had a small revolving platform at the top. He worked in dark grey clay, and I was absolutely enchanted as I watched the likeness of the head emerge from the great mass of soft clay, under the nimble fingers of the sculptor. He came every day for quite a while, and each time the modeling session was over he wrapped the nascent bust in several layers of wet rags. Wald himself suffered from colds, and I remember that on more than one occasion my attention was distracted from the work of his fingers by watching a drop that hung from the tip of his nose for a remarkably long time. After finishing the clay heads, he had plaster casts made of them, which were placed in Father's study. Mother's bust, shellacked to a semigloss finish that gave it a marblelike appearance, was quite large, flamboyant, and impressive. Her head was tilted slightly to one side and back, was crowned with a large halo of hair, and showed her shoulders and draped chest. It contrasted with Father's bald head and severe look, with the shoulders cut off on both sides, showing only the middle part of his chest to a breadth corresponding to the width of his head. This bust was painted dark green in imitation of bronze.

In 1939, when my parents shipped a selection of their furniture and belongings to Palestine, they left these two statues behind in Budapest. My last information concerning them dates from 1980. By that time Father's bust had long since been lost, but Mother's was still in the safekeeping of my cousin Lili in Budapest. As for the sculptor, I have just found a very brief biographical note about him in the *Encyclopaedia Judaica*: "Herman Wald (1906–1970). South African sculptor born in Hungary, the son of a rabbi. He settled in South Africa in 1937. Among his principal works are a monument to martyred European Jewry, "Kria," which stands at the entrance to the Witwatersrand Jewish Aged Home, Johannesburg. His later works include municipal fountains and decorations for synagogues in Johannesburg and Cape Town." The bronze head of my late friend Cecil Roth by Herman Wald, which illustrates Roth's biography in the same *Encyclopaedia*, reminds me of the style of the two heads of my parents.

Observing the birth of two sculptured heads at close quarters created in me the wish to do some sculpting myself. As far as I can remember, I made only two attempts. The first was a small bearded head of Zeus that I fashioned in clay, and once it dried I kept it on my desk until I left for Jerusalem, after which I lost track of it. The second was a life-size head of myself that I also made in clay; under the cut-off neck I fashioned, from the same lump of clay, a cube to serve as a pedestal. When done with the clay model, I wanted to make a plaster cast of it, but had no idea how to go about it. Fortunately, a young budding sculptress, two or three years older than I, lived in an apartment on the ground floor of our house. Her name was Elza Jakobi (not related to my uncle Yóshka Jacobi, the doctor). Her father was a gentlemen's tailor among whose customers was my own father. Once, I remember, my father made Mother very unhappy when he had Mr. Jakobi make him an overcoat and a suit from the same material, which my mother considered to be in very poor taste. She was somewhat mollified when Father explained to her that he did not have to pay anything for that outfit, because Mr. Jakobi ran ads in Father's journal, and the two accounts canceled each other. However, I think that Father never wore that suit and that coat together.

Elza Jakobi was more than willing to help me. She told me what materials to buy, and came up to our apartment, where we set up a workshop in the bathroom. I remember the whole procedure in such sharp detail that I could duplicate it without a moment's hesitation. First she smeared oil all over the clay head, then took small pieces of tin and stuck them into the clay, beginning with the very top of the head, and down the two sides of the face and the neck and the cube under it. Then we mixed the plaster to the proper consistency, and

Elza poured it over the head all around, several times, until she was satisfied with its thickness. Thus we had a mold, divided in two by the tin pieces. When the plaster had hardened, we carefully pulled it off the clay core, removed the tin, fitted the two halves together, and joined them with more layers of plaster poured on the outside. The bottom, of course, remained open. Now the whole inside surface of the mold had to be oiled so as to prevent it from sticking to the plaster that was to be poured into it. The pouring of the positive, which was to be the finished product, into the negative mold was tricky, because, as Elza explained to me, if one simply filled the whole inside of the mold with plaster, it would surely crack while drying. The thing to do was to coat the inside of the mold with the liquid plaster so that it formed a layer of more or less even thickness all around. When she judged the job done, we began to chip away the mold, which was not too difficult to do. However, when the whole mold was removed we found that the cast had some holes in it on one cheek and the chin, which had to be patched up and then carefully smoothed. Therewith Elza's task was finished, and I was left with the unpleasant job of cleaning up the mess we made. Once the cast was thoroughly dry, I coated it with shellac, and painted the cube under the head a dark color to contrast with the eggshell color of the head itself. When my parents moved to Palestine in 1939, they thought this juvenile masterpiece important enough to take along, while as mentioned above, they left behind the two really fine heads by Herman Wald. Incidentally, my head arrived broken in two at the neck and I had quite a job fixing it. It is to this day in the house of my sister in Givatayim, Israel. After these early forays into the plastic arts, I never again dabbled in sculpture.

I have so far not referred to the beginnings of my Zionism that fell in this period and led to my *'aliya* (immigration) to Palestine in the spring of 1933. I can no longer recall when and how I became influenced by the deep-seated Zionist convictions of my father, but I do remember quite distinctly that he never spoke to me about Zionism or the return to Palestine as the ultimate destiny of the Jewish people, just as he never spoke to me about the values of Jewish culture, although his entire life was dedicated to the service of these causes. Still, even without ever touching upon these subjects in the course of the many hours weekly he devoted to teaching me the Talmud or while conversing with me on other issues, it was inevitable that the example of his life and work should impress itself upon me. Thus, during my early teens, as my mind gradually opened up to matters beyond the everyday interests of childhood, I came to take it for granted that it was the sacred duty of every Jew to work for the upbuilding of Palestine, and became seized with a deep desire to make my *'aliya* as soon as possible.

Only one brief but eloquent contemporary document happened to survive from that period of my life—a letter I addressed on May 24, 1926 (when I was fifteen), to my father, who was at the time in Palestine on the second of his frequent visits to the Holy Land. I wrote to him in Hungarian:

> Dear Papa!
>
> I received your postcard from Constanza, and have already sent a drawing to Mr. Halpern.
>
> My teacher Mr. Eckstein said I should ask you to bring me Hebrew school books. From them, in the course of the summer, I could pre-pare myself a little for the year I am to spend there.—Please, don't hesitate concerning my registration, once the matter is settled Mama, too, will give her consent.
>
> I myself would be very miserable if this plan, which has preoccupied me for years, would not be realized now.
>
> Otherwise everything is in order here. In the school there is much work, and I do my best studying Hebrew.
>
> I wish you all the best, and kiss your hands,
>
> > Gyuri
>
> *LaShana haBa'a bIrushalayim* [Next year in Jerusalem].
>
> Mama is in error.

The three Hebrew words I wrote in Hebrew characters. The last line refers to the doubts about my seriousness my mother expressed in a few lines she added to the back of the page. She wrote:

> My sweet, dear Yóshka,
>
> I already mailed a letter to you today, but I must absolutely add to Gyuri's letter that his Palestinian year must still be thought over care-fully. This great yearning is due to the newness, the voyage, the sen-sation—the great seriousness that practically oozes from his letter does not at all reveal itself in everyday life. Although it certainly would not hurt. I am very nervous, I suffer more from your absence this time than two years ago. Strange—I have a thousand things to do, practically every day I go somewhere, and yet—But I don't want to complain,

that would anyhow not change the situation. Indeed, even this only slipped out of my pen —

God be with you, I embrace you many times

Your Edith

The same letter contains also a few lines from my brother Guszti who at the time was two months short of his eighth birthday. He makes a few orthographic errors, but what he writes shows, perhaps even more clearly than my letter, that in our home problems of Palestine were frequently discussed, that consequently we children were surprisingly well informed, and that the desire to go to Palestine was firmly embedded in our consciousness. Guszti wrote:

> Dear Papa!
>   How do you feel? How nice it must be in Palestine! Have you already bathed in the Red Sea? Does Palestine still develop ten times as fast as America? I hope the relations between the Jews and the Arabs are good?! I hope that in 5–6 years I, too, shall be able to go out to Palestine. I can already write in German.
>   I kiss your hand,
>   Guszti

One of the health problems I began to suffer from when I was fifteen or sixteen was recurrent conjunctivitis every spring. Once my eyes not only got bloodshot but the conjunctiva of one eyeball bulged out and impinged on part of the iris. I went several times to an ophthalmologist, Dr. Pál Béla, who was a friend of Father. He treated me with eyedrops and prescribed bathing my eyes three times a day with a warm camomile compress. He also suggested that I wear dark sunglasses. In those days in Hungary sunglasses were worn only for medical reasons and were seen very rarely. I kept them on in school as well, and once, when I was called up by Dr. Latzkó to recite by heart an English poem that he had told us to memorize and I was totally unprepared, I stood up between my seat and my desk, as we were supposed to, adjusted the sunglasses on my nose as best I could so as to be able to look down behind their protective camouflage at the textbook that lay open on my desk, and thus read the poem instead of reciting it by heart. After the period Dr. Latzkó called me and said, "I saw very well that you were reading the poem from under your sunglasses, but did not want to shame you by reprimanding you. I expect you won't do this again." My respect for Dr. Latzkó grew after this encounter, and I began to take my English work more seriously.

Simultaneously with my introduction to English at school I also began to take English lessons at home. Father felt that the language was important enough to have my sister and me tutored by a private teacher. Our first English tutor was a young Englishwoman, Miss Elsie by name. She was blond and blue-eyed, with disproportionately wide nostrils that spoiled her otherwise pretty face. She came twice a week in the afternoon, gave one hour's instruction to my sister and me jointly, and then spent another hour tutoring Father in his study. Father must have been somewhat taken by Miss Elsie, for, as Mother once remarked to us in her characteristic half-humorous and half-serious tone, he shaved before each of his English lessons.

After a while, for reasons unknown, Miss Elsie was replaced by Mr. Árpád Toth, a Hungarian Jew who had spent several years in America, and who, if my memory serves me right, was a more capable teacher than Miss Elsie. The first text we read with Mr. Toth was Oscar Wilde's "The Happy Prince." Mr. Toth tried to improve our pronunciation, and read out the story phrase by phrase, making us repeat the words after him. I still remember the emphasis and enthusiasm with which he scanned the words "For whát is the heárt of a bírd compáred to the heárt of a mán?" "A wonderful line," he said repeatedly. Most of our lessons were spent in practicing conversation, and within a reasonably short time both my sister and I began to speak English, which thus became the fourth language (after Hungarian, German, and Hebrew) I learned to speak.

At the beginning of each lesson Mr. Toth would write the date into a copybook, and then, as we conversed or read, whenever a new word would come up, he would write it into the copybook with its Hungarian translation, and we were supposed to memorize this vocabulary for the next lesson. Every tenth lesson he would draw a little circle after the date and fill it in with his pencil, which, it just comes to me, was a copying pencil that, when wetted, left dark violet-colored inklike lines on the paper. This circle served to remind me that he had to be paid, and, when the hour was finished, I would fetch either my father or my mother to pay Mr. Toth for the past ten lessons.

After a year or two our lessons with Mr. Toth were discontinued because he went back to America. I saw him only once more, some thirty years later, when I was professor of anthropology at Dropsie

College in Philadelphia. One day I got a phone call at the college. The caller identified himself as Mr. Árpád Toth, and to help my memory added that he had been my English teacher in Budapest many years before. I of course remembered him very well, and we made an appointment to meet at the college a week later. When I saw him I recognized him without difficulty, although I remembered him as a vigorous black-haired man of about forty, and he was now a white-haired man in his seventies. But his features had remained basically unchanged, and his mannerisms, too, were the same, except for a certain slowing down. He told me that he was retired and lived in Philadelphia with his son and the latter's family, and then asked about my parents. I told him that my father had died a few years before, and that my mother was well and lived in Israel with my sister. He said he wanted to write to her, and asked me for her address, which I gave him. We parted on a cordial note, and assured each other that we would soon meet again and have a more leisurely chat. That meeting, however, never materialized.

Some weeks later I got a letter from my mother in which she informed me that she had received a note from Mr. Toth telling her that he had just mailed her a carton full of clothes and that if she needed anything she should let him know and he would be glad to send it to her. My mother, as she wrote to me, thanked him kindly and assured him that she was well and needed nothing. I found Mr. Toth's gesture interesting and characteristic. Being a private tutor in our family he must have felt that he occupied an inferior position vis-à-vis my parents. Now, by sending my mother a gift package and offering to give her other things she might need, he must have felt that he reversed the relationship.

One of the results of my private English lessons was that I was soon far ahead of my class. If I nevertheless did not receive "excellent" marks but only "good" ones, this was due to the fact that in school part of the requirement was that we memorize English poems and long passages from Shakespeare, which I was too uninterested, or too lazy, to accomplish to a degree deserving an "excellent." Nevertheless, I still remember major parts of Antony's speech in *Julius Caesar*, of Hamlet's "To be or not to be," as well as quite a number of poems, such as "You must wake and call me early . . . " and "I met a little cottage girl. . . . "

Another, more important, result of my twofold schooling in English was that, after I had studied it for about a year, I began to read English books and journals. One of the first English publications I read—or, rather, tried to read—on my own was an issue of the *Saturday Evening Post* that I bought at a newsstand because I found its title page with a picture showing a scene from the life of an American family very attractive. I suspect it must have been a Norman Rockwell painting, although at the time, even if I had noticed the name, it would have meant nothing to me. I remember nothing at all of the contents of that issue, or of the subsequent ones that I purchased from time to time. What I do remember is the effort, the struggle, to understand the English text. I had, of course, an English-Hungarian dictionary—it must have been the one compiled by Professor Arthur Yolland, whose student I was to become a few years later at the University of Budapest—but even with its help the meaning of many an English phrase or sentence eluded me. I was annoyed but not discouraged, and went on reading, trying to supply from the context and from imagination what I could not understand. Thinking back on the effort it cost me to work myself up to the point where I was able to understand most of what I read, I think I must have been strongly motivated by a goal I wanted to reach. There was, I am sure, absolutely no outside pressure on me to improve my English, and there were the endless Hungarian and German novels that beckoned and enticed and promised more reading pleasure than I could squeeze into a day. I have no precise recollection of what the motivation was, but I strongly suspect that my desire to get acquainted, through journals and books, with the faraway, great world of England and America must have had something to do with it.

Throughout my childhood Hungary was politically dependent on Austria (a country of which I knew next to nothing), and in both my childhood and adolescence it was culturally dominated by the powerful German *Kultur*. In my own family, German culture was as much part of our lives as Hungarian: we children had our German Fräuleins, Father insisted that we speak to him in German, the encyclopaedia in his library was German, although, as I later found out, a perfectly adequate Hungarian encyclopaedia of the same size (twenty volumes) was available, major parts of Father's library were in German, many of the authors whose works I read, first in Hungarian translation and later in the original, were German, most of the films shown in the Budapest motion picture theaters were German, the first modern foreign language we were taught in school was German, and so forth.

I still remember how in my early teens I ranked nations in an ascending order of importance and excellence. Of the nations located to the east and south of Hungary I had such a low opinion that they simply did not count. Of those nations that did count, Hungary, in my estimation, constituted the base line, and the farther away to the north and west of Hungary a country was located the higher the mark I gave it. This meant that immediately above Hungary stood Austria, and above it followed Germany; Hungary, I knew, constituted a kind of cultural dependency of these two countries. The countries to the west of Germany—that is, France and England—ranked higher, but they were so far outside my horizon that I gave them little thought. Of America, in the mythical distance across the ocean, I had no image at all. But still, it must have meant for me, in a very vague and indeterminate way, the great world, with skyscrapers and huge cities (Budapest at the time had barely one million inhabitants), in which, I imagined, events of global importance took place. As for the war (World War I, of course), which ended when I was eight, I knew that Austria, Germany, and Turkey were our allies, and that Russia was our enemy—but that France, England, and later also America were lined up against us, of that I had no knowledge, or, at least, I have no recollection of having been aware of it.

But, to come back to my determination to master English sufficiently to be able to read it without difficulty, its primary source, I think, was the impression English authors made on me when I first read them in Hungarian translations. For some reason that I can no longer fathom, they appealed to me more than writers in other languages whose works I also read in Hungarian. When I left behind the age at which my interest was focused on, and satisfied by, juvenile authors such as Jules Verne and Karl May, I first read German, Russian, Polish, Scandinavian, French, and English authors in Hungarian translation, then the same authors in German, and while doing so I felt an increasing affinity with the English authors. It was not so much that I could distinguish between the literary quality of the English writers and those of other languages; it was rather that I was attracted to the society, the scenery, and the atmosphere presented in the English novel, and, above all, the character of the individuals who peopled its pages. Thus I became an admirer of Conan Doyle, Bernard Shaw, H. G. Wells, and John Galsworthy long before I was able to read them in English, and, once I was, I became a lifelong addict of the English novel.

I had an especially soft spot for Galsworthy. In the fifth or sixth grade our class produced, on the occasion of one of our school performances, a scene from Galsworthy's play *Loyalties*, in Hungarian translation. I did not take part in the performance, but sat in the audience, and while I was not greatly impressed by the acting ability of my classmates, I still remember the thrill I felt when the boy who played the role of the Jewish protagonist in the play belted out the words, "I am proud to be a Jew!" There was an outburst of enthusiastic applause in which I fully participated. Thinking back on that scene of several hundreds of schoolboys wildly applauding those words, I can see today that it manifested something of which I was not at all conscious at the time: namely, that all of us were, deep down, very much aware of being Jewish, and that we were proud to be Jewish. This was the more remarkable since neither at school nor at home did we ever receive even the faintest intimation that Jewishness was something to be proud of. I can only conclude that our pride in our Jewishness grew spontaneously out of our studies of the Bible, the Hebrew language, Jewish literature and history, and Jewish religion with its rather limited practice we were required to observe.

In any case, those words endeared Galsworthy to me. I started to read his plays and his novels, first in Hungarian, then, as soon as I was able to, in English, and for a long time I considered *The Forsyte Saga* the greatest masterpiece in world literature. And as for the society he depicted, with its civility, its cultured tastes, its sincere friendships, the deeply felt emotions it was loath to allow to surface, its love of art, the amenities of its life, its concern for the feelings of fellow men, it was one of which I would have loved to be a part. In reading Galsworthy and the other English authors in their original language I felt I was becoming a participant in the world they described, a world whose life was on a higher level than that of the German lands, and certainly much higher than that of Hungary.

I was also greatly impressed by what I would call today the technological, organizational, and institutional complexity of the environment in which the protagonists of those novels moved, in which they were thoroughly at home, and which they helped to create. I was impressed by the descriptions of the many things that did not exist in Hungary (or, at least, of whose existence in Hungary I was unaware), such as richly endowed research institutes, agencies for the placement of university professors, the stately country homes of dukes and lords, the luxurious town houses of the rich, exclusive clubs, secret societies, and colonial offices. All this I took for manifestations of the superiority of that society over the one I knew in Hungary. I remember being impressed even by the names of thoroughfares, such as "avenue" and "boulevard," while we in Hungary only had such simple and commonplace designations as *út* and *utca*. The words "continental" and "metropolitan" conjured up in my mind images of the great world, compared to which Budapest was small, provincial, and backward. And yet, paradoxically, I loved Budapest, and on the rare occasions that I visited other Hungarian cities I simply could not understand how people chose to live there rather than move to Budapest, which, compared to those places, appeared to me glamorous and containing everything that made life not only worth living, but fascinating, enticing, exciting.

After I entered the fifth grade of the *gimnázium*, in the fall of 1924, when I was two months short of fourteen, I became interested, and engaged in, so many activities outside school that I remember little of what went on in the classroom apart from our unruly behavior during the English periods. In addition to the private lessons I got in English and Hebrew, and the Talmud studies with Father, I began to play tennis, in which (as documented by snapshots contained in my first photo album) my partners were my classmate Imre Angyalfi, his sister, and a second girl of whose identity I have no idea. Of Angyalfi I have only one recollection. When we both began to shave we would frequently cut our faces, although we used safety razors, and when he came to class with highly visible marks on chin and cheek, I would jokingly taunt him, "Your face is a battlefield!" Thereupon he would simulate extreme rage and make as if he were about to attack me, although, as a matter of fact, we both were very proud of these telltale signs of our budding virility. As we grew taller — we both reached the height of six feet about the age of fifteen — the two of us, occasionally accompanied by a third classmate of similar stature, would march down the street with very determined, manly steps, and were filled with the feeling of having, at long last, crossed the threshold of the coveted world of adulthood, at least as far as body size was concerned. After graduating from high school I lost track of Angyalfi, but years later I heard that he had moved to England, got married, and had a child who died in infancy.

I also grew interested in soccer at that time. Soccer, called in Hungary "football," was a national sport in the sense of having been very popular as both a spectator sport and a sportive activity, and the Hungarian teams always gave excellent account of themselves in international matches. One Sabbath I made an appointment with a number of friends to meet them in the City Park, in which there was ample room for amateur soccer practice, and, since the park was quite a distance from our home, I took the subway. There was at the time one single subway line in Budapest, which we all knew was the oldest in Europe, having been built in 1896, on the occasion of the one-thousandth anniversary of the occupation of Hungary by the Magyar tribes under Chief Árpád. The train consisted of one single car, rather small, which even at that time made the impression on me of being a toy train rather than a real one. Once the train reached the City Park it emerged from underground and traversed the last two or three hundred yards at ground level. I liked to ride this train, and took it quite frequently. The reason I remember that particular ride is that I knew that I was committing a sin by taking the train on the Sabbath, since not using a wheeled conveyance on the Sabbath was one of the rules we children were expected to observe. But I was so eager to reach the playing field as quickly as possible that I knowingly transgressed. When I returned home, after several hours, I was so stricken by my conscience that I could barely look Mother in the face. Father must have been out of town at the time, on a lecture tour, or perhaps on one of his annual visits to Palestine; otherwise, I would have had to stay home on the Sabbath afternoon to study Talmud with him.

On only one other occasion, until going to Jerusalem, that is, did I transgress against the prohibition of using a vehicle on the Sabbath, and that was done inadvertently. Mother and we children were at Lake Balaton for our summer vacation, while Father again was away, probably staying in Budapest in connection with his work. We were at the beach where we spent most of our time when I noticed that nearby, at a wooden jetty, a small one-engined hydroplane was tied up. I was, of course, curious, waded over in knee-deep water, and learned that one could sign up for a ten-minute ride for a modest fee. While I watched the plane, several youngsters paid their fare, got into the plane, and took off. Immediately I decided that this was an opportunity I could not miss, ran back to our cabana, got the required amount out of the pocket of my shorts (I received a small allowance even in the summer for incidental expenses), and ran back to the plane, which was just taxiing back to its mooring place. I took my place among the other boys waiting their turn, paid, entered the plane, and off we went. I have no recollection of any sensation as I experienced being airborne for the first time in my life, but I do remember the curious sight of the lakefront far beneath us, with small, antlike people seeming to rush toward the plane and disappear under its wing. The plane banked, turned around, and the flight was soon, too soon, over. We touched down in the water, and, feeling in a mood for bravura, I jumped out of its door into the water while it was still in rapid motion. Exhilarated by the experience, I ran to Mother to tell her about it. She looked at me with consternation and said, "But today is the Sabbath!" I was crestfallen, ashamed, crushed.

For a short while I took fencing lessons. I can no longer remember what made me interested in that sport—perhaps it was the glowing newspaper accounts of Hungarian victories in international fencing championships. The Budapest papers always reported the victories of Hungarian athletes in the most flamboyant and exaggerated terms. Already at the age of fifteen I felt that there was something ridiculous in a headline such as "The Hungarian Wonder-Swimmer Defeats the Japanese Swimming Monster." As for fencing, I knew nothing about it, but simply went to a nearby fencing school of whose existence I knew because I often passed its sign. When I told the first person I found there that I wanted to take fencing lessons, he asked, "Sword or epée?" I had no idea what an epée was and what was the difference between it and a sword, but was too embarrassed to say so, and answered at random, "epée." I was assigned to a group of beginners, and told to bring along a pair of pants and a towel. However, soon after I started to attend classes I began to feel annoyed by the instructor's insistence that we—that is, my five or six fellow students and I—assume a stance that appeared to me twisted and unnatural, and concluded that I would not become a Hungarian wonderfencer. I dropped out, leaving behind my pants and towel.

My interest in photography was more enduring. I think I received my first camera, into which 1 1/2-inch by 2 1/2-inch glass plates or film packs could be inserted, as one of my Bar Mitzva presents. I also was given, or got for myself, darkroom equipment for developing the negatives and making prints, and used our bathroom for this purpose. I took pictures of members of my family, of myself in a mirror, of interesting buildings and streets of Budapest, of groups in school, and of I don't know what else. A few years later I graduated to a larger and finer camera, and at the same time gave up tinkering in the darkroom, and patronized professional photo laboratories instead. I bought heavy dark brown paper to make my first photo album, and when it was full I bought ready-made albums. I maintained the habit of preserving the pictures I took in albums until I started, around 1950, to take color slides instead of black-and-white pictures. I still have my old albums, but many of the pictures have mysteriously disappeared from them. Those that are left are a spotty record of my progress through countries, homes, women friends, men friends, wives, children, and professional engagements.

When I was thirteen or fourteen I began to go to the movies, and this soon became one of my favorite pastimes away from home. There were several motion picture theaters within five or ten minutes' walk from our home. The biggest and most lavishly decorated was the UFA Theater, which, I think, was owned by a German film company. In the 1920s Hungarian moviemaking was in its infancy, and thus practically all the films I saw were German or American. While we were in Swinemünde (when I was thirteen), one day as I was walking along the seashore I came across the shooting of a scene, outdoors, with the available natural light. There were, I believe, two cameras set up in the sand, and in front of them stood Harry Piel, a well-known German film star. I managed to get close enough to see that he wore some kind of dark makeup around the eyes, and that the lower edge of his whiskers in front of his ears was marked with a black painted line so as to set it off clearly from his cheek. The preparations took a long time, and when they finally started to crank the camera, Harry Piel, facing it, spoke, that is, moved his lips, but I could hear no sound emerging from them.

I remember several silent films I saw. One of the them starred Elisabeth Bergner, Conrad Veidt, and Emil Jannings. In it Jannings and Bergner are man and wife, and Veidt is a poet with whom Bergner falls in love. A memorable scene: Veidt writes a poem for Bergner on a ticker tape, and as he writes it he feeds the tape to her, so that she reads the poem almost simultaneously with its birth. She leaves her husband, who at first is heartbroken, but soon finds consolation in the arms of a woman of easy virtue. Another memorable scene: Jannings sees the woman in the street, turns around and follows her, at which point the camera shows only the two pairs of feet walking, those of the woman in front with the man following her, then slowly the distance between them diminishes, until we see the two pairs of feet walking side by side. Soon thereafter the poet tires of Bergner and leaves her, and she, I believe, commits suicide.

I remember two silent films with the Russian-German actor Ivan Mosjoukine. In one he plays a man who buys a secondhand tuxedo in order to be able to attend a dinner party. Memorable scenes: the owner of the used-clothing store brings out a tuxedo for him, but he finds the price marked on the tag too high. The storekeeper returns with it to the back room and turns the tag around, so that it shows a much lower price. The man buys it. At the dinner he is asked to make a speech—it turns out that he has a God-given talent for speech-making (all this in a silent film!). A political organization employs him to make speeches in person and over the radio for its presidential candidate, whose identity, however, remains unknown to him, and, of course, to the public as well. The line he is instructed to take is to praise the anonymous candidate to high heaven and to assure the electorate that his name would be divulged at the last minute before the elections. While our orator is in the middle of his last radio address, the name of the candidate is handed to him on a slip of paper—it is that of a man whom he hates (love rivalry?), and, doing some quick thinking, he announces instead that he himself is the candidate. The party bosses are appalled, but it is too late to do anything about, and our man is elected.

Of the other Ivan Mosjoukine film, in which he starred together with Brigitte Helm, a beautiful, statuesque German actress, I remember only one scene. The two of them sit opposite each other in a train compartment. They do not know each other. Glances are exchanged, and speak volumes. She drops something (the proverbial handkerchief?), and bends forward to pick it up. At the same moment he, too, reaches for the object. His eyes go to the cleft of her breasts. The fade-out indicates that thereupon something intimate happens between them that in those days films were not supposed to show.

One of the finest silent films I remember from those days is *Metropolis*, starring the same Brigitte Helm. It was a futuristic film in which the bosses of the metropolis lord it over the workers. Memorable scenes: a worker stands in front of a huge dial on which he must move two large arms, and do this for many hours. The new shift of workers comes, those of the old shift exit *en masse*; they are so exhausted they can barely walk. An evil genius makes a mechanical woman in order to use her to excite the workers against the bosses. We see a steel figure of a woman, all cogs and gears and wheels and rods, walk up and down in a try-out. In the next scene the robot is finished: she is a beautiful woman (Brigitte Helm), the exact copy of the woman whom the son of the chief boss of the metropolis loves. The next scene I remember is the one in which the robot-woman is being burned at the stake. While the flames lick at her body she continues to go through the motions she has been programmed to do: she smiles, beckons, flails with her arms, even after the flames have consumed her outer skin and the steel mechanism under it is again revealed. At the end, the son of the boss effects a reconciliation between the workers and the lords of the metropolis, and gets the girl — the real one, of course.

In 1927 the first talking films reached Hungary. In that year I saw *The Jazz Singer* with Al Jolson, and in the same year, or perhaps in 1928, the great German film about the sinking of the Titanic in which Fritz Kortner played the role of a crippled writer who is confined to a wheelchair. I remember especially vividly the scene in which, after the ship hits the iceberg, the people continue to talk, until one of them, becoming aware that the ship's engines have stopped, says, "Listen!" They all fall silent. The engines, whose throbbing was a kind of background music throughout the scene, are silent, too. For several seconds there is total silence, and this absence of all sound had a frightening effect on me, and, I imagine, on everybody else in the audience. By cutting out the sound track for a minute, the director gave a masterly demonstration of the power of the newly introduced dimension of sound. The noisy panic of the passengers that followed and the rest of the film was, I felt, anticlimactic.

In 1930 I saw *The Blue Angel* with Marlene Dietrich and the shattering performance of Emil Jannings as "Professor Unrath," but I saw it again in later years several more times, so I cannot be sure which of these viewings I remember. After 1930 I saw so many films in so many countries that they merge in my memory and I can no longer pick out individual ones as being most memorable.

About the age of sixteen, prompted by my interest in drawing and my awakening libido, I enrolled in an art school. I had hoped that in a drawing class I would be able to sketch nude female models, in which I was motivated at least as much by my adolescent desire to see the naked body of a live woman—I had seen enough paintings and statues of female nudes in art books and museums—as by the wish to draw something really interesting and challenging instead of the monotonous and, to my mind, ridiculous tasks we were given in the weekly drawing lessons in school. What we had to do in our drawing classes at school week after week and year after year was to show that we knew what perspective meant by drawing two or three large white cardboard cubes that our teacher set up in front of us placed one on top of the other at various angles. After the first two or three lessons I was so bored by this primitive task, and was able to finish it so quickly, that I looked about for something else to draw during the rest of the period, and hit on the simple solution of drawing the cubes as the teacher required it, and then proceeding to fill in the background as I saw it from my seat. So I drew behind the cubes the figures of the boys who sat opposite me, and behind them whatever was visible of the walls, doors, and windows of the classroom. I expected some praise from my teacher for this special effort, but all I got was a "Hmmm . . . " and an "excellent" grade at the end of each term.

When my dissatisfaction with all this grew to a sufficient extent to motivate me to action, I located an art school not far from our home, which turned out to be the studio of a painter (name long forgotten). I enrolled, without daring to ask the question that was uppermost in my mind, namely, whether in his school I would have the opportunity of sketching nude models. When I appeared for the first class, I found there four or five other young boys, and, to my great disappointment, far from being presented with a live model, let alone a nude female, the maestro placed the plaster cast of a large Greek head in front of us (I think it was that of Apollo Belvedere), and after a few words of explanation set us to work on sketching it in pencil. Despite my disappointment over the absence of live models, I learned a lot from that master. While we worked, he would go around from bench to bench; we would get up and he would sit down in our place and correct our amateurish attempts, calling our attention to a line, a curve, that we had overlooked, and sketching in lights and shadows that brought the head to life. For two or three months, I believe, I went to this studio, and then had enough of plaster heads and signed out. Never again thereafter did I take lessons in the visual arts, and when I entered the eighth (last) form of high school I gave up drawing and painting altogether, and resorted thereafter to this form of self-expression only on the rarest occasions.

However, when I left that studio, I consulted with Mother and explained to her that I wished to attend a real art school in which I could draw real nude models. She did not like the idea, probably because she was afraid that my mores would be corrupted by the bohemian atmosphere of a studio in which presumably sex-starved young men sat around and leered at an enticing nude female model. Instead she offered to sit for me herself, with her back toward me, and letting her clothes down to her hips. Now it was I who, in turn, found this solution unsatisfactory. The idea was dropped, and my plan to paint nude females was never realized.

My mother's concern with keeping me in a state of sexual ignorance and innocence, I can see today, was as touching as it was, of course, futile. But she felt that women constituted a danger from which she must shield me as best and as long as she could. Once, I remember, Mother and I found ourselves in a place where women performed in a state of considerable exposure. Could it have been a cabaret or a nightclub where showgirls danced with nothing but their breasts and crotches covered? It is highly unlikely, for what would Mother and I be doing in such a place? And if not that, where else could we have faced, in public, women in such a state of undress? Much as I strain my memory, I cannot find the answer. But I do remember clearly that, glancing sideways at Mother, I caught her eyes resting on me with a worried expression, as if she were trying to gauge the effect of all that female nudity on my adolescent susceptibilities.

She was also worried lest I entangle myself with women in a different sense. When I was sixteen, my father arranged for me to visit, during a school holiday, his brother Shimshon (Shimshi) Klein in the town of Gyöngyös. My uncle Shimshi was the only one of the Klein siblings to remain, not in the village of Gyöngyöspata itself, where all of them were born, but in the nearby town of Gyöngyös, where he had a grocery store, as had his father before him in the village of Pata. When I left home, Mother said to me half in jest and half in earnest, "Now, don't you get engaged to any girl while you are there!" I had no idea why she found it necesary to sound this warning until I arrived at the home of Uncle Shimshi and found that he had several daughters, the oldest of whom was a year or two younger than I. Much later I understood two more things in connection with that motherly caution: that engagements at a very young age were still quite common in traditional Jewish circles, and that marriages between the children of two brothers were, at least in theory, preferred to other liaisons.

Of my visit to Uncle Shimshi I remember only two things. One is that I had great difficulty in falling asleep because, as soon as the light in the room was turned off, mice began to scutter around on the floor. At first I heard them, then I saw them in the dim light. I was not frightened, but they made me feel acutely uncomfortable.

The other thing I remember is our visit to the village of Pata, to see the house in which Father was born and spent the first ten or eleven years of his life. Uncle Shimshi hired a carriage that took us in about an hour to Pata (the distance is six miles), waited there for us, and then took us back to Gyöngyös. I would no longer remember how the house looked, but luckily I had with me my camera, and in my earliest photo album I find two contact prints of the snapshots I took of Father's birthplace. The pictures, which I myself developed and printed, are very faded, but one can still recognize the house: a simple, square, one-story building, with plaster walls, a slate roof (at the time my father lived there it had, he told me, a thatched roof), windows framed in white, and two large trees before it. In front of the house stand, lined up, two corpulent women and four lean men, evidently the people living in the house at the time. Uncle Shimshi showed me the well in the courtyard that Father had dug when, after earning his doctorate at the University of Budapest, he was able to afford this gift to his parents. When I returned to our apartment on Podmaniczky Street, it seemed opulently luxurious compared to the place where my father had spent his childhood.

To bring to a close what I remember and know of Uncle Shimshi and his family, let me add that he visited us a few times in Budapest, staying overnight, but not eating anything Mother cooked. Although Mother kept a kosher kitchen, her cooking was not kosher enough for Uncle Shimshi and his kind of very Orthodox Jews, because—*horribile dictu*—she wore no *shaytl* (peruke), as required by Orthodox custom, nor did she hide her own hair under a kerchief. Orthodox rigorism considered the cooking of such a woman untrustworthy as far as *kashrut* (kosherness) was concerned, and therefore, when mealtime arrived, Uncle Shimshi spread out a newspaper on the table, put on it two slices of dry bread, and broke open two hard-boiled eggs that he let Mother cook for him, and this was all he ate. In 1944, after the Germans occupied Hungary, he, his wife, and all his children except one became victims of the Holocaust. The only one who survived, Catharine (Kató), was by that time in Sweden. She had contracted tuberculosis as a youngster, and was sent to a Swedish sanatorium before the outbreak of World War II. In the course of time Kató was cured, married a Swedish Gentile, had a son, divorced her husband, and settled with her son in Israel where she remarried and lives to this day.

I have so far not mentioned Freud among the authors whom I read as a teenager. Since I have read Freud on and off in the course of many years—most recently I found it necessary to consult some of his writings while I was working on my book *The Jewish Mind* in the 1970s—I find it difficult to pinpoint the time in my life when I first became aware of him and first read him. However, I am quite sure that I started reading him in Hungarian translation, from which I conclude that I could not have been older than fourteen or fifteen, for after that age I read all German authors in the original. In any case, either before or shortly after that age I read his most popular works, *The Interpretation of Dreams, The Psychopathology of Everyday Life*, and several others.

In 1925 I found in a bookstore a copy of the fourth German edition of Freud's *Totem und Tabu*, which was published that year. I devoured it. It was in it that I first met the names of James George Frazer, Andrew Lang, Ernest Crawley, Wilhelm Wundt, Adolf Bastian, Edward Westermarck, Herbert Spencer, Edward B. Tylor, S. Reinach, R. R. Marett, Spencer and Gillen, Emile Durkheim, William Robertson Smith, C. G. Jung, and others who later became household names for me and many of whose books I was to purchase and cherish for decades as mainstays of my library. To say that I found *Totem und Tabu* an eye-opener would be an understatement. I felt that it opened new horizons for me. It transported me into the midst of worlds whose very existence had been totally unknown to and unsuspected by me. The sweep with which, in order to prove his point, Freud brings together data from primitive peoples in the four corners of the world, the ease with which he lifts out points supporting his argument from what seemed to be a vast literature in many different languages, his occasional interjection of the first person singular in statements such as "I shall now . . . " or "I shall forego . . ." —all this enchanted me, carried me away, and made me feel that by merely reading that book I had embarked upon a great voyage of intellectual adventure across the seven seas.

Needless to say, I read *Totem und Tabu* totally uncritically. I felt that it placed in my hands the key to the understanding of a wide range of basic phenomena in human history and culture, and the working of the human mind. It was only many years later, when I reread *Totem und Tabu* in connection with my own research interests, that I noticed that this idol of my youth had clay feet, and I still remember how this very insight at first seemed to me something of a sacrilege.

My youthful enchantment with Freud, and especially with *Totem und Tabu*, was, even before I finished high school, extended to Frazer, who was Freud's chief authority, and whose *Golden Bough* I first read in an abridged German translation. And as late as 1941, when I was working on my two-volume book *Man and Earth in Hebrew Custom, Belief, and Legend* (published in Hebrew, in 1942 and 1943 by the Hebrew University Press), I wrote to Frazer in Cambridge, described to him what I was doing in that book, and asked him to write a preface for it. Postal communications between Palestine and England were sluggish during the war years, and only much later did I learn that Frazer had died that very year. My admiration for *The Golden Bough* was, among other things, expressed in my insistence that my *Man and Earth* be bound in cloth of the same shade of green that is a hallmark of all the dozens of Frazer volumes published by Macmillan. And—to my great gratification—when Professor William F. Albright reviewed my *Man and Earth*, he termed it the Hebrew-Jewish counterpart of *The Golden Bough*. In later years, as I became acquainted with modern anthropological approaches and perspectives, I grew gradually disillusioned with both Freud's eclectic and selective use of anthropological sources and Frazer's encyclopedic comparativism, but I shall never forget the magic spell *Totem und Tabu* cast upon me.

Throughout my high school years, all my diverse interests, and above all my passion for reading, made me neglect my schoolwork, and my marks deteriorated ominously. I had trouble with several subjects, and barely squeezed through in Latin, nature study, history, and mathematics. I manifested a special antitalent in math.

On one occasion, our math teacher, Dr. Biró, a man with heavy glasses, bushy eyebrows, and an intimidating manner, drew a triangle on the blackboard, then called me up and asked me to use that triangle in presenting the proofs of the Pythagorean theorem. I went to work at the problem; Dr. Biró watched me for a while, then interrupted me and said scathingly, "You forgot one thing. The Pythagorean theorem applies only to a right triangle, and as you can see the one I drew on the blackboard is not a right triangle." Mortified, I went back to my seat, and whatever slight interest I may have had in mathematics was therewith extinguished once and for all.

In addition to my lack of interest in several of the subjects taught at school and my aversion to spending my time memorizing Hungarian, German, English, and Latin poems and the intricacies of Latin syntax, I came to like school less and less because of another circumstance that developed beginning with the fifth grade and that had nothing to do with the school curriculum. I had become a member of the Zionist youth group called Blue-White (*T'khelet Lavan* in Hebrew), and in class I made no secret of my Zionist convictions. This aroused the antagonism of several of my classmates, some of whom engaged in a veritable campaign of persecuting and abusing me. They derided me for being a Zionist, called me names, pushed, shoved, and hit me whenever they could. I, of course, hit back and fought back, and before long I felt I was in an enemy camp. True, I did also have friends in class, some of whom, such as László Schwarz and Imre Angyalfi, I have already mentioned, while of another, Dezső Stern, I shall speak later, but none of these friends shared my Zionist convictions and enthusiasms, so that I felt like a maverick in my almost daily confrontations with my anti-Zionist antagonists. The interesting thing is that we never discussed the issue of Zionism *versus* Hungarian patriotism, which might have cleared the air. It never came to marshaling arguments pro and con, and the differences remained throughout on the level of verbal abuse and fisticuffs.

More peculiar still, despite my fervent Zionism, I cannot remember a single thing about that Blue-White group, neither a single one of the boys who were my co-members and who, of course, shared my views, nor anything of the activities we engaged in. All I can recall is that I did go frequently to the offices of the Hungarian Zionist Organization on Király Street, which also served as the clubhouse for the Zionist youth groups of Budapest, and that we learned to sing Zionist songs in Hungarian and Hebrew. After some time in the Blue-

White I switched to another Zionist group of older boys, called Barissia, of which, too, I remember nothing, except for its marching song, the words of which were written by János Giszkalay, a brother of our teacher Solomon Widder. We sang that song with great enthusiasm and so many times that I still remember most of the words. As I recite them to myself now, they appear to me, to my regret, as very primitive, inferior lyrics, but in those days all I knew was that they spoke of the heroic stand of the last fort in Jerusalem, the Barissia, which resisted—according to the song—the Roman onslaught a long time after the rest of the city had fallen.

In the first six years of high school Mr. Solomon Widder was our teacher in Jewish religion and Hebrew language, to which five periods a week were devoted. When entering the seventh year, we found that Mr. Widder had been replaced by a new teacher. We learned that the powers that be in the Israelite Congregation of Pest, to whom our school belonged and who controlled its curriculum and the employment of teachers, had decided to relieve Mr. Widder of his Hebrew and religion classes because he did not have a rabbinical diploma or a Hebrew teacher's certificate. He was a certified teacher of Hungarian and German, subjects he also taught us and continued to teach us through the seventh and eighth grades. We students liked Mr. Widder, who was a fine teacher and knew Hebrew at least as well as any graduate of the Rabbinical Seminary. In addition, we all felt a certain loyalty to him becuase it was he who had seen us through our Bar Mitzva preparations and celebrations. We were indignant at his removal from the religion and Hebrew classes, although he not only continued to teach us Hungarian and German but also remained our form master. I do not know whether it was as a result of these feelings that we consciously decided to demonstrate our displeasure by making the life of the teacher who took his place, Dr. Mór Fényes, miserable, but we certainly proceeded to do precisely that.

Dr. Fényes, whose biography is contained in the *Hungarian Jewish Lexicon*, was a graduate of the Budapest Rabbinical Seminary and a recognized Jewish scholar. He was the author of a textbook on Jewish religion, an introduction to the Bible (of which I still possess a copy), and numerous other studies on Hebrew language and Jewish religion. At the time he became our teacher he was past sixty, a small, frail man, with glasses and a little goatee, who was totally

unable to impose discipline upon our class of more than fifty sixteen-
and seventeen-year-old boys. As soon as the class noticed his weak-
ness, during the very first moments after he first entered our classroom, we, I am ashamed to say, made the most of it. We were
noisy, unruly, spoke out of turn, and I don't know what else—subsequent embarrassment probably blocked it out of my memory. In
retrospect I wonder whether Dr. Fényes was able to teach us anything at all in that bedlam. Things reached the point where the
chairman of the education department of the Israelite Congregation
of Pest, who was not an educator but a rich Jewish industrialist, felt
constrained to pay us a visit, to reproach us and demand that we
behave properly in the classes taught by Dr. Fényes.

The education chief entered our classroom in the company of
our principal. He was a small, stocky man with a well-rounded stomach and a stance that exuded what we boys all felt was enormous
self-importance, nay, arrogance. He harangued and threatened us
that, unless we mended our ways, "I shall send down my subordi-
nate authorities" (I remember the very words) and have the ring-
leaders summarily expelled. I can no longer remember whether this
stern warning had any effect, probably it had very little if at all, but
I can still remember the rage and loathing I felt, and I know also my
classmates felt, toward that bloated, self-assured, arrogant plutocrat
who, we imagined, was responsible for removing our beloved Mr.
Widder from teaching religion and Hebrew.

I had to stop here to try to remember his name. It took me some
minutes to overcome a memory block. It was Samu Glücksthal. Checking in the *Hungarian Jewish Lexicon* I find that he was born in 1864,
was a lawyer and political leader, and in 1927 was made a member
of the Hungarian Upper House of Parliament, which roughly corresponded to the United States Senate, so that his appearance at our
school took place either directly before or shortly after his appointment to that high position. I also find that he was one of the five
vice-presidents of the Israelite Congregation of Pest. He must have
been, like the entire leadership of the Congregation, an anti-Zionist,
and it is my suspicion that he engineered the suspension of Mr.
Widder from teaching religion and Hebrew not so much because
Widder did not have a rabbinical diploma—nobody could cast any
doubt on his qualifications as a teacher of those subjects—but because
he was known to be a Zionist, whose brother, János Giszkalay, was a
leading Zionist in Rumania, and the leaders of the Congregation no

doubt wanted to prevent him from infecting his students with his Zionist sympathies.

Dr. Fényes frequently spent part of the periods by giving us written tests in class. He probably did this because while we were busy writing we were forced to be quieter than otherwise. He would write a number of questions in Hebrew on the blackboard, and we had to copy them and give the answers in Hebrew. For me, by that time fairly fluent in reading, writing, and speaking Hebrew, the questions were simply too elementary and easy. I finished jotting down the answers in a few minutes and was always the first to hand in my paper to Dr. Fényes. Once, after having given the answers, I wrote on the remaining blank part of my test paper, in Hebrew, "Why do we have to write so much, instead of speaking Hebrew?" And then, overcome by a childish desire to demonstrate to the taecher how well I knew modern Hebrew, I added a total *non sequitur*: "Is it true that they are building a radio station in Palestine?" which gave me the opportunity to use the Hebrew neologism for radio, *al-ḥut* (literally, wireless), which word has long since fallen into disuse. When I got the test paper back, I found that Dr. Fényes, while disregarding my second question, did answer the first. He wrote, in Hebrew, "For the writing is the writing of God" (a quote from Exodus 32:16), by which he seemed to indicate that to know how to write in Hebrew was more important than to know how to speak it.

Undaunted by the treatment he received at the hand of his bosses in the Congregation, or perhaps in defiance of it, Mr. Widder announced at the beginning of the spring term of the seventh grade (in February 1927) that he was planning a summer tour of Palestine, informed us of the details, and asked us to consult with our parents as to whether we could sign up for it. He explained that the forthcoming summer vacation between the seventh and the eighth (the last) year of our *gimnázium* studies would be the last real vacation time in our lives, for after finishing school our summer would be taken up by efforts to get into a university, or to obtain a job, and in no way would resemble the carefree summer vacations between school years to which we had been accustomed. Therefore, he said, the forthcoming vacation was the last opportunity for us to take a trip as a group, and to experience something truly memorable.

Needless to say, I was enthusiastic, and could barely wait to get home and obtain Father's consent (and financing). To my great disappointment, he refused. I no longer recall in detail what he said, but the gist of it was that he planned to let me go to Palestine after I finished high school, for a full year, or as long as I wished, and therefore it made no sense to go that coming summer for a short trip of a few weeks' duration, which was good enough only for tourists. I had no choice but to acquiesce, but the sense of keen disappointment remained with me for a long time.

To my surprise, a considerable number of my classmates, including several of those who used to vilify me as a Zionist, signed up for the trip. What their true motives were in doing so I have long forgotten, or perhaps never knew, but I do remember one of them announcing to a group of friends that he was going because he had learned that the women in Palestine had pointed breasts—a statement that was received with great glee by the others. I kept my peace, but inwardly I was enraged at this vulgarity and concupiscence. I felt that the presence of boys such as these in the hallowed land would somehow desecrate it, and it pained me even more that such contemptible characters would see Palestine, while I, who wished to go there from the loftiest of motives, had to stay behind. When we assembled again after the summer vacation, I must have been still smarting under this affront to my Holy Land by my classmates, and consequently I never asked them a single question about what they saw and did in Palestine.

As the above incident shows, many of my classmates in the seventh grade (when we were sixteen to seventeen years old) had either long passed the stage of initiation into heterosexual activity or, at least, tried to make it appear that they were sexually experienced. But I, after my preadolescent encyclopaedia research on sexual information shared with my friend Laci Schwarz, never again exchanged as much as a single word about sex with any of my classmates throughout the remaining five years of my high school attendance. Whatever my sexual feelings at the time, the atmosphere in which I grew up in my parents' house was such that it seemed absolutely impossible for me not only to seek sexual contact with a woman but also even to discuss sex with my classmates. My normal, regular, and frequent sexual outlet had been, since I was about fourteen, masturbation to orgasm, which was to continue, with lesser frequency, even after I began to have heterosexual relationships at the age of twenty. I still remember having had orgasms, that is, intense sensations of pleasure followed by a feeling of relief and satisfaction, for quite a while before I had ejaculations, and having been surprised, as well as frightened, when I first experienced a discharge of fluid from my penis. I thought I must be bleeding, got out of bed, and turned on the light to inspect myself. When I saw that it was not blood but some kind of whitish fluid, I was reassured, but still did not know what it was until a renewed search in the *Meyers Konversations Lexikon* and some other reliable sources set me straight. Although this manner of providing myself with a sexual outlet never gave me complete satisfaction, it still gave relief and an easing of the sexual tension that was extremely strong in me, and enabled me to engage in no more than moderate flirting, kissing, and necking with girls of my own age, without ever having resorted to prostitutes as, I believe, most of my classmates had.

In the seventh grade the curriculum was enriched by a subject called "health study." I assume that this was in conformity with the study plan developed by the Ministry of Education, whose experts thought that the age of sixteen to seventeen was the time for boys to be told the facts of life. Accordingly, the health study course, to which one hour a week was assigned, consisted mostly of divulging to us the secrets of sex, with which all of us had long been acquainted, and the emphasis was on how to avoid becoming infected by venereal disease and what to do in case one nevertheless did contract it, despite all the precautions that were recommended. This course was taught by our school physician, who once a year examined all of us in the school surgery. We had to undress completely, the doctor looked us over, listened to our heart and lungs, and dictated whatever he found to his assistant who sat behind him at the desk. If he noticed some sprouting of pubic hair, he said "Incipient puberty," which his assistant duly wrote down on the boy's chart. I think he also looked at our eyes, throat, and nose, and palpated the glands in the neck. He was a jolly and friendly man, and probably a competent doctor, but he had not the slightest idea of how to control a class of fifty youngsters, in whom a discussion of sexual matters evoked, to say the least, great hilarity. Although I no longer remember details, I know that what the class did to the poor doctor was even worse than the treatment Dr. Latzkó and Dr. Fényes received at our hands. He was absolutely helpless, although he was a great hulk of a man, and all he could do was to repeat in desperation, "What kind of new swinishness is this?" As for the information he imparted to us, I remember only one concrete detail. He explained that if one of us got infected with syphilis, it was not the end of the world, and, provided one got the proper treatment, one could live even twenty years with it.

At the end of the seventh grade, after which I had only one more year to go before finishing high school and facing the problem of admission to the university, my report card was worse than in any of my previous six years in school. I got a "sufficient"—the lowest passing mark—in Latin, history, and mathematics, "good" in English, physics, and health studies, and "excellent" only in religion, Hebrew, Hungarian, German, and drawing. When I brought home my report card, Father asked me to come into his study, sat down behind his desk, bade me sit opposite him, and proceeded to treat me to a very serious talk. While I no longer remember his words, I do recall what he wished to convey to me. After finishing high school, he said in effect, the next step in my life would be to go on to the university. This had been our understanding for many years—it was so self-evident that we never even had to discuss it. The admission of Jewish students to the university was limited by law, the infamous *numerus clausus*, to 5 percent of the total admissions because the number of Jews in Hungary was 5 percent of the total population. Year after year many more Jewish students applied for admission to the country's universities than were accepted. Naturally, only the best Jewish students were admitted, those with the best *matura* (high school diploma), and not even all of them. Father had friends in high places, and could and would try to pull strings to have me admitted, but he could do nothing at all unless I earned a high school diploma with the highest marks. Therefore he expected me to pull myself together and work hard during the coming school year, because, as I undoubtedly understood, my entire future would depend on my being a *prematurus*, a student who got "excellent" in at least four of the five subjects of the final exam. Judging from the marks I earned in the following year, I must have taken this fatherly admonition to heart, and made a serious and successful effort to upgrade my record. And never again thereafter did I give Father reason to reproach me for neglecting my studies or not working hard enough.

In the eighth grade the unruliness of my class diminished appreciably. We were older, more serious, and felt that we would soon leave the school and that the long period that saw our transformation from children to adults was drawing to a close. And there were, of course, the impending and dreaded final exams, which cast their shadow over us and loomed before us as a painful ordeal we had to weather. In addition, two of the three teachers who were unable to discipline the class, the school physician and Dr. Fényes, no longer taught us in the eighth grade, and the only remaining weak link in the chain of strict disciplinarians. Dr. Latzkó, seemed to reap some benefits from the consequent general improvement in class behavior.

Dr. Fényes was replaced by Dr. Miksa Weisz as our teacher of religion and Hebrew. The *Hungarian Jewish Lexicon* informs me that Dr. Weisz, born in 1872, was a graduate of the Budapest Rabbinical Seminary, the rabbi of one of the district synagogues in the city, a leader in reorganizing Jewish religious education in Hungary, and the author of numerous important Jewish scholarly studies. Shortly after he became our teacher in the high school, he was appointed professor at the Rabbinical Seminary, where I became his student. At the time I knew nothing of Dr. Weisz's scholarly accomplishments. What impressed me as well as all my classmates was, first of all, his uncanny ability to keep perfect order in class with seemingly no effort at all, and, secondly, his esprit, his humor, and his knack of making every subject he discussed interesting, in fact, riveting. He was a small, stocky man, whose eyes sparkled behind his glasses, and it was in him that I first encountered the phenomena of male charm and prepossessing personality.

The religion and Hebrew classes of Dr. Weisz were always the last periods in the school day, and when he finished his class he would ask me to go down to the street corner and fetch a fiacre, while he went to the teachers' room to get his hat and coat. He lived just a few blocks away from our house—we lived at no. 6, and he at no. 39, Podmaniczky Street. By the time I arrived back with the carriage, he was waiting at the school entrance. He would climb up into the fiacre (by the way: the New York Central Park carriages are the exact duplicates of those fiacres in Budapest) and sit down next to me, and we would ride in state to his apartment house. During the ride, which may have lasted about twenty minutes, he would engage me in conversation, and although I remember nothing of what we talked about, he must have known how to draw me out and make me tell him what I thought of various subjects, for once my father reported to me that he had run into Dr. Weisz at a meeting, and that Dr. Weisz had told him that I "had quite a world view." This compliment made me very proud, although I am not at all sure that I knew what precisely was meant by a world view.

My efforts to improve my marks bore fruit, and at the end of the first term of the eighth grade I earned five "excellent" and seven "goods," with not a single "sufficient." At the end of the second term, which was the end of my last year in the high school, I added two more "excellents," and reduced my merely "good" grades to five. That last term at school was entirely overshadowed by the impending *matura* exam, scheduled to take place within a few days after the end of the term. In contrast to all the previous school years, which ended on June 29, the eighth grade concluded its term on May 14 (1928). The *matura* examination, which alone qualified a high school student for admission to a university or other institution of higher learning, was not an internal affair of the school, as were all the preceding exams, but an official state examination, supervised by a school inspector delegated by the Ministry of Education. Since the standing of a school in the educational hierarchy of the country depended to a great extent on the performance of its students at these *matura* exams in the presence of the inspector, the policy of the school was to make sure, as far as possible, that the students gave a good account of themselves at these all-important orals. Fortunately, the putting of test questions to the students was left entirely to the teachers of the subjects in which they were examined, while the inspector merely sat there observing the proceedings. This made it possible for those teachers who were so inclined to let their students know in advance, in an indirect way, what kind of questions they planned to ask them, and thus to enable the students to prepare themselves.

The *matura* exams included only five of the twelve subjects we had studied in the eighth and preceding grades. They were Hungarian, Latin, German, physics, and mathematics, I believe. I remember nothing of how we prepared for four of these five subjects, but I do remember the proceedings in the Hungarian language and literature course taught by Mr. Widder. In the last few weeks prior to the end of the term he said he would review with us the material we had to know for the *matura*. He proceeded by naming a subject, and asking for a volunteer to review it then and there in the class. Then he went on to another subject, and another student volunteered to review it. When he asked for a review of the descriptive poetry of Sándor Petőfi (Petőfi was one of the greatest Hungarian poets, who died at the age of twenty-seven in the 1848 Hungarian revolution against Austria), I held up my hand, Mr. Widder called upon me, and I presented what I knew of the subject. Somehow all of us knew, without ever being told so by Mr. Widder, that the question a student volunteered to discuss would be the one Mr. Widder would put to him at the *matura* exams. This gave the student ample opportunity to read up on his subject and to prepare himself thoroughly. I passed the exam in Hungarian with flying colors, getting an "excellent" in it, and also did so in three of the other four subjects, although I do not remember having received any such helpful hint as given us by Mr. Widder. The only subject in which I got a "good" was Latin. Since four *A*s and one *B* made a student a *prematurus*, the road was now open before me to apply for admission to an institution of higher learning.

Although under the pressure of the approaching *matura* I spent most of my time in the eighth grade studying, I nevertheless found it possible to devote a few hours every day to reading. By that time I read only a few books in Hungarian, more in German, and most of them in English. Since I knew of no public library in Budapest from which I could have borrowed English books, if I wanted to read an English book I had to buy it. Fortunately, most of the books I was interested in reading were available in paperback, which cost relatively little. They were published by the great German publishing house Tauchnitz, whose name became synonymous for me, as for thousands of English readers outside England, with the English novel.

Besides studying and reading there were girls, who by that time played an important role in my mental world. Almost all of the girls I knew were classmates of my sister, which meant that, apart from mild flirtation, there was nothing doing with them. So I did engage in mild flirtation with several of them, without becoming emotionally involved, as proven by the fact that I no longer remember, with the exception of one, either their names or their faces. In those days my sister and I were frequently invited to house parties, which were all-night affairs given mostly by one of her classmates. The parents of the hostess were usually absent, or, after greeting the guests, discreetly retired to their bedroom. The parties would begin with a buffet dinner, then followed hours of dancing to music supplied by a phonograph. Of the popular tunes I remember the one whose lyrics were in German and started with *Valencia, deine Augen glühn und saugen mir die Seele aus dem Leib. . . .* (Valencia, your eyes glow and suck the soul out of my body . . .), and another one whose lyrics were in Hungarian: *Szép, gyönyörű város Barcelóna, de nem az a fő, hanem a nő* . . . (A beautiful, splendid city is Barcelona, but that's not the main thing but the woman . . .). At a typical house party the rooms were very dimly lighted and there were cushions around the walls on which we could sit when we got tired of dancing, and where kissing and light necking could be engaged in. If the party did not break up until dawn it was a sign of success.

Once at such a party a girl (name forgotten), with whom I danced and sat in a corner, surprised me by putting her head on my shoulder and saying, "Gyuri, love me." Could it be, I thought, that here was a girl who had fallen in love with me, and who, moreover, was willing to go further than the usual kissing and teasing? I took her phone number, called her, and went to see her with great anticipation. The visit turned out to be a disappointment. She behaved as if she had never uttered those inflaming words, and I, in my habitual shyness, did not dare even to kiss her. I never saw her again.

It was the custom in those days that after one was invited the first time to a house party one would, a few days later, pay a return visit to the hostess. This visit was called *reconnaissance*, which, for us, meant "getting acquainted again." I have a vague recollection of several such visits, and in all of them I found the hostess to be more reticent than she had been at the party itself.

The one girl who constitutes an exception among the many whose names and faces I have long forgotten was Rózsi Csányi. I was in love with her for a while, although she did not stir me as deeply as Lilla Rozsnyai had five years earlier. Rózsi was a classmate of my sister, a blonde with straight silky hair parted on the left side of her head and falling to her shoulders, with light blue eyes, white skin with large pores, a broad face, and a cast of features that vaguely reminded me of a Greek head. My sister, Rózsi, and a third girl, Ilus Schäfer, formed a trio of best friends. Rózsi had a cousin, a few years older, by the name of Péter Somlyó, who courted my sister in the same innocent and ineffectual way, I believe, in which I courted Rózsi. We used to take walks as a foursome on the Margaret Island, with Peter and my sister either walking ahead of me and Rózsi, or lagging behind us at some distance, along deserted paths under the huge wild-chestnut trees, so as to allow each of us to enjoy some privacy. Or else the four of us would go to the movies, or to house parties. I gradually overcame my shyness, and tried to make use of whatever privacy these outings afforded us to kiss and hug Rózsi, but she was a rather reluctant partner who invariably rebuffed my timid approaches. Once, in a movie house, when under the cover of darkness I put my hand on her knee and began to caress her naked thigh, she tolerated it for a moment or two, and then whispered to me, "If you don't stop this I shall move away to another seat." In brief, she always managed to keep me to strict limits. This relationship between me and Rózsi did not change even in my college years when I again courted her for a while.

Looking back at these two experiences with Lilla and Rózsi, which must have been the most important ones for me or else I would not remember precisely them while having forgotten the others, I can see that they not only contributed to my shyness with girls in general, but created in me the conviction that decent girls simply did not allow boys to come near them physically, even to the extent of kissing and hugging them. Thus it was not until the age of twenty, when I went to Breslau and there met German Jewish girls who were much freer in their relations to boys, that I first had sexual intercourse. And it took me quite a while to digest the idea that a girl could have sex with a boy and yet remain a "decent" girl.

As far as I remember, and as far as I can ascertain by going through the volumes of Father's monthly, my first piece of writing was published when I was seventeen. It was a brief review of the novel about Shabbatai Zevi by the Russian Jewish author S. Poljakoff, which was published at that time in a German translation. The review, signed modestly, or more probably by Father's decision, only *P. Gy.*, the initials of my Hungarian name Patai György, appeared in the January 1928 issue of *Mult és Jövő*.

Some time before that, probably at the age of sixteen or seventeen, I began to write poetry, in Hungarian, of course, the bulk of which is lost, but several examples of which have survived in a copybook I subsequently took with me to Jerusalem and from there to New York. It gives me a peculiar feeling to see my immature handwriting and to read those juvenile poetic attempts, which—and of this I am quite sure—I never showed anybody. In fact, I would have been mortified had my parents, both of whom were accomplished poets of genuine talent, found out that I dabbled in versifying. It was part of my most private life, of which, I felt, nobody must know.

The poems themselves, as I can judge them from this time-distance, are less than mediocre at best. They show the unmistakable influence of Endre Ady, the great early-twentieth-century Hungarian poet. Incidentally, it was characteristic of the highly conservative nature of my high school, which in this respect differed in no way from all the other Hungarian schools of the time, that Hungarian literature, as far as the school was concerned, ended in 1900 and that the name of Ady was never even mentioned. But at home, where the atmosphere was suffused with an appreciation of art and literature, I inevitably not only learned about Ady but acquired a deep admiration for his poetry, which I have retained to this very day. (I still have a volume of his collected poems on the nightstand next to my bed.) Ady, who lived for years in Paris and was influenced by Baudelaire, Verlaine, and Rimbaud, was certainly as great a poet as the author of *Les fleurs du mal*, and in relation to the Hungarian poetry before him was a much more significant figure, towering high above his predecessors and contemporaries. He was and remained the unequaled master of mood, evocation, conjuring-up of images, and, above all, he was able to play with the language with a gripping mastery and originality, molding and kneading it at will as a sculptor does with clay, which only those who can read it in Hungarian can appreciate. Occasionally at night when I cannot sleep I still recite to myself an Ady poem I know by heart, and try, not in writing but in my mind, to translate it into English, invariably to my deep dissatisfaction with the result.

Just as it was inevitable in the Patai family in the 1920s to acquire an admiration for Endre Ady, so it was inevitable that when I tried my hand at poetry I should do so under his influence. That a poem had to have rhyme and rhythm went without saying. That it had to express thoughts and feelings in intense or even exaggerated imagery was likewise a *conditio sine qua non*. My early poetic attempts had a goodly share of these features. Actually, the only thing I can say for those juvenile efforts is that behind and beneath all that extravagant Adyesque verbiage and cadence, the poems of sixteen- and seventeen-year-old György Patai express the restlessness, the impatience, the ambitions, the expectations, the *Sturm and Drang* of a youth who did not know where he was heading, but was convinced that he was destined to reach commanding heights in life. Thus, while I don't consider those early poetic attempts in Hungarian (or those that were to follow them, from 1929 on, in German) worth remembering *per se*, they do have a meaning for me as a singular and eloquent witness of the mental state I was in (at least from time to time) in those years.

The copybook, which somehow escaped getting lost in the course of my moves from country to country and from home to home, contains a miscellany of drawings and writings from the year 1928. On the first page there is a pen drawing of a nude male figure, stepping forcefully forward, with his left arm raised high above his head, while his right arm, as counterbalance, is swung sharply back, so that the whole body gives, or tries to give, the impression of motion, thrust, tension, impetus. This is followed by three brief essays, one on the Spanish Jews, the second on the biblical Moses (which concludes with the words, "Moses the man died on Mount Nebo, but Moses the liberator, the lawgiver, Moses our teacher, lives forever!"), and the third on the renaissance of the Hebrew language (whose upbeat finale is, "The Hebrew language has already been renewed. This renewal is the harbinger of the national revival of Jewry, which is an event of the greatest global historical significance in the post war period").

The next few pages contain thoughts and aphorisms, such as:

> Aristocracy is the class composed of those who excel over their fellow men through a divine gift. And a divine gift is something that can be acquired neither by physical nor by mental exertion, nor by any other means. I know of only two kinds of aristocracy: that of talent and that of beauty.
>
> There is only one certainty in life: death.
>
> Happy are the poor in spirit for theirs is the kingdom of heaven— happy are the rich in spirit for theirs is the kingdom of thought.
>
> A poem is like a pearl. A pearl is genuine only if it is the fruit of the oyster's malady. A poem is genuine only if it is the fruit of the soul's malady. Fortunately, much of both is counterfeit.
>
> Human life is like a lightning that flashes between two great nothingnesses. Most lightnings disappear without a trace. But some strike the earth and leave behind a gigantic spoor. That is the life of a person of value.
>
> Happiness is creating.
>
> God = nature + something that is still unknown.
>
> A beautiful woman is like a glittering stone. If it is soulless, it is mere glass, and its glitter is false, empty. If it has a soul, if it is animated by an internal fire, it is a true gem, an immeasurable treasure.

Following these aphorisms there is a quatrain that reads in literal translation:

Today György Patai began to sing,
The song-spring burst forth from his soul,
An artesian well had to be sunk
So difficult it was to find this spring.

Finally, there are several poems in the copybook, all dated 1928, which show that I was preoccupied with problems of life and death, with breaking out of the confines of the present and conquering the future, and that I saw myself in a cosmic perspective. Conspicuously absent are love poems, despite the fact that in that very year I was in love with Rózsi Csányi, and, more briefly, with other girls as well.

However, since Rózsi refused to let herself be drawn into even the mildest form of necking, in my frustration I conceived the idea that I would write an erotic fairy tale, read it out to her, and thus arouse in her a positive response to my ardor. So, on January 29, 1929 (I know the date because I jotted it down on the opus itself), I wrote what at the time appeared to me a most daring erotic fantasy. I titled it "Pagan Symphony." Written in the first person, it tells how through the forest of death I approach the gate of the garden of life, which I find locked behind a wall. Through a peephole I see that the garden of life is dead, too. The gate is guarded by a dragon (detailed description of its huge size, its fiery breath, etc.). I kill it by shooting an arrow into its heart. Thereupon the gate of the garden springs open, and the garden itself comes to life. A description of the wonderful flowers, birds, and so forth, in the garden follows. Then—I encounter you. I look into your eyes, and know yearning, pain, and love. We walk amidst red roses, white lilies, pink flamingos, and golden peacocks. Nightingales sing to us, we see naked nymphs cavorting with goat-legged fauns, and on a faraway hilltop we see the great Pan himself playing his daring tunes on his seven-throated flute. At the foot of the garden the blue sea awaits us.

A fresh, sweet wind blows, and the white crests of the waves open as if about to give birth to a new Aphrodite. White-bodied Nereids and dark-skinned Tritons embrace playfully on the backs of the billows, and the powerful symphony of life rings in our ears.

And I put my strong arm around your waist, and lift you into my softly dancing boat. The fresh wind puffs out the sail, and lets the little ship soar ahead. And the waves rock and the breeze lulls, and the boat glides silently over the blue waters. Frolicsome dolphins race us, and white gulls flit about in the air. And the waves rock and the breeze lulls, and the boat glides silently over the blue waters.

The sun sinks red into the sea, and we look up to the thousand-colored sky. And, behold, the firmament splits open above us, and amidst the clouds we glimpse the splendid assembly of the Olympian gods. And our lips fuse in a divine kiss, and I know happiness.

I shall refrain from giving any expression of my present opinion about the literary quality of this early attempt. I shall instead report only that as an effort at literary seduction it was a total failure. I can still quite clearly remember what happened. I went to visit Rózsi; we sat down in the elegantly furnished living room of her parents' apartment, and I read out to her what I had written. I had planned in advance that when I read the words, "And I put my strong arm around your waist . . ." (I even remember that I had considered writing "slender waist," which would have sounded better in conjunction with "my strong arm," but then, since Rózsi's waist was anything but slender, decided against it), I would actually put my arm around her waist. When I did, I noticed a slight stiffening in her attitude, but, undaunted, I read on. And when I reached the punch line, "And our lips fuse in a divine kiss . . ." I tried to fuse our lips, but the kiss turned out to be anything but divine, for she turned her head away, and all I could do was to plant a peck on her cheek, catching a whiff of the medicinal cream she used to improve her complexion. She immediately stood up, and therewith my magic garden, blue sea, birds of paradise, and Olympic company disintegrated before a frustrating reality.

Nevertheless, I did continue to see Rózsi, on and off, for more than a year. One evening she and I took a walk along the Danube embankment, and stopped at a place where there was a narrow cobbled walkway between the water and the long riverside warehouses. I kissed her, and she, while not exactly responding, did not seem to object. Neither of us noticed that a policeman had come around the corner of the warehouse and approached us. When he was but a few steps from us, he startled us by addressing us sternly, "Hey, what are you two doing there?" What mumbling answer I managed to give I forget, but I remember that the cop came up to us, bent sort of forward and down to see whether we were in any way indecently exposed, which would have told him that we were engaged in something more than kissing—of course we were not—and then ordered us to leave the place forthwith. It was an unpleasant scene. Rózsi silently cried all the way home. I said good-bye to her at the street door of her apartment house, and walked home quite depressed. I confided to my sister what had happened. She advised me to send or take Rózsi a bunch of roses, which I duly did the very next day. I enclosed a poem I wrote in the dead of the night, the last poem I wrote to her, and, I believe, the last one I ever wrote in Hungarian. I said above that I never showed my poems to anybody. In writing that I had members of my family in mind. Let me qualify that statement by adding that I did show some of them to the girls to whom they were addressed.

I still remember in connection with the poems I wrote, first in Hungarian, and later in German, that when ever I worked on a poem I felt challenged by the task of finding an appropriate expression for my thoughts and feelings, and, at the same time, of putting what I wanted to say in rhyme and rhythm. It was, in fact, more than a challenge, it was a struggle that often kept me absorbed for hours. But then, when I did find what I considered the right form, I was overcome by a feeling of a veritably sensuous satisfaction, and I repeated the rhythmical and rhyming lines several times, actually reading them aloud to myself, although in barely more than a whisper, letting the rhymes roll back and forth on my tongue, like a connoisseur who tastes a new wine. This simile, incidentally, is anachronistic, for I had to reach the age of fifty before I started to enjoy wine.

7

At the Technical University: 1928

I have not the slightest recollection either of my "maturity" exams themselves or of the summer of 1928 that followed it. As for my plans for higher studies, after repeated discussions with Father, we reached an understanding to the effect that I would apply for admission to the Mechanical Engineering Department of the Budapest Műegyetem, the Technical University. This came about in a rather roundabout way. My father wanted me to study at the Rabbinical Seminary, of which he himself had been a student for a short while. By the time I finished high school I knew modern Hebrew quite well, and had a passable familiarity with the Bible, thanks to the efforts of Mr. Eckstein, and with the Talmud, to which I was introduced by Father. I was also used to observing the basic rules of religion, which were part of our home life. In addition, I was tall and of a slender stature, possessed a certain self-assurance in demeanor, had a pleasant baritone voice, and was the opposite of tongue-tied. Conclusion—a fine career as a rabbi seemed to be a good prospect for me.

But I thought otherwise. I had strong objections to a rabbinical career, not so much because of what I would have to do as a rabbi, but because of what I would have to forego. In those days a Hungarian rabbi, even one of the Neolog congregation (there were no Reform congregations in Hungary), had to lead a rather restricted and austere life. All the rabbis I knew wore only black or dark grey suits, could not—or, at any rate, did not—attend any public gathering except for those of a most serious nature—they were never seen in a movie house, a concert hall, a theater, or an opera, not to mention such "lewd" places of entertainment as cabarets or dances; nor did they engage in such sports as tennis, skiing, swimming, sailing, horseback riding, and the like. Not that I had done much of any of these things up to that point in my life (nor, for that matter, thereafter), but the very idea that by becoming a rabbi I would cut myself off from the possibility of engaging in such pleasurable activities was sufficient for me to take a very dim view of the rabbinate as a career.

One detail reemerges in my memory as I think about my reluctance to embark on a rabbinical career. In my last few years as a high school student I loved to dance. To dance with a girl was for me the greatest, in fact, the only, erotic pleasure I could derive from the opposite sex. When I put my arms around a girl's waist, pressed my body against hers, and moved in unison with her to the rhythm of a tango or a fox-trot, I got a taste of what it would be like to have sexual relations with a woman. One of the things a rabbi in those days in Hungary definitely could not do was to dance, and when I contemplated a rabbinical career what came foremost into my mind was that it would mean giving up this one and only enjoyment that the mysterious world of girls held for me.

To these negative considerations was added one of quite a different nature. I had a modicum of talent for drawing and painting. Although I did not practice these arts assiduously, I liked to draw, and when the opportunity arose I did engage in sketching people, figures, heads, and landscapes, and I fancied myself a potential painter. I still have in my possession several small sketches I made of my classmates in the last few years at school, showing them standing at attention while being quizzed by a teacher; while I have no way of judging whether these drawings were good likenesses, they are of sufficiently individual character to make me believe that they were.

By a coincidence I had in the junior or senior year of my high school studies an opportunity to get closely acquainted with architectural drawing. Some years earlier Father had purchased a sizable building plot in Buda, at the corner of Nyúl (Rabbit) and Fillér (Penny) streets, in one of the finest residential sections, located on a gently sloping hillside from which there was a broad view of the Pest side of the city. Some time later he sold one half of it, and planned to build a small apartment house on the remaining half. For several months there were intensive and pleasurable consultations with architects (I even remember the names of two of them: Mr. Bodánszki and Mr. Irsai) who submitted plans. Father, Mother, and I studied these plans closely, suggesting some changes, and I prepared sketches

of these suggestions. I even participated in negotiations with prospective tenants. I remember one woman who came to our apartment in Podmaniczky Street, very elegantly dressed and beautifully
made-up. She was, it soon transpired, an avid tennis player, and
since I also liked to play tennis at the time, we discussed the possibility of having a tennis court on the top of the building we were
planning. She was enthusiastic, and asked me to show her a plan so
as to give her an idea of how that could be accomplished. A few
days later, plan in hand, I went to her apartment, and was sorely
disappointed, in fact, shocked, when the door was opened by a
middle-aged woman with no makeup, with a wrinkled face and stringy
hair, in whom I barely recognized the glamorous lady who had visited us a few days earlier.

In any case, my ability to draw, and my interest in architecture,
made me decide that I wanted to become an architect. Father reluctantly agreed, and Mother talked it over with her brother.

Mother's brother, Dr. Bertalan Ehrenfeld (Uncle Berti), two years
younger than she, was a highly successful corporation lawyer, and in
that capacity sat on the boards of several large Hungarian banks. I
remember that he once told us that he had five desks in the city. He
was a friendly, good-natured man, always dressed elegantly, used a
walking cane, and wore black-rimmed glasses that gave him a certain resemblance to Harold Lloyd, whose movies were popular in
those days in Budapest. There was a strong mutual liking between
Uncle Berti and me. When I was still a small boy, I remember that
whenever he came to visit us he would turn to me and say, *Na te kis
ember*?! (Well, little man?!). One of the desks Uncle Berti had was
that of legal counsel to Ganz-Danubius, the largest machine factory
in Hungary, which had its main plant on the island of Csepel, just
outside Budapest. Founded by two Jews, Berthold Weiss de Csepel
and his younger brother, Baron Manfred Weiss de Csepel, this factory started out by producing canned food, then branched out into
munitions, employing 30,000 workers during World War I; after
the war it built agricultural machinery and other iron and metal
products.

When Mother discussed with Uncle Berti the question of what
kind of studies I should choose, he suggested that instead of taking
architecture, in which field I would have to struggle hard to make a
living and get ahead, I should study mechanical engineering. Once I
had my degree in that field, he said, he could get me a fine position

with Ganz-Danubius, and my career would be assured. The advice seemed to make sense, and Father, undoubtedly with some reluctance, agreed. As for me I had no clear picture of the difference between the study of architecture and mechanical engineering, but the prospect held out before me by Uncle Berti was enticing, and so I, too, agreed. I duly submitted my application to the Technical University, asking for admission to its department of mechanical engineering.

Since I was a *prematurus*, that is, had the highest grades in my high school diploma, Father assumed that this would be sufficient to secure my admission. He turned out to be mistaken. My application was rejected, which came as a shock to both Father and me. Now Father had no choice but to start pulling strings in order to have my rejection reversed. I have no idea what he did, whom he contacted, and what influences he was able to bring to bear on the University authorities, who, although all Hungarian universities were state institutions, were supposed to be totally autonomous. I suspect, although I have no basis to do so, that he must have spoken to Professor Ignác Pfeiffer, who was his good friend and co-leader of the Pro Palestine Federation of Hungarian Jews, and was a full professor of chemical technology at the Technical University.

Whatever happened behind the scenes, after a delay of perhaps three weeks, I was admitted. The registration book that I still have in my possession states that on October 9, 1928, "Mr. Ervin György Patai, born in the city of Budapest in November 1910, of the Israelite religion, was admitted to the Royal Hungarian Joseph Technical University as a regular student" in the division of mechanical engineering. On October 11 the dean signed my registration book, attesting that I had been duly registered, and the page facing his signature contains those of the professors, which students had to obtain both at the beginning of the term and at its end, the latter attesting that they had indeed attended classes. Attendance was obligatory and was strictly monitored. I remember that when I went to my medical examination, which all students had to undergo at the beginning of each year, and I therefore had to miss a class, the doctor reassured me that being in his office constituted a valid excuse for not attending class.

During my short stay at this school I had no contact whatsoever with students or teachers. I found the atmosphere in the huge cold marble halls, corridors, and classrooms of the building most oppressive. Anti-Semitism was rampant in those years at Hungarian universities, and Jewish students were beaten up with almost clockwork regularity within a few days after the annual fall registration period had come to an end. Apart from this situation, which made me expect any minute to be, at least, accosted by "race-protector" rowdies among the Christian students, there was an adulation of authority that, already at that time, I found ridiculous. What I mean can best be illustrated by an incident my brother Saul related to me some ten years later, after he had come to Jerusalem. He was sitting in the classroom waiting for Professor Ilosvay, who was also the author of the introductory textbook of chemistry used in his classes. My brother was studying, in preparation for the class, the internationally known chemistry text by Treadwell, when the professor's assistant happened to pass by, and, seeing Treadwell's book in my brother's hand, said to him indignantly, "What, you believe Treadwell rather than the *Méltóságos Ur* [Dignified Sir]?!" referring to the professor by the title all full professors were accorded. The title alone placed its bearer on a pedestal high above the run-of-the-mill assistants, not to mention the lowly students.

While obtaining the signature of the dean I underwent what to this day has remained the most humiliating experience in my life. We stood there, some ten or twelve students—I assume the others were latecomers like me—in a line, waiting for the dean to enter. It was a large room, with a high ceiling and huge windows. The very fact that I had to line up among students whom I knew to be Christians and assumed to be anti-Semitic filled me with unease. Finally the dean entered, and asked each of us two questions: "What is your name?" and "From which high school did you graduate?" I was frightened. I thought that if I answered that I was a graduate of the high school of the Israelite Congregation of Pest, the other students would, after being dismissed by the dean, waylay me in the corridor and beat me up. So when my turn came, I answered, "I graduated from the Abonyi Street High School." Abonyi Street was the street on which my high school was located, and numerous high schools in the city had, in fact, no special name but were called after their street. The dean was puzzled, and said, "I don't know of such a high school." I timidly repeated that I was indeed a graduate of that high school, whereupon the dean pointed to the phone book that lay on his desk, and said, "Show me the name of that school in the phone book." I stepped over to the desk, and found, of course, no such high school listed in the directory, whereupon I turned to the letter "p" and found there listed "Pesti Izraelita Hitközség Reálgimnáziuma," that is, Real-Gymnasium of the Israelite Congregation of Pest, with the address, Abonyi Street. I pointed out the entry to the dean, whereupon he gave me a scornful dressing-down right there in front of all those Gentile boys who by that time, I was convinced, were my sworn enemies. "Being Jewish," said the dean, "is nothing to be ashamed of," and he went on berating me for quite a while. I felt annihilated. I was unable to utter a word, let alone explain to him that I was not at all ashamed of being Jewish, that I was simply afraid of being beaten up by anti-Semitic students who roamed the corridors in packs and fell upon every Jewish student they encountered. When the dean dismissed us, I slunk away mortified, and hurried out of the building as fast as I could.

Before leaving this painful subject, I think I should explain how the anti-Semitic students knew who was Jewish. In appearance, clothing, demeanor and speech most Jewish students were indistinguishable from the Gentiles. Still, there was no need to resort to pulling off pants and examining penises, as was done occasionally in the heyday of the White Terror of the early 1920s. (In Hungary only Jews were circumcised.) All these "race-protector" students had to do was to demand to see the university identity card that every student had to carry, which stated, as did the registration book and other documents, the religion of the bearer. There it was written clearly, "Religion: Israelite." If a student refused to produce his card, they knew he was Jewish and beat him up; if he did show it, and it read "Israelite," they beat him up.

It so happened that nobody beat me up that day, nor on any other day during my years of study, but that was a matter of sheer luck. One morning, soon after the incident with the dean, I entered the huge amphitheater-like hall in which another "Dignified Sir" gave his lecture on general mechanics, and, as I was about to sit down in one of the back benches, as was my wont, my eyes caught two handwritten notices tacked to the back well. One read, "I shall come tomorrow," and was signed "Simon Hirig." *Hirig* was a Hungarian slang word, derived, through the Yiddish, from the Hebrew *hereg*, meaning killing, slaughter. In Hungarian it was used in the sense of beating up, and there was even a Hungarian verb derived from it, *hirigelni*, to beat up, the equivalent of the Yiddish *hargenen*. (Both words are contained in the great Hungarian-English dictionary of László Országh, published in 1963 and reprinted many times thereafter). I had never before heard of Simon Hirig, but, since the term *hirig* was familiar to me, I understood it instantly. Simon Hirig, I instinctively grasped, was the quasi-mythical person-ification of the Gentile Hungarian "race-protector" student, out to beat up Jews. The second notice read, *ÉME a zsidó fiuk réme* (ÉME, the dread of the Jew-boys). ÉME was the well-known acronym of Ébredő Magyarok Egyesülete, the Union of Awakening Hungarians, a right-wing, strongly anti-Semitic organization, which not only was dreaded by "Jew-boys," but was perceived as a serious threat by Hungarian Jewry as a whole.

Since the beating of Jewish students in the Hungarian universi-ties was an annual ritual, I knew I had to take the warning seriously. But, I thought, if Simon Hirig says he will come tomorrow, then today there will be no attack on Jews. What I did not take into account was that the notice might have been posted a day earlier, and I simply had not seen it. Thus, after the class I went to a draft-ing room, located in a remote wing of the building, and sat down to work on some mechanical drawing I had to prepare. I was all alone in the room, and worked for several hours. Late in the afternoon I finished, packed up my gear, and left. In the long corridor, on the huge stairway leading down to the main gate, I met not a soul, which was quite unusual. When I reached the main entrance door, I found that it was locked. I knew that there was a side entrance at one corner of the building, went there, and was relieved to find the door unlocked. I exited, and went around on the outside to the main entrance. There, tacked to the middle of the huge bronze door, was a proclamation by the rector stating that because of dis-turbances that had taken place on the premises that noon, the insti-tution was closed with immediate effect until further notice. I hur-ried home. Next day I read in the papers that several Jewish students had been seriously beaten, two of them thrown down the stairs, one suffering a broken arm.

In addition to these painful and discouraging incidents, my inter-est in being a student in that school greatly diminished when I found that, having missed the first three weeks of classes, I was unable to understand much of what the teachers discussed. As for approaching an assistant or a fellow student and asking for help, what I had experienced at the school made me too timid to make such a bold move. In general I was not shy, but the atmosphere of the huge building, with its broad and menacing marble stairway, its endless corridors, and the crowd of students among whom there was not a single face I knew and all of whom I imagined to be hostile, overwhelmed and intimidated me. I had spent the preceding eight years of my life in a Jewish high school, the people whom I met in my parents' house were almost exclusively Jewish, and this meant that, with one or two rare exceptions, such as an occasional Gentile visitor, and the super of our house, I had not had a personal conversation with a single person of my age or older who was non-Jewish. And now I was suddenly thrown into a Gentile environment in which, although there must have been a few Jewish students and teachers, I had not met any, and where any group of colleagues I encountered would, as likely as not, be looking for an opportunity to beat up a Jew. I therefore felt I must make myself as inconspicuous as possible, and I was simply unable to address another student with a request.

In circumstances such as these must lie at least a partial explanation of the pursuit of anonymity, the desire not to be recognized as a Jew—much later I was to term it Marranism—that was a general trait of the Jews of Budapest, with the exception of the Hasidic Jews, who wore long beards and sidelocks, long black kaftans, and black velour hats with a broad rim and low crown, all of which advertised their Jewishness from a distance. These, however, were a small minority among the Jews of the capital city, many of them new arrivals from East Europe. They were looked down upon by the native (or assimilated) Hungarian Jews, and derided as *Galizianer*, Galicia being the easternmost province of Austria, which after World War I became a part of Czechoslovakia, and from which, in fact, at least some of the Hasidic Jews had come. *Galizianer* was a term of contempt; it meant a Jew who was unkempt, dishonest, sly, and untrustworthy, who spoke Hungarian, if he spoke it at all, with an ugly foreign accent, and whose presence in Hungary, as the "native" Hungarian Jews liked to assert, created, or at least contributed to, Hungarian anti-Semitism. *Galizianer* would have been the designation unhesitatingly applied by assimilated Hungarian Jews to my paternal grandfather, R. Moshe Klein of Pata, although in fact he and his father before him were natives of Hungary.

I remember Father once telling me that whenever his father came to Budapest to visit him (which happened very rarely), he, of course, would go to meet him at the railway station, which was at a distance from our home. He did not take a cab back home but walked with his father all the way carrying his suitcase, lest his father think that he was ashamed to be seen in the street with an old, bearded, sidelocked and kaftaned Jew, in a word, with a *Galizianer*. I was duly impressed, and still am, by Father's sensitivity in sparing his father's feelings. But today I recognize that, in addition to filial respect, this act was also a demonstrative protest on Father's part against the generally prevalent Marranistic attitude of Hungarian Jews, for whom not being recognized as Jewish was a dominant concern.

I, on the other hand, I must confess, was sufficiently intimidated by the atmosphere at the Technical University to fall into line, during my brief few weeks as a student there, with precisely that typical behavior pattern of the average Hungarian Jew. But even so, the situation became so oppressive that a week or two after the experiences described I began to consider withdrawing from the institution. After all, I rationalized, I originally wanted to study architecture, and now I found myself a student of mechanical engineering, which evidently was not my cup of tea. Why, then, continue to struggle against unfavorable odds? Then something happened that, so to speak, took the decision out of my hands. Late in 1928 Uncle Berti died, at the age of forty. With his death, which was a tragedy for his parents, his wife, and his two sisters—his three children were still too small to feel the full impact of having lost their father—the main basis for my studying mechanical engineering suddenly disappeared.

Uncle Berti was sick for only a few weeks before he succumbed to what I believe must have been some intestinal disorder. I remember being told that his belly had swollen to huge dimensions and that the fluid accumulating in it had to be drained off several times, which was done through a tube inserted into his abdominal wall. I also remember the last time I saw him. I went to visit him in the hospital, and was waiting in the corridor. He was brought out from a room in a wheelchair, looked at me, smiled sadly, without saying a word, and then was wheeled on and disappeared behind another door.

A few days later my sister and I were at a house party. Those were still the days when we gave, and went to, parties that began in the evening after supper and lasted until daybreak. At about two in the morning, just as we were becoming tired of dancing and settled down in the almost entirely dark rooms on cushions along the walls, the phone rang. Our hostess, who was present in order to keep a wary eye on what was going on at her daughter's party, answered it, then called me to the phone. It was Mother. She sounded terribly upset and said that Uncle Berti was extremely ill and we should come home right away. We did, of course, and went to bed, and I still remember how, in a mixture of fear and rage, I stormed heaven, repeating voicelessly again and again, "O God, don't let him die!" In the morning I was awakened by our grandparents coming into our apartment, Grandmother crying silently, and Grandfather sobbing aloud, unrestrained, with tears running down his cheeks. Uncle Berti, we were told, had died in the early hours of the morning.

I don't remember his funeral. But I do remember my grandparents and other members of Uncle Berti's immediate family sitting *shive* (as the Hebrew word *shiv'a*, seven, was pronounced), observing the traditional Jewish mourning ritual, which, in the main, consists of sitting on the floor, or on a low stool, from morning to evening for seven days after the funeral (except on the Sabbath), receiving visits of condolence from friends and relatives, praying every morning and evening with a quorum of ten men gathered for the occasion, and, in the course of those prayers, reciting the kaddish, as the prayer for the dead is called in Hebrew. I also remember very vividly the difference between the reaction of Grandfather and Grandmother to losing their only son so suddenly and at such a young age. Perhaps a mother's love for her son is deeper than a father's, and for this reason Grandmother was more devastated by Uncle Berti's death than Grandfather. But there was undoubtedly also another factor that made Grandfather less, and Grandmother more, smitten by the death of their son. Grandfather was a deeply religious man; for him it was axiomatic that God's ways are inscrutable, that whatever happens to us is willed by God, and that we must accept and acquiesce in God's will. Grandmother, although she, too, observed scrupulously all the precepts of Orthodox Judaism, had a more questioning mind, and I suspect that she was not as readily able to accept that it was the will of God that her son should die. Hence Grandmother suffered more than Grandfather, and was not able to recover from the blow as fully as he did.

One scene from those seven days of the *shive* has remained in my memory. It was the entrance of Uncle Ede into the room where the mourners sat. As he came through the door and saw his sister and brother-in-law and his nephew's widow and sisters sitting on their low stools in the traditional, age-old Jewish posture of deep mourning, he stopped for a moment, and burst into a deep bellow, an animal cry the like of which I have never heard in my entire life. Later somebody, I don't remember who, but certainly a person with an evil tongue, said that the great pain displayed by Uncle Ede was at least partly due to the fact that, always being in straitened financial circumstances, he either actually did receive, or felt he could always count on receiving, some financial support from his nephew Berti, who was by far the most well-to-do member of the family.

At this point I stopped writing and phoned my aunt Ruth, the widow of Uncle Berti, to get some more concrete details about him. Aunt Ruth, née Frank, born and bred in Frankfurt on Main, lived in Manhattan and was eighty-five years old in 1984, but her memory was perfect to the extent of being able to recall the smallest details of events that took place more than sixty years ago. She was glad to receive my call (I had not spoken to her for several months), and we started to chat by bringing each other up to date about our children and grandchildren. Then, in reply to my questions, she told me that she and Uncle Berti were married on August 31, 1921, and that Uncle Berti died of peritonitis (she gave the name of the illness in German, *Bauchfellentzündung*), on October 28, 1928. She remembered that he had four (and not five) desks, one in his own law office, the second as attorney of the Hitelbank (Credit Bank), one of the largest banks in Budapest, for which he had organized an international department, the third as legal counsel to the Hungarian automobile dealers' association, and the fourth as attorney of the Yugoslav consulate in the city. He was not, she said, counsel of Ganz-Danubius, but the director-general of that great industrial complex, Paul Prager, was his best friend. In fact, it was from Prager that Uncle Berti bought the plot on which he built his villa on Maros Street, in Buda, while Prager retained the other part of the same plot and built his own villa on it, so that they were next-door neighbors. And she added, without my asking, that she still believed that Uncle Berti's death was a fated thing. Had the same illness struck him just a few years later, he could have been saved with antibiotics. It was precisely in 1928 that Sir Alexander Fleming discovered penicillin.

After I said thank you and good-bye to Aunt Ruth and hung up, I considered for a moment checking over what I had written before I called her, and correcting some factual details in the light of what she had just told me. But, on second thought, I decided that I would rather leave my version unchanged so that it remains an account of what I have retained in my memory from those days, even if it does not tally exactly with the historical facts.

Although the death of Uncle Berti was my first experience of what it meant to lose a loved one (the death of my paternal grandfather a year earlier did not touch me closely since I barely knew him), I have no recollection of how I felt when it happened. Still, it must have affected me deeply, not only because his memory was to remain with me all my life, but also because, on and off, I had a recurrent dream about him for decades after his death. In my dream Uncle Berti suddenly returned. One day he simply walked in and continued his life with his wife and children as before. His return filled me in my dream with a feeling of great joy. At the same time I wanted to ask him where he had been and why he had stayed away for so long, but somehow I never had the opportunity or the courage to put the question to him. Always after this dream when I woke up and realized that Uncle Berti was, after all, dead, I was overcome by a feeling of great sadness.

After Uncle Berti's death, which suddenly made my studies of mechanical engineering seem pointless, I could have switched to architecture, which I had originally planned to study. But my experiences at the Technical University up to that point had been so unpleasant, indeed so painful, that to study anything, even architecture, in that institution had lost all attraction for me, and all I wanted was to get out of there as quickly as possible. A family palaver duly ensued, and it was decided, with my concurrence, that I would do what Father had wanted me to do for a long time: I would take up rabbinical studies at the Francis Joseph I National Rabbinical Seminary. However, I made Father understand one thing clearly: engaging in Jewish studies did not mean that I obliged myself to embark upon a rabbinical career. What I would do once I completed my studies at the Seminary was left in abeyance. Since all students of the Seminary also had to study at the Faculty of Philosophy of the University of Budapest and earn their Dr. Phil. degree, there seemed to be other possibilities as well. This decision determined once and for all the framework and direction of my entire future life.

The first thing I did after this decision had been reached was to stop attending classes at the Technical University. I dropped out several weeks before the end of the first term, which lasted until the middle of December 1928. Only once thereafter did I again set foot in that forbidding building: I was required, in order to keep my record in order, to notify the registrar's office in person that I withdrew. I postponed this as long as possible, and finally took care of it on May 5, 1930.

8

Swiss Interlude: 1929

I have absolutely no recollection of how I spent my days from December 1928, when I stopped attending classes at the Technical University, until May 1929, when I went to the yeshiva in Montreux. It is probable, but this is merely a conjecture, that under the guidance of Father I studied the subjects constituting the Jewish part of the curriculum in the lower division of the Rabbinical Seminary, which was a kind of prep school for its college division. The course of study in the lower division took five years, although its secular studies corresponded to the four upper years of an academic high school. The fifth year was added in order to make up for the fewer weekly hours devoted to secular subjects, since about half of the daily periods were given over to courses in Hebrew, Bible, Talmud, Jewish history, and so forth. The one thing I seem to recall is that during those months I read all or most of the German three-volume abridged edition of *The History of the Jews* by Heinrich Graetz; at least I remember the peculiar smell of the printed pages of those volumes, and the interest I took in Graetz's vivid descriptions of the literary and scholarly achievements and of the vicissitudes of the Jews through the three millennia of their history.

Despite my long Sabbath-afternoon sessions with Father over the course of many years, which amounted to an excellent introduction to the Talmud, he felt that I was still not sufficiently grounded in my grasp of that huge compendium of Jewish law, lore, and life. He therefore suggested that I spend a term at the yeshiva of Montreux that had been established a year or two earlier by a rabbi of Russian extraction by the name of Eliahu Botschko. Father's plan was for me to spend some three months at that yeshiva, and thereafter to meet him and Mother in Zurich, where Father was to attend the Sixteenth

Zionist Congress and the founding convention of the Jewish Agency that was to follow it. The idea appealed to me, and early in May, I believe, I took the train to Montreux. This was the first time that I traveled abroad alone, and I felt very grown up and independent.

Upon arriving in Montreux I was, at first sight, most favorably impressed with the town, which I glimpsed as the taxi took me from the railway station up the hillside. As the view expanded, and my eyes could take in the beautiful sight of the curving shoreline, the blue waters of the Lake of Geneva, the romantic Chateau Chillon at some distance, and the magnificent white serrated peaks of the Dents du Midi beckoning from afar, I felt I was in a wonderland, so different was it from anything I had seen before. I also liked very much the luxurious and spacious villa high up on the hillside that the yeshiva occupied. It stood on its own grounds, surrounded by a good-sized garden with evergreens and leafy trees and a number of flower beds. Most of the rooms on the ground floor were used as classrooms; one of them served as the dining room, another as Rabbi Botschko's office. An impressive curved stairway with heavy wrought-iron balustrades led up to the second and third floors, where the students' rooms were located. At the back of the stairway there was a large stained-glass window showing a female figure surrounded by thick foliage, the originally nude upper part of her body pasted over with thick black paper. A few days later, while walking about in the garden, I discovered the statue of a nude female that had been pushed back deep into the midst of a cluster of tall and dense bushes. The purpose of both concealments was, of course, immediately obvious: the religious sensitivities of the management of the yeshiva were offended by pictorial and plastic representations of female nudity, and it took steps to prevent its charges from laying eyes on these manifestations of un-Jewish immorality.

Those charges, as I soon found out, were thirteen- to fifteen-year-old boys, all from Orthodox Jewish families from Central and Western Europe, whose parents had sent them to the new Montreux institution because it offered a traditional East European type of yeshiva education coupled with all the amenities of a modern Swiss boarding school. As soon as I got to know my fellow students and my teachers, I felt again, as at the Budapest Technical University, an outsider, although this time for quite a different set of reasons. First of all, I was eighteen, some two years older than the oldest of the other students, and at that age two years really made quite a lot of difference: compared to them I was a mature young man. Also, I had a far more liberal attitude to religion than the students and the teachers and was the proud possessor of a more advanced secular education and of what I considered a superior knowledge of Jewish history and the historical development of Jewish religious literature.

The room I was assigned was already occupied by two boys of about fourteen. It had three beds, ample closet space, and an enchanting view of the lake. As for my studies, I was put into the most advanced Talmud class taught by a young rabbi from Frankfurt on Main, a certain Mr. Schwab. He was a somewhat corpulent young man of perhaps twenty-five, and, in keeping with the type of Judaism represented by the Frankfurt *Trennungsorthodoxie*, or Secession Orthodoxy, as it was called because it separated itself from the less observant majority, he struck me as extremely Orthodox in both outlook and deportment. The only concession he made to modernism was that he shaved his beard, no doubt by using a chemical depilatory approved by Orthodox rabbis, and thus made quite a contrast to Rabbi Botschko, who had an untrimmed, flowing black beard. Since I was older than the other boys, and probably also in order to prevent them, as far as possible, from being contaminated by the less-than-Orthodox views that I was suspected of harboring, I was seated in the dining room not at one of the students' tables, but at the table occupied by Mr. Botschko himself and his faculty of five or six young talmudic luminaries.

At first everything seemed to be going well. We spent all day, and I mean literally *all* day, with the exception of time out for the morning and afternoon-evening prayers, studying the Talmud, as this was done in the most conservative East European yeshivot. Although I remember nothing of what precisely we studied, which tractate of the Talmud was our subject, and what method was used by the instructors, I am sure that my knowledge of the Talmud must have increased to no small extent during the weeks I spent in the institution.

Once in a while, under the supervision of one or two instructors, we were taken on trips. I remember one of these excursions in particular: we took a boat from Montreux across the lake to its southern shore, to St. Gingolph, which straddled the Swiss-French border. The ship laid to on the Swiss side of the town, and from there we took a stroll across the border, guarded by a single Swiss and a single French soldier, neither of whom took the slightest notice of us. We explored the French town, where—how memory retains insignificant little incidents!—I bought a bottle of French eu de cologne, which, I thought, must be much cheaper in France than in Switzerland. I did, of course, not know the prices of such items in Switzerland, and I have long forgotten why I was interested in buying eau de cologne at all. Another time we went to Evian, again by boat.

On other occasions, two or three fellow students and I undertook shorter private excursions to the immediate vicinity of Montreux, such as the famous Chateau Chillon, which I had espied in the first hour of my arrival and which was familiar to me from Byron's "The Prisoner of Chillon." I had read it perhaps two or three years before, and although my English had been not quite up to understanding all of it, it made a tremendous impression on me. I also went a few times up into the mountains overlooking Montreux, and I still remember the surprise I felt when, on the way up, I saw large, silvery aluminum milk cans along the street, deposited in front of the gates leading into the gardens that surrounded the beautifully kept villas. How remarkable, I thought: anybody passing by could pick up these cans and walk away with them. People in this country must be both very well-to-do and very honest. In Budapest, such a can, whether full or empty, would disappear within a few minutes after being left unsupervised in the street. What I do not remember, and I am sorry I don't, is how and from whom I got permission to take these walks, which surely meant missing classes.

A snapshot, dated Vaux, June 1929, which I find in one of my photo albums, shows me and three other boys, all obviously younger, sitting around a table on the terrace of a café or hotel, and enjoying what, to judge from the shape of the glasses before us, must have been ice cream. Each of us wears a hat, obviously in deference to the religious custom we all observed even when away from the yeshiva itself. I took the picture, using an automatic exposure device I was very proud to possess.

Soon after my arrival in Montreux I went down to the business section of the town and had my head shaved. I no longer remember why I did it. It could be that I noticed the first signs of thinning at the hairline over my forehead, and since both Father and Uncle Berti were bald, I may have thought that the same fate awaited me unless I did something about it. Cutting the hair short, I may have heard or read somewhere, could prevent baldness. On the other hand, it is quite possible that the instructors at the yeshiva had reminded me of the ritual rule that required that an observant Jew wear his hair short, so that, when putting the *tefillin* (phylactery) on his head there should be no *meḥitza*, separation, between it and his head.

Some time after I had subjected myself to this prophylactic or ritual hair cutting, I received a phone call at the yeshiva. The caller was a Mrs. Krausz, one of Mother's good friends. She said she and her daughter Kató—whom I had met a number of times in Budapest—were passing through Montreux, and she had promised Mother to call and find out how I was. If I was free, they would be glad to see me. I was, of course, free, and the same afternoon I walked down to the lakeshore and met Mrs. Krausz and Kató in a café. The only thing I can recall from the meeting is that throughout the hour or so we spent together sitting at one of the terrace tables, I never once removed my cap, because I was embarrassed to let them see my shaved head.

In the midst of my term at the yeshiva the town of Montreux celebrated its annual *Narzissenfest*, Feast of the Narcissuses. It was held, I believe, on the first of June, and it was (possibly still is) a kind of carnival on a minor scale, to mark the full flowering of the narcissuses that grew wild and covered large fields on the slopes above Montreux. Many posters with beautiful pictures advertised the feast well in advance, and I decided that I must go and see for myself what goes on at such a *Volksfest*, the like of which I had never seen before but of whose observance in Nice I knew from my reading. The trouble was that, as the posters stated, the parade of floats, the bands, the fireworks, and the dancing in the streets were all to take place late in the evening, and the yeshiva regimen called for students to be in bed by nine o'clock. Evidently, special preparations were required for a nocturnal absence. I reconnoitered the whole building and found that, in addition to the main front entrance, there was a small service entrance at the back from which a second stairway led to the upper floors. This back door, like the main entrance, was locked for the night; although it was possible to exit through it, once one pulled the door shut, the latch would automatically engage, and one could not reenter. I must have read somewhere how to overcome such an obstacle: when nobody was around, I took a small piece of cardboard and jammed it into the socket in which the latch moved back and forth, so that it could not spring forward but remained flush with the door jamb—and, behold, the problem was solved. I could go out that way, and when I came back, the door, although shut, would not be locked.

When the time came for us to retire, I went to bed as usual, and waited. Soon the quiet breathing of the two boys who were my roommates indicated that they were asleep. I got up quietly, dressed without turning on the light, sneaked out of the room, and went down the back stairs and out the service entrance, making sure that the cardboard was in place and the latch immobile in the open position. I carefully pulled the door shut after me, and was on my way. In fifteen or twenty minutes I was down in the main street where the merrymaking was just beginning. I have a vague picture in my memory of dense crowds pushing and milling up and down the street, of some fancy costumes, of floats decorated with lots of narcissuses, of loud music, of confetti, of streamers. I mixed happily in the crowd, but I do not remember having spoken to anybody. I was in the carnival but not of it. I was an outsider. I do not remember how long I stayed, but it could not have been much longer than an hour, or two at the utmost. My return to the yeshiva was uneventful. The door opened smoothly, I removed the cardboard, let the latch fall in place, went up to my room, undressed in the dark, and fell asleep.

Since I went to bed much later than usual, I overslept, and when I awoke I saw my two roommates looking at the floor near my bed and giggling. I looked down and saw there on the floor, where I had taken my clothes off, a sprinkling of confetti. Some of the confetti lavishly thrown around by the revelers got stuck in my clothes, and when I undressed it dropped to the floor. For a moment I did not know what to do, then I thought that the only way to stop these kids from telling on me was to threaten them. So I said to them, "If you dare to say a word of this to anybody, I shall break your bones!" This was the only time I remember having made use of my superior size and strength to threaten anybody. Then I swept up all the confetti I could find and flushed it down the toilet. The two boys did keep quiet, and thus nobody else found out about my nocturnal excursion.

Nevertheless, I was to run into trouble in the yeshiva, which ended, if not with my actual expulsion, with my being excluded from class work. A minor clash between me and one of the instructors occurred on the first Sabbath after my arrival. I still suffered frequently from conjunctivitis that used to be especially bad in the spring. During the week, when we spent all day inside the building studying, I did not wear my sunglasses, but on the Sabbath, when we went out to take a walk, I put them on to protect my eyes from the glaring sunlight. One of the teachers who was with us, when he saw me putting on the dark glasses, remarked that, since on the Sabbath it was forbidden to carry anything, I would have to leave my glasses at home, because wearing them would be tantamount to transgressing this Sabbath prohibition. I demurred, saying that I must wear the sunglasses for medical reasons, just as some others wore optical glasses, which was halakhically permitted. The teacher did not insist, so that I won my point, but after this little run-in I felt that I was suspect of being nonobservant, which, of course, I was when measured by the standards of the yeshiva.

Serious trouble erupted in the first week of July. As I mentioned earlier, I took my meals at the table of the instructors; after the first few days, I lost my initial hesitancy, and freely participated in their conversation. The language was German, in which I was quite fluent, and when it came to Jewish historical topics, or questions of Hebrew grammar, I quite often had something to contribute. On the day in question, at the lunch table, somebody referred to the Song of Deborah (Judges 5), with which I happened to be quite familiar. I was too immature to keep under the bushel whatever light I had, and so I remarked, without in the least suspecting that I would unleash a storm, that the words *'ad shaqamti D'vora, shaqamti em b'Yisrael*, usually translated as "until I Deborah arose, until I arose, mother in Israel," did not at all mean that, because the verb *shaqamti* was an archaic form of the second person singular feminine, so that the verse actually meant, "until that thou didst arise, Deborah, that thou didst arise, a mother in Israel," which also made much better sense because it exonerates Deborah from immodest boasting. When making this factual observation on a grammatical form, I had no idea that it would be interpreted as an expression of unbelief in the divine origin and sanctity of the Bible. But that, precisely, was what happened. Most vehement in his reaction was my own instructor, Mr. Schwab. He got red in the face, and sputtered: "You are an *epikoyres*, an unbeliever, who holds that the Song of Deborah is older than the Five Books of Moses . . . who denies that the Tora was given to Moses by God . . . I shall not teach you any more!" Therewith he jumped up from the table as fast as his bulk permitted, and marched out of the room.

The same afternoon Rabbi Botschko, who was not present at this exchange, asked me to come to his office, and spoke to me in a conciliatory tone. He said he regretted the incident, but he could not force Mr. Schwab to admit me to his class. In the circumstances all he could suggest was that I stay at the yeshiva until the end of the term, which was not far off, but without attending classes.

This was fine with me. I was due to leave Montreux in the last week of July to meet my parents in Zurich. After what had happened, I decided to leave several days earlier and to see something of Switzerland before going to Zurich. I stayed on at the yeshiva for another eight or ten days, during which I considered it nothing more than a boardinghouse where I slept and took my meals. During the day I explored Montreux and its environs. I sat around on the lakeshore, even tried to swim, but the water was much too cold for my taste. I took the narrow-gauge electric train with its blue cars and went up to the highest point above Montreux, and even visited a nearby glacier. On one occasion I plucked a large bundle of narcissuses, bought a box for them, and mailed them to Kató Krausz in Budapest. In general, I enjoyed myself, although the mealtimes, at the instructors' table, were somewhat tense since they completely ignored me.

Despite my less than honorable discharge from the Montreux yeshiva, Rabbi Botschko gave me a rather flattering certificate (in German) which, although I left the institution before the end of July, he dated August 30, so as, I believe, to correspond to the date of the official end of the summer term.

SCHWEIZ, THORA-LEHRANSTALT JESCHIWAH "EZ-CHAYIM" MONTREUX

Montreux, August 30, 1929

Certificate for Mr. Georg Patai

We are pleased to certify herewith that Mr. Georg Patai studied at our Yeshiva in the summer semester of 1929, and during this time delved diligently into the material, and profited and took along in knowlege as much as was possible for him in this time. He devoted himself willingly and joyfully to his studies, followed the *shiurim* [lessons] with the greatest attention, so that we are convinced that with his thirst for knowledge and his great talents he will be able to achieve much in continued studies for Judaism and the Tora.

We wish him much luck in his future, and sign for the management of the Yeshiva,

R. Eliahu Botschko
Director of the Yeshiva

Leaving Montreux, I took the train in the direction of Zurich, stopping on the way in several towns, of which I remember only Bern with its *Zwinger*, or bear pit, in the middle of town, and Lucerne with the bas-relief showing a lion. In one of the towns I thus passed through, I ran into a group of five or six Palestinian students and coeds, whose Hebrew rang out loudly across the street. I approached them, addressed them in Hebrew, introduced myself, and joined them for a couple of hours, immensely enjoying the opportunity to converse in Hebrew, and with an uncovered head, with young people from Palestine.

Having finished the foregoing pages, I went to the New York Public Library for the purpose of perusing my father's monthly to supplement my recollections with concrete data. While doing so, I found, to my surprise, two articles dealing with the Montreux yeshiva. The first, written by a certain Dénes Láczer, was published in the November 1928 issue. It describes the yeshiva, states that its founder and principal was Mr. R. E. Botschko, of Lithuanian origin, who went to Switzerland as a merchant, and, as a matter of Jewish duty, founded, financed, and managed the yeshiva, whose name, which I had completely forgotten, was Yeshiva 'Etz Ḥayyim, that is, Yeshiva Tree of Life. A photograph of the building, illustrating the article, bore out my memories of it. But the statement that the six to eight hours of daily Talmud study left time for the students to engage in sports definitely had no foundation in fact. Then, in the June 1929 issue—published at the time I was actually at the yeshiva—I found a short notice to the effect that the yeshiva had recently moved into the former villa of an Egyptian princess, that Mr. S. Schwab had joined the faculty, and that the latest term opened on May 12. The first of these two articles answers a question I have asked myself since I began jotting down what I remembered of the Montreux yeshiva: how did Father learn about the existence of this small and newly founded institution? Now I suspect that Mr. Láczer, about whom I know nothing, must have spontaneously sent in his article assuming that Father would find it interesting enough to print it, and that Father must have liked the account sufficiently to decide to send me to Montreux. These, then, were the antecedents of my becoming a student at the Montreux yeshiva, the only traditional talmudic academy I ever attended.

The Sixteenth Zionist Congress (July 29–August 10, 1929) and the subsequent constituent conference of the enlarged Jewish Agency for Palestine, which my parents and I attended in Zurich, represented a great moment in the history of Zionism. At this gathering the Zionist leadership, long prodded by Dr. Chaim Weizmann, its venerable president, to do so, decided to form an expanded Jewish Agency in which the non-Zionist sympathizers with the Jewish upbuilding of Palestine should be able to participate as equal partners with the Zionists. The Congress was followed by the constituent assembly of the Jewish Agency, whose governing bodies were composed of 50 percent Zionists and 50 percent non-Zionists, the latter prominent Jewish leaders supporting the building of the national home in Palestine without identifying themselves with the political aspirations of the Zionist movement. Father must have attended these deliberations and watched the resolutions with special interest and satisfaction, for what the Jewish Agency for Palestine was supposed to be and to do on a global scale he had achieved two years earlier in Hungary by founding the Pro Palestine Federation of Hungarian Jews.

As for me, at the time I took little interest in the political problems faced by world Zionism, and the manner in which Chaim Weizmann and his colleagues went about solving them. It was not until almost forty years later that, in my capacity as editor of the two-volume *Encyclopaedia of Zionism and Israel* in New York, I acquired a close familiarity with the Zionist Congresses, the struggles that went on in them and behind the scenes, the significance of the resolutions passed, and the roles of the leaders of the various Zionist parties participating in them. Because of this subsequent overlay of factual and detailed information, it is almost impossible for me to be sure what are my actual recollections of those days in July and August 1929 in Zurich, and of the great debates that took place at that historic Zionist Congress, and the perhaps even more historic constituent assembly of the Jewish Agency. All I can do is to conjure up, from a distance of more than half a century, the images of the leaders of the Jewish people, Zionists and non-Zionists, who mounted the rostrum and addressed the usually packed hall.

The greatest impression was made on me by Rabbi Stephen Wise with his magnificent, organlike voice, his impassioned oratory, and his imposing, leonine presence. He spoke in German, this I remember clearly, the *lingua franca* of the Zionist Congresses in those days, of which he had no full mastery, so that, every now and then, he had to pause, searching for a word, and, not finding it, he said it in

English, whereupon some people on the dais hastened to supply him with its equivalent in German. I also remember Chaim Weizmann, Nahum Sokolow, Louis Marshall, Albert Einstein, Leo Motzkin—not what they said but the mere fact that they spoke, and that I, together with hundreds in the audience, listened spellbound to this rare galaxy of great Jews from all over the world. And, although the meetings often ran late into the night, I stayed and listened; had I left, I thought I would miss something important, for I was convinced that I was witnessing Jewish history in the making.

While I was in Zurich I became acquainted with a Jewish girl from St. Gallen, Switzerland, who also attended the meetings. Her name was Judith Kimche, and I remember asking her whether her family descended from the famous medieval Sephardi Kimhis, and if so, why and when they changed the spelling to Kimche. She did not know the answer. She was a tall girl with dark hair, an elongated oval face and prominent nose, broad hips and a slender torso, and a manner that at the time I found outgoing and attractive. We took walks around the city, preferring the parks in which we could engage in some groping and kissing. I was somewhat saddened when she left Zurich, and I had to say good-bye to her, because I thought I would never see her again. But, some five or six years later, to my great surprise and delight, we ran into each other in Jerusalem. In the intervening years we both had lost our teenage naiveté and inexperience, and so, when we did meet again, the love affair that had broken off in 1929 even before it could start was this time tempestuously consummated. I lived at the time in a separate little pavilion in the garden of the house that belonged to the widow of Boris Schatz, the late founder and director of the Bezalel Art School. One apartment in the main building was occupied by my sister and her husband, while the other apartment, which included Boris Schatz's original large studio, was occupied by the graphic artist Jacob Steinhardt, who lived there with his wife and their little daughter, Josepha.

I enjoyed the privacy my separate pavilion provided me, but one day I invited Judith to have lunch with my sister and me. Mother happened to be present, and it was instantly evident to me that all she had to do was to have a brief look at Miss Kimche to decide that she did not like what she saw. I noticed in her face a worried look that told me that she was apprehensive lest this entirely unsuitable female entice me into marrying her (ever since I was an adolescent

Mother had been worried that I might marry someone unsuitable). Well, she need not have worried. Within a week or two Judith simply disappeared. Without even hinting at what she intended to do, she moved out of the furnished room she had rented nearby, leaving no forwarding address, and I never saw her again.

When the constituent assembly of the Jewish Agency was over, Father took us to Interlaken for a brief rest. One day, while taking a stroll with him in the forest that surrounded the resort town, we encountered Chaim Weizmann. He was walking alone along the narrow path leading through the wood. My father greeted him respectfully, although I don't think they had been introduced. Weizmann returned the greeting. Neither of them stopped or addressed a word to the other. As we passed Weizmann I sensed in his face a sadness, a pensive preoccupation that, I felt, must be the reflection of the great burden he was carrying as president of the newly formed Jewish Agency—the fate of the *yishuv* in Palestine, of Zionism, and of the Jewish people as a whole.

While we were still in Interlaken, the local papers reported the outbreak of Arab riots in Palestine. When Father read the news he turned deadly pale—I had never seen him react like that to anything. I do not know whether the paper reported the casualty figures, but the fact is that in those bloody attacks on the Jews of Jerusalem, Hebron, and Safed, 133 Jews were killed and 400 wounded. It is also a fact that the 1929 riots led to the appeasement of the Arabs by the British Mandatory Government with a limitation of Jewish immigration to Palestine.

From Interlaken we went on to a few other places in Switzerland of which I have no recollection, although I still have photographs I took of the whole family standing on a glacier, sitting in a café in front of a huge statue of Rübezahl, a hero of Swiss folklore, and in other places. By the time the school year started, we were back in Budapest.

9

Freshman at the Seminary and the University: 1929–1930

At some point, I cannot remember exactly when, but it must have been shortly after my return from Switzerland, I sat for, and passed with flying colors, the entrance examinations at the Rabbinical Seminary. I can no longer recall any of the questions the examiners put to me, but I do remember that when Professor Ludwig Blau, the rector of the Seminary, who chaired the exam, informed me that I had passed, I thanked him and then, right away, handed him a brief Hebrew article with the request that he consider it for publication in *HaTzofe l'Hokhmat Yisrael* (Review of the Science of Israel), the Hebrew scholarly journal of the Seminary, of which he was editor. The article was entitled "M'shorer 'Ivri-Hungari Bilti Noda'" (An Unknown Hebrew Hungarian Poet), and it contained a few Hebrew verses, written sometime in the nineteenth century, by an otherwise unknown person, with my brief introduction and notes. The holograph poems had been in the possession of Father, who gave them to me and suggested that I use them for an article. Professor Blau accepted the article and published it in one of the 1929 issues of *HaTzofe*. Thus at the very time I started my studies at the Seminary, I became a contributor to its scholarly Hebrew journal, which, understandably, filled me with quite some pride.

Studies in the college department of the Seminary, to which I was admitted on September 1, 1929, were conducted in one single classroom. All the students, irrespective of whether they were in the first, second, third, fourth, or fifth year of their studies, sat in one room and received the same instruction. This meant that each student went through the same curriculum, the same five-year course of studies, but not in the same sequence. The subject matter that I studied in my freshman year in 1929–1930 constituted for a fifth-year senior the concluding part of his studies. That this rotation system caused no problems was due to the fact that the material we studied was not progressively more advanced, but was basically of one and the same level.

Take, for instance, the main course in Talmud, called *Talmud statarie*, to which five hours weekly were devoted in each of the five years. This course was designed to cover a certain amount of the Babylonian Talmud. The sequence in which the various tractates of the Talmud that formed the texts for this course were studied was immaterial. Nor did the fact that nineteen-year-old freshmen studied side by side with twenty-four-year-old seniors cause any problem. At least I felt none, and, from the very first moment, I felt that I was in a congenial environment.

Our classroom was located on the third floor of the Seminary building on Rökk Szilárd Street, next to József Boulevard. On the ground floor was the Seminary's synagogue and the apartment of the caretaker; on the second, the premises of the Jewish Teachers Institute and of the high school division of the Seminary. The third floor was occupied, in addition to our classroom, by the spacious office of the rector, and the library that took up most of it. The classroom had a large desk that served as the cathedra of the teacher, and several rows of benches with each row built up somewhat higher than the one before it, with a total seating capacity of about sixty. In the years I attended there were about thirty to forty students in all, which meant that in those years the Seminary graduated six to eight rabbis annually, who, upon graduation, either found positions as rabbis in one of the Neolog congregations in Hungary or became teachers of Jewish religion. I usually occupied a seat in the second row, not far from the entrance door.

Consulting my old registration book, I find that we had to attend no less than thirty weekly periods, that is to say, five hours of fifty minutes each, for six days a week, including Sunday, but, of course, not Saturday. The classes were all concentrated in the mornings, from 8 A.M. to 1 P.M., so as to enable the students to attend classes at the University in the afternoon. The course offerings remained largely the same throughout my years of study, with but minor variations. They comprised five weekly hours of *Talmud statarie*, three hours each of *Talmud cursorie* and liturgy, two hours each of Jewish his-

tory, introduction to the Bible, Bible, readings in religious philosophy, style exercises, and German seminar; and one period each week
in Jerusalem Talmud, historical sources, exegetical readings, Codes,
homiletics, religious philosophy, and Midrash.

Of my teachers in my freshman year, Professor Ludwig Blau
(1861–1936), the rector of the Seminary, made the greatest impression on me. He was a large, sturdy man, with a powerful round
head covered with dense, closely cropped grey-black hair, a bulging
forehead, penetrating black eyes, and a pug nose—a face remarkably like that shown in the busts of Socrates. Among my papers I
still have a pencil sketch I drew of him while listening to his lectures. His main subject was *Talmud statarie*, that is, freely translated, Talmud in depth. And, truly, what depths of the Talmud he
opened up for us! He taught it in German—it was taken for granted
that students had to know German—and used the talmudic text as a
key to open up before us the history and culture of the talmudic
period, of which he was past master. He spoke in a high-pitched,
whining voice, but every word he uttered was a pearl. I remember
one phrase he must have repeated whenever he came across a passage that gave him an insight into the life and thought of the Jews
of Palestine and Babylonia. He would slightly raise his right hand
from the Talmud folio that lay open before him on the desk, and
with the palm turned inward toward himself, he would move it
twice or three times up and down, and say in his typical, nasal
twang, *Es durchschimmern hier die Jahrtausende* (The millennia gleam
through here), and then continue to draw surprising conclusions
from the sparse talmudic statement.

On another occasion—this may have been not in his Talmud
class but in his course on Jewish history—he quoted the talmudic
passage that reports how frightened Rabbi Yehuda Hanasi, the head
of the Palestinian Jewish community, got when they informed him
that "Huna is coming." Huna was the exilarch, the powerful leader
of Babylonian Jewry. Then the messenger added, "In his coffin,"
that is, the body of Huna was being brought to be buried in Palestine. This little incident, Blau explained, shows that the leaders of
Babylonian Jewry were more powerful than those of Palestinian Jewry:
the arrival of Huna alive would have jeopardized the position of
Rabbi Yehuda the Prince, the head of the Palestinian Jews.

After writing the above paragraph based only on my memory, I
could not resist the temptation to check how the talmudic sources

actually describe the incident that, after fifty-five years, I still remember as having been referred to by Professor Blau. I find the story told in the Jerusalem Talmud, tractate Kilayim 9:4, folio 32b mid., and give it here in my literal translation from the Aramaic original: "At one time Rabbi Hiyya went to him [to Rabbi Yehuda Hanasi] and said to him: 'Behold, Rav Huna is outside!' The face of Rabbi [Yehuda] turned pale. [Thereupon Rabbi Hiyya] said to him: 'His coffin came. . . .' "

I don't know whether other Jewish historians before Blau or after him have paid attention to this little incident and interpreted it as Blau did, but in any case it shows the acuity of his perception, the sharpness of his powers of deduction, and the method he used in teaching us.

To my great regret, I had the privilege of studying under Blau for less than one full term. Before the end of the fall 1929 semester he fell ill, and Professor Armin Hoffer took over his courses in the Babylonian and Palestinian Talmuds, while Professor Miksa Weisz filled in for him in Jewish history and historical sources. Once, I remember, I visited him in his home in a garden suburb of Budapest, where he had moved after his retirement. He died in 1936, but for me he remained alive in his books (all of them in German), which for many years were a source of enlightenment for me. Two years after his death a volume of scholarly studies was published in his memory, to which I contributed an article on *T'khelet*, the precious blue dye, in biblical and talmudic folklore, having found this subject most suitable to a memorial volume dedicated to Ludwig Blau, whose last name meant blue in German.

However, the teacher who influenced me most was not Blau but Professor Bernard Heller (1871–1943). Heller, whom I first met when I was a first-grade pupil in the *gimnázium* of the Israelite Congregation of Pest, of which he was principal, in 1922 was appointed professor of Bible at the Seminary, a post he filled for ten years, until he resigned before the end of the fall 1931 semester because of a disagreement with Blau. Heller was small of stature, of lean build, and wore both his hair and his beard closely cropped; he had blue eyes and narrow lips that he had a knack of pursing and pulling inward when speaking. He had a high-pitched voice, but, in contrast to Blau's whining mannerism, he spoke in clipped tones, with brief pauses between rapidly ejaculated phrases. He was a strict taskmaster, treated his students as if they were high school pupils, and called upon us several times a term to come up to the blackboard to answer his questions, precisely as was done in high school.

Despite Heller's somewhat peculiar mannerisms, I liked him, enjoyed his classes, and made sure I was always well prepared in case he called upon me. It was evident that he liked me, too, and, perhaps remembering that he first knew me when I was a child of ten, he called me *Gyuri fiam* (my son Gyuri), although as a rule he, like all the other teachers, called the students by their family names. I remember that on one occasion, when Heller called upon me for an impromptu oral exam, I feigned ignorance because I was embarrassed to show that I knew all the details concerning a biblical passage that had sexual connotations. Professor Heller asked me to explain Ezekiel 8:17, a passage he had discussed in his lectures, which reads in the Masoretic text, "Then He [God] said unto me: 'Hast thou seen this, O son of man? Is it a light thing to the house of Judah that they commit the abominations which they commit here in that they fill the land with violence, and provoke Me still more, and, lo, they put the branch to their nose?" I remembered precisely everything Professor Heller had told us about this verse: that "the branch" the prophet speaks about was a euphemism for a phallic image, and that the expression "to their nose" was again a euphemistic device, for what the prophet actually said was that God reproached the idolatrous Judahites with symbolically raising the phallus toward *his*, God's nose. I explained all this, mentioning that the "branch" corresponded to the Greek cultic use of phallus images. I also remembered Heller telling us that the ancient Persians, too, had a similar ritual object called *barezma*—I remember the term even now, after all these years. Heller prompted me by asking what was the Persian equivalent of the phallus, but I just could not say it. I felt that if I should mention *barezma* in addition to phallus, it would indicate that I was too greatly interested in sexual matters, which of course I was. After waiting for a moment, Heller pursed his lips and said, *"barezma,"* and I could see that he was dissatisfied with my ignorance of this important detail.

After my return from Breslau, where I acquired a good working knowledge of Arabic, I definitely became one of Heller's favorite students. In addition to Bible, Heller also taught a seminar course of readings in religious philosophy. In the fall term of 1931 the text we read was the *Guide of the Perplexed* of Maimonides. The manner in which Heller conducted this class was to call upon one student after another to read a few sentences from the medieval Hebrew translation of this greatest classic of Jewish philosophy, to translate and explain it.

Knowing that Heller himself had a fine command of Arabic, I asked him whether, when my turn came, I could read, instead of the Hebrew translation, the original Arabic text of Maimonides. He was delighted with the suggestion, whereupon I borrowed from the Seminary's library the Munk edition of the *Dalālat al-Ḥā'irīn* in Arabic, printed in Hebrew characters as Maimonides originally wrote it, and conscientiously prepared several pages every week for this seminar. I still remember that it was not easy to do this, despite the fact that the Hebrew translation, which I kept next to the Arabic version, gave me the meaning of the Arabic text. I had to refer frequently to the Arabic-German dictionary of Adolf Wahrmund, a copy of which my fellow student, Joseph Klein, had given me as a present, and which I still have and use to this day. (Checking the title page of the first volume I notice that it is inscribed "Hatala Péter, 1877." Hatala was appointed professor of Arabic at the University of Budapest in 1874, to the great chagrin of Ignaz Goldziher, who had been practically promised that position. Evidently, three years later Hatala bought his copy of the dictionary, which was published that very year. I wonder how that particular copy got into the possession of Joseph Klein. Probably, after Hatala's death his heirs sold it to a secondhand bookshop, and Joseph Klein picked it up there. He gave me the dictionary because he decided not to study Arabic, after all.) To make sure that I would read the Arabic text fluently and correctly—Arabic, like Hebrew, is usually printed without the vowel marks—I added those marks in pencil over and under the letters. These exercises added considerably to my knowledge of Arabic, and especially of its Judeo-Arabic variety.

In another respect, too, I had a special position in Professor Heller's classes. In the Seminary, as in other institutions of Jewish learning all over Europe and America, Hebrew was read with the Ashkenazic pronunciation, used, albeit with considerable variations, in the synagogues of all Ashkenazi communities. In the *yishuv* of modern Palestine, however, Hebrew was spoken with the Sephardic pronunciation, and Father had insisted from the very beginning that my Hebrew tutors should use this pronunciation in teaching me. The difference between the Hungarian Ashkenazic and the Sephardic pronunciations is not great, and can be summed up in a very few points: (1) the *qametz gadol* is pronounced *o* (as in *on*) in Ashkenazic, and *a* (as in *heart*) in Sephardic; (2) the *ḥolam* is *au* (as in *house*) in Ashkenazic, *o* in Sephardic; (3) the *tav r'fuya* is *s* in Ashkenazic, and *t* in Sephardic; (4) the Sephardic observes the rules of the ultimate and penultimate accent of words, while in Ashkenazic the accent tends to shift toward the beginning of the word; for example, Sephardic *breshít bará Elohím* (in the beginning God created) becomes in Ashkenazic *bréshis bóro Eláuhim*. Either Professor Heller or I must have suggested that when my turn came to read out of a Hebrew text, I should use the Sephardic pronunciation, which I did, the only one in class to do so.

The influence of Heller's interest in Jewish and Arabic folklore, and especially the Hebrew and Arabic folktale, remained with me long after I left Budapest and became a "research student" at the Jerusalem University. Heller himself was not a very prolific writer, but he certainly made up in erudition, thoroughness, and meticulousness what he lacked in volume. It was characteristic of his modesty, or, perhaps, rather of his formalistic correctness, that he never mentioned his own scholarly studies in his classes, despite the fact that he published his two most important works during the year that I was his student at the Seminary. He probably felt that it was not good form to refer to his own writings in class, even though there were enough occasions for him to do so. Thus all my colleagues and I remained ignorant in 1929–1930 of the fact that in that very year appeared his 100-page contribution on the Hebrew and the Arabic folktale in volume 4 of Johannes Bolte's and Georg Polivka's classic *Anmerkungen zu den Kinder- und Hausmärchen der Brüder Grimm* (Notes on the Children's and Domestic Tales of the Brothers Grimm; Leipzig: Dieterich'sche Verlagsbuchhandlung, 1930, pp. 315–418), and that he must have received advance copies of his 500-page monograph *Die Bedeutung des arabischen 'Antar-Romans für die vergleichende Litteraturkunde* (The Significance of the Arabic 'Antar-Romance for the Comparative Study of Literature, Leipzig: Hermann Eichblatt Verlag, 1931), which was an expanded version of his book on the same subject published in Hungarian in 1918 by the Hungarian Academy of Sciences and reviewed enthusiastically by Heller's former teacher Ignaz Goldziher in the *Pester Lloyd*.

My own interest in scholarship was at the time still rather rudimentary, and it never occurred to me to look up in the catalog of the Seminary's library what books authored by my teachers were available in it, let alone to take out any of their books and read them. Still, I was not entirely unaware of Heller's work due to the fact that I occasionally encountered his name in Father's monthly, for which he wrote articles and book reviews. In any case, while I had not read the major works of Heller, his interest in Jewish and Arab folklore somehow communicated itself to me, so that by the time I left for Jerusalem I had a definite plan to write a study on ancient Palestinian folklore as my Ph.D. thesis at the Hebrew University. About my continuing contact with Professor Heller while I was working on my Jerusalem dissertation, and the detailed and friendly review he gave it in the *Revue des Etudes Juives*, I shall report in due course.

But to return to my first year at the Seminary and my teachers at that institution, which in those days was still a major center of Jewish scholarship, next to Blau and Heller I remember most clearly Professor Armin Hoffer, who taught Talmud and Codes. Hoffer was, in addition to being a full professor at the Seminary, rabbi of one of the synagogues of the Israelite Congregation of Pest located not far from our home in Podmaniczky Street. Occasionally, on Friday evenings, I would attend services in Hoffer's synagogue.

He was a smallish, rotund man, with a little goatee, a ducklike gait, and a Hungarian accent like that of a peasant. His speaking style, too, had something peasantish about it, which we students found rather amusing. The relationship between him and us was cordial, almost one of camaraderie, very different from the respect we showed Blau and Heller. Hoffer would joke with us, and never object to being spoken to jokingly by us. As far as his scholarship is concerned, I am not aware of any scholarly publication by him (which, of course, does not necessarily mean that he did not have any to his credit), but he undoubtedly had great mastery of the Talmud and the Jewish religious Codes based on it, beginning with Yitzḥaq Alfasi's eleventh-century code, and ending with Yosef Caro's *Shulḥan 'Arukh* of the sixteenth, which has remained authoritative to this day for tradition-abiding Jews.

Of the material covered by Professor Hoffer in his courses I remember especially the parts dealing with the laws of *kashrut* and the signs of sickness in the inner organs of cattle that rendered them *t'refa*, unfit for consumption. In order to be able to explain these matters more clearly, Professor Hoffer used a sculptured figure of a cow, about twenty inches in height and about thirty from head to tail. It was a nicely turned out little animal, probably made of wood or plastic. One side of its body was open, that is, it presented a view of the inner organs laid bare, with the heart, lungs, stomach, intestines, and so forth all colored differently. I think some of these organs could even be removed for closer inspection. The purpose of studying that particular part of the *Shulḥan 'Arukh* was to enable the student, once he occupied the position of rabbi in a congregation, to decide whether a slaughtered animal, of which there was some question, was or was not kosher. However, since in every Hungarian Jewish congregation to which a graduate of the Seminary could ever expect to be appointed there was a *shoḥet*, a ritual slaughterer, who had to be an expert in scrutinizing the internal organs of the animals he slaughtered, and fully capable of deciding whether there was any abnormality in them that would render the animal *t'refa*, we all considered these studies an exercise in futility, and received Professor Hoffer's instruction with a mixture of frustration and restrained hilarity. In addition, his rustic speech mannerisms prompted us to entertain ourselves by imitating him more frequently than our other teachers.

The rusticity of Professor Hoffer's personality and speech came through especially strongly in his sermons. On Friday evenings in his synagogue, as I witnessed several times, he would greet the mourners, who had lost a loved one in the course of the preceding week, with a brief address of welcome and comfort. After reading out the names of the mourners, who would come and line up in front of him, facing the Holy Ark, he would quote, first in Hebrew, then in his own inimitable Hungarian translation, the passage from Jeremiah's Lamentations (2:13), *godaul kayom shivrekh*, which means "great like the sea is thy breach," but which he translated into Hungarian as *tengernagy az önök romlása*, that is, "sea-great is your ruination." The Hungarian word he used, *tengernagy*, although it is composed of the two elements *tenger* (sea), and *nagy* (great), is used in proper Hungarian only in the sense of "admiral," so that what he actually said was "admiral is your ruination." At a time when Admiral Horthy was the regent of Hungary, this sounded to me (and perhaps to others as well) like a rather risky statement that could easily be misunderstood, but I was afraid that, should I point it out to Professor Hoffer, he would take it as a disrespectful criticism.

As it was, Hoffer sensed that the Codes were not one of my favorite subjects. It so happened that his course on Codes was given

Sunday mornings, taking up three full hours. No other courses were scheduled on the same day. Once I suggested to him that perhaps he would consider moving the course to another day, and thus enable us poor students to have a day of rest, since the Sabbath, the traditional day of rest, was for us, as for all rabbis, a working day: we all had to spend the morning in the synagogue, they to preach and lead in the prayers, we to listen and learn, not to mention the duty of praying. Hoffer rejected the suggestion in his usual gruff and bantering manner, but thereafter he seemed to pay special attention to whether or not I attended his Sunday classes.

That winter I decided to go skiing. I acquired a pair of skis, ski boots, poles, and suitable clothing, and the first Sunday morning when the snow conditions were good I took the rack-railway that climbed up Mount Sváb on the outskirts of the city. I spent several hours teaching myself how to ski, gliding down gentle slopes and climbing up again, and although I fell several times, I got through the day without any mishap. When I came to Professor Hoffer's class the next day or the day thereafter, he said nothing. Next week I again went skiing, this time with a friend of whom I remember only that he was not a student at the Seminary or a former classmate of mine in high school. He in turn brought along his girl friend, a pretty girl with dark hair whose cheeks became very red in the cold. For quite a while everything went fine, and my friend, who had quite a good voice, sang love songs to his lady friend, of which I remember one: the "Siciliana" from Mascagni's *Cavalleria Rusticana*, which he sang, in Hungarian translation, with great passion, and which made me envious and sad, because I did not have a girl friend whom I could have entertained with love songs. . . .

When we started down a narrow path leading between steep banks on either side — my friend first, then the girl, and then myself — she stumbled and fell. Following too closely behind her, from lack of experience, I was unable to stop. She lay there, taking up all the space from snow-wall to snow-wall, and all I could do to stop myself from crashing into her was to turn my skis sharply sideways. But the path was narrower than the length of my skis, so that one of them got caught and broke, about a foot from its front end, just as I hit the ground right behind the girl. We got up, and I, of course, had to remove my skis. All three of us walked quite a distance until we found a repair shop where my broken ski was fixed with a sheet of tin nailed around it. We then went on skiing, but the repaired ski scraped against the snow and made me veer to the side. The accident materially diminished the attraction skiing had for me, to which was added the unpleasantness of being reproached in front of the class by Professor Hoffer, in a half-bantering and half-serious and indignant tone, for preferring to go skiing rather than attend his class. It seems that when Hoffer noticed that I was absent a second Sunday, he asked where I was, and one of my less than loving classmates volunteered the information that I had gone skiing — I probably had made no secret of my intention of doing so. So this was the end of my short-lived attempt to become a champion skier.

At the time I shared with my colleagues the view that there was little value in what Professor Hoffer taught us, but years later, when I began to peruse the *Shulḥan 'Arukh* and the other Jewish codes for the purpose of extracting from them information about differing Ashkenazi and Sephardi customs, I felt grateful to Professor Hoffer for having given me instruction in them and thus having enabled me to find my way in their labyrinthine minutiae.

Two of my other teachers, Dr. Gyula (Julius) Fischer (1861–1944) and Dr. Simon Hevesi (1868–1943), were both chief rabbis at the main synagogue of the Israelite Congregation of Pest, the *Dohány Templom* (Tobacco Synagogue), so called because it was located on Dohány Street in central Budapest. That synagogue was, and still is, as far as I know, the largest in the world, with 3,000 seats and two rows of galleries, one on top of the other, where the women were seated. It was built in a pseudo-Moorish style, and boasted two tall minaretlike towers at its front facade topped with two somewhat bulbous domes. It had a fine choir of men and women. The inclusion of women was a concession to modernity, as was the magnificent organ. This combination of adherence to tradition and concessions to modernism was characteristic of the Neolog congregations of Hungary in many other respects as well. Another example in the synagogue itself was the seating of the women in the galleries, separate from the men, in obedience to tradition, but without putting up any curtain or latticework to hide the women from the sight of the men as tradition would have required, because that would have been offensive to modernist sensibilities.

The two chief rabbis, as I found out later, had been invited to become rabbis of the grand synagogue simultaneously, in 1905, and a keen competition instantly developed between them. They preached on alternate Saturdays, each from his own pulpit affixed to a column on opposite sides of the nave, high above the heads of the congregation. Both were truly great orators, both could spellbind the audience, both had powerful voices that could be heard clearly in the farthest corners of the nave and in the backmost benches of the second gallery. The oratorical competition between the two chief rabbis was the chief attraction of the Sabbath morning services, and whenever I attended them I could not help noticing that the synagogue filled up shortly before the sermon was due to begin, and that after its conclusion the audience thinned out considerably. The two rabbis' competition was duplicated by the rivalry between the two chief cantors of the synagogue, the tenor Linetzki and the base Abrahamsohn, each of whom had his enthusiastic partisans just as the two rabbis had. Finally, just about the time when I was a freshman in the Seminary, Dr. Hevesi achieved a signal victory over his older colleague: he was given the title *vezető főrabbi* (leading chief rabbi) by the Governing Board of the Congregation, while Dr. Fischer remained simply chief rabbi.

During the first year of my attendance at the Seminary Dr. Fischer taught Midrash and conducted a weekly German seminar; then, after Heller's resignation, he also took over Heller's Bible and Jewish philosophy classes. If I remember correctly, he objected to my reading the Bible text with the Sephardic pronunciation, so I had to practice Ashkenazic reading. He could not have made a deep impression on me, for I remember absolutely nothing of what transpired in his classes, except for the fact that he often was strongly indignant, I no longer remember about what.

Dr. Hevesi taught us homiletics and Jewish religious philosophy in my first year, and after Heller's resignation also took over the readings in religious philosophy. Hevesi was not an Arabist, so my exercises in reading medieval Jewish philosophical texts in the original Arabic came to an end. Hevesi was an extremely impressive person: tall, stately, with a large oval face, regular features, big blue eyes, and the barest trace of a beard on his chin. He was dignified and managed always to be both friendly and reserved. He always wore a black suit with a clerical collar and a knee-length double-breasted frock coat, called in Hungarian *ferencjóska* after King Francis Joseph, and known in the English-speaking world as Prince Albert. In his religious philosophy course he spent much time on Ḥasdai Crescas, who seems to have been his favorite philosopher — I remember once visiting him in his home and finding him reading Crescas.

His homiletics classes consisted of having one student after the other prepare a sermon, memorize it word by word, and deliver it in class, after which he subjected it to painstaking, or rather pain-giving, criticism. He also supervised, or was in some way responsible for, the sermons we students gave in the synagogue of the Seminary on Friday evenings. From Dr. Hevesi's attestations in my registration book I learn that in each of the two terms of my freshman year I delivered one practice sermon and one synagogue sermon. In his classes Hevesi never tired of reiterating that a good sermon had to catch the imagination of the audience, had to appeal to its sentiments, had to contain religious and moral teaching, and had to be encouraging. I certainly learned a lot from him, although I remember that when I sweated over composing my first sermon I finally had to turn to Father for help.

Once, I remember listening to a sermon by Dr. Hevesi in the Dohány Temple, which began with the words "On dark waters swims the swan and sings . . . "—I can recall nothing else of it, although while listening to it, it made a tremendous impression. When we met next time in class I asked him whether he wrote down and memorized his sermons. "No," he answered, "all I do is consider in advance the main theme, the important points I want to make, and then go up to the pulpit and speak." When I expressed my admiration at his being able to deliver a thirty- or forty-minute sermon without even as much as a written outline, he smiled and said, "A few years' practice, and you will be able to do the same." And right he was; I, too, was to develop the same ability, although not in sermonizing, but in public lecturing.

But that was still far in the future. In my Seminary years, learning the sermon by heart was the rule. When I prepared my first sermon, I composed it carefully, asked Father to correct it, learned it by heart, and went to the Seminary synagogue with considerable trepidation. In the vestry, Samuel Löwinger, an older colleague, who soon thereafter was to become a professor at the Seminary and later its director, helped me select one of the black brocade robes kept there, which was long enough for my height, and one of the black velvet five- or six-cornered birettas that fitted my head size, and then walked next to me down the aisle leading from the back entrance door of the synagogue to its front, where the Holy Ark was and where the rabbi of the occasion and visiting dignitaries had their seats. As I entered the synagogue, I felt my heart throb, and, in order to overcome, or at least mask, my mounting stage fever, I stepped out with determination, hitting the wooden floor with the heels of my shoes. Shamu (as we called him) hissed at me from the corner of his mouth, and bade me walk quietly, which I shame-facedly did.

At the front of the synagogue, just before the Holy Ark, was the reader's desk, upon which, in the course of the Sabbath morning services, the Tora scroll was laid for the reading of the weekly por-tion, and at which the cantor stood while leading the congregation in prayer. This desk was quite a contraption. It looked like an ordi-nary, big, solid cube with a somewhat slanting top, usually covered by a velvet burgundy embroidered coverlet. But there was more to it than met the eye. It could be opened up vertically, so that it became transformed into a pulpit with stairs leading up to it from behind, and standing high above the congregation assembled in the small sanctuary. Before I climbed up the stairs, Shamu whispered to me, "Mind the *Ner Tamid* [Eternal Light]." And it is good that he did so, for the Eternal Light, with its oil-filled glass container and burn-ing wick, hung perilously low above the improvised pulpit. Had he not warned me, I would certainly have knocked my biretta against it and enjoyed an impromptu anointing with the oil contained in it.

I seem to have been able to control my internal agitation, for the sermon was a resounding success. Teachers and colleagues who were present congratulated me and Father, who had come along, for this was a great event for him, too. Dr. Miklós Hajdu, a good friend of Father and a frequent contributor of sentimental articles to *Mult és Jövő*, came up to me and said, "You will be a great orator!" And then he added, "I was worried when I saw you going up there with-out any notes in your hand. You should always have some paper with you, you know," and here he switched to German, "*es kann einem immer etwas menschliches passieren*" (any moment something human can happen to you).

It must have been about eight in the evening when Father and I finally set out for home. The weather was dry and not too cold, and we strolled along in a leisurely fashion on the Körút, the boulevard that was one of the busiest thoroughfares of the city. We discussed my sermon, and Father broached the subject of sending me to Breslau for my sophomore year. As we walked, two prostitutes approached us, and as they passed us, they slowed down, and one of them said provocatively, "We, too, are two . . . " Father and I continued to walk and talk as if we simply had not noticed the two women. This mutual reticence was characteristic of my relationship with Father. Never was as much as a single word exchanged between us about sex. It was as if that area of life simply did not exist. I would have been mortified if Father had any inkling of the burning importance sex had in my secret life, of the compelling force that drove me to seek solitary relief at night, and the even more irresistible lure of the psychological satisfaction I found in fantasizing about women, not to mention the actual timid and unsuccessful attempts I made to meet women with whom I could translate my obsessive phantasms into palpable reality. Only on one single occasion did Father violate his unwritten but no less inviolate rule of never speaking to me about sex. He did it at the railroad station just before I boarded the train that was going to take me to Breslau. At that time, I remember, I was acutely embarrassed. Today, thinking back on that scene, I understand that it must have cost Father an extraordinary effort to surmount the long-standing barricade of silence he had erected between us on this subject.

But, to finish up my recollections about my teachers at the Seminary in my first year of study, there was one more, Dr. Miksa (Max) Weisz (1872–1931), of whom I have already spoken earlier in connection with my senior high school year, and for whom I had deep affection. As a seventeen-year-old boy I was not yet able fully to appreciate either the charm and wit or the scholarship of Dr. Weisz. A year and a half later, when I became his student at the Seminary, where he greeted me as an old friend, I instantly became his admirer. In the fall of 1929 he taught only one course of two hours weekly, called style exercise, of which I remember nothing except the fact that I enjoyed listening to his witty, occasionally somewhat cynical, delivery. He liked to tell jokes, and then, catching himself in the act, as it were, he would say, as if referring to an established and well-known fact, "You know, don't you, that a Jew will sell his mother for the sake of a joke."

Toward the end of the term, when Professor Blau fell ill, Dr. Weisz took over his courses in Jewish history and historical sources. Not only was his approach to history quite different from that of Blau, but he was interested in a different period. Blau covered the talmudic period in the two courses mentioned. Weisz had collaborated with Blau and Hevesi on an important volume entitled *Ethics in the Talmud* (in Hungarian, 1920), worked on Geniza texts, edited an Italian-Jewish book of customs, and wrote several other books in various fields of Jewish scholarship. But his great love was the history of the Jews in Renaissance Italy, and his courses were devoted largely to that subject. It seems that professors had considerable academic freedom at the Seminary: under the same course title they could treat widely differing subjects. Once, I remember, Dr. Weisz told us in class, "If you want to go in for studying Jewish history, don't waste your time with the history of the Jews in Hungary. Study Italian Jewish history. There you will find any number of fascinating subjects." I think that this advice from Dr. Weisz influenced me in copying at the Breslau Rabbinical Seminary the following year the autograph manuscript collection of poems by the eighteenth-century Italian rabbi Israel Berekhya Fontanella, which eventually became the subject of my Budapest doctoral thesis, although it was actually Dr. Samuel Löwinger who suggested that I look into that manuscript, which had caught his attention when, a year or two earlier, he had worked on cataloging the Hebrew manuscripts in the library of the Breslau Seminary.

Before leaving for Breslau in the fall of 1930, I went to say goodbye to Dr. Weisz. He said to me in his usual humorous way, "I know you are well supplied with good advice as to what to do in Breslau, what to study at the Seminary, what courses to take at the University, and the like. I want to give you only one piece of practical advice: while there, you will take your meals in restaurants. Don't eat minced meat." I still remember the Hungarian words he used: *Ne egyél fasirtot.* Since I had been a pupil of his in high school, he continued to address me with the familiar *te* (the equivalent of the German *Du* or the French *tu*) instead of the formal *maga* (you, *Sie, vous*), customarily used by teachers in colleges and universities when speaking to their students. I also remember that I did, indeed, follow his advice, which, of course, was easier to do than to obey the caution about sex that Father tried to impress upon me. To my great regret and shock, when I returned from my year in Breslau, Dr. Weisz was no longer alive.

Before going on to describe my studies at Budapest University, I must discuss at least briefly the status of the Rabbinical Seminary within the network of higher education in Hungary. The Seminary was (and still is) a state institution, the only one of its kind in the world. It functioned under the Hungarian Ministry of Education, which appointed a twenty-four-member governing board to supervise it. This board, in turn, appointed the teachers, subject to the approval of the minister of education. The professors of the Seminary were government employees just as were all the teachers in all the universities and colleges in the country. This official status of the Seminary was the result of its historical origins. When the Hungarian revolution of 1848 was defeated by Austria, the Austrian government imposed a special fine of 2.3 million florins on the Jews of Hungary as a punishment for their participation in the revolution. In 1856 the Emperor Francis Joseph I placed this amount, or whatever was actually paid in by that time, at the disposal of the Hungarian Jews for the purpose of using it as a fund for financing Jewish religious and educational institutions, primarily, the establishment of a rabbinical seminary. After several years of discussions and preparations, the Seminary opened its doors in 1877. The successor of Francis Joseph, Charles IV, permitted the incorporation of the name of the late ruler into the name of the Seminary, thenceforth officially called the Francis Joseph I National Rabbinical Institute.

One of the rules governing the Seminary was that its students had to attend the faculty of philosophy at Budapest University. Only a candidate in possession of a Dr. Phil. from the University could be ordained as a rabbi by the Seminary. When the infamous *numerus clausus* law was passed by the Hungarian Parliament (in September 1920), it provided, in essence, that the proportion of Jewish students admitted to Hungarian universities and colleges in relation to the total number of students could not exceed the proportion of Jews in the total population of the country. Hungarian Jewish leaders engaged in an energetic but unsuccessful fight against the *numerus clausus*, although because of their patriotic scruples they refrained from bringing the problem to the attention of either international bodies or Jewish organizations outside Hungary. Nevertheless, the injustice and inequity of the law were recognized by the British Jewish Board of Deputies, the Anglo-Jewish Association, and the Alliance Israélite Universelle, and these organizations submitted a complaint to the League of Nations. The Hungarian Jewish leadership, in its fight against the *numerus clausus*, had two basic arguments: first, that the Jews were not a race, or a racial minority in Hungary, as the law treated them, but a religious denomination, just like the Catholics, the Calvinists, the Protestants, and so forth. Second, they pointed out that the Jews were a pronouncedly urban element—in Budapest, for instance, they constituted about 25 percent of the total population—and university students were, and always had been, recruited primarily from the urban population; hence the limitation of Jewish students to the proportion of Jews in the country as a whole was patently unjust. However, all the efforts, whether in Hungary or abroad, were of no avail, and the *numerus clausus* remained in effect, albeit with some insignificant, largely cosmetic, modifications.

There was only one exception to the quota system introduced by the *numerus clausus*: all the students of the National Rabbinical Institute were admitted to the University of Budapest over and above the "closed number." However, the studies they were allowed to take were limited to two fields: either philosophy proper, or ancient Near Eastern languages and literatures, including (in alphabetic order) Arabic, Aramaic, Assyrian-Babylonian, Egyptian, Hebrew, Persian, and related history courses. The logic behind this limitation was that these studies had a close relationship to the various Jewish subjects a rabbinical student was expected to take, and that the earning of a Dr. Phil. degree in these fields would not qualify the Jewish graduates to become competitors of Christian Hungarian students, who, evidently, were not supposed to take an interest in such esoterica.

Of the two fields open to them, most students of the Seminary opted for ancient Near Eastern languages and literatures. I, too, was inclined to "Semitics" rather than philosophy, but circumstances I can no longer recall enabled me to take any courses I wanted, and so, for the first term of my freshman year (fall of 1929), I registered for only four weekly periods in that field. My University registration book informs me that I took one hour of Arabic for beginners and one hour of Syriac grammar, both taught by Professor Mihály Kmoskó, and two hours of general chronology, taught by Professor Ede (Eduard) Mahler. As against this, I took a full complement of courses in German and English—German Historical Grammar, Old High German Grammar and Texts, Schiller and His Times, The Faust Legend and Goethe's Faust, The German Novel, German Language Exercises for Beginners, as well as Survey of English Literature, Readings in Old and Middle English, The Development of the English Novel, Shakespeare's Tragedies, The Life and Poetry of Petőfi (the great Hungarian nineteenth-century poet), and, for good measure, Italian Sculpture in the Fifteenth Century. All in all I registered for no less than twenty-eight weekly periods at the University, which, added to the thirty weekly periods we had to take at the Seminary, amounted to fifty-eight hours a week, or roughly ten hours per day.

Evidently, it would have been physically impossible to attend this many classes, but, fortunately, academic freedom at the faculty of philosophy, which contrasted sharply to the strict attendance requirements of the Technical University, included the freedom of not attending classes. Actually, the only duty of a student was to obtain at the end of each term the signature of the professors for whose courses he had registered at the beginning of the term. Since class attendance was not a requirement, a student, if he wished, could go through his four years of study without ever setting foot in a class. Once he had accumulated the requisite number of credits, he could ask one of the professors to serve as supervisor of his doctoral thesis, agree with him on a thesis subject, write the thesis, submit it to him, and, if the thesis was accepted by him, have it printed at his own expense. Once all this was done, the student could sit for the doctoral examination at the end of his fourth year, pass it, and in this manner "earn" his Dr. Phil. degree. In practice, the students did attend at least those classes that were relevant to their doctoral work; this was certainly the case with the students who took Oriental studies. The other courses were only window dressing, and served to satisfy the formal requirement of accumulating a certain number of credits. The seminaries of both Budapest and Breslau were, of course, quite a different thing: in them one could not skip classes with impunity.

Nevertheless, in the first few weeks of my combined Seminary and University attendance in Budapest I worked very hard. Every morning, including Sundays, I attended classes at the Seminary from 8 A.M. to 1 P.M., then rushed to the University, located, fortunately, not too far away, so that, if one stepped out energetically, one could reach it in some fifteen minutes. Since all the classes I attended at the University were scheduled for the afternoon, there was no problem of having to miss periods in one school because of attendance in the other. What puzzles me in retrospect is when, where, and how my colleagues and I had lunch in the midst of those busy days, and especially so since at the time lunch was the main meal in Hungary and consisted of several courses.

The German offerings at the University, whether historical grammar or modern literature, did not hold much interest for me. This I know because I remember nothing either of the material my teachers covered or of the proceedings in class. The reason for this must have been that the intricacies of Old High German grammar left me entirely cold, and when it came to the modern German novel, or to Goethe and Schiller, the teachers covered territory with which I was quite familiar from my private reading in the course of the preceding four or five years. So, while sitting in the few sessions I did attend, I entertained myself with making pencil sketches of my teachers: Professor Gedeon Petz, who a year later became rector of the University, and Professor Jakab Bleyer, who a few years earlier had filled the post of minister of education in the Hungarian government.

Incidentally, about Bleyer an anecdote circulated among the students that both illustrated and mocked the rank consciousness characteristic of Hungarian society in general, and of the civil servants, including university professors, in particular. It is difficult to render the story into English because in English we don't have anything like the Hungarian range of forms of address according to rank. All the full professors at Hungarian universities had the title *Méltóságos Uram*, which the largest and best Hungarian-English dictionary (that of László Országh, published in Budapest in 1977) renders very inadequately with "Milord," or "Your Lordship," but which could better be translated with something like "Your Dignity." Bleyer, however, as a former government minister, was entitled to being addressed with the much more lofty title of *Kegyelmes Uram*, or "Your Excellency." At the other end of the title scale was *Tekintetes Ur*, something like "Squire," which even the lowest village official or burgher could and did claim. Some students, especially the more obsequious among them, were not satisfied with addressing their teachers as *Professzor Ur* (Mr. Professor), but would address them as "Your Dignity." But woe to the hapless students who thus addressed Professor Bleyer, forgetting, or perhaps not knowing, that he was the proud possessor of the exalted rank of "Excellency." Bleyer would snap back, "Why don't you rather address me as 'Squire' "?

I took more interest in the English classes, all of which, a total of six periods weekly, were given by Professor Arthur Yolland. Yolland had what I at the time believed to be the typical British physiognomy. In fact, having seen shortly before I first set eyes on him a photograph of John Galsworthy (probably in a volume of his *Forsyte Saga*), I discovered a definite resemblance between the tight-lipped, pronouncedly orthognathous, profiles of Galsworthy and Yolland. My impression of Yolland can be seen in a pencil sketch I made of him while listening to his lectures. Student gossip had a story to tell about how Yolland got to Budapest University. He was originally, so the story went, brought from England to Hungary by a certain Count Zichy, one of the great Hungarian magnates, to be tennis instructor for his two sons, and, at the same time, to teach the young counts English. When the boys reached university age, Count Zichy, who wanted Yolland to continue keeping an eye on his sons, had him appointed professor of English.

In fact, Arthur Battishill Yolland, as the *Révay Nagy Lexikona* (Révay's Great Encyclopaedia; Budapest, 1926, 19:612) informs me, came to Budapest as a young man of twenty-two, after having studied in Cambridge, and immediately became a teacher at the Francis Joseph Institute and at the University of Budapest. He was a scholar, the author of, I think, the first English-Hungarian dictionary, and, as I remember from attending his classes, he was a man of great erudition and an excellent lecturer who could capture and hold the attention of his students, some fifty or sixty of whom filled his classes period after period. He lectured in English, and even at that early and rudimentary stage of my familiarity with the language I noticed that he had a much more English-sounding accent than my erstwhile English tutor, Mr. Árpád Toth, who was a Hungarian-American. Whenever, in the course of his lectures, Yolland used a word he had reason to assume the students would not understand, he stopped and gave it in Hungarian translation, whereby his foreign-accented pronunciation of Hungarian struck us as rather funny—this was the typical Hungarian reaction on the very rare occasions when we happened to hear a foreigner speak Hungarian.

For me, Professor Yolland appeared to be the representative of the great English-speaking world, compared to which, I felt rather than knew, Hungary was a cultural backwater. I took notes of his lectures, writing furiously in order to keep up with him, but all of them have since been lost somewhere in transit, with the exception of one single page, dated September 27, 1929, on which day Yolland seems to have begun his course on The Story of the English Novel. My English orthography was somewhat shaky, but I succeeded in jotting down much of what Yolland had to say about the beginnings of the novel in England. That first period he devoted to the medieval romance, and one of the observations he made I copied as follows: "The change came from Spain, the romantic mysticism. In 1556 a book appeared, *Lazarillo de Tormes*, the first picaresque romance [here Professor Yolland inserted the Hungarian translation of this term, *selmaregény*, which, however, we understood as little as its English equivalent], adventures in the slums (Hungarian *sikátor*, he added], the adventures of very common and uncultured people, adventures that touch on realism. . . . "

Much of what Yolland was talking about I could not grasp, since the concepts he operated with were new and strange to me, but I still had the feeling that I was being given a glimpse of world literature, in which a Spanish novel genre influenced English writers, at a time when Hungarian literature could boast of nothing more than a few rather simple pieces of poetry.

Despite my interest in English literature, I gravitated toward Semitic languages and the ancient Near East. Before the end of the first term I decided to reduce my other courses and concentrate on Semitics. Thus in the spring 1930 semester, of the twenty-eight weekly periods for which I registered, twenty-one dealt with Semitics, the ancient Near East, and related subjects, including Arabic and Syriac Grammar, Readings in the Koran, History of Arabic Literature, History of the Ancient Near East, General Chronology, Persian Language, State and Society in China, Ancient General History, Greek History, and the Economic Life of Ancient Egypt.

The Arabist of the University was Professor Mihály Kmoskó, a priest, a kind and unpretentious man, who died the next year while I was in Breslau. During my first year, of the thirteen teachers for whose courses I registered, Kmoskó was the only one who was not satisfied at the term's end with simply attesting to my attendance with his signature in the registration book, but entered the word *jeles* (excellent) in the column headed "Notes." Of my other teachers at the University my memories date back, not to my freshman year, but to my junior and senior years, and I shall therefore leave my references to them to a later chapter.

During that first year at the Seminary and the University I wrote my first serious study and the first for which I got an author's fee. The Jüdischer Verlag in Berlin was preparing the fifth volume of the *Jüdisches Lexikon*, and the editor wrote to Father asking him to write the article on the history of the Jews in Hungary that was to be published under the title "Ungarn." Father, in turn, passed on the assignment to me—I don't know when and how he cleared it with the editor—and I got to work on it right away. The task was not easy, but it taught me how to use sources, how to compress a long and complex history into a relatively short narrative, and how to give it continuity, and make it readable. Nor did my German come without a struggle. But, when I got stuck, Father was there, willing and able to help. I was in Breslau when the article appeared in the concluding volume of the *Jüdisches Lexikon*, in which it took up twenty-five tightly printed columns. When a copy of it was received in the library of the Breslau Seminary, I proudly pointed out my contribution to my friends. And when I received the fee of RM 120, I promptly spent it on a tuxedo I bought in one of the city's big department stores.

The same year I also wrote several shorter articles, and reviewed a number of English and Hebrew books, in Hebrew for *HaTzofe*, and in Hungarian for Father's monthly.

Much of what I wrote during my student years in Budapest remained unpublished, and I have long forgotten what the pieces were. But I remember that I was greatly attracted to translating Hungarian writings into Hebrew, a language I felt I had mastered to a degree sufficient for such undertakings. Since I was a great admirer of Endre Ady, I tried my hand at translating some of his poems, but I was so dissatisfied with the results that I destroyed them.

Prose pieces seemed easier to cope with. When I finished translating one of Father's short stories, I felt my Hebrew version was good enough to show him. The story was titled "Thousand and One Nights," and it was contained in the volume of Father's Hasidic short stories, *Kabbala: Lelkek és Titkok* (*Kabbala: Souls and Secrets*), which subsequently also appeared in a German translation by Dr. Leo Singer under the title *Kabbala: Seelen und Welten* (Berlin: Jüdischer Verlag, 1919). One evening I entered Father's study to ask him whether he had time to listen to my translation. I found him sitting, as usual, behind his big mahogany desk. He bade me sit down and put aside the writing he was engaged in, and I read the story. He interrupted me a few times, correcting an awkward expression here, or suggesting some improvement there.

The story was about the *tzaddiq*, the miracle-working rabbi, of Belz, who is seized with the idea of building in his city a great temple, a new sanctuary for the *Shekhina*, the divine Matron wandering in exile. He spends a thousand nights poring over the sacred texts in order to find the secret of the exact spot on earth that corresponds to the heavenly temple, so as to locate his sacred edifice there. His wife Rachel sits next to him night after night, holding the candle to shed light upon his books. As the nights grow into years, Rachel becomes more and more desirous of sharing the secret learning with her husband, and at last asks him to let her enter the mysteries that absorb him. The *tzaddiq* demurs, saying that in a few more nights the vigil will be over, and Rachel bursts out bitterly: "A few more nights, and your beard, Rabbi, has become like your white robe, and the white of your hair merges with the white velvet of your skullcap. . . . " The rabbi relents, and reads to his wife the mysterious passages from the holy books telling about the love between God the King and His Spouse, the *Shekhina*, about their separation, and about the Matron's fathomless sorrow in her exile.

On the 1001st night, the *tzaddiq*, accompanied by his wife, proceeds by torchlight to the sacred spot, and there he begins the great work of building the new sanctuary by trying to push the cornerstone into its place. The heavy stone refuses to move, and Rachel bends down to help her husband push it. But the exertion is too much for her: she collapses and dies. The *tzaddiq*, heartbroken, throws himself upon the body of his wife. He remains prostrate for hours, and finally, when midnight, the sacred hour of laments, arrives, he rises, lifts his arms heavenward, and cries: "Lord of the Universe! She kept vigil with me through a thousand nights, and shed Your light upon me. . . . Were I able to, I would raise up my dear spouse and bring her back to life. But I am powerless, a broken vessel. . . . But You, Lord of the Universe, You are almighty, why don't You raise up Your dear Matron, Israel? . . . "

When I finished reading the story, Father said: "You know, I wrote this story when I first noticed white strands in my hair. This is reflected in Rachel's words about the *tzaddiq*'s hair having turned white."

I was deeply touched. This was one of the very few occasions when Father spoke to me of his personal feelings. Although he was only in his late forties, I felt that he must have been greatly saddened by those telltale signs of approaching old age, and my heart overflowed with love and pity for him.

That story was to have considerable significance for my scholarly interest in later years. In Father's story the tragedy of the *tzaddiq* and his wife served merely as the framework; the gist and kernel of the story, as I later came to understand it, were the passages that the *tzaddiq*, in response to his wife's entreaty, reads to her from the Kabbalistic literature. The relationship between God the King and

His Spouse the *Shekhina*, the Matron, who is also the symbolic personification of the Community of Israel, is one of the great themes of the Kabbala. Most touching are the pages that tell about the catastrophic separation of the divine couple, which comes about when the Temple, their bedchamber, is destroyed. Father in his story did not give a literal translation of these passages, but rendered them freely, poetically, impressively.

At the time I translated the story into Hebrew, I was, as far as I can remember, not particularly impressed by these passages. My interest was rather focused on the human tragedy of Rachel's death. I did not even know whether the passages about the divine couple were the invention of Father's poetic imagination or actual quotations from ancient texts, nor did I care. Nevertheless, they must have made a deep impression on me, which was to remain buried in my unconscious for forty years, until the 1960s, when I started working on my book *The Hebrew Goddess*. At that time, while I was gathering material for the image of the *Shekhina-Matronit*, the spouse of God the King, from the mythical-mystical passages of the Zohar and other Kabbalistic sources, I came across the original of Father's quotations, and suddenly felt as if I had been hurled back into a landscape that had been familiar to me in the days of my youth, but had long since been forgotten. More than that: I believe that seeds of my interest in the Hebrew Goddess were sown in me at that early date, and that I carried them in me during a remarkably long period of gestation, until they finally germinated and brought belated fruit.

The only actual encounter I had with a Hasidic rabbi showed him to me in a light very different from the picture Father painted of the *tzaddiq* of Belz. It happened in the summer of 1930, after I finished my freshman year, when Father took the whole family to Marienbad for our annual vacation. While there, Father took me along to neighboring Karlsbad, to visit Bialik, the famous Hebrew poet, who had gone there from Tel Aviv. I listened with awe to Bialik's anecdotes, stories, and comments. The very next day Bialik returned the visit, and came over to Marienbad in the company of Yitzhak Leib Goldberg, the Palestinian orchard owner and Maecenas of Hebrew literature, whose granddaughter I was to marry ten years later in Tel Aviv. At Father's suggestion I described the two meetings in an article he published in the September 1930 issue of his journal.

While we were in Marienbad, the Rebbe of Munkács (Mukačevo) was also there, taking the famous waters. One Sabbath morning Father and I went to attend the services held in a room in the Rebbe's temporary apartment. Checking in the *Encyclopaedia Judaica* (s.v. Mukachevo), I find that in 1930 the rabbi of Munkács was Ḥayyim Eleazar Shapira, who had succeeded his father in 1913. The article on the Shapira family states that Ḥayyim Eleazar was "an extremist opponent of Zionism, Mizrachi, and Agudat Israel, [and] regarded every organization engaged in the colonization of Erez Israel to be inspired by heresy and atheism," and this despite the fact that the Agudat Israel organization was headed by rabbis no less religious than himself.

What I remember from that visit is this: in the course of the Sabbath morning service the Rebbe gave a brief Yiddish sermon, in which at one point he said, *Di Agudisten, yimakh sh'mom v'zikhrom, vos zenen erger als di k'lovem di Zionisten* . . . (The Agudists, may their name and memory be blotted out, who are worse than those dogs the Zionists . . .). At another point he referred to Lord Balfour, the famous author of the Balfour Declaration of 1917 in which the British government promised its support to the establishment of a Jewish national home in Palestine, as *Baal Peor*, distorting the British peer's name to that of the Canaanite idol after whom the Children of Israel went awhoring. After the service Father stepped up to the Rebbe and asked him why he was so bitterly opposed to the upbuilding of the Holy Land. His answer was that in our prayers we entreat God that He should restore Zion to us, and that therefore any human effort to achieve that goal was sinful. "But," countered Father, "we also pray 'Heal us, O God, and we shall be healed,' and yet, you yourself, Rebbe, come here to Marienbad to seek human help for your ailment." The Rebbe's answer was a laconic, *Dos iz epes anders* (That is something else), and he moved away so as to cut short any further argument.

After our return from Marienbad I had a few weeks before leaving for Breslau, and I made use of the time to prepare a lengthy article in Hungarian on "The Image of Shabbatai Zevi in Modern Jewish Literature." In that essay I attempted a literary analysis of the Turkish false Messiah as seen by four modern authors: Israel Zangwill, Sholem Asch, Solomon L. Polyakoff, and Joseph Kastein. Of the four, Polyakoff (1875–1945) is the least known today. He was a Russian Jewish author whose long novel about Shabbatai Zevi was

Rector Ludwig Blau

Chief Rabbi Gyula Fischer

Professor Armin Hoffer

Professor Samuel Löwinger

Rabbi Miksa Weisz

Professor Jakab Bleyer

Professor Mihály Kmoskó

Professor Gedeon Petz

Professor Arthur Yolland

originally written in Russian, then translated into Yiddish (1926) and German (1927). My essay was published in the 1931 yearbook of the Izraelita Magyar Irodalmi Társulat (Israelite Hungarian Literary Society), known from its initial as IMIT. My style was unbelievably flowery, but not more so than was the accepted Hungarian style of the period. It began: "The writer performs a creative task when he fixes upon paper the shapes that flicker in his soul, and makes them come alive, existent. This is creation even if he brings up from the depths of history some faintly outlined figures, and, with the power of his imagination, lifts the puppets idling in the mist of the past into palpable, plastic, moving reality. . . . " Such bombastic style was a hallmark of Hungarian writing. This is why it is so difficult to translate Hungarian *belles lettres* into English. You either retain the phraseology, which makes it sound ridiculous in English, or tone it down, which renders it flat, colorless.

To conclude this chapter with yet another recollection that belongs to my freshman year rather than to the months that followed it, let me tell about the exams all students had to take at the end of their first year in the Seminary. In 1930 they were held on June 19, and I took them in the company of some six or seven other freshmen. We were given three hours to answer in writing the questions in Bible, Talmud, Codes, and Jewish history handed us by one of our teachers, who also acted as proctor for the duration of the test. I can no longer remember who he was, but I can still see him sitting down at the desk, opening a book he had brought along with him, losing himself in it, and raising his eyes only from time to time to make sure that everything in the classroom was as it should be. Since we could have no idea in advance as to the nature of the questions that were to be put to us, we could not make special preparations for these exams. All we could do was review the material we covered during the year, memorize as much as we were able to, and trust our luck. Needless to say, we were not allowed to use any books or notes while working on the exam questions.

However, since only freshmen had to take the exams, the sophomores and other older students had the morning off. In fact, they were banned not only from the classroom itself, but also from the third-floor corridor in front of it. But several of them did not simply go away; instead they stuck around on the ground floor, ready to help. Since upperclassmen, and especially those who had just finished their fourth or fifth year, of course knew much more than we freshmen did, there was a standing arrangement that enabled us to be helped by their superior knowledge. There was always a sufficient number of these advanced students who were willing to sacrifice an hour or so of their time for the benefit of their younger colleagues in the throes of their first exam's rigors. As soon as the questions were distributed by the proctor, one of the examinees would copy them on a small slip of paper, fold it as tightly as possible, and then ask permission to go to the bathroom. The corridor between the classroom and the facilities was patrolled by another teacher, so that any communication there between freshmen and advanced students was impossible. Ah, but the powers that be did not count on the ingenuity of students dreading failure in their exams. The freshman went straight to the bathroom whose window opened to the courtyard, took his copy of the questions from his pocket, made sure that it was well folded up into a small bundle, and threw it out the window. Below, in the courtyard, waited one of the seniors; he retrieved the missile and hurried with it to his colleagues, whereupon they all retired to some place where they would not be disturbed, and went to work answering the questions. With their superior knowledge, some mutual aid, and possibly the use of books and notes, they were able to write out the answers within an hour or so.

After enough time had passed, another freshman asked permission to go to the restroom. He let down a string through the window, to which a senior tied as many versions of the sets of answers as the number of those taking the exams. With this treasure retrieved, the freshman returned to the classroom, and there, surreptitiously, the answers were distributed among the examinees, who, up to that time, only made desultory stabs at writing out their answers to those questions they were able to handle on their own. Now they could copy the answers within a relatively short time. This system was practically fail-safe; in any case, I never heard of any freshman failing his exams. What we thus owed to the seniors, two or three years later we repaid, not to them, but to the new freshmen class.

In telling this story, I certainly do not want to create the impression that the average student at the Seminary was either lazy or ignorant. Far from it. We all worked hard, and frequent informal oral exams, as well as the seminar-style conduct of the classes in several subjects, made it practically impossible for us not to make an all-out effort to meet the demands of our instructors. But the amount of work expected of us, especially in the first year of our studies, was staggering. Thirty hours a week at the Seminary, plus several more at the University, and preparation for these classes were more than enough to keep a student busy from morning to evening. In addition, many of the students also had to earn some money to supplement whatever stipend they had, which they did mostly by tutoring — all this together amounted to considerable pressure, so that some outside help with the first serious exam was felt to be needed, and, in a higher sense, justified.

10

A Year in Breslau: 1930–1931

The institutions of higher learning in Germany started their fall term later than those of Hungary, and thus I could still spend the High Holy Days of 1930 at home with my parents. When the time for my departure approached, I went to take my leave from my teachers at the Seminary and the University, as well as from my grandparents, and, when the day arrived, Father took me to the railroad station from which my train left for Breslau. We arrived well in advance of departure time, and spent some fifteen or twenty minutes walking up and down on the platform next to the train. Father was silent for a while, then turned to me and said: "I want to tell you something about the death of your uncle Berti. You should know that he died of a venereal disease that he had contacted several years earlier. He had a secretary working for him, she became his girl friend, and he was infected by her. He got treatment and was thought to have been cured, but years later the disease came back and killed him. I am telling you this in confidence, so that you should understand how important it is to refrain from that kind of relationship."

I was terribly embarrassed hearing Father talk about things he had never before even touched upon in conversation with me, and all I could say was, "Yes, Father." Soon thereafter the whistle blew, I kissed Father's hand, as I did only on solemn occasions, and boarded the train. As I found out many years later, the disease that took Uncle Berti's life was not at all of a sexual nature, so I have had to conclude that Father simply invented the story in order to impress me with the imperative of abstaining from sexual adventures in the foreign city I was going to.

When I arrived in Breslau, well supplied with both fatherly and professorial advice, I was met at the railroad station by a classmate from the Budapest Seminary, Henrik Fisch, who had gone to Breslau some time earlier. He took me to his room, where I stayed overnight, and the next day he set out with me and another Budapest seminarian who had arrived a day before me, Miklós László, to find lodging for us not far from the Seminary. Before long we did locate a suitable room that was available to two students, and thus László and I became roommates.

My year in Breslau was the first time I was away from home for a long period. However, it was not really like going out into a completely strange world, because the relationship between the Jüdisch-theologisches Seminar in Breslau and the Budapest Seminary was like that of an older brother to a younger one. When the latter opened its doors in 1877, its board of supervisors envisaged it as a Hungarian version of the Breslau Seminary. Established in 1854, with funds bequeathed by Jonas Fraenkel, a prominent Breslau businessman, the Breslau Seminary also served as the prototype for other rabbinical institutions in Europe. Its religious position was neither Reform nor Orthodox but Conservative, which was expressed in the formulation of its basic aim: to teach "positive historical Judaism." In 1921 Dr. Michael Guttmann (1872–1942), who had been professor of Talmud at the Budapest Seminary since 1907, was invited to be professor of Talmud and *Seminarrabbiner* (seminary rabbi) in Breslau, the only person who could ordain the Seminary's graduates as rabbis. Thus there was a personal connection as well between the two institutions, and it became the custom that students of the Budapest Seminary, who could mange it financially or obtain a stipend for the purpose, spent their sophomore year in Breslau.

The date of my admission to the Breslau Seminary, according to my registration book, was October 30, 1930; I was admitted to the Schlesische Friedrich Wilhelms-Universität zu Breslau on November 5. The curriculum of the Seminary, I found, did not differ greatly from that of the Budapest school. There were five teachers who offered a total of twenty-one courses, several of which consisted of only one weekly period. Professor Guttmann taught the tractate *Baba Bathra* of the Babylonian Talmud and the Codes (*Even ha'Ezer*), and also conducted a seminar called Apologetic Exercises. Professor Isaac Heinemann (1876–1957) taught Outline of Medieval Jewish Philosophy, Readings in Maimonides' *Guide of the Perplexed*, Outline of Jewish Homiletics, and Homiletic Exercises. *Dozent* (lecturer) Albert Lewkowitz (1883–1954) gave courses on the Influence of Romanticism on Judaism, the Crisis in the Contemporary Philosophy of Religion, the Great Religions of the East, Exercises in the Philosophy of Romanticism, and Pedagogical Exercises. *Dozent* Israel Rabin (1882–1951) taught the Book of Job, the Bible Commentary of Rashbam, Hebrew Syntax, Jewish History of the Mishnaic Period, and seminars on the famous Epistle of Sherira Gaon and the tractate Horayot of the Babylonian Talmud. *Dozent* H. J. Zimmels (1900–1974) gave courses on the Communal Life of the Jews in the Middle Ages, Readings of Historical Responsa, and Liturgical Rules. In the second term, each of these courses was replaced by a new one from the same general field. As in Budapest, so in Breslau all the students from freshmen to seniors sat together in one and the same classroom, and all our mornings were taken up by these courses, while in the afternoon we attended classes at the University.

At the University my main teacher was Professor Carl Brockelmann (1868–1956), the great Semitic linguist, author of the multivolume *Geschichte der arabischen Literatur* and the *Vergleichende Grammatik der semitischen Sprachen*. His courses were, in the first term, Outline of Hebrew Syntax, Explanation of the Aramaic Texts of the Old Testament, Syriac, and Introduction to Arabic. Actually, in the University catalog that term, Brockelmann listed no Arabic course but an Introduction to New Persian, which I duly entered into my registration book, although I regretted greatly that I would have no chance to have Brockelmann as my teacher in Arabic, the most important modern Semitic language. But when one of my fellow seminarians and I arrived for the first class of that course, we found that we were the only students taking it, and we decided then and there to ask Professor Brockelmann to change the subject to Arabic. Brockelmann said something to the effect that he did not have many opportunities to teach Persian, but nevertheless, he acceded to our request, and right away began to instruct us in Arabic.

Brockelmann was a demanding teacher and a hard taskmaster. Using Socin's *Arabische Grammatik* that he had reedited only the year before in an improved tenth edition, he covered during every period what seemed to me a huge amount of material. He expected us to have memorized all of it by the next session, as well as to have prepared several pages of the exercise texts that were appended to the book. I had to work very hard to keep up with Brockelmann's demands, and I think that if I had not had at least some previous knowledge of the language (after all, I had attended Professor

Kmoskó's Arabic course in Budapest for two terms) I could not have done satisfactory work. As it was, I had to devote two hours every single day of the week to prepare myself for that one Arabic course of two weekly periods.

For my colleague Ziegler, who had never before taken Arabic, the pace proved too strenuous, and he did not register for the continuation of the course in the second term. I was somewhat apprehensive that if I remained the only student in that course it would be canceled, but that did not prove to be the case. Brockelmann continued the course, and thus I was privileged to have been his only student in the Arabic class, which amounted to private instruction by the foremost Arabist of the age. Throughout each of the periods I read and translated Arabic texts, explained the grammatical forms and the syntax, rattled off, in reply to Brockelmann's questions, the various Arabic verbs in their many forms, showed that I knew the almost endless vareties of the noun plurals, and so forth. I worked hard, much harder than for any other course in all my higher studies in five academic institutions (five, not counting my aborted attendance at the Technical University of Budapest), but the price was not too high considering that I did acquire not only a sound foundation in Arabic, but also a great love for that rich and beautiful language that was to remain with me all my life.

Brockelmann looked and behaved like a typical Prussian army officer. On his left cheek he had a long and clearly visible *Schmiss* (cut), proof that in his student days he had belonged to a *schlagende Burschenschaft* (dueling fraternity) whose members were supposed to engage in sword duels, and to sustain at least one such cut across the cheek (the other parts of the head and the body were protected by padding). In the second term of my Breslau year Brockelmann also gave a lecture course entitled Semitic Peoples and Languages, which was attended by some fifteen students. As soon as he entered the classroom, even before he closed the door behind him, he began to speak, with great speed, and continued without interruption until the bell sounded, when, still speaking, he would walk to the door and exit.

Because of his rapid delivery I found it impossible to take notes of what undoubtedly was a comprehensive survey of the subject, but the memory of the course itself, and of the sweeping approach utilized by Brockelmann, remained with me, and many years later, when I gave courses at Dropsie College in Philadelphia and at

Princeton University on Peoples and Cultures of the Middle East, I felt that I was following in his footsteps. I remember, in particular, the feeling I had while listening to Brockelmann that he opened up before me unsuspected vistas, and enabled me, for the first time, to see the Bible and its language as the product of one people among many who in their totality made up the great world of the ancient Near East. In the course of those lectures Brockelmann referred to dozens of other scholars and their work, but there was only one among them whom he described as "great": each time he mentioned Ignaz Goldziher he said *der grosse Goldziher* (the Great Goldziher). I was tempted to tell him that once, in my childhood, I shook hands with Goldziher, but then I thought such a piece of information would mean nothing to him.

When Brockelmann was satisfied with my performance in class, he as a rule did not say so, but it was evident from his demeanor. I remember only one occasion when he uttered the words *sehr gut* (very good). It happened while I was reading an Arabic text, and when I came to a sentence that contained a clause, he asked me what kind of a clause it was, and I answered that it was a *sifa Satz*. Brockelmann said *sehr gut*, and I was swept by a warm feeling of satisfaction.

I remember only one occasion on which I found myself in disagreement (unspoken, of course) with Brockelmann. He asked me to read and translate a passage from the *Kitāb al-Aghānī* (18:209ff.) that tells how the poet Ta'abbata Sharran met a *ghūl* in the desert, struggled with him to subdue and capture him, and, just when he thought that he had him in his power, the evil being urinated on him, whereupon the surprised poet could no longer hold on to him but had to let him go. It was due to this adventure that the poet was given the nickname Ta'abbata Sharran, "He carried evil [in his arm]." When I finished reading and translating the piece, Brockelmann said something to the effect that this story closely paralleled the biblical story of Jacob's encounter with the angel at the Ford of Jabbok. Not yet being a comparative folklorist, and having a strong respect for the sanctity of the Bible, I considered this comparison totally improper, but of course I did not dare to voice my opinion to the *Herr Professor.*

Professor Brockelmann was an extremely conscientious teacher. Although in the summer term of 1931 I was the only student in his Arabic class, he never missed a single period, and, needless to say, neither did I. The Breslau University was a Catholic institution, and it was closed on all Catholic holidays. A number of times, at the conclusion of a period, Brockelmann, who was a Protestant, would say to me, "*Ach*, next week there is again a Catholic holiday. But we shall have our class; come to my office at the usual hour." While the classrooms were closed on Catholic holidays, the professors' offices that served as their studies were open.

Once, and only once, as far as I can remember, I screwed up enough courage to ask Brockelmann a question not related directly to the texts we were studying. Some time prior to my Breslau year, Father was involved in a discussion concerning the meaning of an Aramaic phrase. In his book *Bava Metzia — The Middle Gate*, he translated the first words of the traditional prayer that is printed in all standard editions of the Talmud at the end of each tractate, each time with the name of the appropriate tractate inserted. At the conclusion of the *Bava Metzia*, from which tractate Father took the name of his book, the prayer starts as follows: *Hadran 'alakh mas-sekhet Bava M'tzi'a w'hadrakh 'alan* . . . which was commonly taken to mean, "We shall return to you, O tractate 'The Middle Gate,' and you will return to us. . . . " Father, however, translated it as "Our glory upon you, O tractate 'The Middle Gate,' and your glory upon us. . . . " Some reviewers of his book, which was published shortly before I left for Breslau, trying to parade their erudition, took exception to this translation, and Father, in response, defended it. On that occasion in Breslau, when the bell signaled the end of Brockelmann's class, I asked him whether I could put to him a question of Aramaic grammar. He was, as usual, already on his way to the door, but stopped instantly, and said, "Of course."

I went to the blackboard, and wrote on it the four words in Hebrew characters, הדרן עלך · · · והדרך עלן , mentioned the source from which they came, and told him about the controversy concerning their meaning. He took the chalk, added the vowel signs and explained that while הדרן alone could be read either as *hadarn*, which would mean "we return," or as *hadran*, meaning "our glory," the word *hadrakh* can be read only one way and can mean only "your glory," since "your return" would be *hadret* in Aramaic. Since the two parts of the sentence were evidently parallel, the whole phrase can only mean "our glory upon you . . . and your glory upon us. . . . " Then Brockelmann also added something about the difference between biblical and talmudic Aramaic that, to my regret, I can no longer recall. All in all, he spent some ten or fifteen minutes explaining these things to me, and when he left I understood that his rushing out of the classroom at the sound of the bell did not mean that he was eager to get out of the class, but was simply a manifestation of his Prussian-officer punctuality, and that when he had any academic reason to stay longer he did not begrudge the time. The same evening I wrote Father, telling him that no less an authority than Professor Brockelmann agreed with his interpretation of *hadran 'alakh*.

After leaving Breslau I had no further contact with Brockelmann, but ever since then, and throughout my life, I have often delved into his great works and always found them a rich source of information.

In addition to the classes given by Brockelmann, I also registered, and attended, two one-hour weekly classes given at the University by Dr. Israel Rabin. The courses were the Language of Tannaitic Literature with Selected Readings, and Style Forms of New Hebrew Literature. Part of the tuition fee system at Breslau University was that each student was charged for each course of one hour weekly 2.50 reichsmarks per term, except for those courses that were considered public lectures and covered by a general tuition fee. The 2.50 reichsmarks per student were passed on by the Universitäts-Quästur (bursar's office) to the instructor. At the first meeting of his classes, Dr. Rabin handed 5 reichsmarks to each of the students, explaining that he did not want to take money from us even in this indirect way. I remember one of my colleagues remarking cynically that a few marks did not make any difference for Rabin, and that this was simply his way of attracting students to his classes at the University, in which, for reasons of prestige, he wanted to have as many students as possible.

As far as I remember, Dr. Rabin was the only one among my teachers in Breslau who asked his students to prepare a term paper. The subject he assigned me was "Die poetischen Stücke in den späthistorischen Schriften auf ihren Psalmcharakter untersucht," a rather involved title that roughly meant "An Inquiry into the Psalm-Character of the Poetical Pieces in the Late Historical Writings," of the Bible, that is. By a mere chance, the draft manuscript of this research paper did not get lost in the course of my transcontinental moves, and upon rereading it now it strikes me as showing that, at least, I took my assignment seriously. I started by stating the main

My maternal great-grandmother, Mrs. Raphael Kurländer, ca. 1890.

My paternal grandfather, R. Moshe Klein, ca. 1926. This picture is a drawing my father had made on the basis of an old photograph.

My maternal grandmother, Mrs. Theresa Ehrenfeld, ca. 1926.

My maternal grandfather, Mór (Moshe) Ehrenfeld, ca. 1926.

My father, aged 22 (1905). My father sent this picture as a postcard to my mother to whom he was engaged at the time, and who spent the summer of 1905 with her grandmother in Nagyvárad.

From left to right: My sister Évi, my mother, I, my brother Guszti, ca. 1926.

In Swinemünde, Germany, summer of 1923. From left to right: my father with my brother Guszti in from of him, the famous Hebrew poet Saul Tchernichowsky, Chief Rabbi Adler.

Guszti, Évi, and I, ca. 1928.

My mother at the age of ca. 20 (1906).

My father at the age of ca. 33 (1915).

The Executive Committee of the Pro Palestine Federation of Hungarian Jews, ca. 1928. From left to right: Court Councillor Ferenc Székely, Prof. Ignác Pfeiffer, Chief Rabbi Immanuel Löw, Government Chief Councillor Dr. Ignác Friedmann, Father.

In Zurich, Switzerland, August 1929. From left to right: Father, and unidentified friend, Sholem Asch, the famous Yiddish novelist, Mrs. Asch.

I (standing on the left) with a group of my colleagues from the Budapest
Rabbinical Seminary on a hike, spring, 1930.

Mother and Father in Marienbad, summer 1930.

With Marion in Breslau, winter 1930-31.

In Karlsbad, summer 1930. Seated from left to right: my sister Évi, the famous Hebrew poet Hayyim Nahman Bialik, Mother, Father; I stand behind my sister, my brother Guszti stands behind Father, and to the right stands Yitzhak Leb Goldberg, whose granddaughter, Naomi Tolkowsky, I married ten years later in Tel Aviv.

I, aged 21, as a student of the Budapest Rabbinical Seminary.

My sister Évi, aged ca. 22.

characteristics of biblical poetry (accent rhythm and parallelism of thought), then went on to demonstrate to what extent the few poetical pieces contained in the books Ezra, Nehemiah, and Chronicles evince the same features. Then I adduced all the examples I could find in these late historical books to show similarities and differences between the phraseology and thought-content of their poetical pieces and those of the Psalms. In general, I confined myself to quoting, comparing, and commenting upon the biblical passages themselves, but on one occasion I quoted the contrasting opinions of Wellhausen and Kautzsch, and expressed myself in support of the more conservative view of the latter. I also referred to the comments of C. F. Keil, Kittel, Gunkel, Graetz, and Buhl, and drew my own conclusion that "the Chronist no longer seems to have had a real sense of rhythmical-poetic language," that there were no original poetic pieces preserved in the late historical writings, and that each of the poetical pieces that appear only in these books lacks both the accent-rhythm and the parallelism of thought structure, and that, therefore, strictly speaking, they cannot be termed poetry.

Another of the Seminary professors who gave courses at the University was Professor Heinemann. He lectured on Philo of Alexandria, complementing thereby the courses he gave on Jewish philosophy at the Seminary. He was working at the time on his book *Philons griechische und jüdische Bildung* (Philo's Greek and Jewish Education), in which, when I later read it, I found much that was familiar to me from his lectures. Heinemann was editor of the *Monatschrift für Geschichte und Wissenschaft des Judentums*, well known all over the scholarly world as *MGWJ*, which was founded in 1851 by Zachariah Frankel, just three years before he became the first head of the Breslau Seminary, and which in 1930 was still the most prestigious journal of Jewish studies. As editor of the *MGWJ*, Heinemann was a most influential figure in the world of Jewish scholarship. Only much later did I discover that Heinemann was a significant Jewish philosopher in his own right, whose main contribution, as I understood it, was to uphold the specifically Jewish viewpoint as reflected in, and derived from, the Bible, and to juxtapose it to the Gentile attitudes that stemmed from Greek and Germanic thought and from Christianity. At the same time he emphasized the role of Jewish thought as a link in transmitting Greek influences to the West.

In 1930–1931, when I was his student in Breslau, Heinemann was in his mid-fifties, a slim figure of a man, with a high forehead, a balding head, bushy eyebrows, piercing jet-black eyes covered by thick glasses, a prominent nose with pronounced nostrils, a black moustache, a goatee shot through with grey, and a facial expression of sustained fierce intensity. I remember especially his classes in hom-iletic exercises, held in the synagogue of the Seminary on weekday mornings, as part of his course offerings. The student whose turn it was to deliver the exercise sermon went up to the lectern, and Professor Heinemann, who was hard of hearing, stood next to him to his left, and bent his neck forward so as to catch every word the student uttered. After the student finished, Heinemann would make detailed critical remarks, pointing out both the strengths and the weaknesses of the sermon, and suggesting improvements.

For my exercise sermon I took the easy way out, and translated into German one of the Hungarian sermons I had given the previous year in the synagogue of the Budapest Seminary. My knowledge of German was quite adequate by that time so that the translation caused me no difficulty. What I did not take into account, because I was not sufficiently alerted to it, was that the flowery phrases of the Hungarian did not sit too well in German garb, and that therefore I should have done a good amount of pruning and rewriting instead of translating. Fortunately, we were allowed to read our sermons from the prepared text, so that I was spared the trouble of memo-rizing mine. My Hungarian accent, however, coming as it did on top of the Hungarian phraseology, must have been difficult for Pro-fessor Heinemann to understand, for he bent even closer to me than was his wont, and cupped his right hand around his ear to hear me better. Of the remarks he made after I concluded I remember only two: he pointed out that the proper pronunciation of the word *brachte* (brought) was with a short *a*, and not with a long one as I pronounced it; and, on a more general level, he criticized my hom-iletic effort for having too much poetry and too little thought-content in it. In 1939, just before the outbreak of World War II, Heinemann moved to Jerusalem, where he continued his scholarly work, and wrote and published two books in Hebrew. He died in 1957, at the age of eighty.

Of my other professors at the University I remember little. One of them, Professor Anton Jirku, was a famous biblical scholar, whose course on the Old Testament in the Light of Ancient Near Eastern Culture was well attended. Although I remember nothing of his classes, he must have made an impression on me, because the relationship of the Bible to its contemporary environment and to the modern Middle East subsequently became a subject to which I devoted several studies.

The most popular lecturer at the University was the philosopher Eugen Kühnemann (1868–1946). Professor Kühnemann was an impassioned, excited, and exciting speaker, whose lecture course, entitled On the Struggle for a Modern View of Life, attracted hundreds of students who filled the largest lecture hall of the University to capacity. He was an enthusiastic *Deutschnazionaler* (German nationalist), whose views must have been quite close to those of the National Socialist party of Hitler, which at the time was in ascendancy all over Germany. Student gossip had it that one of Kühnemann's slogans was *Kauft deutsche Ware, trinkt deutsches Bier, hurt deutsche Weiber* (Buy German goods, drink German beer, screw German women). While the authenticity of this quotation is doubtful, it unquestionably reflected Kühnemann's spirit of *Deutschland über Alles*. I myself heard him, in the course of his lectures, say, *Spinoza stand an den Peripherien des Deutschtums* (Spinoza stood on the peripheries of Germandom). Poor, persecuted Sephardi Spinoza: he certainly never dreamt that the fact that he lived in Holland would one day give rise to such an ascription of German affinity to him.

Giving in to my usual curiosity and urge to verify what I remember, I looked up Kühnemann's biography in the *Meyers Lexikon* and the *Brockhaus Enzyklopädie*, and find that he authored numerous books, all in German, of course, among them *The World Reich of the German Spirit (1914), From the World Reich of the Spirit* (1926), and *The German Struggle for Freedom* (1941). He survived the collapse of the German "World Reich" by not more than a year.

As far as my studies were concerned, my life in Breslau closely resembled the routine I had in Budapest: the Seminary in the morning, the University in the afternoon, and studying at the Seminary or in my room in the evenings. Yet the fact that I lived not at home, but in a rented room, made a difference. I had to cope with all kinds of little things to which I had never had to give a thought while at home. I had to take my underwear to a laundry. I had to go out for most of my meals. At home I was never aware that the house was well heated in the winter. In Breslau, I had to make special arrangements to have heat in my room. None of the apartments in which I rented rooms had central heating. There was, to be sure, a big tile stove in the room, but whenever I wanted to have a fire in it, I had to ask the landlady, who, in turn, instructed the maid to start the fire and keep it going as long as a bucketful of coal or coke lasted. Each time a fire was laid, I had to pay an extra amount for it—heating was not included in the monthly rent. My budget was tight, and I could not afford the luxury of a heated room more than once a week. So on many an evening I went to the Seminary library to study, and had to get used to going to bed in a room that was bitterly cold in the winter evenings.

After László and I decided to move into separate rooms, I found lodgings in an apartment in which, next to me, lived a Swiss student of the Seminary by the name of Lothar Rothschild. There was a connecting door between our two rooms, and we made an agreement that each of us would pay our landlady to make a fire in his room once a week, alternatingly, and we would both study in that room that day and the next, when some of the warmth still lingered. The third or fourth day, of course, both rooms were again equally cold. In these circumstances we were literally forced to develop a liking for the library of the Seminary—which was warm, and open in the evenings—where we could study undisturbed. The most difficult moment was to undress in the cold room, and to get into the ice-cold bed, which I did as quickly as possible. Once under the heavy and plump feather-bedding, I got warmed up soon enough, and slept soundly. But in the morning the problem returned. Breslau lying at a more northerly latitude than Budapest, its winter nights were longer, so that when I got up in the morning it was still pitch dark. I would put on the light and wash in the cold room, using the even colder water that I poured from a heavy china pitcher into a china bowl that stood on a sideboard. This was all the washing I could do six days a week. Once a week I took a hot bath in the bathroom of the apartment—that luxury was included in the monthly rent of the room, which also included a change of bed linen once a month. To save on laundry, I, like all my colleagues, wore shirts with detachable celluloid collars and cuffs that could be scrubbed clean with soap and water.

I had a warm winter coat with a large fur collar so that I was relatively well protected from the cold outdoors. In the mornings, on the way to the Seminary—it was usually still half dark—I would stop at a milk bar, where I would get a glass of hot milk and a large hard roll with nothing on it. This was my daily breakfast. Unlike Proust, I do not remember either the taste or the smell of the roll, but I remember that in my hurry to be in time for Professor Guttmann's Talmud class, which was the first period in the morning, I used to drink the milk while it was still too hot, and it often scalded my tongue.

For lunch all the students of the Seminary went to Mr. Kornhäuser's nearby restaurant, which was something like a *mensa academica* for the seminarians, and, I think, had no other guests. The meals—lunch was the main meal of the day—were simple, but good and not expensive. Incidentally, no minced meat was served, as far as I remember, so that I did not have to worry about Dr. Weisz's caution. Two young girls served as waitresses, and the underarm smell that emanated from the prettier of them was interpreted by some of the students as an indication of the girl's excitement in the company of so many young men. I took my evening meals (I cannot call them dinners because they were much too meager for that) in most cases in my room. Once or twice a week, on the way home from the University, I would buy bread, butter, some cheese and some fruit, and that would be my *Abendbrot*. The landlady allowed me to keep the butter in her icebox in the kitchen. It was characteristic of the deprived economic conditions of the household help in the city that the maid who worked for my landlady (I no longer remember whether she slept in or out) stole from my butter, which I noticed since my bar of butter seemed to become shorter from one evening to the next. To make sure what was happening, I cut lines into the butter bar with my knife at about each quarter of an inch, and, to be sure, the next evening there was one line less. I confronted the maid with the evidence, but she, of course, denied being responsible for the diminution of the butter. Nevertheless, thereafter the butter stopped shrinking.

Even though we were being kept very busy with our double schedule at the Seminary and the University, plus the endless preparation for the classes, we somehow found time for social activities as well. First of all, we, that is, one or two colleagues and I, went to the movies, perhaps as frequently as once a week. I can no longer remember whether it was during my year in Breslau that I first saw *The Blue Angel* with Marlene Dietrich and Emil Jannings, but I do recall that it was there that I saw my first French film. In Budapest most of the films shown were German, there was no Hungarian film industry to speak of until 1929, and films from other countries were rarely imported. So when I saw advertised the film *Sous les toits de Paris*, I went to see it. All I remember from it is the melody of the song starting with the same words, and some shots of the Paris roof-tops.

We also went out occasionally to dances. My memory on this point is somewhat hazy, but I do see myself and a friend standing near the wall in a dance hall filled with quite a crowd of young people. A small orchestra is playing, and almost everybody is danc-ing. Among them is a young doctor whom we happened to know from somewhere, dancing with a girl whose image, as I conjure it up in my memory, brings to my mind the expression "Tiger Lily." She is small of stature, with a trim figure and a beautiful face with freck-les and an expression of great intensity. When the orchestra takes a break, the doctor comes over with her and introduces us. We chat for a few minutes, and my friend looks at her with unconcealed admiration. Before one of us can screw up enough courage to ask her to dance, the doctor takes her back to the floor. My friend looks after them with envy and sadness, and says, "Look at Dr. X; he knows how to live. He works hard, but still has time to enjoy him-self. I bet that girl must be a tiger in bed." And then he adds even more sadly, "And we? What do we have of life? We study day and night, and when we are back home in Hungary we shall not even be allowed to have any fun."

One of the places I remember having visited in Breslau was an amusement park set up somewhere on the outskirts of the city for the celebration of the *Johannesfest*, the German Midsummer's Day, on June 24. In this case I don't have to drag my memory for details because on the basis of my impressions I wrote a short short story (in German) that also has survived to this day in manuscript. One of the attractions of the *Johannesfest* was a booth in which the spectators could purchase balls to throw against targets over which, on protrud-ing planks, sat girls clad in bathing suits. Beneath them was a tank of water, and if one hit the target, the plank dipped down, spilling the girl into the water. In my story I described what one such girl felt as she was sitting there, shivering in the cool night air, and hop-ing that her target would not be hit and she would be spared being dunked in the water as long as possible. Drawing on my imagina-tion I described the thoughts that went through the mind of the girl, what she felt about her boyfriend, about her work, which did not give her enough income so that she had to take this additional evening job, about the pregnancy she had to have aborted, and the like. The story ended with the girl falling into the water. I called it *"Das süsse Mädchen"* (The Sweet Girl), the actual name inscribed over that booth.

Soon after my arrival in Breslau I got acquainted with local girls of my own age, or perhaps a year or two younger. I would visit them in their homes (they all lived with their parents), or, either in a twosome or with another couple, we would go to a movie, a dance, a party. The girls were all from middle-class Jewish families; their fathers were businessmen, store owners, or professional men. All the girls had finished high school, but none of them went on to higher studies. In Budapest girls of this class, as I knew from frustrating experiences, were extremely reticent, inhibited, and what I considered rejecting. All one could hope for was to plant a quick kiss on their lips, and even that was considered a most daring act. In Breslau (and in Berlin, where I was to spend ten days during the Christmas vacation) girls of the same social background were much more forthcoming. Here for the first time I met girls who not only did not object to being kissed, but made no bones about liking to kiss and even to pet. This response of theirs made quite a difference in my self-evaluation as a man. I became more self-confident, outgoing, and direct in my approach, not only with girls but with men as well.

The name of my first love in Breslau was Marion. Her father was an accountant, and she had a younger brother who was as tall as I was and even thinner. I must have made Marion's acquaintance immediately after my arrival in Breslau (for the life of me I cannot remember the circumstances), for the first of the many photographs I took of her and still have in a photo album bears the date of October 1930. She was a charming, very pretty girl, tall and slim, with chestnut hair, a round, freckled face, dreamy brown eyes, a short, straight nose, and lovely, full, and sensuous lips. We took to each other instantly, and we were together so often that I wondered why her parents did not object to my practically monopolizing her. I must have visited her several times a week; we went out together, took walks, went swimming and dancing, and when the weather turned colder and snow fell, we took sleigh rides on the mountain slopes around the city. At one time my sister Évi, who was spending some time with our aunt Ruth (the widow of Uncle Berti) in Berlin, passed through Breslau on her way home to Budapest, and stopped over for a day. I took her to meet Marion, and she gave her sisterly approval of the friendship between Marion and me.

Even though our outings were modest, I soon found that my expenditures tended to exceed the allowance Father gave me. Fortunately, I found out from one of my colleagues that the Fraenkel Foundation, which had established the Seminary and still defrayed all its expenses, had earmarked some money to be given as scholarships to its students. I have some vague recollection that those scholarships were given only to students who were in some way related to the founder, and that I was able to furnish proof that I indeed fulfilled this requirement, but I am not at all sure about this. What I do remember with great clarity is that I went to the office of the Fraenkel Foundation (which, I believe, was located in the Seminary building), presented my case, and, without much ado, was allocated a monthly stipend of 150 reichsmarks, thus increasing my budget by 50 percent. I was greatly impressed by this example of German (or, rather, German Jewish) efficiency and promtpness, and, in my mind, compared it with the endless red tape I would have had to disentangle had I submitted a similar request to a Budapest office.

For a while I debated with myself whether I should inform Father of this windfall and suggest that he reduce my allowance by the same amount or part of it. But in the end I found compelling reasons—that is to say, excuses—for not doing so. After all, I said to myself, Father had budgeted my allowance for the Breslau sojourn, and the amount he gave me was certainly small in relation to the total expenses of the family. It was also a fact that prices in Breslau were higher than expected. So I put my mind at rest and kept silent about this increment in my income.

While I enjoyed being with Marion, there was one aspect of the relationship between us that was not satisfactory: it did not solve my sexual problem. Since she was the first German girl I got friendly with, I took it for granted that sex for her was as much a forbidden territory as it was for the girls I knew in Budapest. The relationship between us was purely platonic in practice if not in attitude, and it never occurred to me that I could persuade her to "give herself to me." Hence, even though I loved her, I was constantly on the lookout for girls with whom I could have sex. My hunger in this area increased each time I heard a colleague tell about the easy availability of the German girls. Occasionally I went to one of the big department stores in the inner city, not to buy something but to look at the young salesgirls, and imagined how it would be if I started talking to one of them and asked her, "What are you doing after work?" But I never found enough courage to address any one of them. I was naturally timid, and, in addition, I was afraid that they would scorn me because I was a foreigner and a Jew. So it was only in my imagination that I spoke to them, and engaged them nonchalantly in witty conversation that led to an assignation. I even went so far as to build up in my mind quite a series of false identities for myself, of the kind I thought a salesgirl would find irresistible: a visiting businessman, a sports instructor, an artist. But I never spoke a single word to any of them, and even when I did have to buy something, I transacted my purchase as quickly and with as few words as possible.

Of the dozens of letters I wrote my parents from Breslau only two have survived. They constitute the only contemporary record of what I did and how I felt during the first few months of my sojourn in that city. The opening sentence in the first letter shows that in an earlier one I informed my mother of my intention to move out of the room I shared with my colleague László, and that she inquired why I was planning to do so. I wrote her in German:

Breslau, Nov. 20, 1930

My Dearest Mama:

My decision to move away has only one reason: I don't want to listen any longer to the babble of László. Of course we speak German, but from his German I get nothing, or even less than nothing. Until now it was still pleasant for me to room together with a friend, but now that I already move about quite confidently on this foreign soil I want to room alone, or rather with a German next door. However, I shall move out in all probability only on the first of January.

[Tibor] Fábián arrived and brought along the cakes and the two September issues [of Mult és Jövő]. The first night he slept in our room on the couch. Today, already the whole Seminary laughs at him. One line to his portrait: he accosts girls on the street, some three or four every day, quite unhesitatingly, in the closest proximity of the Seminary.

Thank God, heaven shield us from harm, I look very well, am of good constitution, I sit all day long in the halls of the University and the Seminary, and still am never tired.

Last night I attended a lecture at the local group of the Zionist-Revisionists. Among those present was Mrs. Lachman (she filled half the hall); she spoke to me and said she was very sorry that she was not at home when I called, and would soon invite me for an evening. I thanked her politely.

Just now I received the letter for my birthday and Évi's book. Many heartfelt thanks. Of course, I, too, am a little sorry that I cannot celebrate my birthday at home, in the warm family circle, but am comforted by the thought that I shall learn a lot during this year, that I shall utilize it as fully as possible, and turn it to my advantage.

I repeat now my requests: 20 offprints of my article on Yosef Adler; material for articles about Hungarian Jewry. There is here a Jewish weekly for East Germany, in which I could place an article, and also get some fee for it. (Apropos: what about the fee for my article in the *Jüdisches Lexikon*?)

For Papa: we should get a copy of Goldschmidt's Talmud translation. It is in the process of being published. If we cannot get it fully gratis, we should perhaps buy it at half price. It costs RM 13.50 per volume, and the whole work will consist of 12 volumes (Jüdischer Verlag, Berlin).

The [biblical] *Dictionary of Gesenius* (latest edition, 1921) can be had here for RM 20. I think it is worthwhile to buy it. I would like to pay for it out of the RM 48 the *Lexikon* owes me.

The day before yesterday [Heinrich] Fürst visited me. We had a pleasant time, chatted about various things, he told me how it goes with him at the wine firm.

I shall mail the *Clavis* [*Mafteaḥ haTalmud* by Michael Guttmann] very soon. I think Professor [Bernard] Heller should be asked to review it. The old scholar would be very pleased with that. He is asking for the individual fascicles of the old volume.

Next week I shall get the manuscript of Fontanella from Dr. [Israel] Rabin. As Papa wishes, I shall copy a few [poems] and send them to him.

I ask Évi and the little one to forgive me. I have not enough time to write to them separately.

Please, Mama, would you count how many mistakes I make in this letter and in the subsequent one, and let me know the numbers? Thus I shall pay more attention that they show a decreasing tendency.

Many hearty regards from your twenty-year-old, serious son,

Gyuri

Let the editorial office send out requests for review copies to:

1. *Hebrew Union College Annual* 1924–1929 or 1930. Hebrew Union College, Cincinnati, Ohio, U.S.A.

2. H[annah] Emmrich, *Das Judentum bei Voltaire*, Gesellschaft zur Förderung der Wissenschaft des Judentums, Berlin-Schöneberg 1, Belzigerstr. 46, Aufg. II. 2. (Nathan)

3. To ask exchange copy or review copy of the *Jewish Quarterly Review*, Dropsie College, Cor. Broad and York Streets, Philadelphia, Penn., U.S.A.

4. Emil Vandervelde, *Schaffendes Palästina*, Carl Reissner Verlag, Dresden.
Would Évi ask Dezső [Stern], [László] Salgó, [Pál] Vidor, etc., to forgive me for not writing them? I am much too busy, etc.

The second letter, written four days later, reminds me of something I had entirely forgotten: that I was friendly with Liesl (Lizi) Fischer, who was my great love in the winter and spring of 1933, already in 1930. I shall have more to tell about her in the next chapter.

Breslau, Nov. 24, 1930

My Dear Mama:
I spent my 20th birthday well and joyfully. Saturday the weather was magnificent; in the morning I took a walk, in the afternoon I was together with friends, and in the evening I celebrated by working: I began the compilation of the *Piyyutim* [liturgical poems] about which I have already written. Yesterday, Sunday, the weather turned very bad; in the morning I went to a museum, in the afternoon we studied Arabic, a Polish youth who is also a beginner and I.

Today I received a box of chocolates from Liesl Fischer with birthday greetings. I had to pay 50 pfennigs duty for it, and by this hour (3 o'clock, before the Arabic class at the University) already almost half of it is in my stomach. But now I must write her and express my thanks. Hopefully, Mama has nothing against that.

At 5:30 in the lecture hall of the Seminary I was interrrupted by the entry, or rather rushing in, of [Professor Carl] Brockelmann. Now, with the afternoon mail, I received a long letter from Grandmother.

Tomorrow, as Rabin promised me, I shall get the permission to use the manuscripts. Then I shall mail [Father] the poems of Fontanella.

We received a hundredweight of coal per head. Now we always get a lot of heat. Actually, it is a waste because I spend at home only one hour after lunch and the evening.

Otherwise nothing new. Many regards,

Gyuri

Please send requests for review copies, as usual, for the following:
1. S. Dubnow, *Toldot haHasidut*, D'vir, Tel Aviv.
2. D. Yellin, *HaMelekh Omar al-Nu'man uVanav*, D'vir, Tel Aviv.
3. Moshe Kleinmann, *D'muyot v'Qomot*, R. Mazin & Co. London E.1. 139–141 Whitechapel Road.
4. *Igrot Ahad Ha'Am*, Haolam, London W.C.1, 77 Great Russell Street.
5. A. A. Kabak, *Sh'lomo Molkho* (trilogy), same address.
6. E. b. Yehuda, *Thesaurus VII*, Langenscheidtsche Verlagsbuchhandlung, Berlin-Schöneberg.

7. Felix Goldmann, *Der Jude im deutschen Kulturkreise*, Philo Verlag, Berlin S. W. 68, Lindenstr. 13.

The lists of books appended to the two letters indicate that by the age of twenty my interests covered a wide range of subjects within the general area of Jewish studies. Of the many books whose appearance came to my notice in Breslau I asked my father to obtain review copies only of those in which I was interested and which I intended to read and to review for his journal. In fact, several of the books listed I did subsequently review after my return to Budapest. Moreover, it so developed that after I settled in Jerusalem, I made the personal acquaintance of David Yellin, Moshe Kleinmann, and A. A. Kabak, and became a contributor of articles and book reviews to the *Hebrew Union College Annual*, the *Jewish Quarterly Review*, and *Ha'Olam*, which was edited by Kleinmann.

For the Christmas vacation I was invited to the house of Aunt Ruth, who shortly after the death of Uncle Berti had moved to Berlin, where her three brothers lived. She had a pleasant and spacious apartment in a good section of the city (Charlottenburg?), and her three small children were glad to see their big cousin. I spent most of the time in Berlin seeing the sights of the big city, whose very size amazed and somewhat intimidated me. I had no recollection at all of my former visit to Berlin that had taken place seven years earlier, when I was twelve years old, when Father took the whole family through Berlin to Swinemünde for the summer.

From my 1930 Berlin visit I remember in particular the incomparable head of Nefertiti in the great museum (today in East Berlin), placed on a five-foot stand in a rectangular glass enclosure. To my surprise, there were two identical Nefertiti heads standing one next to the other, each on its own stand and in its own glass enclosure. I asked a guard for an explanation, and he told me that one was the original, while the other was an identical copy, and that the two were placed side by side in order to confuse and discourage would-be burglars. I also remember the Pergamon Museum, where the magnificent marble friezes of the great altar of Pergamon were exhibited in a beautiful setting. I had never before seen the like of it. I visited the Hochschule für die Wissenschaft des Judentums (College of the Science of Judaism), which was officially a scholarly institution for the training of rabbis for all trends of Judaism, but which, in actuality, trained only Reform rabbis. I attended the Sunday morning services in a big Reform synagogue where, for the first time, I saw Jews praying with uncovered heads, and, also for the first time, heard Jewish prayers recited not in Hebrew but in German. It is strange that I do not remember anything of the service of the Reform synagogue in Breslau, which I also must have attended once or twice. But I do remember listening in Berlin to a sermon by Rabbi Joachim Prinz, a graduate of the Breslau Seminary, who at the time was at the height of his popularity as the finest rabbinical orator in Germany. I also explored the huge Berlin department stores, and traveled back and forth on the city's elevated lines to get a feel of the sprawling metropolis, or just walked about along its wide and busy streets. In the evenings I reported to Aunt Ruth what I had done and seen during the day, and she advised me what to take in on the morrow.

One evening Aunt Ruth took me to see the *Dreigroschenoper* (Three-Penny Opera), which was at the time the longest-running musical in Berlin. She proudly explained to me that Kurt Weill, who wrote its music, was a cousin of her brother Gabriel's wife Nellie, née Weill. The performance made a deep impression on me. I found the music irresistible, and despite my tin ear I was never to forget its songs, several of which I can hum — undoubtedly quite out of tune — to this day. I was especially taken by Jennie's song in which the downtrodden scullery maid fantasizes about her pirate lover whose galleon sails into the harbor and bombards the city. In her imagination Jennie watches with glee as the heads of the masters, under whom she had to slave, are cut off, cries "Hoppla" each time a head rolls, and finally is taken triumphantly aboard her pirate lover's ship. On the other hand, my sensibilities were offended by the scene in which Meckie Messer (the German rendering of Mac the Knife) danced with his girl, because the actor-singer who played him at one point grabbed the girl's behind, which, I felt, was just too vulgar. I was astonished to see that Aunt Ruth laughed heartily when she saw that gesture.

On the way back from the theater we saw some women with knee-high red boots loitering in the street. In response to my inquiry Aunt Ruth explained that they were prostitutes whose red boots indicated that they were willing to accommodate sadistic or masochistic clients. (I don't remember whether there was a German term corresponding to the American "johns.") Berlin in those years was a great center of sexual liberty and experimentation. I remember that only a year or two earlier Father once came home from a visit to Berlin and told us that he had been taken to a nightclub in which men, dressed up as women, with painted faces, were dancing with other men. With the mixture of naiveté and skepticism peculiar to him, Father added, "I am sure that when the night was over the transvestite went home, took off his makeup and dress, and said to his wife, 'Well, dearest, I did make quite a bit of money tonight, although these false breasts are mighty uncomfortable.' " From Jakob Wasserman's novels that I read both prior to and during my Breslau year, I got, to be sure, a different picture of German mores of the period.

I no longer remember how, when, and where I made the acquaintance of the daughter of Ossip Dymov during that Berlin visit. The name Ossip Dymov had been known to me from having read, in a Hungarian translation, a piece of writing by him (a novel?) entitled *The Singer of His Sadness*. Looking up his biography in the *Encyclopaedia Judaica*, I now find that Ossip Dymov (1878–1959) was a Russian and Yiddish author and playwright, whose plays were produced by various Russian theaters, by the Hebrew Habimah theater in Bialystock, and, after his emigration to the United States in 1913, by Yiddish and English theaters in New York. The book for which I remembered him is not mentioned. I have not the slightest idea how his daughter came to be in Berlin in December 1930, nor can I recall anything of the conversations we had. I cannot even remember her first name. What I do remember is that she was a very beautiful young girl with black hair, deep violet eyes, and a fine nose of the type usually called Jewish. I visited her in her room, a sublet in an apartment located next to an elevated line. Whenever a train passed, the room shook and its windows rattled. I found Miss Dymov in bed. She had a bad cold. If I had any amorous hopes in visiting her, this threw cold water on them. I sat on a chair facing her bed, and we talked. I was greatly attracted to her, and for the life of me I cannot understand why I did not make another date with her. But I am sure I did not, and I never saw her again.

On New Year's Eve I went to a dance with two girls. I had met one of them earlier and made a date with her—to my annoyance, she brought along a friend. I can recall neither their names nor their looks. Being a stranger in Berlin, I did not know where to go, and the girls suggested a place that turned out to be a large dance hall.

It was crowded, noisy, and hot. A band was playing the raucous dance music of the time, and people were throwing about streams of colored paper tapes, the German equivalent of ticker tapes. Scantily clad girls walked about amid the dancers, carrying trays full of such reels of tapes. In my inexperience I thought that these paper reels were given away free of charge, that they were a courtesy extended by the management in exchange for the entrance fee, so I grabbed two and was about to rush back to the place where my two dates were standing or sitting, when the ticker-tape girl put out her hand and said, "That'll be two marks." My budget was tight, but I was too embarrassed to put the reels back on her tray, so I paid and gave the tapes to the two girls. They immediately let them streak over the heads of the dancers, and I thought, "There go my two marks."

And we danced. I led the two girls to the floor one after the other, and soon felt that the girl who was brought along by my original date snuggled close to me while dancing, pressed her whole body against me, and evidently was what in later years came to be termed in colloquial English "hot in the pants." Before long we began kissing and hugging each other tightly, while continuing to dance. Never before had I behaved so uninhibitedly in public, nor have I ever since. But the atmosphere of the place was contagious. Many young couples around me showed me how I was allowed, or perhaps even expected, to behave. At midnight the lights went out for a minute. The crowd burst into great shouts. It was 1931.

At about two in the morning we left the dance hall. But the girls were not yet ready to call it a night. They suggested that we proceed to another place where, they said, things would pick up just about then. I, however, had had enough. I was tired, having danced without a break, while each of the two girls sat for half of the time. It did not seem to be the custom of the place for strangers to ask girls to dance. Also, having paid the entrance fees for three, as well as for drinks, not to mention the ticker tapes, I was down almost to my last mark. So I excused myself, and said good-bye to my dates. They went off quite merrily. I never saw them again.

But the experience did not remain without consequences for me, although only after a period of incubation of three or four months. I felt increasingly that I simply could not go on without having sex with a girl. I loved Marion and would have been only too happy to become her lover, but, having experienced the kisses and passionate wriggles of that girl in Berlin, I became even more convinced that

Marion, whose kisses were meek and mild and restrained, was a virgin and would never consent to sleeping with me or with anyone else until she got married. It was also completely out of the question for me to try to seduce her, or even as much as tell her about my desires.

What I did instead was to pour my love and desires into poems. I had done that earlier in Hungary, where I had written Hungarian poems to several of my loves (all platonic, of course), and now, in the winter of 1930–1931, I wrote German verse to Marion. She was the only girl in Breslau to whom I wrote poems. I found the German language more suitable to my versification than any other language I knew, including my mother tongue, Hungarian. During the two years I spent in Budapest after my return from Breslau, and for several years after I moved to Jerusalem, I celebrated my lady loves in German verse. I don't remember whether I ever showed Marion the poems I wrote her, but I suspect I must have. If so, I have no recollection of her reaction to them. I originally used to write my poems on any slip of paper that happened to be handy, but then I copied them into a notebook I still have, so that my recollections of my poetic peccadillos are aided by genuine contemporary documentation. The poems are immature, incurably romantic, and occasionally embarrassing. One does not have to be a connoisseur to see that they don't show traces of true talent. But, and this is why I mention them at all, the very process of writing poems gave me the feeling that I, too, was a poet, and filled me with a satisfaction I did not derive from my scholarly writing. It also lifted up, or so I felt, my infatuations with girls to a poetic, and hence higher, level.

The winter term ended late in February, and on February 26 I took the train back to Budapest. The intersession lasted eight weeks. I spent them at home, but they are a complete blank in my memory except for the fact that halfway through them I made a long-distance phone call to Marion. We spoke at length, and in retrospect I must recognize the generosity of my parents, who never said a word to me when they received the bill for that call. Looking back, I can see what happened after my return to Breslau toward the end of April. I was still in love with Marion, but my sexual drive was too strong to resist any longer. So the first thing I did was to look for a new room, and this time for one that was *sturmfrei*—a good Germany literary word that the dictionary translates as "sheltered from the storm." But in the life of the students it had a different and very important meaning. It meant a room in which the landlady tolerated women visitors to the tenant until the late hours of the evening, without coming storming in to see whether anything untoward was going on. Planning to be sexually active, I needed such a room where I could bring my future girl friends. I found one in a beautiful, ivy-covered house, in a wide, tree-lined residential street. It was a modern building, and the apartment in which the room was available was on the second floor. It opened from the entrance hall, just a step or two from the front door that led from the landing into the apartment. I fell in love with the house and the room, and, although I did not have the courage to put to the landlady the crucial question of whether or not the room was *sturmfrei*, I took it because I assumed that the advantageous location of the room at the very entrance of the apartment would make it possible to have female visitors without attracting her attention or provoking her ire.

I returned to my studies at the Seminary and the University with the assurance of an experienced old-timer. Everything was familiar, and I enjoyed resuming the old routine and rhythm.

Within a few days after moving into my new room I found out that another room in the same apartment — large and beautifully furnished, as I espied once when its door was left open — was rented to the leading lady of the Breslau theater. I no longer remember her name. What I do remember is that I once forgot my key so that I had to ring the bell, and it was she who opened the door. She was tall, something of a Brunhilde, blue-eyed, with a big shock of blonde hair. She somehow made the impression of being larger than life. Now in Hungarian the proper address of an actress was *művésznő*, which in literal German translation is *Künstlerin* (something like "Mme. Artist"), but which is never used in addressing an actress. In my surprise at being confronted by her I stammered, "Thank you, *Künstlerin*. I forgot my key. I am sorry to have bothered you." She only smiled. She must have thought, "These foreigners are surely peculiar." In the course of those months I took one or two of my girl friends to plays in which this actress had the leading roles, and, of course, did not neglect to inform them that she shared an apartment with me.

It did not take me long to find a girl for whose visits a *sturmfrei* room was required, but it so happened that she had an apartment at her disposal. She must have been my age, perhaps a year older, of middle height and somewhat sturdily built. I remember nothing about her, not even her name—I shall call her Hilda—except for a curious little detail: her eyebrows were stiff and rich, so that when I touched them with my lips or cheek they gave me a strange and somewhat unpleasant sensation. After one or two dates she invited me to her home. She lived with her mother, who was either divorced or widowed, and was a commercial traveler, rarely at home. In fact, on none of my visits did I meet the mother. The living room was filled with old-fashioned overstuffed furniture, and although at the time I did not have much of an eye for class differences as manifested in home furnishings, I could not help noticing that it was a poorer apartment than that of Marion. The next thing I remember is that we were in Hilda's bedroom, sitting, then lying on her bed. She undressed, but I was inhibited and reluctant to do likewise, and Hilda had to prod me to take off my jacket, trousers, and underpants. She urged me to take off my shoes, too, but for some reason I refused to do so. I think I was afraid that her mother might unexpectedly come home, and I would not be able to get dressed quickly enough. If I was to be caught with my pants off, I did not want to be caught with my shoes off as well.

My first lovemaking was accomplished with but minor difficulties. At the time of course I did not know, but later experience told me that Hilda was built extremely tightly. So I fumbled, but she helped me. I knew from conversation with experienced friends that in relations with girls, in contrast to older women and prostitutes, one was supposed to practice *coitus interruptus*. What the term meant I had known even before they spoke to me about it, because I had read, and had not forgotten, the biblical story of Onan who "spilled his seed on the ground." It was, of course, over too quickly. The sensation I had at the climax was not appreciably different from what I had experienced without the assistance of girls. Nor did I feel too great a measure of postcoital *tristesse*. A friend of mine had told me that after he had sex the first time, with a prostitute, he was seized with such revulsion that he vomited right then and there. Fortunately, I was spared that reaction. Still, I felt I did not want to, I could not, see Hilda again. I made no new date with her, nor did I contact her. But about two weeks later we ran into each other in the street. To my surprise, she was neither embarrassed nor angry. "Why didn't you come to see me?" she asked. We made a date. Things went much better. I no longer objected to taking my shoes off. We began to meet frequently. Since then sex has been an important part of my life. I have always been like my ancestor Jacob, about whom the Midrash says that it was his nature to be constantly attracted to women.

At the beginning of the term I still met Marion a few times, but having found release elsewhere, my interest in her cooled, and after a while I stopped seeing her altogether. Later I came to regret this, but at the time I was like someone acting under compulsion. For some thirty-five years thereafter I neither saw her nor heard of her, until, one day, I passed a woman on Fifth Avenue in New York whom I thought I recognized as Marion. Since I had believed that she, like almost all the 20,000 Jews of Breslau, had perished in the Holocaust, I was stunned, and it took me more than a moment to recover. She did not notice me, or did not recognize me, and did not stop. I hesitated for a moment, since at first I was not sure that it was indeed Marion, and let her pass. I turned and looked after her, and her gait—her left leg was turned a little bit outward from the knee down—made me sure that it was. Still, something kept me from rushing after her and speaking to her. I remained frozen, standing where I was until she disappeared in the crowd.

At that moment I did not know what prevented me from stopping her, approaching her, embracing her. Today, thinking back on that encounter that was a nonencounter, and that itself is now twenty years in the past, I think I know. That summer of 1965, just two or three months earlier, during a visit to London, I went to see a woman whom I had known in Breslau at the same time as Marion. I shall call her Freda. She was in 1930–1931 a simple, pleasant girl with a somewhat ample figure, black hair, dark brown eyes, olive skin, and a sulky expression. I cannot recall how and when I first met her, but I know that one day she invited me to visit her in her room. Since I was not in the mood for the intimacies such a visit was likely to lead to, I asked my friend Tibor Fábián, another Hungarian student at the Seminary, to come with me. I rang the bell, Freda opened the door, and I shall never forget the expression of disappointment, nay dismay, when she saw that I was not alone. The visit could not have lasted long, and I don't remember whether I saw her again in Breslau. Years later I met her brother, who worked as a doctor in Jerusalem, and from him I learned that Freda was in London. She had been in a concentration camp, but somehow survived. There is here a hiatus of several years in my memory, but the fact is that on that visit to London I knew how to get in touch with Freda, phoned her, and on

July 26, 1965, at 6:30 in the evening, I went to see her. The address she gave me was in a suburb of London, and it turned out to be that of a Jewish institution in which persons not able to live alone and to fend for themselves were provided with room and board. It was not unlike other institutions of this kind: clean, very simply furnished, cheerless, drab. The room into which Freda led me was a sitting room of sorts, with wooden chairs and tables covered with oilcloth.

The Freda who opened the door for me was a wreck of her former self. I did not recognize her at first. No traces of the charm, even of the features, of the twenty-year-old girl remained in the fifty-five-year-old woman. She had white hair, rather unkempt, and her skin had turned grey; her black eyes were sunken, her cheeks wrinkled, her body a shapeless spread. She said she would have recognized me anywhere, and I, as I sat there and watched her, began to see some faint resemblances between the two creatures separated by thirty-five years. She told me about her life in the home, how kind and considerate the people were, mentioned proudly that she was one of the few who were able to go out to work every day, that she was working for a furrier, and that she thus earned enough money to cover her expenses in the home. She also told me that she had had what she called a nervous breakdown, after which she had to stay for a long time in a hospital, but that now she felt so much, so much better. Smiling happily, she introduced me to a few people who were sitting around in the room as "my friend," and then went into the kitchen to bring us cups of tea and biscuits. My visit was a joyous event for her. It made her day and raised her in the regard of the others.

For me the visit was a shock, an experience of grief, of great sadness. I commiserated with Freda, I was filled with a wrenching pity for her for what life and German inhumanity had done to her, for what she had become. I asked myself, can it be that this is still the same person she was thirty-five years earlier, or is it somebody entirely different who happens to inhabit an aged and deformed version of the same body? And, inevitably, my thoughts turned to myself, and I asked, is there anything but the most tenuous connection between me as I was in Breslau thirty-five years ago, and as I am now? Or is it only the thin threads of memory in my mind that connect me with that twenty-year-old youngster I was so long, so long ago? The question remained not only unanswered but largely also unasked while I sat there and chatted with Freda. Before I left,

I asked her whether I could do anything for her. She shook her head, looked around with an expression I could not decipher, and said, "No, thank you. I have everything I need." When I left I had the feeling that I had performed a small *mitzva*, and this itself gave an added edge to my sadness.

This experience was still very much with me when I saw Marion that day on Fifth Avenue. I did not stop her because I was afraid that the person I would find if I looked at her closely, if I talked to her, would be the same kind of sad, faded, ruined facsimile of the Breslau Marion as Freda was of her former *alter ego*. If seeing Freda, whom I had known only superficially in Breslau, pained that much when I was confronted with what she had become after going through the wringer of thirty-five cruel years, seeing a similar change in Marion whom I had loved would have a devastating effect on me. If I did not stop her, did not speak to her, did not face her and tell her that we had known each other thirty-five years earlier, it was because I felt I must keep her old image as intact as I had carried it all those years in my memory. I wanted to be able to continue remembering her as she was in Breslau: a young, sweet thing, with a softness in her eyes and mouth, a doll's freckled face, the girl I loved and abandoned because I felt that to seduce her would have been a sin.

However, back in my salad days in Breslau such thoughts were far beyond my mental horizon. *Carpe diem* was the slogan, and I went at it with gusto. After my first tumble with Hilda, next morning I told my friend Tibor Fábián, who was six years my senior and hence hence more experienced in many respects, what had happened. He looked at me sharply, and said: "Yes. I can see it in your eyes that you finally had a woman. You do look different. You look like a man."

Tibor was a peculiar character. He was a good-looking man with a head of wavy gold-blonde hair, eyes like those of Robert Mitchum, a hooked nose, and sensuous red lips. His finances were always shaky, and once I lent him a few marks that he never repaid. His German was rudimentary, and when his turn came to preach his exercise sermon, I translated it for him from Hungarian, and then practiced German pronunciation with him. Because of his poor German he often did not find the proper expression for what he wanted to say. Once he said to *Dozent* Lewkowitz: "Your lecture was like a great theater," when what he intended to say, as a compliment to Dr. Lewkowitz, was, "Your lecture was most dramatic."

Tibor had an impulsive personality. One evening, as we were strolling on a street in the inner city, we heard from a distance a woman's voice that sounded like the cry of somebody in trouble. While I was looking around and straining my eyes to see where the cry came from, Tibor was already running toward the voice, ready to defend a damsel in distress if that turned out to be the case. Another evening he, I, and a third student stopped to look at the brightly lighted shop window of one of the big department stores — it may have been a Schocken store — when several young Nazis stopped near us, and one of them said with loud derision: "The Jew-boys are looking at the store of their grandfather!" Tibor turned and wanted to punch the nose of the one who said it, and we were able to restrain him only with difficulty.

Tibor also had a strong liking for salacious humor with a bent to the scatological. One of his favorites was to ask, "What is horrible?" We would, of course, answer, "We don't know," whereupon he would say, "If you push an umbrella into the ass of a donkey, and then open it inside, that is horrible." Or he would ask, "What is ḥutzpe [impudence]?" And would answer, "If you do your duty in front of Professor Guttmann's door, and then ring the bell and ask for toilet paper, that is impudence." Imagining the very dignified *Seminar-rabbiner* answering the doorbell sent us into paroxysms of laughter. Years later Tibor became the rabbi of a lakeside community in Hungary, and his colleagues, creating a new variant of the title *Grand Rabbiner*, promptly dubbed him *Strand Rabbiner*. In the last years of his life he was rabbi of a congregation in America.

The German students at the Seminary, in general, kept their distance from us foreigners. In addition to Hungarians, there were also Polish, Rumanian, Czechoslovakian, and other East European students at the Seminary, all of whom, including the Hungarians, were considered by the German students *Ostjuden* (Eastern Jews).

I knew only too well what *Ostjuden* meant, for I had many times heard Jews in Hungary speak disdainfully of them, or, more precisely, of the *Galizianers*, the *Polaks*, the *Litvaks*. All these were considered to be a low type of Jew with whom a true Hungarian Jew had little in common and as little to do as possible. I remember having heard, from Father, I believe, that during World War I, when parts of East Europe were contested between the German and Austro-Hungarian allies on the one hand and the Russians on the other, and large territories were captured once by this side and then by the other, resulting in a large number of Jewish refugees knocking on the doors of Hungary, the leaders of the Budapest Jews asked the government not to let them enter the country. Later, when my father told me about this incident, I shared his outrage at this un-Jewish and inhuman act, but still could not help feeling that an East European Jewish refugee was somehow different from and inferior to an autochthonous Hungarian Jew. Now, in Breslau, for the first time in my life I got a slight taste of what it meant to be looked down upon by other Jews who held themselves to be superior.

Not that there was any overt act, such as rudeness or snubbing. But I had enough sensitivity to feel that the German Jewish students were a shade less friendly to us *Ostjuden* than they were to their compatriots, that we were not included in their social activities, and that by design or happenstance our friendships and contacts were largely confined to our own numbers. There were a few German Jewish students who constituted exceptions to this general reticence to fraternize with us foreigners. One of them was my roommate, Lothar Rothschild, but he was Swiss and not German. The other was Bernhard Brilling, who was somewhat older (he was born in 1906), and who, while a student at the Seminary, was also archival assistant to the Breslau Jewish Community. In 1960 he was to publish his important *History of the Jews of Breslau* (in German). I still have some snapshots showing me in the company of these two colleagues.

A third colleague was Max (Meir) Brafmann, one year ahead of me in his studies and a far more advanced student of Brockelmann, under whom he took his doctorate two years later. Brafmann was even more shy than I was, and although of old German Jewish stock— he was born in a small town near Heidelberg—he had no close friends among the other German students. He and I became friendly due to our common interest in Arabic, and occasionally, when something baffled me in an Arabic text I had to prepare for my class with Brockelmann, I would ask his help, which he always most willingly extended. Brafmann and I were to remain lifelong friends. Shortly after I settled in Jerusalem, he also arrived there, and worked in the Arabic department of the Hebrew University on a scholarly edition of the great Arab historian Balādhurī. Then we met again in New York, and it was at my recommendation that he was appointed professor of Arabic at Dropsie College in Philadelphia, where I served as professor of anthropology, and where we remained colleagues for nine years. In the last years of his life Brafmann was cataloguer of

Oriental books and lecturer in Arabic at Columbia University. He was a great scholar in the Brockelmann tradition, but he never received the recognition he deserved. I reviewed one of his last books in the *American Anthropologist* and expressed my admiration for his work. He never married, and lived in a sublet room on the upper West Side; his work was the only interest in his life. When he died, his sister had his body taken to Israel for burial.

There were several others with whom I was friendly in Breslau and then maintained contact with or met occasionally in later life. One of them was Max Nussbaum, originally from Bessarabia (another *Ostjude*), who after his ordination in 1933 served as rabbi in Berlin, and, from 1942 on, was rabbi of Temple Israel in Hollywood. He was for a number of years president of the Zionist Organization of America, and in connection with my work at the Herzl Institute and the Herzl Press in New York I had meetings with him from time to time. There was Béla Presser, who subsequently Magyarized his name to Béla Berend, became rabbi in Hungary, and after World War II was accused of having collaborated with the Hungarian Nazis. He was tried in the Hungarian courts, was acquitted, came to America, changed his name again, to Albert Belton, and worked for a while for the American Council of Judaism and the City of New York. There was Emil Feuerstein, who later became a well-known journalist in Palestine-Israel, where I used to meet him either in Jerusalem or in Tel Aviv. He was a nephew of the Hebrew poet and novelist Avigdor Hameiri, whose original name was also Feuerstein, and who in his youth in Hungary was a disciple and protégé of Father. There was Ephraim Urbach, somewhat younger than I, who later became lecturer at the Breslau Seminary (in the tragic closing years of the life of that venerable institution), then moved to Palestine, where he became professor of Talmud at the Hebrew University and chairman of the Jewish section of the Israel Academy of Sciences and Humanities. And there were several others, whose names I cannot recall at the moment.

In 1930–1931 Hitler's ominous shadow was lengthening over Germany. The country was in the throes of depression. In the national elections of September 1930 the National Socialist party garnered more than 18 percent of the votes. Hitler's anti-Jewish views were, of course, well known from his book *Mein Kampf*, published several years earlier, but after the success of his party at the polls he publicly embraced a policy of legality, therewith placing himself and his party within the framework of the democratic political process. While his demagoguery appealed to the unemployed and the victims of the depression, his insistence on legality served to make him acceptable to the military, the conservatives, and, above all, the nationalists.

During my year in Breslau, practically every Sunday there was a political parade in the main thoroughfares of the city. One Sunday the Nazi party would march, preceded and flanked by the police to make sure that law and order were observed; next Sunday the same police contingents escorted in the same manner a parade of the Communists, who had polled 13 percent in the September elections. I do not remember having seen, or heard, parades organized by other parties.

Despite the Nazi ascendancy, the German Jews, as far I could see, were not worried in the slightest. Life, whether private, business, academic, or communal, went on as usual, and nobody seemed to give a thought to what could happen in the unlikely event that at some remote future date the Nazi party should gain the majority. There were even some Jews who sympathized with the officially proclaimed program of the Nazi party. In the Seminary itself there were two among the fifty or so students who were Nazi sympathizers, and who, if I remember correctly, participated in the Nazi party's Sunday parades. Looking back at this strange phenomenon, I can only assume that they were ignorant, callous young men, who were impressed by the Nazi paraphernalia, and never took the trouble of familiarizing themselves with Hitler's *Mein Kampf* or with the program of the Nazi party. I have a vague recollection that they even used to appear at the Seminary with the Nazi armband displaying the swastika, and greet the others with upraised arms and the "Heil Hitler" salute. The other students considered them not quite right in the head.

But those two were not alone among the German Jews. The *Verband Nationaldeutschen Juden* (Association of National-German Jews), headed by a certain Max Naumann, strongly opposed Zionism and admitted as members only "Germans of Jewish descent who . . . felt so completely rooted in German culture and essence [*Wesen*] that they could not but think and feel as Germans." Not satisfied with this, it called upon the Jews to acknowledge the truth of some anti-Semitic charges, and to shed all traces of Jewish nationalism. It identified itself with the German right and center parties, and for years tried, in vain, to find a *modus vivendi* with the Nazis. It even advocated that the Zionists be deprived of their German citizenship and be allowed to reside in Germany only as aliens, and it rejected all cooperation with non-German Jews. Only a minuscule minority of German Jews supported the *Verband*, but when I got acquainted with its program I had the uncanny feeling that the distance between it and the Hungarian equivalent of its position as represented by the official leadership of the Israelite Congregation of Pest, the largest by far in Hungary, was not too great. Those were the days when some Nazi marchers began to carry banners reading "The Jews are our misfortune. Out with the Jews!"; and the students of the Seminary would tease their two pro-Nazi colleagues by telling them that they saw a contingent of National-German Jews march after the Nazis with banners that read, "We are our misfortune. Out with us!" It was a time when it was still possible to crack jokes about the Nazis.

As I said, life still flowed in its wonted channels. The police kept law and order. The German sense of lawful behavior and respect for authority—so painfully satirized in the figure of Professor Unrath in Heinrich Mann's novel and in the film *The Blue Angel* based on it that precipitated Marlene Dietrich to fame in 1930, while I was in Breslau—still prevented violent acts against Jews. We seminarians lived the normal lives of students, studied, ran after girls, studied, went to movies, studied, studied. To me as a foreigner, Jewish life in the city appeared to be very orderly, very well organized, very sedate. In order to get acquainted with various aspects of it, I occasionally attended the Friday evening services at the major Reform synagogue of Rabbi Hermann Vogelstein (1870–1942), whose name I knew as that of a Jewish scholar and author of several important books on Jewish history. Soon after my arrival in Breslau I went to pay my respects to the *mara diatra*, the master of the place, as Jewish tradition recommended it, and I still remember that he received me with the same friendly coolness that characterized Chief Rabbi Hevesi's attitude to his students. In 1938 Dr. Vogelstein immigrated to the United States, where he died a few years later. I also remember a visit I paid to Dr. Hugo Schachtel (1876–1949), although that was not a social call, but a visit to his dentist's office. I developed a cavity in one of my molars, and he took care of it most expeditiously, albeit a little roughly, drilling and filling it in one rather unpleasant sitting. He charged all seminarians only a very nominal fee. He had known Herzl in his youth, and remained an active Zionist all his life. In 1932 he settled in Haifa, and died there in 1949.

About halfway through the summer term I got acquainted with a new girl whom I shall call Erika, and almost instantly she and I became lovers. I found her much more attractive than Hilda, whom I felt I had to stop seeing. Not wishing to hurt her, I told her a white lie: now that the term was nearing its end, I had to prepare for my exams and concentrate on my studies, and therefore, to my regret, I could not go on seeing her. She was unhappy, but, I believe, not unduly so. Having thus got rid of my previous amorous entanglement, I could devote myself to Erika, which I did quite intensively. She was a lively, outgoing girl, tall and slender, with dark hair that she wore cut straight across her forehead, and dark brown eyes in which there was always a hint of a roguish expression. She was rather uneducated, and I am not sure whether she had finished high school. I remember that on one occasion when I visited her — she lived with her parents — I noticed that among the books in the living room there was the great Brockhaus encyclopaedia, and I suggested to Erika that we look up this or that subject in the Brockhaus. To my great consternation it appeared that she did not know how to find an entry in the encyclopaedia. I was very disappointed, but patiently explained to her the simple secret of alphabetic arrangement. Still this did not diminish my interest in her, which was clearly more erotic than intellectual.

Our first union almost ended in a disaster. She came up to my room — I remember clearly that it was the first time that I made use of its presumably *sturmfrei* character — we undressed, and went to bed. She was willing and ready, and, in contrast to Hilda, so open in her proportions and so well supplied with natural lubricants that, in the intensity of my passion, I was simply unable to withdraw in time. A moment later I came to my senses, and told Erika what I did. She said in quiet resentment, "I thought I could trust you." I was remorseful, and said to her, "You stay here, and I shall go down to a pharmacy and get something." In my inexperience I had no idea as to what could be done *post facto* to prevent impregnation. I quickly got dressed, ran down the stairs, and went to the nearest pharmacy. By then it was about ten o'clock at night, and the pharmacy was closed, but on its door there was a sign saying that the nearest pharmacy on night duty was located at number so-and-so of

X Street. I ran all the way, entered the pharmacy, and, having no choice, was forced to overcome my embarrassment and stammered out to the clerk on duty my story and request. He seemed to find nothing unusual in the situation, removed a white enameled cylindrical container from one of the shelves, and said quite matter-of-factly, "Here, take this *Klistier-Spritze* [douche]." Then he gave me some stuff to be dissolved in the water, and explained quite casually what had to be done. Since I did not feel that I could let Erika use the bathroom in the middle of the night, I also bought a washbowl and, thus equipped, rushed back to my room. The procedure was somewhat messy; some water did spill on the floor, but I carefully mopped it up, and when everything was done I felt that we did the best we could in the circumstances. I hid the vessels in the bottom of the wardrobe, and took Erika back to her apartment.

The next several days were full of tension, apprehension, and waiting. A week or so later Erika informed me that her menses had come on time. My relief was enormous. When we resumed sex, I was careful, and everything was fine. We enjoyed each other greatly and frequently. The room proved to be *sturmfrei*, at least in the sense that we never encountered my landlady either coming or going. Never, that is, until the very day on which I left Breslau at the end of the term. During all that time I never was "unfaithful" to Erika.

On the day of my departure from Breslau my train was scheduled to leave at noon. The day before I packed all my things and said good-bye to my teachers and friends. In the morning I went to fetch Erika and brought her to my room. It seemed terribly important to make love to her once more, a last time, before leaving and perhaps never seeing her again. As we were leaving my room we ran into the landlady in the hall. She said nothing, and we quickly went out, to find a taxi. I directed the cabbie to my place, and Erika waited in the car while I went up to fetch my luggage. The landlady was waiting for me at the door. She accosted me angrily. How could I do such a thing, to bring a girl to my room? This was an affrontery, and so forth. It was a painful scene, but I was leaving anyway. I said I was sorry this had to happen, and left. Erika came with me to the station and we walked up and down the platform until it was time for the train to leave. I was reminded of walking like that with Father on the platform in the Budapest railway station almost a year earlier. It seemed so far away, as if it had happened in another life. I can still recall the feeling that the person going back to Budapest was very, very different from the one who had left his native city at that remote time. As against this, I remember nothing of what I felt about having to part from Erika.

There is a short postscript to this story. After settling in at home again I exchanged one or two letters with Erika. As time passed, and I found no other girl to take her place, I missed her more and more. Finally, I told Father that I thought it would be advantageous to my studies if I went back to Breslau for another year. He gave an evasive answer, which, I thought, indicated that if I insisted he would agree. I wrote to Erika that I planned to come back to Breslau, and how much I looked forward to a reunion. Her answer was late in coming, and when it came it contained the information that for the next year she would have to be in Hamburg. I understood. I did not write to her again, nor have I ever again visited Breslau.

There was one more girl with whom I got acquainted during my summer term in Breslau. All I can recall about her is that her name was Eva Perl, and that she was a very serious young art student. She studied painting. Once I went to the beach with her, and when she came out of the cabana in her bathing suit I saw that she had a big red birthmark on her left leg just above the knee. This birthmark stamped her in my eyes as something particular. I was fascinated with her, at least for a while, and wrote a short story in which the heroine had a birthmark just like hers. What role the birthmark played in the story I no longer remember. That story, incidentally, was the only nonscholarly piece of writing I ever showed Father. He was not particularly impressed by it, and suggested that I change the ending. I had the impression that his lukewarm reaction was due, not so much to the inferior quality of the writing, as to his dissatisfaction with the very fact that I had spent my time writing a story instead of a scholarly paper.

In the midst of all my manifold activites and preoccupations I still found the time to copy, as I have mentioned, the poems of R. Israel Berekhya Fontanella from the manuscript preserved in the library of the Breslau Seminary. It was Dr. Rabin who was in charge of the manuscripts, and he put the handwritten volume at my disposal, and gave me permission not only to copy it but also to publish it. The manuscript consisted of forty-five folios, of which twenty contained Fontanella's poems. Fontanella, who died in 1763, was rabbi in Reggio Emilia in Italy and was known as the author of a book titled *Maftehot haZohar* (Keys to the Zohar). That he also wrote

Hebrew poetry was unknown. The manuscript was in an Italian-Hebrew cursive hand that differs considerably from the Ashkenazic Hebrew script with which I was familiar. Hence my first task was to learn the Italian-Hebrew cursive writing.

The way I went about it was to list the Hebrew alphabet, and then write next to each letter its Italian-Hebrew form once I was able to ascertain it. The first clues were supplied by the name "Israel Berekhya Fontanella" that was stated to be the author's in the catalog of the Breslau manuscripts, and was signed under the first poem. The three names alone supplied me with the Italian cursive form of twelve Hebrew characters, leaving only ten more to be identified. After struggling with the problem for perhaps two or three hours, I had the complete alphabet, and from then on it was only a question of gaining some fluency in reading it. Once I was able to read the manuscript, I enjoyed the task of copying it, which I did during several evenings in the well-heated reading room of the library. In the course of this work I decided that I would indeed use this manusript as the basis for my doctoral dissertation at the University of Budapest. When I finished the copying, I put aside my copy for future use, and did not look at it again until about a year later, when it was time to start working on my thesis.

What did I learn during the two semesters I spent in Breslau? Needless to say, I learned a lot from my teachers at the Seminary and from Carl Brockelmann at the University. I deepened my knowledge of Jewish subjects, and became an incipient Arabist. I also matured in the sense in which sex, based on mutual attraction, ripens a youth into a man. I learned to get along on my own, without the protective shield that a loving Jewish family constitutes for a child, an adolescent, and even a youth. Although I was still financially dependent on Father, as I was to remain, more or less, for another five years, I acquired a sense of independence, a conviction that, should it become necessary, I could stand on my own feet financially as well, as I did during that year in all other respects.

And, last but not least, my horizon had broadened considerably. I looked at the world, that of both the Jews and the Gentiles, from a new angle, an observation point that differed materially from the view I had as long as I lived in Budapest. Although Breslau had only about half as many inhabitants as Budapest, it was a German city, and, as such, part and parcel of the great, culture-rich Western world, which, as long as I had lived in Budapest, I had known only from books, films, and such mediators as the British Professor Yolland. In Breslau I learned that I could hold my own in a cultural environment other than Hungarian, that I could communicate and establish relationships in German with people of both sexes and all ages with no more problems than I had in my social contacts at home in Hungarian. If until that time I still had my misgivings about how I would fit into the very different society of the *yishuv* in Palestine, after my Breslau year all doubts were eliminated, and I was determined more than ever that my future would lie not in Hungary but in Eretz Yisrael.

11

The Last Two Years in Budapest: 1931–1933

Life at the Seminary

When I returned to the Seminary, after a year's absence, I found many things changed. Professor Blau had retired, and Professor Hoffer had taken over his Talmud courses. Dr. Weisz had died—how I missed his kindness, his spirit, and the glimmer in his eyes!—and his Jewish history courses were taught by Dr. Zsigmond Grossman, who also introduced a new course, on Legal Relations of the Israelite Denomination in Hungary. Professor Heller was still teaching at the beginning of the fall 1931 term, but in the middle of that term he resigned, and his classes in Bible, Introduction to the Bible, and Readings in Religious Philosophy were taken over by Dr. Gyula Fischer, while his seminar on exegetical readings was continued by Dr. Simon Hevesi. Homiletics and Religious Philosophy continued to be Dr. Hevesi's subjects, and Dr. Fischer continued with his Midrash course and his German seminar. A new instructor, Dr. Bertalan Edelstein, introduced a new subject, Liturgy, and in the subsequent year he taught Methodology of Religious Instruction. I missed not only Dr. Weisz, but also Professor Heller and Rector Blau, and felt that the Seminary as a whole had lost stature with their departure.

These changes in the faculty, however, did not mean any change in the daily schedule of the students. We still had to spend thirty solid hours every week at the Seminary. In contrast to the cavalier attitude toward attendance that characterized our University studies, at the Seminary absence from classes was frowned upon. The fact that most fourth-year students were working on their dissertations for the University, and had to study hard for the comprehensive oral examinations that preceded the formal awarding of the doctoral diploma, did not constitute a valid excuse for absences in the eyes of our teachers.

As for my University studies, I increasingly had the feeling that I would waste my time if I attended courses that had no relations to Semitics and the ancient Near East. I still registered for courses such as Yolland's Survey of English Literature, Dr. Ákos Pauler's History of Ancient Philosophy, Dr. László Négyesi's Artistic Creativity, and Dr. Károly (Karl) Kerényi's Greek Religion (Kerényi later achieved great renown in the field of the psychological study of classical religions), but attended them only sporadically. I definitely became the student of two teachers, Professor Vilmos Pröhle, who took over the Arabic courses after Kmoskó's death, while also continuing his old classes in Persian and Japanese, and Professor Eduard Mahler, who taught Ancient Oriental History and Chronology, and Ancient Semitic and Egyptian Texts. In the last year of my studies, at the end of the fall 1932 term, both of them noted in my registration book, "Term examination: excellent."

Although the atmosphere at the Faculty of Philosophy was nothing like that at the Technical University, I still had not a single friend among my fellow students, not even an acquaintance with whom I could have exchanged at least casual greetings and remarks. In the courses that were not attended by my Seminary colleagues, such as Yolland's on English literature, I would enter the classroom, sit down somewhere among the fifty or sixty students usually present, and speak not a word to anybody until, at the end of the period, I would get up and exit. In the Semitic and Near Eastern courses, all the students, with one or two exceptions, were my Seminary colleagues. Every day, when our Seminary classes were over, in the early afternoon, we would set out in a group, or in several smaller groups, for the University building, go together to our class, and then leave together.

My best friend throughout my student years in Budapest was not a Seminary colleague, but an old classmate from my high school days, Dezső Stern. Dezső was an extremely serious young man, deeply religious, and with an overriding sense of morality and purposiveness. Despite the *numerus clausus*, which was applied with special rigor to the medical faculty ("there are too many Jewish doctors in Budapest" was the often heard anti-Semitic complaint), Dezső, being an excellent student, managed to be admitted to that faculty. Even though, after we graduated from high school, we both were very busy, Dezső and I met fairly frequently and kept each other informed of the separate worlds we had chosen to enter. And, of course, we discussed intensively the things that preoccupied both of us. In talking to him I felt that I was flighty, where he was solid, sincere, and somewhat plodding. Still, we never had serious differences of opinion, except on the very rare occasions when I tried to convince him that his rigidly Orthodox Jewishness could not be supported by the historical development of Judaism, of which, as my studies progressed, I knew more and more. To my regret, all that has long been obscured by the mist of decades, and there is only one little insignificant incident I remember in which Dezső figured. One day, when we were both freshmen in our respective schools, while Dezső and I were sitting and chatting in my small bedroom-study, my brother Guszti came in to ask me something. He was at the time eleven years old and rather chubby. "Come here," Dezső said to him, "Let me have a look at you." He made Guszti raise his shirt, palpated his belly, and said with the seriousness and the certainty of a first-year medical student, "I think all this fat should be surgically removed." The suggestion was never carried out, and within a few years adolescence took care of Guszti's figure.

I remember of Dezső only one more thing. I asked him about his studies in anatomy, and he told me of the unruliness of his classmates in the dissecting room. "Just the other day," he said with indignation, "they hooked up one end of the small intestines of a cadaver to the faucet, and ran around all over the room with the other end, sprinkling water over the other students, and especially the two girls who are in our class."

After I left for Palestine, I lost contact with Dezső. I don't remember having met him when I went back to Budapest in 1936. Years later I met his father in Palestine, and he told me that Dezső had been taken to one of the Nazi extermination camps, where he treated the sick with self-sacrificing heroism until he, too, was put to death.

In the Seminary, all of us students were a rather fraternal group, all attending the same classes for thirty hours a week, all studying the same material, and all sharing the same attitude toward it and toward our teachers. Occasionally we even went as a group on excursions to the mountains around Budapest. Most of my colleagues also shared the same expectation concerning a career. The common goal was to finish one's studies and to acquire the knowledge a rabbi was expected to have, above all the ability to deliver impressive sermons, which was the major consideration of a congregation in choosing a rabbi. For it was a fact that a rabbi in a Neolog Jewish congregation in Hungary was primarily a preacher.

The task of leading the congregation in prayers in the synagogue services was in most communities taken care of by a *ḥazan* (cantor). A *shoḥet* (ritual slaughterer) saw to it that the members had kosher meat. A *hittanár* (teacher of religion) was employed to teach the children the rudiments of their religion, for which purpose two hours weekly were set aside in every public school. Depending on the size of the congregation, there were one or more other functionaries as well, such as a *mohel* (ritual circumciser), a *liberer* (sexton) who took care of burials, a *shames* (another type of sexton), who took care of the synagogue, and attendants in the *miqve* (ritual bath), if the congregation had one. Thus the rabbi's function as pastor of his flock consisted of little more than delivering a sermon once a week, at either the Friday evening or the Sabbath morning services as well as on the annual holy days; officiating at Bar Mitzvas, weddings, divorces, and funerals, visiting the sick and the bereaved, and giving occasional lectures, or, if he so wished, courses for adults, on Jewish religious and historical subjects. Unless the congregation was large, yet not so large as to warrant the employment of a second rabbi, these functions left the rabbi with enough free time to engage in scholarly research and writing. And, in fact, a surprisingly large number of Hungarian rabbis did produce scholarly works, and some of them, while never giving up their rabbinical position, became the foremost Jewish scholars of their age. Among the rabbis who had pulpits in one of the many synagogues in Budapest, there was an impressive number of scholars, so that the Seminary never had any problem in finding instructors for the courses in its curriculum.

Well, this was the kind of life, position, and occupation for which the Seminary prepared us, and to which its students looked forward. In many cases, if a rabbinical vacancy developed in a congregation, its president would contact the head of the Seminary, and the latter would send one of the fifth-year students, or occasionally even a fourth-year student, to deliver a "test sermon." The test sermon would be given within the framework of the usual Sabbath services; since traveling on the Sabbath is forbidden, this meant that the candidate had to arrive Friday afternoon, and could not leave before Saturday evening. The time the candidate spent in the locality afforded the heads of the congregation an opportunity to become acquainted with him, to see how he comported himself in the company of the local people and their families, and to obtain a general impression of the man. If the impression was overwhelmingly favorable, and the candidate delivered a fine sermon, the congregation's search for a new rabbi would end then and there; if not, they would ask the Seminary for another candidate, or even two or three more, until a decision was reached in favor of one of them.

Among the seminarians many anecdotes, passed along as true stories, circulated about the adventures and misadventures of colleagues in connection with such visits to provincial congregations. One of them was retold by Dr. Arnold Kiss, leading chief rabbi of Buda, himself a magnetic orator and a fine poet, and, incidentally, a good friend of Father and a frequent contributor to Father's monthly journal.

It seems that on one occasion a congregation decided to speed up the procedure of selection, and invited two candidates to preach test sermons, one after the other, the same Sabbath morning. Friday night both of them were put up by the president of the congregation in two adjoining rooms. Both had their prepared sermons with them, and Rabbi Cohen spent the whole night memorizing his by reading it aloud again and again. Rabbi Levi, in the next room, could not help overhearing the oratory of his colleague and competitor, and was forced to recognize that Rabbi Cohen's sermon was much superior to his own. Now it so happened that Rabbi Levi was scheduled to speak first at next morning's services, to be followed immediately by Rabbi Cohen. As Rabbi Levi listened to Rabbi Cohen's sermon, it occurred to him that he could easily memorize the entire speech, and then deliver it in the synagogue, thereby achieving two things: he would give a most effective sermon, and his colleague who was to follow him would be deprived of the sermon he had prepared, and would be left high and dry, figuratively speaking. And so he did.

What Rabbi Cohen felt while he was listening to his sermon being delivered by his colleague the anecdote does not specify. But when Rabbi Levi finished, he went up to the pulpit, and said: "Dearly beloved coreligionists! Any rabbi can preach an impressive sermon, given enough time for its preparation, and for the perusal of the many great ideas contained in our millennial sacred literature. What I want to give you today is something entirely new and different. I shall give you a demonstration that I think you will agree will be an extraordinary feat of memory. We have all just heard for the first time a long and intricate sermon. I shall now proceed to repeat all of it, word by word." And so he did. The impression he made was so overwhelming that the congregation decided the same afternoon to invite Rabbi Cohen to be their rabbi.

My own expectations were different from those of all or most of my colleagues. I say "all or most," because I know that there were two or three among them who, unlike the rest, did not ultimately become rabbis, but I don't know whether this came about fortuitously or was in accordance with the goals they had set themselves while still students, as was the case with me. There was István Hahn, whom I remember as an extremely shy, even awkward young boy (he was a year younger), and who was something of a pet of the other students. When I returned to Budapest in 1976 as the guest of the Hungarian Academy of Sciences, I found that Hahn had become a professor of ancient Near Eastern history at the University of Budapest, but when I met him in his office I still discovered in the man in his sixties traces of his old boyish shyness. On that occasion he told me something that I would otherwise never have known: that when the Hungarian translation of my book *Hebrew Myths* (written jointly with Robert Graves) was published seven years earlier, it was he who was asked to look over and correct the work of the translator. Another of my old Seminary colleagues who did not become a rabbi and whom I met during that visit was Zsigmond Telegdi, who, even as a young student, evinced signs of serious scholarly inclination, and who now was professor of comparative linguistics at Budapest University. A third one, who had left the Seminary before I started to study there, was George Vajda, who became a famous Arabist and professor at the Sorbonne.

But these were the exceptions. By and large, the typical Seminary student wanted to and did become a rabbi. If I remember some of them better than others, this is simply because in a class of some forty students I inevitably had more frequent and closer contact with just a few. Among these was Pál Vidor, the son of a lawyer's clerk (his father had his doctorate in law but, not having gone through his years of probation, worked as an employee in a large lawyers' office). Vidor used to poke fun at the sound of Arabic, which he would hear when, in Professor Heller's class, I would read Maimonides' *Guide of the Perplexed* in the original, and his favorite exclamation was *aber wassatu*, which was the German *aber was* (what else), with the addition of the Arabic feminine noun ending, *-atu*. It was from Vidor that I heard the first time the Hungarian translation of "sympathetic magic" — *szimpatétikus mágia*. At first hearing I thought he was speaking of some sort of pyre or stake, the Hungarian word for which, *máglya*, sounds almost exactly like *mágia*. However, he soon cleared up the misunderstanding, and only then did it dawn on me that I had, of course, encountered the term in Frazer's *Golden Bough*. Later, magic was to occupy an important place in several of my own books and articles.

That Vidor and I were close friends I can conclude from a fragment of a discussion I had with him that I happen to remember. He said that he found it the most delicious thing to kiss a girl on the nape of her neck just below the hairline, which I countered by confessing that for me the most exciting thing was to kiss a girl's eyes. I do not remember having discussed with anybody else such intimate perceptions about contact with the opposite sex.

Sometime during the last years I spent in Budapest occurred the death of a young Jewish poet by the name of Ödön Bölcs. Bölcs, meaning wise in Hungarian, must have been his pen name. I never knew what his original name was. All I remember about him is that he was miserably poor, emaciated, scrawny, sickly, small of stature, and always most shabbily dressed. He was one of Father's protégés, and the author's fees he received for an occasional poem Father published in his journal must have been a substantial part of his income. Of all his poems I can recall only one, and even that only very vaguely. It described an imaginary encounter between the poet and a woman, to whom he refers in the poem as "The Girl." She appears from somewhere, jumps in front of the poet, and then follows the phrase I remember, "her breasts were dancing." Since Father did not consider such erotic imagery admissible to the pages of his monthly, this poem by Bölcs must have been published elsewhere, or perhaps he showed it to me in manuscript.

When Bölcs died — I imagine his resistance was so low that some kind of disease made short shrift of him — Father suggested that I, as an apprentice rabbi, eulogize him at his funeral. I accepted the assignment and prepared a brief eulogy; and Father, Uncle Virág, and I went together to the cemetery. Nobody else was present besides us three. Evidently, Bölcs had no family, no friends. Nor did the Girl appear. I have only the vaguest recollection that I spoke about the fate, the loneliness, of the poet. I remember more distinctly that I was deeply moved, not by my words but by the sadness of this man's life and death. (In a letter dated December 30, 1986, Dr. Joseph Schweitzer, director of the Seminary, informed me that Bölcs died on October 18, 1932, at the St. Ladislaus Hospital in Budapest, at the age of thirty-eight, and that two volumes of his poems were published in 1920 and 1921.)

Girls and Women

When it comes to my relationship to the other sex in those early years of my manhood, I would love to recapture in the net of memory the motivations that were at work in me and governed my behavior. The task, however, is patently impossible to accomplish, for I can barely remember, from a distance of more than fifty years, what I did, and not at all why I did what I did. But some images and names do emerge.

While translating for this book a letter I wrote my sister in 1932, I came across the name Olga Nyiki. At first the name meant absolutely nothing to me. I put down the pen, closed my eyes, and started to cast that ineffective net back into those days of more than half a century ago — and, lo and behold, I began to remember: there were two sisters, one tall, Junoesque, blonde, and very beautiful; the other somewhat smaller in stature, with black hair, also beautiful. The blonde one was Olga. The Nyiki sisters lived with their parents in an apartment in Buda, not far from the Danube, and I visited them a few times. A scene rises before my mind's eye: the three of us are sitting in their living room, in front of the open French window that leads to a small balcony, and overlooks — what? I believe one could get a glimpse of the river between the houses. I remember being attracted by Olga's statuesque beauty, her white skin, blue eyes, curly blonde hair. I don't think I ever went out with her in a twosome. In fact, I can be more positive: I remember never having gone out with her. Why not? Why, if I was as attracted to her as I remember I was, did I not invite her to come with me to a movie, to a concert, to take a walk on the Margaret Island, the favorite haunt of boys and girls, where I would have had a chance to kiss her, or at least to try to kiss her? Why did I not take such initiatives with other girls whom I met, whom I liked, and who, in all probability, would have been responsive to my attentions? Why, during those last two years in Budapest, did I kiss, or do I remember having kissed, only two girls, Guli and Lizi? The images of girls whom I met, and whose loveliness I let slip through my fingers, loom up from the mist that the passage of half a century creates in a man's mind, and I cannot but lament my lack of resolution, my timidity, my inability to catch fire, my unwillingness to make the effort, or whatever else it was that kept me from getting close to those girls whose paths crossed mine for a fleeting moment.

There was, for instance, a young actress, Dóra Kelen by name, whose acquaintance I made when, in November 1932, at the very time from which my letter to my sister dates, she was a performer at one of the cultural evenings organized by Father. I would not remember the date, but I found the fact of her appearance recorded in the November 1932 issue of Father's monthly. She must have recited some poems by Father and other Jewish poets at that evening. She was, and this I do remember, a beautiful young girl with big "soulful" blue eyes. Some time thereafter I ran into her in Váci Street, in the Inner City of Budapest. She was visibly glad to see me, I was glad to see her, and for a while we strolled along that most elegant street, lined with terribly expensive stores, and suffused with what for me at the time was a magic atmosphere. I still remember the proud feeling I had of being the escort, however temporarily, of a beautiful up-and-coming young actress. Would it not have been the natural, the inevitable, thing to do to ask her for a date? But no, I did not. Why? Why? We said good-bye, and I don't remember ever having seen her again.

There were at least another three or four girls whose acquaintance I made through my sister, and with whom I went out once, or at the most twice, and with whom all contact ended even before it began. Why? What was behind this reticence on my part, this hesitancy, reluctance, or timidity, when all the time I was sexually starved and dreamt of intimacy with a woman, any woman? The answer eludes me, and I think I had better abandon the subject.

I have just mentioned Váci Street. I loved to saunter back and forth along its relatively short length, window shop, eye covetously the luxurious clothes, shoes, riding outfits, objets d'art, and beautifully prepared delicacies displayed behind great expanses of plate glass, and observe the elegantly dressed men and women whose stride showed that the street belonged to them. I was enchanted by the ambience of luxury and elegance, and I enjoyed even the smell of the passing automobiles, whose exhausts seemed to give off a pleasant scent in contrast to the foul odor exuded by the motor vehicles in other parts of the city.

Another favorite haunt of mine, when the weather was sunny, was the *Korzó*, as Corso was spelled in Hungarian. It was the promenade on the bank of the Danube between the Chain Bridge and the Elizabeth Bridge. Along it, facing the river, were located splendid buildings, among them the most luxurious hotel of the city, the Danube Palace, with a row of sidewalk cafés in front of them. The *Korzó* was closed to vehicular traffic, so that the people sitting around the tables could watch without any obstruction the milling crowd, the broad Danube with its beautiful white riverboats, and the hills of Buda rising from the opposite bank and crowned by the magnificent royal palace. Every afternoon the *Korzó* was full of strollers who had come to see and be seen, to meet friends, and to enjoy the pleasant surroundings. I was often one of those people, and even though I was mostly by myself, I still remember the pleasure I derived from spending an hour or so promenading and being at least physically present at the scene of what I considered high life.

The two years in Budapest, between my return from Breslau and my departure for Jerusalem, were spent in much work, and, in between, in sporadic and unsuccessful attempts to find a woman whom I could love and to whom I could make love. The difficulty lay in the fact that, while there was no dearth of girls whom I could love, they could not be made love to, and for a young man in my position to find girls to whom he could make love was almost impossible. Having tasted in Breslau the honey of sex, I missed it badly, and those two years could best be described as a long period of acute sexual plight. Yet throughout those months—and in my entire life— I never had contact with a prostitute, and only on one single occasion with a person who might qualify as a girl of "easy virtue."

A small incident that took place toward the end of my sojourn in Budapest vividly illustrates my state of acute longing during those days for female companionship of a different nature from the platonic affairs that always carried within them a kernel of frustration. It was actually not even an incident, but merely a little scene I happened to observe. One day, while I was substituting for Father as editor *pro tem* of his journal, some electrical repairs had to be done in the offices. The electricians, two young men, came at about 4 P.M. and started to work. One of them stood on a ladder and dismantled a faulty ceiling fixture; the other stood on the floor, held the ladder steady, and handed up to him whatever implements he needed. Five o'clock came, and it was time for Uncle Virág, the office manager, and the typists to leave, but the electricians were not yet finished. Since I was always interested in watching electricians, plumbers, and handymen doing their work, I volunteered to stay and lock up after they left.

Some time later a girl arrived, and from the way she and one of the two men greeted each other it was evident that they were lovers. She must have been a working girl herself, and was nothing more than a plain young thing. While the electrician continued to work on his high perch, he and his girl friend exchanged some good-natured banter, and I could sense the hearty belonging-together that was expressed almost palpably in the occasional words they addressed to each other. I sat at my desk and watched the scene, and my heart ached. Oh, what I would not have given to have such a relationship with a girl, a girl who would come to fetch me, with whom I could joke, with whom I could go off to spend the evening together, who would love me, embrace me, make love to me. The proof that I was touched and pained, made envious and unhappy, by the little scene is supplied by the mere fact that even today, after more than fifty years, I can still see the scene: the electrician standing on his ladder, his colleague steadying it, and his girl friend standing somewhat aside and raising her laughing face toward him.

I spent the month of July 1932 at a little resort on the shores of Lake Balaton for the purpose of devoting myself to an intensive study of Greek. I no longer remember how I managed to persuade my parents to let me go alone to a spa, but the fact is that they agreed, and I soon found myself in a small kosher pension a few steps from the lakefront.

To study Greek was not my decision; it was imposed upon me by the rules of the University, which demanded a high school diploma in Greek as a prerequisite for the Dr. Phil. degree. Since the high school of the Israelite Congregation of Pest I had attended was a *reálgimnázium* that placed equal emphasis on the humanities and the sciences, it had offered me Latin (lots of Latin), but no Greek. Students whose high school diploma did not include Greek had to make up the deficiency by passing a special exam. In the spring of 1932 time began to press; I was scheduled to take my doctoral orals in May 1933, and I felt that in the coming academic year I would be too busy to devote the requisite time to cramming in Greek. Hence my plan to separate myself from the distractions of family life and devote one full month to Greek. As it turned out, I ran into more distractions than I would have had I remained with my family.

Since the pension had no single rooms, I agreed to share a room with an eight- or nine-year-old boy who was sent there by his parents into the good care of the landlady. Within a day or two I found out that the wife of a close friend of Father was staying in a neighboring pension with her daughter, who was a year or two younger than I was, whom I had met once or twice at some Zionist affairs or gatherings in Budapest. She was a tall, slender brunette, with a pretty Greek profile, serious, soft-spoken. I went over to see her several times. She evidently liked me, but my inhibitions were too strong for me to be able to catch fire. A few times we sat in the evening on a bench on the lakefront, just above the sandy beach, held hands, and tentatively embraced — and that was all. Since she was the daughter of one of Father's friends, she was, needless to say, out of bounds as far as sex was concerned.

After we both returned to Budapest, I no longer saw her. But a few weeks later, while I was in Bardejov, Czechoslovakia, again together with my family, when I thought back on those evenings at the beach, they appeared to me clad in a veil of romance. I felt that I had been touched by love, and was filled with regret at having let a rare opportunity slip by, not an opportunity to make love to her, which, as I said, was out of the question, but to develop a deeper emotional relationship with her. Much later I was to read somewhere that a situation is never truly romantic while it lasts, but becomes romantic only in retrospect. I still don't know whether this is generally true, but as far as that particular encounter was concerned it undoubtedly appeared to me as a much more romantic happening after it was over than while it lasted. In fact, I was so moved in retrospect that I wrote a poem to that girl. It was a sonnet, and I wrote it in German, the language I had adopted as my language of poetry while I was in Breslau. I still remember that when I wrote it I liked it quite well not so much on account of its rhymes, rhythms, frequent alliterations, and rhapsodic imagery, as for the melancholy mood it conveyed of having missed something beautiful, which, as I still remember well, was precisely my mood that summer in Bardejov.

It was in this despondent mood that, one hot evening, as I was taking a stroll in the park surrounding the spring whose healing waters were the great attraction of the place, I saw a girl ambling about slowly, aimlessly, as if she were at a loss as to what to do. She was dressed simply, almost drably, wore no makeup, and seemed to have no interest in either the place or the people. I don't know what gave me the courage to approach her, but approach her I did, and began to talk to her, first in German, which she did not understand, then in Hungarian, of which she knew a little and which she spoke with a strong foreign accent. She was a Slovak girl from the neighborhood. While talking to her I did not suspect at all that she could be anything else but a simple working girl, out to take the air after a hot day.

We walked about for a while in the park, then I took the direction toward the nearby woods, and when she came along willingly I began to think that perhaps she would be sexually accessible. I definitely remember that I did not associate her in my mind with the concept "prostitute," which had always been repulsive to me. When we were well inside the woods, I drew her to me and hugged her, which she let me do without objection, and I got the feeling that she would be willing to "go all the way." At a secluded and sheltered spot we lay down under the trees; the ground was covered with a thick layer of dry leaves, and I proceeded to do what by then I knew she expected of me, and what in my state of arousal I had no choice but doing. Long before, in Budapest, I had provided myself with a condom that I used to carry around in my wallet — hope springs eternal — and now I used it for the first time in my life. Only when it was over, which was quickly enough, did it dawn on me that a girl who was as willing as she was to let a man whom she had just met make love to her must be used to doing precisely that and would expect some payment. I gave her what in the confusion of the moment I considered an appropriate amount. I said good-bye to her. I never saw her again.

But to return to the previous month on the shores of Lake Balaton, in the same pension in which I stayed, among the other vacationers, there were two women, each with a daughter of six or seven, and each without her husband. They were from the same provincial town in Hungary, which shall remain unnamed, and they were ostensibly friends, although, as I was soon to find out, no love was lost between them. My preoccupation with my Greek studies did not mean that I could not spare two or three hours every morning to go to the beach, swim in the tepid water, and take the sun lying on the sand. Both women were around; inevitably, I began to flirt with them, and they were not unreceptive to my attentions. We would go into the water together—the south shore of the lake was extremely shallow so that one had to wade out perhaps a hundred yards from the shore before the water was deep enough to swim in—and since neither of the two ladies could swim, I volunteered to go out with them, one at a time, to a distance where the water was some three or four feet deep, and give them swimming lessons there. The lessons consisted of holding the lady horizontally in the water, supporting her at the waist or somewhat higher up on the body, and encouraging her to make swimming motions with arms and legs. Before long my hands happened to slip upward, and I supported her body by cupping my hand around her breasts.

One thing led to another, and I made assignations with each of them in turn, which, however, encountered certain logistical difficulties. Since the daughter of each of the two women slept in the same room as her mother, neither of them would risk letting me come to her room after the rest of the people in the hotel had gone to bed. As for my room, since I had not been blessed with foresight, I was saddled with my little roommate, and in the circumstances the women were unwilling to come there. However, their interest in sex was stronger than their caution, and they accepted my assurance that the boy was a sound sleeper who would certainly not wake up unless we shook him or shouted in his ear. The upshot of it was that each of the ladies visited me two or three times during my stay. Both insisted that I promise, as they put it, "to be careful," which method of birth control seems to have been the prevailing one in the Jewish middle class in country towns. Each of the two suspected that I carried on with the other as well, and this prompted them to utter some catty remarks about each other. One of them told me that the other was "pigeon-breasted," and the other opined that her friend had "the body of a cow." It seems that animal imagery was very much part of small-town language in Hungary.

One morning, after the pigeon-breasted lady had visited me, I slept late; when I went out to the porch to have my breakfast, she was sitting there with a middle-aged man. She called to me, "Come here, Gyuri, I want you to meet my husband!" I felt terribly embarrassed and guilty, but managed to keep a straight face, shook hands with the man, and then escaped to the dining room. The same evening the couple and their daughter left, and I never saw them again.

But the woman with "the body of a cow" did continue to see me until I left for Palestine. It is typical that I do not remember her name. I shall call her Julia. She certainly did not have the body of a cow, but had what was referred to as a Junoesque figure. From time to time, once in five or six weeks, Julia would come up to Budapest to do some shopping. She would check in to a hotel and then phone me, and we would make an assignation. Once, I remember, she called relatively early in the morning. The phone was in my parents' bedroom, and they were still in bed when it rang. Mother picked up the phone, and when the caller told her that she wished to speak to Gyuri, she called out to me come in and take my call. I entered, saw my parents lying side by side in their twin beds, answered the phone, and, rather embarrassed, made my assignation with her for the same afternoon, without mentioning her name or saying anything else except "Fine, that will be fine," and "Good-bye." I put down the receiver and quickly exited before my parents could ask anything. In fact, they were very discreet, and never referred to this phone call.

The assignations with Julia always took an identical course. I would show up at her hotel at the appointed hour and call her room on the house phone; she would come down; we would greet each other with formal coolness, walk out of the hotel, take a taxi, drive to another, small hotel on the Buda side of the city, check in as Mr. and Mrs. Klein (I reverted to the original name of my father), go up to our room, which, in anticipation of such guests, was well heated, get undressed, make love (I "was careful") repeatedly, chat in between, get up, get dressed, take a taxi back to her hotel, and there we would say good-bye to each other. I still remember that the expenses of the taxi and the hotel made deep dents in my budget (I did earn some money by lecturing), and I had to skimp all the weeks in between Julia's visits.

Once, I no longer remember for what reason, I took Julia not to that small hotel in Buda, but to a large one in the center of town. She sat down in the lobby while I went to the reception desk, asked for a single room, and registered as Mr. György Klein. Then, having had no prior experience with such arrangements, she and I together followed the bellboy who showed us to the room. A minute after he left, the phone rang. I was surprised, but picked it up, and heard a male voice say, "Mr. Klein? This is the reception desk. Who is the lady who went up with you to your room?" I was taken aback, and managed to answer only with some difficulty, "A friend." "Well," answered the receptionist, "We cannot have women visitors in a single room. I shall send back the bellboy and he will take you to a double room. You can pay him the difference in the rates." This unpleasantness taught me to be satisfied with the small hotel in Buda.

What would Julia and I talk about during the rare and precious hours we spent together? I can barely remember. She would exclaim (at least the first time or so) how wonderful it was to make love to a thin boy instead of a man-mountain like her husband, and would tell me all kinds of intimate details about her husband's sexual preferences, with which, however reluctantly, she had to go along. Later I read somewhere that the ultimate betrayal a married woman commits when she is with her lover is not so much to give herself to him physically as to tell him how her husband behaves in bed. Fortunately, in those early days I was not yet sensitized to these things. Julia would also describe in some detail what she was doing all day long at home, her visits to the local synagogue, her meetings with her girl friends, including the pigeon-breasted one, the books she was reading (made available to her by the local lending library), the dresses she bought or was about to buy in Budapest, and so forth.

In between our meetings we would occasionally write to each other—she gave me the name and address of a woman friend of hers whom she could trust. She, on her part, would address her letters to my home without putting the name of the sender on the envelope. Since until my departure for Palestine in May 1933 Julia was the only woman to whom I was able to make love, both the meetings with her and the exchange of letters between us assumed great significance for me. In fact the letters became something of a substitute for lovemaking, and I could not refrain from erotic outpourings in them.

My relationship with Julia, while it contributed somewhat to the release of tensions in a twenty-one- or twenty-two-year-old youth, and filled me with a certain pride in having a mature woman as my lover, even though a very occasional one, did not involve romantic love or deep emotional attachment on my part, nor, as far as I could judge, on her part either. We both had a need that the other filled to some extent at least. Years later, when the Nazi madness sent four-fifths of all Hungarian Jews to their death, killing off almost all of those who lived outside the capital, I often thought with horror of the fate that must have befallen Julia, her husband, and her daughter whom I knew as a child, who must have been about twenty years of age at the time of the Holocaust. Julia was a simple soul, into whose drab life, I liked to think, the tenuous relationship with me must have introduced patches of color and excitement.

As for the Greek exam in preparation for which I went to Lake Balaton, it was held at the Seminary under the auspices of the Hungarian Ministry of Education, and I failed it ignominiously. This was the only exam I have ever failed. I had no choice but to continue studying Greek, and to sit for the exam again. This time the exam was held in a high school, and it was presided over by Dr. Jenő Pintér, the chief governmental supervisor of secondary schools. The twelve or fourteen students who took the exam were asked to be seated in a row facing the examiners, and each of us was given a Greek textbook in which the passage to be translated was marked. The textbook also contained a glossary, and thus, while I was waiting for my turn, I could look up the words I did not understand. This helped a lot, and I passed the exam with a "good" mark. Dr. Pintér knew Father and had written about him most appreciatively in his *History of Hungarian Literature*, in a chapter entitled "Joseph Patai and His Literary Circle"; when the test was over, he bade me come out with him to the corridor, and there asked me how Father was, and what were my study plans. I remember a peculiar mannerism of his: while standing opposite me, he made a few very small steps sideways, as if he wanted to have a look at my profile, while I, of course, turned my head following him, offering him only a front view.

Today, in retrospect, I wish I had failed that second time, too, and had been forced to go on studying Greek for a third exam. As it is, I never acquired a sufficient mastery of Greek to be able to cope with a Greek text, and in my subsequent scholarly work I often had to resort to the help of a Greek scholar when the understanding of a Greek text or passage was imperative.

When one is twenty it seems desperately important to be older, or, at least, to appear older in order not to be looked down upon by women as a mere boy, and to be accepted by them as a young man who can be considered a potential lover. Such aspirations must have been uppermost in my mind when I began to pay attention to my clothes, with a definite inclination toward elegant attire of a type that made me look older than I was. After my return from Breslau to Budapest I acquired a black winter coat with a narrow black velvet collar and a matching black derby that, I thought, was not only dashing but also most becoming to a young man in the third decade of his life. I no longer remember how I managed to convince Mother— it was she and not Father who supplied me with pocket money—to let me have a special allowance for the purpose; she probably understood how important these props were for my incipient manhood. I do remember, though, how proudly I strutted in the streets of my city in what I believed was a splendid outfit, and one that made me look no longer a mere fledgling, but an impressive young man.

Thus equipped, and whipped by a powerful sex drive, I made several attempts to get acquainted with women who would be willing to become my girl friends. After my experience with Jewish girls of middle-class families in Breslau, with their much freer attitude to sex, the Budapest girls of a similar background, who would go no further than mild flirtation, with kissing, hugging, and the touching of sexual parts through clothing as the absolute limit, left me dissatisfied and frustrated. And I simply did not know other types of girls or women, or, if I did meet them, I was not sufficiently attuned to their behavior patterns to recognize the signs of approachability. I was, I felt, in a desperate situation that called for, if not desperate, at least daring, measures. I took several such steps, always after considerable hesitation, and always with a fiasco as the end result.

One winter day, I remember, I put on my elegant black coat and bowler hat, and went to Margaret Island to the indoor swimming pool that had been opened only a short while previously. While taking my laps in the Olympic-sized heated pool, I noticed a young girl swimming alone whom I found attractive. When she got out of the water and lay down to rest in the area that surrounded the pool, I stretched out not far from her. There were only a few people around—wintertime swimming was not yet popular in Budapest— and I could easily have struck up a conversation with her, but did not have the guts to do so. I just sat there ogling her without making any overt move. When, after a while, she got up and went toward the women's dressing rooms, I rushed to the men's locker room, got into my clothes as quickly as I could, and then went to the entrance hall through which she had to pass in order to get out of the building. I had to wait quite a while, and when she finally appeared, I got up and walked after her. As she approached the ramp that led up from the island to the Margaret Bridge, I looked around carefully to make sure that nobody could observe us, stepped out to overtake her, and, screwing up all my courage, addressed her. I must have said something like, "Would you allow me to accompany you?" The girl gave no sign of having heard me, did not look in my direction, and continued to walk at the same pace. I interpreted this as a haughty refusal on her part even to acknowledge my existence, despite bowler hat and velvet-collared black overcoat, and felt discouraged, embarrassed, and slighted. I slowed down immediately, letting her go ahead, and following her only with my eyes until her figure got lost among the many pedestrians who were crossing the bridge between Buda and Pest.

Another unsuccessful attempt I made about that time to strike up an acquaintance with a young female willing to accommodate my unquenched ardor consisted of placing an ad in a paper. Although I no longer remember the name or the character of the paper, it is still clear in my mind that ads placed by men and women wishing to meet persons of the opposite sex were quite common in the papers of Budapest in those days. After considering the matter carefully, I composed the text of an ad saying something to the effect that "young man wishes to make acquaintance of independent woman with apartment of her own." The latter point was important because, living as I was with my parents, if my would-be woman friend had no apartment of her own, we would have had to meet in a hotel, for which I did not have the money. Even the visits to a hotel with Julia once every five or six weeks were a serious strain on my resources. My ad asked for responses to be addressed to a numbered box at the newspaper's office. The next day I bought the paper and saw that my ad was indeed published, and the day after I went to the paper's office to see whether there were any letters addressed to my box. There were none, nor were there any the next day and the day after. On the fourth day, finally, there was one single letter waiting for me. I tore it open with great impatience, and found that it contained precisely what I had hoped for. A woman, who gave neither her name nor her address, but described herself as slender, of middle height, in her late twenties, was interested in meeting me. Hurray! She named a well-frequented midtown street corner, where I was to wait for her, three days hence, at a certain hour in the early afternoon. To make recognition possible, I was to hold in my hands a copy of the paper in which my ad appeared, and a bunch of violets. She would be wearing a dark mink coat.

My happy excitement was overwhelming, my impatience excruciating. A young woman, with a mink coat! It was as if all my secret dreams were suddenly about to come true. I found her instructions that I should hold a bunch of violets in my hand especially romantic and promising, for in those days one could hear everywhere a popular song with a sweet sentimental air, whose lyrics said (my literal translation), "Violets, purple violets, this is my sin, nothing else/ I love you, I love you very much, if this is a sin, fate is to blame. . . . "

When the appointed hour approached, I dressed carefully, bought a copy of the paper, and went to a flower shop to get a bunch of violets, which the florist wrapped in cream-colored wrapping paper, pinning it carefully at top and bottom so that what I got was a small cone-shaped package. I hurried to the place of rendezvous, arriving there almost half an hour before the time specified, and waited. I considered for a moment whether I should unwrap the violets, but then I decided against it, partly because I felt I would be ridiculous standing at the street corner with a bunch of flowers in my hand, and partly because I thought it would be a more delicate gesture to present the unknown lady with the violets still wrapped up and hidden. I thought that the shape of the package that I held firmly in front of my chest did clearly enough indicate that it contained flowers. I waited. I unfolded the paper and tried to read it, but was too nervous to be able to concentrate and too anxious to take my eyes off the street even for a moment. I wanted to be sure that I would espy her as soon as she appeared from whatever direction she came. I waited. The appointed hour came and went. I waited. A quarter of an hour passed, half an hour, forty, fifty minutes. When a full hour had passed, I knew that she would not come. I threw the violets into the wastebasket that stood at the corner, slammed the paper under my arm, and left.

All the way home I speculated on what could have happened. Was the letter a trick played by the people in the newspaper office, to make a person who had placed an ad believe that there was some response? Or did the unknown woman actually write the letter, come by, dressed not in a mink coat but in quite a different coat, inspect me, and, finding me not to her liking, pass on without making herself known? Was I still too young, too rosy-cheeked, to make women take an interest in me? Or did she pass by, and, not seeing the violets—violets, purple violets—because they were hidden in the wrapping paper, not recognize me as the person with whom she had made the appointment? I was distraught, but nevertheless, for three or four more days thereafter I returned to the newspaper office to inquire whether there were any additional letters addressed to my box number. There were none.

A Month of Funerals

When I was in the fourth year of my studies at the Seminary, my turn came to officiate for one month in the cemetery of the Israelite Congregation of Pest. There was a standing arrangement between the Seminary and the Congregation to the effect that its upperclassmen took turns in officiating in the cemetery at those funerals for which the bereaved family did not request the services of a specified rabbi. The well-to-do people, of course, called upon the rabbi whose synagogue the deceased had attended, and he came out to the Rákoskereszturi cemetery, located in a suburb of Budapest, to eulogize the deceased. Depending on the family's ability and willingness, it could choose among a first-, second-, and third-class burial. Each of the three classes had its own funeral chapel, located in a different part of the sizable building that also housed the offices, and the rooms in which the traditional washing of the dead was performed. The first-class funerals were always conducted by a rabbi whom the family had engaged for the purpose. Most of the second-class burials were also taken care of by rabbis whom the families of the deceased had selected. A few of them, and all the third-class burials, fell to the Seminary student whose turn it was to officiate at the cemetery that month. There were, on an average day, ten to twelve burials—the Israelite Congregation of Pest was a very large one, numbering in the early 1930s something like 200,000 souls, and while it had no less than fifty-six synagogues, this was its only cemetery.

When members of the bereaved family arrived at the cemetery, usually in a few taxis, following the hearse in which the body of the deceased was transported, they would be received by Uncle Salgó, the *liberer* (Yiddish for burial functionary or sexton), whose task it was to supervise the washing of the body, to recite, or rather chant, the prayers for the dead, and to accompany the bier with the family from the funeral chapel to the grave site, which, because of the large size of the cemetery, was inevitably at quite a distance. We all called him *Salgó bácsi* (Uncle Salgó), since his son, László, was our classmate at the Seminary. Uncle Salgó also briefed the bereaved family about the customary fee they would have to hand the officiating rabbi, and then ushered them into the rabbi's office. It was this feature, the fee, that, apart from the pastoral practice represented by some 200 burials in the course of the month, made the tour of duty in the cemetery a very important thing for the rabbinical students, most of whom came from poor families. The fees the student received during that one month in the cemetery were often the only source from which he could defray the cost of printing his doctoral thesis — a *conditio sine qua non* for getting his Dr. Phil. degree.

So there I sat for the first time in the rabbi's office in the cemetery. Uncle Salgó ushered in the first of the bereaved families I was to meet. I was tense, ill at ease, and overwhelmed by the old feeling of dread, of being threatened, even though only at second hand, at having to face people whom death had touched by removing a member of their family, a feeling that I had first experienced when I visited Father while he sat *shiv'a* for his father back in 1928. But this time I had a duty to perform, and had to force myself to face the mourning family, asking them questions about the deceased so as to be able to say something personal about him or her in the brief eulogy, of which I had prepared two or three versions in advance. I asked the name, age, occupation of the deceased, whether he had died suddenly or after a brief or long illness, what family members he had left behind, and something about his personality. I took notes, and closed the interview with a few murmured comforting words. Before they left, one of the mourners placed an envelope on the corner of my desk. After they left I pocketed the envelope, and then had a few minutes to organize my thoughts on how best to incorporate the information I had been given, or at least some of it, into the prepared funeral oration. I put on my rabbinical biretta and shiny black gown, and entered the chapel, where the coffin was already in place in front of the pulpit, and where the mourning family and friends were waiting.

As the days passed, and I went through the same procedure again and again, my confidence grew, and I was better able to communicate with both the bereaved family during the interview and the larger audience in the chapel. Yet, at the same time, I remained as affected by the presence of death, and especially by the tragic death of young people, as I had been on the very first day. I even felt the need to discipline and harden myself; and, since I found that I had an unreasonable fear of looking at a dead body, I forced myself once or twice to enter the room where the *tahara*, the traditional Jewish ritual of washing the dead prior to burial, was performed, and to watch how it was done.

As my days of service at the cemetery accumulated, I became sufficiently used to its atmosphere to be able to make a few observations about the mourners. The concept of pattern was not yet familiar to me at the time, but I began to notice marked differences in the behavior of various types of mourners. At first I thought that the death of an old person, who had lived a long life, would be mourned less vehemently than that of a youngster whose life had been nipped in the bud, or, to put it differently, that children would be affected by the death of their parents less painfully than parents by the death of their children. I did not find this to be the case at all. What I did observe was that it was the death of a breadwinner that evoked the strongest manifestations of despair in the surviving relatives.

Another point that was brought home to me in the cemetery was that there was a definite correlation between the economic status and the behavior of the mourners. People who could afford a second-class funeral (I had no experience with first-class funerals) behaved with decorum. The men looked before them stoically, somberly, sadly; tears were rarely visible in their eyes. The women would, from time to time, sob quietly, hiding their faces behind handkerchiefs. Silence was the rule, and the only voice heard in the chapel was that of my own funeral oration, and the chanting of prayers by Uncle Salgó. In the third-class funerals, especially those of the really poor, the mourners gave unrestrained expression to their grief. The women cried loudly even before I began my eulogy, and when I came to my references to the deceased, there was much shrieking, screaming, and wailing, with heads thrown back and arms raised high. The men exercised more self-control even here, but much less than the men in the second-class funerals. Of course, economic differences went hand in hand with differences in educational level and with what was considered proper behavior in times of stress and grief. I concluded, although at the time I did not formulate the conclusion on this level of generalization, that individual behavior under the stress of acute grief depended not so much on individual temperament as on the environment in which a person grew up and lived, and on the influences absorbed from it.

Two incidents stand out in my memory from that month of rabbinical apprenticeship in the cemetery. One is that, before I started my service, I was told to pay a visit to Mr. Simon Henrik Endrei, the director and chief secretary of the Ḥevra Qadisha, the Holy Society, as the organization within the Jewish congregation responsible for burials and other charities was called, in order to give him an opportunity to look me over and give his approval. At the age of twenty-one or twenty-two I was a clean-shaven, milky-faced youth with a luxuriant mop of dark brown hair. Endrei chatted with me for a few minutes, then, before dismissing me, he brought his thumb and forefinger near my chin, rubbed them together gently, and said, "A little beard would be in place here." I don't remember whether I had anything to reply to this suggestion, which was a late and stunted survival of the old biblical commandment about not cutting the edge of one's beard.

The other incident involved my late arrival at the cemetery on one occasion. I no longer remember why, on that particular morning, I did not go to the cemetery at the usual early hour when the first funerals used to be scheduled. There was, in any case, a standing arrangement that, if the student rabbi happened not to be present, the funeral would be handled by one of the cemetery's permanent employees. At about ten o'clock I got a phone call from Uncle Salgó: a bereaved family had just arrived, and the son of the deceased wanted me to officiate at the funeral. "I am coming right away," I said; I put on my black clerical vest that hugged my collar at my throat and rushed to the corner streetcar stop. It never occurred to me that the call was urgent enough to warrant taking a taxi, which, in any case, would not have cut down the traveling time by much. We lived by that time in Nyúl Street, which was at the opposite end of the city from the district where the cemetery was located, so that the trip by streetcar took a good three-quarters of an hour. By the time I arrived, the chief mourner was furious. He made me understand in no uncertain terms that he no longer required my services, and that he had in the meantime made arrangements with somebody else to eulogize his father. Needless to say, it was a second-class funeral. I apologized, and retired to my office. Uncle Salgó later said, "You should have taken a taxi." And I learned another lesson in human nature.

Guli

One of Father's friends was Dr. Ignác Friedmann (1882–1956), a leading lawyer in Budapest. Dr. Friedmann had represented Hun-

garian interests in the post–World War I negotiations with Czechoslovakia and in the deliberations of the International Mixed Court of
The Hague, where he achieved considerable results in connection
with the settlement of the estates of several Hungarian noblemen
whose properties were located in the territories Hungary had to cede
to the successor states. In recognition of these services Dr. Friedmann
was awarded the title "government chief counselor," which meant
that he had to be addressed as *Méltóságos Uram*, a coveted title. His
wife was the daughter of Simon Gold, another lawyer and government chief counselor.

Friedmann was of the same age as Father and bore a striking
physical resemblance to him. He had the same round, bald head,
the same type of nose that protruded at an angle beneath the forehead, wore the same kind of heavy, black-rimmed glasses, and had
an identically trimmed black moustache. From a distance it was possible to confuse the two men, but when one got nearer one could
not help noticing that Friedmann was heavier and bigger than Father,
his lips were thicker, and his features coarser. There was also considerable difference between them in manners. Father was always kind,
polite, and friendly, while Friedmann was somewhat rough, gruff,
and aggressive—this, at least, is how he struck me, and how I remember him. Father always wore business suits, while Friedmann always
wore a black jacket with grey-and-black striped trousers, and a black
vest lined with a white brocaded material that showed as a thin
stripe at the neck opening. I found the latter so attractive that I once
had a suit tailored for me with that distinguishing white stripe.

Friedmann was a loyal friend and admirer of Father, who succeeded in winning him for the Pro Palestine Federation, and in that
capacity Friedmann became one of the non-Zionist Hungarian signatories of the foundation document of the expanded Jewish Agency
for Palestine in Zurich in 1929.

Friedmann was a very wealthy man. He lived with his wife, two
daughters, and one son in a large and luxurious villa on Stephania
Avenue near the city park, one of the most elegant residential streets
in the city. He was, among other things, a member of the board of
the Czech-Hungarian Chamber, and some time before I left for Palestine he acquired a chateau in the Czech Carpathians, with a chapel
whose upkeep, including the salary of its chaplain, was part of the
estate expenses. When Father told me about this—he in turn had
heard it from Friedmann himself—I found it most remarkable that a

Jew, as lord of the manor, should have a Christian clergyman in his pay.

When Father's biography of Theodor Herzl was published (1931), he dedicated it to Ignác Friedmann. I have a vague suspicion that Friedmann contributed to the cost of publishing the book, which appeared under the imprint of the Pro Palestine Federation of Hungarian Jews. Later the Omanuth Publishing House in Tel Aviv brought out a German and a Hebrew translation of it, and still later a rather unsatisfactory English translation was published in New York under the title *Star over Jordan*.

Friedmann had what was undoubtedly the richest private collection of Jewish ritual and ceremonial objects in the world. According to the *Hungarian Jewish Lexicon*, his collection, which contained mostly liturgical and ritual objects, old silver Tora-crowns, breastplates, pointers, spice-boxes, ethrog-boxes, old parchments, and other valuable Judaica, matched in size and quality the Jewish part of the world-famous Cluny Museum in Paris. It was kept in the Friedmann villa in numerous big glass showcases. I still remember that on the occasion of my visits to the Friedmanns I would be irresistibly drawn to those vitrines, and almost physically ingest the beauty of the one art form in which Jewish artistic talent most intrinsically expressed itself in the centuries prior to Emancipation. In one issue of his monthly Father published an article about the Friedmann collection, written by a noted art historian and illustrated with numerous photographs. Years later, when I asked Ignác Friedmann's son, Andrew Freeman, whom I met from time to time in New York, what had happened to his father's collection during the Nazi period, he said he did not know.

For a time I engaged in a diffident and desultory courting of Hella (called Guli by everybody), the older of the two Friedmann daughters. During that time I was an occasional visitor to the villa on Stephania Avenue, and this is why I remember the Friedmann collection so clearly. The house stood in its own spacious grounds that included a tennis court where I played some matches with Guli. She was a sweet, intelligent, somewhat shy girl, not precisely pretty but with a good figure and a charming expression. She was four years younger than I, and was, I believe, a freshman at the University. If I did not fall in love with her—I was so ready to fall in love with any girl who responded to the interest I showed in her—one of the reasons must have been her ardent Hungarian patriotism, which, in my equally ardent Zionism, I found patently absurd. Once or twice I broached the subject of whether she would consider the possibility of going to Palestine to live, and her answer was a definite no. "I am a Hungarian," she said, "and this is my country." I don't know how and where, but she did survive the Nazi period, and settled in Vienna, where, when I visited her with my wife in 1973, she was a teacher of English at the university, a widow, and a grandmother, living alone.

In the fall of 1932 Lily Montagu (1873–1963), a leader of the Liberal Jewish movement in England, visited Budapest together with Margarethe Goldstein, editor-in-chief of the Berlin Jewish journal *Der Morgen*, for the purpose of creating interest in Liberal Judaism among Hungarian Jews. Lily Montagu had founded the Jewish Religious Union in Britain, which, in 1926, sponsored the World Union for Progressive Judaism. In her capacity as leader of this movement, Miss Montagu visited several countries (a photograph in the *Encyclopaedia Judaica* shows her delivering a sermon in 1928 in the Berlin Reform Synagogue). Dr. Friedmann had been interested in Liberal Judaism for some time, and lectured and wrote about it (see, for example, *Mult és Jövő*, April 1932, p. 117, and May 1932, pp. 137–38). In all probability it must have been he who invited the two ladies to Budapest and, in any case, it was in his home that they addressed a select group of Hungarian Jewish leaders. My parents and I were among those invited to attend the meeting. It was a festive gathering of the rich, the famous, and the intellectual leaders of Budapest Jewry, from which, however, the rabbis of the city were conspicuously absent due to the simple fact that the Neolog congregations of Pest, Buda, and their suburbs were all Conservative in their official stance and hence opposed in principle to Liberal or Reform Judaism.

Lily Montagu, from a distance of more than fifty years, appears to me to have been an elderly, gaunt, sparsely built woman, and what I remember in particular about her is that she was dressed much more simply and austerely than the rich Hungarian Jewish women and their daughters who were present in the Friedmann mansion on that occasion. The most peculiar aspect of the evening, however, was that there was no common language between the speaker and her audience. Dr. Friedmann introduced Miss Montagu in German, she spoke in English, and after her address there were comments from the floor, again in German. It is interesting, and characteristic of the selectivity of memory, that while I remember clearly these details about Lily Montagu, the fact that Margarethe Goldstein was also present and also addressed the gathering had escaped me altogether, and it is only from a news item in *Mult és Jövő* (November 1932, p. 318) that I learn that she was there. Since most of the Budapest Jews knew only one foreign language, German, I suspect that not many of those present could understand Miss Montagu. My own English at the time was quite adequate, but my interest in such an abstruse problem as whether or not an effort should be made to introduce Liberal Judaism into Budapest was minimal, and so I did not speak up, for which lack of participation I was, on our way home, mildly reproached by Mother.

One of those present at the Friedmanns who did speak up, in German, gracefully and with considerable eloquence, was a brilliant young lawyer, Dr. Endre Neugröschl by name, who was extremely good looking to boot. He was, as Mother explained to me during our taxi ride home, one of the most eligible Jewish bachelors in the city, and the Friedmanns would have loved to see him as their son-in-law. "But," said Mother, giving me a rare insight into matrimonial politics in upper-class Budapest Jewry, "Did you notice that Neugröschl paid more attention to the Székely girl than to Guli Friedmann, although Guli is certainly the more intelligent and the prettier of the two? The reason is obvious. Székely is the executive officer of the Hungarian Telephone Factory, has more money than Friedmann, and can be more useful for Neugröschl's career. I am sure he will marry the Székely girl"—which he did.

As far as I know, Lily Montagu's visit remained an isolated incident, and no further attempt was made at launching a Liberal Jewish movement in Budapest in the course of the eight years that still remained of the life of its Jewry until the Holocaust.

There are two little incidents that have remained stuck in my memory in connection with Guli. One is that one winter evening, while she and I were taking a walk in the park near her parents' home, I kissed her. She did not object, did not turn her head away, and did not pull away from me. But, a moment later, she threw up. I was too shy to ask her what was the matter, and she volunteered no explanation. I cannot remember whether thereafter I ever again kissed her. The other thing I remember is that for her birthday I gave her a book as a present. One of my favorites at the time was Oscar Wilde, most of whose writings I had read in English during my college years. And one of my favorites among Wilde's works was the play *Salome*. I read it in English, and was so impressed by it that I translated it into Hebrew. When setting out to do so, I had to consult Father for the very basic reason that I did not know the proper Hebrew form of the name Salome. Father enlightened me: it was *Sh'lomit*. My translation was never published, I did not even dream of submitting it to a publisher, and the manuscript has disappeared long since. I assume it must have been a rather juvenile attempt, if for no other reason than because my Hebrew, prior to my going to Jerusalem, while adequate for conversational purposes and for writing scholarly papers, was far from being of literary quality.

But, to go back to Guli's birthday: I knew, of course, that Wilde had written *Salome* originally in French, and then translated it himself into English, and I took it into my head to give Guli, who spoke French well, the French version of the play. I went to several of the biggest bookstores in the city, until, in one of them, I found the book I wanted. It was a beautifully printed edition with illustrations by a French artist whose name — remarkably — I do remember: it was Alastair. I even remember that the title page said *Dessins d' Alastair*, and that I had to go to my French dictionary to look up the word *Dessins*. But there was a problem with the book — it was available only in paperback, and hence not quite suitable as a birthday present. Still, I bought it, and located a bookbinder whom I entrusted with the task of binding it in burgundy morocco, with a gold design of my own composition to be stamped on its spine and front cover. The binding was completed in time for me to present the book to Guli on her birthday. What her reaction was to being given what for me was quite an extravagant present, I don't recall. But it so happens that a letter I wrote to my sister in that period of my half-hearted involvement with Guli has been preserved, and it opens a window not only on my relations with Guli, but also on my own private universe of thoughts and feelings.

My sister lived at the time in Berlin with Aunt Ruth, and was a student at the University of Berlin. Among her teachers was Wolfgang Köhler (1887–1967), the famous animal psychologist and founder of the school of Gestalt psychology, who in 1935 was to leave his position of director of the Psychological Institute because of Nazi interference with his work, and to become a professor of psychology at Swarthmore, and then at Dartmouth. While in Berlin, my sister also worked for a while in a German office, where, as she later told me, when she tried to do things as expeditiously as she could, her boss would say to her, *Wozu diese unvornehme Hast?* (Why this ungenteel haste?). The original form of this saying referred not to "ungenteel haste" but to "Jewish haste," but her employer was genteel enough not to offend her by referring derogatorily to anything Jewish.

The occasion for my letter was that my sister got acquainted in Berlin with Joseph Kastein (1890–1946), a by then well-known German Jewish writer and biographer, who in 1933 was to leave Germany and settle in Palestine. They became friendly, which development aroused my brotherly worry and misgivings, in view of the great age difference between them (he was forty-two and she twenty) and the fact that Kastein had a stiff leg. So I wrote to her (in German):

Budapest, November 29, 1932

My Dearest Évi:

Today, finally, I can get to fulfilling my promise to write to you at greater length. You can assume that my insignificance reads your letters with interest, and I was very glad when reading your last one. I was glad to know that you were feeling so well in Berlin, that you were meeting interesting and valuable people, and that you have had, let us say, experiences such as one (or more) meetings with Joseph Kastein. But in this connection I must immediately add also words of caution. It is very wrong if somebody, in this case a young girl, lets herself so easily and so deeply be influenced by somebody else. That Mr. Kastein made a very deep impression on you becomes evident not from your aforementioned letter, but from the last but one, which, I believe I can conclude correctly, you wrote after attending his lecture. That letter is full of abstractions, full of higher points of view, full of shifting the level into the intellectual, etc. And all these are precisely the literary qualities of Kastein with which I am familiar from his books. Since I can assume that these also constitute his characteristics when lecturing, it must be they that made such a strong impression on you already then, that is, even before you spoke to him personally. I do not want to enter here into the deeper motivations. . . . I want only to remark quite in general that you, who claim, don't you, to be a person of high intellectual quality, should possess more firmness and self-determination. There is something very wrong in letting yourself go so easily, and allowing yourself to come this quickly under the influence of a man (or, rather, a human being). One must know how to hold one's own in all situations, despite all influences, and vis-à-vis every person, even one of the highest intellectual caliber.

However, apart from this issue, I do like the style of your last letter, and the buoyancy it exudes. Perhaps I like it precisely because I (and herewith we have arrived at the sacred center of the universe, the I) in my contact with Guli, miss in her precisely this style and buoyancy. However, this means only rare and small disturbances at the most. Otherwise we understand each other quite well, and spend, not infrequently, pleasant hours together. She is very sensible and intelligent, and possesses an excellent ability to absorb new things. Besides, it is easy to deal with her. We have so far never quarreled. And, what is quite remarkable and characteristic of her candor toward me, she is the first girl who admitted that she recognized that Eros and Sexus play a much greater role in a woman than in a man. Otherwise, too, she is rather candid with me. Peculiarly, whenever our conversation touches upon intimate themata, we always avail ourselves of the English language. Thus, when a few days ago I presented her with a book on the occasion of her eighteenth birthday (it was an illustrated edition of Wilde's *Salome* in French, which you, too, know, in a red morocco binding, a noble gift, isn't it?), I wrote in it these words, "To Guli, that the fire of strange beauties should shine into her 18-year-old eyes." — It is unnecessary to add that she was very happy with the book. But nevertheless, I don't think that I shall concentrate totally on her. If for no other reason, I shall not, because of the aforementioned self-determination. And, besides, one must, mustn't one, preserve the balance. Thus, e.g., I also devote myself to Lizi Fischer, who lives in enticing proximity, and Olga Nyiki, who presents in every respect a splendid contrast to Guli. And, quite apart from these things (among which I also count the visits of my acquaintance from the country, with whom I have just spent a few jolly and healthful days), which I can consider of secondary importance, I devote myself seriously to my studies. I want to and shall, God willing, take my doctorate in May. And, beyond this, and beyond my hours at the Seminary, I am engaged in something really beautiful: I am working on a study that I shall title "Gotterzeugende Rasse" [more or less, The God-Begetting Race], which will be a comparison between the Aryans and the Semites. Such comparisons have been made so far always in favor of the Aryan peoples. I want to try, on psychological-historical foundations, to point up the higher values of the Semitic peoples, as the only racial community in the circle of the Mediterranean cultures that was able to produce the pure idea of God, that is, to beget a God. I shall, in this study, relate to Freud, Spengler, Wundt, Reik, Frazer, etc. It surely will be quite a thing, if only I shall have the time and disposition to do it. As for talent and ability, there is no lack of that, that we know.

Let me conclude with two requests: 1. Please have the goodness of preserving this letter. Perhaps one day it will be valuable as a *documentum humanum*. 2. If your answer contains anything private concerning me, put it in a separate envelope.

With hearty greetings, your old brother,

Gyuri

Please give my best regards to Aunt Ruth, her children, and relatives.

Well, the letter has been preserved. But the ambitious study never came to be written.

Bishop Baltazár

One of the great events in Hungarian Jewish life took place in the spring of 1933. It was the address given by Protestant Bishop Dezső Baltazár (1871–1936) of Debrecen, under the auspices of the Pro Palestine Federation of Hungarian Jews which Father had organized in 1927, and of whose department of cultural affairs he was chairman. I know little of the antecedents of the lecture, except that Father had maintained for many years friendly relations with the bishop, who was the recognized leader of the Hungarian Protestants. Baltazár also was an outspoken critic of Catholicism. On one occasion he told Father, who, in turn, quoted him to me, that "we Protestants have a hard fight on our hands against Catholic idolatry in this country." Bishop Baltazár played an important role in the social and political life of Hungary, and was a staunch supporter of the counterrevolutionary regime that followed the defeat of the short-lived Communist government in Hungary in 1919. He was not only president of the Reformed National Council, but also a member of the Upper House of the Hungarian Parliament.

When Father approached the bishop with the suggestion that he give a talk to the Pro Palestine Federation, the bishop accepted unhesitatingly, but because of his heavy schedule it took almost two years before he actually could deliver it. During that time, in correspondence, they discussed the subject of the planned lecture, and settled on "Jewry's Mission with a Country and without a Country." Father wanted to publish the text of the lecture in his monthly as soon as possible after it was delivered, and to be able to do so he asked the bishop to let him have the text in advance. Baltazár agreed, on condition that nobody should have a copy of the text in the lecture hall while he was speaking. It was his custom, he wrote Father, to learn by heart his speeches and sermons, and it would disturb him if he knew that some people among his listeners were checking his delivery against the written version. Once this was settled, the bishop mailed in his text, which was duly printed in the March 1933 issue of Father's journal.

The bishop's lecture took place on March 1, 1933, in the Ceremonial Hall of the Israelite Congregation of Pest named after Karl Goldmark (1830–1915), the famous Hungarian Jewish composer. The very fact that the strongly anti-Zionist leadership of the Congregation put its premises at the disposal of the Pro Palestine Federation was a considerable victory for the Zionist cause, which Father was able to achieve only because the featured speaker was Bishop Baltazár. An hour before the scheduled beginning of the event, the hall was filled to capacity, and its doors had to be closed. More people gathered in the street, and the police had their hands full keeping order. Inside, on the dais, sat not only the leaders of Hungarian Zionism, but also the heads of Hungarian Jewry, both rabbis and laymen, including Court Councillor Samu Stern, president of the Israelite Congregation of Pest, and members of its board, who otherwise would never have honored a Zionist gathering with their presence. Bishop Baltazár sat in the middle, Father next to him.

The introductory part of the program consisted of the recital of Palestinian Hebrew songs by uniformed members of Betar, the Zionist-Revisionist youth organization. One of the songs they sang was *HaTiqva*, the Zionist national anthem—another victory for the cause. Then Father introduced the bishop, whom he greeted as a *goy tzaddiq*, a "righteous Gentile." The bishop rose to thunderous applause, and delivered his speech without as much as a slip of paper in his hand. He was a sparse, tall man, dressed in a black frock coat with a clerical collar. His greyish hair was cropped short; his clean-shaven face made the impression (at least on me) of being closed in upon itself. He had an imposing presence, and a grand, self-assured demeanor. There could be no doubt that there stood a prince of the church, even though his church was not Catholic but Protestant.

It is peculiar how memory can retain external images while allowing the essentials to sink into total oblivion. I can still see Bishop Baltazár standing there and speaking, but I remember not a word of what he said. Fortunately, however, in this case I don't have to rely on my memory, because the full text of the address was printed in the *Pester Lloyd* (the foremost Budapest daily, which was published in German), in Mother's German translation, and a few days later in the Hungarian original in Father's journal, the first of which is available in the Library of Congress in Washington, and the second in the New York Public Library.

Based on the latter, I can summarize the bishop's address. He started with a brief review of biblical history. He dwelt on Abraham, the father and founder of the Hebrew people, who as yet had no country of his own. These beginnings, he said, were indicative of Judaism, which was a world view, a universal, all-embracing world view. "Judaism," he said, "began to fulfill its global mission in a state of countrylessness," for which concept he had to coin a new Hungarian word, just as I had to in translating it into English. "It borders on the miraculous," he said, "what an untouchable awesomeness was radiating out of that enormous ideological superiority that made the Jewish people tower high above other Oriental peoples." After the conquest of Canaan, "the Jewish people had the opportunity to fulfill its global mission also with a country." Thereafter, despite all the reversals and misfortunes, Zion "remained the sacred node that tied together the four corners of the earth and all their points with the golden threads of the justification of the chosen people. The international settlement of the Palestine question set the historical demands, in both their theoretical and practical aspects, on the track of right solution that provides favorable possibilities for the rebuilding of the ancient national state and for the placement of all those Jews who in the situation of countrylessness found neither the conditions of subsistence, nor the satisfaction of their religious-national needs, nor the loving hand of brotherly reception." After quoting a number of biblical passages, Baltazár concluded: "Let Jewry fulfill its global mission without a country until the faithfulness of the hands that do not wither rebuild Jerusalem."

The convoluted style of the bishop may have been difficult to follow, but the stature of the man, his striking seriousness, and his impassioned delivery amply made up for the lack of popular home-hitting appeal of his oratory. His address lasted some forty minutes, and the overfull house listened throughout with bated breath. When he finished, he was given a standing ovation that just did not want to subside. It was, as I can still vividly recall, a truly memorable event.

The day after the lecture my parents gave a reception in honor of Bishop Baltazár. It was a sit-down tea to which some twenty leaders of the Pro Palestine Federation were invited, making it an illustrious gathering. Among those present were Professor Ignác Pfeiffer, president of the Pro Palestine; Dr. Arnold Kiss, leading chief rabbi of the Israelite Congregation of Buda; Mr. Jenő Szántó, vice-president of the National Office of Hungarian Israelites; Baron Bertalan Hatvany, industrialist and writer; Professor Lajos Török, a leading dermatologist; Dr. Nison Kahan, lawyer and Zionist leader; Dr. Ignác Friedmann, whom we have already met; Dr. Joseph Schönfeld, editor of the Zionist weekly *Zsidó Szemle*; and several others. Our dining-room table was extended to its full length, and still the seats were crowded around it. Father had offered to arrange transportation for the bishop, but Baltazár said that would not be necessary, since Mr. Samu Stern was in the habit of putting his chauffeur-driven limousine at the bishop's disposal whenever he visited Budapest.

Baltazár arrived punctually, just after the rest of the people were assembled. After a brief interlude of introductions and some conversation in the living room, everybody sat down around the table. Light snacks, coffee, tea, and nonalcoholic beverages were served, and then, one of those present, Chief Rabbi Kiss, rose to greet the bishop. Dr. Kiss was a very small and very rotund man, with a big bald head, topped with a black skullcap. He had a round face and short round nose on which his spectacles kept sliding down. He was a truly great orator—in the opinion of many cognoscenti he was by far the best among the many fine rabbinical preachers of Budapest—the words, the well-rounded phrases, rich with similes and metaphors, flowed from his lips in a torrent that rose to several crescendos before they reached their cadence. He was always able to captivate, nay, enrapture, the audience, so that when listening to him one was spellbound, completely oblivious of the passage of time. He was expansive and voluble, yet so fiery that nobody ever thought him prolix. This time it took a full half hour before the few words of greeting Dr. Kiss addressed to the bishop drew to a close—I timed it—and I could not help noticing that Bishop Baltazár, too, glanced once or twice at his pocket-watch. He evidently had another engagement coming up. As soon as Dr. Kiss finished, Baltazár stood up, thanked him and my parents, said he was sorry that he had to rush away, shook hands with everybody, and left. I went down with him to the street, where President Stern's limousine was waiting for him. When I got back, the party was about to break up.

I wrote the above account of Bishop Baltazár's lecture and visit to our house on the basis of my recollections of the events and what I found about them in Father's journal. It so happens that Mother, in her reminiscences that she started to jot down in 1955, two years after Father's death, described the same events in a few paragraphs that show them from a different angle. She wrote (I translate from her German manuscript):

The fight of official Jewry against the P[alestine] idea was still in full swing. The lords of the Budapest community tried with all means to keep B[altazár] from giving the lecture. . . . B. informed my husband about the diplomatic maneuvers resorted to by the president of the community, but emphasized that he would in no way let himself be dissuaded. When this seemed unalterable, they wanted at least to prevent his appearance at the reception in our house. But that did not succeed either.

The lecture was a sensation. The external framework itself was overwhelming. The hall was fully packed with people who had arrived much earlier in order to secure seats. Even the corridors, the stairways, the entrance hall were filled to capacity, so that we were barely able to reach our seats. I noticed the pallor of Joseph as he sat on the podium. As if every drop of blood had drained from his face. Looking at him, I myself was seized with a nervousness, and glanced about restlessly. Suddenly there arose shouting at the entrance, and I saw with alarm that the wings of one of the entrance doors were lifted out of their hinges. The people in their excitement could no longer control themselves. I don't know what they hoped from that lecture. Perhaps the fact that a Christian prince of the church came to them gave them the illusion of security. They lulled themselves into believing that the brown flood that swept over Germany would not reach Hungary. Thus the groping, insecure people, who in secret trembled for their future, streamed into the hall.

For most of them the lecture was too difficult, too complicated, but that made no difference. They stood squeezed against one another, the hall was overfilled, and no one moved from his spot. When the leaves of the door were lifted out, a tumult arose, but when Dr. B. entered the hall all became suddenly dead quiet. Joseph told me later that he was afraid that the floor would not support the excessive weight. Never have I seen him so beside himself as at that moment. But when B. concluded, and he rose to say the concluding words, he was calm again. . . .

When we arrived home I felt like after a battle. It surely was a battle won by the Zionist cause, we said to ourselves as we finally sat down to tea. But the fear of the future, a formless fear as yet, kept us constrained. Next day I had, of course, much work with the preparations for the reception for B., and that left me little time for brooding. But I already knew from a firsthand source how it looked in Berlin . . . perhaps Évi was already on the way home. . . . Just now when at last she had found satisfactory work. But that did not count next to the gloomy events that darkened the sky. . . .

Meanwhile the small intrigues around B. continued. They could not prevent the lecture, but that he should go to a Zionist house — that was too much. They begged him over the phone, they said it would be exploited for propaganda. But B. could not be deterred. He sent his secretary, a dried-out and extremely matter-of-fact young man, to inform us of the exact time of his arrival. But this was the only formality. B. gave of himself simply, but his whole being was of a certain solemnity brought about by his high office. He was a true humanist, and it was in the spirit of humanism that he viewed the Jewish question. He never dabbled in politics, and one could see that the machinations of the [Jewish] community were almost incomprehensible for him.

By arranging for Bishop Baltazár's lecture, Father achieved two results. First, that a Zionist gathering should take place on the premises of the Israelite Congregation of Pest, which until that event were out of bounds for Zionists, and that the official leadership of the Congregation, for the first time in history, should attend such a gathering. Second, that one of the most influential Christian church leaders went on record, both orally and in writing, in support of the Zionist endeavor of building a national home for the Jews in Palestine.

Reading, Writing, Redacting

If the stories told in the earlier sections of this chapter created the impression that running after, or planning to meet, women and girls took up most or much of my time, in truth that was not at all the case. Although the other sex may have been much in my thoughts, most of my time was devoted throughout my college years to studying, reading, and writing. As for studying, the routine established in my freshman year at the Seminary and the University continued, except that gradually, as I advanced in my studies, I became more and more aware of how little I knew and how much more there was to learn. As for reading, there was a constant struggle going on in me between wanting to read books I enjoyed and the dutiful feeling that I should use all the time I had to get acquainted with as many books as I could making up the practically limitless library of basic texts in the fields to which my studies were devoted. It happened only rarely that I found satisfaction of both desires in one and the same book.

And then there was writing. Up to the end of 1931, by the time I reached the age of twenty-one, I had published twenty-three items in Hungarian, German, Yiddish, and Hebrew. In 1932 and 1933, ninety-two additional pieces of mine were published, most of them in Father's journal, whose main book reviewer I had become, others in the Jewish press of Budapest, Rumania, Austria, Germany, Palestine, and the United States. As for reviews and book notes, I wrote about everything that interested me: scholarly books on Jewish history, philosophy, religion, linguistics, politics, and also novels, poetry, humor, and so forth. Most of my writings were brief book notes, but some were lengthy and detailed criticisms of important books. For example, about Dubnow's two-volume *History of Hasidism* I wrote an eight-page review in two installments in the *Magyar Zsidó Szemle*, the scholarly journal published by the Budapest Seminary. I also planned to review Dubnow's ten-volume *Weltgeschichte des Jüdischen Volkes* (World History of the Jewish People), but gave up the idea when I heard Professor Blau say in his caustic way, "The title itself contains two mistakes: the Jews have no world history, and they are not a people." The way I obtained books for reviewing was simple. I had Father print up a form letter requesting "a review copy of the book . . . by . . . recently published by you, which we would like to review in *Mult és Jövő*." Whenever I saw an announcement of the publication of a book in which I was interested, I sent off such a form letter to the publisher. From the potpourri of the books I reviewed, I must say that my interest was eclectic, and my reading habit voracious.

Apart from the book reviews, I also wrote in those two years between Breslau and Jerusalem a number of essays. I wrote, for instance, an article on the court Jew Koppel Theben on the occasion of his 200th birthday, which was published in German in the Jewish journals *Die Stimme* of Vienna and *Der Israelit* of Frankfurt on Main, and in a Yiddish translation in the *Jewish World* of Cleveland-Cincinnati-Columbus, Ohio. These papers published my article in September, October, and November 1932, respectively, and in December of the same year the New York–Chicago Jewish daily *Forward* plagiarized it: it published a practically identical article signed "by our Viennese correspondent Maskof," containing, well hidden in the middle of the article, the statement (my translation from the Yiddish), "in such cases of persecutions of Jews—tells the Jewish-Hungarian writer Ervin Georg Patai in an article—the Shtadlan R. Koppel Theben would travel in his carriage to Vienna, to the Emperor." (Let me add here in parentheses that only now, while working on these memoirs, did I discover that Koppel Theben was one of my paternal ancestors.)

I wrote an article on "The Messianic Idea" that was published in the *Uj Kor* (New Age), a Jewish political weekly of Timisoara, Rumania (in Hungarian), and a sharp polemical article (published in the

Budapest Zionist weekly *Zsidó Szemle* [Jewish Review]), in defense of the Seminary against an anonymous author who had attacked it, in an article published in another Jewish paper, from an Orthodox point of view, and, what was worse, in a tendentious manner. In my article I demolished the author of the attack by showing his ignorance and pointing out his many mistakes in elementary Jewish matters, and rose to a spirited defense of the Seminary, its methods of instruction, its scholarly level, its teacher-luminaries. I signed the article "Erwin George Patai, Student at the Rabbinical Seminary." The only reaction to my article that I can recall was that of Professor Hoffer, who mildly rebuked me, saying that I should not have dignified the attack by a response.

In addition to these occasional pieces of writing, attendance at the Seminary and the University, and preparations for my doctoral examination, I had an additional task to shoulder during the last two months I spent in Budapest. As already mentioned, one of the many activities Father was engaged in was organizing and conducting tours to Palestine. In the spring of 1933, for reasons I can no longer recall, he planned to remain in the Holy Land longer than on other occasions, and this meant that somebody had to substitute for him in putting the finishing touches on the May issue of *Mult és Jövő* and seeing it through the press. While preparing for his tour of Palestine—this must have been early in April—Father told me that he had decided to entrust me with these tasks. I was greatly flattered that he deemed me knowledgeable enough to shoulder these responsibilities, and undertook them gladly, although I was quite busy with my own affairs. To be left in charge of editing an issue of the most prestigious Hungarian Jewish periodical filled me with pride, and I felt that I had suddenly become an influential personage on the Hungarian Jewish intellectual scene.

The editorial offices of Father's journal were located in the central part of the city at a distance of some thirty minutes by streetcar from our home, but not too far from either the Rabbinical Seminary or the University. The premises consisted of one large loft, in which two cubicles were marked off by glass enclosures. One of these cubicles was the office of the editor (or rather editor-in-chief, as he was invariably styled), and I would take my seat there, behind Father's desk, in the early afternoon, after leaving my classes at the Seminary and after having a full-course lunch in a nearby kosher restaurant. On those days of the week when I had classes at the University as well—these were held from 1 or 2 P.M. to 3 or 4 P.M.—I would show up in the office later in the afternoon.

In the other cubicle sat the office manager, Mr. Gyula Virág, who must have been in his early sixties at the time. He and his wife, Aunt Szeréna, lived not far from the office, so it was not difficult for Uncle Gyula, who had lost the toes of one of his feet in a traffic accident some years earlier, to cover the distance between home and office on foot. The Virágs had a small apartment, in one room of which they boarded two boys, usually students at the Franz Liszt Academy of Music, which was located nearby. The street on which the Virágs lived was at night a favorite beat of prostitutes, but this did not seem to have prevented the parents of aspiring young musicians from entrusting their boys to the Virágs' care. It is also possible that, being from country towns, the parents had never seen that street at night.

During the weeks that I substituted for Father as the *pro tempore* editor of *Mult és Jövő*, I had personal contact with many of the regular contributors of the monthly. The phone rang incessantly, and every day a few writers would come to the office to bring an article, a short story, a poem, or simply to talk about plans they had for a piece of writing. Of course, all I could do was to assure them that Father would be back soon, and that all decisions had to wait for his return. Since my time was very limited, I could not stay long with any visitor, and within a few days I learned how to get to the point expeditiously, and then usher out the visitor politely but firmly. Uncle Gyula, from his glass enclosure, could observe everything that went on in my section, and once he remarked, "I see, Gyurikám, that you manage to spend much less time with a visitor than is the wont of the editor-in-chief." At the time I felt that he meant this as a compliment, a praise of my efficiency. Today, thinking back on that scene, I suspect that it was rather a veiled criticism. Whatever his reaction was, I did learn during those weeks that, in addition to assembling articles and other contributions to the journal, editing them (in most cases abridging them), and seeing the issues through the press, a major part of an editor's work consisted of maintaining personal contact with the contributors. Fortunately, I had nothing to do with the business side of the journal, the dealings with the agents who worked for the paper soliciting and renewing subscriptions, the settling of the printer's bills and so forth—all that was competently handled by Uncle Gyula.

Apart from Uncle Gyula, the office staff consisted of two secretary-typists. One of them, at the time I am talking about, was a sister of Dr. Ernő Molnár, my mother's sister's husband. She was a spinster, perhaps thirty-five years of age, and rather unattractive, being endowed with the same large and sharp nose as was Uncle Ernő, on whom, however, that pronounced feature did not look bad. The other one was a young girl of perhaps twenty, whose name I have long since forgotten, but who, I remember, had a slim figure and a pretty face with curly blond hair. Once or twice, when we both left the office at the same time, I walked with her several blocks — perhaps even as far as the house in which she lived? — this is the only thing I remember in connection with her. After the second or third of these walks, Mother spoke to me with consternation and visible embarrassment. "Aunt Szeréna called me today," she said, "and told me that she had seen you accompanying Miss. . . . " She quoted Aunt Szeréna as having said, "I don't know how far they went . . . " and having left the sentence unfinished in its ambiguity, but then having added, "Why doesn't he rather go out with Miss Molnár?" Then Mother spoke to me very seriously, explaining in some detail that such things just aren't done, the boss's son simply does not go out with a typist, this is, or can be, nothing but sordid, and so forth. I had great respect for Mother, was easily influenced by her, and, besides, had not the faintest interest in the girl, so from that day on I politely said good-bye to her when I left the office, and walked alone to my streetcar stop.

I remember that the May issue of *Mult és Jövő* came off the press about the same time as my doctoral dissertation. When I held in my hands the two publications, the journal I edited and the book I authored — my first — I had a sense of accomplishment that was never duplicated when any of the numerous subsequent books I wrote and edited was published.

My Doctoral Thesis and Exam

In the midst of my many and varied preoccupations I still had to find the time to write my doctoral disssertation. Having copied in Breslau the manuscript of Israel Berekhya Fontanella's poems, I had to write an introduction to them and to annotate them. Dissertations of this type, consisting of the publication of a manuscript text or part of it, with annotations, were favored by most of the students of the Seminary. For example, single chapters from a book by Yūsuf al-Baṣīr, the eleventh-century Karaite philosopher, whose manuscript (or one of whose manuscripts) was preserved in Budapest, provided dozens of dissertation topics. Thus, by publishing an annotated edition of a collection of poems, instead of doing a research paper, I followed a well-trodden path. I wrote the preface and the introduction in both Hungarian and Hebrew, published the poems in their original Hebrew, and wrote my annotations in Hebrew. In my preface I characterized Fontanella in the usual flowery style of Hungarian letters in the 1920s and 1930s: "Fontanella lived in an age in which the old, powerful stream of Hebrew poetry only trickled like a rivulet of scanty water, like the wadis of Palestine at Tammuz time. Among the poets of the Arab-Spanish Golden Age Fontanella would have had little significance. But in his own age his poems represent unquestionable values."

Then I went on to point out that Fontanella, who died in 1763, paved the way for Moses Ḥayyim Luzzatto (1707–1746), who was some twenty-five years younger, and the greatest Hebrew poet of eighteenth-century Italy. In the introduction I presented what I could find about Fontanella's life, his Kabbalism, and his book *Mafteḥot haZohar* (Keys to the Zohar), which was printed in Venice in 1744. In this connection I dared to criticize the attitude of Heinrich Graetz, the great Jewish historian, toward the Kabbala. I quoted a statement by Graetz: "Luzzatto's teacher in his youth, Isaiah Bassan of Padua, was an empty-headed Kabbalist, a disciple and son-in-law of the half-Sabbataian Rabbi Benjamin Cohen of Reggio. Bassan injected mystical poison into his healthy humors." Then, in a footnote, I added, "It is quite peculiar to what extent Graetz, the great master of Jewish historiography, misunderstood the influence and meaning of the Kabbala. He saw a veritable curse in the Kabbala and the Zohar, and could speak only disparagingly about the Kabbalistic masters. The position of Graetz on the Kabbala is a typical example of the extent to which a one-sided point of view and a lack of understanding of the spirit of the age can lead to the presentation of a false picture."

In other sections of my introduction I pointed out biblical and talmudic elements in Fontanella's poems and the influence on him of the Spanish Jewish poets, and discussed the meters and rhymes he used. However, more interesting for me than the poems themselves were the introductoy statements Fontanella wrote to his poems in the traditional *maqāma* (rhymed prose) style. These brief introductions stated in whose honor and on what occasion the poems were written. The occasions were mostly weddings or funerals, and the individuals honored by the verses were, as a rule, members of Fontanella's own community. The introductory *maqāmas* to the thirty-six poems in their totality mention close to a hundred individuals, among them numerous Ottolenghis, Bassans, Vitales, Luzzattos, Modonas, Foas, Fontanellas, Sanguinettis, Rovigos, and, of course, Cohens and Levis. My self-imposed task was to identify as many of these as possible. This required quite some digging into Italian Jewish historical sources, and, to be able to do this, I had to acquire a minimal ability to read Italian. This was the first time I tasted the excitement of scholarly detective work, whose attraction was to remain with me all my life.

Since I did not feel quite at home in Italian Jewish history, despite diligent reading, I wrote to Professor Umberto Cassuto (1883–1951), the foremost Italian Jewish scholar of the age, who at the time was professor of Hebrew at the University of Rome, whose Bible classes I was to attend later at the Hebrew University of Jerusalem, and whose studies on the early chapters of Genesis I was to use later still to great advantage. Cassuto had written a brief entry about Fontanella in the German *Encyclopaedia Judaica*, which was being published at the time in Berlin, and in my letter I asked him how it could be that none of the sources I could locate about Fontanella, including his own *Encyclopaedia* article, mentioned that the author of the *Maftehot haZohar* also wrote poems. I wrote to Cassuto in Hebrew, and it was, I believe, one of the first times that I made use of, and appreciated, the fact that Jewish scholars could correspond in Hebrew across international boundaries and thus easily surmount the language barrier that hampered communication between Gentile scholars. In his reply Professor Cassuto stated that in the catalog of the manuscripts in the library of the Breslau Seminary, prepared by B. Zuckerman in 1870, the author of the poems is identified only as Israel Fontanella, without the second name Berekhya and without his father's name, and therefore "I was not sure whether or not the author was Israel Berekhya Fontanella. . . . In the other sources I used there is no mention of the poems of Israel Berekhya." This letter reinforced in me the feeling that by publishing Fontanella's poems I performed a small service for Jewish scholarship.

Once my thesis was finished, I typed it, and then took my manuscript to Professor Pröhle, who was supposed to act as my major advisor. I don't know whether he read it or not, but a few days later he returned the manuscript to me with one single correction: in the Hungarian title of the thesis he made a slight stylistic improvement. Other than this, I got no help whatsoever in writing my thesis from my teachers, either in the University or in the Seminary. This I remember clearly, and it is confirmed by the fact that in the preface I expressed my thanks to Professor Samuel Löwinger, who called my attention to the Fontanella manuscript, to Dr. Israel Rabin, who permitted me to copy and publish it, to Professor Cassuto for the information he supplied, and to Dr. Jacob Teicher of Florence, who copied for me the data about Fontanella contained in *Il Vessillo Israelitico*, the Turin Jewish monthly review, but not to any of my teachers in Budapest.

What was left now was to see the thesis through the press, since the rules of the University demanded that doctoral dissertations be printed prior to the oral exams. Since very few of the theses were of a quality that warranted their acceptance for publication by a scholarly journal, most of the candidates had to print their theses at their own expense, which was no small problem for the impecunious rabbinical students. I was exceptionally fortunate in this respect, for Father was both able and willing to foot the printer's bill. As for the technical side of the printing process, the preparation of the manuscript for the press, proofreading, and so forth, I already had some experience, so that this caused no difficulty either. However, I had to divide the typesetting and printing between two printers, a Hungarian and a Hebrew. The Hungarian part, which ran to only thirty-one pages, I gave to the printer of Father's journal, the Hungaria Nyomda, while the larger Hebrew part, eighty-two pages long, I entrusted to the press that printed *HaTzofe l'Hokhmat Yisrael*, the scholarly Hebrew journal of the Seminary, in which by that time two articles of mine had been published. The dissertation had to be printed by May 1933, and this urgency in timing prevented me from suggesting that *HaTzofe* should publish my dissertation, quite apart from the fact that it was too long for the modest-sized journal. When the Hebrew printer was finished with his part, he delivered the folded sheets to the Hungarian printer, and the latter bound them together with the Hungarian pages into a handsome soft-cover volume. I no longer remember how many copies I had to submit to the University.

There was an explicit understanding with Father that I would go to Palestine only after having earned my Dr. Phil. degree at Budapest University. Thereafter he would take care of my travel expenses and support me during the additional few years I needed to take a Ph.D. also at the Hebrew University of Jerusalem. I think I should explain the difference between the two doctorates. In Hungary, where in this respect as in many others the Austrian and German systems were followed, a Dr. Phil. degree could be earned at any university after a total of sixteen years of schooling: four years in elementary school (from age six to ten), eight years in a *gimnázium* or other academic secondary school (age ten to eighteen), and then four years of university studies (age eighteen to twenty-two). The doctorate was the only degree awarded by the Faculties of Philosophy of the universities. There were no degrees corresponding to the B.A. and M.A. of the British and American universities. The latter system, however, was adopted by the young Hebrew University (founded in 1924), so that a Hungarian doctorate was considered in Jerusalem nothing more than the equivalent of a B.A. degree. Having earned my Hungarian doctorate, I could apply to the Hebrew University to be admitted as a "research student" (as graduate students were called at the time), and after two or three years of additional study I could earn a Jerusalem Ph.D.

In any case, I both wanted and had to take my doctorate at Budapest University before departing for my Land of Promise. Class attendance at that concluding stage of my studies was not onerous. In general, as already mentioned, academic freedom was taken to mean that a student was free not to attend classes. If he duly registered for eight consecutive semesters, found a professor who was willing to sponsor his dissertation, wrote his dissertation, had it approved by his professor, had it printed, and then passed his orals, he got his doctorate, and at the next commencement exercises his diploma was handed him by the rector. Thereafter he was officially entitled to be addressed as *Doktor Úr* (Mr. Doctor).

If I nevertheless did attend my last classes, I did so not because I had to, but because I was interested in the subject matter and wanted to be well thought of by my teachers, who, at the term's end, would sit in judgment over me. At the conclusion of the fall 1932 term that ended with the Christmas–New Year vacation, I passed exams in reading the Koran and the *Shahname* of Firdausi, and received an "excellent" in both from Professor Pröhle. I also sat for tests in three courses given by Professor Mahler (Introduction to the History of the Ancient Near Eastern Peoples, the Development of the Calendar, and Old Semitic Texts), again receiving "excellent" in each. In the second term, which began on January 11, 1933, I attended only classes given by the same two teachers. Pröhle continued his Koran and Firdausi courses, and added one more, Medieval Japanese Authors. Mahler's courses were Assyrian and Hieroglyphic Texts, History of Babylonia and Assyria, and a seminar in Ancient Oriental History. These six courses together amounted to twelve hours weekly, and I attended them most conscientiously. To bring my weekly credits up to the required minimum, I also registered for another ten hours on Principles of Cultural Politics, Child Psychology, Ancient General History, and History of Modern Philosophy, but did not attend them. Since I had acquired quite a good working knowledge of Arabic during my year with Brockelmann in Breslau, I was Pröhle's star student, and anticipated no trouble in my orals in that language, nor, for that matter, in Persian, in which I was not too bad either.

As for Professor Eduard Mahler, by 1933 he was quite an old man. (I have just looked up his biography in the *Hungarian Jewish Lexicon*, and found that he was born in 1857, so that in 1933 he was seventy-six years old.) He had retired officially in 1928, but the University enabled, or asked, him to continue to teach. His specialization was in ancient Near Eastern history in general, and chronology in particular, and his books in these fields had brought him world renown in scholarly circles. He was a charming man, warm, friendly, informal with his students, with a fatherly, or rather grandfatherly, attitude to us.

Mahler had spent his childhood and youth in Pressburg, where his father was the rabbi of the Neolog Jewish congregation, which was totally overshadowed by the Orthodox community led by the renowned Sofer-Schreiber dynasty. His mother tongue was German. He took his doctorate at the University of Vienna, and lived in Vienna until the age of thirty-nine, when he moved to Budapest. He became *Privatdozent* at Budapest University, and it was not until 1914 (when he was fifty-seven years old) that he became full professor. Mahler had also studied at the University of Budapest in his youth, so that he must have learned Hungarian at that time, but even in his old age he still spoke Hungarian with a pronounced German accent, which we students thought extremely funny. In America people are used to hearing English spoken with all kinds of foreign accents; in Hungary, foreigners who learned Hungarian and hence spoke it with an accent were practically nonexistent, for what foreigner would come to settle in Hungary? Ergo: a foreign accent was something ridiculous for us. In addition, Professor Mahler also made occasional mistakes in Hungarian grammar and syntax, but all this only served to endear him to us. I always thought that Professor Mahler's smooth, rosy cheeks endowed him with a childlike appearance, and the white goatee under his red lips looked, I thought, like a bib tied around a baby's neck.

The only subjects in which I anticipated some difficulty were Egyptian hieroglyphics and Assyrian cuneiform texts. Although I had no special interest in these subjects, I did register for them and attended Mahler's seminars devoted to reading them. On the basis of my performance at the December exams, Mahler considered me a good student, and wanted to show me off at the doctoral orals in front of the dean who *ex officio* chaired the examination committee. Several weeks before the scheduled orals, Mahler asked me to visit him at his home. He took me to his study, and asked me how I stood with hieroglyphics and cuneiform. When I shamefacedly admitted that my familiarity with them was minimal, he took from his library two volumes containing selections of such texts, leafed through them slowly, then pointed out a page in each of them and said, "Study these pages." Without exchanging a further word on the subject, I knew what he meant: at the doctoral exam he would ask me to read and translate those passages. Then he asked me about my plans after the doctorate, and told me to give his regards to a friend (or former pupil? I can no longer remember) who lived in Jerusalem. Needless to say, my affection for Professor Mahler increased after this conversation. Although I had other teachers from whom I learned more, there was none whose memory I have retained with more love. He died in 1945 at the age of eighty-eight.

Of my doctoral examination at the University I don't remember much. It was, like all doctoral exams, open to the public. The examining committee, headed by the dean of the faculty, sat behind a long table. I, the candidate, sat on a chair facing them, and behind me, at a goodly distance, sat the interested public, almost all of them my colleagues from the Seminary, whose turn to face the ordeal would come later that term, or within a year or two. My memory retained nothing of the two hours I spent on the "hot seat," answering the questions put to me by one after the other of my teachers. Nor do I remember whether I was excited, nervous, shy, afraid, or whatever. I cannot even recall whether Professor Mahler asked me to read and translate those passages of hieroglyphic and cuneiform texts that he had bidden me to study, but I assume that he must have. In fact, I do not even know who the members of the examining committee were, except that Pröhle and Mahler must have been among them. What I do know, but not because I remember it, is that I must have given a good account of myself, for my doctoral diploma states that I passed my exam *summa cum laude*.

Lizi

Over and above everything else that kept me busy during that winter and spring of 1933, my life was dominated by my restrained but haunting, heady but wrenching, love affair with Lizi Fischer.

Lizi was two or three years younger. Our love, like all my other, lesser loves of the period, was strictly platonic. The one factor that distinguished it among all the others was that from the very beginning we both knew that it was inevitably doomed and soon to come to an end. There were two external circumstances that, we felt, were an unalterable *terminus ad quem*. The question was only which of the two impending events would occur first.

The Fischers were, not precisely friends, but acquaintances of my parents. I no longer remember what Mr. Fischer's occupation was, but I can still recall that both he and his wife, who was originally from Germany or Austria, were very handsome people. They had two daughters, of whom the elder was Lizi. Her sister, whose name escapes me, was perhaps two years younger than she was. They lived in a villa in Buda, not far from our own home. It was a pleasant house, surrounded by a garden, but it had no street front: between two other houses (each with its own garden) that fronted the street, there was a footpath with tall hedges on both sides, leading to the Fischer house, which stood behind them. The first floor consisted not only of the usual entrance hall, living room, dining room, and study, but also of the parents' bedroom. On the smaller second floor there were the rooms of the two girls with their bathroom. The bathroom, I remember, had an unusual feature: next to the wash basin there was a much smaller basin with separate hot and cold faucets that served as a spittoon for brushing the teeth. Mr. Fischer's study was lined with books, among them, this, too, I can recall distinctly, a multivolume German Bible commentary in which I would occasionally browse while waiting for Lizi to come down, or to call me to come up to her room.

I no longer remember when and how I met Lizi the first time. My first memory of her stems from the time when we were very much in love and tried to spend as much time together as possible. I cannot recall what she did during the day—I believe she worked in the office of her father, who must have been a businessman. She was a lovely girl, with a charming face and a smile that totally captivated me and that even today, after more than fifty years, still makes my heart ache when I conjure it up in my memory. She had a sweet, natural charm, the like of which I was never again to find in another woman. She was of somewhat less than medium height, with a curvaceous, full figure. Her great sorrow was that her breasts were very large—this was considered a defect in those days—and she tried one thing after the other in order to reduce their size, including a kind of suction pump that she conscientiously applied every day, without any visible success.

From the very beginning of our friendship I knew that Lizi was engaged to be married to a young businessman who lived in Prague, and who came to visit her once every several weeks. Now that I am writing these lines it occurs to me that there was a certain parallelism between Lizi's periodic meetings with her fiancé and mine with Julia. We never spoke to each other about these relationships, and while I knew of her fiancé, I don't think she knew about Julia.

We were totally wrapped up in each other, and during the months preceding my departure from Budapest we spent almost every evening together, or so it now seems to me. I usually walked over to the Fischer house after dinner, always a light meal that I took with my family, and went up to Lizi's room; there we talked and kissed, and talked and kissed. Nothing else ever happened between us. One evening, and only once, I remember, when we went, as we frequently did, for a walk, our mutual restraint almost broke down. We strolled in a leisurely manner up a street to a nearby hill where between the houses and trees one had a panoramic view of the city with its myriads of lights and their reflection in the broad ribbon of the Danube. It must have been February or March, for it was cold and snow was still on the ground. We stopped, embraced, and kissed. I opened my heavy overcoat, pressed Lizi against me, and wrapped the coat around her. Then, timidly and hesitatingly, I pulled her hand toward my crotch until I felt the pressure of her fingers through my clothing. We remained like this for a while, pressing against each other, then we got too cold and returned to her house. It never occurred to me to seek closer physical contact with her. Or, perhaps, it did occur to me, but I never acted upon the thought, because I was inhibited and because I was convinced that such a thing simply was not done. I took it for granted that she was a virgin, and one just did not mess around with a virgin.

Nor did it ever occur to me to raise the possibility that, perhaps, we should not resign ourselves to having to give each other up. That she was destined to marry her young man from Prague was considered by both of us an unalterable fact, just as we both knew that all my love for her would not stop me, when the day came, from packing up and going to Palestine. To marry the Prague man was her destiny, and to go to Palestine was mine. For a while the unexpressed question between us was which of the two events would occur first. Then it became clear that I would go first, in May, and her wedding would take place soon thereafter, in June. We never touched, with as much as one word, upon the possibility of changing these destinies. We loved each other, and the fact that our love was doomed to an early end, while it cast its pall over us, made every minute we were together the more precious, the more excruciatingly bittersweet. For me, marriage was a thing far away in the future, and the most passionate love could not make me consider it an actual possibility. Not to mention the fact that I was as yet a student, with no job or income or means of my own, dependent on the support of my father, so how could I think of marrying? And there was, of course, the great dream of Palestine, which was about to be realized and made it absolutely impossible for me to think of any turn in my life that would mean remaining in Hungary or going to any other place than the Land of Promise.

Since we never touched upon the issue, I don't know what Lizi felt about it. Perhaps, had I suggested it, she would have agreed to break up with her Prague fiancé, and come with me to Jerusalem. Today, thinking back on those bittersweet, sad-happy days, I indulge myself in believing that this could have been the case. Why, then, did I never broach the subject? Was I afraid that, with the staid middle-class values of which we both were products, she would have pointed out, perhaps tearfully but nevertheless unarguably, that while she loved me dearly, there was a safe and comfortable future waiting for her in Prague, while I had nothing to offer her except my love and a very uncertain life in a faraway, strange, and primitive country of which she knew little and in which she was interested even less?

How selective is memory! How coolly, unfeelingly, even cruelly selective: how worse than a surgeon's scalpel that, once it lays bare the inner recesses of the body, excises only that which is pathological excrescence! Memory's negative mirror-image, oblivion, lops off so much more than it retains, while remembrance selects only a very few items according to some mysterious criteria that remain forever hidden to the conscious mind. By doing this, of how much does oblivion deprive us! How much I would give now to be able to conjure up, and thus relive in detail, everything that happened between Lizi and me in those bitter-sad and yet sweet-happy days, the like of which one can experience only when one is very young, when love itself is a marvel before which one stands dumbfounded, and with which one simply does not know what to do. What did we talk about during those many evenings in Lizi's room, during those many walks in the hilly streets? What did we say to each other, what did we feel, as the day of my departure came nearer and nearer? Were we heartbroken, or did her impending marriage and my impatience to see the land of my dreams overshadow, or at least compensate to some extent for, the loss we must have felt in saying good-bye to each other? Nothing, nothing can I recall of all this. Oblivion's pitiless scalpel cut away everything. *Mene mene tekel ufarsin* — it must have weighed these things and found them wanting, and excised them once and for all.

There were also a number of extraneous things in connection with the relationship between Lizi and me that either my memory did not retain or I never knew. In all probability I never knew what Lizi's parents thought of our evident infatuation with each other at a time when she was about to be married to a young man who, I am sure, must have been highly eligible. Did they express any disapproval to her? I never asked her. To me — this I remember — they never said a word. Whenever they saw me in the house, whether coming or going, they always greeted me kindly and had a few friendly words to say. That is, they behaved toward me as parents in our circles would toward a young man who courted their daughter. Today I find this strange; at the time I never thought about it.

Nor did I give much thought to what today appears to me as a strange silence or noninterference on the part of my mother. She, who so decidedly interfered when she was told that I was seen walking in the street with the young typist from our office, never asked—and this, too, I remember clearly—what was going on between Lizi and me. Her seeming indifference to my involvement with a girl engaged to be married to somebody else should have struck me as peculiar, to say the least. But it did not. Possibly I was too busy with the many different activities that I was engaged in to be aware of Mother's apparent and most unusual unconcern with my relationship to Lizi. With the hindsight I have from today's perspective, I think Mother probably felt it was best to take no notice of a situation that, she knew, would inevitably and before long come to an end. She must have known me well enough not to be worried that my relationship to Lizi could make me change the course planned for my life by my parents and me. So that which was foreordained took its inevitable course, and one day the end of my time in Budapest had suddenly come.

There was one more activity, of which I have so far not spoken, in which I was engaged during those last few months in the city of my birth. Among the tasks Father left me to complete when he sailed for the Holy Land that spring was to conclude all the arrangements for a second group of tourists who signed up to visit Palestine with a tour organized under the aegis of Father's journal. The first tour, with which Father left for Palestine in April, I believe, had been duly advertised in two or three of the winter 1932–1933 issues of *Mult és Jövő*. Now, after Hitler's coming into power in Germany, the interest in visiting Palestine and possibly settling there had increased among Hungarian Jews. Hence the number of those wishing to join was so large that they could not all be accommodated in one group but had to be divided into two. After the first group had left with Father, the date for the second group was set for the latter half of May, so as to enable me to sit for my doctoral exam at the University, and then go as leader of the group.

There were some thirty people who signed up, and it was my job to be available to them, consult with them, answer their questions, and give advice as best as I could, and to see to it that all paid their round-trip fare at least four weeks in advance of departure date. It so happened that, in contrast to all the previous tours that included land arrangements in Palestine, hotels, meals, and land transportation for sightseeing, for this group no such arrangements were made for the simple reason that all the participants stated that they preferred to tour the country on their own. I, of course, knew well what this meant: their true intention was to use the tour for getting into Palestine without having first to obtain an immigration certificate, which, by that time, was almost impossible to come by, and then to remain in the country as illegal immigrants. Although Hitler's rise to power in Germany reached Hungary only as distant rumbling from beyond the horizon, and the Nazis' anti-Jewish measures had hardly been initiated, so that it was too early even for the "it can't happen here" mentality to develop in Hungary, still there were already quite a few among the Hungarian Jews, most of them unattached young people, who preferred to infiltrate Palestine rather than wait and see what was going to happen in Hungary. Officially, as the tour leader, I knew nothing of what the individual members of the group planned; each of them bought his round-trip ticket from Lloyd Triestino, which, on that basis, obtained tourists' visas for the participants from the British Consulate in Budapest. Thus, neither the Lloyd nor *Mult és Jövő* could be held responsible if, after landing in Palestine, some members of the group, or all of them for that matter, did not utilize their return ticket but instead disappeared ashore.

Three days after passing my orals at the University, I boarded the train and "led" my group of tourists from Budapest to Trieste, from whence we sailed for Palestine. What I remember of the trip, of my arrival in the land about which I had dreamt for so long, of the impression it made on me, and of the experiences I had there will have to wait to be told elsewhere. I know that soon after settling in Jerusalem I wrote to Lizi, because I remember distinctly the excitement I felt when I got a reply from her. She addressed me as "Dear Ching Chung Chan," this being the nickname by which she, I don't know why, used to call me. Of the contents of the letter I remember only one thing: she wrote that she had received my letter just as she was about to leave her house, took out the letter from the envelope, and in her hurry stuck both in her handbag. After she returned home, she sat down to read the letter, but found only the envelope in her bag. The letter itself must have dropped out from her bag somewhere on the way. The envelope had my return address, and so she was able to write to me, even though she did not know what I had written to her. I remember this detail with uncanny clarity, while I remember nothing else of what she wrote. I never again heard from her.

But, some three or four months later, in one of the many letters Mother wrote to me, she informed me that Lizi Fischer had died in Prague, of leukemia. I was heartbroken. I was unable to accept that the vibrant, vital, scintillating creature I had left behind should be no more. For days I simply ceased functioning. Although the subject of my Jerusalem doctoral dissertation was well mapped out by that time, I was unable to concentrate on my studies. I stopped seeing the girl friend whom I had succeeded in winning only a short while earlier. I barely moved out of my room. For the first time in my life I knew the real meaning of bereavement. It was as if death had torn a pound of flesh out of my chest. A few months later, Mother wrote that Lizi's husband had married his deceased wife's younger sister.

12

Budapest Revisited: 1936

Return to Budapest

When I made my move from Budapest to Jerusalem, in May 1933, I left behind several pieces of unfinished business. Having passed my doctoral exam, I still had to be personally present at the commencement exercises to be handed my Dr. Phil. diploma. Equally importantly, I had to sit for the final examinations at the Rabbinical Seminary in order to get my rabbinical diploma, and to receive, again in person, that traditional document attesting that I was found deserving of becoming a "Master and Teacher in Israel."

Accordingly, having passed my doctoral exam at the Hebrew University of Jerusalem, in June 1936, and received, in Hebrew and Latin, the first Ph.D. diploma to be awarded by that young university, I boarded, together with my parents, an Italian liner in Haifa, and sailed for Trieste. From there we took the train to Budapest. Soon I was back, together with my parents, in the same comfortable, beautifully furnished, and efficiently run home on Nyúl Street to which we had moved some two or three years prior to my departure for Palestine.

My brother Guszti, grown in the three years since I had seen him to a young man of eighteen, was there, all ready to start his studies at Budapest University. He still had the room adjoining mine, just as in the old days. Our maternal grandparents, with their daughter, my aunt Dóra, and her husband Ernő and daughter Juci (now a tall and pretty adolescent of fifteen), lived in the same apartment on the other side of town in which I had last seen them. Thus my return meant a kind of family reunion, although not a complete one, because my sister Évi had remained in Jerusalem with her husband.

To speak of generalities first, upon arriving back in Budapest I found no change in the physical aspect of the city. It was for me still the same beautiful place that throughout my youth had held me captive until I succumbed to the great lure of an imaginary Palestine. Nor did I perceive any change in the manifestations of its vibrant culture; the theaters, the movies, the concerts, the opera, the papers, the literary journals (including the monthly edited by Father), the bookstores, the cafés with their gypsy orchestras and their literary circles, all seemed the same, all had the same old fascination. The city as a whole still appeared to me the hub and center of Hungarian culture, as it had always been in my eyes and was, of course, in reality.

Of *Hungarian* culture. There was the rub that had not existed for me before. Budapest now impressed me, as it never had while it was the only hometown I knew, as beclouded by something provincial in its atmosphere. In Jerusalem, although it was a much smaller city, one met people from all over the world. There were Jews from many countries of Europe and America, Asia and Africa, there were Muslim and Christian Arabs, there were people of all hues, including Sudanese and Ethiopians, there were Eastern Christians of various denominations, each with its own complement of priests garbed in their distinctive robes. There was the British presence, the uniformed soldiers and the always impeccably dressed civilians, both of whom impressed me, if for no other reason than because as Britishers they were the representatives of the empire that, prior to World War II, ruled the waves and much of the world.

That is to say, Jerusalem, while certainly not a metropolis—that status it was to achieve, according to the Talmud, only in the messianic age ("In the Future Jerusalem will be the metropolis of all the countries")—was a cosmopolitan, colorful, fascinating city. Compared to it, Budapest in 1936, with its million-plus inhabitants, seemed a homogeneous and monotonous place for the simple reason that everybody in it was Hungarian, few people spoke any language other than Hungarian, and its pervasive Magyardom had isolated it from the rest of the world. The homogenizing influence of Hungarian culture, I now felt, coupled with the language barrier, effectively cut off the entire population of the country, including the Jews, from the rest of Europe. Moreover I now sensed, as I never had prior to

1933, that the Jews were motivated by a pathetic ambition to hide their Jewishness when appearing in public and in contact with non-Jews, that they practiced a form of Marranism that, with my newly acquired Palestinian-Hebrew-Jewish self-assurance, I found unpalatable. In brief, even if the city had not changed in the three years of my absence, the perspective from which I looked at it and its Jews was now a completely different one.

Also, it was unmistakable that the shadow of Hitler had crept closer to Hungary in the three years of my absence. There was a faint, but clearly perceptible, unease among the Jews of Budapest, attested, among other things, by the very fact that one could hear quite frequently, in discussions among friends, the statement that "it can't happen here." I no longer remember much of the arguments marshaled by my interlocutors to prove to me and to themselves that the position of the Jews in Hungary was better than that of the Jews in Germany, and that the attitude of the Hungarians to the Jews was so positive that the type of discrimination (it was only discrimination in 1936, persecution was to come later) that was being introduced at the time in Germany against the Jews was simply unthinkable in Hungary. Were not the Hungarian Jews even more patriotic than the Christians? Were not the Hungarian Jews in the territories torn away from Hungary after World War I and annexed by Czechoslovakia, Rumania, and Yugoslavia the one population element that maintained its Magyardom and preserved the Hungarian language more staunchly than the Christian Hungarians in the same areas? Had it not been a basic Jewish conviction ever since the Emancipation in Hungary that the Jews did not constitute a national minority but were true Hungarians who differed from the Christian majority to no greater degree than did the Protestant Hungarians from the Catholics?

Arguments such as these left me unconvinced, and I doubt whether they gave more than momentary reassurance to my Hungarian Jewish friends themselves. I know that they in no way convinced me because one of the clearest memories I have retained from those six months I spent in Hungary in 1936 is the acute feeling of *Unbehagen*, discomfort, unease, bordering on apprehension, that I had throughout my stay. During the working day this feeling did not bother me too much, at least not consciously, but it must have been present in my subconscious, for I repeatedly had a dream of which I no longer remember the details but which sums itself up in my memory to this day in the fearsome feeling that for some obscure reason, because of government regulation or the like, I was unable to leave Hungary and was doomed to remain a prisoner in an increasingly inimical country.

All this, however, did not keep me from following the appointed rounds of affairs that were important enough to make me leave my beloved Jerusalem and return to the Galuth, even if only for a few months. Much of my time was taken up with preparations for my final examinations at the Rabbinical Seminary. Of the five-year course of studies in the college division of the Seminary I had actually spent only three years at the school itself. I had spent the second year in Breslau, Germany. For that year, like all other students of the Budapest Seminary who spent a year in Breslau, I received credit automatically from our *alma mater*. But when I left for Jerusalem, in the spring of 1933, immediately after passing my Dr. Phil. orals at the University, I still owed the Seminary one year of attendance. The rector of the Seminary agreed that my studies at the Hebrew University of Jerusalem would be considered the equivalent of a year's study at the Seminary. In fact, they were both more and less than that. In Jerusalem I studied mainly the historical geography of Palestine and Arabic language, and also attended classes in Palestinian archaeology, albeit somewhat irregularly. My interest became more and more focused on the historical and contemporary folk culture of the Jews and Arabs of Palestine, and I attended only sporadically classes in Bible, Talmud, and Jewish history and philosophy, which would have made up the bulk of my studies had I remained at the Seminary for my fifth and last year.

This having been the case, I was somewhat apprehensive about my impending exams. I felt that, in order to enhance my chances, I had better consult my teachers about the material they wanted me to survey in preparation for the exams. So, first of all, I went to pay my respects to Professor Michael Guttmann, who had become the rector of the Seminary in 1933. Fortunately, Dr. Guttmann knew me from 1930–1931, when he was the head of the Jewish Theological Seminary of Breslau, and I one of his students. I had last seen him in the spring of 1931, before my return from Breslau to Budapest. In the few years that had passed since, he had perceptibly aged, being even more heavy-set, more stooped, and the vertical furrows between his eyebrows cut deeper. He received me in the most friendly manner, and spent quite some time inquiring and hearing from me about his former colleagues at the Hebrew University of Jerusalem, where he had taught Talmud in 1924–1925, the year the University first opened its doors to students. I reported to him also about the development of the University in the decade that had passed since, and pointed out to him the crucial role Hungarian scholars played in the history of that young institution: the first three professors invited to teach were Hungarians—Professor Andor Fodor (chemistry), Professor Samuel Klein (Palestinian studies), and, of course, Guttmann himself (Talmud). Then, somewhat diffidently, I added that now the first graduate student to earn his Ph.D. at the University was yet another Hungarian—me. Before I left, Professor Guttmann told me to review certain chapters from two or three tractates of the Talmud, and set the date for my exam.

My meetings with the other professors took a similar course. I missed, regretfully, Professor Heller, the teacher to whom I was closest of all. He had retired even before I left Budapest, so I went to visit him in his apartment in Buda to thank him personally as well for his letters containing advice and friendly, constructive, and detailed criticism of my Jerusalem doctoral dissertation, parts of which I had mailed to him while I was still working on it.

I no longer remember my preexam conversations with my teachers, but I imagine that in the course of them they must have indicated the general areas within which they intended to put questions to me. Such a delimitation was, in fact, inevitable. The amount of the material covered in the five years of study at the Seminary, in forty weeks a year, and thirty hours every week, was so huge that it was simply impossible for the candidate to review all of it in the course of a few weeks or even months. Nor was it really necessary for the teachers to probe too intensively into the degree of preparedness of the students. Each of us had to pass rigorous tests in every subject at the end of each semester, and, besides, most of the classes were held seminar-style, so that the participation of the students in class work gave our teachers a fair idea of what and how much we knew. Hence the final examinations were little more than formalities, or at the utmost general and rapid reviews, in which there was, as a rule, a friendly give-and-take between teacher and student, and what the student had to show was that, once he knew what material to review for the exam, he was able to answer questions pertaining to it cogently, intelligently, and with a good measure of understanding. Nevertheless, I do remember that until my exam I spent a major portion of my time in preparation for it. I do not think that I have ever studied so intensively and with such sustained effort and concentration either before or after.

Characteristically, I remember absolutely nothing of the studies themselves, nor of the exams, although they were undoubtedly the most comprehensive orals I took in all my life. The *hattarat hora'a*, or rabbinical diploma, which I still have, is proof that I passed them, but I have no idea whether my teachers were, in fact, satisfied with my performance, or whether they just let me pass, as was their wont with every student who had accumulated all the required credits and got to that final point in his studies. Whichever was the case, I was now in the possession of a diploma that qualified me to fill a rabbinical position in any Neolog congregation in Hungary, or in any Jewish congregation abroad that had a similar religious orientation. The only problem in this connection was that I was determined not to become a rabbi, but to devote myself to the pursuit of scholarship.

Miscellaneous Brief Encounters

As soon as I arrived in Budapest, I began to meet again several of my old colleagues and friends, but with none of them was I able to reestablish the warm camaraderie of our student years. In most cases, I suspect, the fault must have been mine, for, having become emotionally part and parcel of the *yishuv* in the course of the preceding three years, having acquired a mastery of what Immanuel Löw termed in his *MGWJ* review of my Jerusalem doctoral dissertation *Palästina-Hebräisch* (Palestine-Hebrew), and having achieved something of a scholarly status, I felt superior to them and considered them provincial, as I did the city of Budapest as a whole.

During my repeated visits to the Seminary I met several of the new students, and I could not help feeling that they and I belonged to two different worlds. Those of my old colleagues whom I did meet manifested the not-so-subtle transformation from penniless and skinny students to relatively well-to-do, stout, and well-emolumented members of the Jewish establishment, which they had become as a result of having succeeded in their quest for a rabbinical position in an established community. A parallel transformation could be observed in their mental outlook as well. As students they had been dissatisfied, probing, questioning, critical; now they were supporters of the establishment, satisfied with the *status quo ante*, and sedate carriers of a quiescent tradition.

I remember in particular the consternation I felt when, by a pure chance, I ran in the street into Pál Vidor, who throughout the three years of my attendance at the Seminary had sat next to me in the classroom, and had been one of my best friends among my colleagues. He had been one of the very few students of the Seminary who had opted for studying philosophy, and not Semitic languages and literatures, at the University, and I had admired him because of his intelligence, humor, quick wit, and wide reading. I no longer know why, but when I arrived back in Budapest after an absence of three years, I did not look up my old friend Pali, nor, in fact, any of my other friends among my former classmates. I suspect that the reason must have been the same that made my attitude to the Hungarian Jewish scene as a whole pronouncedly negative. During my three years' sojourn in Jerusalem I had become so thoroughly imbued with the spirit of the young Palestinian Hebrew generation that I could not help feeling a certain disaffection for the young people in the Hungarian Jewish community, who, of their own free will, chose to remain in the Diaspora. This feeling of mine must have been especially strong toward my erstwhile colleagues at the Rabbinical Seminary, who had devoted their lives to the service of Jewry, and yet did not draw the ultimate conclusion of joining their brethren in Palestine, the only place, I felt, where a Jew could live a fully Jewish life. Added to this was a certain pity for these rabbinical students and young rabbis, and even for the professors at the Seminary, who, despite all their scholarship, would have been unable to understand the Hebrew prattle of a three-year-old Palestinian child.

In any case, I did not seek out Pál Vidor, although I learned, during one of my visits to the Seminary, that he had been appointed rabbi in Buda, and that he had married the daughter of Dr. Ödön Kálmán, chief rabbi of Kőbánya, a suburb of Budapest. Our meeting came about fortuitously. We encountered each other in the tree-lined promenade in front of the Lucas Baths in Buda—for the life of me I cannot recall what I was doing in that neighborhood; perhaps I was simply taking an aimless stroll, although that would have been quite out of character for me at the time. Suddenly I noticed a stately, dignified, and rather corpulent couple approaching me, and, as they came nearer, I recognized, despite his greatly changed appearance, my old friend Pali, and next to him his wife, whom I remembered having met once or twice when Pali and I were students. What struck me most in Pali was not so much the gross filling out of his frame, but the consequent change in his gait. As the emaciated student I remembered, his typical stance was somewhat forward leaning, and when he walked, his elongated head, seemingly precariously balanced on his long scrawny neck, preceded his midriff by a good foot or so. Now, to balance the bulge he carried in front, his posture had a backward tilt, which gave him the appearance of self-assurance and pomposity, of satiety in more sense than one.

When we were but one or two steps from each other, we stopped, and as we shook hands I could not help scanning his face, which appeared to me to be curiously composed of two incongruous parts: the forehead, eyes, and nose were still those of my friend of 1933, but the puffed-up cheeks, the double chin, and the thick neck were those of a stranger, of the man Pál Vidor had become since I had last seen him. Nevertheless, seeing him before me, the warm feelings of our old friendship welled up in me, and I was suddenly sorry that I had not called him to tell him of my return and to set up a meeting. Somewhat embarrassed by this thought, I slowly raised my left arm in order to clap him on the shoulder as we had done on innumerable occasions back in our student years, when I noticed a slight stiffening in his posture, a small increase in the backward tilt of his body. It was barely perceptible, but it was sufficient for me to stop my arm in mid-air, and let it fall back to my side. I greeted his wife with due respect, and, although I don't remember a word of what we said to each other, we must have exchanged a few customary questions and answers, after which, within a very short time, we said good-bye without making any appointment to meet again. Walking on alone under the yellowing trees, I was overcome by a feeling of sadness at the evident and senseless death of a friendship. Some eight years later both Pál Vidor and his wife were among the half-million Hungarian Jews killed by the Nazis.

Another meeting I remember from about the same time was with a spastic girl whose parents must have been friends of my parents. One day Mother asked me whether I would be willing to visit a girl who was very nice in every respect except that she suffered from a terrible disease. I no longer remember how Mother described the girl and her affliction, but the manner in which she put it to me made me feel that I would perform a real *mitzva* (good deed) in spending an hour or so with that unfortunate girl. I can no longer recall who made the arrangements and how, but at the appointed hour a limousine arrived at our house, and took me to the Svábhegy (Swabians' Mountain), to a villa much grander than that of the Friedmanns, with a curved driveway leading up to the front entrance. The door was opened by a uniformed maid, and immediately thereafter the lady of the house appeared, greeted me as if I were an old acquaintance, and said, "My daughter is on the terrace. Let me take you to her." We passed a series of sumptuous rooms and exited through French windows to a large terrace at the back of the house, overlooking the garden. There, next to a table, in a wheelchair, sat the girl. She was beautiful, very carefully made up, and dressed in some kind of loose lacy dress. Since I cannot remember her name, let me call her by a typical Hungarian name, Magda.

"Magda, dear," her mother addressed her in cheerful tones, "look, Gyuri Patai has come to see you!"

The girl, with a visible effort, raised her right hand for me to shake, and said something I could not understand. Her mother ordered the maid to bring us coffee and cakes, then sat down next to Magda, so that when I spoke I could address myself to both of them simultaneously. I cannot recall whether Magda said anything at all during the hour or so we sat there on the terrace, but I do remember that it was the mother who carried the ball of our conversation, and managed to put me at my ease with her obvious interest in my studies, plans, writings, lecturings, and the like. From time to time she turned to Magda and asked her a question that required nothing more than a nod as an answer but made the poor girl appear to take part in the conversation. It was a masterly performance on the mother's part, carried off with seemingly perfect ease, although I could, if not sense, at least imagine, the effort it must have cost her. On my part, I am afraid, I contributed little, although I answered her questions willingly and in as much detail as I was able to. But I was unable to bring myself to ask any of the questions that were on my mind, which would have shown a human interest on my part in the tragic predicament to which both the mother and the daughter were condemned, and which, I now believe, both of them would have liked to hear: how and when did Magda's illness strike her, how did she spend her day, what treatment did she get, and, most importantly, what were her chances of improvement? But I was tongue-tied, and took refuge in the silly make-believe that Magda's illness simply did not exist, that is, played the role assigned to me, at least on the surface of it, by the mother.

When I felt that I could leave without being impolite or seeming to be in undue haste, I mumbled some excuse, rose, shook hands with mother and daughter, and was escorted by the former to the front door. Before depositing me in the car, she said, "I hope you will be able to come again. Your visit meant a lot to my daughter."

While being driven back to our modest home in the luxurious limousine, the thought crossed my mind that if I could put up with living with that seriously handicapped girl, I could have a carefree, luxurious life, enjoy whatever work or hobbies gave me the greatest pleasure, and could even have as many girlfriends as I desired. It was a fleeting thought that immediately ended with my shaking my head and shoulders convulsively. It came to me as a great surge that what I was after in life was to make my own way, to struggle, to achieve, to go back to Palestine, to be part of the great venture of nation-building that was going on there, and to find there the girl I would fall in love with. Poor Magda. I never saw her again, nor heard about her.

While I was in Budapest I decided that it was time to do something about my hair. My father had a totally bald pate with nothing more than a wreath of hair between his temples and occiput, which he always kept closely shaved. While in Jerusalem I noticed that my hairline had begun to recede, which at the time meant only that my forehead grew higher—I was reminded of the Hungarian ditty, "There is no bald head anymore, only a forehead reaching to the back." I had at the time little knowledge of the mysteries of heredity, but still became apprehensive that baldness was one of the traits I might have inherited from Father. So, after my arrival in Budapest I decided to see a dermatologist. I called Uncle Yóshka, our family physician, and he gave me the name of a skin specialist. When I went to see the latter, he had a good look at my hair, poked around on my scalp, and pronounced the verdict: I would grow bald, and nothing could be done to prevent it. It was unpleasant news, but it certainly did not come as a shock.

Then the doctor asked me about Palestine, and, after answering his questions, I told him, as was my wont to tell everybody who showed interest in "the Holy Land," that he should go and see the country for himself. I mentioned that in third-class cabin, in which I had traveled and which I had found completely satisfactory, the fare was quite low. He smiled and said that third class was all right for a young student, but as a married man he wanted to have his comfort. I could not quite understand the imperative of comfort, but left it at that. When I asked him what I owed him, the doctor, remaining seated at his desk, pointed to a small table next to the door, and said, "Put down there whatever amount you want. I won't even look at it." I did as he suggested, and, of course, no longer remember the amount I considered appropriate. As for his prognosis, it proved to be correct. My hair went on thinning, but it was a very slow, gradual process, and even today, at the age of seventy-five, it has not yet reached the stage of total baldness that characterized my father's head from the earliest time I can remember him.

Ordination

My rabbinical ordination ceremony at the Seminary was scheduled to take place on October 12, 1936. The usual ordinations took place in June, at the end of the academic year, and these extraordinary exercises were scheduled for October as a special accommodation for me, since I explained to Professor Guttmann that it was imperative for me to return to Jerusalem as soon as possible. In addition to me there was only one other candidate who was to receive his diploma at the same time. He was Dr. István Molnár, about whom I remember nothing, but written sources tell me that he was born in Hódmezővársáhely in 1908, after graduation became assistant rabbi and teacher of religion in Pesterzsébet, and perished in the Holocaust in 1944, in the Červenka forced labor camp.

The ordinations at the Seminary consisted, as a rule, of one or more speeches given by members of the faculty, and then a brief response by one of the graduating students. Between my colleague Molnár and me, I was chosen for the honor, and Dr. Simon Hevesi, the "leading chief rabbi" of the Neolog Congregation of Pest, who was not only a professor at the Seminary but also a member of its Board of Governors, told me that he wanted to see the text of my address before I delivered it. To this day I do not know in what capacity Dr. Hevesi put that demand to me, and whether he had the consent of Professor Guttmann, the rector of the Seminary, in doing so. Perhaps Hevesi simply relied on the power of his personality, which, indeed, was such that it never occurred to me for a moment to object to what in effect amounted to advance censorship.

When I was ready with my speech, I took the typescript to Dr. Hevesi's apartment. He lived in a big and luxurious apartment house near the Dohány Temple. Although the Israelite Congregation of Pest, of which Dr. Hevesi was the highest-ranking spiritual leader, was Neolog, its rabbis observed the Sabbath, and thus had to live within easy walking distance of the synagogue. I was ushered into his large and beautifully furnished study, where Dr. Hevesi sat behind a big, and evidently very fine, desk. When I entered, he put aside the book he was reading, greeted me in his usual reserved-friendly-dignified manner, mentioned that he was just rereading the *Or Adonai* (Light of the Lord) by Ḥasdai Crescas (the fourteenth-century Spanish Jewish philosopher), and bade me sit down across from him. I handed him my speech; he reached for a pen, and began to read it and to cross out several sentences, and even entire paragraphs. While doing this, he occasionally made comments to explain to me what he was doing and why. When he reached the point where I excoriated the indifference and "tepid obtuseness" of today's Jewish youth, he remarked, "There is no point in assailing the Jewish youth, which today faces very hard times. It is all right to denounce the present generation in general terms, but let the youth be." And he struck the two or three lines I had devoted to the subject.

Apart from several more such deletions, Dr. Hevesi introduced a few subtle changes toning down the Zionist enthusiasm that prompted me to some rather turgid phraseology. Where I wrote that the roots of Jewish culture "draw their strength from the ancestral land that for millennia has radiated its spirit into each country of the Diaspora," he changed my present tense "draw" to past tense "drew," and for "Diaspora" substituted "the globe." And, reflecting his own anti-Zionist and Hungarian patriotic stance, which he shared with most members of the Jewish establishment, he added two sentences. Where I wrote that it was our task as young rabbis to make our brethren "understand the age-old message that 'out of Zion cometh forth the law, and the word of the Lord from Jerusalem' (Isa. 2:3)," he inserted, "understand the age-old message that teaches that we should expect the message from Zion and the teaching of God from Jerusalem, for 'out of Zion cometh forth the Law and the word of the Lord from Jerusalem,'" thus adding a delicate spiritual emphasis to that ancient and proverbial proclamation, and effectively eliminating the allusion

I intended—namely, that Zion and Jerusalem had a meaningful message *today* for world Jewry. And then he added one more crucial sentence: " . . . and that, living in our faith, we should love the fatherland into which God planted us, and serve faithfully its welfare."

When Dr. Hevesi finished his Draconian editing of my speech, he handed me back the corrected text and bade me read it then and there, while he watched me with his big, cold, and penetrating grey eyes.

The passage of decades has totally eliminated from my memory the content of that short speech (although I do remember that I labored mightily on it), but I never forgot that scene in Dr. Hevesi's study, nor the sentence he added about our duty to love the Hungarian fatherland. Now, in the course of this writing, I succeeded in locating the original typescript of the speech with Dr. Hevesi's deletions, and the additions he made in his own hand. Here it is, with the passages he struck put in parentheses, and the sentences he added set in italics:

My Masters and Teachers!

Let words of remembrance be the first words in this festive hour of our lives. I remember our departed masters, Ludwig Blau, Bertalan Edelstein, and Miksa Weisz, who planted into our souls the pure seeds of Jewish thought, etched into the tablets of our hearts their words of instruction and their guiding exhortations. I remember them, and pray that the Almighty grant me that the great tradition of their knowledge, their faith, their Jewishness, and humanity continue in me.

And toward you, my Masters and Teachers, at whose feet I sat for five years, toward you I turn with feelings of gratitude, humility, and a disciple's love.

I do not want to come before you in this festive hour of my life with the dazzle of high-soaring rainbow-hued thoughts. When the glittering mountaintops of dreams, the unfolding longings and plans, are surrounded by such deep, such dark valleys of reality, it is not the time to sing of the road of the rabbi's vocation that leads up to Sinai's peaks, of the fires set burning in the priestly soul by a view of Horeb's crests. Our way cannot rise up to the heights of fiery summits when it is not granted to us to take up with us our brethren, because the shadows of the black vales of the real world hold them captive. We ourselves, too, must walk down here below, and it is down here that we must cut a path for ourselves, a path that can be followed by those who struggle in the valleys' depths.

For it is with a bleeding heart that we, young rabbis, who are called to accompany this generation on the thorny path of its life, see this great, salvationless vale of darkness, this sad greyness, in which today's generation (today's Jewish youth, has sunk, that tepid obtuseness whose walls of indifference can be penetrated by nothing noble, beautiful, and good, not even the sacred ideas of our ancestral faith. We look with desperation at this generation) *lives* whose soul, ignorant of true treasures, disintegrates in a struggle for existence that stifles existence, because the daily bending and stooping in drudgery prevents our souls from straightening up toward that which is better and more beautiful. (And if, nevertheless, the desire stirs in them to draw away a little from the colorless rhythm of the everyday, this stirring, too, is swallowed up by the dubious beauty that loudly advertises its cheap availability on billboards of theaters and posters of popular books, so that it becomes, not an uprise, but mere entertainment.) Where is (here) left *for them* the time and the energy for the beautiful and the good that religion offers modestly and quietly, whose acquisition demands the inner strength, the guided effort, of the soul?

It pains us that the great masses of our brethren take trouble only over prying open the external wrappings of existence, and it pains us doubly that in the bitterness of the day-to-day struggle, the fighting for everyday results, they do not even know, do not even see, that deep beneath the wrappings lies hidden the core of being, the sacredness of spiritual uplift, the meaning and eternal center of life.

We cannot fault our age for being confused about the direction of development, for we ourselves cannot even weigh with the scale of appraisal the benefits and losses of the various trends, we cannot know what is of greater value: the emotional surges, the artistic peaks of times past, or the technical accomplishments, the scientific breakthroughs, of the present age. The life, the fate of cultures, the progress of nations, are beyond our small compass of influence; the human mind has only in recent times begun to attempt timidly to apply its constantly improving distinctions also to these grandest manifestations of life. There can be no doubt that the (awe-inspiring) will of a higher Guide manifests itself in these great sea-surges, and yet it is our feeling that man, whose will, our religion teaches us, is free and independent, (overshot the mark,) has become one-sided, and, suffering from the daily drudgery, strives only to ease it by perfecting technology. In this connection he has become profoundly absorbed in researching the infinite world of nature, has begun to nibble also at the world of the psyche with the methods of natural science, and, intoxicated by his successes, does not perceive that all these are merely husks, that he had achieved nothing but peeling away a few, cutting up others, without getting nearer to the core of being. In the rich branchings-out of science man has lost that which alone is capable of unifying the sciences into knowledge—he lost the faith.

We here, between the walls of this institution, have not only acquired sciences from our masters, but also drew knowledge, religion, and faith from their souls. And I feel that first of all it is our task to pour faith into the souls of our brethren who do not even disbelieve, are not even opposed to faith, but simply have no faith, because they don't know what faith is . . .

(But to inculcate faith into others is possible only for Moses-like personalities. It is a path that rises to truly Sinaitic heights, and a task close to the creative work of God, because it creates man anew. We, who have not been granted such exceptional powers, we must find the way that leads through the dark valley, and must attempt to let the rays of faith illuminate the hearts of those not susceptible to sentience and intuition by means of the gradual cognition and understanding to which they are accustomed.)

One of the ways of this is the learning of our Jewish culture (is one of these ways). There is no other people on earth whose culture is as saturated with the idea of God as is ours. The ideas of Jewish religion, our religious laws, and the beauty of our customs, the nobility of our ethic, the wonderful consecution of our history, all these are factors capable of being acquired through study and comprehension, whose acquisition opens up many new channels for faith in the human soul. And the eternal foundation of our culture is the Bible, (this hundred-visaged manifestation of the soul of believing man, which nourishes like an ancestral root the spreading branches of Jewish culture and religion,) *this nourisher of the soul of believing man, this sustainer of the vast branches of Jewish culture and religion.* These roots (draw) *drew* their strength from the ancestral land, from that ancestral land that through the millennia radiated its spirit into all countries of the (Diaspora) *globe.* The fiery breath of that land carried in it the word of the living God, and I saw that its faith-giving power was unbroken even today.

(I sat among the Hebrew peasants of the Valley of Jezreel, and felt among them the power of living faith with which they strove to adjust the commandments of our ancient religion to the demands of changed conditions.

I sojourned among the Bedouins of Beer Sheba, and listened in the evenings to their colorful tales in which Allah-Eloah lived, appeared, and acted.

I sat among the Oriental Jews of Jerusalem, on whose lips the Hebrew word has lived ever since antiquity as the mother tongue, and recognized their deep religiosity.

I stood on Mount Scopus before the masters of the Hebrew University of Jerusalem, while outside were fought the sacrificial battles of the rebirth of the Jewish land and the Jewish faith, and with my head bowed I received the word of the dedicatory message, about the shreds of parchments that, like unto protecting and shielding wings, carried aloft and preserved Jewry during the storms of millennia.

It is this faith, contained in the living Jewish culture, contained in the rebirth of the Holy Land and of the Jewish people, that we, young rabbis, must bring to the faithless and roadless Jewish youth of the Diaspora, so that they see and recognize the seed of Jewish life hidden in themselves.) *And with gratitude in my heart I bless in my name and the name of my colleague, this mother-institute that taught and educated us to be preachers of the faith of Israel. It is this faith that we must bring to our brethren so that they recognize the Jewish life-force hidden in it,* the beautiful and the good, so that they who tread the depths of the valleys of daily drudgery should be able to (straighten up, and should be able to) rise up, so that the fiery summit of the Horeb of sacred beauties should flash up in their sight, and they should understand and fathom the ancient word that (today again travels across the world of the Jewish dispersion with the power of truth and reality) *teaches us that we expect the word from Zion and the teaching of God from Jerusalem, for* "From Zion issues forth the teaching and the word of God from Jerusalem." *And that living in our faith we should love the fatherland into which God planted us, and serve its welfare faithfully.*

It is for this work, for the work of implanting Jewish faith into Jewish hearts, that I ask, my Masters, your consecrating blessing!

(Then I continued in Hebrew:)

My Masters and Teachers!

With a thirsty soul we stand here before you and wait for your blessings. Our hearts are full of gratitude for the past. May it be God's will that we should walk the way you have taught us, for the benefit of our people and our faith. With a yearning soul we wait, and ask that your full blessing accompany us!

(Turning to Professor Guttmann, I concluded:)

And you, my Teacher and Master, who had the privilege of spreading your Tora also from Mount Scopus, at the Hebrew University, place your hand upon us in this House of Study, this glorious house of Hungarian Jewry and the Science of Judaism. My Teacher and Master, bless us, bless us!

Looking back at this oratorical effort from the distance of fifty years I think that, although it certainly contained nothing new or original as far as Hungarian rabbinical sermonizing went, it is something of a historical document, as an example of Hungarian rabbinical style. Its phraseology, peculiar though it appears in English in my painstakingly literal translation, was strictly in line with the tradition of Hungarian rabbinical homiletics, which, to a lesser extent, also characterized secular speech-making. Using two or three synonyms wherever possible, referring repeatedly to the "soul," heaping adjectives, all this was *de rigueur*. To allude to, rather than name explicitly, issues and problems, to speak of the "dark valleys of the real world" in which people struggle, of "fires implanted into the soul," of "fiery summits," to pass sweeping judgment over trends in art, literature, science, technology, and whatever, to bemoan the Jewish lack of faith and ignorance of religion, all this was nothing more than the expected ingredients of a good sermon.

As far as Dr. Hevesi's emendations are concerned, they, too, are historical data, since they illustrate the prevalent attitude of the Hungarian Jewish leadership toward Zionism and Magyardom in the 1920s and 1930s. Some of Dr. Hevesi's deletions, of course, merely testify to his riper stylistic sensitivity as against my youthful exuberance. He certainly had a better sense of what was and what was not fitting in a synagogal oration. However, other changes he introduced betrayed his antagonism to Zionism and the building of a Jewish Palestine, and manifested his conviction that the Jews have to demonstrate vociferously, on every conceivable occasion, their fervent Hungarian patriotism.

As I sat there, facing Dr. Hevesi and reading what I considered an emasculated version of my speech, I would have dearly loved to rise up in indignation and tell him that I would rather have my colleague Dr. Molnár take over the task of expressing our thanks to our teachers than read the version containing Hevesi's emendations. But, of course, such a step was utterly impossible. So I remained silent. Dr. Hevesi seemed to have sensed something in my demeanor, perhaps a cloud that passed over my face, for, as I stood up to take my leave, he said, "Now, do I have your promise to deliver the speech exactly as it now stands, without deleting or adding anything?" I could say nothing but, "You have it, Mr. Professor." Then I thanked him and left.

Apropos of this incident, let me add here that, with the exception of Professor Heller, who was retired by that time, none of my teachers at the Seminary showed the slightest interest in the *yishuv* in general, or the Hebrew University in particular. And this was in 1936, when in neighboring Germany Hitler had been in power for three years, and daily more and more anti-Semitic measures were put into effect, when every month thousands of German Jews fled their "fatherland," and sought refuse in Palestine. Yet Hungarian Jewry was still practically monolithic in its Hungarian patriotism, in its faith in the unassailability of the Jewish position in Hungary, and in its indifference bordering on antagonism toward the *yishuv*.

Of course, once I gave my word I felt obliged to keep it. But I felt disinclined to memorize a speech that was no longer mine in its entirety, and I informed my friend Samu Löwinger, who during my absence was appointed to the faculty of the Seminary and was in charge of the technicalities of the graduation exercises, that I would deviate from the old-established custom of the institution and would *read* my speech from my notes. And that was what I did.

The graduation ceremony itself, which took place a few days later, is a complete blank in my memory. However, both the Jewish and the general press reported it, and the *Pester Lloyd* carried this account in its October 18, 1936, issue:

> *Rabbinical Ordination.* In the temple of the Franz Joseph Rabbinical Seminary Dr. Stephen Molnár and Dr. Raphael Patai were recently ordained as rabbis in a festive ceremony. After a recital of Psalms and patriotic songs by Chief Cantor Abrahamsohn and the choir, Chief Rabbi Dr. Simon Hevesi spoke to the two candidates in an affectionate address in which he quoted passages from the Hebrew doctoral thesis of Dr. Patai on the hydrography of Palestine, which he had presented to the Jerusalem University, and pointed out the deep thought-content of the rich halakhic and agadic material contained in it. Then Dr. Hevesi spoke of the rabbinical and pedagogic mission in which Dr. Molnár already is engaged, and of the calling whose path often leads through thorns and thistles, yet whose tasks are comparable to the creation of worlds. In the name of the candidates Dr. Patai replied, speaking of the lofty mission of the rabbi. Then he turned in classical Hebrew to his masters, and requested them to ordain him and his fellow-student as rabbis. The Rector of the Seminary, Prof. Dr. Michael Guttmann, emphasized in his ordination speech that the personality and the acts of the rabbi must be in harmony with his pronouncements, and then gave the new rabbis the priestly benediction. Court Councillor Samuel Stern transmitted the felicitations of the Jewish National Office, and spoke of the lofty moral watchtower of the rabbinical vocation. Then he greeted the newly elected president of the Seminary's Board of Governors, Adolf Wertheimer, who responded, deeply touched. Finally, Chief Rabbi Dr. Hevesi greeted presidents Stern and Wertheimer, and asked for God's blessing for the institution and its important work.

As one can see from this brief account, the reporter of the *Pester Lloyd* was twice caught between alternating depths and loftinesses, yet withal he did not overlook or fail to mention the recital of patriotic songs in the introductory part of the ceremony. Moreover, if one can trust the accuracy of his report—and it is difficult to imagine that he would have attributed words to Dr. Hevesi he did not actually utter—the chief rabbi utilized in his address at least one thought that he had struck from mine. I wrote that the inculcation of faith into others was "a task close to the creative work of God," and this idea, deleted by Dr. Hevesi from my speech, recurred in his: that the tasks rabbis must shoulder "are comparable to the creation of worlds." Also, his reference to the path of rabbinical calling that "often leads through thorns and thistles" sounds rather similar to my statement—not deleted by Dr. Hevesi—that it was the rabbi's duty "to accompany this generation on the thorny path of its life." However, orators have always been known to take their inspiration from the greatest variety of sources.

The day after my ordination I was handed my rabbinical diplomas, one in Hebrew, the other in Hungarian. The Hebrew diploma, handwritten in beautiful traditional Hebrew calligraphy by a fellow student at the Seminary, reads as follows in my literal translation, in which I am reproducing the original with the most scrupulous accuracy, down to its lack of punctuation:

> We the undersigned teachers of the Tora of the Lord the written and the oral Tora here in the house of study of rabbis of our country the country of Hagar [Hungary] in the capital city of Budapest came herewith to attest and to make public concerning the dear man our teacher and master Rabbi RAPHAEL son of our master and teacher JOSEPH PATAI a native of Budapest who studied and persevered in our house of study three years and one year in the house of study of rabbis that is in Breslau and one year at the Hebrew University of Jerusalem and listened to instruction in all branches of the science of Israel during that time he rose higher higher and showed his diligence and his talents he succeeded to deepen research in the words of Scripture and its commentators and learned several tractates of the Talmud and thought and was meticulous in the words of our sages of blessed memory and their commentators and his hand reaches to clarify the law and to clarify the Halakha according to first sources and the great ones of the decisors and their commentators also we saw the ways of his life and knew that he is an honest man and pure of heart he is clean in his acts and honest in the traits of his soul the fear of heaven is planted into his heart and he is worthy and deserves to serve in holiness and to perform the guard-duty of rabbi and teacher in Israel and today after he came for the last time in the crucible of examination and passed the test in all his studies behold we authorize him and crown him with the name of rabbi and teacher LET HIM TEACH LET HIM TEACH LET HIM JUDGE LET HIM JUDGE in prohibition and permission and in the rest of religious matters and questions of Israel let his springs be

dispersed abroad let him preach the Tora of the LORD in public and instruct in his community the Children of Israel in the paths of the faith and the ethics and may the purpose of the LORD prosper by his hand in witness whereof we came to sign here in Budapest may our city be rebuilt amen on the 28th day of the month of Elul 5696

Abraham Hoffer   David Samuel Löwinger   Yehiel Mikhael haKohen Guttmann director   Tzadoq ben Avraham Mord'khai head of the rabbinical court of the holy community of Pest teacher of religious philosophy   Shalom Y'huda son of my lord father teacher and master Sh'lomo Fischer

Let me add that Tzadoq ben Avraham was the Hebrew name of Dr. Hevesi; that the phrase "let his springs be dispersed abroad" is a quotation from Proverbs 5:16 with a change of the original second person to third; and that the words "may the purpose of the Lord prosper in his hand" are taken from Isaiah 53:10. The Hebrew date corresponds to September 15, 1936.

Compared to the flourish of this Hebrew rabbinical diploma, whose wording goes back many generations, the Hungarian certificate is pale and prosaic. It reads, again in my literal translation:

CERTIFICATE OF RABBINICAL QUALIFICATION

We the examining committee consisting of the delegated members of the board of directors of the Francis Joseph National Rabbinical Institute established on the basis of the most gracious decision of his Imperial and Apostolic Royal Majesty, and of the professors of the college division of the same institution, endow

Mr. Dr. Ervin George Patai
who was born in Budapest on November 22, 1910
completed his theological studies in the 1929/1930 and 1931/1933 school years at the Francis Joseph National Rabbinical Institute, in the 1930/31 school year at the Jüdisch Theologisches Seminar in Breslau, and in the 1933/34 school year at the Hebrew University of Jerusalem and was examined by us in the rabbinical examination prescribed in the statutes of the institution, on the basis of the results of the examination and of his preaching ability, by virtue of the rights appertaining to us in accordance with the bylaws of the institution approved by the Hungarian Royal Ministry of Religion and Public Instruction with the title RABBI and proclaim him to be QUALIFIED to fill a rabbinical office and perform all the functions consequent upon that office.

In witness whereof we issued, together with the HATTARA issued in the Hebrew language, this rabbinical diploma, which entitles him to the rights given to Hungarian clergymen by national laws now existing, or still to be formulated and by decrees presently valid as well as those still to be issued, and confirmed it with the seal of the Francis

Joseph National Rabbinical Institute as well as with our own signatures.

Dated Budapest, Sept. 14, 1936
Signed: Dr. Michael Guttmann, director of the institute, professor of Talmud
Dr. Simon Hevesi, president of the examining committee
Dr. Armin Hoffer, professor of Codes
Dr. Samuel Löwinger, professor of Jewish History

The other main official purpose of my visit to Hungary was to get my Dr. Phil. diploma from Budapest University. I had passed my orals in May 1933 with flying colors, and had my doctoral dissertation printed at the same time, but still had to be present personally to receive the diploma from the hands of the rector of the University. It took me several visits to the Faculty of Philosophy to find out when the next commencement exercises were to be held and to make the necessary arrangements so that I should be among those handed their Dr. Phil. diplomas on that occasion, and therewith officially declared doctors of the University. The wheels of academic bureaucracy ground notoriously slowly, but finally everything was settled and I was told to report on October 3 for the ceremony. Of the proceedings themselves I remember nothing except that the rector wore a heavy chain around his neck, composed of what seemed to be large and flat medallions, hanging down to the middle of his stomach. I also remember that I was one of some thirty or forty doctoral candidates, and that we had to line up to await our turn, which, when it came, meant that we had to step up to the rector, who shook our hand and handed us the diploma, which was in Latin. Mine read as follows (in my literal translation):

We the Rector
and the bountiful and most celebrated
Royal Hungarian University of Sciences
Named after its founder Péter Pázmány
Greeting to the reader
Whereas the most honored and most learned master
Ervinus Georgius Patai
twenty-six years of age, of the Mosaic religion, born in Budapest the capital of Hungary, had in this Budapest Royal University of Sciences proved his erudition and knowledge in Semitic Philology as principal, and likewise in Persian philology and in the History of Ancient Oriental Peoples as subsidiary, studies *summa cum laude*: we have created,

pronounced, and declared the same most honored and most learned master

Ervinus Georgius Patai
Doctor of Philosophy

In witness whereof we caused *this Diploma*, attested by the greater seal of the University and affirmed by the approved signatures, to be given to him.

In Budapest in Hungary, on the third day of October in the one thousand nine hundred and thirty-sixth A.D.

Dr. Arnoldus Pataky de Pujon   Dr. Stephanus Rybár
            Rector   Dean of the Faculty of Philosophy
                        Seal of the university

Articles and Lectures

Much of my time in Budapest in 1936 was taken up with writing articles and preparing and delivering lectures. I wrote a dozen or two short notes and book reviews for Father's journal, among them a brief appreciation of Freud on the occasion of his eightieth birthday; a notice on the death of Nahum Sokolow; comments about photographs showing French prime minister Léon Blum in action, and so forth.

Among the books I reviewed were Franz Kafka's *Beschreibung eines Kampfes*, the Bible commentary of British chief rabbi J. H. Hertz, Thomas Mann's *Joseph In Ägypten*, Marvin Lowenthal's *The Jews of Germany*, the book *Judaism in Life and Literature* by South African chief rabbi I. L. Landau, Elias Auerbach's *Wüste und Gelobtes Land*, a volume of the *Hebrew Union College Annual*, Joseph Kastein's *Jerusalem: Die Geschichte eines Landes*, and several Hebrew and Hungarian books.

Among the articles I remember especially two that I wrote in German, which were published in *Pester Lloyd*. The *Lloyd*, as its faithful readers usually called it, appeared twice daily, in the morning and in the evening. Since it was published in German, it was considered outside of Hungary the authoritative source on Hungarian events and opinions.

The first article was titled "Vorspiel und Auswirkungen der arabischen Unruhen in Palästina" (Prelude and Effects of the Arab Disturbances in Palestine). In it, rather too optimistically, I spoke about the approaching end of the Arab unrest and strikes in Palestine. I stated that the Arabs had not achieved their demands, for the British Mandatory Government of the country did not stop Jewish immigration and Jewish land purchases. I explained that the Arab working population had greatly benefited economically from the Jewish construction work; that the same held good for the Bedouins and the Arab villagers as well. I commented on the increase in Arab literacy, which was an outcome of the improved conditions of the Arab population, on the struggles between the Husayni and Nashashibi parties, between whom there was agreement only on one thing: an anti-Jewish stand.

I stated, however, that the Arabs were sincere patriots who loved the country and opposed the Jews not only for political but also for moral-ideological reasons. For instance, they considered the freedom enjoyed by Jewish woman highly immoral and a danger to traditional Arab family mores. The temporary successes of the anti-French strikes in neighboring Syria encouraged the Palestinian Arabs to launch hit-and-run attacks against the British and the Jews, and to organize strikes of dockworkers in Jaffa and of drivers and workers in Arab-owned bus companies. In these actions the Palestinian Arabs received, however, no encouragement from their Arab neighbors. The strikes in Jaffa enabled the Jews to open a competing harbor in Tel Aviv. Despite all tension, manifestations of Arab-Jewish friendship continued; for example, there was no interruption in the meetings of the Rotary Club in which both Arabs and Jews participated. All in all, the balance of the Arab rioting and striking was decidedly negative as far as the Arab leadership was concerned. I concluded by expressing the hope that the Arabs would recognize that only friendly cooperation between them and the Jews could be to the advantage of their common homeland.

When I finished writing the article, I phoned the managing editor of the *Lloyd*, Dr. Georg Kecskeméti (1901–1944), who happened to be the son of Rabbi Ármin Kecskeméti, and nephew of Rabbi Lipót Kecskeméti, whose three-volume Hungarian commentary on Jeremiah I had reviewed quite enthusiastically in the July–August 1932 issue of Father's journal. Shortly before I left Jerusalem I had sent the *Lloyd* a review-article about a book of addresses by Dr. Judah L. Magnes, the chancellor of the Hebrew University, a German translation of which was published at that time; that review appeared in the June 9, 1936, issue of the *Lloyd*. I thus had reason to hope that my name would not be entirely unknown to Dr. Kecskeméti, and this gave me the courage to call him and tell him that I would like to submit an article to him. He gave me an appointment for next day, and I went to see him in the impressive offices of the *Lloyd*.

When I was ushered into the editorial presence, I found Dr. Kecskeméti to be a small, stocky man, friendly and informal. He devoted several minutes to talking with me about Palestine, and promised to read my article within a few days. To my great surprise, instead of calling me and telling me his impression of my article, he published it within three days. When I opened the August 2, 1936, morning issue of the *Lloyd* (to which my father subscribed), to my delight I found in it my article, without any deletions, although it was quite lengthy, and practically without any stylistic corrections. I should add that the *Pester Lloyd*, in the good old tradition of the Viennese *Neue Freie Presse*, published every day a *feuilleton*, which contained comments or opinions on current affairs, or reviews or analyses of general interest. To have become a *feuilletonist* of the *Lloyd* filled me with no small pride, and already I saw myself following in the footsteps of Theodor Herzl, who was *feuilletonist* and later the *feuilleton* editor of the famed Viennese daily.

A few weeks later I wrote another German article entitled "Die Versäumnisse der Palästina-Regierung" (Omissions of the Palestinian Government), and took it again to Dr. Kecskeméti, who published it in the September 8, 1936, issue of the *Lloyd*. In this article I was rather critical of the British Mandatory Government of Palestine for its handling of Arab-Jewish relations in the country. Among the omissions and administrative errors I attributed to the Mandatory were its failure to disarm the population; the mild punishments given to those caught in the possession of illegal arms; the wide publicity given over the radio to Arab attacks against the Jews and the British and to bombings and sabotage carried out by the Arabs; the lack of any effort to influence Arab public opinion; and more of the like. In the article I quoted the August 19, 1936, issues of the *London Times* and *Daily Telegraph*, which shows that during my stay in Budapest I followed the British press, and that the writing of my article took no more than about two weeks.

My outspoken criticism of the British authorities did not sit well with the Hungarian Jewish leaders, who, as a rule, were highly respectful of authority. I remember in particular a phone call from Dr. Ignác Friedmann, whom we have already met in the preceding chapter in which I describe my courting his daughter Guli. He called to tell me that while he liked my first article very much, this second one was a *faux pas*. I can no longer recall what he found wrong with it, or what was my response, but I do remember that, not being as yet inured to adverse criticism, I was rather upset.

On the other hand I was gratified to receive positive responses to my *Lloyd* articles. People whom I met mentioned them favorably and quite a few phoned to say they would want to see more articles by me. The editor of the small Jewish review, *Szombat* (Saturday), Dr. Ede Kenéz-Kurländer, of whom I have spoken repeatedly earlier in this book, took my August 2 article in the *Pester Lloyd* as the basis of a page-long note he wrote and published in the September 15, 1936, issue of his journal under the title "Objective Lines about Palestine," which he concluded with the parenthetical remark, "This lesson can be drawn by everyone reading Dr. Raphael Patai's article published just now in the *Pester Lloyd*."

Apart from these German articles, I wrote several shorter ones in Hungarian, and a considerable number of book reviews for Father's journal. Among the former let me mention only one. It was titled "On the Margin of a Joke," and was published in the August 14, 1936, issue of *Zsidó Szemle* (Jewish Review), the official weekly of the Hungarian Zionist Organization. I started by quoting a joke that was current in those days in Jewish Palestine. It told of a delegation sent by the Palestinian Arabs to the high commissioner of Palestine. "Your Excellency," they said to him, "We came to make you an offer. We are willing to restore order in the country, if you give us three days in which to do as we want. Thereafter, we guarantee, there will be order." "Gentlemen," replied the high commissioner, "I would be glad to do as you suggest, but I regret to have to tell you that only a few minutes ago I had here a Jewish delegation that asked for only one day to accomplish the same purpose."

In my "marginal comments" accompanying the anecdote I pointed out the differences between it and the typical Jewish jokes current in the Diaspora. The Diaspora Jewish joke, I wrote,

> is bitter self-mockery . . . whose effect is based on the observation that the Jews are provoked to laughter when they are shown how shrewd, sly, and cowardly, in effect how ridiculous and pitiable, is the figure cut by the Jew. The psychological basis of the effectiveness of these jokes lies in the phenomenon of assimilation: the assimilant Jew loves to put to ridicule those Jewish traits, or rather those traits that he holds typically Jewish, which are found in his own personality, produced by his own disposition to assimilate, by his striving to model his conduct after that of his Gentile environment, and which he thinks he can get

rid of by bestowing them collectively on little Moritz, or Grün and Kohn, who meet in the street, or on Weisz who travels in the company of *goys*, and, then, by demonstrating with uproarious laughter how far he himself stands from these characters, and to what extent he can grasp the ridiculousness of their appearance, behavior, mentality, the awkwardness and absurdity of their relationship to the outer world.

Then, having thus taken to task my Hungarian coreligionists, to whom these strictures were, of course, directed, I went on to analyze the contrasting qualities revealed in the joke about the two delegations to the high commissioner of Palestine. I discerned in it a quiet self-assurance, a sense of power, a reassuring feeling that "we are stronger than they." I found that the anecdote also reflected the great self-control exercised by the Jews of Palestine in the face of almost unbearable provocation, a self-control that stemmed from being revolted at the very thought of desecrating, defiling, and devastating their Palestinian motherland. And I concluded with typical Hungarian oratorical and journalistic grandiloquence, of which three years in a Hebrew-speaking environment were evidently insufficient to divest myself:

> This self-control, this patient bearing, this wordless locking-of-the-jaws, with which Palestinian Jewry endures the wrongs, the attacks, the murders, confining itself to self-defense, attacking nowhere, taking vengeance nowhere, not destroying forest for forest, not killing soul for soul, this proclaims more loudly than any demanding or shouting that this land, whose children and trees are being destroyed by the hands of murderers, belong not to them, to the murderers who trumpet abroad that the country is theirs alone and that they won't tolerate any other master over it, but to these, to the defenders, who bury with pain and love their fallen men and their trees—and heal the bleeding wounds inflicted on the body of the motherland with new plantings of trees and of men.

As for the lectures, which, in general, were much better remunerated than the articles, they were so numerous that I remember distinctly and separately only a very few of them. Nor do I recall any longer whether I had given any lectures (apart from obligatory practice sermons) prior to my leaving Budapest in May 1933. But, once I arrived back in the city with the prestige of my Jerusalem doctorate, my three years of scholarly apprenticeship in the Holy City, and my published writings, I was, so to speak, a "natural" for the Hungarian Jewish lecture circuit. I also could count on the unstinting help of Father, who was a much sought after lecturer and had connections all over the country, and thus I received numerous invitations to speak, both in Budapest and in provincial towns. The subjects of my talks were, of course, various aspects of the life of the *yishuv*, its development, its cultural activities, and the like. Occasionally I spoke of the city of Jerusalem, and, to students or youth organizations, of the Hebrew University. Before my Hungarian stint was over, I was an experienced speaker, and had acquired the knack of giving vivid expression to my thoughts and feelings. Due to my sincere conviction that Palestine was *the* place for Jews to live, I must have been quite an effective Zionist propagandist.

My lectures on the Hebrew University were noted in Jerusalem as well. The November 1936 issue of the mimeographed *Bulletin of the Hebrew University Jerusalem*, published in a Hebrew and a German edition by the University's Department of Organization and Publicity, carried two items in which references were made to me. One described "The First Doctoral Graduation at the Hebrew University," the other, under the title "Hungary," reported as follows:

> At the intiative of our devoted and active friend in the field of university work, Dr. Joseph Patai, an interesting meeting was held in Budapest in connection with the visit of Mr. [Dr. Kurt] Blumenfeld in the home of Prof. Julius Donat. Even though a number of important personalities were absent from Budapest in the month of July, many people attended the meeting. After a talk by Mr. Blumenfeld on the value of the Hebrew University, there followed a lively discussion.
>
> In a series of discussions with the members of the committee and the new friends of the University, Mr. Blumenfeld outlined a great plan for the fall fundraising drive.
>
> We note with special appreciation the help of Dr. Raphael Patai (the first to receive, a short time ago, the degree of doctor from the Hebrew University) in connection with his sojourn in Budapest.

I remember one or two of the lectures I gave because of special circumstances attached to them. One was my lecture in Szeged, the second-largest city in Hungary, which I recall because there I met Immanuel Löw (1854–1944), the most respected rabbi and the grand old man of Jewish scholarship in Hungary. His unequaled prestige was due to two factors: one was that he had been chosen to be the representative of Hungarian Neolog Jewry in the Upper House of the Hungarian Parliament, and the other was his great scholarship. Rumor had it that his election to the Upper House was greatly resented by Dr. Simon Hevesi, who was unquestionably a greater orator than Löw and would certainly have been more effective in representing the majority of Hungarian Jewry in that legislative body. As for Löw's scholarship, his *magnum opus* was his multivolume *Flora der Juden* (published in 1924–1934), of which my father had a copy in his library and which had filled me with great admiration when, as a student, I perused it or looked something up in it. It was a real *tour de force*, in which Löw presented, in a systematized form, all the data pertaining to plants contained in the enormously voluminous Jewish literature (written in Hebrew, Aramaic, Syriac, Greek, Arabic, etc.). He was, incidentally, one of the representatives of Hungarian Jewry at the 1929 Zurich foundation meeting of the expanded Jewish Agency for Palestine.

Yet despite the unique position he occupied in public life, and the great respect he enjoyed, Löw was a very modest and kind man. When I arrived in Szeged for my lecture, I was a twenty-five-year-old youngster whose scholarship was as yet little more than a promise, but the eighty-two-year-old master spent several hours with me. He gave me, to begin with, a conducted tour of his synagogue, one of the finest architectural monuments in Hungary, which had been built under his guidance, and whose many stained-glass windows contained pictures of plants identified by Löw in his *Flora der Juden*, so that the synagogue as a whole was an illustration of his scholarship. I can still vividly remember with what youthful fervor the octogenarian scholar pointed out to me minute details in the flowers depicted on the windows, and with what visible enjoyment he viewed "his" flora so beautifully displayed.

After the visit to the synagogue, Löw took me to his book-lined study, and chatted with me for an hour or so, mentioning that he had received a copy of my Jerusalem doctoral dissertation and that he would review it in the prestigious *Monatschrift für Geschichte und Wissenschaft des Judentums*. The review appeared in 1937 and testified to Löw's generosity in judging my juvenile effort. "The young author," he wrote, "shows great *Arbeitsfreudigkeit* [joy in work] and many-sided reading." After stating briefly what my book was about, Löw continued: "In the choice of his subject matter the author was fortunate. The solution of his tasks is accompanied by a success worthy of appreciation. The Palestine-Hebrew of the author is readable and clear. . . . Print and production are excellent, printer's errors extremely few. . . . "

But, to return to my lecture in Szeged, it was part of the annual meeting of the local chapter of the Zionist Organization, and was titled "Peace in the Holy Land"—a remote desideratum at the time. I can recall nothing of the lecture, but I can imagine that, in accordance with the uplifting character of all the talks I gave about the "Holy Land," it must have discussed the chances for peace, and painted a glowing picture of the great economic, social, and cultural developments the country was bound to experience once peace was restored between the Arabs and the Jews. The next thing I remember is that after the lecture, late in the evening, I was taken by the son of Immanuel Löw (he was, if I remember correctly, a lawyer in Szeged) to the railroad station, where I got into my reserved roomette, undressed, and promptly fell asleep. When I woke up next morning, the car was standing on a siding in the Budapest terminal, waiting for the overnight passengers to get up and get off.

I was never to see Immanuel Löw again. Many years later I learned that when the Germans entered Hungary in 1944, they put the ninety-year-old man, who by that time was totally blind and very feeble, on a train to be sent to Auschwitz; but when the train passed through Budapest, Jewish leaders succeeded in taking him off and sending him to a hospital, where he died shortly thereafter.

Of another lecture I gave in the city of Hatvan I retained no recollection whatsoever, and it is only due to a newspaper clipping I preserved that I know about it at all. The news item, published in the December 26, 1936, issue of the *Hatvani Ujság* (Journal of Hatvan) strikes me today as so peculiar, and so characteristic of the turgid style of Hungarian journalism of the time, that I want to present an excerpt from it here in my literal translation. It is entitled "Patai-Evening (About the Holy Land)," and it reads partly as follows:

> The young scholar, upon his arrival in the jam-packed hall, was greeted by Béla Blumenthal, president of the congregation, with a pithy speech that was received by the audience with great enthusiasm. Dr. Raphael Patai, in his wide-ranging and lofty free lecture, led his audience to the Holy Land, and to its most memorable place, Jerusalem, introduced his audience to the old and new Jerusalem, its culture, its university, its people, and the cultural work, literature, and more notable institutions of the Israelites there. In his almost hour-long speech of elevated spirit, in which he also gave a colorful milieu-picture of Jerusalem, he brought the Holy Land and Jerusalem nearer to the heart of his audience. After his very impressive lecture his audience gave a warm ovation to the young, scholarly, sympathetic-looking rabbi, who, we are informed, has received invitations from several large congregations of our fatherland to give lectures.

Dr. Vilmos Adler, chief rabbi of the Israelite Congregation of Hatvan, thanked his young colleague for his valuable speech, while he himself, too, rendered homage in a poetically soaring speech to the sanctified noble traditions of the Holy Land. They continued to converse convivially with the young scholar-rabbi who had found a second home in the Holy Land, and who proved to be just as witty a lecturer at the white table as he gave evidence of his outstanding oratorical abilities and of his great and thorough grounding at the lecturer's table.

Well, well, how pithy, wide-ranging, lofty, elevated, colorful, impressive, valuable, poetically soaring, witty, outstanding, thorough can you get!

Of all my lectures, the one that stirred up the greatest interest in both Jewish and non-Jewish circles was the one I delivered over the Hungarian state radio. There was only one broadcasting network at the time in Hungary, and, like the railway, the universities, and the mail, it was a governmental institution. As such, it was accorded considerable respect, and everything it put on the air had quasi-official sanction. If I remember correctly, the Budapest radio began to broadcast regular transmissions in 1925 or thereabouts, and, again, if I remember correctly, until my 1936 talk no "Jewish" subject had ever been aired by it. As for the antecedents of the lecture, I remember nothing, but a rather enigmatic reference in one of my mother's letters addressed from Budapest to my sister Évi in Jerusalem and dated only "Thursday," but evidently written in December 1936, indicates that it grew out of a chance meeting aboard the train we took from Trieste to Budapest after we had returned from Haifa to Trieste in June of that year. She wrote:

> . . . in our financial situation, which is becoming daily more difficult, it depressed all of us very much that Gyuri stands here and does not know what to do. In the meantime he has been invited to give lectures, and indeed, with the help of that reporter of the [Hungarian] News Service who was our travel companion from Trieste to Budapest, we succeeded in achieving that he should give a lecture in the Hungarian radio. Apart from the usual 80 *pengő* fee, this has great significance, because, naturally, he will speak of Palestine under the title "Holy Land Panorama." László Szabó, the man of the radio, was difficult to persuade, he cited today's anti-Semitic wave, etc.

Peculiarly, although I must have followed or conducted those prelecture negotiations with considerable excitement, I remember nothing of all this. What I do remember with great clarity is that, since the lecture was to be broadcast live, several days prior to it I had to go to the studios for a voice audition. The man in charge wanted to make sure that my Hungarian pronunciation was satisfactory. It was, but he found that the way I pronounced the *r* was not perfect. "You *raccsol* [burr your *r*'s] just a little bit," he said. "But it does not matter." The Hungarian *r* is pronounced with a rich roll of the tongue, not unlike the Italian, and the inability to pronounce it that way was considered a serious phonetic blemish. I was surprised to hear that I burred my *r*'s, since I had been convinced that my Hungarian pronunciation was perfect. But then I comforted myself with the thought that in Hebrew as spoken in Palestine, which was to be the language of my future life, there was no rolled *r*, and therefore it did not matter in the least whether or not I was able to pronounce the Hungarian *r* to perfection. As it turned out, it was somewhat ironic that in English and in all the other languages I subsequently learned to speak, it was precisely that *r* that unfailingly gave away my Hungarian origin.

There were at the time two illustrated radio weeklies in Budapest, both somewhat similar in content and format to the American *TV Guide*, and both printed illustrated write-ups in advance of my talk. They even printed my picture. One of them, *Rádióélet* (Radio Life), misspelled my name "Patay," thereby inadvertently endowing me with Hungarian nobility. It also asked me to write a brief article, which I did, telling about my forthcoming lecture, the latest cultural developments in Jewish Palestine, and the economic and cultural relations between it and Hungary. The lecture, being a "first," was noted not only in the Hungarian Jewish papers, but also in the German Jewish press (which still existed at the time), and in Palestine. It was broadcast on short-wave as well, and thus it could also be listened to in Palestine, where my teacher, Professor Samuel Klein, subsequently told me that it was a veritable *Qiddush haShem*, "sanctification of God's Name," the highest accolade that can be given to an act reflecting honorably on Jews and Judaism.

The broadcast took place on January 8, 1937, and the next day *Pester Lloyd* printed an article about it entitled "First Lecture about Palestine on Hungarian Radio." After the lecture I rewrote its text and submitted it to Professor Samu Szemere, editor of the *Yearbook* of the Israelite Hungarian Literary Society. He accepted it and published it in the 1937 volume.

My Sister's Novel

While I was busy taking care of my affairs in Budapest and trying to build up something for my future in Jerusalem, two important developments took place in the life of my sister Évi back in the "Holy City."

Aboard the ship sailing from Trieste to Haifa, in the spring of 1933, my sister met Alfred Leon Hirsch, a German Jewish engineer ten years her senior. Emil Hirsch, Leon's father, was a retired engineer and a well-known Jewish art collector. He was among the all too few German Jews who recognized the handwriting on the wall as early as 1933, and moved to Palestine without delay. He was able to get out of Germany and bring along his entire collection of Jewish ceremonial objects and works of Jewish and non-Jewish painters. He rented a beautiful apartment in one of the finest residential areas of Tel Aviv, spacious enough to house his collections, and lived comfortably in a manner essentially similar to the life he had lived in Berlin as a well-to-do, cultured, retired professional man. Leon, the only son of Emil and Jennie Hirsch and a graduate of the Berlin Polytechnic in civil engineering, found employment in Jerusalem with the Public Works Department of the British Mandatory Government. He and Évi fell in love, and, despite the uncertainty of Leon's professional future, they married a few weeks later.

As time passed, Évi began to suffer from the fact that she did not become pregnant. She developed a consuming yearning for motherhood, and as the third year of her marriage drew to a close she was practically obsessed with the imperative of pregnancy. Finally, in the summer of 1936, she did become pregnant. It was an enormous relief and an immense satisfaction for her. Soon after my return from Budapest to Jerusalem, in March 1937, she gave birth to a daughter whom she called Tirzah, who now lives with her husband and three children next door to Évi's house, at 8 Patai Street, Givatayim.

Évi's physical fruitfulness seems to have released her literary creativity, and as soon as her pregnancy was confirmed she embarked on writing a novel that had an autobiographical basis. Since her knowledge of Hebrew was as yet insufficient, and writing in an insular language such as Hungarian while living in Palestine would have made little sense, she wrote in German, a language she had learned in early childhood when we were cared for by a succession of German Fräuleins.

Now it so happened that Mother, too, had written a novel, in Hungarian. It is quite possible that Évi was motivated and encouraged in writing her own story by the knowledge that Mother, who up to that time had written only poems and art criticism, was working on a major literary venture and had finished it by the spring of 1936. The title of Mother's novel was *Szent Szomjuság* (Sacred Thirst), and Father published it while I was in Budapest, in October 1936, under the imprint of his journal. *Mult és Jövő* was both the title of his monthly and the name of his publishing house, whose activity was largely confined to issuing his own books. Shortly before my arrival in Budapest Father also published under the same imprint a volume of poems by Mother, entitled *Engem is hív a föld* (The Land Calls Me, Too), and a pamphlet containing a lengthy essay about Mother's poems, entitled *Patai Edith a költő* (Edith Patai the Poet) written by Isaac Pap, who was a rabbi and himself a respected Hungarian poet.

Mother's novel, which, as the title page states, was crowned with the novel prize of the Israelite Hungarian Literary Society (known by the acrostic of its Hungarian name as IMIT), was published in paperback; it ran to 242 pages plus a glossary that gave the Hungarian explanation of the Hebrew words and phrases appearing in it. It was set in Jewish Palestine, and its story line revolved around the experiences, adventures, and loves of about a dozen characters, some of them visitors from America and Europe, others natives or permanent residents of the country. It was full of local color, reflecting partly Mother's impressions of Palestine, which by 1936 she had visited several times, and partly, no doubt, the deeper familiarity with the *yishuv* possessed by Father, who certainly had made no small contribution to it. I myself saw the novel the first time when I read it in page proof after my arrival in Budapest. Soon thereafter its printing was completed, and thus Mother's own authorship did not interfere with the attention she paid to Évi's novel. In fact, she was preoccupied with Évi's *opus* quite intensively. She discussed it in several of her letters to Évi, which she, as was her wont, did not date except for jotting down the day of the week on top of the first page. One of these letters, dated only "Tuesday," must have been written at the end of July because in it she mentions that I went to the *Pester*

Lloyd and was well received and was promised that my article would appear next Sunday, which it did, on August 2. Mother wrote:

> In the meantime I, too, read *The Street of the Fishing Cat* [by the Hungarian novelist Jolán Földes], and even if its global success is not totally justified, one cannot deny that it is alive, that there are well-observed and well-drawn figures in it. The soft voice is no drawback; it would be a drawback only if it was boring. Conversely, your novel has some sensational details, but there is also much immaturity in it. Father today sent somebody to Dr. Nádas[?] to get back your manuscript. Nádas enclosed also his opinion, but I cannot as yet tell you about it, for I spoke with Father only over the phone. Next time I shall send it to you. But no outside opinion is needed, since Father and I and Gyuri all agree that there is still much to be polished in it. Especially in view of its great values, its interesting theme, one must undertake that polishing. One must also write additions to it without fail, for, according to Mr. Nádas, this is a question of proportions. Even Mr. [Béla] Szegő [?] made correct criticisms, and it would not be wise to disregard the opinions of others, especially since the success of the novel depends on those others. Father wants me to tell you that you should mail us the corrections and additions, we shall type them and insert them in their proper places. . . .

After reporting about an operation she underwent and about all the relatives and friends who had come to visit her in the hospital and filled her room with flowers, in a P.S. Mother returns to Évi's novel:

> Yesterday Béla Szegő brought Father and Gyuri home from the office in his car. He said that if you would expand the beginning of the novel, then the many births would not be so conspicuous. That is to say, the people are for expansion. Perhaps Father will write the chapter about Jericho. Perhaps one should describe the past of the *Wunderdoktor* [one of the chief characters in the novel]. Possibly he could come from Russia, and reminisce about the sea voyage, and there you could weave in the impressions you gained aboard ship. I don't find the characterization stereotyped. Rather, it is incomplete. We know nothing of the past of either Dolla or Herbert [the two chief protagonists]; perhaps this is why their characters are not sufficiently thrown into relief. They hang in the air somewhat. In any case, Nádas is intelligent and well-meaning; he promised that he would have another look at the novel in its corrected form. Precisely because of this one must listen to everything he wrote. Don't think that in place of improvements and additions you could write a new book. This one contains such a lot of experiences, has so much power, the topic is so interesting, that it is not possible to shake out another one like it. Do expand it, and you will see what a success it will be.

Father wrote in a similar vein and in even greater detail, specifying what he thought should be corrected in the novel and how it should be expanded. In a long letter of about 2,000 words, undated, but evidently written about the same time, he let Évi have the benefit of his advice and editorial experience:

My dear Évikém,

Since you left Mother and I have continued to be occupied with you, at least through your novel, apart from your private affairs. I have read the entire text carefully and in one stretch, and I find that Szegő is right, the course of the novel is uneven, and not all parts are on the level of the Fatma story [a story within the story about the tragedy of an Arab woman]. No wonder. One cannot shake out a novel in a few weeks. Such a thing can, at the utmost, be considered a draft, which comes into being in the first inspiration, but which must thereafter be carved and polished, like every work of art, none of which ever bursts forth fully finished. Mother and I discussed some smaller improvements, but it would be the right thing if you, too, would make some additions, improvements. And only after we have looked over the corrected manuscript can it be sent either to the Nekudah Publishers who have asked for it, or to the Hungarian publishers, one after the other; and it should be shown also to Palestinian publishers only thereafter. A few weeks don't count in immortality.

Father's tightly typed letter (Mother must have typed it) goes on to discuss specific improvements in the novel, and shows with what concentrated attention he read it, how seriously he took it, and how thoroughly he went into suggesting changes, improvements, additions, and, rather rarely, deletions.

One would have imagined that under the impact of all this expert advice and in the possession of detailed pointers as to what to do to improve her novel, Évi went to work introducing at least some of the scenarios suggested by Father. But this was not the case. In her letters to the family in Budapest, no longer extant, she must have reiterated her unwillingness to return to work on the novel, which, in turn, motivated me to add my voice to that of our parents. It would seem I took it for granted that I had inherited from them, if not a talent for writing *belles lettres*, at least an ability to pass critical judgment on literary attempts—that I was a better judge of what was right and what was wrong with a piece of fiction than its author. I wrote a lengthy critical analysis (in Hungarian) of my sister's novel and mailed it to her on November 1, 1936.

It is possible that my sister was discouraged by all this criticism, or perhaps in the advanced stages of her pregnancy she had no patience to return to working on her novel. Moreover, in order to supplement the modest salary of her husband, she engaged in drawing commercial posters, for each of which she got paid one Palestinian pound, at the time the equivalent of five dollars. When she informed us about the various activities that kept her busy, I wrote to her on December 8, 1936:

> I got very upset when I gathered from your letters that not only are you not working on finishing your novel, but do not even intend to do so in the near future. You really cannot expect the family to finish it for you, for, after all, the family is not able to do it as well as you could if only you would ovecome your accursed laziness and inertness. I know that such reworkings and improvements often mean serious torture, but you surely know that without work there is no result, and that without suffering there is no happiness. Just recently I read in a biography of Jakob Wassermann that he rewrote the first 50 pages of his novel *Christian Wahnschaffe* 25 times until finally he found that it was good. This alone meant writing 1,250 pages! You can imagine how much time and energy this required! And you, you want to dash off your brainchild in a few weeks, and then want no longer to deal with it!

While I confined myself to criticism and advice, and while Évi herself reiterated her reluctance to change, or to add to, her first draft, Mother continued to work patiently on improving and augmenting her daughter's novel. She wrote several chapters (in German) and sent them to Évi to be reworked and put into the novel.

Even while the Hitlerite menace was steadily reducing the number of subscribers to Father's journal, and thus eroding the family's livelihood, Mother continued to be preoccupied with Évi's novel. In December 1936 she touched upon the economic problems faced by the family in a letter to Évi:

> In the last several weeks, alas, the financial situation has seriously deteriorated, as a result of several factors. The fact that the price of paper rose by 50% (and of this nothing can be passed along to the subscribers) is only a minor factor. The fact is that Father severely reduced the allowance for household expenses, so severely that I don't know whether it will be possible to manage even half decently from it. According to Father, from now on we can spend only 300 *pengős* monthly, including all outside expenses, clothing, lighting, heating. For me, of course, even more difficult than all this is the fact that it

was necessary to curtail the allowance of my parents, precisely now, when Ruth [the widow of Mother's brother Berti] did the same. But this is what usually happens, trouble does not come alone. Only let us all be healthy, then it is not so tragic if one must live quite modestly. . . . Grandmother is here with us; alas, she is very, very weak, looks bad, and is so thin that it is a pity, and still I had to tell her cruelly that we are reducing the monthly money. Truly, these are bitter days, especially the first few months, until I see how I can manage with this small amount, and my parents with their small amount. According to Father we *must* manage with this, because there is simply no more. But, believe me, my little Évi, that although these things preoccupy me, and I know that they are important, nevertheless they don't touch me in the deepest—there, deep down, you are there, and your future fate—if only that were in order, how easily I could bear the rest, especially that which touches my own person! Such is life. Grandmother says she grieves much more over us having to reduce our standard so radically than over herself, and I on my part worry much more over my parents and you than over myself. But if only the situation in Palestine were solved, everything could so easily be well again. Thank God, that which, according to Gyuri, one cannot acquire—talent, ability to work—you have it, and only a little bit of luck is needed. . . . I am typing your novel so diligently that I am almost at the half way mark. Even while I type, I enjoy the beautiful details, and I rejoice with it as with a property that cannot be lost. . . .

My impending return to Jerusalem filled Mother with great anxiety, and the Arab riots in Palestine, which continued despite my optimistic appraisal of the situation in the *Lloyd*, supplied her with a more than sufficient basis for worries. The contents of the few of her letters that survived the various intercontinental moves of the family, which I still have in my possession, are about evenly divided between expressions of anxiety about the general situation in Palestine and the Middle East and utterances of worry about the personal problems of each member of her family. For instance, early in January 1937 she wrote my sister:

My dear Évi:

I live again in constant tension and excitement because of the renewed news in the papers. They write that if the [Peel] Commission leaves, in the middle of February, new riots can be expected. In Iraq, Transjordan, the Arabs are making preparations with well-equipped armies. You can imagine what these news mean for me. . . . When I read the news I don't even want to think about Gyuri, that he, too, will leave [Budapest], and then one will have to worry about him too. . . . Of course, the papers write also about the great national movement of the Near

East, etc., so that in the end one sees Palestine as a small island in the midst of a great Arab sea. . . . It is not easy when politics touches one's own skin. . . . Gyuri's picture and article appeared in *Radio Life*. His lecture "is anticipated with great interest," at least in the bosom of the family. For New Year's Eve only Guszti went off to make merry. Gyuri sits constantly at home, types, writes, corresponds, and looks rather poorly. But what can one do?

Again, on January 7, 1937 (the letter is dated only "Thursday," but its content makes the date certain) she wrote my sister first about my impending departure from Budapest, then about Évi's novel:

. . . Gyuri already is preparing to leave. There is only one comforting moment: that there he will be with you, which, in view of the many absences of Leon, will be very good. . . . One of Gyuri's eyes was again bloodshot for three days, but I could not prevail on him to go to the doctor. Please, pay attention to it when he is there. Otherwise, too, I beg you to keep an eye on Gyuri, that he should eat properly. Indeed, he is not at all strong, the moment he tires himself it is visible on him as on a young girl. Tomorrow will be his radio lecture, for which there is really great advance interest. Yesterday he visited the Bechs [?], both of them got with him on a "thee" and "thou" footing, and gave him great *koved* [honor]. Gyuri tries to get something from them for the [Hebrew] University. Perhaps something will come of it. Today I finished looking over your novel. I shall send you the amplified copy with Gyuri, so that you can merge the new parts into your own style. I am still not entirely satisfied with its beginning, despite the united labor of the whole family, but the other new chapters, I believe, are quite good. . . .

These letters show not only that Father, Mother, and I spent much time on Évi's novel and willingly lent a hand to improve it and add parts to it, but also that we all made sustained efforts to persuade her to continue working on it. Ultimately, it seems, entire chapters were added by Mother, with the active participation of Father, and a goodly share by myself. Évi herself was much too busy with her daily life, with watching the child grow in her womb, and, beyond all that, she lacked the perseverance, the ability to sit and sweat *à la* Jakob Wassermann, over a piece of writing, going over it again and again, polishing and improving it, considering and reconsidering the best way of saying what she wanted to say. This is why, despite her considerable talent — in her youth she had written some marvelous poetry in Hungarian — she never became a writer, and, after having been prodded by all of us into finishing her novel, she never again wrote anything but a few brief articles about our par-

ents. Nor did she take into account most of the constructive suggestions my parents and I communicated to her, and while she agreed
to the inclusion of some additional scenes written by Mother, she
left her novel substantially in the same shape that it had when it first
emerged from her hasty pen.

Nevertheless, I felt that the novel was good and should be published. I arranged with Dov Kimhi (1889–1961), a respected Hebrew
author and translator, to render Évi's German manuscript into Hebrew.
The novel was published under the title *Bifro'a Pra'ot* (When Riots
Swept the Land) by Yavne Publishers of Tel Aviv, in 1938. It received
favorable notices in the Hebrew press, and then shared the fate of
many others: it was forgotten.

"Titlemania" and Jewish Excellence

An old adage, much circulated among Jewish critics of the Jews, had
it that in every country the Jews were like the Gentiles only more so.
I have spoken elsewhere about the patriotism that was an outstanding characteristic of the Hungarians, and the corresponding super-
patriotism of the Hungarian Jews. Another example of the Jewish
"more so" was the Hungarian proclivity to using the prefix *fő-* meaning "chief," in combination with as many terms designating titles,
ranks, and positions as at all possible. Thus the coveted title that
quite a number of wealthy Christians and Jews acquired (it was
awarded by the government) was "government chief counsellor,"
although there was no such title as "government counsellor." After
World War I, when the Austro-Hungarian monarchy fell apart and
Admiral Nicholas Horthy became the head of the Hungarian state,
his official title was "chief regent," although there were no "regents"
under him. The waiters in restaurants were addressed as *Főúr*, literally "chief mister," even though no servitors of lower rank functioned under them. To call a waiter simply *Pincér* (waiter) was considered rude.

Even educational institutions suffered from the same "titlemania."
The dictionary term for an academic secondary school, in which pupils
aged ten to eighteen were enrolled, was *gimnázium*, but in actuality
all secondary schools of that type were called *főgimnázium* (chief
gimnázium). In other countries a Catholic cardinal is called "primate";
the title of the Hungarian cardinal was "prince primate"—evidently
even "chief primate" would have been considered insufficient. Sim-

ilarly, the conductor of a gypsy band, a familiar appurtenance in all larger Hungarian cafés, was called "gypsy primate." This Hungarian titlemania was well known to, and cleverly utilized by, panhandlers, who addressed people from whom they solicited handouts by all kinds of gratuitous titles. I remember one occasion when I was sitting in a park on top of Mount Gellért in Budapest with Hedy Feuerstein (a niece of the Hungarian-Israeli poet Avigdor Hameiri), one of the girls to whom I briefly paid attention, when we were approached by one of these characters who addressed me as "Mr. Chief Director." On another occasion I was styled "Mr. Chief Secretary." That titles should be a preoccupation in the army should surprise no one. But in Hungary officers' titles were used by adolescent street gangs, which were gently satirized by Ferenc Molnár, the famous Hungarian Jewish playwright, in his very popular juvenile novel *The Boys of Pál Street*. In it he describes the organization of boys who imitate the military, each of whom assumes an officer's rank: one of them is a general, others are colonels, majors, captains, and so forth. Finally, there is one single boy, the most timid and insignificant among them, who is the hero of the novel, and who has to be satisfied with being a lowly private.

The same hankering after titles characterized the village people as well. Householders in the village were addressed as *Tekintetes Úr*, which can only roughly be translated as "respected Mr." The corresponding title for a woman was *Tekintetes Asszony*, "respected Mrs." The middle-class men in the cities were addressed as *Nagyságos Úr*, which originally had meant something like "grandiose sir," but whose meaning paled by the twentieth century into the insignificant equivalent of "Mr." Correspondingly, middle-class women were addressed as *Nagyságos Asszony*, which had long lost its original meaning of "grandiose lady," and meant nothing more than "Mrs." High-ranking government officials, including full professors of the universities, as well as persons decorated by the title "government chief counsellor," were addressed as *Méltóságos Úr*, or "dignified sir"; their wives enjoyed the title "dignified lady." After World War I, when there were no Habsburg kings around anymore to award titles of nobility, the great ambition of many Jews who had attained wealth and achieved distinction was to become a "dignified sir."

The language, of course, both reflected and perpetuated the Hungarian predilection for "chief" titles. In the Hungarian-English dictionary of László Országh (published in Budapest in 1963) no less than eight tightly printed columns contain the listings of Hungarian words compounded with the prefix *fő-*, of which a few will have to suffice as illustrations. Thus abbot is *főapát* (literally, chief abbot); tenant, *főbérlő* (chief renter); nave of a church, *főhajó* (chief ship); street front, *főhomlokzat* (chief front); protagonist, *főhős* (chief hero); college, *főiskola* (chief school); town clerk, *főjegyző* (chief notary); ledger, *főkönyv* (chief book); aristocrat, *főnemes* (chief noble); noun, *főnév* (chief name), and so on.

The Jews, of course, used all these terms, and added to them quite a few more. Thus the secretary of a Jewish community had the title "chief secretary," even though no other secretaries worked under him. All rabbis were addressed as *Főtisztelendő Úr,* or "Very Reverend Mr.," and not merely as "Reverend Mr.," which title was sufficient for the Christian clergy. The spiritual leaders of all the Jewish congregations, even the smallest ones, were styled "chief rabbi," even though they had no other rabbi functioning under them. Only a very few large congregations, such as those of Pest, Buda, and Szeged, in addition to their "chief rabbi" also had a clergyman of lower rank, who had to be satisfied with the title "rabbi." The Dohány Temple of Budapest had, in addition to its two chief rabbis, also two "chief cantors." All the congregations that employed cantors gave them the title "chief cantor," although most of them were the only cantors in their synagogues.

The Jewish press, too, abounded in "chiefs." Every Jewish paper, even the smallest one, had an "editor-in-chief," even though no "editor" was working under him. In a word, while Hungarian society as a whole was enamored of titles, the Jews were even more so.

The foregoing remarks must by no means be interpreted as indicating a negative attitude on my part to Hungarian Jewry as a whole. True, I found quite a number of things to criticize in its thinking and acting, especially the opposition of its majority to Zionism, its hesitance in joining forces with world Jewry, its Marranistic assimilationism to Magyardom, its almost compulsive need unceasingly to emphasize its overriding Hungarian patriotism, and, on a different level, its tireless chasing after titles and servile respect for them. But all this impinged no more than marginally on my attitude to Hungarian Jewry, which, on the whole, was one of admiration. I admired it, because, from whatever perspective I possessed at the time, I saw it as one of the most talented constituent communities of the Jewish people, and the front-runner in all Hungarian cultural, economic, scientific, scholarly, literary, and artistic endeavors.

I took great pride in the fact that Theodor Herzl, the founder of political Zionism, was born and grew up in Budapest, and that his first lieutenant and heir as president of the World Zionist Organization, Max Nordau, who was, in addition, one of the great figures on the European literary scene, was also born and bred in the Hungarian capital. I took pleasure in finding evidence for the role Hungarian Jews played in Jewish scholarship, and that the heads of the leading Jewish theological schools in Europe — Samuel Krauss in Vienna, Michael Guttmann in Breslau, and Adolf Büchler in London — were graduates of my own *alma mater*, the Budapest Rabbinical Seminary, and thus, in a sense, colleagues of mine. When I became a student at the universities of Budapest, Breslau, and Jerusalem, I noted with satisfaction that in all three of those seats of learning the names of Armin Vámbéry and Ignaz Goldziher, both Jews and professors at the Budapest University, were often mentioned, and always with the greatest respect. And, of course, I delighted in the fact that, as already mentioned, the first three professors at the Hebrew University were Hungarian Jews. To be a son of this particular tribe of the Jewish people meant a lot to me, and when the resolve matured in me to become a scholar, the images of the great Hungarian Jewish masters of the past two generations were before my eyes, and they were the great exemplars whom I wanted to follow.

My admiration for the Hungarian Jewish cultural achievement was, of course, nurtured by the atmosphere in Father's house, in which Jewish writers, scholars, and artists were frequent visitors. I mentioned earlier in this book the artistic evenings organized by Father several times every year, in which some of the foremost Hungarian Jewish and non-Jewish musicians, singers, and actors participated. For months prior to each of those evenings our house was the scene of intensive consultations between Father and the performers who were to appear in them, and of informal rehearsals at which, whenever possible, I sat in. Thus I got to know, or at least see at close quarters, artists whose names shone brightest on the horizon of Hungarian performing arts.

Likewise, through the editorial work of Father, I got acquainted with Jewish poets, including József Kiss, Lajos Palágyi, Henrik Lenkei,

Andor Vér, Zseni Várnai and her husband, Andor Peterdi, Zoltán Somlyó, Mózes Bolgár, and Joseph Holder; and the writers Gyula Csermely, Miklós Hajdu, Andor Gábor, and Jenő Heltai (a cousin of Theodor Herzl). I also met many of the most outstanding Hungarian Jewish painters, among them Gusztáv Magyar-Mannheimer, Mozart Rottman (whose portrait of Mother still hangs in my living room in New York), Lipót Herman and Nándor Katona (both of whose works I still possess), Fülöp Szenes (whose large portrait of Mother decorates the home of my sister in Givatayim, Israel), Armand Schönberger (whose portrait of Father is in my brother Saul's house in Jerusalem); as well as graphic artists including István Zádor, Gyula Zilzer, and Miklós Szines-Sternberg (the works of all three of whom hang in my house in New York), and sculptors Joseph Róna and Ede Telcs (a statue of the latter stands in my sister's house). Among the composers I met I remember Oszkár Dienzl, who set Father's poems to music, and Hugó Kelen, who did the same for some of my sister's verse. And, last but not least, I met several of the leading Hungarian scholars, among them the Islamologist Ignaz Goldziher, the Turcologist Ignác Kúnos, the historian Henrik Marczali, the chemist Ignác Pfeiffer, and the linguist Bernát Munkácsi (whose wife was Mother's cousin).

Growing up as I did in such a culturally saturated home environment I developed not only an appreciation of the artistic, literary, and scholarly world, but also a sense of enjoyment at being, however peripherally, part of it, and, later, a resolve to do my utmost to achieve something in the scholarly field to which I became increasingly committed.

As for the general picture, that is, the share of Jews in the cultural life of Hungary, in the academic professions, and in industry, I could not help becoming aware of it in the last few years of my high school studies, and concerned about it in my senior year (1927–1928). In that year, as the time of our university studies drew nearer, all of us seniors began to worry about our chances of being admitted within the narrow limits of the *numerus clausus*. At the time I was not interested in statistics, and was concerned only about my own chances of admission, but when I returned from Jerusalem to Budapest in 1936, with strong feelings of loyalty to the Hebrew University, I felt I should look into the issue in order to ascertain whether it was possible on that basis to recruit students for what at the time was the only Jewish university in the world.

I found, first of all, that the *numerus clausus* was still in force, although actually the number of Jewish students had not been reduced to the 5 percent mandated by that law. The relevant data were conveniently presented in the *Hungarian Jewish Lexicon* (published in 1929), from which I learned that, in 1924–1925, of the total of 8,544 students at the four Hungarian universities, 1,027, or 12 percent, were Jewish; while at the Technical University of Budapest, of the total of 2,152 students, 194, or 9 percent, were of the "Mosaic faith." Still, the number of Jews who gained admission to the Hungarian institutions of higher learning was grossly inadequate, which became apparent when one considered that of the total of 6,233 students who passed the high school examination in that year no less than 1,593, or 25.5 percent, were Jews, most of whom planned to go on to higher studies, but were barred by the *numerus clausus* law. As a result, a large number of Hungarian Jewish high school graduates went to study abroad, and in 1925 some 1,200 of them were enrolled in universities in Austria, Germany, France, Belgium, Switzerland, Italy, and Czechoslovakia. Most of these, after earning their diplomas, did not return to Hungary, either because they had difficulties with the "nostrification" (the process of acceptance and validation) of their foreign degrees, or because, having tasted life outside Hungary, they preferred to remain abroad. In any case, what the *numerus clausus* actually amounted to was a brain-drain that deprived Hungary of much of its young Jewish talent.

I was aware of this process already in my student days, since several of my classmates who had passed their high school exams together with me in the spring of 1928 had to go abroad to study, and some of them I met during the summer vacations when they returned to their families. I also knew that the work of Hungarian Jewish artists constituted the major channel through which the art of the great world penetrated Hungary. Almost all of them spent shorter or longer periods of their lives abroad, absorbing artistic influences in Austria, Germany, and so forth. After their return they continued to build on the experiences they gained in their contacts with the new artistic directions in those countries, and thus enriched Hungarian art with works that, although often derivative, were original within the Hungarian artistic scene. There were, of course, also many Hungarian Jewish artists who, at an early stage of their career, left Hungary for good, and settled abroad. As the *Hungarian Jewish Lexicon* explained apologetically (on p. 465)—let us remember that to emigrate was considered an unpatriotic act—some of them "when already mature artists, were forced to develop their artistic activities abroad, without, however, severing their connection with the soil of the fatherland. But we also encounter names of others whom the harsh circumstances or the chances of fate swept into *strange lands* [emphasis in the original] already in their early youth, before opportunity opened up at home for unfolding their artistic activity, and who, although of Hungarian origin, did barely or not at all maintain connection with the art of their native land, and exerted no influence on it."

In the *Hungarian Jewish Lexicon* I found that in the 1920s, Hungarian Jewry, which constituted 5 percent of the total population, provided 50.6 percent of all the lawyers in the country, 46.3 percent of the physicians, 41.3 percent of the veterinarians, 34.3 percent of the newspaper editors and journalists, 39.1 percent of the engineers and chemists, 24.5 percent of the singers and musicians, 22.7 percent of the actors, and 16.8 percent of the painters and sculptors. No less than 40.5 percent of all industrial firms were owned by Jews, as were 19.6 percent of the large landed estates, while 26.4 percent of those who either owned or rented small estates were Jews.

No article in the *Lexicon* deals with the emigration of Hungarian Jews, although it was an important sociological phenomenon in the interwar years. Motivating factors were, in addition to the *numerus clausus*, the anti-Semitic waves that ever and again swept over Hungary, and the economic problems faced by the country, which, after World War I, was reduced to about one-third of its former size. Hungary's loss, as far as Jewish emigration was concerned, became the gain of other countries. I was convinced of two things: that the Jews were the economically and culturally most active element in Hungary, playing a role by far exceeding their proportion in the general population; and that, in a global perspective, Hungarian Jewry was the most talented group among all the Jewish communities of the world.

Literary Contacts

One of the brightest rising stars on the Hungarian literary horizon whose acquaintance I made in those months in Budapest was Károly Pap (1897–1945), who, in the course of the few years still left him between 1936 and the Nazi Holocaust, came to be recognized as one of the foremost novelists of the new generation. When I met him I did not know how old he was; his youthful looks and demeanor made me feel that we were more or less of the same age; in fact, he was thirteen years older. He had published, just a year prior to our meeting in my parents' house, an essay of eighty-seven pages entitled *Zsidó sebek és bűnök* (Jewish Wounds and Sins: A Polemical Essay with Special Reference to Hungary; Budapest: Cosmos Publishers, 1935), in which he ruthlessly exposed and castigated the self-deception practiced by the Hungarian Jews, which was manifested in their constantly reiterated assertion that they were fully accepted in Hungary as Hungarians in every respect, and that they differed from the Christian Hungarians in nothing but religion.

In that rather peculiar piece of writing, Károly Pap first reviewed, from a highly individual point of view, biblical history and the role of the major biblical figures such as Moses and Ezra in the foundation of Judaism, then went on to devote quite some space to Jesus, and finally offered some highly critical observations on both Hungarians and Jews. He wrote (in my literal translation from the Hungarian):

> The role of Jews in the history of Magyardom is the faithful reflection of the deficiencies of Magyardom.
> That is to say:
> The leading role of Jewry in Hungarian economic life is the reflection of the economic impotence of Magyardom.
> The leading role of Jewry in the organization of Hungarian culture of the most recent age is the reflection of the impotence of Magyardom in cultural organization.
> Finally:
> The leading role of Jewry in the Hungarian revolutions of the modern period is naturally a consequence of the preceding two:
> A nation that is impotent in economic and cultural organization is incapable of renascence.

Károly Pap's attitude to Zionism was humanitarian, idealistic, and unrealistic. After criticizing the motivations of Hungarian Jews in going to Palestine, he stated in one sentence what the role of "the New Zion" should be. What he had to say on this subject he considered so basic that he put it in italics: *"I cannot imagine the new Zion in any other manner but as a country that, on a small scale, will first bring into being the United World States, where the Hungarian Jew together with the Rumanian and the Czech Jew, the German Jew with the French Jew, will, in a small country, first attempt world harmony."*

As for the Jewish problem in Hungary, the only solution for it envisaged by Károly was the acceptance of the fate of a national minority, as was done in countries to the east of Hungary. Needless to say, such views were anathema for the Hungarian Jewish leaders, who rejected and condemned them with great indignation. They also caused no little tension between Károly and his father, Dr. Miksa Pollák (1868–1944), who was the chief rabbi of Sopron, a noted historian of Hungarian Jewry, and a student of the influence of the Bible on Hungarian poets.

Károly, who had Magyarized his name from Pollák to Pap, had, by 1936, an eventful life behind him that included precipitous ups and downs. As a very young man he had become an officer in the Austro-Hungarian army and was decorated for bravery in World War I. After his demobilization he joined the Communist revolution led by Béla Kún, and became an officer in the Hungarian Red Army. When the short-lived Hungarian Soviet Republic of 1919 collapsed, Károly was arrested, tried, and condemned to eighteen months' imprisonment. Following his release he left Hungary, and lived abroad until 1925. Returning to Budapest, he began to publish poetry and stories, and soon made himself a name in literary circles. His first novel, *Megszabaditottál a haláltól* (You Have Delivered Me from Death), published in 1932, dealt with a Jewish Messiah in the days of Jesus, was acclaimed by Hungarian critics, and won him the friendship and encouragement of Zsigmond Móritz, the celebrated Hungarian writer. My father, too, was impressed by Károly, and published several of his short stories from 1934 on.

In 1937 Károly Pap published what came to be generally considered his most important book, *Azarel*, an autobiographical novel that pictured his father's house as seen through the eyes of a child. Again, the cruel frankness of this book aroused much antagonism, and Károly became definitely a *persona non grata* as far as the Jewish establishment was concerned. Nevertheless, during World War II, two of his plays were performed by the Budapest Jewish Theater. In 1944, when the Germans occupied Hungary, Károly was sent to a labor camp, where he refused to make use of an opportunity to escape. He was deported to Buchenwald, and is presumed to have died in Bergen-Belsen in 1945. His father had perished a year earlier in Auschwitz.

During my stay in Budapest I read one of Károly's stories, but beyond the fact that it had a biblical theme I remember only that I disliked it because in it God was referred to as "the Thunderer," "the Avenger," or by other such names, and appeared as a sinister deity against whose wrath the chief protagonist of the story battled in vain. One day, while Károly visited Father, we were introduced, and, inevitably, started to discuss his story. I criticized the manner in which it depicted God within a biblical context, as a wrathful, merciless, in fact cruel, deity. I told Károly that from what I gathered from my reading of the Bible—and, in case he was unaware of it, I let him know in no uncertain terms that I was quite a student of the Bible—God was shown in it to be *ḥanun w'raḥum*, merciful and compassionate, that the relationship between God and the people of Israel was one of mutual love, that the two pivotal commandments in the Bible were "love thy neighbor as thyself" and "love the Lord thy God with all thy heart, all thy soul, and all thy being," and that the single sentence "He [God] visiteth the sins of the fathers upon the sons" in no way invalidated the general picture of a people loving its God and firmly believing that God loved the people. I concluded by asserting firmly that therefore Károly's Thunderer-God, of whom the people in his story lived in utter terror, simply did not exist. Regrettably, I can no longer remember what he replied and how he defended his depiction of the biblical God as a menace.

Among the writers of the older generation whose acquaintance I made during those six months of my sojourn in Budapest were the cousins Baron Lajos (Ludwig) and Baron Bertalan (Bertram) Hatvany. The very numerous and prominent Hatvany family traced its descent to Ignác Deutsch (1803–1873), who in the 1820s established a sugar refinery in Arad. He had two sons, Bernát and Joseph. Joseph's son Sándor (1852–1912), and Bernát's son Joseph II (1858–1913) collaborated in developing the firm, originally called Ignác Deutsch and Sons, not only into one of Hungary's most important industries with numerous plants all over the country but also into a power in the world sugar market. Together with other cousins, these third-generation Deutsches also founded and developed dozens of large breweries, tanneries, and steam mills. Sándor Deutsch also founded the Union of Hungarian Manufacturers. For these achievements, both he and Joseph II were first granted nobility ("de Hatvan") by King-Emperor Francis Joseph I, and subsequently created barons, and made members of the Upper House of the Hungarian Parliament. Both cousins used much of the huge fortunes they accumulated to support Hungarian literary, artistic, and cultural endeavors, and also generously contributed to Jewish charitable and cultural institutions. Baron Sándor Hatvany-Deutsch de Hatvan was also a writer himself; his studies on economic problems were published in the foremost periodicals of Hungary.

While the Barons Sándor and Joseph II remained faithful to Judaism, they did not transmit the same loyalties to their children. The two sons of Sándor, Baron Lajos Hatvany (1880–1961) and the painter and art collector Baron Ferenc Hatvany (1881–1958), not only dropped the "Deutsch" part from their names, but also converted to Christianity. The same step was taken by two daughters of Baron Joseph Hatvany, the author and playwright Baroness Lili Hatvany and the political writer Baroness Antonia Hatvany-Deutsch, several of whose books, written jointly with Frances Alice Kellor, and dealing with the League of Nations, were published in English in New York. Only their younger brother, the industrialist and writer Baron Bertalan Hatvany (1900–1980), remained Jewish. Of Lili Hatvany let me mention only that her first play, performed in the prestigious Inner City Theater of Budapest in 1918, when she was but twenty-eight years old, was a sensational success. It was followed by several similarly successful plays that secured her an outstanding place in the Hungarian theater, second only to that of another Hungarian Jewish playwright, the world-famous Ferenc Molnár. Some of Lili Hatvany's plays were translated into German and English, while she herself translated into Hungarian Anita Loos's *Gentlemen Prefer Blondes*.

Of the entire highly talented and successful Hatvany clan the most famous and acclaimed was the playwright, novelist, and literary historian Baron Lajos Hatvany. When still young he was one of the founders of *Nyugat* (West), the monthly that, under the editorship of Hugó Ignotus (pen name of Hugó Veigelsberg, 1869–1949), yet another Hungarian Jewish writer of prominence, became the foremost literary journal in Hungary and the forum for young writers and poets, including Endre Ady, the greatest modern Hungarian poet. Before and during World War I, Lajos Hatvany himself edited several Hungarian dailies and journals, and under the short-lived Károlyi regime of 1918 he became a member of the National Council. At the outbreak of the Communist revolution of 1919, Hatvany left for Vienna, where he published critical articles about the reactionary "White" Hungarian government that came into power after the defeat of the Communists. This government considered Hatvany's articles treasonous and an "offense against the nation," which meant that return to Hungary was tantamount to certain arrest and probable conviction for Hatvany. Nevertheless, return he did, voluntarily, in 1927; he stood trial, and was sentenced to four years in prison, which the high court reduced to eighteen months. While in Vienna, and also after his return to Budapest, Hatvany wrote numerous articles on the relationship of Jewry to Magyardom, and on the problems of Zionism, assimilation, and conversion. He also authored numerous plays and novels in both German and Hungarian, including his *magnum opus*, the trilogy entitled *Urak és emberek* (Lords and Men), which was published from 1927 on, and whose first volume also appeared in an English translation in 1931 under the title of *Bondy Jr.* This trilogy is semiautobiographical, depicting the rise and the struggle for assimilation of a Hungarian Jewish family. In the preface to the first volume, titled *Zsiga in the Family*, Hatvany wrote:

> Principally, however, I want to write about the Jews, the most vividly seething inhabitants of the capital city, who, on the basis of their birth, their programmatic education that made them into zealous Hungarians, and their activity that, according to the contemporary newspapers, was proclaimed to be "patriotic, in the public interest, and beneficial," claimed the right to the happy self-deception that they could proclaim the Hungarian land, forced into increased production, their sweet homeland. . . .

The trilogy is written in a bittersweet tone in which the author combines a critical appraisal of the Bondy family's foibles with an apparent personal fondness for its members. The second and third books of the trilogy, which were to be titled *Zsiga in Life*, and *Zsiga in the Castle*, were never completed, but fragments of them were published in 1963 together with the first book, accompanied by a highly appreciative postscript by the Hungarian literary critic László Bóka. Bóka acclaims the novel as the only portrait of the rise of the Hungarian Jewish upper middle class, its struggle with the decadent Hungarian aristocracy, and the ultimate cooperation between the two.

In 1938, because of the growing Nazi threat, Hatvany again emigrated, this time to London, where he spent the years of World War II. Succumbing again to the attraction of Budapest, he returned in 1947, only to be condemned to silence. Some years later he was finally rehabilitated, and even awarded the prestigious Kossuth Prize by the Hungarian Academy of Science.

From 1929 to 1938 Hatvany's home in Budapest was the meeting place for the most outstanding writers, artists, and intellectuals of the period. It was there that Thomas Mann met the Hungarian composer Béla Bartók, to mention only one example of the role his "salon" played in establishing contacts between the Hungarian and foreign intelligentsia. Well known also was the generosity with which Hatvany supported Hungarian poets and writers. One of his most famous protégés, who also enjoyed the support of his cousin Bertalan, was the poet Attila József (1905–1937).

In 1936 Hatvany was working on the second (or perhaps third) volume of his trilogy. Wishing to be authentic in giving details of the Jewish aspects of the life of the family portrayed, Hatvany sought help from Father, and in the first few days of January 1937 came to our home to consult him and to borrow some books. I happened to be present on that occasion, and Hatvany was interested to learn that I was a resident of Jerusalem. Before he left he invited me to pay him a visit on a certain evening a few days later. He lived in a centuries-old house on Castle Hill overlooking the Danube and the Pest side of the city. At the appointed hour I took a bus from our home up the hill. When I arrived at the Hatvany residence, I was first of all impressed by the thick walls and vaulted ceilings of the sixteenth- or seventeenth-century house, its spaciousness, and the fine antique furniture. (It was just the time when I was beginning to have an eye for antiques.) I was led into the "salon" by a footman, and was received in the most friendly and informal manner by the baron and the baroness. Apart from me there was only one other guest present, Béla Reinitz, the well-known composer who had set to music many of the poems of Endre Ady.

What we discussed during the evening has long ago escaped me, except for two scenes. One was that, at the request of our hostess, Reinitz sat down to the piano and recited some of his Ady songs, accompanying himself as he sang. He had a rough, hoarse voice, probably ruined by years of smoking, but the pathos of his delivery was irresistible. Some of those melodies still reverberate somewhere in the back of my mind. At one point the young son of the Hatvanys, clad in pajamas, came in, sat down and listened for a while, and then politely said good night, and withdrew. After he left, Baroness Hatvany told me that some years earlier, when the boy was four or five, he had done the same thing, and had come in as Reinitz was singing an Ady poem that tells about the poet passing a wheat field and seeing the peasant women working with their sickles. The poem ends with the outcry, *S a lábuk térdig meztelen* (And their legs are naked to the knee), which in Reinitz's musical setting is repeated with a resounding *crescendo* of pain and passion. When the song was finished, the boy said, to nobody in particular, "But why must one yell so loudly that their legs are naked to the knee?" The baroness's presentation of the childish incomprehension of the desire surging out of the line created considerable hilarity in the little company.

The other moment I remember is that at one juncture, while the baroness and Reinitz were discussing some musical point, I asked Lajos Hatvany whether he would mind answering a somewhat personal question that had bothered me ever since I had first read him and learned about his life. "Not at all," he answered, and I asked, with some diffidence, why he had returned voluntarily to Hungary, knowing that he would have to face trial and a possible jail sentence. Instead of answering directly, Hatvany said, "Come with me!" and led me to one of the windows, drew aside its heavy burgundy velvet drapes, and pointed to the fabulous vista of the broad Danube with the pearllike strings of lights along its banks and the glittering rows of lamps marking the avenues and boulevards of the city. The nocturnal panorama spread out below us like a fairyland. For a moment both of us stood still, drinking in the magic of the scene, and then Hatvany said, "I just could not continue to live without all this!" What he meant by "all this" was not at all clear, but I was too shy to ask. Was it merely the beauty of the cityscape, or life in the Hungarian capital, in which he was one of the most celebrated authors and in which his fortune enabled him to live like a prince? I shall never know. What I do know, having since read his brief biographical entries in the Hungarian encyclopaedias, is that he was irresistibly drawn back to Budapest not once but several times, and was unable to keep away from the city even though returning to it meant hardship, humiliation, and loss of liberty in more senses than one. The last time, after having survived World War II in England, the sixty-seven-year-old Hatvany again felt impelled to return to a Hungary in the grip of a Communist regime that was opposed to everything he had stood for all his life and that for years was to deprive him, if not of physical freedom, of the freedom to speak and to publish. This irresistible attraction that Hungary exercised upon some of its emigrant sons was, incidentally, given wonderful poetic expression by Endre Ady in one of his famous poems in which he compares himself to a stone that, even though flung up into the air again and again, inevitably falls to earth. In the last two years of his life Hatvany had at least the satisfaction of being granted recognition by the Communist incarnation of his beloved country.

My brief encounter with Lajos's cousin, Baron Bertalan Hatvany, was of an entirely different nature. While I was only superficially acquainted with the novels of Lajos Hatvany, and even had I known them better I would have had little to say about the work of one of Hungary's most acclaimed novelists, Bertalan Hatvany worked in a field in which I was much more at home, or at least felt I was — the cultural history of the East, including that of the Jews. Also, for some reason I cannot fathom, while I have retained no visual memory at all of Baron Lajos and his wife, I would still instantly recognize Baron Bertalan if I were to meet him today, after the passage of fifty years. He was a tall, heavyset man, in his mid-thirties at the time, with a somewhat stooping posture that gave the impression that his head was too heavy for him to hold up, and massive and pudgy facial features with a nose that was aquiline, large, and fleshy.

Bertalan had not only remained Jewish, but was a member of the Pro Palestine Federation of Hungarian Jews organized by Father in the 1920s. As far as Palestine and Zionism were concerned, he exemplified that type of Hungarian Jew to attract whom and to gain whose support Father had organized the Federation. Hungarian Jews, such as Bertalan Hatvany, would never have become members or supporters of the Zionist organization, because their entrenched Hungarian patriotism forced upon them a narrow view that made it psychologically impossible for them to identify with Zionism's political aims. But they could be interested in the cultural work of the *yishuv*, and could be persuaded to support it with their name and money. Typical of Baron Bertalan's position was the statement he made in the course of a lecture he gave in the fall of 1929 to the OMIKE (initials of the Hungarian name of the National Hungarian Israelite Educational Union), an organization of the official Hungarian Jewish establishment. The lecture was subsequently published by Father in the December 1929 issue of his journal under the title "Impressions of Jews, Arabs, and Others from an Oriental Journey." Hatvany's credo was contained in the following statement:

I emphasize repeatedly that this new Jewish nation (which is being born in Palestine) does not comprise, cannot comprise, that part of Jewry that today is Jewish purely religiously, and therefore the fact that that nation is taking shape down there cannot clash with the patriotic feelings of anybody, for Palestine does not deprive the European nations of their Jewish members who are deeply rooted in them, but, on the contrary, Zionism wants to ease their situation by putting the unabsorbable elements down there to the service of new and great human goals.

According to Baron Bertalan, Zionism was for the "unabsorbable elements" (read: the Jews of East Europe), but certainly not for the Hungarian Jews, who were "deeply rooted" in their Hungarian patriotism. And yet, *nota bene*, Bertalan Hatvany was one of the best of the Hungarian Jewish aristocracy, one of the few who, within their self-imposed limits, were willing to lend their support to the *yishuv*, to the "new Jewish nation," which was "taking shape down there," as long as it did not interfere with their own commitment to Magyardom. This was the kind of human material with which Father had to work, and from which he extracted a grudging consent to help the cultural work being done by Jews in "the Holy Land."

As was to be expected, Bertalan Hatvany and his ilk held views close to those of the B'rit Shalom which at the time advocated an Arab-Jewish binational state in Palestine. His interest in Jewish Palestine extended so far that he took Hebrew lessons, one of the very few Hungarian Jews to do so. My good friend Illés Tisbi (who later, as Isaiah Tishby, was to become a professor of Jewish mysticism at the Hebrew University of Jerusalem) tutored him in private lessons, at the recommendation of Father. Bertalan Hatvany was interested in Asia, traveled in various parts of that continent including China and Palestine, and wrote several books on its culture and history. At the time I met him in Budapest he had just finished writing a major work, a 450-page book (in Hungarian) entitled *Ázsia lelke* (The Soul of Asia), in which, as he stated in the introduction, he intended "to mirror the spirit of Asia not with the means of strict science, but in pen-pictures. The methods of science result in a photograph. The writer of these lines wants to paint the soul." And he added, "If this book succeeds in advancing the understanding of the cultures that are rooted in a millennial past and of the soul of integral Asia, then, the author believes, he has fulfilled his duty." The book as a whole is the result of the literary wanderings of a well-informed and level-headed dilettante across the breadth and width of Asia, scanning its history from earliest times to the present, with brief stopovers in those places and periods that attracted him and that he thought significant. Mesopotamia, Iran, India, Tibet, China, the Arab world, and Japan all have their moments in the book, in which vague generalizations alternate with good insights, but which nevertheless is unified by the sincere endeavor to understand and to present the essential elements underlying the many cultural manifestations of that huge continent.

One day in 1936 my parents and I attended a lecture given by Bertalan Hatvany. I recall nothing of his talk, but I do remember that, when he finished, the floor was thrown open to questions and comments, and that I contributed my two bits' worth by pointing out that Oswald Spengler in his *Decline of the West* said this and that, which had such and such a bearing on certain issues raised by the speaker. Had this scene not remained in my memory, I would have no recollection at all that by the age of twenty-five I had read Spengler.

After the lecture, Hatvany, my parents, and I stood around for a while, engaging in further discussions of his talk, and it turned out that he had read, and remembered the contents of, my articles that were published shortly before in the *Pester Lloyd*. He seems to have been impressed by them, and asked me whether I would be interested in reading, and commenting upon, the chapter on the Jews and their return to Palestine that formed part of his book *The Soul of Asia*. I willingly agreed, and within two or three days I received the manuscript of the chapter entitled "The Wandering People Returns Home." It comprised some thirty typewritten pages, which I read rapidly, finding some things in it to which I took exception, but, all in all, I liked it quite well. I was especially impressed by his presentation, in the brief compass of four or five pages, of the ideas of the two great eighteenth-century reformers of Judaism, Yisrael Baal Shem Tov, the founder of Hasidism, and Moses Mendelssohn, the originator of the *Haskala*, the Jewish Enlightenment.

The last ten pages of the chapter dealt with Zionism, and in them Hatvany revealed himself as a full adherent of the cultural and sociological aspects of that movement, and, with certain modifications, also embraced the political ideology underlying it. He wrote (pp. 390–91):

After the tragic exhaustion of the absorptive power of the central European nations, the only remedy for the radicalization of Jewry is the development of the Jewish people of the Holy Land. Thereafter, the number of Jews remaining in Europe will no longer be so great that it should not be possible to cope with it by means of the hoped-for resuscitation of the absorptive capacity of the peoples. With hatred, persecution, it is not possible to achieve beneficial results in this question. Only intellectual and economic development, and the striving for understanding, can yield satisfactory results.

The clarification of the questions is in the interest equally of Jewry and of the European peoples. The peoples cannot bear the unnatural situation in which a disproportionate share of their economic life and intellectual manifestations should be in Jewish hands; while Jewry cannot bear the likewise impossible situation that its social structure should be based almost exclusively upon men who have found — or can no longer even find — positions in commercial life and in the liberal professions. . . . The task of Jewry cannot be that, over and above a certain intellectual importation — which only enriches the mother-people — it should exert a decisive influence on the fate and development of the European nations. The task of the Jews is to find the path leading back to themselves and to the Jewish soul, and to reciprocate with their own spiritual values for the human rights accorded them by the mother-peoples. Mainly, it cannot be the task of the Jewry of the future to deny itself and to make itself the object of public hatred by loudly propagating a muddy and harmful materialism. *The so-called "Jewish materialism" is not a Jewish idea, but a product of Jewish disintegration* [emphasis in the original] that not only poisons European thought but also attacks the healthy Asiatic roots of Judaism. The aim of Judaism is to serve humanity; it can pursue this aim only if it remains faithful to itself, and not if it becomes the unbidden pettifogger of confused revolutionary ideas. Jewry should become a bridge between Asian tradition and European civilization (Zionism, in fact, aspires to filling this role), and not a bridge between the past and the future of Europe. The European Jew should strive to *understand* [emphasis in the original] the mentality of his fatherland a hundred percent, for he has no title at all to changing it. A human group that has come from a strange country can serve a nation even if it does not strive to hide under a bushel its own mental dissimilitude. What should become common is not the effectuation of half-baked assimilation, but the straightforward and honest application of values, and thus a Jewish nation developing in Palestine and the honest labor of men of the Jewish religion living amongst the European peoples could make possible, with the elimination of all rootless and harmful half-products, the solution of the Jewish question. How did Theodor Herzl say? "If you will it, it is no tale."

If we make the effort to penetrate behind the less than felicitous style and the convoluted manner in which Bertalan Hatvany expresses his ideas, we find that his thinking stood halfway between that of Jacob Klatzkin and Simon Dubnow, although I doubt that he was familiar with the writings of either of them. Klatzkin's "negation of the Galuth" denied the possibility of any future for Jews as a national group in the countries of the Diaspora, while Dubnow and Chaim Zhitlowsky were the fathers of the ideology of "Galuth nationalism," which held that the Jews the world over constituted a nation and that they must be recognized as such and given cultural autonomy by the states in which they lived. Hatvany advocated a retention of the Jewish mental specificity in the European countries (America at the time was beyond his ken), but felt that the number of Jews in them should be reduced, and that the surplus—the "unassimilables"—should go and build their own nation in Palestine. He viewed the "settlement work in the Holy Land" with sympathy and even pride, described it in glowing colors in his book, and expressed the conviction that it redounded to the advantage of both the Jews and the European nations.

After reading the chapter he gave me, I met Hatvany once more, in the editorial offices of Father's journal. I gave him my comments, suggested some changes, mostly in emphasis, and complimented him on his understanding of the complex issues of the differences between Jewish identity in Eastern and West-Central Europe. Soon thereafter I left for Palestine, and it was some two years later that I obtained a copy of his book and read it in its entirety. By that time I had forgotten my comments, and thus I was not able to tell whether or not Hatvany had taken them into account.

Let me add here the little I know of what happened to Bertalan Hatvany in the ensuing years. His book *Ázsia lelke* was published in Budapest. The year of publication is stated nowhere in the book, but it must have been 1938. Hatvany left Hungary in 1939 (as did, coincidentally, my parents), spent some time in Australia, and then settled in Paris. As late as in 1957 his Hungarian translation of *Tao-te-Ching* was published under the title *The Book of the Way and the World*. I do not know what happened to him thereafter, except that he died in 1980 in Paris.

In an earlier chapter of this book I spoke about the memorable lecture on Jewry and the Land of Israel given by Protestant Bishop Dezső Baltazár in 1933. Following that lecture Father, who continued to maintain contact with him, raised the idea that the bishop should visit Palestine and be awarded, on that occasion, an honorary degree by the Hebrew University. Baltazár responded to the idea enthusiastically, but his failing health prevented the plan from coming to fruition. In the spring of 1936 I took a group of Hungarian tourists to the Holy Land, and, probably at Father's suggestion, sent a greeting to the ailing bishop in the name of the Hungarian "pilgrims." It was during my stay in Budapest later that year that Baltazár's reply, forwarded from Jerusalem, reached me. It was dated Debrecen, July 12, 1936, and read as follows (in my literal translation):

My Dear Scholarly Friend:

The greetings and blessings that you so kindly sent me in the name of the Hungarian sons of the Holy Land's Jewry were like the balm of Gilead on the wounds I had sustained in the many great fights I fought in defense of the eternal truths of the Holy Scripture and of the heirs of those truths. What I was I am, and remain, and [here the bishop quoted in Hebrew Psalms 27:1 and 3] "The Lord is my light and my salvation; whom shall I fear? The Lord is the stronghold of my life; of whom shall I be afraid? . . . Though a host should encamp against me, my heart shall not fear, though war should rise up against me, even then will I be confident." [Then he continued in Hungarian:]

May the Lord, our common God, the one and same Father of all peoples, bless all of you, and may He grant you that [and here again follows a quote in Hebrew from Psalm 126:5] "They that sow in tears shall reap in joy."

With love and blessings,

Dr. Dezső Baltazár

Father published the letter in the September 1936 issue of *Mult és Jövő*, and in the same issue he printed a brief notice about the death of the bishop, who had succumbed to a lingering illness a few weeks earlier. In the October issue Father published a selection from the letters Bishop Baltazár had written him in the course of eighteen years, from 1918 to 1936. Apart from the one occasion in 1933 when my parents gave a reception for the bishop and when I attended his lecture, I never met him personally. Nor did I at the time, preoccupied as I was with my own problems and plans, take an interest in the remote and rather forbidding figure of that Protestant prince of the church. But now, rereading his 1933 address about the Jews and the Land of Israel, and the letters he wrote to Father, I get a belated sense of a man of sincere humanity, and a deeply religious believer in the one God whose common fatherhood inevitably renders all men brothers.

What to Do Next?

What to do next was the most serious problem that preoccupied my brother Guszti at the time I arrived back in Budapest in June 1936, and it was to become an increasingly burning issue for me as the months of my visit to my hometown drew to a close.

My brother, eight years my junior, had started to attend the *reálgimnázium* of the Israelite Congregation of Pest in the fall of 1928, just a few months after I myself had finished my studies at the same school. Eight years later, in the spring of 1936, he duly passed his high school exams, and was faced with the question of what career to choose. That he would have to go on to university studies was a foregone conclusion, but what field to select was a problem, and a very serious one at that. For reasons I no longer recall he had no inclination to go in for the humanities or social sciences, which left the exact or natural sciences among which to make his selection. What I still remember is that after my return to the bosom of the family, Guszti and I spent many hours discussing the choices that lay open before him, and poring over the catalog of courses offered by the Faculty of Philosophy or the Royal Hungarian Pázmány Péter University of Budapest, trying to decide on his future studies and therewith on the direction his entire life would take. After careful consideration of all the possibilities, it was decided that he would study chemistry.

After writing the foregoing lines I found that Mother in her 1955 reminiscences referred to one such discussion between her and Guszti:

> I remember a stifling summer evening when I went with my son Shaul [in retrospect she calls him Shaul, although at that time all of us still called him Guszti] to take a walk in the nearby park. I told him that we should actually be in Eretz Israel, and asked whether he would want to devote himself, together with a literary editor, to the journal, which one could not simply give up. Without a moment's hesitation he answered with a decisive "no." No, no, no, no, Europe was sick, and he wanted to go to Jerusalem to study chemistry. Enough of literature in the family! Enough, he added as if in conclusion. In me there was a vague fear, a terrible insecurity. Yes, one should finish and be done with Europe, with this mendacious liberalism that was breathing its last.

However, in 1936 it was not yet feasible for Guszti to enroll at the Hebrew University. Although Dr. Andor Fodor had been professor of chemistry ever since it first admitted students in 1925, there was, even ten years later, as yet no complete department of chemistry in which a student could get a well-rounded education in the most important branches of that rich science. So, as far as choosing a school was concerned, there was no feasible alternative to Budapest. Guszti duly submitted his application, was admitted, and studied for two years at the Faculty of Philosophy there. A few pages later Mother describes a painful experience Guszti had that took place at an unspecified time during his two years at Budapest University:

> Shaul as a rule returned late from the University, so that we did not wait for him with the lunch. But one day he came home much earlier than usual. His face was deadly pale, he seemed to have aged years. There was a brawl, a Jew-baiting that, although it ended without bloodshed, was demeaning and shattering. He himself was in the thick of things, but was not personally attacked. A powerful giant of a youth, whose parents had converted long before, stood next to him, and, beating with his fist on his breast, cried, "Hit me, hit me, I, too, am of Jewish descent!" But his voice was swallowed up in the general tumult, and his friends pulled him away. "Are you crazy?" they whispered to him. "Keep quiet, for goodness sake!" Shaul emerged, untouched in body, but so depressed that we were worried about him. "You see, Mother," he said bitterly, "this is how the Galuth [exile] looks. Now we see its true face. . . . There are those who want to hold out, perhaps they will even succeed, but I don't want to, I cannot. . . . " So Shaul too went. . . . Now our house was empty. . . .

Guszti finished his sophomore year just a few weeks after the *Anschluss* of Austria by Hitler (which took place on March 13, 1938), and this ominous political development could not fail to impress those among the Hungarian Jews who were not completely under the spell of wishful thinking with the dangers a common border with Nazi Germany meant for Hungary's Jews. Although Father himself was not yet ready to leave Hungary even after the *Anschluss*, he had no objection when Guszti announced that he wanted to go to Palestine without further delay.

As for my own problem of what to do next, it was, of course, no longer one of what to study, but of how and where to find employment. As the weeks and months passed, I became increasingly uneasy about how I would earn a living once I passed my exams, received my diplomas, and thus brought to a close my formal education of twenty years. There were many talks on the subject with my parents, in which many avenues were considered only to be dismissed. It is characteristic of the atmosphere both in Hungary in general and in my parents' house in particular that in the course of these discussions never was even a moment's consideration given to the possibility of finding a position for me in Budapest or elsewhere within the borders of Hungary. The immediate reason for this may have been my determination not to take a rabbinical post, which reduced my chances in Hungary to practically nil. But I suspect that there was more to it, and that both my parents and I ruled out Hungary because of the uncertainty that beclouded the future of Hungarian Israel. Still, the same *a priori* exclusion did not seem to apply to neighboring countries, which, in the event, fell victim to Hitler's aggression years before Hungary.

Thus one of Father's ideas that we discussed briefly was that he would contact Abraham Stiebel, the Polish Jewish industrialist who was a generous supporter of Hebrew literature, and founder-owner of the Stiebel Publishing Company in Warsaw, an illustrious name in the Hebrew book world. During the early part of my sojourn in Budapest Mr. Stiebel and his wife Svetlana paid a visit to the city, met Father and me, and seemed to have been impressed with me as a young Jewish scholar and Hebrew *littérateur*. Now Father suggested that he would make a long-distance phone call to Warsaw to talk to Mr. Stiebel about my career plans. This, Father thought, would certainly result in an offer to me of a position in his publishing house. I, however, turned down the idea, and told Father that I would like to quote to him the talmudic saying I had quoted shortly before to Dr. Magnes, the chancellor of the Hebrew University, when he suggested that, having become the first doctor of the University, I should now seek a position in Hungary, where I could be a leading spokesman of Zionism and the *yishuv*. My answer to Dr. Magnes was, "Our sages said, 'Better to live in the deserts of the Land of Israel than in palaces abroad.' " I repeated the quotation to Father, who, of course, had no argument against a position that he himself had brought me up to embrace. So the Warsaw idea was dropped. Some five or six years later, when news of the fate of Polish Jewry after the German invasion of Poland began to reach Palestine, I more than once reflected that had the "Stiebel connection" worked out, I would, in all probability, have been one of the victims of the Nazi Holocaust.

A second idea that was considered, again briefly, in the Patai family council in that fall of 1936 was that I go to Karlsbad, Czechoslovakia, to serve as assistant rabbi to Chief Rabbi Ignaz Ziegler (1861–1948). Dr. Ziegler, a fellow graduate of the Budapest Rabbinical Seminary, was getting on in years, was about to retire (or, perhaps, having reached the age of seventy-five, had already retired), and Father judged my chances excellent to win the position, and then to succeed Dr. Ziegler within a foreseeably short time. The position of chief rabbi of Karlsbad was a very highly regarded one; the congregation was German-speaking and thus there would have been no language problem for me. To overcome my persistent reluctance to occupy a pulpit, Father pointed out that Dr. Ziegler was a respected Jewish scholar, the author of several important books, including his most famous *Die Königsgleichnisse im Talmud und Midrash.* "You could preach whenever you chose, and could spend as much time as you wished with your research," Father argued. I must have been tempted, at least to some extent, by these possibilities, for otherwise I would not remember the discussions about them. But in the end my desire to live in Palestine outweighed all other considerations, and I remained unshakable in my resolve to return to Jerusalem as soon as possible. I do not have to point out that the fate that overtook Czechoslovakia's Jewry was scarcely better than that of the Polish Jews.

A third idea of Father's that also was not followed up was to try to find a place for me at the Jews' College in London. Professor Adolf Büchler, principal of Jews' College, was a Hungarian, a graduate of the Budapest Seminary, and a personal acquaintance of Father, who, I believe, published an article about him in his journal. London, I still remember, interested me more than either Warsaw or Karlsbad; to teach at the renowned Jews' College was certainly a more attractive proposition than working in a publishing house or filling a rabbinical position, however respected. In fact, from a letter Mother wrote at that time to my sister in Jerusalem it appears that I mentioned my interest in going to London to Mr. Fischer, the father of Lizi Fischer, whom I had dearly loved and who had died so tragically in 1933 at the age of twenty. Mr. Fischer, in turn, seems to have suggested that I write to a relative of his who lived in London, and Mother, in her letter (left undated, as was her wont) says, "The London relative of the Fischers wrote Gyuri a very friendly letter saying that if he comes to London he can stay with him, and that he will help him in everything. Since there is anyway no longer a chance of a position in Jerusalem for Gyuri, perhaps the opportunity should be taken to acquire a good command of English."

This entire episode had completely escaped me, and had I not happened to find Mother's letter, I should have been sure that I made no move at all in the direction of London. In any case, as far as I remember, we (that is, Father and I) did not follow up the London idea.

What remains interesting in connection with these abortive plans, beyond the personal tribulations they occasioned in the family, is the very fact that they could be broached and discussed at all. They show to what extent Jewish scholarship and rabbinical education were international in character in the pre-World War II period. Linguistic boundaries did, of course, exist, but to overcome them was no great problem for a young Jewish scholar. In fact, graduates of the Budapest and Breslau rabbinical seminaries found their way not only to all German-speaking lands, but also beyond them, to France, Italy, England, and America. But, as far as I was concerned, the only place in the sun I wanted for myself was under the hot sky of Palestine.

Seeing that I could not be swayed from my determination to return to Jerusalem, Father thenceforward tried to find a way of securing for me some kind of a scholarly position at the Hebrew University. That, however, was an extremely difficult task. In 1936 the Hebrew University was still a very small institution with no more than perhaps two dozen faculty members, and practically no provisions (except in the exact sciences) for employing young scholars as assistants or in similar initial academic positions. True, I was the first doctor of the University and my doctoral thesis was generally acclaimed as a respectable scholarly achievement, but the reality was that there I stood without any chance to continue my academic career within the narrow framework of the University, at the time the only institution of higher learning in Palestine apart from the Haifa Technion, which offered only technical and engineering courses of study.

But Father was an exceptionally resourceful man, and he found a way to secure for me at least one more year of grace. One day he informed me that he would try to obtain for me a stipend from a private donor that would be given to the Hebrew University as a research fellowship earmarked for me. This, finally, was a plan to which my reaction was enthusiastically positive, and Father proceeded forthwith to put it into effect. Among Father's many admirers in

Hungary was a wealthy Jewish businessman in the provincial town of Kiskunhalas, the owner of a large food-producing and processing establishment. His name, I believe, was Breuer. I don't know his first name. Father phoned him and made an appointment with him for the two of us. A few days later we took a morning train, were met at the Kiskunhalas station by Mr. Breuer with his chauffeur-driven car, and at his suggestion were taken, first of all, to have a look at his plant. It was, I still remember clearly, an astoundingly large factory that must have occupied several acres. We spent quite a long time walking around in it, and I can recall in particular one of its departments in which eggs were preserved prior to sale and shipping. It consisted of dozens of huge open vats or tanks, rising some four feet above the ground, which, at first glance, seemed to be filled with milk. But Mr. Breuer explained that the white liquid was a solution of lime into which the eggs were placed and thus kept fresh for months on end. To demonstrate, he motioned to one of the workers, who thereupon dipped a big ladle into the liquid and fished out a few eggs. There must have been thousands of eggs in each vat.

After the tour of his plant Mr. Breuer took us to lunch, in the course of which Father broached the subject that was the purpose of our visit. He had two suggestions: one, that Mr. Breuer donate a certain amount to the Hebrew University for the purpose of awarding me a research fellowship; and two, that he arrange with the local Jewish community, of which Mr. Breuer seems to have been the president or some other high honorary official, to invite me to give a lecture on Palestine. I remember how impressed I was with Father's ability to present in a most dignified manner what in effect was a request for a sizable donation for personal purposes. That he was able to do this showed his great self-confidence, and that Mr. Breuer readily agreed in principle testified to the great respect and admiration Hungarian Jews in general had for Father. Thereafter Breuer and Father must have discussed the amount in question, but of that I remember nothing. However, I figure that, since the stipend, when I began to receive it from the Hebrew University soon after my return to Jerusalem in January 1937, covered my living expenses for one whole year, it must have been the equivalent of some $5,000 in 1986 money.

Once this matter was settled, the luncheon was a leisurely and protracted one, and at its conclusion it was time for us to return to the railroad station to catch the train back to Budapest. Mr. Breuer took us again in his car, and said he would let me know the date of my lecture. He did, and I duly gave my talk on January 10, 1937, just a day or two before I left Budapest to return to Jerusalem. I do not know what happened to Mr. Breuer subsequently, but I am afraid that he must have been among the victims of the German-Hungarian Holocaust in which some 90 percent of all the Jews of Hungary outside Budapest perished in 1944. After postal communication was restored between Jerusalem and Hungary, I once wrote him a letter, but it remained unanswered, nor was my letter returned to me.

As for the fellowship, it was expeditiously approved by the Hebrew University, the money was transferred from Hungary to Jerusalem — such transfers were still legal at the time in Hungary — and the February 1, 1937, issue of the Tel Aviv daily *Davar* and the February 4 issue of the *Palestine Post* carried brief items to the effect that a research fellowship in Palestinology was established at the Hebrew University, and Dr. Raphael Patai, the first doctor of the University, was selected as its recipient. The name of the donor who endowed the fellowship was not mentioned.

The Hungarian Israelite Society for the Support of Holy Land and Other Settlements

Coincidentally with my visit to Budapest a shift took place in the attitude of the Hungarian Jewish establishment with reference to the problems the young Jewish generation increasingly faced in Hungary. Its leadership at long last was forced to recognize that the position of the Jews in the country was not as solidly entrenched as it had believed — and proclaimed even more fervently than believed — ever since the emancipation of Hungarian Jewry in 1867, or, at least, since its "Reception" in 1895 as a legally recognized religious denomination. The catalyst for the change was, of course, the German Jewish debacle — up to 1936 it was merely a debacle, the catastrophe was to come later — which left the Hungarian Jewish leadership no choice but to sit up and take notice, although it could still point out with considerable self-assurance that the position of the Jews in Hungary was much better than that of their coreligionists in Germany, and could persist in maintaining that the Hungarian Jews were a more integral part of the Hungarian nation than were the German Jews of the German Reich.

This had been for decades the traditional position of the Hungarian Jewish establishment. It was embraced, in the first place, by the leadership of the Neolog Israelite Congregation of Pest, by far the largest and most influential in the country, accounting as it did for about one-third of all the Jews in Hungary. Psychologically, the patriotic identification of the Jews with the Hungarian nation was made inevitable by that outgrowth of the Jewish proclivity to assimilate to the host-nations that was often commented upon and disparagingly characterized in the old adage that the Jews in every country were like the Gentiles but even more so. Nowhere was this as apparent as in Hungary with reference to patriotic fervor. In the specific Hungarian context it meant that Magyar patriotism was given greater emphasis among the Jewish than among the Christian Hungarians. If the Hungarian attitude was that the Hungarians, as their national anthem put it, had no place in the great world outside Hungary, and that "should the hand of fate bless you or smite you, here you must live and die," this was echoed even more fervently by the Jewish leadership. As early as 1848, when the emancipation of Hungarian Jews was still far in the future, a Hungarian Jew, Sándor Herczfeld by name, published a book entitled *Mi nem megyünk Amerikába, hanem itt fogunk maradni!* (We Don't Go to America, But Shall Remain Here!). A twentieth-century example of the same attitude is represented by the memorial tablet affixed to the house in Budapest in which Ignaz Goldziher made his home in the latter half of his life. It reads (my translation from the Hungarian, in which the quatrain is in hexameter):

> In this house lived for a generation
> Ignácz Goldziher
> university professor

> Night and day here worked, researched the great scholar of the East
> Here matured quietly the great works of his genius
> And while his name spread brilliantly conquering the whole world
> He himself stayed put faithfully on this native soil.

I don't know whether these lines were composed by a Jewish or Christian poet, but, in any case, it was found necessary to mention that the great man "stayed put faithfully on this native soil." To stay at home was considered something laudable, patriotic, and more worth including than a reference to Goldziher's great works that were his equivalents of Virgil's *pascua, rura, duces.*

This remained the often and loudly acclaimed and declaimed posture of "Hungarian Israel," despite the *numerus clausus* law of 1920, the White Terror of the early 1920s, and other painful manifestations of anti-Semitism. It was only the undeniable increase in Jewish emigration, including, in the first place, that of many young Jewish intellectuals and academically trained men, that finally forced the Jewish leadership to take notice of the problem.

Ever since its emancipation, the official position of Hungarian Jewry was that the Jews in Hungary were a religious denomination and nothing else. In this atmosphere Zionism, whose aim was to build a national home for the Jews in Palestine, was doubly anathema: first, because it advocated the emigration of Jews from the countries of their birth to Palestine; and second, because it embraced the doctrine that the Jews were not merely a religious community, but a people dispersed all over the world whose final destiny must be the reestablishment of its ancestral state.

Now, because for many of the young Hungarian Jews emigration was made impossible by insurmountable financial problems, the leadership of the Congregation concluded that it would be a humanitarian act to help them. However, since Zionism still remained the *bête noire* of the Jewish establishment, it did not find it possible to agree to any kind of cooperation with the Hungarian Zionist Organization, or with the Pro Palestine Federation of Hungarian Jews, in which Father was the moving spirit. Instead, Samu Stern, the powerful and autocratic president of the Israelite Congregation of Pest and of the National Bureau of Hungarian Israelites, decided to organize a new body with the avowed purpose of aiding Hungarian Jews who planned to emigrate. The name first considered for the new body was "Society for Settlement in the Holy Land."

Preparations for the establishment of the new society got underway in 1936, while I was still in Budapest. At first it looked as if, finally, the Hungarian Jewish establishment was ready to undertake something akin, at least in its practical aims, to the work pursued by the Zionists. President Stern initiated meetings between leaders of the Israelite Congregation of Pest and those of the Pro Palestine Federation. In the course of these meetings it became evident that the Congregation leaders had several objections to the fund-raising efforts as they were carried out by the Zionist Organization and the Pro Palestine. The objections were partly political and partly organizational. Politically, the position of the Congregation was that there was an irreconcilable contradiction between the Zionist ideology and Hungarian patriotism, and that this made participation by the Congregation in Zionist work impossible. The organizational objection was centered on the question of the right to decide on the disposition of funds raised in Hungary. Monies raised in any country for the Zionist cause were transferred to the Jerusalem headquarters of the Keren Kayemeth (Jewish National Fund) and the Keren Hayesod (Palestine Foundation Fund), whose directorates decided on the manner in which the funds flowing from all parts of the Jewish world were to be utilized. Jerusalem decided who was to be settled on Keren Kayemeth lands, and who was to get financial aid from the Keren Hayesod in building a home and establishing a farm. The leaders of the Pest Congregation found this unacceptable. They argued that those who raised the funds should have the right to dispose of them within the general program of the Jewish national institutions of the *yishuv*.

It so happened that in the spring of 1936 Dr. Sándor Eppler, secretary-general of the Pest Congregation, was a member of the group of tourists led by Father to the Holy Land. On that occasion, Father and Eppler had a meeting with Menahem M. Ussishkin, president of the Keren Kayemeth. At that meeting, Ussishkin, taking into account the special conditions and wishes of Hungarian Jewry, showed himself inclined to have the major part of the monies to be collected in Hungary earmarked for the funding and maintenance of Hungarian Jewish settlements in Palestine. Eppler duly reported back to his president about the understanding with Ussishkin, and this concession on the part of the Keren Kayemeth may have been a factor in Stern's decision to move for talks with the leaders of the Hungarian Pro Palestine Federation, under whose aegis the Zionist fundraising work was conducted.

The best-known symbol of willingness to support this work was the blue money-box of the Keren Kayemeth that was found in many a Jewish household all over the world, including Hungary. Many families that, because of political misgivings, would have been reluctant to join the Zionist Organization accepted the blue boxes, and their small donations added up to quite a respectable amount. The Hungarian Zionist Organization fully cooperated with the Pro Palestine, delegating its best men to the board of directors of the Federation, "through whose intermediacy," as Dr. Julius Miklós, president of the Hungarian Zionist Organization, put it in a letter published in the January 5, 1937, issue of the Berlin *Jüdische Rundschau*, "it actually often found the way to the non-Zionist masses. . . ."

When President Stern initiated consultations with the Pro Palestine, the Zionists welcomed it as a manifestation of a long overdue interest on the part of the Pest Congregation in participating in the "Palestine work." As Father expressed it in an interview with the Budapest correspondent of the *Jüdische Rundschau* (published in its December 30, 1936, issue), he originally "welcomed the initiative that, hopefully, was to realize an idea I had propagated for almost thirty years: to introduce the Palestine idea into Hungarian Jewry that was a stranger to it, and to interest wider circles in the practical aspects of the upbuilding of the Land." Dr. Miklós likewise expressed his willingness to do what he could in order to draw official Hungarian Jewry into the Palestine work.

In the ensuing negotiations President Stern and Dr. Eppler represented the Pest Congregation, while Professor Ignác Pfeiffer, president, Dr. Joseph Patai, executive vice-president, and Baron Bertalan Hatvany, board member, represented the Pro Palestine Federation, and Dr. Miklós represented the Hungarian Zionist Organization. As the negotiations proceeded, however, it became evident that no agreement between the two sides was possible. Stern insisted that the Zionists withdraw from the leadership of the Pro Palestine Federation; that the Pro Palestine desist from fund-raising for the two national funds of the *yishuv*; and that the Pro Palestine cease using the widely known blue collection boxes of the Keren Kayemeth, and instead use its own boxes. The Pro Palestine found these conditions unacceptable. It was forced to recognize that Stern's intention was to gain control of the Pro Palestine Federation, and to make Zionist fund-raising in Hungary difficult, if not impossible. Moreover, as Father stated in the *Rundschau* interview quoted above, "Court Councillor Stern coupled the announcement of the new society with attacks on the Zionists, arguing that the Zionists had launched the fight against the Congregation, and that he would take up the gauntlet."

It so happened that a few weeks prior to these developments, in the fall of 1936, Dr. Arthur Hantke (1874–1955), managing director of the Jerusalem head office of the Keren Hayesod, had visited Budapest and met with President Stern with a view to working out a *modus vivendi* between the Pro Palestine and the new society planned by Stern. However, after the meeting Dr. Hantke had come to the conclusion that, because of the rigid position of the Congregation, collaboration with it seemed impossible.

Unable to bend the Pro Palestine and the Zionists to his will, President Stern proceeded with his plan to set up a new, independent organization in behalf of the Congregation for the support of emigrants. Part of his plan was to introduce new collection boxes, clearly marked as those of the new organization. He took the requisite steps to obtain a permit from the Hungarian authorities for the placing of such boxes in Jewish homes. This step alone was, if not directly calculated, at least liable, to endanger the continuation of the distribution of Keren Kayemeth boxes. For decades, the ministerial permit for these boxes had been renewed from year to year, but, by December 1936, for some unknown reason, it had not yet been issued for 1937. It was to be feared that if the Stern society did succeed in obtaining a permit for its own boxes, the ministry would not issue another permit for an analogous cause, and that, for all intents and purposes, would have meant the end of the Keren Kayemeth collections in Hungary whose main source of income was its blue boxes.

Despite these disquieting developments that took place during the very last days of my sojourn in Budapest, Father had not yet given up hope that an accommodation could be reached between Stern and the Pro Palestine. In any case, he entrusted me, probably with the consent of the other active leaders of the Pro Palestine, with the mission of informing, immediately upon my return to Jerusalem, the Zionist leadership there, as well as the board of the Hitaḥdut 'Ole Hungaria (HOH, Union of Hungarian Immigrants), of which I was a member, of what had transpired in Budapest. Coincidentally, before I arrived back in Jerusalem, the HOH board had received word of the Stern initiative, and, impressed by its seemingly positive orientation, had sent off, early in January, a welcoming and congratulatory cable to Budapest. In the meantime, Dr. Hantke, who already several weeks earlier had come to the conclusion that cooperation with Stern was impossible, had informed Dr. Kurt Blumenfeld (1884–1963), the most influential member of the Keren Hayesod directorate, and one of the most energetic Zionist leaders, first in Germany and then in Palestine, of the Budapest developments. When Hantke and Blumenfeld were notified of the cable and the position of the HOH, they strongly disapproved, and asked for an urgent meeting with the board in order to convince it that it was a grave mistake to approve of an initiative that, as they saw it, was clearly directed against Hungarian Zionism.

The meeting took place on Saturday, January 23, 1937, in the apartment of Dr. Szamecz, a physician and member of the HOH board, in Jerusalem. Present were Chief Engineer Asher (Andor) Koch, director of the Jerusalem waterworks, Dr. Michael Fekete, professor of mathematics at the Hebrew University, and some five or six others whose names I no longer remember. Blumenfeld, Hantke, and I were also present. There was heated discussion about whether the step taken was right or wrong, and I was asked to report about the situation in Budapest, the aims of President Stern, and the reaction of the Hungarian Zionists. In my report, which I gave in Hebrew, I developed the position that I considered the right one and that Father, too shared: that the Zionists must not take any steps against the new society, and therewith *ab ovo* alienate its organizers, but, on the contrary, we should try with gentle persuasion to direct them and lead them toward a constructive participation in the work of settling and building Palestine. After me somebody else (I do not remember who) took the floor, and while he spoke, Dr. Blumenfeld, who happened to sit next to me, whispered in my ear, in German, while his whole body (he was a small and rather corpulent man) shook with excitement and anger, "I cannot understand your position. I am boiling with anger. This is an ideological betrayal. I am ashamed that such a person is our first doctor. I shall fight you as long as I live." I remember the exact words of the last sentence as he spat out the words in German: *Ich werde Sie bekämpfen solange ich lebe!* Then, taking the floor, he said that there had always been Zionists who supported the Palestine actions undertaken by non-Zionists—these were the grave-diggers of Zionism, and true Zionism emerged only from a fight against them.

When the meeting ended, as we were taking leave of one another, Blumenfeld said to me that he wanted to see me before leaving in a few days for Europe, that he wanted to give me a good talking-to; he wanted "to screw off your head; you would remain tall enough even without a head," and added some more such pleasantries. It seemed that he regretted his outburst, and tried to make a jest out of it.

What was the upshot of the meeting? Nothing much concrete. It was resolved to call a general meeting of the HOH, to which a draft letter addressed to Budapest would be submitted for approval.

The letter would state that the sense of the HOH's cable had been that it welcomed the constructive work that the Israelite Congregation of Pest had embarked upon, and hoped that it would conform to the Zionist aims of rebuilding the Holy Land.

The day after the meeting I wrote to my parents describing in detail what had transpired, and asked Father to tell President Stern and Dr. Sándor Eppler that I saved the situation at the meeting, declaring myself for them, and so forth. I told Father that I did not want to write to Stern and Eppler directly, lest the HOH leadership take umbrage at such personal communication. To reassure Mother I added that "one must not take Blumenfeld's outburst seriously, he makes a terribly nervous, almost crazed, impression."

By the time my letter arrived in Budapest, developments had taken place there in connection with the new society that justified Blumenfeld's wrath. In January 1937 the Pest Congregation published in its official organ an appeal in which it invited people to join the new society, informed the public that its program included not only the placement of Hungarian Jewish youth in Palestine, but also the support of emigrants to other countries, and emphasized that the new "action" was totally free of Zionism. This was followed a week later (as reported in the January 15, 1937, issue of the *Jüdische Rundschau*) by the announcement of the definitive name of the new society. It was to be "Hungarian Israelite Society for the Support of Holy Land and Other Settlements."

Although the addition of the words "and other" clearly indicated the intention of the organizers of the new society to put a distance between themselves and Zionism, Father still felt that conciliation was better than fighting, and he told the Budapest correspondent of the *Jüdische Rundschau* that "whether this way or that way, the main thing remains that, instead of discussions, henceforth there should follow work: work for Palestine." Dr. Miklós by that time was totally disillusioned, and stated that he saw in the new society an anti-Zionist demonstration by the Pest Congregation.

Alas, it was again the pessimists who proved right. In the January 22, 1937, issue of the *Rundschau* its Budapest correspondent reported on the constituent meeting of the new society. The great hall of the congregation was filled to capacity. President Stern described the aims of the new society as follows: (1) to support emigration of Hungarian (*sic!*) unemployed to Palestine, and to create agricultural and industrial settlements for them; (2) to support Hungarians who have settled in Palestine; (3) to develop economic ties between Hungary and Palestine; (4) to promote and support emigration of unemployed Hungarians also to other countries. Then, as if the substitution of "Hungarian unemployed" for "Hungarian Jews" were not enough to make the anti-Zionist character of the new society evident, Stern added that with these aims the society wanted to serve, above all, the interests of our native land, without, however, denying its solidarity with the whole of Jewry. He concluded by stating that the first appeal had already resulted in hundreds of applications, and that the organization of provincial chapters was proceeding apace.

After Stern, Dr. Géza Dési, a former member of the Hungarian Parliament, who a few months later was to become the supervisor of education for the Pest Congregation, addressed the gathering, assuring it that the emigrants would remain faithful Hungarian patriots abroad, and would thus serve the homeland there also.

Chief Rabbi Hevesi, who was elected president of the new society, made in his acceptance speech a veiled anti-Zionist comment: "If we are a people, as some maintain, we have the right as a people to work and succeed in Palestine; if we are a denomination, as the Hungarian state laws and legal decisions have it, we can and must secure ourselves a place in Zion at the side of the other denominations."

The pro-Zionist reports in the *Rundschau* of what was going on in Budapest did not, of course, escape the eye of President Stern, who, on January 10, 1937, sent its editor a letter (published in the January 26 issue) in which he marshaled a number of rather ineffective and unimpressive arguments in defense of his point of view. Arguing that he was for unity among all Hungarian Israelites, he said, among other statements, "I subsidized the press organ of the Zionists." In its editorial comment the *Rundschau* pointed out the peculiar mentality underlying this first person singular usage on the part of an elected official of the Congregation, and also took exception to the phrase "unemployed Hungarians" used in the description of the aims of the new society.

The launching of the new society served as an occasion for the leaders of the Israelite Congregation of Pest to attack the Zionists. In its January 12, 1937, issue the *Pester Lloyd* reported that a general meeting of the Congregation had taken place (it does not give the date, but it must have been a day or two earlier) in which Court Councillor Stern played the central role. In his address, Stern

> protested against the Zionist agitation in Hungary, because that was calculated to further the separatist endeavors that were anyhow intent on setting apart Hungarian Jewry from the body of the nation. Hungarian Jews consider themselves, as this has already been stated innumerable times, Hungarian citizens of the Jewish faith, and even if they related to Palestine with the veneration stemming from Jewish tradition, they wished to continue the work of upbuilding of Palestine in the first place for the benefit of those Hungarian coreligionists who wanted to emigrate there. Therefore the official leaders of Hungarian Jewry were now taking over the leadership of the Palestine work, and creating a new organization that will participate in the Palestine work for the support of the interests of Hungarian coreligionists. . . .

The allegation that the Zionists and Zionism were creating a separation between Hungarian Jewry and the Hungarian nation was not only unjust and unfounded, but its purpose was defamatory. The coupling of this accusation with the announcement that from now on the official leaders of Hungarian Jewry would "take over" the leadership of the Palestine work was clearly intended to make the continuation of the activities of the Hungarian Zionist Organization and of the Pro Palestine in support of the *yishuv* difficult if not impossible. What Stern tried to implant into the Jewish consciousness of the country was that the Zionist support of the *yishuv* was unpatriotic, while the "Palestine work" of the new society would redound to the benefit of our "Hungarian coreligionists," and hence of Hungary as a whole.

These developments caused great embitterment in the Zionist leadership of Hungary, and were a great disappointment for Father, who had hoped for many years that the leadership of the Pest Congregation would undergo a change of heart and had worked tirelessly to bring it about. He was too restrained to discuss the matter in detail in his letters to me during that period, but he did refer briefly to the sorry affair in one letter in which he expressed his dissatisfaction with the ineffectual attempts made by Palestinian emissaries to propagate Zionism and raise funds in Hungary for various Palestinian Jewish institutions, mainly for the Hebrew University of Jerusalem. This, incidentally, was one of the few letters Father wrote me in Hungarian (most of his letters to me are in Hebrew and in his own handwriting). It is typewritten, and I assume that he must have dictated it to Mother, who added to it a few lines of her own. Father cautioned me to treat the things he told me in the letter with the utmost discretion.

About the same time Mother, too, discussed the new society in one of her letters. She was both more wordy and more outspoken than Father, and wrote:

> . . . alas, it is not easy to have dealings with Hungarian Jews. Since you left, they launched an attack against the Zionists in their meeting. Géza Dézsi [Dési] said that those young Jews whom they will send to Palestine will remain Hungarians also there, so that this will be a patriotic act. Simon Hevesi became president, little [József] Katona [a young rabbi], secretary. For the time being they do nothing, but they submitted the statutes [to the Ministry of the Interior], and are waiting for their approval. In the meantime their fight against the Zionists has sharpened. On Thursday Stern phoned Father, he wanted to talk to him, and on that occasion he promised that at the statutory meeting they would not attack the Zionists. Nevertheless, on Sunday, both he and Dézsi [Dési] did precisely that. Stern alleges that he merely responded to the attack that was published in the *Jüdische Rundschau*. Prior to the meeting he also said that [Leó] Budai Goldberger [a leader of Hungarian Jewry and friend of Stern] wanted to write a big article against the Zionists, but that he [Stern] prevented it. Despite this, however, a week after the formation [of the new society] B. Goldberger published an infamous article in the *Egyenlőség* [Equality, the anti-Zionist Budapest weekly that had the backing of the official Jewish establishment] and in the *Lloyd*, alleging that the Zionists were anti-national, etc. The lesson from all this is that you must be very cautious in voicing your opinion about all this, since they are totally unreliable, and it is really doubtful whether they will do anything. Thus they included in the name of their society "Society for the Support of Holy Land and Other Emigrants"—that is to say, by now not only is there no reference to the K.K.L. [Jewish National Fund] and the K.H. [Palestine Foundation Fund] as they had promised up to the last minute, but under the title "and Other" Madagascar and South America also find place. Father spoke today with Eppler, according to whom hundreds of new members are registering daily. He says that a respectable amount will be collected. In any case, wait-and-see is the only right thing in relation to them. There is no point in fighting them here; after all, they have the right to form a society, and, possibly, with the right policy one can nevertheless direct them to the useful path. On the other hand, you must not take up their cause, especially not publicly, until we see what direction they take, and whether they achieve any result. Father did not even mention your remarks there, because he did not want it to be treated here as if they received from us information about negotiations there. Blumenfeld, it seems, has sufficient

experience with promises of help made by non-Zionists, and this is why he is so nervous. On the other hand, the basis of the Jewish Agency [for Palestine] is, after all, collaboration [with non-Zionists]. In any case, his vehemence was not justified, and it would be the right thing for you to do to explain to him that it is our opinion that we should not give them the excuse that the Zionists have hindered them. If it shrivels up of itself, then, at all events, that will be a verification of what Hantke said to Samu Stern, namely, that no Palestine work can be done without ideology. Stern says it can be done, well then, let him try. The fact is that already it has become evident that they misled not only Pfeiffer and Hatvany, but even Father, as becomes clear from their present behavior. You could explain this to Blumenfeld and Hantke, adding that nevertheless our opinion is that one should take a wait-and-see position; perhaps, despite everything, a miracle will happen and money will begin to come in. In any case, it is also important that all the bodies there, that is, including the Ole Hungaria, should declare most decisively that they don't welcome the kind of help that wants to shake with calumnies the foundations of Zionism that does the work of upbuilding. . . .

After discussing several other matters, Mother at the end of her letter again returns to my run-in with Blumenfeld, and writes that "although basically and in principle he was not right in his outburst, concerning the Hungarian situation, alas, he was."

Some two or three weeks after my return to Jerusalem, Father again referred in one of his letters to the wrangle between the Pest Congregation and the Zionists. He wrote:

In recent days the quarrel between the Congregation and the Zionists has intensified. Budai Goldberger wrote a terrible article in *Egyenlőség*, and I, too, came out against him in a sharp article to be published in the February [1937] issue [of *Mult és Jövő*] that you will soon see. In any case, if you [plural] write in the name of the Organization of Hungarian Immigrants, you must emphasize to the Congregation that such a quarrel makes a bad impression in Eretz Israel and abroad, and that you ask "in the name of the Land of the Prophets" that they should strive to make peace.

Father's article did in fact appear in the February 1937 issue of *Mult és Jövő*, and it was really quite sharp. I am unable to obtain a copy of the *Egyenlőség* in which Leó Budai Goldberger's article appeared, but from Father's rejoinder one can form a good idea of its tone and content. Budai Goldberger (more correctly Leó Goldberger de Buda) was the scion of a Jewish family of industrialists that received Hungarian nobility in 1867 from King Francis Joseph I. He was active in Jewish life, and took a special interest in the welfare of Jewish youth in Budapest. Father took him to task for his short-sighted rejection—in the fourth year of the German Third Reich—of the Zionist work in Palestine that alone made it possible for tens of thousands of German Jews to find a refuge from the German persecution. "How could you," Father writes, "say with puffed-up self-importance that 'in the midst of the university youth whose care I consider my mission in life, I shall not tolerate that Zionist, and therefore antinational, ideas should become implanted' "?

At a time when all kinds of anti-Semitic groups are busy undermining the much lacerated remaining positions of Hungarian Jewry, when the Jewish youth contemplates in despair its uncertain future, when apostasy begins again to reach the dimensions it had in the days after Communism [that is, after 1919], when tens of thousands of Budapest Jews are able to defray neither their congregational taxes nor their burial expenses—you found no more urgent "work of rescue" than to sound the alarm bells against Zionism and Zionists, who, according to you, "are apt to plunge Hungarian Jewry into mortal danger."

From where do you take the right and the temerity to dispose thus, from on high, of a question over which great masters, deeply concerned about their people, have agonized with a humble soul, eating their hearts out? Herzl, Hess, Nordau, Ahad Haam, Bialik, Buber, Dubnow, Gordon have brooded and labored over the great and difficult problems, and you nonchalantly throw out the *schneidig* [smart] remark, "I reject this Zionist world of ideas. Of this we have no need."

Then Father goes on to give his own view of one of the chief causes of anti-Semitism in Hungary:

. . . anti-Semitism is created by everyone who wants to play the first violin. And, in the first place, by those overzealous Jews who believe that their task here is to instruct the entire nation in patriotism, and to do it as loudly as possible. . . . In all the Catholic, Protestant, Reformed, Evangelical, and Unitarian gatherings together they do not speak as much about the fatherland as in some Jewish congregations. Even if this zealotry arises from the heart, it produces anti-Semitism! Because it creates the impression that the Jews want to reserve for themselves both the fatherland and patriotism.

Touching upon the newly created society, Father says that Budai Goldberger wrote that for emigration, for the rebuilding of the Holy Land, there was no need of Zionism. "But then, right away, you contradict yourself in the very next sentence [in which you write] 'Although it is my belief and conviction that all those who are able to do so should sacrifice first of all for the alleviation of Hungarian misery.' Here you appear to embrace openly a position against the action Samu Stern initiated in the matter of Palestine."

In January 1937 Professor Ignác Pfeiffer, having reached the age of seventy, resigned the presidency of the Pro Palestine Federation of Hungarian Jews. At the annual general meeting, held in February, Father, who up to that time had been the executive vice-president, was elected president. In this new capacity he again approached the Congregation, and in a letter he wrote me that month—typically he did not mention his election—he informed me that the executive of the Congregation was ready to receive Mr. Berger, the director of public relations at the Hebrew University, and to arrange a public meeting for him. And he asked, "Do you know whether he is a good speaker?" In the same letter Father also reported about various donations the Pro Palestine had received for the Hebrew University.

In the remaining weeks of the winter and in the spring of 1937 the news reaching Jerusalem from Budapest was not encouraging. Disturbances and demonstrations directed against Jewish students took place at various universities, and the demand was voiced that the *numerus clausus* should be reduced to a *numerus nullus*, in other words, that no Jews at all should be admitted to Hungarian institutions of higher learning. In Jerusalem the leaders of the Jewish Agency and the Keren Kayemeth and Keren Hayesod continued to be concerned about the new society organized by the Pest Congregation, and its effect on Zionist activities. I was again consulted by them on this issue, but, of course, there was little we or they could do about it. On February 24, I informed Father that the day before I had had another conference at the Jewish Agency with Dr. Hantke, Dr. Lauterbach, and others, but that the only conclusion reached was that the board of the Hungarian Immigrants' Society should write a somewhat more energetic letter to Chief Rabbi Hevesi, president of the new society, and inform him that we insist on cooperation between his group and the Pro Palestine.

In fact, we need not have been concerned. The Hungarian Israelite Society for the Support of Holy Land and Other Settlements fizzled out within a few short weeks, and to the best of my knowledge it did not help a single emigrant to settle either in the Holy Land or elsewhere.

toward Budapest. I could never forget that Mother was, until 1939, consumed with worry about the safety of her two children in Palestine, torn as the country was by Arab riots, Jewish resistance, and futile, but occasionally brutal, British efforts to keep the peace between the two warring peoples. Whether Father had the same fears I could not know, for he rarely if ever gave the slightest indication of his personal feelings on this score, or on anything else, for that matter. In any case, parental worries about us were amply reciprocated by my sister and me: from the perspective we had from Palestine we saw more clearly than our parents did in Budapest that the storm was rapidly gathering over Europe, and, in correspondence with our parents, we engaged in an energetic campaign to make them come to Palestine while it was still possible.

Nor was it easy for me to make a break with Hungarian Jews in a general sense. During my sojourn in Budapest Father gradually introduced me into the secrets of fund-raising for Palestinian Jewish cultural institutions, and, although it was a purely voluntary, unpaid activity on my part, I did not hesitate to do the best I could, because I felt it was my moral and Zionist duty. The lectures I gave in Budapest and dozens of country towns on the cultural life of the *yishuv*, as well as the articles I wrote, served the purpose of arousing interest in, and sympathy with, Jewish Palestine, and prepared the ground for professional fund-raisers sent over by the Hebrew University and other Palestinian Jewish institutions.

In January 1937, when I arrived back in Jerusalem, Mr. Berger (his first name escapes me), director of what was then the department of organization and publicity of the Hebrew University, invited me to work one day a week in his office, pursuing through correspondence the contacts I had established in Hungary, and in this manner to help raise funds for the University. For this work I was to be paid three Palestinian pounds a month, the equivalent at the time of $15 (something like $300 in today's money). I hesitated before accepting this arrangement, for I had inherited from Father the conviction that we Patais were duty and honor bound to volunteer our services to all Zionist causes. In the end, financial pressures prevailed, and, for a number of months, I worked in Mr. Berger's department engaging in a lively correspondence (having to type all my Hungarian letters myself) with heads and officials of Hungarian Jewish communities, and with individual wealthy Hungarian Jews. I have no recollection of the actual income this work produced for the

University, nor do I remember when and why it came to an end. In any case, while it lasted my relationship with Hungary and its Jews remained intensive.

It was only after my work for Mr. Berger was discontinued, and after the Holy Land and Other Settlements society folded, that my efforts to gain the support of Hungarian Jews ceased, and therewith my contacts with the land of my birth became confined to my parents and brother as long as they remained in Budapest. The more the focus of my attention shifted from Budapest to Jerusalem, the more I felt that the years of my apprenticeship had come to an end, and that I was entering a new phase of my life, that of a scholarly journeyman.